Seaforth WORLD NAVAL REVIEW 2012

Seaforth

WORLD NAVAL REVIEW

2012

Editor
CONRAD WATERS

Seaforth
PUBLISHING

Frontispiece: The *Anzac* class frigate *Warramunga* seen early in February 2010. The *Anzac* class form the core surface component of the Royal Australian Navy's current fleet, which is described in some detail in Chapter 2.2A. *(Royal Australian Navy)*

The editor welcomes correspondence and suggestions from readers.
Please contact him via Seaforth at **info@seaforthpublishing.com**.
All correspondence should be marked **FAO: Conrad Waters**.

First published in Great Britain in 2011 by
Seaforth Publishing
An imprint of Pen & Sword Books Ltd.
47 Church Street, Barnsley
S Yorkshire S70 2AS

www.seaforthpublishing.com
Email info@seaforthpublishing.com

British Library Cataloguing in Publication Data
A CIP data record for this book is available from the British Library

ISBN 978-1-84832-120-5

Typeset and designed by Stephen Dent
Printed in China by 1010 Printing International Ltd.

CONTENTS

Note on Tables: Tables are provided to give a broad indication of fleet sizes and other key information but should be regarded only as a general guide. For example, many published sources differ significantly on the principal particulars of ships, whilst even governmental information can be subject to contradiction. In general terms, the data contained in these tables is based on official information updated as of June 2011, supplemented by reference to a wide range of secondary and corporate sources, such as shipbuilder websites.

1 OVERVIEW

INTRODUCTION

'Quick decisions are unsafe decisions' wrote the Ancient Greek playwright Sophocles, one of the three Greek tragedians of that period whose plays have survived to modern times. These words are particularly appropriate in the context of this introduction to the 2012 edition of the *Seaforth World Naval Review*, which is written against a backdrop of significant reductions to the strength of many of Europe's major fleets. Possibly the hardest hit has been the British Royal Navy. It emerged as the main loser from the UK Government's 2010 Strategic Defence and Security Review (SDSR), which was completed in rapid order between May and October 2010. Faced with an overly-extended defence budget, an urgent need to reduce government expenditure and a medium-term commitment to land-based operations in Afghanistan, the new Conservative–Liberal Democrat Coalition implemented a series of cutbacks to maritime forces. Amongst the most prominent were the abandonment of maritime aerial reconnaissance with the termination of the Nimrod MRA4 programme and acceptance of a lengthy gap in fixed-wing carrier operations due to premature withdrawal of the iconic Harrier aircraft. The wisdom of some of these decisions was subsequently drawn into question by the outbreak of revolution in Libya and, particularly, the use of some assets slated for early withdrawal as part of Britain's contribution to the United Nations' response.[1]

The question of what to cut – and at what speed – is not solely a British dilemma. Amongst Continental European nations, Denmark, Germany and the Netherlands have all announced or implemented significant reductions in naval and broader defence forces over the past twelve months.[2] Others in the region look to set follow. However, the greatest potential uncertainty is faced by the United States' military. US defence expenditures seem likely – at best – to stabilise after more than a decade of increases driven by the interventions in Afghanistan and Iraq. Historic and planned US Department of Defense funding is set out in Table 1.0.1. Even excluding overseas contingency operations funding, the department's base budget increased by approximately two-thirds over the rate of inflation in the decade since FY2001, a trend which seems unsustainable in the light of the substantial federal deficit. Resolution of the protracted and partisan deliberations over the FY2011 US federal budget has already seen current-year defence funding take a c. US$20bn budget haircut from that requested to US$688bn, of which US$530bn relates to core funding. The FY2012 budget request, released in February 2011, envisages a further US$78bn fall in spending compared with previous plans over the five years to FY2016, limiting real terms growth in base funding to less than 1 per cent. However, worse may follow. In April, US President Barack Obama announced plans for additional defence cutbacks of c. US$400bn over the ten years to 2023 as part of a broader deficit-reduction strategy. The direction taken by these economies – which will start to be felt from 2013 onwards – will have significant implications for the future US Navy.

The potential direction in future US defence spending needs to be analysed in the context of overall global trends. On an absolute basis, the US Department of Defense is still allocated considerably more resources than any other defence ministry, as Table 1.0.2 on countries with significant military expenditure makes clear. It accounts for over 40 per cent of total global defence spending and around six times that of China, its nearest rival, on the basis of current exchange rates. However, this is not the whole story. Even discounting the fact that 'real world' purchasing power parity exchange rates – that reflect the greater amount of goods that can be acquired for a given sum of money in lower-cost developing countries – considerably narrow the US's

Table 1.0.1: HISTORIC AND FUTURE US DEPARTMENT OF DEFENSE (DOD) BUDGET TRENDS FY2001-16

YEAR	FY01	FY02	FY03	FY04	FY05	FY06	FY07	FY08	FY09	FY10	FY11	FY12F	FY13F	FY14F	FY15F	FY16F
Base Budget	297	328	365	377	400	411	432	480	513	528	530	553	571	586	598	611
Supplementary Funding	20	17	72	91	79	124	169	187	153	163	158	119	50	50	50	50
Total	**316**	**345**	**437**	**468**	**479**	**535**	**601**	**667**	**667**	**691**	**688**	**671**	**621**	**636**	**648**	**661**

Information from the DOD Fiscal 2012 Budget Proposal, with FY2011 adjusted for the April 2011 resolution of the administration's budget request.
All figures in US$bn. Some totals do not reconcile precisely due to rounding

Notes:
1. The Base Budget includes military construction and armed forces housing appropriations.
2. Supplementary Funding largely comprises Overseas Contingency Operations (OCO) appropriations in support of the interventions in Afghanistan and Iraq.
3. The FY2011 DOD budget request was originally US$708bn. The amount authorised was reduced by nearly US$20.0bn by Congress.
4. Figures for FY2012 and beyond represent the administration's proposal for FY2012 and future plans. Figures for FY2013 and beyond are likely to see further adjustment.

The US Navy destroyer *Forrest Sherman* (DDG-98) passes the Royal Navy's Type 45 destroyers *Daring* and *Diamond* as she departs Portsmouth Naval Base on Good Friday, 22 April 2011. Both of the leading Anglo-Saxon navies face challenges as their respective governments adjust to the aftermath of the global credit crunch. *(Conrad Waters)*

headline advantage, the country's likely economic performance is simply not strong enough to allow it to maintain its relative position indefinitely. As demonstrated by Table 1.0.3 on the current economic strength and future growth prospects of the world's major maritime powers, rapidly-expanding levels of economic activity in emergent countries such as China and India are progressively lessening American financial hegemony. This change in relative economic power will inevitably also be reflected in the military – and hence naval – balance of power over time. This fact is already apparent in the way the expanding Chinese and Indian 'blue water' fleets are rivalling those of established European maritime nations such as France and the United Kingdom. Whilst the United States is unlikely to face a similar

Table 1.0.2: COUNTRIES WITH HIGH NATIONAL DEFENCE EXPENDITURES – 2010

RANK	COUNTRY	TOTAL: US$	SHARE OF GDP: %	CHANGE 2009–10
1	United States	698.0bn	4.8%	2.8%
2	China	119.0bn	2.1%	3.8%
3	United Kingdom	59.6bn	2.7%	-0.8%
4	France	59.3bn	2.3%	-8.4%
5	Russian Federation	58.7bn	4.0%	-1.4%
6	Japan	54.5bn	1.0%	0.8%
7	Saudi Arabia	45.2bn	10.4%	4.0%
8	Germany	45.2bn	1.3%	-1.3%
9	India	41.3bn	2.7%	-2.8%
10	Italy	37.0bn	1.8%	0.3%
	World	**1,630.0bn**	**2.6%**	**1.3%**

Information from the Stockholm International Peace Research Institute (SIPRI) – http://milexdata.sipri.org
The SIPRI Military Expenditure Database contains data on 171 countries over the period 1988–2010.

Notes:
1 Spending figures are at current prices and market exchange rates.
2 Figures for China, Germany, Italy and the Russian Federation are estimates.
3 Data on military expenditure as a share of GDP (Gross Domestic Product) relates to GDP estimates for 2010 from the IMF World Economic Outlook, October 2010.

Table 1.0.3: ECONOMIC STRENGTH AND GROWTH PROSPECTS FOR MAJOR NAVAL POWERS

COUNTRY	ABSOLUTE GDP (US$BN) END 2010	FORECAST CHANGE 2011	FORECAST CHANGE 2012	FORECAST CHANGE 2013	FORECAST CHANGE 2014	FORECAST CHANGE 2015
United States	14,119	2.76%	2.87%	2.72%	2.73%	2.73%
Japan	5,459	1.40%	2.07%	1.69%	1.51%	1.28%
China	4,990	9.59%	9.52%	9.48%	9.52%	9.46%
France	2,583	1.65%	1.78%	2.00%	2.07%	2.07%
United Kingdom	2,248	1.66%	2.33%	2.50%	2.49%	2.56%
Italy	2,055	1.05%	1.30%	1.37%	1.38%	1.40%
India	1,538	8.24%	7.82%	8.17%	8.14%	8.12%
Russia	1,465 (Forecast)	4.83%	4.51%	4.34%	4.24%	4.00%
Spain	1,410	0.83%	1.61%	1.77%	1.94%	1.83%
South Korea	1,007 (Forecast)	4.46%	4.18%	4.17%	4.05%	4.04%

Information from the International Monetary Fund's World Economic Outlook April 2011 Database.

Notes:
1. Absolute GDP figures – the most widely used measure of national economic output – are based on current prices and market exchange rates.
2. Forecast growth is based on constant prices, i.e. adjusted to exclude the impact of inflation.

A number of European fleets are suffering from cutbacks as the continent's governments seek to reduce their expenditure. Here, the German Type 206 submarine *U18* leads the remaining members of her class into retirement on 30 August 2010. *(German Navy)*

situation in the immediate future, it is clear from developments such as ongoing refinement of the 'Air-Sea Battle' concept that considerable thought is being given to how the US will maintain its current maritime supremacy in an age when its relative quantitative and qualitative edge will be in decline.

FLEET REVIEWS

For the time being, current estimates of fleet strengths are set out in Table 1.0.4. This also contains the equivalent figures contained in *Seaforth World Naval Review 2011* by way of comparison.[3] Although significant movement over the previous year is inevitably limited, a number of features are worthy of comment:

- Whilst the table shows little in the way of quantitative adjustment in most cases, this tends to mask underlying qualitative changes. For example, the numerical strength of China's People's Liberation Army Navy is largely unchanged year-on-year. However, series production of modern vessels such as Type 054A 'Jiangkai II' frigates and Type 041 'Yuan' class AIP-equipped submarines in replacement for obsolete Cold War 'Jianghu' and 'Romeo' types paints an entirely different picture. As referenced in previous editions of the *Seaforth World Naval Review*, pure numerical comparisons are subject to considerable hazard.
- The annual comparative figures provided also reveal little about current construction programmes and, hence, likely changes in comparative strengths over the next few years. This is particularly the case with India. Here, a recent uplift in defence expenditure in recent years has yet to stabilise a decline in the number of major units in service, partly due to delays in the country's relatively inefficient shipyards. This position will start to reverse over the next few years as completion of new indigenous construction is supplemented

Table 1.0.4: MAJOR FLEET STRENGTHS 2010-2011

COUNTRY	USA		UK		FRANCE		ITALY		SPAIN		RUSSIA[2]		INDIA		CHINA[2]		JAPAN		S KOREA	
Year[1]	2010	2011	2010	2011	2010	2011	2010	2011	2010	2011	2010	2011	2010	2011	2010	2011	2010	2011	2010	2011
Aircraft Carrier (CVN/CV)	11	11	–	–	1	1	–	–	–	–	1	1	–	–	–	–	–	–	–	–
Support Carrier (CVS/CVH)	–	–	3	1	–	–	2	2	1	1	–	–	1	1	–	–	1	2	–	–
Strategic Missile Sub (SSBN)	14	14	4	4	4	4	–	–	–	–	15	15	–	–	3	3	–	–	–	–
Attack Submarine (SSGN/SSN)	57	57	8	7	6	6	–	–	–	–	20	20	–	–	5	5	–	–	–	–
Patrol Submarine (SSK)	–	–	–	–	–	–	6	6	4	4	20	20	16	14	55	55	16	16	12	12
Battleships/Battlecruisers (BB/BC)	–	–	–	–	–	–	–	–	–	–	2	2	–	–	–	–	–	–	–	–
Fleet Escort (CGN/CG/DDG/FFG)	109	109	24	19	18	17	16	16	10	10	30	30	21	19	45	50	41	40	19	20
Patrol Escort (DD/FFG/FSG/FS)	2	2	–	–	15	15	8	8	–	–	55	55	8	8	30	45	6	6	25	23
Missile Attack Craft (PGG/PTG)	–	–	–	–	–	–	–	–	–	–	50	50	12	12	75	75	6	6	1	5
Mine Countermeasures (MCMV)	14	14	15	15	14	14	12	12	6	6	45	45	8	8	20	20	30	30	9	9
Major Amp (LHD/LPD/LPH/LSD)	31	30	7	6	4	4	3	3	3	3	1	1	1	1	1	2	3	3	1	1

Notes:

1 Data refers to fleet strengths as of mid-year 2010 and 2011.

2 Figures for Russia and China are approximate.

by the arrival of ships ordered from overseas.

- Conversely, the stability achieved by other nations potentially downplays increasing problems ahead. France's *Marine Nationale* is just one country wrestling with the challenge of block obsolescence. Although the FREMM multi-mission frigate programme provides for renewal of the front-rank escort fleet, many of its patrol frigates are due for withdrawal in the 2013–18 timeframe and no replacements are in sight. Even the US Navy's apparent success in halting the long, post-Cold War decline in operational numbers will only be sustained by the pending arrival of arguably second-tier Littoral Combat Ships in substitution for first-rate fleet escorts.
- The most obvious decline in relative fleet strength over the past twelve months has been that suffered by Britain's Royal Navy as the cutbacks announced in the SDSR were implemented in rapid order.

Given the significant changes imposed on the Royal Navy's future plans by the SDSR, these are the subject of one of the specific Fleet Reviews that supplement our broader regional overviews. In this, Richard Beedall revisits the chapter on the Royal Navy's transformational construction programme he contributed to *Seaforth World Naval Review 2010* and examines its likely composition under the new 'Future Force 2020' structure established for the British Armed Forces. The other specific Fleet Reviews also examine fleets that have long associations with the British Royal Navy. Ross Gillett's upbeat review of the Royal Australian Navy demonstrates what can be achieved when a long-term maritime strategy is backed by a broad level of political consensus. By way of contrast, Mrityunjoy Mazumdar's discussion of the Pakistan Navy indicates the practical difficulties faced by a fleet playing a secondary role to the land-based arm of the military against a backdrop of political instability. The highly-regarded *Armada de Chile* falls somewhere between these two extremes. However, changes to the favourable funding regime provided to the country's armed forces under the so-called 'Copper Law' give rise to uncertainty as to whether recent progress can be maintained, as set out by Juan Carlos Arancibia in his first contribution to this annual.

SIGNIFICANT SHIPS

Our second main section follows the pattern established by previous editions in examining a number of significant new warship classes. The time between a project being initiated and the delivery of a full operational capability can be protracted, as Guy Toremans' description of Sweden's innovative *Visby* class makes clear. Tracing its origins to concept work carried out in the late 1980s, a combination of capability changes, role adjustments and budgetary restrictions – not to mention the challenges involved in commissioning a wide range of new technology – means that it is only now that the Royal Swedish Navy is able to deploy these revolutionary vessels. Of course, not all warship designs are as radical as *Visby* and her sisters. Edward Feege's and Scott Truver's review of the USN's amphibious assault ship *Makin Island* (LHD-8) demonstrates the advantages to be gained by an evolutionary design process. Whilst externally similar to members of the *Wasp* (LHD-1) class, a new propulsion system and other modifications will provide substantial operational and cost-efficiency benefits over her earlier half-sisters.

The Royal Navy Type 45 destroyer *Dauntless* (foreground) operating with Spain's F-100 type frigate *Almirante Juan de Borbón* (middle) and the USN *Ticonderoga* (CG-47) class cruiser *Gettysburg* (CG-64) on 20 May 2011 whilst participating in Exercise Saxon Warrior. The different classifications applied to three ships of broadly similar size and capability demonstrates the difficulties inherent in tabular comparisons. *(US Navy)*

The USN amphibious assault ship *Makin Island* (LHD-8) pictured passing under San Francisco's Golden Gate Bridge in October 2010. She represents some of the advantages of adopting an evolutionary approach to warship design. *(Mrityunjoy Mazumdar)*

An image of the revolutionary Swedish stealth corvette *Visby* whilst undergoing trials. First ordered in 1995, the class is only now entering full operational service. *(Kockums)*

The search for affordability is also demonstrated in the chapter on recent British-built offshore patrol vessels. In addition to the widespread use of modular design techniques to reduce construction costs, the United Kingdom's BAE Systems is in the forefront of introducing contractor logistical support (CLS) arrangements. These allow navies to acquire not just a warship but also a guaranteed level of operational availability. Already widely available in commercial environments, the CLS concept has proved itself in the contractual arrangements implemented for the Royal Navy's 'River' class vessels and is being adopted in a modified form for other British warship types.[4] Given ongoing cost pressures across the world's fleets, such cradle-to-grave support contracts that offer defined availability at a pre-agreed cost have the potential to become increasingly widespread in the years ahead.

TECHNOLOGICAL DEVELOPMENTS

The concluding section of this review looks at technological developments. With the end of the Cold War, the sophisticated and specialised skills needed for the successful prosecution of anti-submarine warfare have fallen somewhat out of vogue. In contrast, the attraction of possessing underwater capabilities seems undiminished. Thailand is reportedly the latest South East Asian nation – joining Malaysia and Vietnam – acquiring diesel-electric submarines and even the relatively impoverished Philippines are said to be considering their options. The loss of South Korea's corvette *Cheonan* to a suspected North Korean submarine attack on 26 March 2010 was something of a wake-up call, particularly to those 'blue water' fleets transitioning from an emphasis on oceanic to littoral operations. Norman Friedman's summary of recent sonar technology is therefore timely. Finally, David Hobbs supplements his annual round-up of developments in the area of naval aviation with an overview of maritime unmanned aerial vehicles. As in so many fields, the US Navy is blazing a trail in its unmanned carrier-launched surveillance and strike (UCLASS) project that aims to deploy a squadron of unmanned aircraft as part of a carrier wing by 2018.

SUMMARY

The last twelve months have seen some of the trends heralded in the initial two editions of the *Seaforth World Naval Review* become more defined. The aftermath of the global 'credit crunch' has started to impact the fleets of some of the European countries that suffered most during the economic downturn. Conversely, the emergence of the new Asian economic and maritime powers – most notably China – is becoming more apparent with the advent of a new spurt of naval construction after a couple of relatively quiet years and the probable commencement of sea trials for the reconstructed carrier *Varyag* in the second half of 2011. Meanwhile, rival India's naval modernisation should receive a boost over the year ahead with final completion of the modernised *Vikramaditya* (the former Soviet *Admiral Gorshkov*), the commissioning of the first Project 15A destroyer *Kolkata* and the arrival of the delayed project 971 'Akula' class submarine *Chakra* (ex *Nerpa*) from Russia.

The medium-term outlook remains more uncertain. The US Navy retains its clear technological leadership and has – at least temporarily – stemmed its previous numerical decline. It has met a long-held ambition to double submarine production to two boats p.a. and also determined a way ahead for the hugely important Littoral Combat Ship programme over the last year. However, new construction programmes remain beset by cost overruns and quality problems, whilst the future budgetary situation is far from positive. Much will undoubtedly depend – both in the United States and the United Kingdom – on whether a bloated and inefficient procurement structure can be efficiently reformed. It remains an interesting time for the student of world naval affairs.

ACKNOWLEDGEMENTS

The survival of the *Seaforth World Naval Review* into its third year of publication – and beyond – inevitably rests on its ability to attract a large and diverse readership. This year we are pleased to welcome access to a much broader American audience through the conclusion of co-publication arrangements with the US Naval Institute Press. When taken together with our Chinese–language edition, *Seaforth World Naval Review* is now in the fortunate position of being published on three continents, albeit increased exposure to a knowledgeable and well-informed US readership brings its own challenges to which the editor hopes to rise.

Success is dependent on the continued support of a large number of people, most prominent of whom are publishing editor Rob Gardiner and designer Steve Dent. Both have been instrumental in giving the book its current form. Special mention must also be made of the contributions of a strong and growing contingent of expert authors, to which must be added the clear and accurate technical drawings supplied by John Jordan. They supplement the illustrations provided by the public relations officers of a broad range of defence companies and government ministries, of which the assistance of Kristina Crowe of BAE Systems, Ute Arriens of HDW, Samuel Danofsky of Kockums, Esther Benito Lope of Navantia and Frank van de Wiel of Thales Nederland has been particularly significant over the past year. Finally, I must continue to acknowledge the ongoing support of my family, most notably my wife Susan, for undertaking much of the initial proof-reading.

The comments, criticisms and suggestions of all readers remain welcome. Please forward these to the editor via the contact address detailed opposite the contents page.

Conrad Waters, Editor
30 June 2011

The US *Arleigh Burke* (DDG-51) class destroyer *Hopper* (DDG-70) operating in company with her sister–ship *Benfold* (DDG-65) and the JMSDF destroyer *Atago*. The USN retains a clear technological advantage over all potential adversaries and has stemmed its recent numerical decline. However, it faces a major challenge to retain its relative advantage to the emergent Asian powers. *(Royal Australian Navy)*

Boeing's Phantom Ray prototype unmanned aerial vehicle pictured immediately before its first flight on 27 April 2011. The development of unmanned aircraft is likely to have a significant impact on naval aviation as the decade progresses. *(Boeing)*

Notes

1. Amongst the warships most actively involved in initial operations was the Type 22 frigate *Cumberland*. She was diverted to participate in the Libyan mission whilst on her way back to the UK to pay off.

2. Germany's *Deutsche Marine* said goodbye to its last Type 206 submarines in August 2010, whilst the majority of Denmark's remaining revolutionary Stanflex 300 patrol vessels were paid off in October 2010 as part of economy measures. Significant reductions to the Royal Netherlands Navy were announced as part of a package of defence cutbacks on 8 April 2011.

3. This table – along with the additional, more detailed tables in the Regional Reviews – is based on official published information updated as of June 2011, supplemented by access to a wide range of secondary sources. The availability and accuracy of information varies widely dependent on the country under consideration and is inevitably subject to a considerable degree of interpretation and inevitable inaccuracy. Data should therefore only be considered as providing a general guide.

4. Availability-based contracts are increasingly common in commercial shipping and other transportation businesses. Amongst the most successful has been Rolls Royce 'power by the hour' concept for commercial jet engines under its 'TotalCare' engine support service.

2.1 REGIONAL REVIEW

NORTH AND SOUTH AMERICA

Author:
Conrad Waters

INTRODUCTION

Navies in the Americas have benefited from a relatively buoyant environment for military expenditure in recent years. This positive backdrop has largely been driven by the ramp-up in US spending devoted to prosecuting the 'war against terror'. However, defence budgets in Latin America have also seen something of a recent upsurge. Whilst, in the words of the Stockholm International Peace Research Institute (SIPRI), the increase 'is surprising given the lack of real military threats to most states in the region', SIPRI does list several factors behind this apparent anomaly.[1] These encompass the combined impact of positive economic growth, a need to combat internal security threats and the desire of the region's major powers – particularly Brazil – to exert greater influence in international affairs.

Whatever the reasons, higher defence spending is feeding through to greater investment in naval assets. A number of Latin American countries are already in the middle of new projects or dusting off previous acquisition plans. These range from the procurement of essentially constabulary-orientated offshore patrol ships by nations such as Argentina, Colombia and Venezuela to the rather more extensive PROSUPER (*Programa de Obtenção de Meios de Superfície*) programme being embarked on by Brazil. Supplementing a new submarine construction project already underway in conjunction with France's DCNS, this envisages the acquisition of five surface escorts, five oceanic patrol vessels and a replenishment ship as the initial phase of an ambitious twenty-year strategic maritime plan.

Brazil's ambitions have attracted keen interest from many of Europe's leading shipbuilders, which hope to supplement somewhat depleted order books by forming partnerships with local industry to take a share of the c. US$5bn PROSUPER contract. They have been joined in the competition by South Korea in the clearest signal to date of the emergent Asian naval construction sector's growing international importance. However, the realisation of Brazil's maritime strategy will depend on long-term commitment to a significant elevation of defence spending over historic levels. Given that there are already signs that the new administration of President Dilma Rousseff will give greater priority to social programmes, it seems unlikely that the navy's aspirations will be achieved in their entirety. In these circumstances, it may be more realistic to supplement a more limited new construction programme with the acquisition of less expensive second-hand tonnage from overseas navies. This is a policy which regional counterpart Chile has already adopted with considerable success over the past decade.

Whilst the significance of the principal Latin American navies looks set to grow, it is inevitably the activities of the US Navy that continue to dominate regional – and international – maritime developments. The most potent demonstration of the far-reaching nature of its influence was undoubtedly the death of al-Qaeda leader Osama bin Laden on 2 May 2011. He died at the hands of a team of US Navy SEALS from the United States Naval Special Warfare Development Group in Pakistan's landlocked Abbottabad. The success of the mission, code-named Operation 'Neptune Spear', marks a major step forward in the post 9/11 campaign against militant Islamic terrorism. It could well facilitate a more rapid drawdown than previously envisaged of forces involved in Overseas Contingency Operations in Afghanistan and elsewhere. This would, in turn, allow the US military to channel greater resources towards the Pacific, where China's steadily expanding 'anti-access' capabilities threaten the US Navy's ability to support key allies in the Western Pacific basin. The past year has seen further refinement of the Air-Sea Battle concept first originated in 2009. This aims to counterbalance the Chinese threat by achieving greater collaboration between USN and United States Air Force (USAF) assets in the region. In a speech given in February 2011, Admiral Robert F Willard, Head of the US Pacific Command, revealed that US Marine Corps assets were now being integrated into plans that also envisage the hardening of facilities on Guam against the threat of long-range Chinese missile attack.[2] The US is also persisting with efforts to link India more closely into its network of regional alliances. However, India remains cautious on placing too much reliance on such bilateral ties in spite of steadily increasing naval collaboration.

Table 2.1.1 provides a summary of major regional fleet strengths as of mid-2011.

Naval expenditure in the Americas is relatively buoyant. This image shows the Mexican offshore patrol vessel *Baja California*, the US Coast Guard cutter *Escanaba* (WMEC-907) and the Brazilian frigate *Independência* alongside at Rio Grande, Brazil, on 9 May 2011. The latter two ships are scheduled for replacement by new tonnage within the next few years. *(US Navy)*

Table 2.1.1: FLEET STRENGTHS IN THE AMERICAS – LARGER NAVIES (MID-2011)

COUNTRY	ARGENTINA	BRAZIL	CANADA	CHILE	ECUADOR	PERU	USA	VENEZUELA
Aircraft Carrier (CVN/CV)	–	1	–	–	–	–	11	–
Strategic Missile Submarine (SSBN)	–	–	–	–	–	–	14	–
Attack Submarine (SSN/SSGN)	–	–	–	–	–	–	57	–
Patrol Submarine (SSK)	3	5	4	4	2	6	–	2
Fleet Escort (CG/DDG/FFG)	4	9	15	8	2	9	109	6
Patrol Escort/Corvette (FFG/FSG/FS)	9	5	–	–	6	–	2	–
Missile Armed Attack Craft (PGG/PTG)	2	–	–	7	3	6	–	6
Mine Countermeasures Vessel (MCMV)	–	6	12	–	–	–	14	–
Major Amphibious Units (LHD/LPD/LPH/LSD)	–	2	–	–	–	–	30	–

The German Type 702 *Berlin* class fleet replenishment ship is one of two designs being considered for the Canadian Navy's long-delayed joint support ship project. This view shows the *Frankfurt am Main* operating alongside the air-defence frigate *Hessen* in March 2007. *(German Navy)*

MAJOR NORTH AMERICAN NAVIES – CANADA

The Canadian Forces Maritime Command's current major fleet units are set out in Table 2.1.2. Long-delayed modernisation plans currently await realisation of the new National Shipbuilding Procurement Strategy that was announced on 3 June 2010. The strategy envisages construction of major vessels – those displacing more than 1,000 tons – being channelled to two Canadian shipyards. One of these will build combat ships and the other non-combatants. Five yards were short-listed for selection in October 2010 and a final decision is expected in mid-2011. Once a conclusion has been reached, the way will be clear to move forward with a number of new construction programmes. The most significant of these are:

Arctic Offshore Patrol Vessels: This project envisages the construction of between six and eight ice-capable patrol vessels at a cost of C$3.1bn (US$3.2bn). The new ships are intended to strengthen Canada's ability to police its northern

Table 2.1.2: CANADIAN NAVY: PRINCIPAL UNITS AS AT MID-2011

TYPE	CLASS	NUMBER	TONNAGE	DIMENSIONS	PROPULSION	CREW	DATE
Principal Surface Escorts							
Destroyer – DDG	**IROQUOIS**	3	5,100 tons	130m x 15m x 5m	COGOG, 29 knots	280	1972
Frigate – FFG	**HALIFAX**	12	4,800 tons	134m x 16m x 5m	CODOG, 29 knots	225	1992
Submarines							
Submarine – SSK	**VICTORIA** (UPHOLDER)	4	2,500 tons	70m x 8m x 6m	Diesel-electric, 20+ knots	50	1990

waters. Technical specifications drafted by BMT Fleet Technology suggest an essentially constabulary design for service in a non-military threat environment. Accordingly, main armament will be limited to a 25mm gun, although capability to operate helicopters up to the size of a CH-148 Cyclone is also specified. Maximum speed will be at least 17 knots, endurance is a minimum 6,800 nautical miles (12,594km) whilst core crew numbers are set at a maximum forty-five personnel. The current procurement schedule anticipates contract award during 2012.

Joint Support Ships: Plans for the C$2.6bn (US$2.7bn) acquisition of at least two JSS joint support ships were confirmed on 14 July 2010. This followed postponement of the previous three-ship plan in August 2008 after the short-listed contractors were unable to meet the planned specification within budget. The revised programme appears to downgrade the previous design requirement that envisaged combining replenishment, sealift and logistical support capabilities in a c. 28,000-ton, 200m hull. The new specification will be more focused towards the replenishment role. Designs adapted from Germany's Type 702 *Berlin* class and Spain's new *Cantabria* are being considered alongside an in-house design drawn up with the help of BMT Fleet Technology. A contract for the selected ships should be signed before the end of 2013.

Below: The Canadian Navy's *Halifax* class frigates *Charlottetown* and *Montreal* operating in company on 8 November 2010. The twelve-strong class has recently commenced a rolling mid-life upgrade programme. *(Canadian Navy)*

Single Class Surface Combatant: A longer-term programme likely to commence around 2015 envisages replacing Canada's three *Iroquois* class destroyers and twelve *Halifax* class frigates with a common hull. It appears that Canada has rebuffed a British invitation to collaborate on the Type 26 Global Combat Ship project. As such, a purely national design is likely to be preferred. Given the remaining ships of the *Iroquois* class are already approaching their fortieth birthdays, surface fleet numbers may well fall before their replacements start to be delivered.

In the meantime, a number of other much-needed modernisation projects are drawing closer to fruition. These will support a force that continues to be stretched supporting a wide range of Coalition operations, most recently through participation of a *Halifax* class frigate in NATO's Operation 'United Protector' off Libya. The entire *Halifax* class has recently commenced a rolling mid-life upgrade programme under a combined C$3.1bn (US$3.2bn) package of improvements known as the *Halifax* Class Modernisation/Frigate Life Extension (HCM/FELIX) project. Work will include a series of combat systems improvements under the leadership of Lockheed Martin Canada. It was announced on 1 October 2010 that the programme was formally underway with commencement on schedule of the eighteen-month refit of lead ship *Halifax* at east coast Halifax Shipyards Inc. Refits will be shared with Seaspan Marine Corporation's Victoria Shipyard on Canada's west coast. It is scheduled to commence a similar work package on Calgary by mid-2011. Meanwhile the first of twenty-eight new Sikorsky CH-148 Cyclone helicopters that will eventually replace the elderly CH-128 Sea Kings currently operated from the frigates arrived in Canada on 13 May 2011. This will allow training on the new type to commence shortly.

Progress is also finally being made with modernising the four *Victoria* (former *Upholder*) class submarines acquired from the United Kingdom in 1998. *Victoria* herself is close to completing a significantly delayed, six-year long refit at the west coast base of Esquimalt. Sister boat *Windsor* should also finish a similarly overdue refurbishment at Halifax by the end of 2011. Completion will allow the sole operational submarine, *Corner Brook*, to enter the refit programme, whilst providing an operational underwater capability off both Canadian coasts. Work is also well underway in returning the fourth class member *Chicoutimi* – inoperative since a fatal fire during her delivery voyage to Canada in 2004 – to the fleet as the *Victoria* In-Service Support Contract signed in 2008 finally gets to grips with a previously troubled and controversial acquisition.

The first of twenty-eight new Sikorsky CH-148 Cyclone helicopters has now arrived in Canada and will deploy on the navy's surface warships in due course. *(Sikorsky)*

MAJOR NORTH AMERICAN NAVIES – UNITED STATES

The long-term outlook for USN force levels is somewhat clouded by the potential reductions to US defence expenditure highlighted in the Introduction. However, much success is being achieved in sustaining current front-line fleet numbers – ship battle forces – at c. 290 vessels. This is reflected both in Table 2.1.3, which shows very little overall year-on-year change in major units, as well as in future shipbuilding plans. The overall framework for USN force levels and associated shipbuilding construction is contained in the Long-Range Shipbuilding Plan for FY2011, a document that is now only fully updated every four years in line with the Quadrennial Defense Review cycle. The present plan establishes a long-term requirement of around 322–323 ship battle forces, albeit with considerable fluctuations over the plan's thirty-year lifespan. This requirement translates into a shipbuilding programme of 276 vessels over the same period, representing orders for an average of 9.2 ships each year.

The plan – and similar predecessors – has attracted considerable scepticism given it implies warship construction rates not achieved since the end of the Cold War. However, recent shipbuilding requests have reached the new levels of activity that are necessary. Indeed, the recent FY2012 Five-Year Shipbuilding Plan released with the USN's FY2012 budget request envisages some stepping up in orders compared with previous plans. This is set out in more detail in Table 2.1.4. It should be noted, however, that much of the headline progress is achieved by the acquisition of large numbers of relatively cheap ships, such as the small joint high-speed vessel (JHSV) troop transports and the two Littoral Combat Ship (LCS) variants. There remains considerable uncertainty whether construction rates can be maintained when more sophisticated and, therefore, expensive warships fall due for replacement. There is a particular concern about the affordability of the longer-term plan when the new SSBN(X) strategic missile submarines enter the programme at the end of the present decade.[3]

Whatever the future holds, the FY2012 budget

Construction of the first *Ford* class carrier *Gerald R Ford* (CVN-78) is now well underway at the newly-formed Huntington Ingalls Industries' Newport News shipyard. This view shows one of the stern construction blocks being craned into place in May 2011. *(Huntington Ingalls Industries)*

request does reflect the progress that is being made in bringing current USN construction projects onto a more rational and sustainable footing. Having previously restructured the procurement of major surface units away from the DDG-1000 *Zumwalt* class in favour of renewed construction of the more affordable *Arleigh Burke* (DDG-51) design, the last twelve months has also seen the USN agree a way ahead for smaller surface warships in the form of revised arrangements for the Littoral Combat Ship programme. A 'winner takes all' competition had been set up between the alternative Lockheed Martin *Freedom* (LCS-1) and General Dynamics/Austal USA *Independence* (LCS-2) Littoral Combat Ship designs that would have seen just one variant selected for series production over the FY2010–FY2014 timescale. However, the success of both competitors to reduce their bids significantly below a Congressional cost-cap of US$480m per ship resulted in the navy seeking authorisation for an alternative strategy that would see continued production of both designs. The way ahead was cleared with the receipt of Congressional approval for the new arrangements in December 2010. Contracts with both Lockheed Martin and Austal were signed on 29 December of that year. The new contracts provided for the immediate allocation of one ship to each bidder from FY2010 funds, with a further vessel following shortly after from FY2011 funds and an additional two ships p.a. between 2012 and 2015 for a total twenty-ship buy. The cost of the two immediate ships was US$437m for the LCS-1 design and US$432m for the LCS-2 type but these figures are expected to fall as the programme moves forward. The new ships are to be named *Milwaukee* (LCS-5) and *Jackson* (LCS-6).

Another notable success over the past year has been the long-awaited increase in the rate of nuclear-powered attack submarine orders to two boats each year. The political impasse over the US budget had threatened to delay the move to a two boat p.a. construction drumbeat but an order for the second FY2011 boat – and fourteenth in the *Virginia* (SSN-774) class – SSN-787 was finally announced by General Dynamics Electric Boat on 28 April 2011.

The first US Littoral Combat Ship *Freedom* (LCS-1). A decision in 2010 means that both the LCS-1 and LCS-2 *Independence* Littoral Combat Ship variants will enter series production. *(Lockheed Martin)*

The US Marine Corps is suffering delays and cancellations to some of its projects, most notably termination of the expeditionary fighting vehicle (EFV) programme. A prototype is pictured during early tests. *(US Marine Corps)*

A conceptual image of the new joint high-speed vessel (JHSV) being constructed by Austal US. A May 2011 decision means that all these ships will be operated by the US Navy. *(Austal)*

Table 2.1.3: UNITED STATES NAVY: PRINCIPAL UNITS AS AT MID-2011

TYPE	CLASS	NUMBER	TONNAGE	DIMENSIONS	PROPULSION	CREW	DATE
Aircraft Carriers							
Aircraft Carrier – CVN	**NIMITZ** (CVN-68)	10	101,000 tons	340m x 41/78m x 12m	Nuclear, 30+ knots	5,700	1975
Aircraft Carrier – CVN	**ENTERPRISE** (CVN-65)	1	93,000 tons	342m x 41/76m x 12m	Nuclear, 30+ knots	5,900	1961
Principal Surface Escorts							
Cruiser – CG	**TICONDEROGA** (CG-47)	22	9,900 tons	173m x 17m x 7m	COGAG, 30+ knots	365	1983
Destroyer – DDG	**ARLEIGH BURKE** (DDG-51) – Flight IIA	32	9,200 tons	155m x 20m x 7m	COGAG, 30 knots	380	2000
Destroyer – DDG	**ARLEIGH BURKE** (DDG-51) – Flights I/II	28	8,800 tons	154m x 20m x 7m	COGAG, 30+ knots	340	1991
Frigate – FFG	**OLIVER HAZARD PERRY** (FFG-7)	27	4,100 tons	143m x 14m x 5m	COGAG, 30 knots	215	1977
Littoral Combat Ship – FSG	**FREEDOM** (LCS-1)	1	3,100 tons	115m x 17m x 4m	CODAG, 45+ knots	<50[1]	2008
Littoral Combat Ship – FSG	**INDEPENDENCE** (LCS-2)	1	2,800 tons	127m x 32m x 5m	CODAG, 45+ knots	<50[1]	2010
Submarines							
Submarine – SSBN	**OHIO** (SSBN-726)	14	18,800 tons	171m x 13m x 12m	Nuclear, 20+ knots	155	1981
Submarine – SSGN	**OHIO** (SSGN-726)	4	18,800 tons	171m x 13m x 12m	Nuclear, 20+ knots	160	1981
Submarine – SSN	**VIRGINIA** (SSN-774)	7	8,000 tons	115m x 10m x 9m	Nuclear, 25+ knots	135	2004
Submarine – SSN	**SEAWOLF** (SSN-21)	3[2]	9,000 tons	108m x 12m x 11m	Nuclear, 25+ knots	140	1997
Submarine SSN	**LOS ANGELES** (SSN-688)	43	7,000 tons	110m x 10m x 9m	Nuclear, 25+ knots	145	1976
Major Amphibious Units							
Amph Assault Ship – LHD	**WASP** (LHD-1)	8[3]	41,000 tons	253m x 32/42m x 9m	Steam, 20+ knots	1,100	1989
Amph Assault Ship – LHD	**TARAWA** (LHA-1)	1	40,000 tons	250m x 32/38m x 8m	Steam, 24 knots	975	1976
Landing Platform Dock – LPD	**SAN ANTONIO** (LPD-17)	5	25,000 tons	209m x 32m x 7m	Diesel, 22+ knots	360	2005
Landing Platform Dock – LPD	**AUSTIN** (LPD-4)	4	17,000 tons	171m x 25m x 7m	Steam, 21 knots	420	1965
Landing Ship Dock – LSD	**WHIDBEY ISLAND** (LSD-41)	12[4]	16,000 tons	186m x 26m x 6m	Diesel, 20 knots	420	1985

Notes:

1 Plus mission-related crew.

2 Third of class, SSN-23 is longer and heavier.

3 LHD-8 has many differences.

4 Includes four LSD-49 HARPERS FERRY variants.

Agreement on defence funding also allows FY2011 orders for two DDG-51 type destroyers, as well as for the new mobile landing platform ships that are intended to operate as a floating base for amphibious operations. A total of three ships – based on a commercial 'Alaska' class design – are scheduled to be built at General Dynamics NASSCO in San Diego at a total cost of c. US$1.5bn. NASSCO announced a contract for the first two vessels on 27 May 2011. They will become operational from 2015 onwards.

In the meantime, the current steady state both of overall fleet numbers and of the numbers of the fleet's principal warship types masks some significant underlying changes. Some of the major developments of the past twelve months – subdivided into the principal warship categories operated by the USN – are therefore detailed below.

Aircraft Carriers: The ultimate *Nimitz* (CVN-68) class carrier, *George H W Bush* (CVN-77), departed Norfolk on its maiden operational deployment on 11 May 2011, initially participating in the UK-lead Saxon Warrior training exercises. Construction of the lead ship of the follow-on class, *Gerald R Ford* (CVN-78), is progressing well at the newly-formed Huntington Ingalls Industries group's Newport News facility in line with a planned 2015 delivery date.[4] The new electro-magnetic aircraft launch system (EMALS) destined for the ship was successfully tested with a manned aircraft on 18 December 2010, further de-risking one of a number of items of new technology planned for first-time installation in the carrier. Long-lead items for the second *Ford* class vessel have already been placed prior to a formal order under the FY2013 budget and a first steel cutting ceremony was held in February 2011. On 29 May 2011 it was announced that this vessel would be named *John F Kennedy* (CVN-79) in honour of the former President.

Surface Combatants: Construction of the originally programmed *Arleigh Burke* (DDG-51) class destroyers is winding down, with *Gravely* (DDG-107), *Jason Dunham* (DDG-109) and *William P Lawrence* (DDG-110) all commissioned over the past twelve months. *Spruance* (DDG-111) suffered a minor fire whilst undergoing final trials at General Dynamics' Bath Iron Works facility on 20 May 2011 and a planned autumn commissioning may therefore be delayed. Meanwhile, the sixty-second and final ship of the original programme,

Table 2.1.4: USN FY2012 FIVE YEAR SHIPBUILDING PLAN (FY2012-FY2016)

SHIP TYPE	FY2011: ACTUAL	FY2012: REQUEST	FY2013: PLAN	FY2014: PLAN	FY2015: PLAN	FY2016: PLAN
Aircraft Carrier (CVN-78)	Nil (Nil)	Nil (Nil)	1 (1)	Nil (Nil)	Nil (Nil)	Nil (Nil)
Attack Submarine (SSN-774)	2 (2)	2 (2)	2 (2)	2 (2)	2 (2)	2 (2)
Destroyer (DDG-51)	2 (2)	1 (1)	2 (2)	2 (1)	2 (2)	1 (1)
Littoral Combat Ship (LCS-1/2)	2 (2)	4 (3)	4 (4)	4 (4)	4 (4)	3 (3)
Amphibious Assault Ship (LHA-6)	1 (1)	Nil (Nil)	Nil (Nil)	Nil (Nil)	Nil (Nil)	1 (1)
Amphibious Transport Dock (LPD-17)	Nil (Nil)	1 (1)	Nil (Nil)	Nil (Nil)	Nil (Nil)	Nil (Nil)
Joint High Speed Vessel (JHSV-1)	1 (1)	1 (1)	2 (2)	2 (2)	2 (2)	1 (2)
Mobile Landing Platform (MLP-1)	1 (1)	1 (Nil)	1 (1)	Nil (Nil)	Nil (1)	Nil (Nil)
Replenishment Oiler (TAO(X))	Nil (Nil)	Nil (Nil)	Nil (Nil)	1 (Nil)	1 (Nil)	1 (Nil)
Fleet Tug (TAFT)	Nil (Nil)	Nil (Nil)	Nil (Nil)	Nil (Nil)	1 (1)	Nil (Nil)
Surveillance Ship (TAGOS)	Nil (Nil)	Nil (Nil)	1 (Nil)	Nil (Nil)	Nil (Nil)	Nil (Nil)
Total	9 (9)	10 (8)	13 (12)	11 (9)	12 (12)	9 (9)

Notes:
1 Figures in brackets relate to previous FY2011 Budget Request and Shipbuilding Plan.
2 Figures relate to Ship Battle Forces – other ships are not included.

Series construction of *Arleigh Burke* (DDG-51) class destroyers continues to maintain US fleet numbers. However, imminent completion of the original building programme will result in a pause in activity until new construction gets underway. This image shows *Gravely* (DDG-107) on sea trials during June 2010. *(Huntington Ingalls Industries)*

Michael Murphy (DDG-112), was christened at the same yard earlier in the month on 7 May. There will now be a hiatus in construction whilst preparations are finished for resumption of the programme pursuant to the FY2010 budget approval to restart fabrication of the class in preference to the DDG-1000 design. An order for the new DDG-113 was confirmed on 15 June 2011. Ships ordered through to FY2015 will be built to the existing Flight IIA specification after which construction of a revised Flight III variant is planned. The FY2012 budget request includes funding for preliminary work on the new design, which will incorporate an upgraded AMDR Air and Missile Defence Radar.

The second-tier escort force is starting to see the withdrawal of the remaining FFG-7 type frigates. *McInerney* (FFG-8) was transferred to Pakistan on 31 August 2010, *Hawes* (FFG-53) and *Jarrett* (FG-33) were decommissioned in December 2010 and May 2011 respectively and *Doyle* (FFG-39) will go soon. Their replacements will effectively be the new Littoral Combat Ships. The second LCS-1 variant, *Fort Worth* (LCS-3), was launched in December 2010. Together with *Coronado* (LCS-4), she is expected to enter service during 2012. Agreement of the way forward for the programme has seen construction quickly ramp up, with orders for the two FY2011–funded ships – one of each variant – being placed on 17 March 2011. The contracted prices were US$376.6m for Lockheed Martin's *Detroit* (LCS-7) and US$368.6m for Austal's *Montgomery* (LCS-8), reflecting the considerable economies arising from the revised purchasing strategy. In spite of this, the programme still has many detractors, with remaining concerns including the technical maturity of the mission packages that form the ships' primary war-fighting capabilities, the relatively low level of survivability accepted for both designs and the emergence of hull cracks on LCS-1.[5]

Amphibious Shipping: The US Navy's core amphibious force of thirty front-line units – excluding the two specialised command ships – remains somewhat removed from its planned 33-ship goal. This will be achieved around FY2015 as new vessels enter service. The last year has seen the withdrawal of the penultimate *Tarawa* (LHA-1) class amphibious assault ship, *Nassau* (LHA-4), leaving just *Peleliu* (LHA-5) in commission. By way of compensation, *Makin Island* (LHD-8) is now fully operational, whilst work on the new *America* (LHA-6) is progressing well after earlier delays. In contrast with previous designs, she lacks a well dock for landing craft, a design feature which will be reinstated in the planned LHA-8 and subsequent ships. *America*'s design was influenced by the emphasis placed on F-35B Lightning II and other aviation operations. However, the former aircraft's future is by no means secure after a series of problems on early trials resulted in it being put on two-year probation for potential cancellation in January 2011. The same problems might delay a programme of 'at sea' tests of the aircraft on *Wasp* (LHD-1) scheduled for late 2011.

The US Navy played a lead role in the initial intervention against the Gadaffi regime in Libya in Operation 'Odyssey Dawn'. A notable participant was the reconfigured *Ohio* class guided-missile submarine *Florida* (SSGN-728), which fired over ninety Tomahawk cruise missiles in her first combat mission. *(US Navy)*

Future amphibious operations will also be impacted by the proposed cancellation of the US Marine Corp's expeditionary fighting vehicle (EFV) programme that was heralded by the same series of announcements that revealed the F-35B's probation. Estimated costs reported at US$18m per unit were deemed unaffordable and existing AAV amphibious assault vehicles will be upgraded until a cheaper alternative can be procured. Further efficiencies are being created by the transfer of all the new JHSV troop transports to US Navy control following an agreement reached with the army on 2 May 2011. The original plan was to split the first ten vessels equally between the two services but the revised arrangement will save money. Construction of *Spearhead* (JHSV-1) is well underway at Austal USA and her delivery is expected by the start of 2012.

The most significant amphibious construction programme currently underway is for the remaining *San Antonio* (LPD-17) amphibious transport docks. Authorisation for the eleventh – and final – member of the class has been sought in the FY2012 estimates. Meanwhile, construction of the tenth ship, *John P Murtha* (LPD-26), got underway at Pascagoula on 25 May 2011 and two previously-ordered ships were launched over the past twelve months. The earlier ships in the class have been plagued by construction faults that have taken sustained efforts to remedy. There was consequently some relief when *San*

The new Mexican Navy *Oaxaca* class offshore patrol vessel *Independencia* photographed in April 2010. Mexican naval procurement continues to be focused on the indigenous construction of relatively unsophisticated warships for constabulary missions. *(Mexican Navy)*

Antonio reportedly performed well during May 2011 sea trials that followed nearly two years of repairs to a defective propulsion plant.[6]

Submarines: Submarine service developments continue to be dominated by the progressive introduction of *Virginia* (SSN-774) class boats. *Missouri* (SSN-780) was commissioned in July 2010, whilst delivery of both *California* (SSN-781) and *Mississippi* (SSN-782) is expected over the next year. This is allowing withdrawal of the older *Los Angeles* (SSN-688) class submarines at a broadly equivalent rate, allowing overall force levels to be maintained for the time being. However, a progressive fall in numbers is expected from the middle of the decade as large numbers of boats built in the later years of the Cold War are withdrawn from service. The doubling of *Virginia* class production to two boats p.a. will only partially alleviate this problem and there have been reports that life-extension of some of the younger *Los Angeles* class is being mooted. Meanwhile, development work has begun on the replacement SSBN(X) strategic missile submarines that will begin replacing the existing *Ohio* (SSBN-726) class from the middle of the next decade.

Operationally, the US Navy remains actively involved in missions ranging from the provision of humanitarian relief following the March 2011 Japanese earthquake and tsunami under Operation 'Tomodachi' to participation in the initial military operations against the Gadaffi regime's military in Libya during the same month under Operation 'Odyssey Dawn'. A notable participant in the latter mission was the modernised *Ohio* class guided missile submarine *Florida* (SSGN-728), one of four boats modified from an original strategic role to act as a platform for cruise missile strikes and clandestine operations. In her first combat mission, she fired over ninety Tomahawk cruise missiles, thereby making a significant contribution to the suppression of the overall Gadaffi defence network. More broadly, the navy remains in the forefront of expanding ballistic missile defence (BMD) capabilities. The development of a theatre ballistic missile defence capability in the western Pacific in conjunction with Japan is now being followed by the deployment of BMD-equipped assets to Europe as part of the Phased Adaptive Approach announced by President Obama in September 2009. The Aegis cruiser *Monterey* (CG-61) – equipped with the Standard SM-3 missile – has been deployed to the Mediterranean as the first component of this European 'missile shield'.

The US Coast Guard's national security cutter programme is moving ahead with the christening of the third of class, *Stratton* (WMSL-752), by First Lady Michelle Obama on 23 July 2010. She will be delivered by the end of 2011 and commission in 2012. The fourth of a planned eight-ship class was ordered in November 2010 and options taken for long-lead items for the fifth and sixth ships. The first of the new fast response cutters – *Bernard C Webber* – was launched on 21 April 2011, whilst orders for a further four (making eight in total) were placed in September 2010. Preliminary design contracts for the intermediate offshore patrol cutter are planned within the next year.

OTHER NORTH AND CENTRAL AMERICAN NAVIES

With little to face in the way of external threats, the Mexican and other Central American fleets continue to focus their operations towards constabulary missions. These are driven largely by the need to police natural resources and to counter the local narcotics trade. The *Armada de México*, particularly, has taken an active role in the war against the drugs cartels, albeit ongoing news reports of cartel leaders arrested and vast quantities of illegal substances

The Mexican fleet's front-line surface force continues to be formed of an increasingly elderly flotilla of former US Navy frigates. This is the *Bronstein* class frigate *Nicolas Bravo*, formerly *McCloy* (FF-1038), on 22 June 2010. She was first commissioned forty-seven years earlier in June 1963. *(US Navy)*

destroyed seems to have little overall impact on the underlying problem. Mexican procurement continues to be focused on the indigenous construction of offshore patrol vessels, with the fourth *Oaxaca* class unit, *Centenario de la Revolución* (PO-164), commissioned on 23 November 2010. An additional locally-built but Swedish-designed CB-90 fast patrol boat was inducted on the same day. Further vessels of both types are planned. No apparent replacements are in sight for Mexico's increasingly elderly flotilla of former US navy surface escorts, although the acquisition of surplus FFG-7 frigates must remain a possibility.

Elsewhere in the region, Trinidad and Tobago's ambitious expansion plans have been derailed by the cancellation of its offshore patrol vessel contract with Britain's BAE Systems following a change in political administration.[7]

MAJOR SOUTH AMERICAN NAVIES – ARGENTINA

Details of the current main units of the *Armada Argentina* are set out in Table 2.1.5. There have been no significant alterations to fleet strength over the last year. The current focus appears to be on modernising dockyard infrastructure and completing existing modernisation work, most notably on the TR-1700 patrol submarine *San Juan*. The pressure hull of the submarine was rejoined at the Astillero Almirante Storni (previously the Astillero Domecq Garcia) shipyard in the first half of 2011 following the refurbishment of propulsion and electronic systems. Argentina is looking at the feasibility of restarting construction of the TR-1700 type once *San Juan*'s refit is complete, as material for several additional boats had been acquired and partly assembled before construction ceased in the mid-1990s. There are ambitious plans to develop nuclear-powered boats, possibly in conjunction with Brazil, in due course.

Meanwhile, refurbishment and modernisation of the fire-damaged ice breaker *Almirante Irizar* at neighbouring Astilleros Tanador is reportedly running behind schedule and will not be completed in time for deployment during the 2011/12

Table 2.1.5: ARGENTINEAN NAVY: PRINCIPAL UNITS AS AT MID-2011

TYPE	CLASS	NUMBER	TONNAGE	DIMENSIONS	PROPULSION	CREW	DATE
Principal Surface Escorts							
Destroyer – DDG	**ALMIRANTE BROWN** (MEKO 360)	4	3,600 tons	126m x 14m x 4m	COGOG, 30 knots	200	1983
Frigate – FFG	**ESPORA** (MEKO 140)	6	1,800 tons	91m x 11m x 3m	Diesel, 27 knots	100	1985
Corvette – FSG	**DRUMMOND** (A-69)	3	1,200 tons	80m x 10m x 3m	Diesel, 24 knots	95	1978
Submarines							
Submarine – SSK	**SANTA CRUZ** (TR 1700)	2	2,300 tons	65m x 7m x 7m	Diesel-electric, 25 knots	30	1984
Submarine – SSK	**SALTA** (Type 209)	1	1,200 tons	54m x 6m x 6m	Diesel-electric, 22 knots	30	1974

Antarctic summer season. The extensive reconstruction should help prepare workers at the facility for construction of Fassmer-designed OPV80 type patrol vessels, five of which were approved in 2010.

The Argentine MEKO 360 type frigate *Almirante Brown* pictured during the UNITAS 52 exercise in the Atlantic. The country's navy has seen few changes in principal units in recent years. *(US Navy)*

MAJOR SOUTH AMERICAN NAVIES – BRAZIL

The *Marina do Brasil* currently has the most extensive procurement ambitions of any of the Latin American fleets. Carried out under the framework of the 2008 National Defence Strategy and the associated twenty-year 'PEAMB' naval organisation and equipment plan, the initial acquisition programme envisages renewal of both the submarine and surface forces under, respectively, the PROSUB (*Programa de Desenvolvimento de Submarinos*) and PROSUPER projects. Having concluded the PROSUB element of the plan with a contract for the local construction of French-designed 'Scorpène' submarines in 2009, recent attention has been on renewal of the surface fleet under the PROSUPER modernisation programme. Shipyards from France, Germany, Italy, South Korea, Spain

Table 2.1.6: BRAZILIAN NAVY: PRINCIPAL UNITS AS AT MID-2011

TYPE	CLASS	NUMBER	TONNAGE	DIMENSIONS	PROPULSION	CREW	DATE
Aircraft Carriers							
Aircraft Carrier – CV	**SÃO PAULO** (FOCH)	1	33,500 tons	265m x 32/51m x 9m	Steam, 30 knots	1,700	1963
Principal Surface Escorts							
Frigate – FFG	**GREENHALGH** (Type 22-Batch 1)	3	4,700 tons	131m x 15m x 4m	COGOG, 30 knots	270	1979
Frigate – FFG	**NITERÓI**	6	3,700 tons	129m x 14m x 4m	CODOG, 30 knots	220	1976
Corvette – FSG	**INHAÚMA**	4	2,100 tons	96m x 11m x 4m	CODOG, 27 knots	120	1989
Corvette – FSG	**BARROSO**	1	2,400 tons	103m x 11m x 4m	CODOG, 30 knots	145	2008
Submarines							
Submarine – SSK	**TIKUNA** (Type 209 – modified)	1	1,600 tons	62m x 6m x 6m	Diesel-electric, 22 knots	40	2005
Submarine – SSK	**TUPI** (Type 209)	4	1,500 tons	61m x 6m x 6m	Diesel-electric, 22+ knots	30	1989
Major Amphibious Units							
Landing Ship Dock – LSD	**CEARÁ** (LSD-28)	2	12,000 tons	156m x 26m x 6m	Steam, 22 knots	345	1956

and the United Kingdom have all submitted proposals for the project, which is aimed at delivering five surface escorts, five offshore patrol vessels and a replenishment tanker from 2017 onwards. As for the submarine contract, the programme envisages substantial technological transfer to assist the expansion of the domestic shipbuilding industry. Local content for the offshore patrol vessels must be at least 60 per cent, with an indigenous share of at least 40 per cent for each frigate. However, the first vessels of each of the two principal surface classes may be built abroad.[8]

As is often the case with medium-term naval acquisition programmes, a potential stumbling-block is the availability of funding. Brazil's previously buoyant defence budget has already experienced significant short-term cuts under the new presidential administration that may impact the schedule of the PROSUB programme and recast PROSUPER in its entirety. In this environment, the United Kingdom has attempted to steal a march on the competition with an offer to transfer second-hand Batch III Type 22 frigates paid off under the Strategic Defence and Security Review reductions. As well as offering the prospect of short-term savings, this could add to the attraction of British proposals to share development of the Type 26 Global Combat Ship, which is not due for completion until early in the following decade. The deal could also encompass the *Port of Spain* class offshore patrol vessels rejected by Trinidad and Tobago, as well as the decommissioned replenishment oiler *Fort George*.

Given future acquisition decisions are largely tied to the resolution of the PROSUPER competition, there have been few material changes to current fleet composition. As such, the details set out in Table 2.1.6 are unchanged over the past twelve months. Construction of NPA-500 type patrol vessels based on the French CMN 'Vigilante 400' design continues, with second of class *Macau* delivered towards the end of November 2010. Four further units were ordered in 2009 but the navy's ambitions for more may have to wait until funding improves. The importance of riverine operations to the Brazilian Navy was emphasised by the award of a contract for four river-based 25-metre hydrographic vessels on 26 May 2011.

MAJOR SOUTH AMERICAN NAVIES – CHILE

A full review of the *Armada de Chile* is contained in Chapter 2.1A, whilst a summary of principal units is set out on Table 2.1.7. Recent efforts have been directed at repairing the significant destruction at the ASMAR yard at Talcahuano resulting from the February 2010 earthquake and tsunami. As such, the previous healthy flow of new acquisition and modernisation has slowed down. Repairs to earthquake damage are ongoing under a programme that also has one eye to a substantial upgrade in indigenous construction capabilities. The return of the fast attack craft *Chipana* to the fleet at Punta Arenas on 13 April 2011, following completion of repairs at ASMAR to significant damage sustained by the tsunami, marked a major step forward in a return to normality. New construction should resume at the yard during 2012 following financial approval for a third *Piloto Pardo* class offshore patrol vessel of the Fassmer OPV80 design.

Future acquisition plans also envisage a replacement amphibious ship for the former tank landing ship *Valdivia* – the former *San Bernardino* (LST-1189) – that was decommissioned in January 2011. A replacement is also urgently required for the Antarctic survey ship *Almirante Oscar Viel*, which is approaching retirement. Meanwhile, support assets have been bolstered by the arrival of a commercial tanker, renamed *Araucano*, to act as an auxiliary oiler. She supplements the *Almirante Montt* – formerly the *Andrew J Higgins* (T-AO-190) – acquired from the United States in 2009.

MAJOR SOUTH AMERICAN NAVIES – PERU

The principal units of the *Marina de Guerra de Perú* are set out in Table 2.1.8. There have been no material changes to force structure year-on-year. The fleet's main strength continues to be focused on its submarine flotilla, which comprises six Type 209 submarines of different variants. The submarine service reached its centennial on 19 August 2011 and a review was held in June, also involving Brazilian and US Navy boats, to celebrate the event. Mid-life upgrades for the increasingly elderly submarines are planned in due course but, for the time being, modernisation of the existing eight-strong flotilla of Italian-built *Lupo* class frigates is taking priority. Recent acquisitions have been confined to two new Griffon hovercraft delivered in 2010 for riverine operations, as well as Fokker F-60 maritime patrol aircraft and UH-3H Sea King helicopters. The proposed acquisition of two former *Newport* (LST-1179) tank landing ships was announced in 2009 but the ships had not been delivered as of mid-2011.

OTHER SOUTH AMERICAN NAVIES

Amongst the other South American fleets, the *Armada Nacional de la República de Colombia* has one of the more active investment programmes. Some of this funding is being channelled towards mid-life upgrades of existing front-line units, with both the four FS-1500 *Almirante Padilla* light frigates and the two Type 209 submarines benefiting. News reports suggest that the frigates are being fitted with new electronics from DCNS, as well as Thales' radar and fire-control systems. The

Table 2.1.7: CHILEAN NAVY: PRINCIPAL UNITS AS AT MID-2011

TYPE	CLASS	NUMBER	TONNAGE	DIMENSIONS	PROPULSION	CREW	DATE
Principal Surface Escorts							
Frigate – FFG	**ALMIRANTE WILLIAMS** (Batch II Type 22)	1	5,500 tons	148m x 14m x 5m	COGOG, 30+ knots	260	1988
Frigate – FFG	**ALMIRANTE COCHRANE** (Type 23)	3	4,800 tons	133m x 16m x 5m	CODLAG, 28 knots	185	1990
Frigate – FFG	**CAPITÁN PRAT** (L class)	2	3,800 tons	131m x 15m x 4m	COGOG, 30 knots	200	1986
Frigate – FFG	**ALMIRANTE RIVEROS** (M class)	2	3,300 tons	122m x 14m x 4m	CODOG, 30 knots	160	1992
Submarines							
Submarine – SSK	**O'HIGGINS** ('Scorpène')	2	1,700 tons	66m x 6m x 6m	Diesel-electric, 22 knots	30	2005
Submarine – SSK	**THOMSON** (Type 209)	2	1,400 tons	60m x 6m x 6m	Diesel-electric, 22 knots	35	1984

Above: One of the more interesting warships in active service is the world's last all-gun-armed cruiser, Peru's *Almirante Grau*. Laid down in the Netherlands in September 1939, she was launched by German occupation forces for possible use as a block-ship in December 1944 but subsequently commissioned into the Royal Netherlands Navy in November 1953. Transferred to Peru in 1973, she is now approaching sixty years of operational service. *(Peruvian Navy)*

Right: Peru's submarine service celebrated its 100th anniversary during 2011. This earlier, July 2010, view shows its Type 209/1200 submarine *Angamos* arriving at US Naval Station Norfolk for exercises with the US Navy. *(US Navy)*

submarines are scheduled to receive ISUS 90 combat systems from Atlas Elektronik under a modernisation programme being overseen by HDW. Another element of the modernisation is the construction of new Fassmer-designed OPV80 and

Table 2.1.8: PERUVIAN NAVY: PRINCIPAL UNITS AS AT MID-2011

TYPE	CLASS	NUMBER	TONNAGE	DIMENSIONS	PROPULSION	CREW	DATE
Principal Surface Escorts							
Cruiser – CL	**ALMIRANTE GRAU** (DE RUYTER)	1	12,200 tons	187m x 17m x 7m	Steam, 32 knots	950	1953
Frigate – FFG	**CARVAJAL** (LUPO)	8	2,500 tons	112m x 12m x 4m	CODOG, 35 knots	185	1977
Submarines							
Submarine – SSK	**ANGAMOS** (Type 209)	6[1]	1,200 tons	54m x 6m x 6m	Diesel-electric, 22 knots	30	1980

Notes:

1 Peru operates both T209/1100 and T209/1200 submarines. Details refer to the Type 209/1100 variant.

Colombia is investing significant sums in renewing its naval forces. The coastal patrol vessel *11 de Noviembre* was delivered by Germany's Fassmer in 2011 and is intended to be the first of a class built for service in the Caribbean. *(Fassmer)*

The modernisation of Venezuela's constabulary forces is drawing to a close with the delivery of 2,400-ton POVZEE type oceanic patrol vessels from Spain's Navantia. This is first of class *Guaiqueri* pictured on sea trials in Spanish waters. *(Navantia)*

CPV40 patrol vessels as part of a wholesale renewal of littoral surveillance capabilities. *20 de Julio*, the first of a planned total of five locally-built offshore patrol vessels, should be delivered around the end of 2011. Meanwhile, *11 de Noviembre*, the first CPV40 type, departed Fassmer's shipyard at Berne on 10 May 2011 for the six-week voyage to Colombia's Caribbean coast. It is likely that further vessels of this type will also be built locally under licence.[9]

Neighbouring Venezuela is close to completing naval modernisation plans. Three of the four 1,500-ton 'BVL' littoral patrol ships ordered from Spain's Navantia have now been handed over to the Venezuelan Coast Guard with the delivery of *Naiguatá* on 1 February 2011. Blocks for the fourth are also under construction in Spain prior to planned local assembly in Venezuela. Progress has also been made with the larger, 2,400-ton POVZEE type intended for oceanic operations and first of class *Guaiqueri* was handed over on 14 April 2011. A further three vessels of this type are close to completion and all should be in Venezuelan hands by the end of the year. With a length of 99m and a maximum speed of around 24 knots, these ships have a maximum range of 3,500 nautical miles (6,482km) and are suitable for a wide range of constabulary duties. Venezuela is also close to completing mid-life upgrades to its two Type 209 submarines following the return of *Sábalo* to the fleet in January 2011 on completion of extended sea trials that commenced in November 2009. Attention has now turned to finishing the modernisation of sister boat *Caribé* under a project that has involved Germany's HDW in a major sub-contracting capacity.

Notes

1. For further detail, please see *Background paper on SIPRI military expenditure data 2010* (Stockholm, SIPRI, 2011). This can be found at the Institute's website: sipri.org. The background paper is based on more detailed data and analysis published in *SIPRI Yearbook 2011* (Oxford, Oxford University Press, 2011).

2. Admiral Willard's comments to the Asia Society were commented on in detail in an article by Bill Gertz in the 18 February 2011 edition of *The Washington Times* (Washington, The Washington Times LLC, 2011).

3. A useful overview on the USN's current shipbuilding plans and the potential challenges they face is contained in Ronald O Rourke's regularly updated *Navy Force Structure and Shipbuilding Plans: Background and Issues for Congress* (Washington DC, Congressional Research Service) at opencrs.com. The Congressional Budget Office has also produced an interesting analysis of the Long-Range Shipbuilding Plan but this had not been updated to take account of the FY2012 adjustments at the time of writing. Please refer to *An Analysis of the Navy's Fiscal Year 2011 Shipbuilding Plan* (Washington DC, Congressional Budget Office, 2010) on the ww.cbo.gov website.

4. Huntington Ingalls Industries commenced operation as an independently-listed company on 31 March 2011 following Northrop Grumman's decision to divest its former shipbuilding division. Employing nearly 38,000 workers, it is the United States' largest shipbuilding group. Its main facilities are the 550-acre Newport News facility in Virginia, where 19,000 workers are employed, and the 800-acre Ingalls site at Pascagoula, Mississippi, home to some 11,000 employees.

5. Another invaluable series of reports by Ronald O Rourke, *Navy Littoral Combat Ship (LCS) Program: Background and Issues for Congress* (Washington DC, Congressional Research Service) provides a comprehensive discussion of the project's current status. The latest edition at the time of writing – dated 29 April 2011 – also provides an interesting review of US Navy ship survivability requirements in pp 14–24.

6. A more detailed report of the sea trials is contained in Sam LaGrone's '*San Antonio* sails through engine tests', *Jane's Defence Weekly* – 1 June 2011 (Coulsdon, HIS Jane's, 2011), p 8.

7. An overview of this programme is contained in Chapter 3.1.

8. The Portuguese-language *Poder Naval* website at www.naval.com.br remains an excellent source of information on Brazilian naval developments.

9. The Spanish-language *Base Naval* website at www.basenaval.com provides a broad range of press reports and other news from which some of the material used for this summary of the minor Latin American fleets has been drawn.

2.1A Fleet Review

Author:
Juan C Arancibia

CHILE Reaping the Benefits of the Copper Law

INTRODUCTION

Stretching more than 2,600 miles (4,184km) from north to south along South America's west coast but only 160 miles (257km) broad at its widest point, Chile is linked to the sea like few nations are. Little wonder then, that the Pacific Ocean has always been a critical element of Chile's defence thinking. If a study of a map doesn't make the point obvious, history certainly has. Chile's most significant war was decided largely thanks to its control of the sea. The War of the Pacific (1879–83) saw Chile fight an alliance of Peru and Bolivia over the nitrate-rich northern desert. With no roads in the region and the massive Andes Mountains to the east, it was the Pacific Ocean that became the pivotal battlefield. Chile's navy eventually defeated Peru's navy and gained control of the ocean. Once that was achieved, Chile was able to freely supply its army and wreak havoc along Peru's coastline, gaining the strategic leverage to win the war.

The consequences of the War of the Pacific dramatically changed the fortunes of the three countries involved. Bolivia became a landlocked country; Peru lost valuable territory and prestige. Chile, on the other hand, enriched itself with its vast land acquisition, which gave it a bountiful source of minerals – most notably copper. Today, Chile has become the world's largest producer of copper, which accounts for its largest export commodity. Indeed, copper is king in Chile: it is one of the country's largest industries and it provides the government with roughly one-third of its revenue each year. This copper wealth extends to the military, which for decades has enjoyed a cut of the government's copper pie. This has happened thanks to the so-called Copper Law, which mandates that 10 per cent of export sales by the state-owned copper company, Codelco, must be earmarked for weapons purchases. The law was enacted in 1958 and for most of its history has provided modest amounts. In the 1990s, the annual sum was around US$200m. That changed sharply starting in 2004. As major emerging markets such as China and India started taking off in the new millennium, demand for copper – used for plumbing, electronics and many other products – started booming. The price of copper responded accordingly, soaring from under US$1 a pound in 2001 to above U$4 in early 2011. Even after the global financial crisis of 2008 took down the price by nearly 70 per cent, copper rallied to erase the entire drop and to reach new highs.

The Chilean Navy frigate *Almirante Riveros* (the former Dutch *Tjerk Hiddes*) pictured operating in the Pacific during 2008. The Chilean military was able to use windfall funding obtained from the global boom in copper prices to renew its force of principal surface combatants from 2003 onwards. *(US Navy)*

The Copper Law, therefore, has given Chile's armed forces a huge windfall in the past decade. While the armed forces' coffers swelled, Western nations found themselves with vast amounts of surplus weapons from their Cold War build-ups, and offered them to other nations at attractive prices. This confluence of trends was ideal for Chile. In the past decade it has embarked on the largest military spending-spree the country has ever seen. The result so far has included a total renovation of Chile's surface fleet, an ongoing modernisation of naval aviation and ambitious plans for the acquisition of force projection assets.

STRATEGIC SITUATION

With a coastline stretching nearly 4,000 miles (6,435 kilometres) and a 200-mile exclusive economic zone (EEZ), Chile has about 10.4 million square miles (approximately 27 million square kilometres) of ocean under its responsibility. That corresponds to about five times more surface area than Chile's entire land mass. The Pacific provides Chile with an ample fishing industry and a range of tourist attractions. But the most critical strategic aspect is Chile's lucrative export trade, of which 80 per cent moves by ship. Therefore, one of the navy's main roles is keeping sea lanes open, with the need to keep the fisheries safe from illegal fishing, environmental dangers and other threats an important secondary responsibility. The Chilean Navy also acts as the coast guard for Chile, being responsible for the rescue of vessels in distress and for policing the shoreline.

Of course, the navy must guard territorial waters against any aggression, and the balance of power with neighbouring countries factors into the navy's structural make-up. Until the past decade, Chile's navy lagged behind the firepower of its two most likely rivals at sea: Peru and Argentina. Both had acquired modern warships, whilst Peru's potent submarine force grew to as many as twelve boats for a time. However, defence spending was cut sharply in both nations under civilian governments and as a result of economic crises. Meanwhile, Chile used the large treasury it built up after the millennium to update its fleet to the point where Chile leapfrogged both Peru and Argentina in terms of technology and firepower. Although the governments of Chile and Peru maintain cordial relations, the two have traditionally eyed each other warily. Anti-Chile sentiment still resonates in parts of Peruvian and Bolivian politics. And while Chile and its northern neighbours have been at peace since the War of the Pacific, tensions still flare up from time to time. For example, Peru has taken Chile to the International Court of Justice at The Hague over their ocean border. By contrast, Chile's relations with Argentina today are quite cosy. In 1978, the two countries stared each other down in a dispute over three small islands at the southern tip of the continent. Over time, a rapprochement developed that has blossomed into a close relationship between the two country's armed forces. Both have worked together in United Nations' missions, and have set up a joint peacekeeping force, the Southern Cross team. Thus, any conflict with Argentina is viewed as a remote possibility. Consequently, the border along the Andes is lightly defended.

Beyond regional issues, Chile has also forged international alliances to coordinate the defence of commercial sea lanes according to Daniel Prieto Vial, a leading Chilean expert on defence and foreign affairs. That, he adds, resulted in Chile leading the formation of the annual PANAMAX war games, in which forces from Chile, the United States and many other countries train to protect the Panama Canal from terrorists, drug trafficking, disasters and other threats. Chile also participates in UNITAS, a large-scale exercise with naval forces from Chile, the US, Argentina, Peru, Brazil and other nations. Chile also is a regular participant of RIMPAC, a biannual exercise with naval forces from the US, Canada, Japan,

Chile has been an active participant in international exercises designed to ensure the security of Latin America's commercial sea lanes, along which the vast bulk of its lucrative export trade moves. This image shows ships of the US, Brazilian and Chilean Navy manoeuvring in formation during the 2009 UNITAS Gold exercise. *(US Navy)*

The Chilean Navy's 'M' class multi-purpose frigate *Almirante Blanco Encalada* (the former Dutch *Abraham van der Hulst*) departing Pearl Harbor in July 2006 at the start of the Rim of the Pacific (RIMPAC) exercises. Chile is a regular participant in RIMPAC. *(US Navy)*

Singapore, Peru and other Pacific Rim countries.

Despite the improvements, some analysts question whether Chile's force structure is adequate for the tasks demanded of it. For example, Chile's eight major surface warships are too few for the country's needs, whilst the Navy sorely needs to bulk up on its amphibious forces, according to Jose Miguel Pizarro, a defence analyst who served in the Chilean Army and US Marine Corps. 'Clearly, the first step is for the Chilean navy to realize that Blue Water operations... may never happen and focus instead on meeting the Chilean armed forces' most compelling operational needs – winning the war by conducting successful amphibious operations,' he adds.

FLEET STRUCTURE AND MODERNISATION

Submarines: The first step in Chile's naval renovation occurred before the copper boom. In 1997, Chile ordered a pair of 'Scorpène' diesel-electric submarines from a joint consortium of France's

In addition to two 'Scorpène' type submarines, Chile's navy also operates a pair of older Type 209 boats constructed in Germany during the early 1980s. This photograph of *Simpson* was taken in June 2004. *(US Navy)*

Table 2.1A.1: CHILEAN NAVY FLEET COMPOSITION – MID–2011

TYPE	CLASS	NUMBER	TONNAGE	SERVICE DATE[1]	NOTES
Principal Surface Escorts					
Frigate (FFG)	**ALMIRANTE WILLIAMS** (Type 22-2)	1	5,500 tons	1988 (2003)	Former British Royal Navy SHEFFIELD. Modernised.
Frigate (FFG)	**ALMIRANTE COCHRANE** (Type 23)	3	4,800 tons	1990-97 (2005)	Acquired from the British Royal Navy. Arrived Chile 2007-08.
Frigate (FFG)	**CAPITÁN PRAT** (L Class)	2	3,800 tons	1986 (2004)	Acquired from the Netherlands. Arrived Chile 2006.
Frigate (FFG)	**ALMIRANTE RIVEROS** (M Class)	2	3,300 tons	1992-93 (2004)	Acquired from the Netherlands. Arrived Chile 2006-07.
Submarines					
Submarine (SSK)	**O'HIGGINS** ('Scorpène')	2	1,700 tons	2005-06	Newly built by DCNS and Navantia in France and Spain.
Submarine (SSK)	**THOMSON** (Type 209)	2	1,400 tons	1984	Newly built by HDW in Germany. Modernised.
Fast Attack Craft					
Fast Attack Craft (PGG)	**CASMA** (SAAR 4)	3	450 tons	1973-74 (1979-97)	Acquired from Israeli Navy. Survivors of four acquired.
Fast Attack Craft (PGG)	**RIQUELME** (Type 148)	4	250 tons	1972-75 (1997-98)	Acquired from German Navy. Survivors of six acquired.
Amphibious Ships					
Tank Landing Ship (LST)	**RANCAGUA** ('BATRAL')	2	1,400 tons	1983-85	Built at ASMAR to French BATRAL design.
Landing Ship (LSM)	**ELICURA**	2	800 tons	1964-68	Commercial design for coastal use.
Transport (AP)	**AQUILES**	1	5,000 tons	1998	Built at ASMAR. Incorporates a helicopter platform.
Minor War Vessels[2]					
Offshore Patrol Vessel (OPV)	**PILOTO PARDO** (OPV 80)	2	1,700 tons	2008-09	Fassmer OPV80 design built at ASMAR. Three more planned.
Support Ships					
Replenishment Tanker (AOR)	**ALMIRANTE MONTT** (KAISER)	1	42,000 tons	1987 (2009)	Former US Military Sealift Command tanker. Chile's largest ship
Replenishment Tanker (AOR)	**ARAUCANO**	1	12,500 tons	1984 (2010)	Former commercial tanker built in Sweden.

Notes:

1 Relates to first commissioning dates of remaining ships in class. Dates in brackets relate to acquisition by the Chilean Navy when the ship served elsewhere previously.

2 Other minor war vessels include six large and c. twenty-five smaller patrol ships, a depot ship, an ice breaker, a surveillance ship and a sail training vessel.

A Navantia-built 'Scorpène' type submarine. Chile ordered two boats of this type from the former DCNS-Navantia submarine partnership in 1997 to replace its elderly *Oberon* class. They form the core of the country's underwater forces. *(Navantia)*

The Chilean Navy entered the new millennium faced with the block obsolescence of a surface fleet comprised of British-built 'County' class destroyers and *Leander* class frigates. This picture shows the previous *Blanco Encalada* (formerly *Fife*) docked in San Francisco in October 1997. *(Marc Piché)*

DCNS (formerly DCN) and Spain's Navantia (known at the time as Bazán). The 'Scorpènes' replaced two British-made *Oberon* class submarines that were retired in 1998 and 2003. The first 'Scorpène' to join the Chilean fleet was christened *O'Higgins*. It was commissioned in 2005 and arrived in Chile around the end of the year. The second, named *Carrera*, arrived at its homeport in December 2006. The 'Scorpènes' represented a leap forward in technology for Chile's submarine force. The new submarines have a hull-mounted active/passive sonar and are armed with the Black Shark, a wire-guided torpedo fitted with an ASTRA active/passive acoustic head and a multi-target guidance and control unit that includes a countermeasures-defeating system. The 'Scorpènes' six torpedo tubes can also launch SM-39 Exocet anti-ship missiles from underwater and Chile has purchased a small quantity of these. The centrepiece of the 'Scorpènes' is the SUBTICS combat management system, composed of a command and tactical data-handling system, a weapon control system and an integrated suite of acoustic sensors with an interface to a set of air surface detection sensors and to the navigation system. The 'Scorpènes' gauge seawater density and temperature and their own noise signature. Chile also still operates a pair of older Type 209 German-built submarines that were acquired in the early 1980s. Each is equipped with eight 21in (533mm) torpedo tubes. Both have undergone upgrades and are expected to remain operational for many more years. However, it should be noted that both the 'Scorpènes' and Type 209 boats were designed largely for close-to-shore operations and therefore have more limited abilities in terms of force projection.

Surface Fleet: In the early part of the past decade, the navy's high command had an ambitious plan to build up to eight frigates based on the German MEKO A-200 design. By this time, Chile's surface fleet (mainly ex-British 'County' class destroyers and *Leander* class frigates originally built in the 1960s and early 1970s) was reaching obsolescence. By 2003, only three destroyers and three frigates remained operational. Under Plan Tridente, half the replacement ships would be built in Germany and the rest in Chile under license. But the staggeringly high cost (US$1.3bn just for four ships by some accounts) and the fact that a number of cheaper, used warships were coming onto the market forced Chile to rethink its strategy.

In 2003, Chile took the first step in its surface fleet update when it acquired a used Type 22 frigate from Britain, its long-time ally and provider of warships. The former *Sheffield*, launched in 1986, was bought for US$45m. Renamed *Almirante Williams*, the 5,500-ton ship has recently completed a refit that has included the installation of Harpoon missiles, an Oto Melara 76mm main gun and the Israel-made Barak air-defence missile system – the latter apparently recycled from a retired ship. *Almirante Williams* is also fitted with 324mm Plessey torpedo tubes.

Subsequently, in 2004, Chile agreed to purchase four used frigates from the Netherlands for US$350m. Two of these were 3,800-ton 'L' class ships – completed in 1986 and refurbished in 2000 – that were principally designed for the air defence role. They are equipped with a Mk13 launcher for up to forty Standard SM-1 long-range surface-to-air missiles and an octuple Mk29 launcher for shorter-ranged Sea Sparrow missiles in this role. Other armament includes eight Harpoon anti-ship missiles, two

Right: The modernisation of the Chilean Navy's surface forces received a major boost with the acquisition of four former Royal Netherlands Navy frigates in 2004. This included two 'M' class air-defence frigates, one of which was *Almirante Latorre* (previously *Jacob van Heemskerck*). *(US Navy)*

twin torpedo tubes and a Goalkeeper 30mm close-in weapons system. They have been named *Almirante Latorre* (formerly *Jacob van Heemskerck*) and *Capitán Prat* (ex *Witte de With*) in Chilean service. The other pair were 'M' class multi-purpose frigates. These 3,300-ton vessels also have Harpoon missiles, twin torpedo launchers and Sea Sparrow missiles but also benefit from an Oto Melara Compact 76mm gun and a hangar and flight deck for an embarked helicopter. *Almirante Riveros* was originally commissioned as the *Tjerk Hiddes* in 1992, whilst the *Almirante Blanco Encalada* was completed as the *Abraham van der Hulst* in 1993.

In 2005, the modernisation of the surface flotilla was completed when Chile purchased three Type 23 frigates from Britain, which had put a number of its warships up for sale amid a force reduction programme. The former *Norfolk*, *Grafton* and *Marlborough* were acquired for a combined total of US$348m. The three ships were completed between 1990 and 1997 and have been renamed *Almirante Cochrane*, *Almirante Lynch* and *Almirante Condell* by Chile. Each 4,800-ton ship is equipped with eight Harpoon missiles and the Sea Wolf anti-missile system, as well as a 4.5in (114mm) Mk8 main gun and two twin 324mm torpedo tubes. They can also land and support a medium-sized helicopter. With the exception of the *Almirante Williams*, the crew size for all of the newly-acquired frigates is fewer than 200, a key consideration given that the Chilean Navy wanted to reduce personnel expenses at the time of the purchases. The average age of the ships was around just fourteen years when they were purchased and the navy estimates that they will remain operational until 2026.[1]

After acquiring the submarines and frigates, the Chilean Navy turned its attention to support vessels and littoral defence ships. The navy-owned shipyard, ASMAR, got into the act with a licence to build up to five offshore patrol vessels based on the German

Renewal of Chile's surface forces was completed with the purchase of three former British Royal Navy frigates. This included the lead ship of the class, *Norfolk*, which has been named *Almirante Cochrane*. This photograph was taken whilst she was undergoing trials in British waters following refurbishment. *(Conrad Waters)*

Right: *Almirante Lynch*, the former British *Grafton*. She was one of a package of three frigates transferred to Chile for c. US$350m after the 2004 round of British defence reductions. *(BAE Systems)*

A detailed June 2008 view of the Type 23 frigate *Almirante Condell*, which started life as the British Swan Hunter-built *Marlborough* in 1991. The last ship of the class to be handed over, she arrived at Valparaiso on 21 October 2008. *(Conrad Waters)*

Chile's flotillas of second-hand fast attack craft are divided between the north and south of the country. *Orella* is one of four former German Type 148 vessels acquired in 1997 that are deployed in the north. *(US Navy)*

Fassmer OPV80 design. Two of the ships are operational; the first – *Piloto Pardo* – joined the fleet in 2008, the second – *Comandante Toro* – in 2009. The 1,700-ton ships are capable of patrolling the sprawling national territorial waters and are lightly armed with a 40mm main gun and machine guns. A landing pad and hangar make it possible to operate a light helicopter. The vessels not only conduct patrol missions but can also carry out search-and-rescue and environmental protection tasks.

The Navy's littoral combat force also counts on four ex-German 'Tiger' class missile boats, each with four MM-38 Exocet missiles and 76mm and 40mm guns. These are based in the north. In the southern Punta Arenas base, three ex-Israeli SAAR 4 type missile boats are each armed with eight Gabriel anti-ship missiles and a pair of 76mm guns. All missile boats were built in the first half of the 1970s and have undergone refits in Chile.

In 2010, Chile acquired a tanker ship from US Navy surplus to replace a 46-year-old oiler. The *Kaiser* class oiler *Andrew J Higgins* (T-AO-190), displacing 42,000 tons, became the largest ship ever in Chile's navy when she was recommissioned as *Almirante Montt*. The only icebreaker is due to be retired in four years, and a replacement is being studied.

MARINES

The Chilean Navy currently deploys its Marines in detachments in defence of key port facilities in the cities of Iquique, Concón, Talcahuano and Punta Arenas. Each detachment is kitted out with standard infantry equipment plus batteries of 105mm and 120mm artillery pieces for coastal defence. A few Excalibur systems (land-based Exocet anti-ship missiles) are also in use. An embarked battalion that includes Scorpion light tanks (for reconnaissance) makes up the rest of the force. In addition, the Marines have a Special Forces unit trained for interdiction, rescues and commando operations.

NAVAL AVIATION

Just as warships became aged and in need of replacement, Chile's naval aviation is in need of fresh wings. After studying its options (including extensive airframe repairs), the Chilean Navy decided to replace its entire fleet of Lockheed P-3ACH Orion and Embraer P-111 maritime patrol and CASA C-212 light transport aircraft with new planes. In a competition for a plane capable of conducting reconnaissance, search and anti-submarine missions, Chile

Three fast attack craft of the Israeli SAAR 4 type – *Casma* is pictured here – are maintained in the south. *(US Navy)*

A US-built P-3 Orion maritime patrol aircraft. The Chilean Navy retains three in operational service pending replacement by additional EADS C-295 Persuaders in the medium term. *(Lockheed Martin)*

selected, in 2007, the C-295 Persuader built by EADS/CASA. The C-295 is a twin-turboprop aircraft whose electronic backbone is the Fully Integrated Tactical System (FITS). The system is capable of handling patrol, attack and other roles. The Persuader has an operating endurance of eleven hours (similar to the Orion's) and can operate from short runways. Chile made an initial order for three C-295s – reportedly for US$120m, including anti-ship missiles and torpedoes – with options for five more. The first two have been delivered. The first is equipped for maritime reconnaissance and the second for anti-submarine warfare. Analyst Prieto Vial has reported that the options for the five additional planes have not yet been exercised. They were not urgently needed because the Orions remained in acceptable condition. However, emerging problems with life extensions may cause a change in approach.[2]

The helicopter fleet also is being updated, with several Eurocopter Dauphin units purchased in the second-hand market to replace BO-105 choppers. The main naval helicopter is the Cougar SH-32, also built by Eurocopter. It serves as a ship-borne helicopter, with search-and-rescue, anti-ship and anti-

The Eurocopter Cougar – also known as the SH-32 in the Chilean Navy – is the fleet's main naval helicopter and can be used in both anti-submarine and anti-surface roles. *(US Navy)*

submarine equipment, including the air-launched Exocet AM-39 missile. The electronic suite includes over-the-horizon targeting system, surface-scan radar and dipping sonar. These aircraft – about a half-dozen in service – have been upgraded with electronics, infrared vision cameras and structural improvements over the past several years.

IMPACT OF THE FEBRUARY 2010 EARTHQUAKE

Chile's armed forces form part of the country's response team in the event of earthquakes or other natural disasters. And they have had plenty of opportunities to put their skills to work. In the past four years, Chile has faced a major volcanic eruption, a sizeable earthquake in the north and a massive earthquake and tsunami in the south. The navy itself became a casualty of the most recent catastrophe, the 27 February 2010 8.8-magnitude earthquake and ensuing tsunami. The tsunami swept through the Chilean Navy's key base in Talcahuano, destroying its principal repair and construction yard. ASMAR, the navy-owned shipyard, sustained more than US$450m in damage. An oceanographic research ship that was nearly ready for launch was damaged, as were other vessels. Fortunately, the major combat ships in the submarine and surface escort flotillas escaped major damage.

El Mercurio, the Chilean broadsheet newspaper, has reported that US$200m from Copper Law funds has already been allocated towards the reconstruction of ASMAR. In April 2011, the yard awarded a U$170m contract to Dragados-COM for the first two phases of the Talcahuano reconstruction. Designs to blunt the effect of natural disasters – borrowing ideas from engineers who helped rebuild post-Katrina New Orleans – should mitigate the damage from a repeat of the 2010 disaster. In May 2011 ASMAR reached a milestone in its recovery as it delivered a fishing boat to an Iceland-based company, the first delivery since the quake. Prieto Vial, the defence analyst, believes it could take until 2013 or 2014 to complete repairs, although the work is being eyed as a launching pad for a longer-term modernisation of the facility.

The Chilean Navy also took a blow to its reputation from the 2010 quake. The agency in charge of tsunami warnings initially told the government there was no tsunami looming. It soon changed its mind, issuing an alert that came too late to save many lives. Last February, after an inquiry into the fumbled alert, the head of the Chilean Navy's Hydrographic and Oceanographic Service was dismissed.

The disaster also underscored Chile's need for more aircraft and ships, particularly those with transport and amphibious capabilities. Currently, the navy is seeking to purchase at least one multi-role amphibious vessel capable of transporting trucks, relief supplies and helicopters to a disaster zone. A ship-borne relief force makes good sense for Chile's angular geography, in which most populated areas are on or within a reasonable distance of the coast. The Chilean Navy's Commander-in-Chief, Admiral Edmundo Gonzalez Robles, has said a multi-role ship could quickly evacuate isolated areas – a job that in recent disasters required multiple missions by the navy's smaller landing ships. Of course, such a ship would also serve as an amphibious assault vessel, with the potential to project forces farther and with more muscle than currently possible. Several second-hand ships have been mentioned in press reports as possible acquisitions. Recent reports have noted that Chilean officers examined France's surplus *Foudre* LPD-type amphibious transport dock in February 2011. The 12,000-ton *Foudre* can carry a normal load of up to 470 troops or up to 2,000 people, including crew, in a disaster scenario. Its dock can transport vehicles or landing craft, and its deck can handle several medium-sized helicopters. At the same time, press reports suggest the navy is also considering buying six used Super Puma helicopters for troop transportation, as well as General Dynamics LAV III eight-wheeled armoured fighting vehicles or possibly AAV7 tracked amphibious assault vehicles. All would dramatically increase the Chilean Navy's force projection capabilities. A more capable amphibious assault ship of the LHA/LHD type akin to France's *Mistral* or Spain's *Juan Carlos I* would offer more potential – but at a higher cost.

Lack of an amphibious assault ship is certainly one of the gaps in Chile's naval force, analysts say. Prieto Vial is a long-time proponent of a ship capable of carrying some 600 troops and several helicopters. He also sees a need for a squadron of vertical-takeoff combat planes, such as Harriers, to provide air cover over a large area. Ideally, two ships of this type would prevent Chile from having all its eggs in one basket. However, he acknowledges that political considerations make it more likely that a multi-role ship for troop transport and disaster relief is the most realistic option. Pizarro, the other analyst, agrees that Chile requires 'a robust amphibious force capable of projecting a decisive force from the sea'.[3]

THE FUTURE PROCUREMENT BUDGET

The impact on the armed forces of the transition to civilian power that began with Chile's 1990 elections continues to evolve. The biggest change looming is the proposed elimination of the Copper Law, the military's multi-billion-dollar weapons acquisition

Development of a domestic warship-building industry is one of Chile's medium-term objectives. This October 2009 image shows the offshore patrol vessel, *Comandante Toro*, one of two ships constructed by the ASMAR facility at Talcahuano to the popular Fassmer OPV80 design. ASMAR was severely damaged in the February 2010 earthquake and tsunami, but the disaster has provided an opportunity to modernise the yard. *(Fassmer)*

mechanism. The law currently mandates that 10 per cent of all foreign sales by the state-owned copper company, Codelco, must be allocated to weapons purchases. Proceeds from Codelco have enabled Chile to become one of the largest buyers of military equipment in Latin America over the past decade. In 2003 the sum allocated from Codelco was US$249m; in 2004 it grew to US$598m; and by 2005 it was US$826m. In 2006, it topped the US$1bn mark for the first time, totalling US$1.31bn. It peaked at US$1.39bn in 2007. Last year, the sum amounted to US$1.27bn. Only part of the money has been spent, and much of it has gone to pay off debt. Additionally, analysts estimate US$3bn to US$4.5bn had accumulated before some US$1.2bn was used to finance post-earthquake reconstruction projects, according to the daily *El Mercurio*.

The law had its origins in 1958, after many years during which Chile neglected defence spending. The mandate has been revised from time to time. For example, in 1973 the set-aside was reduced to 10 per cent from 15 per cent and US$90m was set as an annual minimum contribution. In support of his current proposal to rid the country of the Copper Law, current Chilean President Sebastian Piñera has argued that the law has become archaic. Defence needs are not correlated to the world price of copper, and the current mechanism unfairly punishes Codelco. The copper company – a huge source of government revenue, with more than US$6bn sent to the national treasury last year alone, including defence payments – is in dire need of modernisation. However, many Chileans worry that Chile is ridding itself of an important support for its national defence at a sensitive time. For example, just as the bill for the eradication of the law headed to Chile's legislature, Peru's leftist presidential candidate Ollanta Humala, who had become popular in part for his anti-Chilean rhetoric, was elected as the ninety-fourth president of Peru.

Although the new funding mechanism still has to work itself through Chile's legislature, the broad framework involves a twelve-year master plan in which the needs of each service would be decided. The plan would be subject to revision under each four-year presidential term, with a more granular review each year. As far as money is concerned, there would be a minimum acquisition budget amounting to 70 per cent of the average sums the Copper Law provided from 2001–10, according to *El Mercurio*. That works out to about US$600m a year. Besides curtailing the amount of money spent on defence, the abandonment of the Copper Law also means a reduction in the armed forces' power over acquisitions. What was once a largely secretive process will become much more transparent, allowing civilian leaders to exercise greater authority.

Spain's new amphibious assault ship, *Juan Carlos I*, pictured off Istanbul during a marketing visit to Turkey in June 2011. Such a ship would fill a major gap in Chile's naval and amphibious capabilities but a less-sophisticated acquisition seems more likely. *(Navantia)*

CONCLUSION

Chile acted successfully to replenish its fleet between 2003 and 2005 with the assistance of Copper Law funding, providing a relatively modern core force structure which is amongst the strongest in the region. Today the navy finds itself in a different phase of modernisation. This involves a focus on its aviation arm, as well as the development of domestic warship construction. If Chile goes forward with the purchase of a multi-role amphibious warfare ship, it would give the navy a new dimension and elevate its influence as both a peacekeeping and potential war-fighting force. However, the navy, like the other branches of the military, faces a more uncertain future as the government develops a new procurement mechanism and a long-range strategy for weapons programmes in replacement of the Copper Law. With armed conflict in the region unlikely, the Chilean Navy's role will be largely defined by its domestic policing responsibilities and by its participation in peace-keeping missions overseas. Yet, the ocean is so crucial to Chile's economy and culture that the country has little choice but to maintain as strong a navy as possible.

Notes:

1. The Type 23 frigates underwent a period of modernisation after their purchase. As a result, the acquisition programme was not completed until the arrival of *Almirante Condell* in Valparaiso on 21 October 2008.

2. Chile acquired eight Orions from US surplus inventories during 1992–4. Four have been used for spares and one converted to a transport, leaving three for maritime patrol. They were modernised with AN/APS-115 radars in 2003. Recent refits undertaken by New Zealand company Safe Air were intended to keep the planes in service for some time but the first encountered more problems than anticipated. As such, the programme may be curtailed in favour of more C-295 Persuaders.

3. The need for an upgraded amphibious capability has been reinforced by the decommissioning of Chile's most important existing amphibious asset, the tank landing ship *Valdivia* on 14 January 2011. Formerly the US Navy's *Newport* (LST-1179) class *San Bernardino* (LST-1189), she was withdrawn from service when the work required in respect of a planned refit was found to be too extensive to be economic. More information is provided in José Higuera's 'Chile eyes new amphibious transport ship', *Janes's Defence Weekly* – 26 January 2011 (Couldson, HIS Jane's, 2011), p.6.

4. Printed English-language sources on the Chilean Navy are somewhat limited and the Internet offers more possibilities. The Chilean Navy publishes part of its own website in English – please refer to www.armada.cl. The author's own 'Chile's Defense & Military' blog provides regular updates on the broader Chilean military scene at chiledefense.blog-spot.com.

2.2 REGIONAL REVIEW

ASIA AND THE PACIFIC

Author:
Conrad Waters

INTRODUCTION

2011 has seen renewed focus on the ongoing build-up of Chinese naval capabilities after the brief interlude during 2010 when tensions on and around the Korean peninsula, most notably the sinking of the South Korean corvette *Cheonan*, were foremost in the news. Press attention has inevitably been heavily skewed by the obvious progress achieved with the refurbishment of the former Soviet Project 1143.5/6 *Kuznetsov*-type carrier *Varyag* at Dalian in northern China. By early 2011, the installation of electronic equipment and close-in weapons systems was quite far advanced and initial quay-side testing of generation plant was also evident. As such, it seems probable that preliminary sea trials will be underway within the next twelve months. Considerable effort is also being made to establish the extensive infrastructure required to support carrier operations. Additionally, an indigenous carrier-based fighter in the form of the Shenyang J-15 is in development. On 7 June 2011, General Chen Bingde, Chief of the General Staff of the People's Liberation Army, became the most senior Chinese official to date to confirm the obvious when he was quoted in the *Hong Kong Commercial Daily* newspaper as saying that reconstruction work on the carrier was underway.

The development of an effective carrier force and associated 'blue water' power projection capabilities is certainly a logical objective given China's reliance on extended – and potentially vulnerable – sea lines of communication for the raw materials upon which her industrial economy depends. It fits closely with some other recent Chinese maritime developments. These include the People's Liberation Army Navy's (PLAN) involvement in anti-piracy operations off the Horn of Africa, as well as its reported ambitions to obtain basing rights at the Pakistan port of Gwadar. At the same time, it seems probable that the Western media's fascination with the PLAN's development as a symbol of China's emergent 'superpower' status overlooks the more immediate aim of Chinese naval expansion, namely the ability to control the country's littoral waters of the Yellow Sea, the East China Sea and the South China Sea. In a recent well-reasoned article in *Jane's Defence Weekly*, analyst Trefor Moss argues that the development of comprehensive anti-access/area denial capabilities is currently the PLAN's paramount objective.[1] This is evidenced by the channelling of the vast bulk of the country's naval investment into the platforms – patrol submarines, fast attack craft and anti-surface oriented escorts – and equipment – sophisticated mines, anti-ship cruise missiles and surface-to-air missiles – required for this task. Certainly, it is China's increasing ability to dominate the waters around a number of disputed island and islets in this littoral zone that is of most cause for concern to neighbouring Asian countries.

The PLAN's increased capabilities are inevitably drawing a response across the region. For example, the new Japanese Mid-Term Defence Programme for 2011–15 approved on 17 December 2010 envisages a significant increase in operational submarine forces to supplement recent investment in light aircraft carriers (nominally 'helicopter-carrying destroyers') and theatre ballistic missile defence (TBMD) capable, Aegis-equipped destroyers. The regionally-deployed escort flotillas will also be re-organised to allow for more flexible and mobile operations. The focus on deploying underwater forces noted in last year's *Seaforth World Naval Review* has also continued elsewhere. For example, Thailand has confirmed it is in discussions to purchase some of the former German Type 206A submarines decommissioned in 2010. Even the cash-strapped Philippine Navy is looking at the feasibility of deploying underwater forces by 2020. However, the acquisition of additional *Hamilton* (WHEC-715) class cutters from the US Coast Guard looks a more realistic aim in the immediate term.

The response to China's emerging naval influence is inevitably tinged with ambivalence. Many of the countries that most fear the possible consequences of their neighbour's increasing military capabilities also look to China as an important trading partner. This inherent contradiction poses significant challenges to the United States, which remains the dominant power in the Asia-Pacific area and faces a difficult balancing act. Whilst the emerging 'Air-Sea Battle' concept referenced elsewhere is seen as the ultimate strategic counterweight to growing Chinese anti-access capabilities, enhanced day-to-day engagement with navies in the region is also being pursued as an important stabilising initiative. Measures to enhance the local US footprint, for example through the mooted forward deployment of Littoral Combat Ships to Singapore, can be seen in this light.

Table 2.2.1 provides a summary of the more significant regional fleets as of mid-2011.

The new Japanese 'helicopter-carrying destroyer' *Ise* (DDH-182) pictured shortly after her commissioning in March 2011. Although China's reconstruction of the former Soviet carrier *Varyag* has been the focal point of media attention, other Asian fleets are also boosting their capabilities and response. *(JMSDF)*

Table 2.2.1: FLEET STRENGTHS IN ASIA AND THE PACIFIC – LARGER NAVIES (MID-2011)

COUNTRY	AUSTRALIA	CHINA	INDONESIA	JAPAN	S KOREA	SINGAPORE	TAIWAN	THAILAND
Support/Helicopter Carrier (CVS/CVH)	–	–	–	2	–	–	–	1
Strategic Missile Submarine (SSBN)	–	3	–	–	–	–	–	–
Attack Submarine (SSN)	–	5	–	–	–	–	–	–
Patrol Submarine (SSK/SS)	6	55	2	16	12	4	4	–
Fleet Escort (DDG/FFG)	12	50	6	40	20	6	26	8
Patrol Escort/Corvette (FFG/FSG/FS)	–	45	24	6	23	6	–	11
Missile Armed Attack Craft (PGG/PTG)	–	75	7	6	5	–	c.50	6
Mine Countermeasures Vessel (MCMV)	6	20	12	30	9	4	8	6
Major Amphibious Units (LHD/LPD/LSD)	–	2	5	3	1	4	1	–

Note: Chinese numbers approximate; Taiwanese fast attack craft numbers are fluctuating as new KH-6 class replaces many of the existing 'Hai Ou' type.

MAJOR REGIONAL NAVAL POWERS – AUSTRALIA

The Royal Australian Navy is in the middle of an ambitious fleet renewal programme that will see a major uplift in capabilities from around the middle of the current decade onwards. Current fleet structure and future plans are described in detail in Chapter 2.2A, which provides a broadly positive prognosis. In the meantime, principal fleet numbers remain stable, as set out in Table 2.2.2.

The Royal Australian Navy's modernisation is not, however, proving altogether straightforward. There are particular concerns surrounding the local construction of three *Hobart* class destroyers by the Air Warfare Destroyer (AWD) alliance to the Spanish Navantia F-100 design under project SEA 4000. Each destroyer is being constructed in thirty-one prefabricated blocks in three shipyards around the country prior to final assembly by ASC in Adelaide. Problems started to emerge in October 2010 when it was reported that the central keel block for the first destroyer had been constructed to inaccurate dimensions by BAE Systems' shipyard in Melbourne.[2] At that stage, it was estimated the resulting delay to the programme would be around six months. However, it seems that the problem is greater than first estimated. A ministerial statement in May 2011 revealed that some of BAE Systems' blocks were being re-allocated to other Australian shipyards and to Navantia's facility at Ferrol in Spain to minimise delays that had escalated to at least a year. As such, the existing FFG-7 *Adelaide* class frigates are likely to have to soldier on for longer than first anticipated before their replacements arrive.

The other major challenge faced by the Royal Australian Navy is maintaining the operational availability of the six *Collins* class boats that comprise its submarine flotilla. Problems arising from maintenance issues and crew shortages have regularly featured in the Australian press for years. However, a new low was reached in June 2011 when propulsion systems problems reportedly took both operational boats – *Waller* and *Dechaineux* – temporarily out of service. *Dechaineux* – only recently returned to the fleet in May 2010 after a major overhaul – was forced to cancel its involvement in 'Five Power' defence exercises also involving Malaysia, New Zealand, Singapore and the United Kingdom, leaving a major gap in the training programme. Although the navy was quick to deny that there were no seaworthy submarines, it seems clear that the situation remains far from satisfactory. However, considerable investment is being made in upgrading the support infrastructure available to ASC – which built and now maintains the boats – and this may improve reliability as a rolling programme of refits continue.

The Australian *Collins* class submarines *Dechaineux* and *Waller* sailing in company in July 2010. With the low availability of Australia's submarine fleet drawing adverse media attention, the sight of two Australian submarines operating together could be a rare one. *(Royal Australian Navy)*

MAJOR REGIONAL NAVAL POWERS – CHINA

After a short downturn in the acquisition of new equipment over the past couple of years, the PLAN is seeing a renewed burst of procurement activity. To a large extent, this pause would seem to have been a reflection of a need to gain operational experience with many of the new classes introduced towards the end of the last decade. With this process apparently now completed, it seems that there is sufficient confidence to move forward to series production of a number of vessels. As such, Table 2.2.3 setting out principal fleet units is likely to see considerable adjustment in the next twelve months.

Table 2.2.2: ROYAL AUSTRALIAN NAVY: PRINCIPAL UNITS AS AT MID-2011

TYPE	CLASS	NUMBER	TONNAGE	DIMENSIONS	PROPULSION	CREW	DATE
Principal Surface Escorts							
Frigate – FFG	ADELAIDE (FFG-7)	4	4,200 tons	138m x 14m x 5m	COGAG, 30 knots	210	1980
Frigate – FFG	ANZAC	8	3,600 tons	118m x 15m x 4m	CODOG, 28 knots	175	1996
Submarines							
Submarine – SSK	COLLINS	6	3,400 tons	78m x 8m x 7m	Diesel-electric, 20 knots	45	1996

Table 2.2.3: PEOPLE'S LIBERATION ARMY NAVY: PRINCIPAL UNITS AS AT MID-2011

TYPE	CLASS	NUMBER	TONNAGE	DIMENSIONS	PROPULSION	CREW	DATE
Principal Surface Escorts							
Destroyer – DDG	Type 051C **SHENYANG** ('Luzhou')	2	7,100 tons	155m x 17m x 6m	Steam, 29 knots	Unknown	2006
Destroyer – DDG	Type 052C **LANZHOU** ('Luyang II')	2	6,500 tons	154m x 17m x 6m	CODOG, 28 knots	280	2004
Destroyer – DDG	Type 052B **GUANGZHOU** ('Luyang I')	2	6,000 tons	154m x 17m x 6m	CODOG, 29 knots	280	2004
Destroyer – DDG	Project 956E/EM **HANGZHOU** (Sovremenny)	4	8,000 tons	156m x 17m x 6m	Steam, 32 knots	300	1999
Destroyer – DDG	Type 051B **SHENZHEN** ('Luhai')	1	6,000 tons	154m x 16m x 6m	Steam, 31 knots	250	1998
Destroyer – DDG	Type 052 **HARBIN** ('Luhu')	2	4,800 tons	143m x 15m x 5m	CODOG, 31 knots	260	1994
Plus c. 10 additional obsolescent destroyers of Type 051 **JINAN** ('Luda') class							
Frigate – FFG	Type 054A **XUZHOU** ('Jiangkai II')	9	4,100 tons	132m x 15m x 5m	CODAD, 28 knots	190	2008
Frigate – FFG	Type 054 **MA'ANSHAN** ('Jiangkai I')	2	4,000 tons	132m x 15m x 5m	CODAD, 28 knots	190	2005
Frigate – FFG	Type 053 H2G/H3 **ANQING** ('Jiangwei I/II')	14	2,500 tons	112m x 12m x 5m	CODAD, 27 knots	170	1992
Plus c.25-30 additional obsolescent frigates of Type 053 H/H1/H1G/H2 **XIAMEN** ('Jianghu') classes							
Submarines							
Submarine – SSBN	Type 094 ('Jin')	2+	9,000 tons	133m x 11m x 8m	Nuclear, 20+ knots	Unknown	2008
Submarine – SSBN	Type 092 XIA ('Xia')	1	6,500 tons	120m x 10m x 8m	Nuclear, 22 knots	140	1987
Submarine – SSN	Type 093 ('Shang')	2+	6,000 tons	107m x 11m x 8m	Nuclear, 30 knots	100	2006
Submarine – SSN	Type 091 ('Han')	3	5,500 tons	106m x 10m x 7m	Nuclear, 25 knots	75	1974
Submarine – SSK	Type 039A/Type 041 ('Yuan')	5	2,500 tons	75m x 8m x 5m	AIP, 20+ knots	Unknown	2006
Submarine – SSK	Type 039/039G ('Song')	10-16	2,300 tons	75m x 8m x 5m	Diesel-electric, 22 knots	60	1999
Submarine – SSK	Project 877 EKM/636 ('Kilo')	12	3,000 tons	73m x 10m x 7m	Diesel-electric, 20 knots	55	1995
Plus c. 25 obsolescent patrol submarines of the Project 033 ('Romeo' Class) and Type 035 ('Ming' Class) designs.							
Major Amphibious Units							
Landing Platform Dock	Type 071 **KULUN SHAN** (Yuzhao)	2	18,000 tons	210m x 27m x 7m	CODAD, 20 knots	Unknown	2007

Reference has already been made to the considerable progress made with refurbishing the aircraft carrier *Varyag*, which may be renamed *Shi Lang* in Chinese service. Details of programme developments in respect of some of the other principal warship categories are set out below.[3]

Major Surface Combatants: It seems that there are currently two principal classes of major surface vessel under construction. The most numerous are the Type 054A 'Jiangkai II' general-purpose frigates that started to enter service with the commissioning of lead ship *Xuzhou* at the start of 2008. As of mid-2011, a total of nine were in service and another two had been launched from production lines at the China State Shipbuilding Corporatuion's Huangpu Shipyard in Guangzhou and its Hudong-Zhonghua facility in Shanghai. Displacing 4,100 tons and featuring an all-diesel CODAD power arrangement of French design, they feature a mixture of indigenous weaponry and Russian-designed sensors, as well as extensive stealth features said to originate from the *Marine Nationale's La Fayette* class. They are supplemented by the two earlier Type 054 'Jiangkai' class ships that were commissioned between 2005 and 2006. The two classes are effectively the PLAN's 'jack of all trades' and have deployed on anti-piracy missions to the Indian Ocean.

The 'higher end' of surface fleet modernisation is represented by the Type 052C 'Luyang II' destroyers. These are also known as the *Lanzhou* class after the lead ship. Two of these ships were one of three pairs of air-defence destroyers – the others being the Type 052B and Type 051C classes – delivered in rapid order between 2004 and 2006. The design has now been selected for series production. At least four further examples, quite possibly built to a modified design, were under construction as of June 2011. Featuring Aegis-like fixed phased-array panels and the indigenous HQ-9 surface-to-air missile system, they are effectively the PLAN's equivalent of the US Navy's *Arleigh Burke* (DDG-51) class, albeit somewhat smaller at around 7,000 tons full load displacement.

Submarines: Submarines have always played an important role in China's anti-access strategy and series production has also been renewed here after a brief interlude. The current main production variant is the Type 039A/Type 041 'Yuan' class of diesel-electric patrol submarine, which is reportedly AIP-equipped. The first entered service around 2006 in succession to the earlier Type 039/39G 'Song' boats and to a design influenced by the twelve 'Kilo' class submarines purchased from Russia. This initial boat was followed by a batch of three more around 2008 and has now been followed by series production. One of this new batch has already entered service and at least two more are under construction at the Wuchang Shipyard in the inland city of Wuhan. The shipyard is also building a much larger conventionally-powered submarine of a new class, the purpose of which has caused much speculation. There appears to have been less progress with either the Type 094 'Jin' class nuclear-powered strategic submarines or their Type 093 'Shang' class nuclear-powered attack counterparts following sightings of

The People's Liberation Army Navy Type 053H3 'Jiangwei II' class frigate *Mianyang* and the training ship *Zhenghe* enter Sydney Harbour on a goodwill visit in September 2010. In comparison with the large quantities of new tonnage joining the Chinese fleet, both these vessels are relatively obsolescent. *(Royal Australian Navy)*

versions of both types in the 2006–8 timeframe. This might be explained by the more complicated nature of the technology involved and the longer time needed to progress to bulk production.

Amphibious Shipping and Other Categories: A wide range of other construction is also underway, of which there is only space to cover the main highlights. The previous pattern of proving a prototype design in actual service before moving to bulk production has also been seen with amphibious shipping. Here, the initial Type 071 amphibious transport dock, reportedly named *Kulun Shan*, which was delivered in 2007, has been followed by at least two further examples. The first of these was launched in November 2010 and will enter service shortly. Further investment is being made in the acquisition of new replenishment ships, doubtless reflecting experience gained from the Indian Ocean deployments. However, in light of the focus being placed on anti-access capabilities, littoral units have not been forgotten. In addition to ongoing construction of Type 022 'Houbei' class catamaran missile fast attack craft, there have also been reports of a new Type 056 corvette that will fill the gap between the catamarans and the larger frigates. These might be similar to two 'stealth' missile boats ordered by Pakistan, although other reports suggest a larger ship is likely. A new class of mine-countermeasures vessels has also entered series production, addressing an area where the PLAN has hitherto been weak.

Away from new construction, most attention has focused on the 'Dongfeng' DF-21D anti-ship ballistic missile, which was reported as having achieved initial operating capability early in January 2011.[4] Regarded as posing a particular threat to the US Navy's carrier task groups, the new missile adds to the range of asymmetric capabilities developed to deny China's littoral waters to likely enemies, potentially overwhelming their defences with a variety of saturation attacks. Whilst it is by no means clear that China has yet overcome the challenge of tracking and targeting a moving task force with such a long-range weapon, the missile is certainly having an influence on US military thinking.

MAJOR REGIONAL NAVAL POWERS – JAPAN

Japan surrendered its status as the world's second largest economy to China during 2010. This changed economic balance is also reflected in a swing in the comparative strength of the two countries' armed forces in China's favour, albeit Japan's self-defence forces still retain a significant technological edge. The proximity of an unstable North Korea remains Japan's main concern, although how best to counter the capabilities of a growing PLAN seems to be an increasingly important consideration. The problem Japan faces is how to achieve this objective on a static defence budget, itself a reflection of the relative deterioration in Japan's overall economic strength. The National Defence Programme Guidelines for FY2011 and beyond and associated 2011–15 Japanese Mid Term Defence Programme attempts to square the circle with an increased emphasis on the modernisation and retention of existing naval equipment. However, it is uncertain how successful this approach will be in the longer term.

Japan's new five-year defence guidelines envisage maintaining a fleet of forty-eight front-line surface ships through life-extension programmes for older vessels. Here, the 25-year-old air-defence destroyer *Hatakaze* (DDG-171) is seen passing the 21-year-old general-purpose destroyer *Hamagiri* (DD-155) during exercises with the US Navy. *(US Navy)*

The new guidelines establish a projected strength of forty-eight destroyers and twenty-two submarines for the Japan Maritime Self Defence Force (JMSDF). This compares with forty-seven destroyers and sixteen submarines previously. Four of these 'destroyers' will be helicopter-carrying light aircraft carriers of the *Hyuga* and enlarged 22DDH classes. The slight increase in escort forces appears to be driven by a change in the structure of the regional escort flotillas that are deployed for local defence from five divisions of three ships to four divisions of four vessels. This is intended to make them more flexible in supporting the four eight-ship destroyer flotillas that comprise the JMSDF's principal surface strength. The difficulty is that new construction will actually fall to a total of thirteen warships over the next five years compared with fifteen vessels during the comparative previous period, with destroyer construction particularly impacted. It is envisaged that life extension of some of the existing *Asagiri* and *Hatsuyuki* class vessels will fill the gap, although the older members of the latter class are already approaching their thirtieth birthdays.

Expansion of the submarine flotillas should be an easier proposition, as the JMSDF has historically

Table 2.2.4: JAPAN MARITIME SELF-DEFENCE FORCE: PRINCIPAL UNITS AS AT MID-2011

TYPE	CLASS	NUMBER	TONNAGE	DIMENSIONS	PROPULSION	CREW	DATE
Support and Helicopter Carriers							
Helicopter Carrier – DDH	**HYUGA** (DDH-181)	2	18,000 tons	197m x 33m x 7m	COGAG, 30 knots	340	2009
Principal Surface Escorts							
Helicopter Destroyer – DDH	**SHIRANE** (DDH-143)	2	7,500 tons	159m x 18m x 5m	Steam, 32 knots	350	1980
Destroyer – DDG	**ATAGO** (DDG-177)	2	10,000 tons	165m x 21m x 6m	COGAG, 30 knots	300	2007
Destroyer – DDG	**KONGOU** (DDG-173)	4	9,500 tons	161m x 21m x 6m	COGAG, 30 knots	300	1993
Destroyer – DDG	**HATAKAZE** (DDG-171)	2	6,300 tons	150m x 16m x 5m	COGAG, 30 knots	260	1986
Destroyer – DDG	**TAKANAMI** (DD-110)	5	5,300 tons	151m x 17m x 5m	COGAG, 30 knots	175	2003
Destroyer – DDG	**MURASAME** (DD-101)	9	5,200 tons	151m x 17m x 5m	COGAG, 30 knots	165	1996
Destroyer – DDG	**ASAGIRI** (DD-151)	7 (1)	4,300 tons	137m x 15m x 5m	COGAG, 30 knots	220	1988
Destroyer – DDG	**HATSUYUKI** (DD-122)	9 (2)	3,800 tons	130m x 14m x 4m	COGOG, 30 knots	200	1982
Frigate – FFG	**ABUKUMA** (DE-229)	6	2,500 tons	109m x 13m x 4m	CODOG, 27 knots	120	1989
Submarines							
Submarine – SSK	**SORYU** (SS-501)	2	4,200 tons	84m x 9m x 8m	AIP, 20 knots+	65	2009
Submarine – SSK	**OYASHIO** (SS-590)	11	4,000 tons	82m x 9m x 8m	Diesel-electric, 20 knots+	70	1998
Submarine – SSK	**HARUSHIO** (SS-583)	2 (3)	3,300 tons	77m x 10m x 8m	Diesel-electric, 20 knots+	75	1990
Major Amphibious Units							
Landing Platform Dock – LPD	**OSUMI** (LST-4001)	3	14,000 tons	178m x 26m x 6m	Diesel, 22 knots	135	1998

Note: Figures in brackets refer to trials or training ships.

Above: The first new 19DD type destroyer *Akizuki* (DD-115) was launched in October 2010. With a full load displacement approaching 7,000 tons, she has a general-purpose orientation and is intended to supplement the Aegis-equipped destroyers in the four mobile escort flotillas. *(JMSDF)*

Above: The Japan Maritime Self Defence Force's future plans target an increase in underwater forces from sixteen to twenty-two operational submarines as part of efforts to strengthen maritime defences. The most modern will be AIP-equipped boats of the new *Soryu* class that are entering service at the rate of one every year – *Soryu* herself is seen here. *(JMSDF)*

adopted a policy of withdrawing its boats from front-line service after only around sixteen years in the fleet, far before the end of their potential lifespan. The new five-year construction plan envisages a new submarine being ordered each year so this should enable total numbers to be gradually increased. However, more submariners will need to be recruited and trained to man the enlarged fleet and these crewmembers will have to be found from a service that will see stable overall numbers. This will all take time. An increasing proportion of the submarine force will comprise the AIP-equipped *Soryu* class, in which a Kockums-developed Stirling engine is fitted. A seventh member of the class was authorised in the FY2011 defence budget at a cost of 56.4bn Japanese yen (US$700m) – she will incorporate an improved satellite communications system.

Key highlights over the past year have included delivery of the second *Hyuga* class helicopter carrier *Ise* on 16 March 2011 and the third *Soryu* class submarine, *Hakruyu*, two days previously. The first of the new 19DD type destroyers, *Akizuki* (DD-115), was launched in October 2010. With a full load displacement approaching 7,000 tons, the new design has a general-purpose orientation that includes the FCS-3A weapons system. This is built around an indigenously-developed multifunction radar reportedly derived from Thales' APAR and installed in an earlier FCS-3 variant in the *Hyuga* class. A total of four ships of the class are currently under construction, with *Akizuki* scheduled to commission in March 2012. They are intended to supplement the Aegis-equipped destroyers in the mobile escort flotillas, allowing the latter to concentrate on the TBMD role.

Effective ballistic missile defence remains a key Japanese objective in view of North Korea's nuclear weapons programme. Accordingly, the new FY2011 guidelines allow for modification of the two newest Aegis-equipped destroyers of the *Atago* class for TBMD, joining the four earlier *Kongou* class destroyers that have already been upgraded to deploy the enhanced Standard SM-3 missile. *Kirishima*, the

Left: The development of theatre ballistic missile defence (TBMD) capabilities has been a key Japanese defence objective in view of the potential threat from North Korea's nuclear weapons programme. The *Kongou* class Aegis-equipped destroyer *Kirishima* (DDG-174) is pictured firing a Standard SM-3 missile at a ballistic missile target on 29 October 2010 after completing the necessary modifications. *(US Navy)*

last of these vessels to be modernised, successfully intercepted a ballistic missile target at the American Pacific Missile Range Facility at Barking Sands, Kauai, Hawaii on 29 October 2010, thus marking the end of the earlier modification programme. Japan is holding out the possibility of acquiring additional Aegis-equipped destroyers if the international situation warrants it but these would be included within the 48-strong projected escort force.

MAJOR REGIONAL NAVAL POWERS – SOUTH KOREA

The destruction of the *Po Hang* class corvette *Cheonan* on 26 March 2010 and continued tensions with North Korea appear to be having significant ramifications for South Korean naval strategy. These were exacerbated as a result of the subsequent bombardment of Yeonpyeong Island by Northern artillery on 23 November 2010 that added a further four deaths to the lives of the forty-six sailors lost with *Cheonan*. Even before the latter incident, the Republic of Korea Navy's Chief of Naval Operations, Admiral Kim Sung-Chan, had been reported as directing a change of emphasis towards deterring North Korean operations in littoral warfare.[5] Doubtless, the most recent provocation will only have strengthened this conviction. As such, previous plans emphasising the acquisition of 'blue water' naval units such as KDX-III Aegis-equipped destroyers and LPX type *Dokdo* class amphibious assault ships are likely to be recast in favour of increased anti-submarine and anti-mine warfare capabilities.

A taste of the future was provided on 29 April 2011 when Hyundai Heavy Industries launched the first new FFX patrol frigate, *Incheon*, at its Ulsan shipyard. The prototype for a class of up to twenty vessels intended to replace the elderly *Dong Hae* and *Po Hang* corvettes and *Ulsan* class frigates, she displaces 2,300 tons in standard condition and is well-suited for littoral operations. Anti-submarine warfare equipment includes a bow-mounted sonar and provision for a future indigenous towed array, supplemented by ship mounted torpedo tubes and at least one embarked helicopter. Other weapons include a BAE Systems Mk45 5in (127mm) gun, surface-to-surface missiles and both RAM and Vulcan Phalanx close-in weapons systems. Current plans envisage entry into service at the end of 2012. Contracts with Hyundai Heavy Industries for a two further vessels have been reported. Also under construction is the 400-ton PKX type fast attack craft, being built both by Hanjin Heavy Industries and STX Shipbuilding. Five have been completed to date and a further two were launched in July 2010.

Hyundai Heavy Industries is also bringing construction of the KDX-III destroyers to a close with the launch of *Ryu Sung-ryong* on 24 March 2011. The third of three 166m long Aegis-equipped ships with a full load displacement in excess of

The Republic of Korea Navy's amphibious assault ship *Dokdo* on exercises with the US carrier *George Washington* (CVN-73). Recent developments suggest the fleet will return to a greater emphasis on littoral waters. *(US Navy)*

Table 2.2.5: REPUBLIC OF KOREA NAVY: PRINCIPAL UNITS AS AT MID-2011

TYPE	CLASS	NUMBER	TONNAGE	DIMENSIONS	PROPULSION	CREW	DATE
Principal Surface Escorts							
Destroyer – DDG	KDX-III **SEJONGDAEWANG-HAM**	2	10,000 tons	166m x 21m x 6m	COGAG, 30 knots	300	2008
Destroyer – DDG	KDX-II **CHUNGMUGONG YI SUN-SHIN**	6	5,500 tons	150m x 17m x 5m	CODOG, 30 knots	200	2003
Destroyer – DDG	KDX-I **GWANGGAETO-DAEWANG**	3	3,900 tons	135m x 14m x 4m	CODOG, 30 knots	170	1998
Frigate – FFG	**ULSAN**	9	2,300 tons	102m x 12m x 4m	CODOG, 35 knots	150	1981
Corvette – FSG	**PO HANG**	22	1,200 tons	88m x 10m x 3m	CODOG, 32 knots	95	1984
Corvette – FS	**DONG HAE**	1	1,100 tons	78m x 10m x 3m	CODOG, 32 knots	95	1982
Submarines							
Submarine – SSK	KSS-2 **SON WON-IL** (Type 214)	3	1,800 tons	65m x 6m x 6m	AIP, 20+ knots	30	2007
Submarine – SSK	KSS-1 **CHANG BOGO** (Type 209)	9	1,300 tons	56m x 6m x 6m	Diesel-electric, 22 knots	35	1993
Major Amphibious Units							
Amph. Assault Ship – LHD	LPX **DOKDO**	1	18,900 tons	200m x 32m x 7m	Diesel, 22 knots	425	2007

South Korea's Hyundai Heavy Industries had a busy start to 2011. These pictures show the launches of the third KDX-III destroyer *Ryu Sung-ryong* on 24 March 2011 followed by the launch of the first FFX patrol frigate, *Incheon*, on 29 April. *(Courtesy Hyundai Heavy Industries)*

10,000 tons, she is essentially a slightly modified and enlarged variant of the US Navy's Flight IIA *Arleigh Burke* (DDG-51) class destroyers. Recent reports suggest that they will be equipped to fire the new 'Cheon Ryong' (Sky Dragon) land attack cruise missile, which is capable of delivering a 500kg warhead to a a range of 500km and would therefore increase the vulnerability of North Korea's nuclear installations. There were embryonic plans for a smaller, follow-on KDX-IIA destroyer of similar size to the six existing KDX-II ships but these may, at best, have been postponed by the renewed emphasis on littoral operations. Meanwhile, submarine production remains focused on a second batch of the German Type 214 class prior to transition to a larger domestic design towards the end of the decade.

OTHER REGIONAL FLEETS

Brunei: The Royal Brunei Navy's fleet renewal plan is making good progress. Following the cancelled acquisition of three *Nakhoda Ragam* class corvettes from the UK's BAE Systems, Germany's Lürssen was contracted for the supply of three 80m offshore patrol vessels and four smaller 41m coastal craft. The first two of the three larger vessels – *Darussalam* and *Darulehsan* – were delivered at Bremen on 7 January 2011 and will be followed by *Darulaman* before the end of the year. They are armed with a BAE Systems Bofors 57mm/70 Mk3 gun and Exocet surface-to-surface missiles and there is also a platform for a medium-sized helicopter. Meanwhile, all four of the smaller *Itjihad* class are already in commission, having been delivered in two separate batches during 2010.

Indonesia: The Indonesian Navy continues to prioritise the development of indigenous construction capabilities as it seeks to modernise a largely obsolescent fleet. The front-line surface force remains dominated by the six former Dutch *Leander / Van Speijk* class frigates acquired in the late 1980s and which have all now passed their fortieth birthdays. They are supplemented by the four 90m 'Sigma' type *Diponegoro* class corvettes also completed in the Netherlands by the Damen group during 2007–9 and which has now been selected as the basis for future local construction. An announcement on 16 August 2010 confirmed that local shipbuilder PT PAL had been contracted to construct a larger, 105m variation of the design under a technology transfer arrangement. The new ship will be similar in size to the 2,300-ton light frigate 'Sigma' variant Damen Schelde Naval Shipbuilding are currently completing for the Royal Moroccan Navy but seems to have significant detailed differences. If all goes well, the new ship should be delivered in the 2015–16 timeframe and could be subject to series production. Meanwhile PT PAL has finished construction of *Banda Aceh*, the second domestically-produced multi-role amphibious transport dock. She was delivered on 21 March 2011 and follows the locally-built *Banjarmasin* and two sister-ships previously completed in South Korea into service.

The next priority is modernisation of the submarine service. The acquisition of new tonnage to reinforce the two current Type 209/1300 boats has been under consideration for years but a likely increase in the defence budget to c. US$7bn by 2012 on the back of an improving economy is now starting to make this a more realistic proposition. Reports suggest the current shortlist is based on the French 'Scorpène' or the German Type 209 or Type 214 designs, the last two possibly license-produced by South Korea. Published plans envisage an initial order for a pair of the new submarines to be built in the successful contractor's own facilities followed by the production of further boats at an Indonesian yard. The existing *Nanggala*, first commissioned in 1981, is currently being refurbished in South Korea by Daewoo and should return to the fleet early in 2012.

Patrol forces remain an important area of focus given the difficulties inherent in policing the vast waters of the Indonesian archipelago. Local-built construction has been slowly bringing some homogeneity to what was previously a diverse collection of second-hand vessels, albeit there is still a long way to go. A new development was the commissioning of *Clurit,* first of a new class of 44m missile-armed fast attack craft in April 2011. Built by PT Palindo Marine Batam, she is relatively simply armed with Chinese C-705 surface-to-surface missiles along with close–in weapons systems. Two further sisters are under construction and up to twenty of the class are ultimately envisaged. Indonesia's strike forces have also been reinforced by the arrival on 15 April 2011 of two *Waspada* class fast attack craft donated by Brunei.

Malaysia: The Royal Malaysian Navy has reached something of a pause in its development within the conclusion of two important programmes in the last twelve months. The most important of these has been the establishment of a small submarine flotilla. This process which was brought to a satisfactory conclusion with the arrival of *Tun Razak*, the second of two 'Scorpène' boats built by the Franco-Spanish consortium of DCNS and Navantia, in Malaysian waters on 2 July 2010. Subsequently, at the end of the year, the previously troubled acquisition of MEKO A-100 type *Kedah* class offshore patrol vessels was completed with the commissioning of the sixth and final ship, *Selangor*, on 28 December 2010.[6] The class joins the two more sophisticated *Lekiu* class frigates and the older but still effective *Kasturi* and *Laksamana* class corvettes at the core of Malaysia's surface forces.

Looking forward, the next major procurement project planned is the acquisition of six additional offshore patrol vessels for littoral protection that – as for the previous *Kedah* class – are likely to resemble light frigates in all but name. Boustead Naval Shipyard, which completed the previous programme, will be the main contractor but will probably rely on a foreign design that has yet to be selected. The projected c. US$2bn cost of the programme has already drawn criticism from Malaysian opposition politicians. Boustead are also undertaking service life extension work on the two *Kasturi* class corvettes at a further cost of US$225m following cancellation of plans to build a further batch of *Lekiu* class frigates.

New Zealand: The Royal New Zealand Navy is in a somewhat similar position to its Malaysian counterpart in experiencing a pause in procurement: in its case following the acquisition of new patrol vessels under the US$350m Project Protector. Future plans are set out in the *Defence White Paper 2010*, which was published on 2 November of that year.[7] The first

The Indonesian Navy desperately requires modern warships to bolster its front-line naval forces. The four 'Sigma' type *Diponegoro* class corvettes built in the Netherlands represent a potential means of recapitalising the fleet and licensed production of an enlarged variant in Indonesia has been agreed. *Sultan Iskandar Muda* is seen here in August 2009. *(Royal Australian Navy)*

The Royal Malaysian Navy frigate *Lekiu* operating with a *Laksamana* class corvette in August 2009. These form two of the four main types operated by Malaysia's effective surface fleet. *(Royal Australian Navy)*

The Malaysian MEKO A-100 type *Kedah* class offshore patrol vessel *Kelantan* pictured with an AgustaWestland Super Lynx helicopter embarked in January 2011. The fifth of six members of the class, she was completed by Boustead Naval Shipyard in Penang in May 2010. *(US Navy)*

The Philippine Navy is about to take delivery of the 44-year-old former US Coast Guard cutter *Hamilton* (WHEC-715) in replacement of Second World War tonnage. To be renamed *Gregorio del Pilar*, this June 2011 picture shows her alongside the new national security cutter *Waesche* (WMSL-751). *(Mrityunjoy Mazumdar)*

The frigate *Steadfast* and corvette *Vigilance* represent two of the Republic of Singapore Navy's principal surface classes. This picture dates from July 2010. *(US Navy)*

comprehensive review of defence forces for over ten years, it looks at New Zealand's strategic outlook as far ahead as 2035. In the short term, investment will be concentrated on the replacement of the fleet tanker *Endeavour* by 2013, the acquisition of a new multi-role ship to carry out the duties assigned to the existing survey and diving support vessels, and purchases of short-range maritime patrol aircraft to supplement the six longer-range P-3 Orions. Self-defence upgrades of the two *Anzac* class frigates are also planned, whilst the armament and sensors of the new patrol vessels could be upgraded. Replacement of the *Anzac* class will take place when they reach the end of their projected service lives in around 2030, most likely in conjunction with the Royal Australian Navy's eventual plans for its own successor to the class.

The Philippines: The Armed Forces of the Philippines suffer from the lowest defence budget amongst comparably-sized Asian countries, with the Philippine Navy doubly impacted by the fact that most available funding is directed towards the army for counter-insurgency operations in the south of the country. The result is a fleet that includes the world's largest collection of former Second World War vessels and one that is woefully inadequate for the task of policing the country's 7,107 islands, not to mention any need to deter external aggression. The acquisition of the 44-year-old former US Coast Guard cutter *Hamilton* (WHEC-715) therefore marks a major step forward in naval capabilities, albeit from a very low base. Purchased in March 2011 on decommissioning from US service, she has been renamed *Gregorio del Pilar* after a Filipino revolutionary general. The Philippines hopes to obtain more ships of the class as they are replaced by the new *Bertholf* (WMSL-750) cutters, thereby creating the core of a more credible fleet.

Singapore: By way of contrast, Singapore has traditionally been a high-spending country on defence. Indeed, a budget approaching US$10bn provides funding in excess of that available to the militaries of much larger neighbours such as Indonesia, Malaysia and Thailand. This has allowed the creation of a numerically small but technologically advanced surface fleet built around six *Formidable* class stealth frigates – designed in France but largely indigenously-built – and four *Endurance* class amphibious transport docks, as well as supporting missile-armed corvettes, patrol vessels and minehunters. The 6,000-ton *Endurance* class has been particularly useful supporting out-of-area missions. Individual ships have been deployed to the Gulf of Aden between April and July 2009 and between June and October 2010 to participate in Combined Task Force 151 (CTF 151) anti-piracy operations.

The main modernisation project currently underway remains the 'Northern Lights' programme. This involves the modernisation of – and installation of Stirling AIP-equipment in – two former Swedish A-17 *Västergötland* class submarines that have been renamed the *Archer* class by their new owners. The second boat, *Swordsman*, was re-launched on 20 October 2010 and delivery to Singapore is likely around the end of 2011. The new submarines will probably replace some of the quartet of older *Challenger* (former Swedish A-12 *Sjöormen*) boats purchased in the 1990s prior to the acquisition of new construction, possibly the planned Swedish A-26 class.

Taiwan: Developments in the Republic of China Navy's fleet continue to be overshadowed by the expansion of its communist rival as its relative decline continues. With the procurement of new submarines still stalled, acquisition activity remains focused on deploying the new 170-ton 'Kuang-Hua' (KH-6) fast attack craft in replacement of older vessels. Over twenty out of a planned total of thirty of the new vessels are now in service, with a second ten-strong squadron inaugurated on 7 April 2011. A further squadron will probably be stood up during 2012, leaving twenty of the older 'Hai Ou' class forming the balance of the fast attack strike force. A larger c. 500-ton stealth corvette with a more powerful missile armament is reportedly under development and construction of a prototype could start in 2012. Remaining procurement seems to be directed towards obtaining second hand tonnage from the United States to replace obsolete Second World War and 1950s construction, with mine-warfare vessels and minor amphibious ships particularly in need of renewal. An indigenous minehunter design is also under consideration.

Thailand: The Royal Thai Navy's procurement plans are dominated by its desire to create a submarine flotilla following similar moves by regional neighbours Malaysia and Vietnam. Provisional agreement has been obtained to acquire the six elderly but

Vietnam has taken delivery of two new Project 1166.1 'Gepard' class light frigates from Tatartstan's Zelenodolsk shipyard. The ships had to pass along Russia's internal waterways before commencing trials in the Baltic. *(Zelenodolsk Shipyard)*

modernised German Type 206A submarines that were decommissioned prematurely in 2010 and which therefore have several years of life remaining. It is unlikely that all six would be returned to operational status, as some would undoubtedly be kept for spares. The design would seem to be well-suited for deployment in Thailand's relatively shallow coastal waters but will likely require replacement by a more modern type within due course.

Surface procurement is focused on the acquisition of an *Endurance* class amphibious transport dock from Singapore and the local construction of both offshore and coastal patrol craft.[8] Mid-life upgrades are also being rolled out across major surface combatants, including installation of Evolved Sea Sparrow Missiles (ESSM) to the two Chinese-built Type 25T *Naresuan* class patrol frigates.

Vietnam: The Socialist Republic of Vietnam is one of the South East Asian countries most exposed to the growth of Chinese military power. Tensions in the South China Sea have been increasing in recent months, particularly around the disputed Spratly Islands. The consequence has been a steady expansion in investment in the Vietnam People's Navy, with a force previously built around Soviet-era corvettes, patrol and fast attack craft being reinforced by rather more sophisticated weaponry. In spite of discussions with other countries, Russia remains the country's preferred supplier.

The two most important acquisition programmes are for Project 1166.1 'Gepard' class frigates and Project 636 'Kilo' class patrol submarines. The former are the more advanced, with the first of an initial batch of two ships commissioned as *Dinh Tien Hoang* at Cam Ranh naval base on 5 March 2011 following sea trials in the Baltic during 2010.[9] The second ship, reportedly called *Ngo Quyen*, was handed over to the customer in late May 2011 prior to being transported to Vietnam by heavy-lift ship. A variant of the *Tatarstan* that serves as the flagship of Russia's Caspian Sea flotilla, the two ships were built at the land-locked Zelenodolsk shipyard on the Volga River under a contract reportedly valued at US$350m that was awarded in December 2006. Displacing around 2,000 tons and featuring stealth technology, a powerful armament includes a 76mm gun, KH-35E 'Uran' anti-ship missiles, the 'Osa-M' air-defence system, close-in weapons systems, anti-submarine torpedo tubes and provision for embarking and supporting a medium-sized helicopter. Two further ships could be locally built in Vietnam. The 'Kilo' class acquisition is an altogether more expensive venture, costing over US$3.2bn according to some reports. A total of six submarines are being purchased, with delivery expected from late 2012 onwards.

Notes:

1. Trefor Moss's analysis can be found in 'PLAN of Action', *Jane's Defence Weekly* – 9 February 2011 (Coulsdon, HIS Jane's, 2011), pp 42–7.

2. *The Australian* newspaper (Sydney, News Limited) has covered the problems with the AWD destroyer programme in some detail. These can be found on its website at www.theaustralian.com.au.

3. The best source of information on ongoing PLAN developments is possibly the China Air and Naval Power blog, which can be found at china-pla.blogspot.com. Dawei Xia's sinodefence.com provides a more structured overview of the Chinese military.

4. Kathrin Hille is one of a number of journalists to cover this story in 'Chinese wonder missile to test US supremacy', *Financial Times* – 19 January 2011 (London, Pearson Plc, 2011).

5. The Admiral's comments were reported by Jung Sung-ki in 'Navy to focus on littoral warfare', *The Korea Times* – 15 September 2010 (Seoul, The Korea Times Company, 2010).

6. The contract for six *Kedah* class vessels was originally signed with a consortium of German shipbuilders in the late 1990s. It envisaged the first two ships being constructed in Germany before final outfitting at the Penang Shipbuilding and Construction-Naval Dockyard (PSC-ND) in Malaysia, where the remaining four vessels would be fabricated. The local outfitting of the first ships encountered technical difficulties amidst allegations of financial irregularities, leading to a wholesale reorganisation and the acquisition of PSC-ND by the Boustead group. The first two vessels were eventually completed some eighteen months late in 2006, with the four locally built ships following at roughly six-monthly intervals between June 2009 and December 2010.

7. Please see *Defence White Paper 2010* (Wellington, New Zealand Ministry of Defence, 2010). A copy can be found at www.beehive.govt.nz/feature/defence-white-paper-2010.

8. An overview of the *Port of Spain* derivative being constructed in Bangkok to meet the offshore patrol vessel requirement is contained in Chapter 3.1.

9. A good review of the Project 1166.1 acquisition is contained in 'Vietnam commissions Gepard light frigate', Editor David Foxwell, *Warship Technology* – May 2011 (London, RINA, 2011), p 24.

2.2A Fleet Review

Author:
Ross Gillett

AUSTRALIA

The Royal Australian Navy in Transition

INTRODUCTION

The year 2012 is a vitally important twelve-month period for the Royal Australian Navy (RAN), the 'senior' member of the Australian Defence Force (ADF). Not only does the year fall between the centenaries of the granting of the Royal title to the Navy on 10 July 1911 and the arrival of the first RAN Fleet unit on 4 October 1913, it also heralds the continuing development of the 21st-century Australian fleet.

The RAN in 2012 is a five-'ocean' navy, operating in the neighbouring Pacific, Indian and Great Southern Oceans, as well as the important seas of South East Asia and the north-west Indian Ocean. Overseas, Australia and the RAN have been long-term supporters of the United Nations' and other Allied activities in the Middle East and – in particular – the Persian Gulf. Originally two (on some occasions up to three) major surface vessels, and in recent years one, have operated in the region, working closely with other Allied naval forces. At the time of writing, the RAN was maintaining its presence in the Middle East through the *Anzac* class frigate *Toowoomba*, which arrived 'on station' in mid 2011. This was the RAN's twenty-sixth such ship rotation since September 2001.

To accomplish the numerous tasks allotted to the navy by the Federal Government, the RAN currently operates a force of around fifty ships of various sizes and complexity, with a small number of older vessels held in reserve. It is a medium-sized group composed both of recent construction and modernised warships, operating thirteen classes of front line and major support ships. It is also an 'international' navy, with a fleet comprised of a variety of naval and commercial ship designs from Australian, European, Asian and US sources.

CURRENT FRIGATES AND SUBMARINES

The 'workhorses' of the Australian Navy in 2012 are its force of twelve surface escorts. These comprise the four recently-upgraded *Adelaide* (US FFG-7) class guided-missile frigates and the eight more recent *Anzac* class FFH-type helicopter-equipped vessels.

The *Anzac* class, based on the German MEKO 200 design but locally built by Tenix Defence Systems (now BAE Systems Australia) at Williamstown, Victoria, are home-ported at the Fleet Base East (FBE) in Sydney and at Fleet Base West (FBW), south of Fremantle in Western Australia. After more

The *Anzac* class frigate *Warramunga* seen in an August 2010 image. Based on a German MEKO 200 design, the class is benefiting from a progressive series of capability enhancements. *(Royal Australian Navy)*

Table 2.2A.1: ROYAL AUSTRALIAN NAVY FLEET COMPOSITION – MID-2011

TYPE	CLASS	NUMBER	TONNAGE	SERVICE DATE[1]	NOTES
Principal Surface Escorts					
Frigate (FFG)	ADELAIDE (FFG-7)	4	4,200 tons	1983-93	Two sister-ships disposed of. Reminder upgraded to serve until 2015-19.
Frigate (FFG)	ANZAC	8	3,600 tons	1996-2006	RAN designation FFH. Two sister-ships in Royal New Zealand Navy.
Submarines					
Submarine (SSK)	COLLINS	6	3,400 tons	1996-2003	RAN designation SSG. Equipped with Sub Harpoon anti-surface missiles.
Amphibious Ships					
Landing Ship Dock (LSD-A)	LARGS BAY	1	16,200 tons	2006 (2011)	In course of transfer from the United Kingdom.
Amphibious Transport (LPA)	KANIMBLA (LST-1179)	1	8,500 tons	1971 (1994)	Sister MANOORA withdrawn 2011. May be replaced by LARGS BAY.
Logistic Landing Ship (LSL)	TOBRUK	1	5,800 tons	1981	RAN designation LSH. May be replaced by LARGS BAY.
Landing Craft Heavy (LCH)	BALIKPAPAN	6	500 tons	1971(73)-74	Some recently laid up in reserve for a period.
Minor War Vessels					
Minehunter (MCMV)	HUON	6	700 tons	1999-2003	RAN designation MCH. Some temporarily in reserve.
Patrol Ships (PB)	ARMIDALE	14	300 tons	2005-08	RAN designation ACPB.
Survey Ship (AGS)	LEEUWIN	2	2,600 tons	2000	Also employed as patrol vessels.
Survey Ship (AGSC)	PALUMA	4	300 tons	1989-90	Catamaran design. Also employed as patrol vessels.
Support Ships					
Replenishment Tanker (AOR)	SUCCESS (DURANCE)	1	18,000 tons	1986	Locally–built version of French DURANCE class.
Replenishment Tanker (AOR)	SIRIUS	1	25,000 tons	1996	Converted double-hulled commercial tanker.

Notes:
1 Relates to first commissioning dates of remaining ships in class. Dates in brackets relate to entry into RAN service when the ship served elsewhere previously.

than fifteen years since the commissioning of the lead ship, *Anzac*, in May 1996, a progressive series of modifications and upgrades is underway that will see these frigates emerge as a new generation of fighting ship. Improvements that include the installation of Evolved Sea Sparrow surface-to-air missiles (ESSM), launchers for Harpoon anti-ship missiles, additional close-range guns for self-defence and a new set of electronics and combat systems will ensure the effectiveness of these ships until their replacements begin to arrive in the late 2020s.

The most significant element of this ongoing modernisation programme is probably the Anti-Ship Missile Defence (ASMD) upgrade being undertaken under Projects SEA 1448 Phases 2A and 2B.[1] In late 2010, the youngest of the *Anzac* class FFHs, *Perth*,

The *Anzac* class frigate *Ballarat* pictured in company with the *Adelaide* (US FFG-7) class frigate *Sydney* in the North Atlantic whilst participating in the Northern Trident deployment. In addition to significant commitments in Australia's neighbouring oceans, the Royal Australian Navy frequently deploys further afield. *(US Navy)*

emerged from this upgrade to her weapons and combat systems. It included installation of the Australian-designed and built CEAFAR active phased-array radar, associated CEAMOUNT illuminators, Infra-Red Search and Track (IRST) systems and an updated combat management system and operations room. To accommodate these new systems, the profile of the ship, inside and out, was changed dramatically. The modernised ship commenced sea trials on 21 February 2011 and a decision will be taken in mid-2011 to extend the upgrade to the rest of the class if these prove successful.

Following an upgrade to four of the original six older *Adelaide* class frigates between September 2003 (*Sydney*) and late 2009 (*Newcastle*) under Project SEA1390, the class can now lay claim as the 'best re-armed' and 'best equipped' *Oliver Hazard Perry* (FFG-7) class guided-missile frigates in service in any of the nine navies that operate the type. Originally conceived as patrol frigates for the USN, they were built as low cost/large scale construction ships. The four remaining Australian vessels have been significantly modified to operate as effective fleet units until the arrival of the trio of more-capable *Hobart* class destroyers. Improvements include new surveillance, fire control and sonar systems, installation of an eight-cell Mk41 vertical launch system for ESSM and upgrade of the existing Mk31 launcher to allow use of the Standard SM-2 surface-to-air missile.

The surface escorts are supplemented by the *Collins* class of six guided-missile submarines (SSGs). Like several other recent warship designs, they have suffered a number of setbacks since their introduction into service. But despite these challenges, the navy has stood by its Australian-built boats and, with the decision to fit new American sourced BYG-1 combat systems in September 2002, the days of the original unreliable combat suites were numbered. *Waller*, in May 2008, became the first of the six boats to receive the new equipment. In mid-2011 three of the class were active. Coupled with a new drive to recruit additional submariners to crew the force, the *Collins* class submarines are capable of providing a

Four of the Royal Australian Navy's original six *Adelaide* (US FFG-7) class frigates have undergone a significant upgrade to improve fleet anti-submarine and anti-air capabilities prior to arrival of the new *Hobart* class destroyers. This 2008 image shows *Newcastle* shortly after modernisation, which included the installation of an eight-cell vertical launch system for ESSM on the forecastle. *(Royal Australian Navy)*

The four *Adelaide* (US FFG-7) and eight *Anzac* type class frigates form the core of the Royal Australian Navy's surface fleet. This early 2010 image shows two Australian *Adelaide* class vessels on exercise with neighbouring New Zealand's *Te Mana*, one of two additional *Anzac* type ships purchased by the Royal New Zealand Navy. *(Royal Australian Navy)*

very effective and stealthy force for current and future RAN operations and exercises. The submarine arm is a very important Force Element Group (FEG) within the Australian Fleet and will continue to be so, as plans are put into motion to design, build locally and then introduce into service a new generation of submarines from the mid-2020s.[2]

CURRENT AMPHIBIOUS SHIPS

Until recently, the core amphibious units in the RAN were the landing platform amphibious (LPA) type transports *Kanimbla* and *Manoora.* Despite initial criticism of their purchase, these two former USN tank landing ships have provided valuable service to the RAN. Now both forty years old, the ships remained effective in their roles until September/ October 2010, when onboard problems necessitated urgent repairs be considered. The two ships, members of the original twenty-strong *Newport* (LST-1179) class, were the most modified from the original American design. Ten sister-ships also served with seven other navies across the globe including Brazil, Chile, Malaysia, Mexico, Morocco, Spain and Taiwan. In modern terms, the two RAN units could not be classified as large amphibious ships; medium-size would be more appropriate. However, they and the heavy landing ship (LSH) *Tobruk* were the only defence assets that could carry substantial loads of Army and other ADF equipment over long distances and within the times required.

In early February 2011, the Minister for Defence announced that *Manoora* would be decommissioned in May 2011. She had been placed on operational pause by the Seaworthiness Board the previous September. A detailed examination revealed that she required remediation of significant hull corrosion and the replacement of both gearboxes. It was estimated this work would have cost over AU$20m (US$22m) and taken until April 2012 to complete. It was quickly and sensibly decided that refitting was not value for money given final decommissioning was scheduled by 2013 in any event. However, with *Kanimbla* due to be docked for repairs for at least eighteen months until mid-2012, a search was undertaken for an immediate replacement for both ships.

Also operating as major elements of the amphibious force are the thirty-year-old *Tobruk* and the equally hard-working *Balikpapan* class heavy landing craft (LCHs), the latter soon completing their fourth decade of service. Both types have provided staunch and valuable service to the RAN. Working

Two images of the modernised *Anzac* class frigate *Perth* on trials during March 2011 incorporating Anti-Ship Missile Defence (ASMD) programme upgrades. Prominent is the new mainmast for CEA Technologies new six-faced CEAFAR E/F (US S-band) active phased-array radar. The CEAMOUNT I/J (US X-band) illuminators for ESSM guidance can also be seen in the close-up image. *(CEA Technologies)*

together, these two types of vessels have enabled the RAN to provide excellent support to other ADF units, and have become the modern-day equivalents of the old Second World War corvettes, the 'maids of all work'. However, the careers of all seven vessels are also fast approaching an end, with *Tobruk* due to be decommissioned in late 2012 and a new class of larger heavy landing craft expected to be ordered for entry into service at the start of the next decade.

Future plans envisaged that the replacement for *Tobruk* would be a strategic sealift ship that could augment the two large amphibious assault ships (LHDs) being built as LPA replacements. The new ship could be provided by new construction or the transfer of an existing unit from an Allied navy. One such vessel, a 'Bay' class LSD(A) operated by the British Royal Fleet Auxiliary (RFA), was paid off in April 2011 as a result of the defence budget cuts implemented by the UK Government's October 2010 Strategic Defence and Security Review (SDSR). Ironically, *Tobruk*'s five older RFA sister-ships were replaced by the four-strong 'Bay' class. Her availability made it possible to consider her acquisition as both a short-term replacement for the LPAs and a potential longer-term candidate for the strategic sealift ship, thereby satisfying the two main requirements of the amphibious force.

Australian Navy officials travelled to Britain in December 2010 to inspect *Largs Bay* and ministerial confirmation that her acquisition was being considered followed shortly afterwards. On 6 April, it was formally announced that the decommissioned *Largs Bay* would be transferred to the RAN for a purchase price of AU$100m (US$110m), the six-year-old ship being seen as now meeting the strategic sealift ship requirement as the ultimate replacement for *Tobruk*, as well as facilitating the transition to the new amphibious force structure. At the time of writing *Kanimbla* is still in refit but to what level this is completed is still unknown. The Antarctic support ship *Aurora Australis* is to be leased for five months as an interim measure during 2011 to maintain a basic amphibious capability whilst *Tobruk* undergoes maintenance and before *Largs Bay* arrives.

CURRENT MINOR WAR VESSELS

Another important member of the RAN is the FEG based around the six *Huon* class minehunters (designated MHC). Having proved themselves in the mine warfare role, a number of the class have also undertaken patrol boat duties. The vessels have now been in use for a period of eight to twelve years and are likely to remain as the RAN's main anti-mine assets for many years into the future. However to secure personnel for new construction now being built, some of the class were 'cocooned' in 2010. The two auxiliary minesweepers, *Bandicoot* and *Wallaroo*,

The LPA type amphibious transport *Kanimbla* pictured whilst on exercise with the US Marine Corps off the Hawaiian island of Oahu in July 2010 as part of RIMPAC 2010. The ship was declared unseaworthy shortly afterwards and is currently under repair. *(Royal Australian Navy)*

The six *Balikpapan* class heavy landing craft are the 'maids of all work' of the Royal Australian Navy's amphibious forces but will soon have completed forty years of service. Replacements are envisaged under Phase 5 of Joint Project 2048 but it is likely to be over ten years before these enter service. *(Chris Sattler)*

The *Huon* class minehunter *Diamantina*. Based on the Italian *Gaeta* class, some of the six *Huons* have also been earmarked for patrol duties from time to time. *(Royal Australian Navy)*

were also laid up at forty days notice. However, in April of 2011, *Wallaroo* was again seen underway.

The replacements for the east coast tugs (auxiliary minesweepers) *Bandicoot* and *Wallaroo* is covered by Project SEA 1351. This will ensure that tug services are still available to support the visits of nuclear powered warships in designated Australian ports throughout the duration of such visits. These tugs will need to be available to move such ships at short notice. The project is focused on the provision of tug services, rather than the acquisition of such vessels. Initial operating capability (IOC) is planned for 2012–14.

In 2011–12 the RAN possesses – in its fourteen *Armidale* class patrol vessels – its most effective force of patrol boats since its creation 100 years ago. In the sixty-six years since the end of the Second World War, the size and complexity of the patrol boats has grown considerably; their armaments increased in firepower, onboard living conditions vastly improved, endurance stretched and their manning made more efficient, with multiple crews to allow for longer deployments, coupled with fewer hours dedicated to maintenance. Unlike the older-generation patrol boats (with their open manned 40mm Bofors), the new style *Armidales* are equipped with a Rafael Typhoon stabilised 25mm gun mount that is fitted with an M242 Bushmaster cannon firing an impressive 200 rounds per minute. This weapon is controlled from the bridge for safety from local retaliatory fire and for protection from harsh weather conditions.

A significant feature of present-day RAN operations has been the employment of additional units as (auxiliary) patrol vessels. In recent times, this has included the two *Leeuwin* and four *Paluma* class hydrographic ships, along with two *Huon* class minehunters, *Huon* and *Hawkesbury*. This move has therefore seen the force of fourteen *Armidale* class boats augmented by as many as eight additional boats for patrolling duties, a 50+ per cent increase in available hulls for such tasks.

The growth in the number of available patrol craft in the past few years has been warranted, especially, by the arrival of dozens of illegal refugee boats onto the north-west coast of Australia and nearby offshore islands. In this regard, RAN patrol boats operate in close liaison with other units of Border Protection Command, including the larger patrol vessels *Ocean Protector* (in service since 2010), the *Ashmore Guardian* (since 2004) and the *Triton* (since 2006), as well as the eight smaller *Bay* class patrol boats active from 1999.[3] All are manned by personnel from Australian Customs. The *Bay* class are planned for replacement from 2013–15 by eight new *Cape* class. The three leased Customs craft, *Ocean Protector*, *Triton* and *Ashmore Guardian*, have in recent times become the important stop-gap patrol vessels and have been retained longer than originally planned.

CURRENT MAJOR SUPPORT SHIPS

The RAN must be capable of supporting itself on both independent and coalition operations. In the current climate of tensions in the Middle East and occasional disturbances in the Pacific theatre and South East Asia, the Navy is maintained at sea through the services of the two principal support ships, *Success* and *Sirius*. These two effective ships ensure an Australian task force can remain self-sufficient, acting as major force multipliers to the overall fleet effort.

With twenty-six years afloat, *Success* is the oldest of the pair. A variant of the French *Durance* design, she was built between 1980 and 1986 at Sydney's former Cockatoo Island Dockyard. Despite her many years of service, she continues to replenish the other ships in both a timely and efficient manner. A new tanker is planned to replace the veteran *Success*, but is not expected to enter service until later this decade. In 2010, to ensure her continuing service, it was decided to refit the ship with a double hull to meet International Maritime Organisation standards for environmental protection against oil spills. This work was performed in Singapore during a regular deployment to the region.

The newer *Sirius* was acquired from South Korea in 2004 (as a replacement for the older *Westralia*), having been laid down as a commercial tanker. After a suitable refit to raise her to naval standards, she now performs similar duties to her purpose-built running mate, but operating from Fleet Base West.

THE WAY AHEAD

For 2012 and the years thereafter, the planned future of the RAN was set out in the 2009 Defence White Paper and associated Defence Capability Plan (DCP). The latter was last updated during December

The Royal Australian Navy maintains two replenishment tankers to support deployments relating to both national and coalition operations. This is the *Sirius*, which was built in South Korea to commercial standards before undertaking conversion to a military role in Australia. *(Royal Australian Navy)*

2010.[4] As part of this very detailed overall plan for the ADF, the RAN has been allotted the resources to acquire and in some cases, build locally, a new force of surface and sub-surface combatants. This overall plan for the ADF will witness a dramatic and positive influence upon the navy, supplementing the three new air-warfare destroyers (AWDs) and two landing helicopter dock (LHD) type amphibious assault ships that are already under construction with additional vessels. Foremost amongst these ships will be a future submarine class – with potentially as many as twelve new boats – and twenty large (corvette-size) offshore combatant vessels (OCVs). The latter will undertake a variety of roles when they begin to replace the existing six *Huon* class minehunters, fourteen *Armidale* class patrol boats and the six hydrographic vessels. The amphibious sphere of operations will also receive an additional boost through the order for up to twelve LCM1E equivalent landing craft (for use with the LHDs *Canberra* and *Adelaide*), the April 2011 decision to acquire the former RFA *Largs Bay* and the eventual acquisition of six new design heavy landing craft (LCH) replacements.

Both sides of the Federal Parliament, the Government and Opposition, are strong supporters of the overall defence effort, and in particular, a viable Australian fleet. They both advocate construction of the new warship classes in local yards, including the very sophisticated *Hobart* class AWDs at Port Adelaide in South Australia and the new submarine class, at the same location. Although the two *Canberra* class LHDs are being built in Spain, their fitting–out is to be undertaken at Williamstown in the southern state of Victoria. In addition, many sections of the *Hobart* class AWDs are being built in Newcastle, New South Wales, and Williamstown, Victoria.[5]

FUTURE DESTROYERS (PROJECT SEA 4000)

The three *Hobart* class air-warfare destroyers will be the largest destroyers ever to serve in the RAN. Ordered in 2007, these very effective Spanish-designed warships are slightly modified variants of the F-100 *Álvaro de Bazán* air-defence frigates. They will no doubt quickly establish themselves as the modern front-line fighting ships of the Australian fleet. With a displacement of over 6,000 tonnes and equipped with the Aegis combat system and its associated AN/SPY-1D phased arrays, the AWDs will ensure a proper and effective level of offensive and defensive capability is maintained in the future fleet, including their role as escorts for the pair of *Canberra* class amphibious warfare ships. The *Hobart* class has been designed with sufficient space and weight margin for future upgrades to both armament and sensors, with all three expected to remain at the forefront of naval technology for decades ahead.

Table 2.2A.2: ROYAL AUSTRALIAN NAVY – MAIN FUTURE PROCUREMENT PROJECTS

PROJECT NUMBER	PROPOSED CAPABILITY (UNITS)	INITIAL APPROVAL[1]	YEAR-OF-DECISION	IOC[2]	COST
SEA 1000 (Phases 1-4)	Future Submarine (12)	2011-12 (Phase 1 – design)	2014-20 (Phase 1 – design)	TBA	>A$12.5bn
SEA 1180	Offshore Combatant Vessel (20)	2015-18	2017-20	2021-24	<A$0.1bn
SEA 1531 (Phase 1)	East Coast Tugs (2)	2011-13	2011-13	2012-15	A$3.0-5.0bn
SEA 1654 (Phase 3)	Replenishment Tanker (1)	2013-15	2016-18	2021-23	A$0.5bn-A$1.0bn
SEA 5000 (Phase 1)	Future Surface Combatant (8)	2018-21	2021-24	2027-30	>A$10.0bn
JP 2048 (Phase 3)	Amphibious Watercraft (12)	Completed	2011-13	2014-16	A$0.3-0.5bn
JP 2048 (Phase 5)	Heavy Landing Craft (6)	2013-15	2016-19	2022-24	A$0.1bn-0.3bn
AIR 9000 (Phase 8)	Sea Control Helicopters (24)	Completed	2010-12	2014-17	A$3.0bn-A$5.0bn

Notes:

1 First Pass Approval in Australian terminology. 2 Initial Operational Capability.

The most expensive Australian naval project currently underway is the acquisition of three new *Hobart* class destroyers, for which a reported A$8bn (US$8.8bn) contract was signed in 2007. These are early images of the new class, which is a slightly modified version of the Spanish F-100 air-defence frigate. *(AWD Alliance)*

After commissioning from 2015 onwards, each *Hobart* class ship will be available to represent the navy and the nation, in conjunction with United Nations and other allied naval forces, when and where required. They will be tomorrow's replacements for the now long retired *Perth* class guided-missile destroyers (1960s–1990s) and the smaller *Adelaide* class guided-missile frigates (1980s–2010s). However, their technology is far ahead of the current generation of warships and will provide a significant uplift in capability with the Australian fleet.

The first major upgrade for the class has already been set out in Phase 4 of Sea Project 4000, which is set to provide for the acquisition of a cruise-missile capability for the ships. This will give the government additional options to conduct long-range precision strike operations against hardened, defended and difficult access targets, while minimising the exposure of naval platforms and their personnel to attack. A decision on the cruise missiles will be taken during 2019–22, with IOC expected from 2022–5. It is possible the government will consider if this strike weapon should be advanced closer to the actual commissioning dates for the destroyers, although budgetary constraints and the development of the required support infrastructure may weigh against such an earlier decision. All AWDs are also expected to be eventually fitted with the Standard SM-6 long-range surface-to-air missile in another project for an extended-range air defence

A mock-up of a *Hobart* class destroyer in Australian service, probably derived from an image of a Spanish F-100 class ship. The three destroyers will be equipped with the Aegis weapon system and associated AN/SPY-1D fixed arrays, which are prominent in this image. *(AWD Alliance)*

It appears the purchase of a fourth AWD is not being pursued by the government. However, such an addition to the force of surface combatants would greatly enhance the fleet's overall operational capabilities. It would also provide extra time before the replacement of the *Anzac* class would need to be considered.

FUTURE FRIGATES (PROJECT SEA 5000)

The Defence White Paper (and its updates) indicated that a separate Next Generation Combatant, Sea Project 5000, comprising eight new and affordable future frigates would be procured. Larger than the *Anzac* class, the new frigates will be equipped with a strong emphasis on the anti-submarine warfare (ASW) role. The new vessels will therefore feature an integrated sonar suite with a long-range active towed array, as well as the ability to embark and support a combination of naval helicopters and maritime unmanned aerial vehicles. The incorporation of a land-attack cruise missile capability will be integral to the design and construction of the chosen frigate type and may, indeed, see this new class classified as more multi-purpose rather than ASW-focused.

Initial operational capability for the first of the future frigates is expected from 2027, when the ages of the *Anzacs* will vary from twenty-one to thirty-one years. Current designs that may be considered include frigates based upon the Franco-Italian FREMM programme or the Royal Navy's new Type 26 class.

The lead ship of Australia's existing six *Collins* class patrol submarines pictured in late 2010. Built to a Swedish design in Australia, they have suffered from poor reliability. A major combat systems upgrade should alleviate many of the remaining problems but – in the medium term – they will be replaced by a more numerous class of larger boats. *(Chris Sattler)*

FUTURE SUBMARINES (PROJECT SEA 1000)

Known as Sea Project 1000 - Future Submarine, the RAN's planned new underwater capability arose from work carried out in advance of the 2009 White Paper to identify and quantify the maritime capability developments that would be required to meet future government expectations. The project aims to provide the RAN with a modern and more potent defence capability available within a larger submarine and able to achieve a greater range, longer patrol endurance and an increased capability than with the existing *Collins* class boats. Key role requirements for the new class will include anti-submarine warfare; anti-surface warfare; strike; intelligence, surveillance and reconnaissance; electronic warfare; mine warfare and the support of both Special Forces and advance force operations. This represents a very large task sheet for any warship!

The cost of this project is considered very high, with many already asking if the planned total of twelve new boats is, in fact, a realistic proposition.

Phase 1 of the project – the design element – should begin from late 2011 onwards, with a final year-of-decision on Phase 2 – acquisition – to be made sometime between 2014 and 2019. A later phase will seek to provide a reserve stockholding of the selected weapons for the future submarine fleet, plus the weapons required for test and evaluation, training and tactical development. Beyond this decision, an underwater strategic strike weapon is planned via the acquisition of maritime-based land-attack cruise missiles, weapon control and mission planning sub-systems for the boats. However, this phase is not expected to be achieved before 2025.

It is highly likely that a totally new design may be selected for the new submarine class, with all current European and Asian conventionally-powered boats considered too small for the level of operations required by the RAN. An enlarged *Collins* class is also believed to have been ruled out of contention, whilst nuclear propulsion is not envisaged. The current capability plan for the new submarines is designed to allow at least eight of the new class to be operational at any one time. Given the demise of the Air Force's force of F-111 swing-wing bombers in late 2010, the future fleet of submarines, supported by RAN surface units, will provide the long-range strategic strike capability of the ADF.

FUTURE AMPHIBIOUS ASSAULT SHIPS (PROJECT JP 2048 –PHASE 4A/B)

One of the most significant decisions made by the Federal Government during the past decade was the 2007 order for two large, highly capable and multi-tasked LHD (landing helicopter dock) type amphibious assault ships. The order had been heralded in Australia's 2000 Defence White Paper and subsequently confirmed in the 2006–16 DCP. As for the *Hobart* class destroyers, they are based on a design by Spanish shipbuilders Navantia, in this case the strategic projection ship *Juan Carlos I*.[6] With their delivery planned for 2014–15, the arrival of the new *Canberra* and *Adelaide* will produce a dramatic and positive leap forward in the overall capabilities of the RAN.

The new amphibious ships will give the RAN the ability to project power ashore throughout the

Two pictures of the first *Canberra* class amphibious assault ship (LHD) prior to and during launch at Navantia's Ferrol shipyard in Northern Spain in February 2011. Sisters of Spain's strategic projection ship *Juan Carlos I*, the two ships will be transported to Australia for the addition of their island superstructure and other fitting out at BAE Systems Australia's Williamstown yard. *(Royal Australian Navy)*

Australasian region. They have the ability to transport a military force of nearly 1,000 troops over a considerable distance and then deploy and support it through embarked helicopters and landing craft. However, *Canberra* and *Adelaide* will be very flexible fleet units that should not be seen simply as platforms to move ADF troops. Another possible use is the conduct of humanitarian missions, not just in the environs of continental Australia but also across the Pacific and into South East Asia. They also offer the potential for supporting a wide range of naval aviation operations

If the sensible decision is made at a later date to purchase a small force of the F-35B STOVL (short take off and vertical landing) variant of the Lightning II Joint Strike Fighter (JSF), these would further enhance the ships' capabilities.[7] Embarking a number of these F-35Bs, whether operated by the RAN or Royal Australian Air Force (RAAF), would particularly increase each ship's effectiveness in projecting power ashore. The Spanish Navy will demonstrate this possibility – initially with the AV-8B Harrier – on board the lead ship of the type, *Juan Carlos I*. Although the two *Canberra* class ships will not – at least initially – embark fixed-wing aircraft, they retain the ski-jump fitted to the Spanish ship.

Despite what many uninformed critics may have previously claimed, the size of a warship does matter. These large warships – displacement is over 27,000 tons in full load condition – will create an aura of power and strength, even more so when attack helicopters or the larger CH-47F Chinooks complement the normally embarked squadrons of Australian Army/RAN MRH90, RAN S-70B-2 Seahawks and – in the future – the planned new fleet of sea control helicopters.

From a local public and media perspective the new *Canberra* class amphibious assault ships are a public relations and recruitment officer's dream. Big impressive ships attract the crowds, ensure media coverage and will accordingly raise the profile of the 'senior service'. The arrival and departure of the ships will be news. Flying and amphibious operations will generate greater interest, providing numerous highlights during the overall naval year.

The two *Canberra* class vessels will each be capable of transporting a force of four mechanised landing craft to enable the transfer of vehicles, troops and other equipment from the ship to shore. These will be integral to the ships' equipment and will operate from the internal docks. Each will also be able to operate in a much wider range of weather conditions, at a higher 20-knot speed and with heavier loads than the older Army LCM 8s that were carried by *Kanimbla* and *Manoora*. The Spanish LCM1-1E design used by *Juan Carlos I* is the front runner for selection under Project JP 2048, Phase 3. The expected service life for each LCM1-E is said to be twenty years.

Phase 5 of Joint Project 2048 for Amphibious Deployment and Sustainment (ADAS), is the plan to acquire six new heavy landing craft with improved speed and sea-keeping capabilities, able to transport armoured vehicles, trucks, stores and personnel, and then land them over the shore. The new craft will also allow a capability to conduct independent small-scale regional amphibious operations, as well as supporting the larger LHDs as part of an amphibious task group. The life-of-type for these new landing craft will also be twenty years.

A decision on the replacement for the forty-year-old *Balikpapan* class LCHs is expected to be made during 2016–18, with entry into service from between 2022 and 2024. However, this programme could be moved to the left to ensure a more timely replacement is available and market proposals have already been solicited. Some of the LCHs have already spent temporary periods in reserve at Cairns and Darwin. The real question is whether they can last until 2022 or whether the navy can forgo this medium-level amphibious capability for those years.

FUTURE OFFSHORE DUTIES (PROJECT SEA 1180)

Despite their relative youth, a replacement for the current minehunters and patrol vessels is on the horizon, with a new-style vessel planned to supersede the *Huons*, plus the fourteen *Armidales* and two classes of hydrographic vessels, six in all. Known as Sea Project 1180, the Patrol Boat, Mine Hunter Coastal and Hydrographic Ship Replacement Project will seek to rationalise these three force elements, potentially into a single modular multi-role class or family of around twenty Offshore Combatant Vessels (OCVs) combining the four existing sets of roles.

The new vessels are likely to be larger (some say up to 2,000 tons) than the current *Armidale* class patrol boats, relying on the use of modular unmanned underwater systems for both mine countermeasures and hydrographic tasks and capable of being deployed independently to any operational area. Whether this is the correct size for this new class is an open question. Some reports have claimed that replacing a small *Armidale* with a large corvette-sized OCV may result in a ship that is too capable for peacetime operational tasks.

The OCV (and its systems) will need to perform various offshore and littoral naval roles, border protection tasks, long-range counter-terrorism and counter-piracy operations, provide support to special forces, and undertake missions in support of security and stability in the immediate regions. Whether or not these vessels will embark a helicopter or UAV will be determined as the project develops. If flexible crewing arrangements are employed, individual ships could maintain a higher operational tempo than the classes they replace.

First pass approval for the new class is currently planned for 2015 to 2017, with an entry-into-service date in the early 2020s.

NAVAL AVIATION

After many years of delays affecting naval aviation, this FEG was re-vitalised from the turn of the decade with the arrival of the first of six MRH90 helicopters as replacements for the venerable but still effective Sea Kings. A Tactical Transport Helicopter (TTH) variant of NH Industries' NH90, the new navy helicopters will serve alongside a further forty of the type ordered by the army.

Later, from 2013, the first of twenty-four new sea-control helicopters for both the *Hobart* air-warfare destroyers and existing frigate classes will enter service. The NFH version of the NH90 was a contender for this requirement but the competing US-built Sikorsky MH-60R Seahawk was ultimately selected in a decision announced on 16 June 2011 in a contract valued at over A$3bn (US$3.2bn). In the meantime, some of the current S-70B-2 Seahawk force of sixteen helicopters is being upgraded to allow the aircraft to remain on the frontline until the new generation machines are delivered.

The navy will need as many aviation assets as possible with the three *Hobart* class and eight *Anzac* class frigates each able to embark one helicopter. The

A NH Industries' MRH90 helicopter in Australian Navy markings. A total of forty-six of these helicopters are being delivered for the Australian Army and Royal Australian Navy, of which forty-two are being manufactured by Eurocopter's Australian Aerospace subsidiary in Brisbane. *(Eurocopter – Patrick Penna)*

Two US Navy MH-60R Seahawk helicopters flying in tandem. The MH-60R has been selected to fill a requirement for twenty-four new sea control helicopters for the Royal Australian Navy. *(US Navy)*

The *Armidale* class patrol vessel *Ararat* sailing in company with the Indonesian *Sultan Nuku* during April 2011 in a coordinated maritime security patrol. Although still relatively new vessels, plans are already underway to replace the *Armidale* class with much larger vessels from the early 2020s. *(Royal Australian Navy)*

support ship *Success* also operates a helicopter and the new LHDs up to twelve mainly Army and Navy crewed machines. Additional aircraft can also be deployed aboard *Largs Bay.*

CONCLUSION

Overall, the Royal Australian Navy enters 2012 in good shape. Its frigates have completed or are undergoing major updates, the amphibious force is in line for renewal from early 2012 onwards, new helicopters are coming on line and a modern fleet of minor war vessels are meeting the tasks allotted to them. Within another five years the navy will boast its new destroyers, as well as the three new amphibious ships. By that time progress will have been made towards replacement of the existing submarines with a larger and more capable underwater flotilla, whilst other longer term projects will also have advanced.

Notes

1. Australian defence procurement is in the hands of its Defence Material Organisation, which lists its major projects under AIR, LAND, SEA and JP (joint) designations. Projects can have a number of distinct phases. For example, the *Anzac* class frigates were acquired under Project SEA 1348 Phase 2 and received surface and underwater war-fighting upgrades under Project SEA 1348 Phases 3A (Harpoon anti-ship missiles) and 3C (mine and obstacle avoidance sonar). Other upgrades to the class have been carried out under Project SEA 1428 (acquisition and integration of ESSM) and the current phases of Project SEA 1448 relating to anti-ship missile defence. Further phases of Project SEA 1448 will encompass electronic support system improvements and air search radar replacement.

2. Until mid-2009, the Royal Australian Navy comprised seven Force Element Groups (FEGS), viz. Surface Combatant; Submarine: Amphibious & Afloat Support; Mine Warfare & Clearance Diving; Patrol Boat; Hydrographic, Meteorological & Oceanographic; and Aviation. A reorganisation has rationalised this structure into six Force Commands with, for example, Mine Warfare & Clearance Diving, Patrol Boat and parts of the Hydrographic, Meteorological & Oceanographic FEG merged into a single unit. However, the FEG terminology is still widely used.

3. The Australian Government's Border Protection Command was established in 2005 to provide security for Australia's offshore maritime areas. It combines resources from the Australian Customs and Boarder Protection Service and Department of Defence to fulfil this mission.

4. The 2009 Defence White Paper, *Defending Australia in the Asia-Pacific Century: Force 2030* (Canberra, Commonwealth of Australia, 2009) can be accessed in full at www.defence.gov.au/whitepaper/. Practical implementation of the procurement decisions required to give effect to the decisions set out in the Defence White Paper is the responsibility of the Defence Material Organisation, which published a Defence Capability Plan in June 2009 describing the major capital projects planned for government approval through to 2013. A second update to this plan released in December 2010 extended this time horizon to 2019. Relevant documentation can be accessed at www.defence.gov.au/dmo/id/dcp/dcp.cfm.

5. The *Hobart* class is being built by the AWD Alliance, which comprises Australia's Defence Material Organisation, the government-owned ASC shipbuilding group and Raytheon Australia, the last-mentioned acting as combat systems system engineer. Key capability partners are Navantia, as platform systems designer, and the US Navy and Lockheed Martin as suppliers of the Aegis weapon system. Whilst ASC is responsible for final assembly at its shipyard at Osborne in Port Adelaide, modular construction means that around 70 per cent of each ship's constituent blocks have been subcontracted to BAE Systems at Williamstown and Forgacs in Newcastle. This has the political advantage of spreading the benefits of construction around the country.

6. A more detailed description of the *Juan Carlos I* design can be found in the editor's 'Modern European Amphibious Assault Ships', *Warship 2011* (London, Anova Books), pp 80–93.

7. The Royal Australian Air Force already plans to acquire at least seventy-five of the F-35A land-based variant of the JSF to equip three operational squadrons. An initial order for fourteen was aircraft approved in November 2009. It would be relatively easy for Australia to acquire a small force of the F-35B STOVL version in a similar way to the approach planned by Italy given commonality in support arrangements. However, this is not under official consideration.

2.3 REGIONAL REVIEW

THE INDIAN OCEAN AND AFRICA

Author:
Conrad Waters

INTRODUCTION

Developments in the Indian Ocean and neighbouring Persian Gulf have exerted considerable influence on international maritime operations in recent years. The significance of the region as the principal transit route for maritime trade between Europe and the Far East, the importance of Middle Eastern oil reserves, the inherent instability of many countries within the area and the associated flourishing of modern-day piracy have all combined to make these waters a focal point of naval activity. However, the first months of 2011 and the advent of the so-called 'Arab Spring' have further increased the impact of the broader Middle East and North Africa on the actions of the world's leading navies. The emergence of a wave of social unrest and political upheaval extending from Bahrain in the east to Morocco in the west has resulted both in an upsurge in maritime activity and a timely reminder of the leverage naval power provides to those countries that possess it.

The most obvious demonstration of this fact has been provided by the NATO-lead intervention in Libya's civil war under the auspices of UN Security Council Resolution 1973. Here, strikes by Tomahawk land-attack cruise missiles deployed from US Navy surface vessels and from both British Royal Navy and US submarines heralded the start of the West's active involvement in the conflict on 19 March 2011. These strikes provided much of the capability required to destroy Libya's air-defence network and open the country's skies to UN aircraft. Subsequently, the ongoing deployment of a carrier task group headed by France's *Charles de Gaulle* has provided what is, perhaps, the most potent single element of an extensive range of aviation and maritime assets assigned to protect Libyan civilians and enforce a no-fly zone. Surface warships have been particularly active. They assisted the withdrawal of Western citizens from the country before UN involvement was authorised and have subsequently facilitated the delivery of humanitarian supplies to the besieged rebel enclave of Misrata.

Elsewhere in the region, fighting in Yemen has resulted in Western nations drawing up contingency plans for the security of their nationals that – in the last resort – rely heavily on a maritime evacuation. More broadly, disturbances in Bahrain – headquarters of the US Navy's Central Command and associated Fifth Fleet – have underlined the vulnerability of land-based facilities located in foreign countries and the options naval forces provide in such circumstances.

Meanwhile, whilst the Indian Ocean has been out of the immediate headlines, it continues to remain central to the ambitions – and fears – of the world's major powers. The depredations of Somali pirates have provided the impetus for many navies to dispatch warships to the region, with the presence of China's People's Liberation Army Navy (PLAN) in its most ambitious and prolonged 'out of area' mission to date being particularly noteworthy. The emergence of an increasingly close strategic relationship with Pakistan has prompted speculation that China will expand the existing commercial facilities at the Arabian Sea port of Gwadar – which it has already largely funded – to provide a local support facility for its warships operating in the area. Whilst China has been quick to play down these suggestions, such a development would help Pakistan counterbalance India's ever-growing regional maritime ascendancy whilst providing the PLAN with enhanced abilities to sustain a presence in a key strategic area. Certainly, the prospect must be viewed with some trepidation by the Indian Navy's planners.

Sub-Saharan African navies have been largely irrelevant in a strategic context, with the small but modern South African Navy being the principal exception. Even here, political inertia has resulted in the navy seeing little use beyond South African waters until recently. However, the spread of piracy as far south as the Mozambique Channel has seen something of a change of approach. Most notably, the frigate *Mendi* was deployed to the area in early 2011 on an anti-piracy mission that could well expand into a longer-term security partnership with Mozambique and other neighbouring countries. At around the same time, the replenishment vessel *Drackensberg* made the lengthy voyage to West Africa – ostensibly on a training cruise – to stand ready to protect South African interests during the conflict in Côte d'Ivoire. The willingness of South Africa to use its navy as a means of greater engagement across a continent not best known for its stability would certainly be a positive development.

Table 2.3.1 provides an overview of the most significant regional navies as of mid-2011.

The United States destroyer *Barry* (DDG-52) launches a Tomahawk land-attack cruise missile against Gadaffi-regime targets in Libya in March 2011. Missile strikes by US and British submarines and US surface warships provided much of the capability required to destroy Libya's air-defence network in the opening days of the West's intervention in the country's civil war. *(US Navy)*

Table 2.3.1: FLEET STRENGTHS IN THE INDIAN OCEAN, AFRICA AND THE MIDDLE EAST – LARGER NAVIES (MID-2011)

COUNTRY	ALGERIA	EGYPT	INDIA	IRAN	ISRAEL	PAKISTAN	SAUDI ARABIA	SOUTH AFRICA
Support/Helicopter Carrier (CVS/CVH)	–	–	1	–	–	–	–	–
Attack Submarine (SSN/SSGN)	–	–	–	–	–	–	–	–
Patrol Submarine (SSK/SS)	4	4	14	3	3	5	–	3
Fleet Escort (DDG/FFG)	–	6	19	–	–	10	6[2]	4
Patrol Escort/Corvette (FFG/FSG/FS)	6	4	8	6	3	–	4	–
Missile Armed Attack Craft (PGG/PTG)	12	30[1]	12	24	10	6	9	3
Mine Countermeasures Vessel (MCMV)	–	14	8	–	–	3	7	3
Major Amphibious (LPD)	–	–	1	–	–	–	–	–

Notes:

1 Egyptian fast attack craft numbers approximate.

2 Status of one Saudi Arabian fleet escort doubtful following grounding damage.

Little excuse is needed to include this fine image of the Bangladeshi Type 41 frigate *Ali Haider* (formerly the British Royal Navy's *Jaguar*) alongside at Southampton Docks awaiting departure to her new home in the summer of 1978. The three Type 41 and 61 frigates acquired from the UK have formed the core of the Bangladesh Navy for most of the country's existence but plans for replacements are now far advanced. *(Editor's collection)*

A refurbished 'Castle' class offshore patrol vessel after handover to the Bangladesh Navy on the River Tyne in September 2010. Bangladesh is adopting a phased approach to expanding naval capabilities with the ultimate aim of creating a 3D force with surface, air and underwater units. *(A&P Tyne)*

INDIAN OCEAN NAVIES

Bangladesh: The Bangladesh Navy has ambitious plans to transform itself into a modern three-dimensional force – including surface, aviation and submarine elements – by the end of the current decade. The ambition is being achieved in stages. 2010–11 has seen the purchase and commissioning of the two former British Royal Navy 'Castle' class offshore patrol vessels as *Bijoy* (ex *Dumbarton Castle*) and *Dhaleshwari* (ex *Leeds Castle*), as well as of the former survey vessel *Roebuck*, now *Anushandhan*. In addition, two new AgustaWestland AW-109 helicopters have been delivered to form the basis of a naval aviation arm. They will principally operate from *Bangabandu*, the most modern of Bangladesh's five frigates, although the 'Castle' class will also provide alternative landing facilities.[1] Meanwhile, construction is underway at the local Khulna Shipyard of a replenishment vessel and five 50m patrol boats, whilst two larger missile-armed patrol craft have reportedly been ordered from China.

The next stage of the modernisation plan envisages the replacement of the navy's three oldest frigates – former British Type 41 and Type 61 frigates originally completed in the late 1950s – with new construction. Discussions have been held with China for the purchase of two new helicopter-equipped frigates, possibly a variant of the F-22P *Zulfiqar* type already commissioned by Pakistan. The status of the existing ships has been open to some speculation, although *Umar Farooq* – the former *Llandaff* – remained operational on training duties as at the end of 2010. The transition to full 3D capability is anticipated to be completed towards the end of the decade, with the establishment of a submarine flotilla and supporting infrastructure by 2019. However, no details of the number or type of boats to be acquired have been revealed and the timetable looks extremely challenging given the difficulties inherent in commissioning an entirely new capability from scratch.

India: The Indian Navy has long been the dominant regional maritime power. Recent growth in the country's defence budget has financed a large acquisition programme aimed at maintaining and expanding this status, with extensive local construction supplemented by overseas imports – largely from Russia. Unfortunately, the execution of this programme has been beset with delays and cost overruns. As a result, India is facing something of a struggle to maintain current fleet strength pending the realisation of a considerable backlog of orders over the next twelve to eighteen months. A major problem has been inadequate infrastructure and inherent inefficiency in the country's state-owned naval shipbuilding sector, which has a long way to go in adopting modern construction techniques. An interesting development has therefore been the award of industrial licenses for the design and construction of warships to two private shipbuilding concerns. One of these, the Pipavav Shipyard, subsequently announced the award of a US$660m contract for five offshore patrol vessels on 30 May 2011.[2] This is reportedly the first time the Indian Navy has placed a major warship order with a commercial facility. The contract will therefore be a litmus test as to whether the private yard's modern infrastructure, most notably the ability to use modular construction and handle large pre-outfitted blocks, will allow the project to progress in a timely manner.

The Indian Navy's current force structure is set out in Table 2.3.2. Details of developments over the last twelve months in respect of the more significant warship categories are set out below:

Aircraft Carriers: It appears that progress is being made with the long-delayed US$2.3bn refurbishment of the carrier *Vikramaditya* – the former Soviet *Admiral Gorshkov* – at Severodvinsk. Indian Navy personnel have started to arrive in Russia for training on operating the new ship and reports suggest sea trials should start by the end of 2011 in line with the revised delivery schedule of late 2012. Deliveries of Mig-29K fighters are also underway. Nine out of a total of forty-five planes ordered were in Indian hands as of mid 2011. A further aircraft crashed during flight-testing on 23 June 2011, killing two Russian aircrew. There has been less news about progress with the indigenous carrier *Vikrant*, which has been under construction at the Cochin Shipyard since 2008. However, it seems that plans for a second member of the class may be delayed due to a higher priority being given to strengthening littoral defences in the aftermath of the Mumbai terrorist atrocities.

The first of the Indian Navy's Project 17 frigates, *Shivalik*, was commissioned in 2010 and is now in operational service. Two additional ships in the class should be delivered to the Indian Navy before the end of 2011 by Mumbai's Mazagon Dock. *(Indian Navy)*

Surface Combatants: Construction of the three 6,800-ton indigenous Project 15A destroyers continues at Mumbai's Mazagon Dock. First of class *Kolkata* is scheduled for delivery in mid-2012 but delays to other ships building at the yard makes this timetable suspect. Mazagon is also completing the second and third 6,100-ton Project 17 frigates, with *Satpura* likely to be commissioned in the summer of 2011 and *Sahyadri* by the end of the year. A March 2011 report by India's Comptroller and Auditor General has suggested that costs for the six ships have reached at least RS197.6bn (US$4.4bn) compared with RS58.3bn (US$1.3bn) first projected, questioning the economics of local construction.[3] However, the follow-on Project 15B (four units) and Project 17A (seven units) classes will all be locally-built. Meanwhile, completion of *Teg*, the first of a modified batch of Russian-built Project 1135.6 *Talwar* class frigates ordered from the Yantar yard in Kaliningrad in 2006, is imminent. *Trikand*, the third and final member of the batch, was launched on 25 May 2011. Her delivery at the end of 2012 will bring the programme to a conclusion.

Table 2.3.2: INDIAN NAVY: PRINCIPAL UNITS AS AT MID-2011

TYPE	CLASS	NUMBER	TONNAGE	DIMENSIONS	PROPULSION	CREW	DATE
Aircraft Carriers							
Aircraft Carrier (CV)	**VIRAAT** (HERMES)	1	29,000 tons	227m x 27/49m x 9m	Steam, 28 knots	1,350	1959
Principal Surface Escorts							
Destroyer – DDG	Project 15 **DELHI**	3	6,700 tons	163m x 17m x 7m	COGAG, 32 knots	350	1997
Destroyer – DDG	Project 61 ME **RAJPUT** ('Kashin')	5	5,000 tons	147m x 16m x 5m	COGAG, 35 knots	320	1980
Frigate – FFG	Project 17 **SHIVALIK**	1	6,100 tons	143m x 17m x 5m	CODOG, 32 knots	265	2010
Frigate – FFG	Project 1135.6 **TALWAR**	3	4,000 tons	125m x 15m x 5m	COGAG, 30 knots	180	2003
Frigate – FFG	Project 16A **BRAHMAPUTRA**	3	4,000 tons	127m x 15m x 5m	Steam, 30 knots	350	2000
Frigate – FFG	Project 16 **GODAVARI**	3	3,850 tons	127m x 15m x 5m	Steam, 30 knots	315	1983
Frigate – FFG	**NILGIRI** (LEANDER)	1	3,000 tons	114m x 13m x 5m	Steam, 28 knots	300	1974
Corvette – FSG	Project 25A **KORA**	4	1,400 tons	91m x 11m x 5m	Diesel, 25 knots	125	1998
Corvette – FSG	Project 25 **KHUKRI**	4	1,400 tons	91m x 11m x 5m	Diesel, 25 knots	110	1989
Submarines							
Submarine – SSK	Project 877 EKM **SINDHUGHOSH** ('Kilo')	10	3,000 tons	73m x 10m x 7m	Diesel-electric, 17 knots	55	1986
Submarine – SSK	**SHISHUMAR** (Type 209)	4	1,900 tons	64m x 7m x 6m	Diesel-electric, 22 knots	40	1986
Major Amphibious Units							
Landing Platform Dock – LPD	**JALASHWA** (AUSTIN)	1	17,000 tons	173m x 26/30m x 7m	Steam, 21 knots	405	1971

Delays in inefficient state-owned shipyards have meant that the Indian Navy's extensive new construction programme continues to face significant delays. In the interim, ships such as the Project 15 *Delhi* class destroyer *Mumbai* (right) and Project 16A *Brahmaputra* class frigate *Beas* (above) are amongst the most modern in the fleet. *(Royal Australian Navy / German Navy)*

The fleet escorts will be supplemented with a numerous flotilla of indigenously-built patrol frigates and offshore patrol vessels. The most important of these are the initial four Project 28 *Kamorta* class anti-submarine corvettes being constructed by Garden Reach Shipbuilders and Engineers (GRSE) of Kolkata. Fabrication of the first ship started as long ago as 2005 and completion is now scheduled for mid–2012 after considerable delays. The 2,500-ton design, featuring stealth technology and an unprecedented amount of locally-produced equipment, could form the basis for an extended class focused towards patrolling India's coastal waters if construction problems can be ironed out. GRSE seems to be making better progress with the smaller and simpler *Car Nicobar* fast attack craft. Eight of these 325-ton vessels are now in service following the induction of *Kabra* on 8 June 2011. She will be joined by a further two vessels before the end of 2011. An intermediate class of four *Saryu* offshore patrol vessels is being built at Goa Shipyard and will be supplanted by the five units ordered from Pipavav in due course. Goa is also likely to be involved in the construction of new minehunters ordered from Korea's Kangnam in a much-needed boost to this crucial capability.

Submarines: India's submarine programme is also beset by delays and cost overruns. The most important project is the licensed construction of six Project 75 'Scorpène' patrol submarines, again at Mazagon Dock. When the contract was announced in 2005, delivery of the first boat was planned for 2012 but

The Indian Navy *Nilgiri* (*Leander*) class frigate *Vindhyagiri* receiving tugboat assistance off Mumbai following a collision with the container ship *Nordlake* on 30 January 2011. Although successfully towed back to Mumbai's naval dockyard, *Vindhyagiri* sank the following day. *(Kapil Chadni)*

this has now been pushed back to 2015 at the earliest. Numbers of operational boats are therefore starting to fall, with the final Project 641 'Foxtrot' class boat *Vagli* decommissioned in December 2010. The four German Type 209 *Shishumar* and eight Russian-built 'Kilo' class boats are also showing their age, albeit that the latter are being progressively modernised. In spite of the problems, it seems that Mazagon may be entrusted with construction of the follow-on Project 75I programme for another six submarines, the design of which has yet to be selected.

The creation of a nuclear-powered underwater fleet is not fairing much better. Commencement of the long-awaited lease of the Russian Project 971 'Akula' class nuclear-powered attack submarine *Nerpa* continues to be pushed back. Latest reports suggest that crew training is underway but that delivery will be delayed until the end of 2011. There has been little further news about the indigenous strategic nuclear submarine, *Arihant*, following her launch in 2009 but final outfitting prior to the start of sea trials is thought to be continuing.

The South African Type 209 submarine *Charlotte Maxeke* pictured on exercises with the US FFG-7 class frigate *Stephen W Groves* in February 2011. The scope of South African naval activity is steadily expanding. *(US Navy)*

Operationally, the Indian Navy remains focused on combating piracy in the Indian Ocean whilst conducting defence diplomacy with regional and visiting fleets. A demonstration of its extended reach was the deployment of the destroyer *Mysore* and amphibious transport dock *Jalashwa* to Libya in February 2011 to assist the evacuation of Indian nationals under Operation 'Safe Homecoming'. Less positively, the *Nilgiri* (*Leander*) class frigate *Vindhyagiri* is expected to be a total loss after a collision with the container ship *Nordlake* off Mumbai on 30 January 2011. The frigate, which was returning from a 'families day' for relatives of the crew, suffered hull damage and a serious engine-room fire. Although successfully towed back to Mumbai's naval dockyard, she sank to the harbour bottom on the following day as a result – at least in part – of flooding from the volume of water needed to extinguish the blaze. Salvage took until mid-June 2011 and it may not be economic to repair the extensive damage to a ship which was due for withdrawal soon in any event. Whilst it was fortunate no lives were lost in the accident, the incident was just the latest in a series of collisions to impact Indian warships and will add impetus to plans to expand the new naval base at Karwar built under Project Seabird so as to reduce reliance on the congested harbour at Mumbai.

Pakistan: A comprehensive overview of the development and current structure of the Pakistan Navy is contained in Chapter 2.3A. Tensions in Pakistan's relationship with the United States and China's growing interest in the Indian Ocean appear to be driving a Sino-Pakistan strategic partnership. The navy is benefiting from new Chinese-built construction as a result. This developing relationship might eventually stabilise Pakistan's relative decline in comparison with neighbouring India's steadily expanding maritime ambitions, although land-based operations and ever-pressing internal requirements security continue to dominate Pakistani military thinking.

Table 2.3.3 summarises current major fleet units.

AFRICAN NAVIES

The twin threats of piracy and terrorism seem to be leading to an up-tick in naval procurement in sub-Saharan Africa. In addition to the increased operational tempo already noted, the spread of pirate activity across the Indian Ocean seems to be lending some urgency to South African naval procurement, which had previously seen little new activity since a contract for the three submarines and four frigates that now form the core of the fleet was signed with Germany in 1999. An updated structural blueprint outlined by the navy at the end of 2010 envisages a

Table 2.3.3: PAKISTAN NAVY: PRINCIPAL UNITS AS AT MID-2011

TYPE	CLASS	NUMBER	TONNAGE	DIMENSIONS	PROPULSION	CREW	DATE
Principal Surface Escorts							
Frigate – FFG	**ZULFIQAR** (F-22P)	3	3,000 tons	118m x 13m x 5m	CODAD, 29 knots	185	2009
Frigate – FFG	**ALAMGIR** (FFG-7)	1	4,100 tons	138m x 14m x 5m	COGAG, 30 knots	215	1977
Frigate – FFG	**TARIQ** (Type 21)	6	3,600 tons	117m x 13m x 5m	COGOG, 32 knots	180	1974
Submarines							
Submarine – SSK	**HAMZA** (AGOSTA 90B/AIP)	1	2,100 tons	76m x 7m x 6m	AIP, 20 knots	40	2008
Submarine – SSK	**KHALID** (AGOSTA 90B)	2	1,800 tons	68m x 7m x 6m	Diesel-electric, 20 knots	40	1999
Submarine – SSK	**HASHMAT** (AGOSTA)	2	1,800 tons	68m x 7m x 6m	Diesel-electric, 20 knots	55	1979

fleet of twenty-two warships by 2030 compared with the eighteen vessels currently in service. Doubtless spurred by the spread of piracy across the Indian Ocean, the main activity will be focused on the realisation of Project Biro, which now envisages procurement of a fleet of three offshore patrol vessels and six inshore patrol vessels from 2013 onwards. Interestingly, the South African Estimates of National Expenditure plan for a significant uplift in naval expenditure to pay for the new vessels from the 2013/14 financial year, suggesting there is a political will to make the programme a reality. Other elements of the structure plan include three new strategic sealift and sustainment vessels under Project Millennium, a replacement survey ship under Project Hotel and the acquisition of a second fleet replenishment vessel.[4]

Nigeria is one of a number of African fleets acquiring elderly second-hand tonnage – in this case the former US Coast Guard cutter *Chase* (WHEC-718), now renamed *Thunder*. It is debateable whether such purchases represent good value. *(Mrityunjoy Mazumdar)*

Other regional economies do not share South Africa's strength and limited defence budgets mean that acquisition of second-hand vessels, often on a subsidised basis, is the norm. For example, France has donated the P400 class patrol vessel *La Rieuse* to Kenya following her withdrawal from the overseas territory of La Réunion in June 2011. Meanwhile, on Africa's west coast, Senegal has taken possession of the former French tank landing ship *Sabre*, whilst Nigeria has obtained the former US Coast Guard *Hamilton* (WHEC-715) class cutter *Chase* (WHEC-718) as part of ongoing efforts to increase stability in the strife-torn Niger Delta region. There has to be a question, however, whether such acquisitions make sense for the new operators given that many have been retired by their former owners because of the crippling operating costs associated with such elderly vessels. The approach adopted by Equatorial Guinea, which took delivery of two new 62m offshore patrol vessels from Israel Shipyards early in 2011, may prove more cost-effective in the long run.

The Royal Moroccan Navy has an ambitious procurement programme that includes the construction of three 'Sigma' type corvettes by Damen Naval Shipbuilding. This image shows the roll-out of the second ship No 614 – possibly to be named *Casablanca* – on 2 February 2011. *(Maritimephoto.com)*

In North Africa, the Libyan civil war has seen the virtual destruction of the country's navy. It was effectively neutralised in a series of air strikes, the most significant of which were lead by Britain's Royal Air Force on 19 May 2011. Amongst the ships that have been left severely damaged were the Project 1159 'Koni' class frigate *Al Ghardabia* and several 'La Combattante' fast attack craft. With *Al Ghardabia*'s sister *Al Hani* and a number of smaller vessels in rebel hands in the east of the country, loyalist Gadaffi troops have been forced to resort to largely ineffectual asymmetrical methods to continue maritime operations. These have included the use of mines to disrupt maritime access to besieged Misrata, as well as small boat operations.

Elsewhere along the North African coastline, neighbouring Algeria is undertaking a progressive modernisation of its navy which has included the doubling of its submarine fleet with the delivery of two further 'Kilo' class submarines in the course of 2010. The upgrade of Soviet-era surface warships at St Petersburg's Severneya Verf is also underway, with delayed work on the Project 1159 'Koni' class frigate *Mourad Rais* and the Project 1234 'Nanuchka' class corvette *Rais Hamidou* finally completed in the first half of 2011. A more significant transformation is planned with the acquisition of a flotilla of modern surface escorts that has attracted bids from shipyards across Europe. No contract had been announced as of mid-2011 in spite of rumours that Germany's Blohm & Voss – with a MEKO A-200 based design – and Russia – with the Project 2038.2 export variant of its *Steregushchy* corvette – had been short-listed. Morocco's fleet modernisation is further advanced and the first of three Dutch-built 'Sigma' type corvettes, possibly to be named *Rabat*, has already started sea trials. A stretched 110m variant of the 90m ships built for Indonesia, she will be followed by two smaller 98m half-sisters. The first – possibly *Casablanca* – was launched on 2 February 2011. A FREMM multi-purpose frigate – to be named *Mohammed V* – and a new class of 70m offshore patrol vessel are also under construction in France. The respected AMI International consultancy has indicated that purchase of a second frigate is also possible to match Algeria's naval build-up. Further east, the Egyptian Navy remains the largest in the area and seems relatively little impacted by the 2011 revolution but has limited resources for new acquisitions. US military aid is significant in this context and it is therefore not surprising that the four-vessel 'Ambassador III' fast attack craft programme at VT Halter Marine in Pascagoula, Mississippi, remains the most significant new procurement.

A US Navy file photo on an Iranian *Alvand* class light frigate. *Alvand* was one of two warships dispatched through the Suez Canal in February 2011 on a training voyage to Syria. *(US Navy)*

MIDDLE EASTERN NAVIES

The Middle East's heady mix of political instability and wealth has always resulted in relatively high levels of military expenditure. The 'Arab Spring' – combined with healthy oil prices – is likely to result in a continuation of this situation. Naval procurement remains buoyant as a result.

Much activity is focused on the United Arab Emirates (UAE), where three significant construction programmes are currently underway. The most advanced is that for the six heavily-armed *Baynunah* class corvettes designed by France's CMN. *Al Hesen*, the second ship – and first to be locally built by Abu Dhabi Shipbuilding – was displayed at the NAVDEX exhibition in February 2011. Third of class, *Al Dhafra*, was subsequently launched in April 2011. Two other projects have been entrusted to Italy's Fincantieri, which commenced work on the first of two 'Falaj 2' stealth patrol ships in November 2010. Work on a derivative of the Italian Navy's 'Comandante' offshore patrol vessel had started earlier. Neighbouring Saudi Arabia also has a long-standing requirement for new surface construction to reinforce both its 'blue water' Western Fleet in the Red Sea and its more littoral-focused Eastern Fleet in the Persian Gulf. A number of potential designs have been mentioned; most notably upgraded variants of both types of US Navy Littoral Combat Ship, but no definitive conclusions have been reached. Meanwhile, Oman is awaiting delivery of the three new corvettes ordered from the United Kingdom under Project Khareef following the emergence of unspecified problems during trials of the lead ship, *Al Shamikh*. More details of this project are contained in Chapter 3.1. Oman is also in the market for three smaller and simpler offshore patrol vessels under Project Ofouq, with yards from India, the Netherlands and South Korea short-listed.

Iran's navy continues to become steadily more ambitious in its deployments. In addition to mounting regular anti-piracy missions in the Gulf of Aden, it despatched the frigate *Alvand* and replenishment ship *Kharg* on a training cruise to its key regional ally Syria in February 2011. This had a high publicity impact but few military implications. Potentially more significant was the announcement in June that an Iranian submarine had been sent to the Red Sea on an intelligence-gathering mission, doubtless in response to similar Israeli underwater deployments in the area. Israel is steadily building up its submarine arm and there have been reports that the country is seeking a sixth Type 800 *Dolphin* class submarine to add to the two current Batch II AIP-equipped boats already being built by HDW in Germany. It has previously been rumoured that at least some of the three existing submarines have been equipped with nuclear-armed cruise missiles as a counter to Iran's own nuclear programme and the Red Sea would be a potential operating area for this mission.

Notes

1. The two new helicopters were inducted on 14 July 2011 according to a report by the United News of Bangladesh Agency. It is likely that the new Naval Aviation Wing will be formally stood up around the end of the year.

2. The contract award was reported in *The Economic Times* (New Delhi, The Times Group, 2011) under the headline 'Pipavav Shipyard gets $660 million Indian navy order; posts FY-11 profit' on 30 May 2011.

3. More information on the ongoing problems facing India's shipbuilding industry can be found in Rahul Bedi's 'Indian auditors warn of navy capability shortfall', *Jane's Defence Weekly* – 30 March 2011 (Coulsdon, HIS Jane's, 2011), p 8.

4. Further details of South African naval developments can be found on the informative *defenceWeb* site at www.defenceweb.co.za.

2.3A Fleet Review

Author:
Mrityunjoy Mazumdar

PAKISTAN Multiplying Limited Resources

INTRODUCTION

Since its inception in August 1947, the development of the Pakistan Navy has been inexorably shaped by responses to the perception of the threat from its neighbour, India, with whom three wars have been fought. It has also been linked to Pakistan's relevance to United States' regional geopolitical strategy, which has ebbed and flowed over time. In effect, United States' military aid has been a double-edged sword. On the one hand, American aid was instrumental in doubling fleet size and enabling major capability upgrades during the 1980s. On the other, shifting geopolitical winds have also meant periodic arms embargoes and withdrawal of support. Notably, the Pressler Amendment enacted in the light of Pakistan's nuclear weapons programme meant that US-supplied assets were removed and sanctions imposed. Predictably, this has had adverse operational consequences for the Pakistan Navy, which lost half its fighting fleet between 1993 and 1994 as leases on former US Navy warships expired.

From early on, the Pakistan Navy sought to mitigate these effects and find more reliable sources for naval equipment by fostering ties with other nations, notably Turkey, France, Italy, Sweden, the Gulf countries and, crucially, China. It has also developed an indigenous warship-building capability. Recent events – particularly the United States' 'direct action' against Osama bin Laden in Abbottabad and a resultant potential souring of relationships – suggest that relationship with China could, indeed, continue to develop, assuming greater strategic importance over time.

The Pakistan Navy's FFG-7 type frigate *Alamgir* – the former *McInerney* (FFG-8) – was acquired in August 2010 and is seen here before her arrival in Pakistan in May 2011. The development of Pakistan's naval forces has been closely linked to the country's shifting relevance to US geopolitical strategy. *(Pakistan Navy)*

HISTORICAL DEVELOPMENT OF THE PAKISTAN NAVY

Early Days: The Pakistan Navy came into being on 14 August 1947 as the Royal Pakistan Navy following the partition of India in 1947 and the creation of West Pakistan and East Pakistan. It had shared the divided Royal Indian Navy's assets – largely minor surface escorts and minesweepers – on a roughly 1:2 basis and commenced operations with a strength of nearly 3,600 personnel. The first commander-in-chief was Rear Admiral J W Jefford, with his headquarters in Karachi and the sloop *Godavari* (later *Sind*) as his flagship. He served until 1953, when the first Pakistani commander-in-chief, Rear Admiral H M S Choudri, assumed the helm. Admiral Choudri remained in office until 1959 when he resigned over serious disagreements with the Pakistan Army leadership. By that time, Pakistan had become a republic and the Royal Pakistan Navy became the Pakistan Navy.[1]

Until the mid-1950s, shortage of money meant that the Pakistan Navy saw only modest growth, largely through the acquisition of a handful of former British Royal Navy destroyers. The primary reason for the service's perennial funding shortages lay in the limited relevance of the navy in the defence strategy of Pakistan which, at the time, was overwhelmingly focused on the air-land battle concept against India, which was seen as the primary threat. Shortly after becoming independent, both countries had fought a land and air war over Kashmir and other wars would ensue. From the Pakistan Army's perspective, the navy was seen to be just a coastal defence force that might also need some submarines.

This situation changed when Pakistan and the United States signed a Mutual Defence Agreement on 19 May 1954. Subsequently Pakistan became a member of two regional security alliances which were formed by the United States as part of the strategy to contain the spread of communism; the South East Asia Treaty Organization (SEATO) and the Central Treaty Organization (CENTO). This brought with it generous funding from the US in the form of the military assistance program (MAP), allowing Pakistan to expand its fleet. Between 1956 and 1964 considerable numbers of surplus platforms were acquired from the United Kingdom and the USA using MAP cash, most notably the Royal Navy's modified *Dido* class cruiser *Diadem* (renamed *Babur*) and several destroyers in 1956. The US Military Aid and Assistance Group (MAAG) also provided assistance for expanding shore facilities. Efforts to acquire a submarine capability were more protracted but came to fruition on 1 June 1964 when the American Second World War era *Tench* class boat, *Diablo* (SS-479), was recommissioned as *Ghazi*. Later, after three years of negotiations, the navy acquired sufficient funds to purchase three *Daphné* class submarines from France. A contract was signed in 1966 and all three boats – *Hangor*, *Shushuk* and *Mangro* – were in commission by the end of 1970.

By this time, Iran's emergence as a bulwark against Communism meant that Pakistan had gradually lost its relevance to American regional strategy as a front-line state. This changing situation, coupled with an arms embargo imposed after the second India-Pakistan War in September 1965, meant that the *Ghazi* was to be the last US-funded transfer until 1977. The net effect was that Pakistan was compelled to seek alternate, more reliable sources of arms elsewhere. It would not be until the Soviet invasion of Afghanistan in 1979 that Pakistan once again became relevant to US strategy in the Persian Gulf. However, although various surface ships were evaluated, the lack of MAP funding meant that the submarines were the only major new acquisitions.

The Royal Navy modified *Black Prince* class cruiser *Diadem* pictured leaving the River Tyne on sea trials in 1944. Sold to Pakistan in 1956 and recommissioned as *Babur* in 1957 on delivery, she played a leading role in the bombardment of the Indian town of Dwarka during the 1965 Indo-Pakistan War. Enjoying a long and eventful career, she was not finally disposed of until the 1980s. *(Crown Copyright)*

The 1965 and 1971 Indo-Pakistan Wars: War with India broke out in 1965 and, for the first time, the Pakistan Navy saw action. The submarine *Ghazi* was deployed off the main Indian naval base at Bombay, while a seven-ship naval task force headed by the cruiser *Babur* bombarded the small Indian coastal town of Dwarka in Gujarat on the night of 7/8 September. Pakistan hoped to draw out the Indian fleet for the *Ghazi* to attack but the raid proved to be of little strategic value, as the Indian Navy chose to keep its fleet – which lacked both submarines and a credible anti-submarine capability bottled up in harbour. Nevertheless, it was a good morale-booster and 8 September is still celebrated as Navy Day in Pakistan.

The aftermath of the war saw a US-imposed arms embargo on both India and Pakistan. Given this situation, Pakistan even approached the Soviet Union for naval equipment but a deal proved elusive. As such, it was only Pakistan's submarine arm that was much modernised by late 1971, when it was becoming increasingly clear that there would be another war over India's support for the Mukti Bahini rebels fighting for the secession of East Pakistan. On the other hand, the Indian Navy had taken the limitations of its performance in 1965 to heart and had made some significant acquisitions, notably of submarines and missile-armed fast attack craft from Soviet sources. War finally broke out on 3 December 1971. All in all, Pakistan – in the midst of political upheaval at the time – did not fare well in a conflict that resulted in the separation of East and West Pakistan, with the former becoming the new state of Bangladesh.

For the Pakistan Navy, things started badly with the loss – even before hostilities commenced – of the submarine *Ghazi* with all hands off India's east-coast naval base of Vishakapatnam. She sank sometime between 29 November and 3 December 1971 although India did not realise this until the following week.[2] *Ghazi* had been deployed to counter India's sole carrier *Vikrant* and the Indian Navy gained uncontested control of the local sea area once her fate became known. The limited number of surface assets in the Eastern theatre – comprising patrol craft and requisitioned troop transports – did not stand much of a chance against Indian naval aircraft thereafter. In the west, the navy proved unable to deter repeated Indian attacks on Karachi. Here, Pakistan suffered two major blows in rapid succession when oil tanks, naval and port facilities, as well as several military and commercial ships, were attacked during two missile strikes by Indian Project 205 'Osa 1' missile boats on the nights of 4 and 8 December. Two warships were sunk in these raids. However, Pakistan's submarine service did score a notable success when the *Daphné* class boat *Hangor*, under the command of Commander Ahmed Tasnim, sank the Indian Type 14 anti-submarine frigate *Khukri* off the Gujarat coast on the night of 9 December. It was also claimed that her sister, *Kirpan*, was damaged in the same attack, although Indian official accounts

The Pakistan Navy *Daphné* class submarine *Ghazi* pictured in January 1991. She was purchased from Portugal in December 1975 to replace the first submarine in the Pakistan Navy, which was sunk with all hands during the 1971 Indo-Pakistan War. Her sister-boat, *Hangor*, sank the Indian frigate *Khukri* in the same conflict. *(US Navy)*

The *Garcia* (FF-1040) class frigate *Aslat* (pennant 265) – formerly *O'Callahan* (FF-1051) – and the *Brooke* (FFG-1) class frigate *Khaibar* (pennant 163) – formerly *Brooke* (FFG-1) – pictured after transfer on lease to the Pakistan Navy. The United States' decision not to renew the leases on these ships in 1993/94 had a significant impact on Pakistan's fleet. *(US Navy)*

An image of the Pakistan Navy Type 21 frigates *Tippu Sultan* and *Shahjahan* operating in company with the US Navy frigate *Reuben James* (FFG-57) in 2002. The class were acquired from the United Kingdom in 1993 after the Pressler Amendment required the return of leased US Navy escorts to the United States. *(US Navy)*

An image of the Pakistan Navy 'Tripartite' minehunter *Munsif* (foreground) taken during Exercise Arabian Gauntlet 2011 on 24 April 2011. Her sister *Muhafiz* is fifth in the line-up. The three ships in the class were commissioned between 1989 and 1998, the last being completed in Karachi. *(US Navy)*

differ. *Khukri* was the first warship sunk by a submarine since the Second World War and her loss had a marked impact on Indian Navy thinking.

The 1971 War was a watershed moment for the Pakistan Navy in terms of its maritime strategy. It no longer had to attempt to protect sea lines of communication spanning the Arabian Sea to the Bay of Bengal that were intersected by a potentially hostile country. At a stroke, the area it had to defend had become vastly more manageable given its limited resources. Maritime strategy clearly evolved to one of sea denial using submarines and long-range maritime patrol aircraft, as well as air force fighters armed with anti-ship missiles. However, the navy also had to contend with problems of filling the gap in trained personnel, many of whom had been from East Pakistan.

Rebuilding the Fleet: The aftermath of the 1971 War saw the development of the strategic alliance with China, which supplied missile- and torpedo-armed fast attack craft. A Pakistan Naval Air Arm was created based on the Mehran Naval Air Station. Westland Sea King helicopters from the UK were joined by French Breguet Br.1150 Atlantique patrol aircraft. This allowed surveillance of an area of up to 150 miles (241km) from the Pakistan coastline. Air-launched AM-39 Exocet anti-surface missiles were also purchased. By 1976, Pakistan had therefore acquired a credible sea-denial capability to prevent a repeat of the December 1971 attacks on Karachi. Additional submarines were also acquired from France.

Major surface forces did not initially do so well. The material condition of many vessels rendered refits prohibitively expensive and two former Royal Navy Type 12 anti-submarine frigates purchased in 1974 were scrapped when refurbishment proved more costly than envisaged. However, renewed US interest in the relationship with Pakistan – strengthened by the loss of Iran as an ally after the 1979 revolution and the subsequent Soviet invasion of Afghanistan – marked something of a revival. The first of an eventual six *Gearing* class destroyers modernised under the fleet rehabilitation and modernisation (FRAM) programme arrived in 1977. Then, in 1982, the US Reagan Administration approved a US$3.2bn military and economic aid package for Pakistan, as the country was once again seen as a front-line state against the Soviets. Four *Garcia* (FF-1040) class anti-submarine and four *Brooke* (FFG-1) class anti-air warfare frigates were acquired from the USN on lease during 1988–9, supplemented by the depot ship *Hector*. Overall, the Pakistan Navy achieved a significant quantitative and qualitative gain, acquiring ships with modern anti-submarine and anti-air warfare capabilities to supplement anti-surface and maritime reconnaissance equipment previously obtained.

However, all was soon to change. The Soviet withdrawal from Afghanistan in 1989, coupled with Pakistan's development of nuclear weapons, resulted in a dramatic re-appraisal of the US relationship. The Pressler Amendment and the renewed arms embargo that followed seriously impaired a Pakistan Navy that depended on US-originated ships for most of its more modern assets. The ships obtained on loan had to be returned to the US Navy upon lease expiry, leaving new options to be explored. Much assistance was obtained from Western European navies in the middle of disarmament after the end of the Cold War, notably the purchase of six former Royal Navy Type 21 *Amazon* class frigates in 1993. Extensively modernised, they formed the core of Pakistan's surface fleet until recently. France was the source of '*Agosta* 90B' type submarines and *Éridan* class minehunters, some of which were built at Karachi under licence. Local shipbuilding capabilities were also demonstrated by the commissioning of the first indigenously-built large patrol craft *Larkana* in 1994. This success resulted in the Pakistan Navy building additional variants of the design armed with surface-to-surface missiles from 1997 to 2006. Chinese influence, which steadily expanded from the 1980s onwards with the supply of more missile-armed attack craft, is also apparent in this design. However, it is only in the past decade that Chinese technology has started to have a dominant impact on Pakistan Navy development.

CURRENT MARITIME STRATEGY

For Pakistan's naval planners, by far the biggest influence has been India and the perceived threat from its much larger navy. Pakistan's maritime strategy and associated force structures are therefore essentially India-centric. However, Pakistan's relevance to US

Images of the Pakistan Navy Type 22 frigates *Badr* and *Tippu Sultan* operating with, respectively, the Royal Australian Navy and United States Coast Guard during 2009. The Pakistan Navy has been an active participant in the US-lead Coalition Maritime Campaign Plan and has commanded both the CTF150 and CTF151 naval task forces established to combat terrorism and piracy. *(Royal Australian Navy / US Navy)*

strategy has remained an important secondary element, a relevance that has been renewed during the so-called Global War on Terror. There has been a pronounced shift towards multinational maritime security operations in and around the waters of the Arabian Peninsula to counter terrorism and piracy through participation in the US-lead Coalition Maritime Campaign Plan. The Pakistan Navy has been active in Combined Task Forces (CTF) 150 and 151, having commanded CTF150 four times and CTF151 once to date. According to the US Navy, Pakistan's involvement and leadership serves to engender trust and confidence among other Islamic nations, encouraging their participation. Besides this, the Pakistan Navy is actively engaged in naval diplomacy with other regional Islamic nations, seeing itself as the guardian navy of the Gulf region. It has strong relations with Gulf fleets such as the Royal Saudi Naval Forces, United Arab Emirates Navy and the Royal Navy of Oman besides South Asian navies such as those of Bangladesh, Malaysia and Brunei. In addition, it has hosted the biennial AMAN multinational exercise since 2007. The most recent – held in March 2011 – saw the participation of thirty-nine regional and extra-regional navies. Pakistan sees AMAN as a successful initiative in bring the navies of East and West together and is particularly proud of facilitating the joint participation of both the Chinese and American navies in an international exercise.

In part because of the size disparity against the much larger Indian Navy and, in part, because of limited resources as a result of a continental mindset amongst Pakistan's political-military elite, Pakistan's naval acquisition strategy can be largely characterised as being proactive and innovative. It has continuously sought to introduce force multipliers – modern weapons and platforms – in an attempt to negate capacity and capability gaps. Whilst India has generally responded in kind, the Pakistan Navy often enjoyed a qualitative advantage for prolonged periods in particular niches until India was able to redress the balance. Key examples are the introduction of submarines, the deployment of air-to-surface missiles, modification of *Agosta* class submarines to fire sub-launched Harpoon anti-ship missiles and, more recently, the introduction of Harpoon-equipped Orion maritime patrol aircraft, to the considerable concern of Indian naval planners.

Pakistan's maritime strategy towards India is essentially based on offensive sea denial along with a localised degree of sea control under local air cover. The enablers for this strategy primarily rest on a triad of (i) an outer ring of missile-armed naval air platforms, (ii) submarines equipped with torpedoes and Exocet and Sub-Harpoon anti-ship missiles and, to a lesser extent, (iii) the use of surface forces supplemented by naval special operations forces to attack Indian warships, shipping and critical national infrastructure. In the unlikely event of a shooting war, the Pakistan Navy might adopt a first-strike approach. Unrestricted submarine warfare would be complemented by anti-surface strikes by missile-equipped platforms. An asymmetric approach could also see the use of small craft attacks against merchant shipping, with mine warfare another distinct possibility. The main challenge is the ongoing build-up of India's naval and coastguard forces, the latter being driven by the response to the November 2008 terrorist attacks on Mumbai, to an extent where the Pakistan Navy will be vastly outnumbered. The sheer quantity of Indian coastguard and naval assets, supported by increasingly networked command-and-control capabilities, would make it difficult for any action to avoid detection.

Table 2.3A.1: PAKISTAN NAVY FLEET COMPOSITION – MID-2011

TYPE	CLASS	NUMBER	TONNAGE	SERVICE DATE[1]	NOTES
Principal Surface Escorts					
Frigate (FFG)	**ZULFIQAR** (F-22P)	3	3,000 tons	2009-10	Newly built by China. A fourth is being built in Pakistan.
Frigate (FFG)	**ALAMGIR** (FFG-7)	1	4,100 tons	1979 (2010)	Formerly the USN's MCINERNEY. More are wanted.
Frigate (FFG)	**TARIQ** (Type 21)	6	3,600 tons	1974-78 (1993-94)	Former British Royal Navy AMAZON class. Modernised.
Submarines					
Submarine (SSK)	**HAMZA** (AGOSTA 90B/AIP)	1	2,100 tons	2008	Built in Pakistan to a DCNS design.
Submarine (SSK)	**KHALID** (AGOSTA 90B)	2	1,800 tons	1999-2003	One built in France, one in Pakistan. To be fitted with AIP.
Submarine (SSK)	**HASHMAT** (AGOSTA)	2	1,800 tons	1979-80	Originally built in France for South Africa but not delivered.
Submarine – Midget (SSW)	**COSMOS**	3	110 tons	1988 onwards	Italian design assembled in Pakistan. Known as X-craft locally.
Fast Attack Craft					
Fast Attack Craft (PGG)	**JALALAT/JURRAT**	4	200 tons	1997-2006	Built locally in two batches to modified designs.
Fast Attack Craft (PGG)	**ZARRAR** (MRTP-33)	2	100 tons	2007-08	Constructed in Turkey.
Minor War Vessels[2]					
Minehunter (MCMV)	**MUNSIF** ('Tripartite')	3	600 tons	1989-98 (1992-98)	First transferred from French Navy. Last built in Pakistan.
Support Ships					
Replenishment Tanker (AOR)	**NASR** (FUQING)	1	22,000 tons	1987	Chinese-built.
Replenishment Tanker (AOR)	**MOAWIN** (POOLSTER)	1	17,000 tons	1964 (1994)	Transferred from the Netherlands.

Notes:

1 Relates to first commissioning dates of remaining ships in class. Dates in brackets relate to entry into Pakistan Navy service when the ship served elsewhere previously.

2 There are also a number of patrol vessels (with more in the coastguard), four hovercraft, a survey ship, a sail training vessel and some coastal tankers and tugs.

The Pakistan Navy AIP-equipped submarine *Hamza* pictured after launch in Karachi in August 2006. The Pakistan Navy is the first fleet in the region to operate AIP-equipped submarines. *(DCNS)*

The Pakistan Navy is increasingly turning to China to modernise its fleet. This image shows *Shamsheer*, the second of four Chinese-designed F-22P frigates that will form the core of the future surface fleet. *Shamsheer* was commissioned in Shanghai in December 2009. *(Pakistan Navy)*

From an Indian Navy perspective, the disparity in numbers means that maritime strategy has been able to move on from a purely Pakistan-centric focus. In fact, if political relations could be normalised between the two countries, the Indian Navy would likely welcome the chance to work with its Pakistani counterpart in enforcing maritime security. However, this could be complicated by Pakistan's growing strategic relationship with China, most notably through the offer of basing rights to Chinese forces in the south-western port of Gwadar.[3] Pakistan has reportedly asked for Chinese help in expanding the existing commercial facilities to provide an additional naval base in an effort to put more of a distance between fleet forces and the not too distant major Indian naval base in Mumbai. The facility would offer the People's Liberation Army Navy the prospect of its first base in the Indian Ocean, close to the strategic sea lanes of the Persian Gulf, in a crucial addition to its 'String of Pearls' ambition.

CURRENT ORGANISATION AND FORCE LEVELS

Today's Pakistan Navy is thought to number over 25,000 personnel including c. 3,000 Marines, as well as an estimated 1,000 in the Special Services Group (Navy) – the SSG(N). Due to the dual influence of British and, later, American naval doctrine, the Pakistan Navy has a unique command structure influenced by these two countries. The navy is headed by the Chief of Naval Staff, currently Admiral Noman Bashir. He is assisted at Naval Headquarters, Islamabad, by the Vice Chief of Naval Staff, as well as by several Deputy Chief of Naval Staff and Assistant Chiefs of Naval Staff. They head various branches and divisions respectively, including Operations, Material, Supply, Training & Personnel, and Projects.

There are at least six operational commands. The main war-fighting command is COMPAK (Commander Pakistan Fleet), with responsibility for the surface, submarine and aviation commands. The submarine service is headed by Commander Submarines (COMSUBS) and the naval air arm by Commander Naval Aviation (COMNAV). Commander Coast (COMCOAST) exercises command over the Pakistan Marines, the Special Services Group and coastal defence installations, including ground-based air-defence and harbour-defence forces. Ensuring that warships and submarines and their crews are fighting fit is the responsibility of FOST (Flag Officer Sea Training), whilst COMLOG (Commander Logistics) is responsible for all repair, maintenance and logistic infrastructure. Geographically, there are three regional commands administering naval installations and training facilities. The major naval base and the bulk of naval infrastructure and training schools are concentrated in and around Karachi under the responsibility of Commander Karachi (COMKAR). Commander North (COMNOR) is responsible for installations in the north of Pakistan, whereas Commander Central Punjab (COMCEP) is responsible for the Pakistan Naval War College and other naval installations in Central Punjab.

Submarine Service: The Pakistan Navy's submarine service is very much an elite group. Formed with the commissioning of *Ghazi* in June 1964, it currently operates at least eight submarines. These comprise three '*Agosta* 90B' *Khalid* class boats, two of the older *Hashmat* (*Agosta*) class and at least three Italian-designed Cosmos midget boats, known locally as X craft. All *Daphné* class submarines were decommissioned on 2 January 2006 after almost forty years of service.

Pakistan purchased the *Agosta* class submarines from France in mid-1978. Originally built for South Africa, they were not delivered due to a United Nations arms embargo on the then pariah country, with its Apartheid policies. The lead boat, *Hashmat*, commissioned in France in February 1979, arriving in Pakistan in October. *Hurmat* commissioned in February 1980, reaching Pakistan in September. They significantly increased Pakistan's maritime

The veteran replenishment tanker *Moawin* was acquired in 1994. She is the former Royal Netherlands Navy *Poolster*. *(Mrityunjoy Mazumdar)*

capabilities due to enhanced endurance, long underwater detection ranges, over-the-horizon targeting ability and increased firepower. A towed-array sonar provided the flexibility to classify contacts at extended ranges. The boats are undergoing an upgrade which includes installation of the DCNS SUBTICS combat system to extend their operational life by around twenty years.

Pakistan subsequently signed a contract for three '*Agosta* 90B' submarines, an improved version of the original *Agosta* type, on 21 September 1994. The contract called for one boat to be built in France with the other two boats to be assembled locally at Karachi Shipyard and Engineering Works (KS&EW) with progressively greater local input. The first boat, *Khalid*, was completed at Cherbourg. Sea trials were conducted at Cherbourg, Brest and Toulon before commissioning on 6 September 1999, followed by induction into Pakistan's fleet on 21 December of that year. The second boat, *Saad*, was assembled at KS&EW from sections built in Cherbourg and commissioned on 12 December 2003. *Hamza*, the final member of the class, was launched by KS&EW in August 2006 and commissioned shortly afterwards, becoming the first submarine equipped with the DCNS MESMA air-independent propulsion (AIP) system to enter operational service. MESMA increases the underwater endurance by a factor of three over a conventional submarine. The other two boats are to be retrofitted with MESMA in due course and it has been reported that DCNS has supplied at least one MESMA kit to Karachi Dockyard at the time of writing. All the Pakistan Navy '*Agosta* 90B' class boats have the SUBTICS combat system and are capable of firing the Exocet SM-39 missile.

An order for the three MG-110 mini-submarines was signed with Italy's Cosmos in 1986. The first was brought to Pakistan partially assembled in 1988; the other boats were assembled locally. Displacing around 110 tons submerged, they can dive to 150m and carry up to twelve commandos. Potential roles include minelaying, torpedo attack, frogman operations and commando landings.

Surface Forces: Ten principal surface combatants are currently operational. The six, elderly – but upgraded – former Royal Navy Type 21 frigates that

Until new ships arrive, the Pakistan Navy will remain heavily reliant on the sextet of Type 22 frigates acquired from the United Kingdom in the 1990s. *Babur*, formerly *Amazon*, is seen here in July 2008 with the replenishment oiler *Nasr* in the background. *(Royal Australian Navy)*

The Pakistan Navy has acquired four British-built Griffon 2000 TD(M) hovercraft to help it police the extensive creeks of the Indus Delta region. *(Pakistan Navy)*

An upgraded P-3C Orion maritime patrol aircraft is prepared for delivery to the Pakistan Navy after the completion of modernisation by Lockheed Martin. Two of these aircraft were destroyed in the terrorist raid on Pakistan's naval air station at Mehran on 22 May 2011. *(Lockheed Martin)*

now comprise the Pakistan Navy's *Tariq* class remain in service with Destroyer Squadron 25. Three are fitted with US Harpoon surface-to-surface missiles, the other three with Chinese LY-60N short-range surface-to-air weaponry. They have recently been supplemented by three new build Chinese F-22P *Zulfiqar* type frigates with eight C-802 surface-to-surface missiles each. They are an improved version of the People's Liberation Army Navy Type 053H3 'Jiangwei II' general-purpose design with many of the stealth features of the newer Type 054.[4] The lead ship was commissioned on 19 September 2009 and all three were operational by the end of 2010. A fourth vessel is under construction at KS&EW in Pakistan and was launched in June 2011 for completion by 2013. The F-22P class serve in the 18th Frigate Squadron, where they have recently been supplemented by the former US Navy FFG-7 frigate *McInerney* (FFG-8), renamed *Alamgir*. She was handed over to her new owners on 31 August 2010, subsequently receiving an extensive overhaul before departing for her new home. Since arriving in Pakistan in May 2011, *Alamgir* has been integrated into the fleet.

Patrol forces comprise a mix of missile boats, small and medium-sized patrol craft, interceptor boats and hovercraft. The missile craft comprise two locally-built *Jalalat* class vessels delivered between 1997 and 1999 and the two modified *Jurrat* class completed in 2006. These displace around 200 tons and are fitted with C-802 missiles. They are supplemented by two Turkish-built MRTP-33 fast attack craft delivered by Yonca-Onuk during 2007-8. Other patrol assets include four British-built Griffon 2000 TD(M) hovercraft and four Thai-built 16m Marsun combat boats used by the Pakistan Marines and two MRTP-15 interceptors for naval Special Forces. In addition, the coastguard like Maritime Security Agency operates a number of patrol assets, largely obsolescent ex-naval vessels including its non-operational flagship, *Nazim*, a *Gearing* class destroyer first transferred to Pakistan over thirty years ago.

Mine warfare forces comprise three *Munsif* (*Éridan*) class minehunters of the Tripartite design ordered from France. Two of these were built at Lorient but the final one was locally assembled in Karachi. These ships are assigned to the 9th Auxiliary and Mine Warfare Squadron although some references suggest they belong to the 21st Mine Countermeasures Squadron. Other auxiliary vessels include the two replenishment tankers *Nasr* – a 22,000-ton Chinese *Fuqing* class variant delivered in 1987 – and *Moawin* – an elderly former Royal Netherlands Navy *Poolster* class vessel transferred in 1994. Both of these ships are fitted with electronic warfare systems, Phalanx CIWS and can carry large helicopters. Smaller ships include two newly delivered 47m 1,600-ton STUS (Small Tanker-cum-Utility Ship) built at KS&EW as well as two small, elderly coastal tankers. The STUSs – named *Madadgar* and *Rasadgar* – will perform replenishment of ships, torpedo recovery, diving support, towed array transportation, minelaying and search-and-rescue.

Naval Aviation: The small but capable Pakistan Naval Air Arm is largely based at Pakistan Naval Station Mehran. The base houses several squadrons, notably:

- **27 Squadron:** Six Fokker F-27 maritime patrol and transport aircraft.
- **28 Squadron:** Three Lockheed P-3C Orion maritime patrol aircraft.
- **29 Squadron:** Two Breguet Br.1150 Atlantique maritime patrol aircraft.
- **111 Squadron:** Six Westland Mk45/45A Sea King helicopters.
- **222 Squadron:** Six newly-acquired Harbin Z-9EC anti-submarine helicopters.
- **333 Squadron:** Approximately seven Alouette III helicopters for training and SAR missions.

There are also a number of unmanned aerial vehicles and a Hawker 850 XP electronic warfare aircraft. Dedicated maritime strike air support is readily available from 8 Squadron, Pakistan Air Force, operating Mirage III/V jets fitted with AM-39 Exocets.

The six Mk45 Westland Sea Kings date to the birth of Pakistan naval aviation in September 1974, when they first entered service with 111 Squadron. However, one was subsequently written off in 1986, being replaced by a Mk45A in 1989. A midlife upgrade of these helicopters is currently underway.

Fixed wing operations commenced when four Dassault Breguet Br.1150 Atlantique maritime patrol aircraft joined 29 Squadron in 1976, so named because it was formed on Pakistan's twenty-ninth anniversary. Six airframes have been acquired in total but only two remain operational. One aircraft was shot down by a R-60 infrared-homing air-to-air missile fired from an Indian Mig-21 fighter aircraft on 10 August 1999 for violating Indian airspace and refusing to land on an Indian airfield. Pakistan has always maintained the aircraft was on a routine training mission and did not violate Indian airspace.

The most potent weapon in the naval air arm is the P-3C Orion. Three aircraft were acquired from the United States in 1990 but not delivered due to the arms embargo until 1996, when they were inducted into 28 Squadron. One was lost due to an accident while carrying out routine exercises on 29 October 1999 and the remainder grounded from 2001 until their reactivation in early 2007. A further eight were donated by the United States in 2005, seven of which were subject to an extensive upgrade by Lockheed Martin. The US Navy formally handed over the first two upgraded planes on 30 April 2010 at Naval Air Station Jacksonville. These aircraft were then inducted into 29 Squadron on 1 June 2010. A total of five aircraft were operational in early 2011, although two were subsequently destroyed during the terrorist attack on Mehran on 22 May 2011.[5]

Marines and Special Forces: Currently brigade-sized and growing, the Pakistan Marines were originally established on 1 June 1971 to support riverine operations in the former East Pakistan and subsequently disbanded in 1974. In 1990, a new Marine Corps with a Marine Battalion, Amphibious Wing and Marine Training Centre was reactivated at Pakistan Naval Station Qasim. The primary roles and tasks of the Marines include defence of Pakistan's creeks in the Indus Delta; protection of high-value assets; amphibious/anti-amphibious operations; special security operations; and humanitarian assistance and disaster relief. There is also a significant Special Forces contingent in the form of the SSG(N) which, together with the Pakistan Marines and army and air force units, makes up the Pakistan Special Operations Command. Based in Karachi and modelled after the US Navy's SEALs and the British Royal Navy's Special Boat Service, the SSG(N)'s responsibilities include covert operations from air, land and sea; protection of critical national infrastructure; maritime counter-terrorism; and maritime interdiction operations. Elements of the group's anti-terrorist team were recently crucial in dislodging terrorists from Pakistan Navy Station Mehran during the May 2011 attack.

PLANNED ACQUISITIONS

Funding procurement has always been an issue for the Pakistan Navy, whilst the political relationship with Western suppliers – particularly the United States – is an added complication. Inevitably, this combination is driving a trend towards China as a major supplier, with domestic sources such as KS&EW also playing an increasingly important role.

An important priority is recapitalising the submarine arm following the retirement of the *Daphné* class. Plans for three new boats, first the French 'Marlin', then the German Type 214, apparently fell through on cost grounds. Consequently, high level inter-governmental talks have been progressing with China since 2009 for the joint development and co production of six AIP-equipped submarines, possibly the Type 041 'Yuan'. In March 2011, Pakistani media reported that the defence ministry had been authorised to sign a mutually-agreed draft protocol for the joint development of six new-generation submarines with China Shipbuilding and Offshore Corporation (CSOC). Four are to be built in China and two in Pakistan. According to 2008 statements by navy officials, a planned force level of between twelve and fourteen boats is targeted, possibly including one or more nuclear-powered submarines.

Meanwhile, future acquisitions for the surface forces are likely to include four larger Chinese frigates, possibly named F-25P. In May 2011, Pakistani media reported that the defence minister had asked China for an estimated US$700m in loans to acquire 4,400-ton frigates, thought to be the Type 054A 'Jiangkai II' frigate that is in series production for the People's Liberation Army Navy. Two 500-ton 'stealth' missile boats incorporating low observable features were also ordered from CSOC in late 2010. The keel of the first was laid down on 1 March 2011 with a delivery date of October. The second vessel

The Pakistan Navy has acquired six Chinese-built Harbin Z-9EC helicopters to operate from its new Chinese-built frigates. *(Pakistan Navy)*

An image of the Pakistan Navy's large coastal patrol vessel *Larkana* operating off Karachi in March 2009. The vessel formed the basis of subsequent Pakistan-built fast attack craft. However, larger and more sophisticated vessels are now being acquired, notably two-Chinese built stealth corvettes. *(US Navy)*

The Pakistan Navy Type 22 frigate *Tippu Sultan* (the former British Royal Navy *Avenger*) receives fuel from the US Military Sealift Command fast combat support ship *Supply* (T-AOE-6) in November 2006. Faced with an on/off relationship from the West, Pakistan is turning towards China for future deliveries of military equipment. *(US Navy)*

The Chinese-built F-22P frigate *Zulfiqar* pictured during a Pakistan Navy training exercise. Recent developments suggest Pakistan is likely to develop a closer strategic relationship with China going forward. *(Pakistan Navy)*

will be constructed by KS&EW. The shipyard will also be involved in the construction of smaller ships and auxiliaries, including a planned fleet oil tanker, hovercraft and small and medium-sized tugs.

Naval aviation plans call for additional Z-9EC helicopters to be procured along with the new Chinese frigates. Further Orion P-3C deliveries appear contingent on the direction of US-Pakistan relations. This could also impact a requirement for further FFG-7 frigates – and associated SH-60F Seahawk helicopters – as an interim step before new construction arrives.

CONCLUSION

The Pakistan Navy has developed into a competent medium-sized fleet that is fully capable of defending its interests. This is certainly recognised by the Indian Navy, with which it has a shared heritage. Throughout its history, it has had to maximise the use of limited resources through the acquisition of force multipliers. Whilst this approach has emphasised niche capabilities at the expense of shortcomings in other areas – for example a lack of long-range surface-to-air-missiles – its submarine force remains its main strength. It is conceivable that this could extend to a nuclear deterrent force over time. The development of an indigenous warship-building capacity is another key aim.

Recent geopolitical developments – and an on/off relationship with the West – suggest the Pakistan Navy will develop a closer strategic partnership with China going forwards. That being said, there are increasing pressures for navies to cooperate for the common maritime good in the present international environment, a role the Pakistan Navy has embraced with some success in its operations in the Arabian Sea. Its relations with the Indian Navy will inevitably continue to be governed by the tone and tenor of the broader relationship between the two states. Much will ultimately depend on developments within Pakistan itself, particularly its success in combating the danger posed by Islamic radicalisation.

Notes

1. Robert Gardiner's (editor) *Conway's All the World's Fighting Ships 1947-1995* (London, Conway Maritime Press, 1995) gives a good overview of Pakistan Navy equipment during its formative years.

2. Accounts vary widely as to what caused the submarine's loss. Until recently, India claimed their destroyer *Rajput* depth-charged the submarine, likely detonating pre-armed ordnance in the boat. However, recent revelations by a senior Indian army theatre commander – as well as the mysterious loss of documents related to the event, including the recovered logbook, from Indian navy archives – suggests otherwise. In addition, accounts by Indian naval divers after the 1971 war suggest an internal explosion took place. The Pakistan Navy maintains the submarine was very likely sunk by one of her own mines.

3. China's interest in establishing a base at Gwadar is described by Farhan Bokhari and Kathrin Hille in 'Pakistan turns to China for naval base', *Financial Times* – 23 May 2011 (London, Pearson Plc, 2011).

4. It is hoped to cover the F-22P design in more detail in a subsequent edition of *Seaforth World Naval Review.*

5. Please see Farhan Bokhari and Alexander von Rosenbach's 'Pakistani P-3C Orions destroyed in Taliban raid', *Jane's Defence Weekly* – 1 June 2011 (Coulsdon, HIS Jane's, 2011), p.5, for a more detailed account.

6. The considerable assistance provided by Captain Bilal Abdul Nasir, PN, Naval Attaché to the Embassy of Pakistan in Washington in the preparation of this article is gratefully acknowledged. However, all views expressed are the author's own.

2.4 REGIONAL REVIEW

EUROPE AND RUSSIA

Author:
Conrad Waters

INTRODUCTION

The last year has seen an acceleration in the relative decline of European maritime power that has been an ongoing theme since the end of the Cold War. The inevitable consequences of the region's weakened economic state have started to feed through to defence budgets, often with significant consequences. In the absence of any direct military threat to Europe's borders, it is unsurprising that military spending is seen as an avoidable extravagance by many of the region's politicians in an era when there is little spare cash for luxuries. Some support remains for limited expeditionary missions in pursuance of stabilisation operations but the willingness to finance such 'discretionary' activity seems much reduced. This political environment is causing friction with the United States, Western Europe's long-time principal ally. It is apparent that the former increasingly sees the continent as hitching a free ride on the back of the United States' considerable defence investment. In a valedictory address to NATO in Brussels in June 2011, retiring US Defence Secretary Robert Gates brought this frustration into the open. He suggested that ongoing cuts to European defence capabilities could ultimately result in the abandonment of the entire NATO alliance, given a backdrop where a new generation of US leaders increasingly lacked an emotional and historical attachment to the partnership.[1]

One consequence of Europe's straightened budgetary position has been a renewed impetus towards defence collaboration. The most developed version of this is typified by the November 2010 Anglo-French defence treaty or 'Declaration on Defence and Security Cooperation' to use its official title. The declaration envisages, *inter alia*, developing the ability to deploy an integrated Anglo-French carrier strike group by the early 2020s, as well as enhanced collaboration in areas such as submarines and maritime mine countermeasures. Whilst such arrangements appear to offer the welcome prospect of allowing more efficient use of the diminished resources available to defence budgets, there is scepticism as to whether the practical reality will match the political rhetoric. For example, whilst sharing Anglo-French carrier assets looks a sensible way forward given it seems that both countries can only afford to operate one carrier each, there are many obstacles to overcome. This includes the subsequent disclosure that a fully-laden F-35B Joint Strike Fighter – selected to become the United Kingdom's future carrier aircraft – is not able to land safely on France's *Charles de Gaulle*.[2]

In spite of the parsimony being displayed in defence allocations, European fleets remain active on a global basis. In addition to ongoing support for anti-piracy and anti-terrorism missions in the Indian Ocean and Mediterranean, NATO's intervention in Libya and more routine defence diplomacy missions are all making demands on a decreasing pool of resources. An emerging requirement is the development of a European-wide theatre ballistic missile defence (TBMD) capability to counter the threat from countries such as Iran. Initially being provided by US Navy Aegis-equipped escorts outfitted with Standard SM-3 interceptors, future burden-sharing could see European warships participate in this shield. In addition to Aegis-equipped ships, a modified extended-long-range variant of the Thales SMART-L surveillance radar fitted to many European air-defence escorts has already demonstrated an ability to track ballistic missile targets in exercises with the US in late 2006. Parallel work is being conducted to give Aster surface-to-air missiles the seeker definition and range necessary to match US advances in this field. It is possible Europe could deploy a combined fleet of around twenty-five TBMD-capable warships within the next decade if money can be found to develop the appropriate modifications.

Russia is one of the few exceptions to the general European rule of declining defence budgets and shrinking maritime aspirations. Unfortunately, its run-down defence industry has proved inadequate to match its leaders' ambitions. They will therefore see conclusion of extended negotiations to purchase *Mistral*-type amphibious assault ships from France as a welcome development. This is particularly the case given the deal seems to envisage the type of technological transfers needed to make Russia's yards more efficient. However, the transaction is unlikely to be sufficient on its own to allow Russia to overcome the huge challenges it faces in modernising its obsolescent Soviet-era fleet. The country's experience is arguably an object lesson to other European countries in demonstrating that maritime capabilities, once lost, are not necessarily easy to regain.

Table 2.4.1 summarises the strengths of the leading Western European fleets as at mid-2011.

The first FREMM multi-mission frigate *Aquitaine* and the *Mistral* class amphibious assault ship *Dixmude* on sea trials off the French coast in April 2011. The *Mistral* design has been selected by Russia to provide a capability its run-down defence industry is unable to provide. *(DCNS)*

TABLE 2.4.1: FLEET STRENGTHS IN WESTERN EUROPE – LARGER NAVIES (MID-2011)

COUNTRY	FRANCE	GERMANY	GREECE	ITALY	NETHERLANDS	SPAIN	TURKEY	UK
Aircraft Carrier (CVN)	1	–	–	–	–	–	–	–
Support/Helicopter Carrier (CVS/CVH)	–	–	–	2	–	1	–	1
Strategic Missile Submarine (SSBN)	4	–	–	–	–	–	–	4
Attack Submarine (SSN)	6	–	–	–	–	–	–	7
Patrol Submarine (SSK)	–	4	8	6	4	4	14	–
Fleet Escort (DDG/FFG)	17	15	14	16	6	10	16	19
Patrol Escort/Corvette (FFG/FSG/FS)	15	[5]	3	8	–	–	6	–
Missile Armed Attack Craft (PGG/PTG)	–	10	17	–	–	–	27	–
Mine Countermeasures Vessel (MCMV)	14	19	9	12	6	6	20	15
Major Amphibious (LHD/LPD/LPH/LSD)	4	–	–	3	2	3	–	6

Note: Five new German K-130 corvettes have been completed but need to complete gearing repairs before they are fully operational.

MAJOR REGIONAL NAVAL POWERS – FRANCE

France's *Marine Nationale* has emerged – at least temporarily – as Europe's pre-eminent fleet in the aftermath of recent cuts to Britain's Royal Navy. However, it wears its new crown by default. On one hand, it enjoys a regionally-unrivalled balance of capabilities provided by its strike carrier and embarked air groups, its force of nuclear-powered strategic missile and attack submarines, flotillas of first and second tier surface escorts and a powerful amphibious component. On the other hand, many core capabilities have been hollowed out and lack the depth needed to sustain independent operations. This is particularly the case in respect of the carrier strike group built around *Charles de Gaulle*, which has been kept remarkably busy since completing refit at the end of 2009 and will inevitably need a period of recuperation soon. Some progress is being achieved in modernising key elements of the front-line fleet but funding is insufficient to meet all requirements.

France's principal naval units are set out in Table 2.4.2. A major problem facing the *Marine Nationale* has been the growing obsolescence of its fleet of surface escorts. Only the two 'Horizon' class air-defence ships and the five smaller *La Fayette* stealth frigates have been completed in the last fifteen years. However, this particular issue is being tackled by the Franco-Italian FREMM (*frégate multi-mission*) programme that will see the bulk of the current front-line escort force replaced by nine anti-submarine and two specialised air-defence frigates over the ten years from 2012. *Aquitaine*, the first of these 6,000-ton ships, commenced three weeks of initial sea trials from DCNS's Lorient yard on 18 April 2011 in advance of her scheduled 2012 delivery. Preliminary reports from DCNS suggest that these were very successful, with a speed in excess of the contracted 27 knots achieved from her combined diesel-electric or gas (CODLOG) propulsion system. Two further members of the class are already under construction at Lorient for the French Navy alongside Morocco's *Mohammed V.* Meanwhile, 16 June 2011 saw the start of the withdrawal of the previous generation of ships with the decommissioning of the FASM-67-type frigate *Tourville.*

The FREMM programme will cost France around US$10bn. A similar amount has been allocated to constructing the six *Suffren* class nuclear-powered attack submarines that are intended to replace the existing *Rubis* class over ten years from 2016/17. This leaves very little money available for other modernisation projects and the strains are beginning to show. For example, the gaps in maritime surveillance around France's overseas territories arising from progressive withdrawal of the P-400 large patrol vessels are being filled by a motley collection of auxiliaries. Refits of some of the remainder are being contemplated to squeeze a few more years of life out of their hulls. Further into the future, there is still no obvious replacement for the A-69 corvettes that are now all more than twenty-five years old. DCNS is keen to promote its new 'Gowind' family of offshore patrol vessels to meet the requirement and has self-funded the construction of a 79m variant of the design – named *L'Adroit* – that will be loaned to the navy for three years to prove the concept. Featuring a 360-degree panoramic bridge, an integrated mast arrangement and a significant degree of automation, the new ship has a light deck for helicopter operation, a stern ramp for launching small boats and can be operated by a core crew of just thirty. Maximum speed is just 21 knots but range is as much as 8,000 nautical miles (14,816km). The new ship was rolled out of her construction hall in May 2011 and will commence sea trials before the year's end.

2011 has been a busy year for France's shipbuilders, as the third *Mistral* class amphibious assault ship *Dixmude* has also made her maiden voyage during the year. The first of a batch of two additional ships heralded in the 2008 White Paper on defence and national security, her order was accelerated as part of the French government's response to the 2008–9 economic crisis. This protected jobs at the Chantiers de l'Atlantique yard in Saint Nazaire that is now owned by the European arm of South Korea's STX. She commenced sea trials at the end of April 2011 and will replace the existing LPD/LSD-type *transport de chalands de débarquement* (TCD) *Foudre*

Images (top) of aircrew on the French carrier *Charles de Gaulle* preparing for operations over Libya in the spring of 2011 and (left) an earlier view of the French ship operating alongside the US carrier *Abraham Lincoln* (CVN-72) in the Arabian Gulf. The French Navy is currently Europe's most powerful but it is being stretched by the current tempo of operations. *(NATO / US Navy)*

TABLE 2.4.2: FRENCH NAVY: PRINCIPAL UNITS AS AT MID-2011

TYPE	CLASS	NUMBER	TONNAGE	DIMENSIONS	PROPULSION	CREW	DATE
Aircraft Carriers							
Aircraft Carrier – CVN	CHARLES DE GAULLE	1	42,000 tons	262m x 33/64m x 9m	Nuclear, 27 knots	1,950	2001
Principal Surface Escorts							
Frigate – FFG	FORBIN	2	7,000 tons	153m x 20m x 5m	CODOG, 29+ knots	195	2008
Frigate – FFG	CASSARD (FAA-70)	2	5,000 tons	139m x 15m x 5m	CODAD, 30 knots	250	1988
Frigate – FFG	TOURVILLE (FASM-67)	1	6,100 tons	153m x 16m x 5m	Steam, 32 knots	300	1974
Frigate – FFG	GEORGES LEYGUES (FASM-70)	7	4,800 tons	139m x 15m x 5m	CODOG, 30 knots	240	1979
Frigate – FFG	LA FAYETTE	5	3,600 tons	125m x 15m x 5m	CODAD, 25 knots	150	1996
Frigate – FSG	FLORÉAL	6	3,000 tons	94m x 14m x 4m	CODAD, 20 knots	90	1992
Frigate – FS[1]	D'ESTIENNE D'ORVES (A-69)	9	1,300 tons	80m x 10m x 3m	Diesel, 24 knots	90	1976
Submarines							
Submarine – SSBN	LE TRIOMPHANT	4	14,400 tons	138m x 13m x 11m	Nuclear, 25 knots	110	1997
Submarine – SSN	RUBIS	6	2,700 tons	74m x 8m x 6m	Nuclear, 25+ knots	70	1983
Major Amphibious Units							
Amph. Assault Ship – LHD	MISTRAL	2	21,500 tons	199m x 32m x 6m	Diesel-electric, 19 knots	160	2006
Landing Platform Dock – LPD	FOUDRE	2	12,000 tons	168m x 24m x 5m	Diesel, 20 knots	225	1990

Note: 1 Now officially reclassified as offshore patrol vessels.

in 2012. An order for a final member of the class is anticipated around 2015 to complete the modernisation of France's amphibious force. Progress has also been made with new EDA-R catamaran landing craft that have been ordered to operate from the class, with trials of the first production version scheduled to take place at Toulon in the second half of 2011. The new vessels are able to transport a maximum load of 100 tons in water of less than 1m deep, whilst Wärtsilä pump jets powered by Tognum diesels permit a maximum speed of around 25 knots in open water. Four have already been ordered for delivery in 2011–12 and a further four are planned.[3]

A key influence on France's ability to fund conventional naval construction programmes is the relatively large proportion of the defence budget allocated to the nuclear deterrent. This currently amounts to around 20 per cent of procurement expenditure. Renewal of the fleet of four strategic missile submarines was completed with the delivery of *Le Terrible* on 20 September 2010 but considerable expenditure is still needed to retrofit the new M-51 ballistic missile into the three earlier class members by 2018. Maintaining the fleet of attack submarines is also seen as key to ensuring the effectiveness of the deterrent and provision was made in the 2011 French Defence Budget for the third *Suffren* class boat. An order with DCNS was placed on 28 June 2011.

France is in desperate need of a new generation of offshore patrol vessels to replace elderly tonnage. DCNS hopes that *L'Adroit* – a variant of its 'Gowind' family of designs – will meet the requirement. *(DCNS)*

MAJOR REGIONAL NAVAL POWERS – ITALY

A summary of the principal units operated by Italy's *Marina Militare* is provided in Table 2.4.3. Italy finds itself in a similar position to France in so far as the bulk of its surface fleet faces block obsolescence. The only really modern surface escorts are the two recently-delivered 'Horizon' class air-defence frigates, with most of the remaining ships being of 1980s origin and due to start paying off over the next few years. As with France, Italy sees the FREMM programme as the solution for reconstituting its front-line surface force, with acquisition of a fleet of more modest offshore patrol vessels planned for secondary duties. The acquisition of six Italian variants of the basic FREMM design has been authorised in two separate batches to date, with work on the first pair now well-advanced. A ceremony marking commencement of work on the third ship was held at Fincantieri's Riva Trigoso yard near Genoa on 14 September 2010, whilst fabrication of the fourth vessel started in the following April. As reported previously, the Italian ships feature significant differences from their French sisters, most notably the incorporation of an active phased array variant of the Italian EMPAR radar compared with the Thales Herakles found on the French ships. Italy eventually wants to field ten ships in anti-submarine and general-purpose versions but funding for the final batch of four looks increasingly uncertain.

Other surface programmes – which include new LHD-type amphibious assault ships and replenishment tankers as well as the offshore patrol vessels – are less well advanced. Design work on the amphibious vessels, which will replace the existing *San Giorgio* class, was authorised in 2010 with a view to fielding the first ship by the middle of the decade, but this seems optimistic. Provisional specifications envisage a 20,000-ton ship which seems very similar to the French *Mistral* class in concept. The offshore patrol vessels will be corvette-type ships of around 2,500 tons full load displacement with a maximum speed of 30 knots on diesel propulsion and the ability to accommodate various mission modules after the fashion of the American Littoral Combat Ship. A total of twelve ships would be required to replace the existing *Minerva* and *Cassiopea* classes on a one-for-one basis by around 2020, although the required funding has yet to be identified.

Italy's aviation arm has been the beneficiary of significant investment in recent years, with the acquisition of the carrier *Cavour* supplemented by orders for new helicopters. The former is still working up to full combat effectiveness, carrying out two successful test-firings of its Aster surface-to-air missile system during May 2011. This left the older

The Italian Navy's *Maestrale* class frigate *Scirocco* on NATO operations. Completed in 1983, she evidences the growing obsolescence of the bulk of Italy's surface fleet. *(NATO)*

Table 2.4.3: ITALIAN NAVY: PRINCIPAL UNITS AS AT MID-2011

TYPE	CLASS	NUMBER	TONNAGE	DIMENSIONS	PROPULSION	CREW	DATE
Aircraft Carriers							
Aircraft Carrier – CV	**CAVOUR**	1	27,100 tons	244m x 30/39m x 9m	COGAG, 29 knots	800	2008
Aircraft Carrier – CVS	**GIUSEPPE GARIBALDI**	1	13,900 tons	180m x 23/31m x 7m	COGAG, 30 knots	825	1985
Principal Surface Escorts							
Frigate – FFG	**ANDREA DORIA**	2	7,100 tons	153m x 20m x 5m	CODOG, 29+ knots	190	2007
Destroyer – DDG	**DE LA PENNE**	2	5,400 tons	148m x 16m x 5m	CODOG, 31 knots	375	1993
Frigate – FFG	**MAESTRALE**	8	3,100 tons	123m x 13m x 4m	CODOG, 30+ knots	225	1982
Frigate – FFG	**ARTIGLIERE**	4	2,500 tons	114m x 12m x 4m	CODOG, 35 knots	185	1994
Frigate – FS	**MINERVA**	8	1,300 tons	87m x 11m x 3m	Diesel, 25 knots	120	1987
Submarines							
Submarine – SSK	**TODARO** (Type 212A)	2	1,800 tons	56m x 7m x 6m	AIP, 20+ knots	30	2006
Submarine – SSK	**PELOSI**	4	1,700 tons	64m x 7m x 6m	Diesel-electric, 20 knots	50	1988
Major Amphibious Units							
Landing Platform Dock – LPD	**SAN GIORGIO**	3	8,000 tons	133m x 21m x 5m	Diesel, 20 knots	165	1987

Giuseppe Garibaldi to head the navy's contribution to the Libyan mission, for which purpose AV8-B Harriers were embarked.[4] The 'Horizon' class air-defence escort *Andrea Doria* is one of a number of other surface vessels that have also been deployed to support operations, protecting Italy's southern airspace from any potential retaliation. Meanwhile rotary assets are set to receive a boost following the long-awaited delivery of the first NH90 NFH helicopter in June 2011. Italy has ordered forty-six units, in addition to ten of the TTH utility variant, making it by far the largest user of the type to date.

MAJOR REGIONAL NAVAL POWERS – SPAIN

The *Armada Española* has made considerable headway in recent years. The commissioning of the four Aegis-equipped F-100 air-defence frigates from 2002 onwards has provided it with one of the most sophisticated fleets of surface vessels in Europe. Progress continued to be made in the latter half of 2010. The new LHD-type strategic projection ship *Juan Carlos I* was formally accepted into the navy on 30 September 2010, whilst the new fleet replenishment tanker *Cantabria* was delivered two months earlier on 29 July. In addition, the fifth – and probably final – F-100 class frigate, *Cristóbal Colón*, was launched at Ferrol in November 2010 prior to sea trials that are expected to commence in the spring of 2012. A slightly improved version of the earlier ships, she shares a number of enhancements incorporated in the *Hobart* class being constructed under licence in Australia. Construction is also proceeding in line with previous plans on all four of the S-80 AIP-equipped submarines at Navantia's facility at Cartagena in spite of rumours that the project might be derailed by Spain's economic problems. All the sections of the first boat are now complete and the AIP module has already been delivered for installation in the second half of 2011. Launch is expected by mid-2012.

Unfortunately, future prospects are much bleaker as it is clear that the Spanish government's financial position will not permit the launch of any additional major procurement for the foreseeable future. In this environment, the only ongoing construction programme is likely to be that for BAM (*buque de acción maritima*) offshore patrol ships. They are badly needed to replace a range of elderly existing vessels that are expensive to maintain and are already starting to decommission. The new ships displace as

Current naval construction in debt-burdened Spain is focused on the new BAM-type offshore patrol vessels that will assume some of the missions previously undertaken by light frigates. These images show the launch of *Relámpago* in October 2010 and first of class *Meteoro* on initial sea trials early in 2011. *(Navantia)*

Table 2.4.4: SPANISH NAVY: PRINCIPAL UNITS AS AT MID-2011

TYPE	CLASS	NUMBER	TONNAGE	DIMENSIONS	PROPULSION	CREW	DATE
Aircraft Carriers							
Aircraft Carrier – CVS	**PRINCIPE DE ASTURIAS**	1	16,700 tons	196m x 24/32m x 7m	COGAG, 25 knots	555	1988
Principal Surface Escorts							
Frigate – FFG	**ÁLVARO DE BAZÁN** (F-100)	4	6,300 tons	147m x 19m x 5m	CODOG, 28 knots	200	2002
Frigate – FFG	**SANTA MARIA** (FFG-7)	6	4,100 tons	138m x 14m x 5m	COGAG, 30 knots	225	1986
Submarines							
Submarine – SSK	**GALERNA** (S-70/AGOSTA)	4	1,800 tons	68m x 7m x 6m	Diesel-electric, 21 knots	60	1983
Major Amphibious Units							
Amph. Assault Ship – LHD	**JUAN CARLOS I**	1	27,100 tons	231m x 32m x 7m	IEP, 21 knots	245	2010
Landing Platform Dock – LPD	**GALICIA**	2	13,000 tons	160m x 25m x 6m	Diesel, 20 knots	185	1998

much as 2,500 tons in full load condition and are 94m long. They are armed with a 76mm Oto Melara compact gun and are able to operate a medium-sized helicopter. Their diesel propulsion provides a maximum speed of over 20 knots and range is around 8,000 nautical miles (14,816km) at 15 knots. Core crew is thirty-five. A first batch of four vessels was ordered in 2006 and all of these have now been launched, with lead ship *Meteoro* likely to be delivered imminently. Acquisition of a further five vessels has already been authorised by the Spanish government and a contract is expected before the end of 2011 to maintain employment in the yards in the Bay of Cadiz that build the ships. Three of these will be standard offshore patrol vessels identical to the initial batch. The other two will be modified, one to act as an oceanographic survey ship and the other as a salvage and rescue vessel.

Table 2.4.4 gives an overview of current Spanish fleet strength.

MAJOR REGIONAL NAVAL POWERS – UNITED KINGDOM

The last twelve months have been difficult ones for the British Royal Navy. The most notable development was the significant reduction in fleet strength announced in October 2010 as a result of the conclusions reached in the Strategic Security and Defence Review (SDSR). The outcome, as well as its implications for future Royal Navy procurement, are analysed in some depth in Chapter 2.4A. The cuts were subsequently carried out in rapid order. The vast majority of the equipment withdrawals envisaged had been implemented by 30 June 2011, when the final operational Batch III Type 22 frigate, *Cornwall*, decommissioned at Devonport. As a result, Table 2.4.5 provides a good indication of the post-SDSR fleet structure. However, it is worth noting that subsequent reports have indicated that the SDSR has not been entirely successful in balancing defence commitments with available resources. As such, the bad news may not be entirely over.

The removal of the Royal Navy's ability to deploy fast jets at sea was one of the most significant – and controversial – elements of the review. With the associated demise of the UK Carrier Strike Group, it has arguably left the United Kingdom with an unbalanced fleet structure until this capability is reconsti-

Table 2.4.5: BRITISH ROYAL NAVY: PRINCIPAL UNITS AS AT MID-2011

TYPE	CLASS	NUMBER	TONNAGE	DIMENSIONS	PROPULSION	CREW	DATE
Aircraft Carriers							
Aircraft Carrier – CVS	**INVINCIBLE**	1	22,000 tons	210m x 31/36m x 8m	COGAG, 30 knots	1,100	1980
Principal Surface Escorts							
Destroyer – DDG	**DARING** (Type 45)	3	7,400 tons	152m x 21m x 5m	IEP, 30 knots	190	2008
Destroyer – DDG	**MANCHESTER** (Batch III Type 42)	2	5,200 tons	141m x 15m x 4m	COGOG, 30+ knots	290	1982
Destroyer – DDG	**EXETER** (Batch II Type 42)	1	4,800 tons	125m x 14m x 4m	COGOG, 30 knots	290	1980
Frigate – FFG	**NORFOLK** (Type 23)	13	4,900 tons	133m x 16m x 5m	CODLAG, 30 knots	185	1990
Submarines							
Submarine – SSBN	**VANGUARD**	4	16,000 tons	150m x 13m x 12m	Nuclear, 25+ knots	135	1993
Submarine – SSN	**ASTUTE**	1	7,800 tons	93m x 11m x 10m	Nuclear, 30+ knots	100	2010
Submarine – SSN	**TRAFALGAR**	6	5,200 tons	85m x 10m x 10m	Nuclear, 30+knots	130	1983
Major Amphibious Units							
Helicopter Carrier – LPH	**OCEAN**	1	22,500 tons	203m x 35m x 7m	Diesel, 18 knots	490	1998
Landing Platform Dock – LPD	**ALBION**	2	18,500 tons	176m x 29m x 7m	IEP, 18 knots	325	2003
Landing Ship Dock – LSD (A)	**LARGS BAY**	3	16,200 tons	176m x 26m x 6m	Diesel-electric, 18 knots	60	2006

tuted at the end of the decade. It would seem that this shortfall is being addressed by evolving the capabilities of the previous UK Amphibious Task Group into a more flexible unit that is better able to respond to a broad range of mission requirements. Renamed the Response Force Task Group (RFTG), it embarked on its first deployment – codenamed Cougar 11 – in the spring of 2011. Although the mission was badly impacted by the diversion of some of its core constituents, most notably the helicopter carrier *Ocean* and the Type 42 destroyer *Liverpool*, to support Libyan operations, its structure provided an interesting indication of how the navy intends to maintain a meaningful expeditionary capability in the next decade.[5] Particularly noteworthy was the deployment of British Army Apache AH1 helicopters on *Ocean* in partial substitution for the loss of the Harriers' strike capability. The helicopters saw active service in Libya from June 2011 onwards alongside similar Eurocopter Tiger attack helicopters deployed from the French amphibious assault ship *Tonnerre.*

In spite of the reductions, the Royal Navy continues to benefit from the arrival of some potent new equipment. The Type 45 *Daring* class destroyer

An image of the naming ceremony for the second *Astute* class submarine *Ambush* at the BAE Systems yard in Barrow-in-Furness on 16 December 2010. The submarine was subsequently rolled out in January 2011 prior to trials. *(BAE Systems)*

The British Royal Navy's Type 45 destroyer programme has made good progress in the last twelve months with the launch of the sixth and final ship, *Duncan*, on 11 October 2010. In addition, both *Dauntless* and *Daring* have carried out successful tests of the new Sea Viper missile system, the latter trial being pictured here. *(BAE Systems / MBDA)*

Astute has continued a somewhat chequered career over the past twelve months, running aground off the Isle of Skye in October 2010 and suffering a fatal shooting incident in April 2011. This view shows the submarine being re-floated on 22 October 2010 with the help of the salvage tug *Anglian Prince*. *(Penumbral.pz)*

programme has made particularly good progress during the last year. The sixth and final ship, *Duncan*, was launched on 11 October 2010, fourth of class *Dragon* commenced sea trials in the following month and third ship *Diamond* commissioned on 6 May 2011. More significantly, perhaps, both *Daring* and *Dauntless* have carried out successful test-firings of their Sea Viper missile system and have entered operational service. Unfortunately, developments with the *Astute* class nuclear-powered attack submarine project were less positive, with the lead boat continuing to hit the headlines for all the wrong reasons. After commissioning on 27 August 2010, she suffered damage in a grounding incident off the Isle of Skye in late October that cost her captain his command and was subsequently the scene of a fatal shooting on 8 April 2011 whilst on a goodwill visit to Southampton.[6] More positively, second of class *Ambush* is now in the water following a naming ceremony at the BAE Systems' yard at Barrow-in-Furness in December 2010 and should commence sea trials by the start of 2012. Work on the fifth boat, *Agamemnon*, is now underway following approval for commencement of work early in 2010.

Other developments have included negotiation of a three-year charter on the Norwegian icebreaker *Polarbjorn* to act as an Antarctic ice patrol ship pending a decision on whether to repair or replace the damaged *Endurance*. She was commissioned at Portsmouth as *Protector* on 23 June 2011, thereby taking the name of a predecessor in the role. Amongst ships returning to the fleet was the sole remaining *Invincible* class carrier, *Illustrious*. She completed a sixteen-month refit at Rosyth at the start of June prior to rejoining the fleet as a helicopter carrier. She will remain in service whilst *Ocean* is refurbished until decommissioning in 2014, when her crew will transfer to the new *Queen Elizabeth* to start preparations for the latter's sea trials.

MID-SIZED REGIONAL FLEETS

Germany: The German armed forces are going through a significant restructuring, with the suspension of conscription from July 2011 and a likely reduction in total force numbers to around 180,000 personnel from a previous level of some 250,000. The idea is to create a more professional and deployable military that is better suited for current operational needs. This objective is well aligned with the *Deutsche Marine*'s own recent direction of travel, which has seen significant involvement in international deployments such as the naval component of the UNIFIL mission off Lebanon and Operation 'Atalanta' in the Indian Ocean. This has been accompanied by a much greater emphasis on investment in deployable naval assets well-suited for stabilisation activity.

It is therefore not surprising that the navy's two most significant current acquisition projects have an expeditionary focus. The most important is the programme for four F-125 frigates. These were contracted with the ARGE F-125 consortium of ThyssenKrupp and Lürssen in June 2007. With a length of 149m and a displacement of 7,000 tons, the new frigates are at the larger end of recent European warship designs and are particularly interesting in so far as their design gives priority to the requirements of extended deployment on medium-intensity operations over absolute war-fighting capabilities. More specifically, they are able to deploy for up to two years in the theatre of operations by using interchangeable crews that can be completely swapped over within forty-eight hours. They are also designed to operate at sea for over 200 days each year – double the current requirement – and to operate

The German Navy has recently seen an upsurge in international deployments, including operational missions in the Mediterranean and Indian Ocean. This image shows the F-122 class frigate *Niedersachsen* squeezing through Greece's Corinth Canal in June 2010. *(German Navy)*

for up to five years between major overhauls. Automation has reduced complement to just 120 core crew but space is available for a further sixty personnel. A combined diesel-electric and gas (CODLAG) propulsion system gives good range and a reasonable maximum speed of around 26 knots. However, armament – focused on a 127mm gun, surface-to-surface missiles, RAM close-in weapons systems and a range of lighter weapons – would be insufficient for a high-threat situation. In spite of rumours that the programme would be reduced in the light of planned defence reductions, it seems that work is going ahead and fabrication of the first ship commenced in Hamburg in May 2011 for delivery in 2016. Construction has also started – in September 2010 – on the third Type 702 *Berlin* class combat support ship, which will be named *Bonn*. Displacing some 20,000 tons, these vessels extend the endurance of German naval task forces from twenty-one to forty-five days and are equipped with extensive medical facilities.

Other construction includes the five K-130 class corvettes, the first two of which were withdrawn from service after design defects resulted in damage to their propulsion systems. Replacement engines have now been manufactured and installed on all five ships and delivery is imminent. Construction of a follow-on K-131 class will depend on the conclusions reached by an ongoing defence review, which may also impact plans for joint logistical support ships. Meanwhile, the two additional Type 212A submarines being built by HDW will be launched in 2012.

Greece: The fast-deteriorating state of the Greek government's finances is inevitably having a significant impact on the Hellenic Navy. Ambitious acquisition plans – most notably for a modernisation of the surface fleet through acquisition of six FREMM type frigates from France's DCNS – have been put

The German Navy's most important current procurement programme is for four F-125 class 'stabilisation' frigates. Work on the first of four 7,000-ton ships commenced in May 2011. *(Blohm & Voss)*

The Greek Type 209/1100 submarine *Glavkos* pictured during her decommissioning ceremony on 9 June 2011. Commissioned in 1971, she was the first of the famous Type 209 submarines to enter service. *(Hellenic Navy)*

on hold. Even more worryingly, existing construction programmes have been put in jeopardy by non-payment to suppliers. In March 2011, it emerged that the UK's BAE Systems had cancelled its contract with Elefsis Shipyards supporting the licensed construction of *Roussen* class fast attack craft on grounds of non-payment, putting construction of the final two members of the class in jeopardy. Subsequently, in May, ThyssenKrupp Marine System's (TKMS) HDW division pulled out of an agreement with its former Hellenic Shipyards subsidiary – only recently sold to Abu Dhabi's MAR group – to provide equipment for a further pair of Type 214 submarines when contractual payments were not forthcoming.

Below: The long-running epic of Greece's acquisition of four Type 214 submarines from Germany's Thyssen Krupp Marine Systems took a step towards a conclusion with delivery of the first boat, *Papanikolis*, towards the end of 2010. She is seen here arriving in Greek waters under escort of the 'La Combattante III' fast attack craft *Ypoploiarchos Troupakis*. *(Hellenic Navy)*

The latter development marked another twist in the lengthy epic of the Hellenic Navy's submarine modernisation ambitions. These were first set out at the start of the new millennium with the signature of the Neptune II and Archimedes projects with TKMS. The former envisaged installation of AIP-equipment in the four existing Type 209/1200 *Poseidon* class boats; the latter the acquisition of four new Type 214 submarines. Three of these were to be assembled at Hellenic Shipyards from German components. Both programmes encountered problems, with Greek claims of poor performance of *Papanikolis* – the German-built unit of the Type 214 contract – being particularly controversial. In retrospect, it seems that many of the difficulties – and associated missed contractual payments – might have had much to do with the poor state of Greek government finances. By early 2010, a deal had been reached by which Greece would commission the three locally-built Type 214 submarines, with *Papanikolis* being sold to a third party. Additionally, the Neptune II contract would be terminated after completion of just one boat – *Okeanos* – but the two additional Type 214 submarines referenced above would be built in Greece instead. It was subsequently decided to accept *Papanikolis* after all and she arrived at her new home at the end of 2010 after a commissioning ceremony in Germany in November. The other three submarines constructed in the first batch are currently in the course of trials and should be commissioned over the next twenty-four months. This will reduce the Hellenic Navy's submarine flotilla to four Type 214 submarines and the modernised *Okeanos*, assuming the remainder of the existing flotilla is withdrawn as expected and it proves impossible to patch up a deal with HDW on the two additional boats. The former process commenced in June 2011 with decommissioning of the elderly *Glavkos*.

Meanwhile, it seems that considerable efforts are being devoted to maintain the strength of the existing fleet, particularly given the long history of tension with Turkey and the latter's ongoing fleet modernisation. However, some reductions are inevitable and three of the six 'La Combattante IIa' type fast attack craft acquired second-hand from Germany in the 1990s were also retired in June. Given the imposition of further austerity measures on the Greek budget in mid-2011 it seems likely the coming year will see further force depletion.

The Netherlands: The Royal Netherlands Navy is another force feeling the chill winds of austerity. Whilst the navy was spared the worst of a €1bn package of cuts announced in April 2011 that envisaged the loss of 12,000 jobs over four years and which included the disbandment of the army's two remaining tank battalions, there will be further depletions to a structure that has already suffered substantial losses since the end of the Cold War. Four of the remaining ten 'Tripartite' type minehunters of the *Alkmaar* class were decommissioned immediately. The fleet replenishment oiler *Zuiderkruis* will follow at the end of 2011 when she completes a deployment in support of the European Union's Operation 'Atalanta' anti-piracy mission in the Indian Ocean. In the longer term, the remaining replenishment ship *Amsterdam* will be replaced by the recently-ordered JSS joint logistics support ship, whilst the original plan also envisaged only two of the four new *Holland* class offshore patrol vessels being commissioned. Interestingly, this last-mentioned reduction was a step too far for the Dutch parliament and alternative cuts are being explored to enable all four vessels to enter Dutch service.

The *Holland* class construction programme is now well advanced and the lead ship was handed over to the Dutch Materiel Organisation in April 2011. With a full load displacement in the region of 3,750 tons and a length of 108m, the new ships are considerably larger than other offshore patrol vessels being deployed around the world but are similar in being able to operate with a relatively small crew and being equipped with a modest armament. A key differential is the sophistication of their electronics outfit, which is focused on the new Thales IM-400 integrated mast. This pyramidal structure features fixed, four-faced arrays for each of its two active phased-array radar systems and also incorporates electro-optical and communications equipment. The mast is

The first of the Royal Netherlands Navy's four *Holland* class offshore patrol vessels has now been delivered to the Dutch Materiel Organisation. She is seen here on trials in April 2011 before installation of the new Thales IM-400 integrated mast, which is a key design feature. The artist's impression (right) shows her final configuration. *(Royal Netherlands Navy)*

completed as a separate structure before being bolted onto the ship. *Holland* will only receive hers towards the end of 2011 once tests of other equipment have been completed. The second ship, *Zeeland*, was launched at Vlissingen on 20 November 2010. The other two vessels are being fabricated in Damen Schelde Naval Shipbuilding's Galati yard in Romania prior to final outfitting in the Netherlands. *Friesland* was launched there on 4 November 2010, with *Groningen* following on 21 April 2011.

Turkey: Turkey's fleet is something of an exception within Europe in so far as its relative ambitions and capabilities continue to grow. In addition to maintaining a strong presence along Turkey's Black Sea and Mediterranean coastlines, the navy has been consistent in its support for Coalition anti-piracy and anti-terrorism deployments in the Indian Ocean and was active in ensuring the safe evacuation of Turkish and other refugees from Libya on the outbreak of that country's civil war. Meanwhile, a focus on developing a strong and technologically-advanced defence industry has resulted in ongoing support for indigenous naval programmes, including the modernisation of existing ships and the development of new designs. Recent projects have included the upgrading of the country's 'G' (FFG-7) class frigates with the domestically produced GENESIS combat management system and the introduction of new indigenously-designed and manufactured corvettes, coastal patrol vessels and coast guard search-and-rescue ships.[7]

The Turkish Navy has embarked on an ambitious programme of indigenous construction, of which the most significant project is for the 'Milgem' class of littoral corvettes. This image shows the first ship, *Heybeliada*, on ongoing sea trials in April 2011. *(Devrim Yaylali)*

The most important new project is that for the 'Milgem' class corvettes. *Heybeliada*, the first of a planned total of twelve of these 2,000-ton ships that resemble smaller versions of the US Navy's LCS-1 Littoral Combat Ship, started sea trials in November 2010 and should be delivered by Istanbul Naval Shipyard before the end of 2011. Istanbul Naval Shipyard is also working on a second modified ship, *Büyükada*, which should be launched by mid-2011. Further construction will then be transferred to the private sector. The Dearsan and RMK shipyards have been short-listed for this purpose. Dearsan delivered *Tuzla*, the first of sixteen planned 400-ton coastal patrol vessels, on 4 January 2011 and a further three are in various stages of trials. An additional two slightly modified variants have been sold to Turkmenistan. RMK are building a class of four 1,700-ton search-and-rescue ships for the Turkish Coast Guard. The first of these was undergoing trials as of mid-2011.

Looking forward, considerable attention is being attracted by the Turkish Navy's plans for an LPD-type amphibious transport dock. This forms part of a long-term amphibious road map announced in 2006 that has already seen orders for eight fast tank landing craft and two larger tank landing ships placed with the ADIK shipyard. It seems that ambitions for the LPD have increased, with recent reports suggesting that a through-deck amphibious assault ship displacing around 25,000 tons is now envisaged. Designs based on Spain's *Juan Carlos I*, South Korea's *Dokdo* and an indigenous proposal drawn up by RMK with assistance from Britain's BMT were

As well as the Turkish Navy, the Turkish Coast Guard is also benefiting from new construction. This is *Dost*, first of four new 1,700-ton search-and-rescue ships pictured in May 2011. *(Devrim Yaylali)*

selected for further consideration in May 2011. Other important future projects include plans for a new generation of air-defence destroyer – the much-delayed TF-2000 programme – for which the United Kingdom is pushing joint development of its Type 26 Global Combat Ship. Underneath the waves, there has been little news on progress with the acquisition of six AIP-equipped German Type 214 submarines contracted in 2009. However, a contract for a limited modernisation of the two newest 'Ay' class Type 209/1200 submarines completed in 1984 and 1990 was signed in March 2011.

OTHER REGIONAL FLEETS

Black Sea: The expansion of Turkey's naval capabilities has not been reflected elsewhere in the Black Sea. The small Bulgarian Navy saw the disbandment of its underwater flotilla in the autumn of 2010 with the formal withdrawal of the country's final remaining Project 633 submarine *Slava*. There is insufficient money available for any new orders, although forward procurement plans do envisage modernisation of the *Wielingen* frigates previously acquired from Belgium to incorporate a helicopter capability. These will doubtless be the three AS656 Panther light helicopters that are scheduled for delivery in the second half of 2011 following conclusion of an agreement with Eurocopter to cut previously contracted numbers in half. One of the frigates, *Drazki*, was briefly involved in supporting NATO's Operation 'United Protector' off Libya before lack of funding curtailed the mission. Romania's Batch II Type 22 frigate *Regele Ferdinand* has also been deployed in support of the NATO arms embargo.

Ukraine appears to be benefiting from the recent rapprochement with Russia and there have been reports that its new class of Project 58250 corvettes will be equipped with Russian armament. Four of these vessels were ordered from the Chernomorsky Shipyard in Nikolayev at the end of 2009. However, progress has been slow and it was not until 17 May 2011 that the keel of the first was laid. In an interesting development that might reflect the uncertain nature of the project's funding, the Ukrainian defence minister has reportedly donated one month's salary to support construction and called on the population to make similar donations. However, money has been found to refit the fleet flagship, the Project 1135.1 'Krivak III' frigate *Hetman Sagaidachny*. Overhaul of the country's sole Project 641 'Foxtrot' class submarine *Zaporizhzhya* is also well advanced and she should return to full operational service before the end of 2011.

North Sea and Atlantic: Portugal and Ireland have been amongst the countries worst-impacted by Europe's economic problems and it is therefore surprising that both their fleets are benefiting from new construction. In Portugal's case, the new ships that have recently been delivered were ordered and paid for in better times, most notably two Type 209(PN) submarines authorised in 2004. The first boat, *Tridente*, arrived in Portugal in August 2010, whilst sister-boat *Arpão* was delivered and commissioned at HDW's Kiel yard just before Christmas on

The Portuguese Navy is continuing to commission new warships in spite of the country's significant financial problems. The latter of a pair of Type 209 (PN) AIP-equipped submarines, *Arpão*, was delivered in 2010. *(HDW)*

The first of the Portuguese navy's new NPO2000 offshore patrol vessels *Viana do Castelo* was delivered in December 2010. Sister-ship *Figueira da Foz* should also be commissioned soon and more are planned. *(Portuguese Navy)*

22 December of the same year. The first NPO2000 offshore patrol vessel *Viana do Castelo* was delivered the same month and sister-ship *Figueira da Foz* should also be operational before the end of 2011. Two additional NCP pollution-control variants have also been ordered but the design is being reviewed to assimilate lessons learned from the trials of the first two ships. It seems that a total of class of eight ships is now planned if funding permits, replacing the remaining seven corvettes of the *João Coutinho* and *Baptista de Andrade* classes and some of the older patrol ships.

The Irish Naval Service's replacement plans are being driven by the pressing need to replace the three remaining elderly P-21 class patrol vessels, which have already exceeded their planned thirty-year lifespan. In July 2010, it was announced that Babcock Marine was the preferred bidder to provide two new offshore patrol vessels, with an option for a third, at a cost of just under €100m (US$145m). In spite of Ireland's subsequent financial difficulties, it appears that a contract was subsequently signed with Babcock for construction of the two ships at the Appledore facility that constructed the existing STX Marine PV80 type vessels *Róisín* and *Niamh*. The new PV90 vessels are based on the previous design but will be 10m longer and have 0.6m more draught to improve sea-keeping in the rough waters of the North Atlantic. There will also be modifications to the propulsion arrangements. Work on the first will start early in 2012 with delivery scheduled for 2014; the second will follow a year later.

Scandinavia and the Baltic: The last year has seen the Scandinavian navies make good progress with recapitalisation programmes intended to complete the transformation from Cold War military structures to more flexible deployable forces. Norway remains in the forefront of this process, supported by a c. US$6bn defence budget that remains the highest in the region. Important recent developments have included the delivery of the fifth and final *Fridtjof Nansen* class frigate, *Thor Heyerdahl*, from Navantia on 18 January 2011, bringing to a conclusion a project that commenced with a contract award in June 2000. Attention is now focused on bringing into service the six delayed *Skjold* fast attack craft that will supplement the *Nansen* class in the anti-surface role. The first operational unit, *Storm*, was delivered on 9 September 2010, with *Skudd* and *Steil* following in October 2010 and June 2011 respectively. The others will follow at roughly three-monthly intervals through to mid-2012, concluding with a refitted *Skjold*.[8] These vessels are capable of deploying eight of the new Kongsberg Naval Strike Missiles supplemented by an Oto Melara 76mm gun and are equipped with a DCNS SENIT combat management system. The combination of gas turbine-powered waterjet propulsion and an air-cushion catamaran design allows a top speed of c. 60 knots and it is claimed they are currently the world's fastest warships.

Neighbouring Sweden is in the course of completing delivery of its *Visby* class stealth corvettes, which are described in detail in Chapter 3.3. The next project is for two new A-26 type submarines, for which design work has already been authorised. Two of the existing A-19 *Götland* class

Norway is steadily commissioning the new heavily-armed *Skjold* class fast attack craft. With a maximum speed of approximately 60 knots, they are claimed to be the world's fastest warships. The first operational unit, *Storm*, was delivered on 9 September 2010. *(Royal Norwegian Navy)*

submarines are being modernised in the meantime to bring them up to the standards of the refitted A-17 *Södermanland* class boats.

In Denmark, the major focus is on completing construction of the new *Iver Huitfeldt* class frigates at the Odense Steel Shipyard in Lindø. The lead ship was delivered to the Danish Defence Acquisition and Logistics Organisation (DALO) in January 2011 and commenced a programme of sea trials shortly afterwards prior to planned transfer to the navy in 2012. She will not be fitted with her APAR multifunction radar until 2014 so as to expedite initial evaluation of other systems. The second ship, *Peter Willemoes*, will therefore be the first unit to be completely fitted out. She received her APAR tower in March 2011 and was subsequently officially named by Danish Prime Minister Lars Løkke Rasmussen on Friday 13 May 2011 before delivery and commencement of trials in June. The third and final ship, *Niels Juel*, will be handed over to the DALO early in 2012, after which the shipyard is scheduled to close. The project is being delivered against a backdrop of ongoing reductions to Royal Danish Navy, most notably the decommissioning of most of the remaining Stanflex 300 coastal patrol vessels in light of the ongoing focus on the Arctic, North Atlantic and international operations contained in the Danish 2010–14 Defence Agreement.

In the Eastern Baltic, where the legacy of the extensive minefields laid during the Second World War still remains something of a threat, the emphasis remains on bolstering mine countermeasures assets. The Lithuanian Navy has now taken delivery of the former British 'Hunt' class minehunters *Skalvis* (formerly *Cottesmore*) and *Kursis* (formerly *Dulverton*), whilst Finland is expecting the arrival of the first of three *Katanpää* class vessels from Italy's Intermarine before the end of the year. Poland has also allocated funding for a new 'Kormoran II' type minehunter which seems to have priority over additional MEKO A-100 type Project 621 'Gawron' corvettes and could be built in conjunction with a French or German yard. The overall future for the Polish Navy continues to look relatively bleak, however, given the increasing obsolescence of the two FFG-7 type frigates and four *Sokól* class submarines that form the core of its fleet and the priority being given to financing army and air force modernisation.

RUSSIA

Russia's government has long-heralded and ambitious plans for the wholesale renewal of the country's navy but the reality continues to fall far short of the rhetoric. Orders for new surface warships and submarines bear little resemblance to the numbers contained in published naval plans, building times tend to be considerably extended and much of the new technology that is eventually delivered seemingly fails to perform as planned. An impressive level of international activity is being maintained by a relatively small cadre of the more modern ships remaining from Soviet-era construction programmes but it is difficult to hide the reality of an increasingly ageing and obsolescent fleet. The situation is clearly of concern to the country's leaders and various measures are being adopted to improve the situation. These include a significant uplift in funding for new procurement and associated infrastructure, orders for modified versions of tried-and-tested designs to provide breathing space for the development of more reliable new technology and – most controversially – resort to foreign assistance. The last step is best evidenced by the lengthy discussions with France for the supply of *Mistral* class

Denmark's current major construction programme is for three *Iver Huitfeldt* class frigates. The photograph on the left shows the second ship of the class, *Peter Willemoes*, being fitted with a tower for the APAR radar system at the Odense Steel Shipyard in March 2011. The lead ship (right) was delivered without the tower to expedite trials of other equipment. *(DALO)*

amphibious assault ships that culminated in an order for two of the class from DCNS in June 2011. Whilst this initial pair will be built in France by STX Europe, it is envisaged that further ships might be licence-built in Russia. Interestingly, STX is reportedly a stakeholder in a venture to move St Petersburg's Admiralty Shipyard to a new facility on Kotlin Island that would provide an ideal location for any move to domestic production.

The combination of long-delayed construction, commissioning problems and changes in strategy has resulted in an often confusion of projects being pursued with greater or lesser success across a multitude of shipyards. An overview of the more important surface and underwater programmes is attempted below whilst Table 2.4.6 summarises current fleet strength.

Major Surface Ships: Although previous plans apparently envisaged construction of new surface warships being concentrated on two major projects, the current position is rather more complex. At least four major classes are currently being built and others are, apparently, planned.

- **Project 2235.0 Frigates:** Previously intended to be the Russian Navy's main class of 'blue water' surface escort, this 4.500-ton general purpose frigate was designed by the Severnoye Design Bureau in the early years of the new millennium. First of class, *Admiral Sergei Gorshkov*, was laid down at the Severnaya yard in St Petersburg in February 2006 and was launched on 29 October 2010. It is currently claimed that delivery is due during 2012 but this looks hugely optimistic in the light of the past performance of Russian yards. A second vessel, *Admiral Kasatonov*, was laid down in November 2009 whilst the yard announced orders for a further units in March 2011.
- **Project 1135.6 Frigates:** Based on the 4.000-ton *Talwar* class frigates built for India, three of this class were ordered from Kaliningrad's Yantar Shipyard in a previously unexpected development in October 2010. They are intended to reinforce Russia's ageing Black Sea Fleet, with delivery planned during 2013–14. The selection of a design already in service elsewhere will reduce execution risk and is therefore a sensible counter to the construction delays that have blighted other Russian projects. First of class, *Admiral Grigorovich*, was laid down in December 2010, whilst work on a second vessel, *Admiral Essen*, will start in the second half of 2011. There have been reports that a second batch of three is planned.
- **Project 2038.0 Corvettes:** A 2,200-ton light frigate intended for littoral operations, this class is

TABLE 2.4.6: RUSSIAN NAVY: SELECTED PRINCIPAL UNITS AS AT MID-2011

TYPE	CLASS	NUMBER[1]	TONNAGE	DIMENSIONS	PROPULSION	CREW	DATE
Aircraft carriers							
Aircraft Carrier – CV	Project 1143.5 **KUZNETSOV**	1	60,000 tons	306m x 35/73m x 10m	Steam, 32 knots	2,600	1991
Principal Surface Escorts							
Battlecruiser – BCGN	Project 1144.2 **KIROV**	1 (1)	25,000 tons	252m x 29m x 9m	CONAS, 32 knots	740	1980
Cruiser – CG	Project 1164 **MOSKVA** ('Slava')	3	12,500 tons	186m x 21m x 8m	COGAG, 32 knots	530	1982
Destroyer – DDG	Project 956/956A **SOVREMENNY**	c. 5	8,000 tons	156m x 17m x 6m	Steam, 32 knots	300	1980
Destroyer – DDG	Project 1155.1 **CHABANENKO** ('Udaloy II')	1	9,000 tons	163m x 19m x 6m	COGAG, 29 knots	250	1999
Destroyer – DDG	Project 1155 **UDALOY**	c.8	8,400 tons	163m x 19m x 6m	COGAG, 30 knots	300	1980
Frigate – FFG	Project 1154 **NEUSTRASHIMY**	2	4,400 tons	139m x 16m x 6m	COGAG, 30 knots	210	1993
Frigate – FFG	Project 1135 **BDITELNNY** ('Krivak I/II')	c.4	3,700 tons	123m x 14m x 5m	COGAG, 32 knots	180	1970
Frigate – FFG	Project 2038.0 **STEREGUSHCHY**	1	2,200 tons	105m x 11m x 4m	CODAD, 27 knots[2]	100	2008
Frigate – FFG	Project 1161.1 **TATARSTAN**	1	2,000 tons	102m x 13m x 4m	CODOG, 27 knots	100	2002
Submarines							
Submarine – SSBN	Project 955 **YURY DOLGORUKY** ('Borey')	1	17,000+ tons	170m x 13m x 10m	Nuclear, 25+ knots	110	2010
Submarine – SSBN	Project 941 **DONSKOY** ('Typhoon')	1 (2)	33,000 tons	173m x 23m x 12m	Nuclear, 26 knots	150	1981
Submarine – SSBN	Project 677BDRM **VERKHOTURYE** ('Delta IV')	6	18,000 tons	167m x 12m x 9m	Nuclear, 24 knots	130	1985
Submarine – SSBN	Project 677BDR **ZVEZDA** ('Delta III')	4	12,000 tons	160m x 12m x 9m	Nuclear, 24 knots	130	1976
Submarine – SSGN	Project 949B ('Oscar II')	c.5	17,500 tons	154m x 8m x 9m	Nuclear, 30+ knots	100	1986
Submarine – SSN	Project 971 ('Akula I/II')	c.10	9,500 tons	110m x 14m x 10m	Nuclear, 30+ knots	60	1986
Submarine – SSK	Project 677 **ST PETERSBURG** ('Lada')	1	2,700 tons	72m x 7m x 7m	Diesel-electric, 21 knots	40	2010
Submarine – SSK	Project 877/636 ('Kilo')	c.20	3,000 tons	73m x 10m x 7m	Diesel-electric, 20 knots	55	1981
Major Amphibious Units							
Landing Platform Dock – LPD	Project 1174 **IVAN ROGOV**	1	14,000 tons	157m x 24m x 7m	Gas, 19 knots	240	1978

Notes:

1 Table only includes main types & focuses on operational units: bracketed figures are ships being refurbished or in maintained reserve.

2 Some sources state CODOG propulsion.

The Russian Border Guard's Project 1135 'Krivak III' frigate *Vorovsky* seen whilst operating with the US Coast Guard in August 2009. Commissioned in 1990, she is one of Russia's more modern surface vessels pending the introduction of new frigates and corvettes. *(US Coast Guard)*

also built by the Severnaya shipyard. The lead ship, *Steregushchy*, has been operational since 2008, whilst second of class *Soobrazitelny* should be delivered in the second half of 2011. The third ship, *Boiky*, was launched on 15 April 2011. It seems that construction from the fifth ship onwards – which was laid down in May 2011 – will be to a modified Project 2038.5 design and that a total of at least fifteen ships is planned.

- **Project 1161.1 Corvettes:** Intended largely for operations in the inland Caspian Sea, this class is built by the Zelenodolsk shipyard on the Volga River. The first ship, *Tatarstan*, was completed in 2002 and a further two, modified ships, are currently under construction with a further pair of modified variants recently delivered to Vietnam. The next Russian ship, *Dagestan*, delayed by the priority given to the export contract, was launched on 1 April 2011 and could be delivered in 2012.

The overall 2011–20 construction programme apparently envisages the delivery of a total of fifteen frigates and thirty-five corvettes within a total 100-ship plan. There have been some reports that the Project 2038.0/5 design does not fully meet modern requirements and an alternative class might therefore be sourced. There is also a possibility of a larger, destroyer-sized design emerging, potentially with nuclear propulsion.

Submarines: The submarine force remains core to Russian defence planning, particularly maintenance of the underwater element of the country's nuclear deterrent. This is currently built around fast-aging boats of the Project 677 BDR/M 'Delta III' and 'Delta IV' classes. Four of the former remain in service, each carrying sixteen R-29R (SS-N-18) ballistic missiles with three warheads, whilst there are six of the latter, each equipped with sixteen R-29RM (SS-N-21) ballistic missiles with four nuclear warheads. The entire force is to be replaced by Project 955 'Borey' class submarines armed with the new RSM-56 'Bulava' (SS-NX-30) missile. The 'Bulava' – which translates to 'mace' in English – has had a troubled development history with a series of launch failures. However, recent progress has been more positive. A renewed test programme from the modified Project 941 'Typhoon' class submarine *Dimitry Donskoy* in the second half of 2010 saw two successful launches. These were followed by the first successful test from the initial Project 955 boat, *Yury Dolgoruky*, on 28 June 2011. Additional launches are planned throughout the rest of 2011 prior to declaring the new system operational. A further three Project 955 submarines are in various stages of construction, each capable of deploying sixteen RSM-56 missiles with six nuclear warheads, and a total of up to eight boats is planned.

Work on the strategic missile force is supplemented by a significant programme of conventionally-armed submarines, the most important being:

- **Project 885 Nuclear-Powered Attack Submarines:** Known as the 'Yasen' class, this project dates back to commencement of work on lead boat *Severodvinsk* at the Sevmash yard in late 1993. She was finally launched in June 2010 and should be commissioned by the end of 2011. With a submerged displacement of c. 10,000 tons, she is armed with a mixture of torpedo tubes and vertically-launched missile cells and is likely to approach modern Western standards of overall stealth. Work on a second boat – being built to an improved Project 885.1 design – commenced in 2009 and a class of at least six is planned.

- **Project 677 Patrol Submarines:** Originally intended as a replacement for the Project 636 'Kilo' class, the follow-on 'Lada' class was designed to provide greater stealth and endurance. However, trials of the initial unit, *St Petersburg*, have been protracted and problematic since the boat first went to sea in 2007. She was finally commissioned into the navy in May 2010 and two further members of the class are scheduled for delivery by the Admiralty Shipyard before the end of 2011. However, series production has been postponed until a satisfactory conclusion has been reached to ongoing tests.
- **Project 636 Patrol Submarines:** Formally the mainstay of Russia's patrol submarine flotillas, recent construction of the famous 'Kilo' class has been destined for export. However, slow progress with the Project 677 design resulted in an order for three of an improved Project 636.3 variant, the first of which was laid down in August 2010 for delivery in 2013. Further batches could be ordered if teething troubles with the Project 677 boats cannot be satisfactorily resolved.

The Russian 'Kilo' class submarine *Alrosa* pictured whilst participating in NATO's submarine rescue exercise Bold Monarch 2011. Russia has ordered improved Project 636.3 variants of this class as part of an attempt to sustain overall submarine numbers. *(NATO)*

In addition to the projects highlighted above, further investment is being directed towards classes of smaller patrol craft and amphibious shipping. The programme of new construction is also being supplemented by significant investment in maintaining the existing fleet, which is inevitably becoming more difficult to maintain. The sole carrier *Admiral Kuznetsov* is scheduled to enter an extensive refit at the Sevmash yard in Severodvinsk from the end of 2012 once work on India's *Virkamaditya* has been completed, leaving Russia without a carrier capability for up to five years. Rumours of plans for imminent construction of a new nuclear-powered carrier continue to surface. However, these have been firmly denied by the Russian defence ministry, which has stressed that only preliminary conceptual work is currently authorised.

Notes

1. Amongst many reports covering Robert Gates' speech was Ian Traynor's 'US defence chief blasts Europe over Nato, *The Guardian* – 11 June 2011 (London, Guardian News and Media Ltd, 2011), p 17.

2. This interesting revelation was made by General Sir Nicholas Houghton, Vice Chief of the (British) Defence Staff whilst being questioned by the House of Commons Defence Committee on 22 June 2011.

3. A useful source of information on this and other French procurement projects is the French language *Mer et Marine* website at www.meretmarine.com.

4. Reports differ as to exactly how many Harriers were deployed on *Giuseppe Garibaldi*. Initial Italian statements suggest eight fast jets were embarked but later statements only reference four Harrier aircraft being assigned to the NATO mission.

5. As of 2011, the RFTG comprised the amphibious transport dock, *Albion* (flagship), the helicopter carrier *Ocean*, the auxiliary dock landing ships *Cardigan Bay* and *Mounts Bay*, the Type 42 destroyer *Liverpool*, the Type 23 frigate *Sunderland*, the nuclear-powered attack submarine *Triumph* and four additional Royal Fleet Auxiliaries. Assigned aviation assets included four Sea King Mk4 transport helicopters, three Apache AH1 and three Lynx AH7 attack helicopters, two Lynx Mk8 anti-submarine helicopters and two Sea King ASaC7 battle management rotorcraft. The amphibious element also included 40 Commando Royal Marines and supporting elements.

6. Full details of the unfortunate incident were reported extensively in the UK media at the time. Full details can be found by searching the BBC website.

7. A comprehensive overview of current Turkish procurement programmes was contained in last year's *Seaforth World Naval Review*. Please see Devrim Yaylali's 'The Turkish Navy', *Seaforth World Naval Review 2011* (Barnsley, Seaforth Publishing, 2010). Mr Yaylali's English language 'Bosphorus Naval News' blog at http://turkishnavy.net is an informed source of news on regional naval developments.

8. *Skjold* was first delivered in a trials configuration in 1999 but has subsequently been rebuilt to full operational standard.

2.4A Fleet Review

Author:
Richard Beedall

UNITED KINGDOM

Defence Review Reshapes the Royal Navy

INTRODUCTION

In October 2010 the United Kingdom's new coalition government published the results of its Strategic Defence and Security Review (SDSR). This made significant cuts to a Royal Navy which had already been steadily shrinking since 2004, but also provided a framework for the British Naval Service to plan its future size and structure under 'Future Force 2020'. The policy document 'Securing Britain in an Age of Uncertainty: The Strategic Defence and Security Review' describes the national security capabilities that the United Kingdom will need by 2020, and charts a course for getting there.[1] It also details how the British armed forces will be reshaped in order to tackle emerging and future threats, and brings some badly-needed coherence to the UK's defence plans, commitments and the resources provided to deliver these.

SDSR supersedes the Strategic Defence Review (SDR) conducted in 1998. This document had placed a strong emphasis on expeditionary warfare and maritime force projection. However, its implementation stalled after 2001 when the UK became involved in military operations in Afghanistan and Iraq. As a result, the Royal Navy's vision for a 'Future Navy' became increasingly disconnected from financial realities: for example not a single major warship was ordered in the years 2003 to 2006. A new strategy was required and the development process began in mid-2009.

In May 2010 a new Conservative–Liberal Democrat coalition government was elected. This considered that the existing defence budget of £36.9bn (c. US$60bn) could not be afforded by a country in a financial crisis. The government also decided that achieving success in Afghanistan meant that no changes could be made to the front-line strength of the British Army whilst operations there continued (anticipated to be until 2014). The burden of immediate cuts would thus have to fall upon the Royal Navy (RN) and the Royal Air Force (RAF). This inevitably created tension as the two services strove to justify and preserve their own projects and force levels.

The results of the SDSR process were finally announced by the Prime Minister, David Cameron, on Tuesday 19 October 2010. As expected, the RN was badly affected, but the short-term cuts were mitigated by some positive long-term commitments.[2]

One of the most controversial decisions taken in the UK's 2010 SDSR was the premature decommissioning of the light carrier *Ark Royal* and her fixed-wing air group of Harrier jets. *(Conrad Waters)*

FUTURE FORCE 2020

SDSR envisages that the UK is unlikely to engage in major military operations except as part of a wider coalition. It then establishes a series of defence planning assumptions as to the size and number of conflicts that the UK armed forces should be sized and shaped to conduct. These range from 'three non-enduring operations if … not already engaged in an enduring operation' up to 'committing all our effort to a one-off intervention of up to three brigades, with maritime and air support'. Based upon these assumptions, the document outlines a

Table 2.4A.1: FUTURE FORCE 2020 STRUCTURE

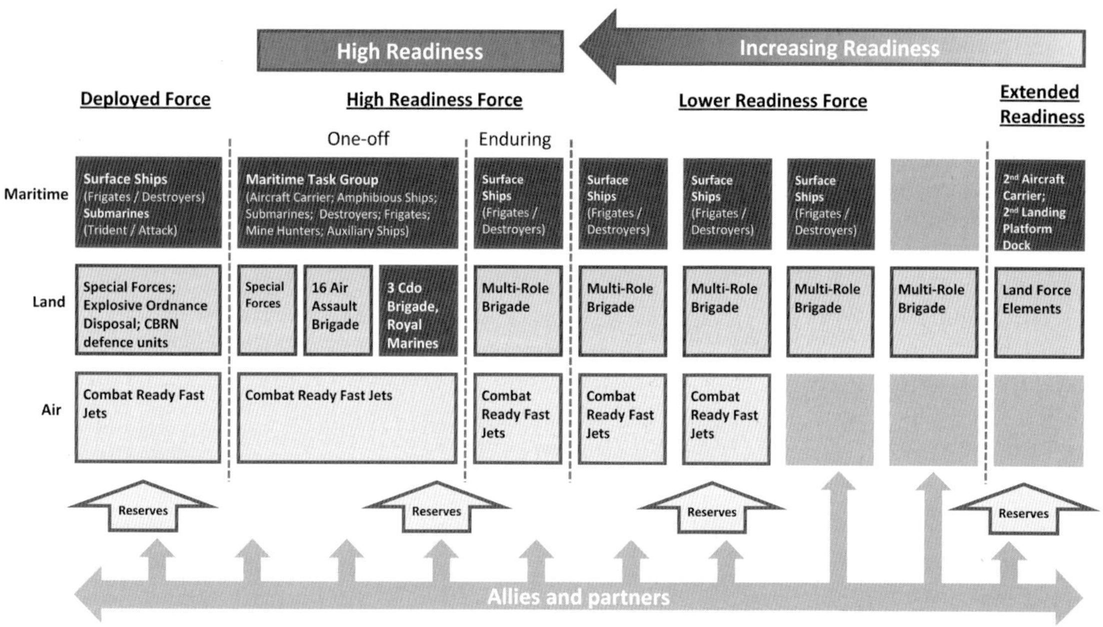

The SDSR places much greater emphasis on any future major military operations taking place in a coalition context. This 2008 image shows the Type 23 frigate *Westminster* being replenished by the US amphibious assault ship *Essex* (LHD-2) whilst on deployment in the Indian Ocean. *(US Navy)*

projected force structure for the armed forces in 2020, which is summarised in Table 2.4A.1.

The correctness of the assumptions contained in the SDSR was challenged in March 2011 when the UK government decided to intervene in Libya whilst still engaged in a large enduring operation in Afghanistan. However, the Secretary of State for Defence, Dr Liam Fox, emphasised that the defence review would not be reopened as 'we would come to the same conclusion[s]'.

STRATEGIC DEFENCE AND SECURITY REVIEW 2015

The UK's Defence Budget will fall to £33.5bn in 2014–15, a reduction of 7.5 per cent in real terms compared to 2010/11. However, because the budget was already insufficient to meet expected expenditure, the actual cut is c. 17.5 per cent. SDSR preserves spending on Afghanistan and maintaining the nuclear deterrent but accepts other risks to make £4.7bn of savings over the next four years. The UK Ministry of Defence (MOD) is still trying to identify additional savings required through base closures and other reductions.

The reduced level of spending is recognised by the government as being insufficient to realise the proposed force structure in 2020. Many major decisions and significant financial commitments – for example the number of Joint Strike Fighters to be ordered – have thus been deliberately deferred.

Another Strategic Defence and Security Review will be held in 2015 and this will consider a long 'shopping list' of equipment projects awaiting approval. It is hoped that the British economy and public sector finances will have recovered sufficiently by that time for an increase in defence spending to be possible. Equally, the ending of UK operations in Afghanistan should permit a reduction in the strength of the army and the reallocation of resources elsewhere.

SDSR AND THE ROYAL NAVY

Under SDSR, the Royal Navy and Royal Marines (collectively the Naval Service) have been tasked with providing the following military capabilities:

- Continuous, at sea, nuclear deterrence.
- Maritime defence of the UK and its South Atlantic Overseas Territories.
- An enduring presence in the waters of priority regions of the world so as to contribute

to conventional deterrence and containment.
- Powerful intervention capabilities from surface and submarine fleets.
- The ability to land forces from the sea by helicopter and over-the-beach with protective vehicles and supplies from specialist ships.
- The ability to command UK and allied naval forces at up to Task Force level.

SDSR envisages that these tasks can be met by a smaller Naval Service and between 2011 and 2015 various cuts will thus be implemented. From 2015 onwards, the RN will transition towards a 'Future Maritime Force'. This will include fully-operational *Astute* submarines and Type 45 destroyers, as well as the introduction of the *Queen Elizabeth* class aircraft carriers, the Type 26 Global Combat Ship, the Joint Strike Fighter, new tankers, new helicopters and, eventually, new nuclear-deterrent submarines.

The first Type 45 destroyer *Daring* alongside the veteran US carrier *Enterprise* (CVN-65) during a training exercise on 19 October 2010 that also involved the Norwegian frigate *Fridtjof Nansen*. Decisions contained in the SDSR that was published on the same day mean that it will be the end of the decade before the Type 45 destroyers serve alongside a British strike carrier. *(US Navy)*

THE FUTURE MARITIME FORCE

SDSR is quite specific as to size and shape of the Naval Service as it moves towards its future force structure. Headcount will fall from 35,000 to 30,000 by April 2015 and 29,000 by 2020, whilst its principal equipment will be as follows:

1. BALLISTIC MISSILE SUBMARINES:

The UK's nuclear deterrent will continue to be provided by the four *Vanguard* class submarines. By 2020 the first of a replacement or 'Successor' class should be under construction.

2. AIRCRAFT CARRIERS:

The most controversial decision made by SDSR was to immediately decommission the RN's only operational fixed-wing aircraft carrier – the relatively small *Ark Royal* – and retire from service the Harrier GR9, the only fast jet that she could operate. This was justified on the basis that the combination had 'a very limited coercive capability', and that there were more cost-effective ways to use the money. However Admiral Sir Mark Stanhope, the First Sea Lord, is reported to have told the Prime Minister, Mr Cameron, that he 'could not endorse [this] as his military advice' and considered it to be a 'political, not military decision'.

The decommissioning of *Ark Royal* will save £10m in 2011–12 and £25m in 2012–13, but has created a ten-year gap during which the UK will have no operational aircraft carriers. SDSR envisages that – by 2020 – a new carrier strike capability will have been created based upon one of the *Queen Elizabeth* class and the Joint Strike Fighter (JSF).

3. FRIGATES AND DESTROYERS:

Under SDSR, the Royal Navy will have just nineteen frigates and destroyers – down from twenty-three in 2010, and thirty-one as recently as 2004. The four Batch III Type 22 frigates were quickly decommissioned without replacement and the frigate force will consist of thirteen Type 23 'Duke' class vessels until the first of a new class, designated the Type 26, enters service around 2021. Meanwhile, the remaining Type 42 destroyers will have been replaced by six Type 45 *Daring* class destroyers by 2013/14.

4. NUCLEAR-POWERED ATTACK SUBMARINES:

The future maritime force will include seven nuclear-powered attack submarines: the same number as in 2010 but down from twelve in 2003. The lead boat of the new *Astute* class entered service in 2010 and these will continue to enter service at the average rate of one every twenty-six months, with the last of the current *Trafalgar* class leaving service in 2022. Six *Astutes* had been ordered in full or part by March 2010, whilst long-lead items for the final boat are expected to be ordered in 2012.

5. ROYAL MARINES AND AMPHIBIOUS SHIPPING:

SDSR makes no significant changes to the Royal Marines Corps, although its numbers will reduce by 600 (from 7,400) by 2015. The Corps will remain part of the Naval Service rather than become part of the Army. Its 3 Commando Brigade will form one of the UK's two very high readiness battle-groups.

The capacity of the amphibious squadron will be reduced from brigade-level lift to that needed to land and support a Commando Group of up 1,800 personnel with helicopters, vehicles, logistics and command-and-control. The required shipping consists of:

- One *Albion* class landing platform dock (LPD) and command ship, with a second available in extended reserve. From November 2011, *Bulwark* will be the high-readiness LPD and fleet flagship, with her sister-ship, *Albion*, held in reserve.
- One landing platform helicopter (LPH). It was decided in December 2010 that the LPH will initially be the converted light aircraft carrier

An image of the Type 45 destroyer *Diamond* on sea trials during May 2010. Commissioned a year later on 6 May 2011, she is one of six ships that – alongside the Type 23 frigates – will form the core of the Royal Navy's fleet for the rest of this decade. *(BAE Systems)*

Illustrious, the sole survivor of the *Invincible* class. She will decommission in mid-2014 when *Ocean* becomes operational after a period in reserve and a major refit.

- Two 'Bay' class auxiliary landing ships (LSD(A)) operated by the Royal Fleet Auxiliary service. A third ship will be held in reserve.
- Six civilian-manned 'Point' class roll-on, roll-off ferries. These are used commercially when not required by the MoD for logistic and re-supply duties.

Before SDSR the RN had been hoping to replace *Ocean* with a new purpose-built ship by 2022, but the MoD is now studying the use of the new aircraft carriers in a secondary LPH role. *Ocean* is thus expected to decommission or go into extended readiness when the first of these becomes operational.

SDSR confirmed that the fast landing craft (FLC) programme will proceed as a replacement for existing Landing Craft Utility Mark 10. The first should enter service in 2014.

6. MINOR WAR VESSELS & HYDROGRAPHIC SHIPS:

SDSR says that the RN will have a force of fourteen mine countermeasures vessels (MCMV). However, this may be a mistake as fifteen were still in service in mid-2011, viz. eight 'Hunt' and seven *Sandown* class.

They will eventually be replaced by a new class resulting from the MCM, Hydrographic and Patrol Capability (MHPC) programme with a self-evident combination of functions. Early MHPC design concepts are the size of a 1960s frigate, and able to carry a range of off-board systems such as unmanned underwater vehicles, unmanned surface vehicles and unmanned aerial vehicles. Up to fourteen may eventually be built, replacing all the existing minehunters, four patrol vessels and the two *Echo* class multi-role survey ships. The Hydrographic Survey Squadron will continue to operate the ocean survey vessel *Scott* and the two *Echo* class until the delivery of MHPC.

A commercial polar research and sub-sea support vessel (*Polarbjørn*, meaning 'Polar Bear') was leased for three years in early 2011. She commissioned on 23 June 2011 as the ice patrol ship *Protector* and will spend nine months a year in the South Atlantic and Antarctic.

7. AFLOAT SUPPORT:

The Royal Fleet Auxiliary (RFA) service provides the RN with re-supply and refuelling shipping. SDSR gives no details as to the service's long term size and composition, as this is subject to a separate review. However, in line with reductions to front-line strength, SDSR proposed the decommissioning of two ships, leaving a flotilla including five tankers, three replenishment ships, an aviation training and casualty support ship, and a forward repair ship.

Three further tankers (*Gold Rover*, *Black Rover* and *Orangeleaf*) are scheduled to leave service between

The *Trafalgar* class submarine *Turbulent* seen in October 2010. The SDSR made no change to planned numbers of Royal Navy nuclear-powered attack submarines, which will remain fixed at seven *Trafalgar* and *Astute* class vessels. *(Conrad Waters)*

2015 and 2017, and the long-delayed Maritime Afloat Reach and Sustainability (MARS) programme has finally gained traction. An order for two tankers is hoped for in 2012, with completion of the first before the end of 2015. The contract is expected to include options for further tankers.

RAPID RESTRUCTURING

In the last months of 2010 and first half of 2011, the cuts in force levels identified by SDSR were implemented at a rapid pace. These included:

- *Ark Royal* arrived at Portsmouth for the last time on 3 December 2010. She paid off on 11 March 2011.
- Joint Force Harrier, including 800 Naval Air Squadron, ceased to be operational on 15 December 2010. Disbandment occurred on 28 January 2011.
- The four Batch III Type 22 frigates decommissioned between February and June 2011.
- The 'Bay' class LSD(A) *Largs Bay* left service in April 2011 and was sold to Australia.
- The RFA tanker *Bayleaf* decommissioned on 20 April 2011. *Fort George*, a replenishment ship previously used to support *Ark Royal*, was also withdrawn in the first half of 2011.

OPERATIONAL STRUCTURE AND BASING

Significant changes are being made to the RN's command structures, reflecting both SDSR and a report from the Defence Reform Unit published in June 2011.

The two highest 4* (i.e. Admiral) posts of First Sea Lord and Commander-in-Chief Fleet (CINCFLEET) will probably be replaced in 2012 by a single 3* (Vice Admiral) Service Chief responsible for the generation and delivery of maritime capabilities. He will head a Battle Staff which includes Commander United Kingdom Maritime Forces (COMUKMARFOR) and Commander UK Amphibious Forces (COMUKAMPHIBFOR). The latter is a Royal Marine.

COMUKMARFOR is the highest sea-going command in the Royal Navy, commanding at sea any naval task forces or task groups formed for specific operations. Before SDSR he had three subordinate commanders; however, with the demise of *Ark Royal*, the post of Commander UK Carrier Strike Group (COMUKCSG) ceased to exist. Additionally, the UK Amphibious Task Group has now been renamed

The force reductions envisaged by the SDSR mean that only one of the two LPD-type amphibious transport docks will remain operational at any one time, with the other being laid up in extended readiness. This view of *Albion* and *Bulwark* operating in concert will therefore be rare in future. *(BAE Systems)*

The naval force reductions envisaged by the SDSR were completed with almost indecent haste. Amongst ships decommissioned were all four remaining Type 22 frigates, with *Cornwall* (pictured here) the last to pay off on 30 June 2011. *(US Navy)*

With the cessation – at least temporarily – of fixed-wing naval operations, the Fleet Air Arm has primarily become a maritime helicopter force. It will be largely comprised of Merlin HM2 (left) and Lynx Wildcat helicopters (as well as marinised Merlin HC3 troop carriers), the Wildcat replacing the existing Lynx HMA8 (right) pictured here. *(Lockheed Martin / AgustaWestland)*

the UK Response Force Task Group (RFTG) to reflect the greater variety of roles that it will be required to undertake. The RFTG is commanded at sea by Commander UK Task Group (COMUKTG), so the appointment of Commander Amphibious Task Group (COMATG) has also gone. An additional officer, UK Maritime Component Commander (UKMCC), is responsible for naval operations in the Middle East.

The ships and submarines of the Royal Navy are divided in to flotillas at the three naval bases: HMNB Portsmouth and HMNB Devonport in Southern England, and HMNB Clyde at Faslane in Scotland. The significant reduction in the size of the Royal Navy since the end of the Cold War means that these bases are all under-utilised, and SDSR commits to rationalising the RN's estate. However, political considerations make it unlikely that any naval base will actually be closed, despite the potential significant savings. Another possible rationalisation is the closure of the underutilised Britannia Royal Naval College at Dartmouth and the moving of officer training to HMS *Raleigh* at Torpoint near Devonport.

Royal Navy minor warfare vessel numbers saw little change as a result of the SDSR. Many of these are deployed far away from home waters. This is the hydrographic survey vessel *Echo* pictured at the Indonesian Fleet Review held in August 2008. An Indian Navy Project 25 *Khukri* class corvette is behind her, *(Royal Australian Navy)*

NAVAL AIRPOWER

The last decade has been difficult for the Fleet Air Arm (FAA), a branch of the Royal Navy that is more correctly referred to as Naval Aviation. The FAA had once expected to start replacing its Sea Harrier FA2 fighter with a new Joint Combat Aircraft (JCA) in 2012. Instead the Sea Harrier was retired in 2006 and the Harrier is also now gone, leaving it with no jet combat aircraft. In April 2011 the FAA made redundant fifteen of its once-precious pool of fifty-nine Harrier pilots.

SDSR envisages that the FAA will be primarily a maritime helicopter force based around Lynx Wildcat and Merlin helicopters – both manufactured by AgustaWestland. The existing fleet of Lynx HMA8 rotorcraft will be replaced in RN service from 2015 by twenty-eight Lynx Wildcat helicopters at a cost of c. £400m (US$650m). A slight puzzle is why SDSR did not cancel the Wildcat order given that all remaining RN warships can operate the larger and more capable Merlin. The FAA has about forty Merlin HM1 anti-submarine helicopters, thirty of which are being upgraded to the HM2 standard. In addition twenty-eight of the troop-carrying HC3 variant will be transferred from the RAF and upgraded to a marinised HC4 standard: these will replace the old Sea King HC4 helicopters currently operated by the FAA as part of the Joint Helicopter Command and which are due to retire by 2016. It is not yet clear how the two year gap will be filled.

With SDSR 2015 in mind, the Royal Navy and FAA are already starting to advocate several initiatives to revitalise maritime air capabilities in general, and regenerate a carrier strike capability in particular.

In 2001 the Lockheed Martin Joint Strike Fighter (JSF) was selected to meet the UK's JCA requirement. Originally it was envisaged to be a Harrier/Sea Harrier replacement and the F-35B Short Take Off and Vertical Landing (STOVL) variant was favoured. However SDSR confirmed a switch to the F-35C carrier variant, stating that 'this version of the jet has a longer range and greater payload ... [and] will be cheaper, reducing through-life costs by around 25%'. The UK had once planned to buy 'up to 150' F-35 aircraft, but no more than fifty now seems likely. Current planning is for the first frontline JSF squadron to become operational by 2020. The RN would ideally like this to be a naval air squadron dedicated to carrier-based operations and manned largely by FAA personnel. Experience with Joint Force Harrier has shown how difficult it is to 'swing role' squadrons between land and carrier based operations over the long term, rather than in a crisis (e.g. the successful operation of RAF Harriers from RN aircraft carriers during the Falklands War in 1982). As the RAF wants the same JSF aircraft to replace its Tornado GR4A strike aircraft, a compromise looks inevitable.

The FAA is currently operating Sea King Mark 7 Airborne Surveillance and Control helicopters. These had been purchased for carrier-based operations but are now primarily used to support operations in Afghanistan. They are due to leave service by 2015/16 and a replacement is being studied. The baseline is the conversion of existing Merlin helicopters, fitting them with Searchwater radars and Cerebus mission systems taken from the existing Sea Kings. However, the RN would prefer to buy a small number of the far more capable Northrop Grumman E-2D Advanced Hawkeye aircraft that is being built for the US Navy. The French Navy already operates the earlier E-2C variant, so opportunities for co-operation with two navies closely aligned with the UK are obvious.

SDSR cancelled the RAF's Nimrod MRA4 Maritime Reconnaissance Aircraft. Alternative measures using helicopters, attack submarines and frigates are proving to be unsatisfactory in some circumstances, lacking the speed, endurance and rapid

A view of the Taurus 09 deployment of the Royal Navy's Amphibious Task Group. With the demise of the carrier strike force, the group has been renamed the UK Response Force Task Group and is the navy's most potent deployable force. *(Crown Copyright)*

A particularly significant change to the future construction programme has been the plan to convert at least one of the two new *Queen Elizabeth* class aircraft carriers to CATOBAR operations, as depicted in this computer-generated image. *(Aircraft Carrier Alliance)*

Construction of the first *Queen Elizabeth* class carrier is progressing rapidly, as pictured in these February 2011 images of lower hull 'rings' being assembled at Govan on the Clyde and at Portsmouth. *(BAE Systems)*

response times of an aircraft. Reliance on the USA and other NATO allies is also sometimes undesirable, e.g. in relation to safeguarding the transit of *Vanguard* ballistic submarines. The eventual purchase of a few Boeing P-3A Poseidon patrol aircraft seems possible and the RN is advocating that these should be operated by the FAA.

Finally, the RN is rather belatedly looking at the possibilities offered by unmanned air vehicles (UAV). Huge strides have been made in this area over the last decade, and the options are extensive, including:

- Long-range maritime surveillance from land bases.
- Attacking well-defended targets using stealthy UAVs launched from aircraft carriers.
- Rapid-reaction maritime search-and-destroy missions launched from escorts and minor warships, including the Type 26 frigate.

FUTURE WARSHIP PROGRAMMES

1. CARRIER STRIKE AND THE *QUEEN ELIZABETH* CLASS:

Since SDR in 1998, a centrepiece of RN planning has been 'carrier strike' – the deployment of offensive air power from aircraft carriers in support of UK military operations around the world. Whilst the RN now lacks a carrier strike capability, in 2008 two new aircraft carriers were ordered at an expected cost that had reached £5.9bn (c. US$9.5bn) by January 2010. These ships, *Queen Elizabeth* and *Prince of Wales* (likely to be renamed *Ark Royal*), will be the largest warships ever operated by the Royal Navy. First steel was cut for *Queen Elizabeth* at the BAE Systems Govan shipyard in July 2009 and for *Prince of Wales* in May 2011. The ships are being built in blocks weighing up to 11,500 tons by shipyards around the UK. When completed, these are being transported to Babcock's Rosyth dockyard for the final assembly and fitting out of the ships.

SDSR re-examined the carrier strike concept and concluded that that there was a requirement for a future capability, but the cost of the *Queen Elizabeth* class and associated programmes was deemed to be 'crowding out' other important investments. It decided that only one new aircraft carrier was needed and that the UK would work with France to minimise the risks this caused. The Anglo-French Defence and Security Co-operation Treaty signed in November 2010 states: 'Building primarily on initial maritime task group co-operation around the French carrier, *Charles de Gaulle*, the UK and France will aim to have the ability, by the early 2020s, to deploy a UK-French integrated carrier strike group incorporating assets from both countries. There will be co-ordination of aircraft carriers to ensure that there is always a British or French vessel available for joint operations.'

During the SDSR process the government considered cancelling one of the new carriers. However, the contracts with the BAE Systems and the Aircraft Carrier Alliance were found to be so tightly written that it would cost more to cancel than build. SDSR thus confirms that both carriers will be completed but that one will be held in reserve and could be made available for sale; potential buyers include India, Brazil and France.

The *Queen Elizabeth* class was designed to operate the F-35B STOVL variant of the JSF. However, SDSR decided that the F-35C variant would be purchased instead and this uses the CATOBAR (Catapult Assisted Take Off But Arrested Recovery) system for launch and recovery.[3] The Aircraft Carrier Alliance is currently studying the changes that will need to be made to the carriers to operate in this revised configuration, as well as the cost associated with these: expected to be £600m–£800m (US$950m–US$1300m) per ship. The MOD will make a decision in late 2012 as to whether one or both carriers will be converted to a 'cat and trap' configuration and, if only one, which one. It is likely but not certain that the MOD will decide to adopt the least-costly option of converting just *Prince of Wales*, whose construction is the least advanced.[4]

On that basis, *Queen Elizabeth* will probably be completed in 2016, entering service as a helicopter carrier and LPH the following year. Her air group will include up to twelve Chinook or Merlin transports plus additional Apache attack helicopters. She will be able to support a range of operations such as landing a Royal Marines Commando Group or a Special Forces Squadron conducting a counter-terrorism strike, and assist with humanitarian crises or the evacuation of UK nationals.

Prince of Wales will then complete in 2019 and *Queen Elizabeth* will go in to extended readiness. if she has not been sold. *Prince of Wales* will enter service as a strike carrier the next year, although, in practice, it will take far longer for the RN to fully regain its atrophied skills in fixed-wing carrier operations. As the core of a Maritime Task Group, the carrier will in the words of Dr Liam Fox,'have the ability to combine fast jet … and amphibious capabilities – a floating piece of sovereign British territory which we can use as

A Royal Navy *Vanguard* class nuclear-powered strategic missile submarine. Work on its 'Successor' replacement is already underway to meet a planned 2028 commissioning date. It seems unlikely that there will be much room for other naval programmes in the meantime unless mooted increases in the defence budget become a reality. *(This photograph is reproduced with the permission of Rolls-Royce plc, copyright © Rolls-Royce plc 2010)*

The Type 23 frigate *Kent* pictured leaving Portsmouth Harbour during 2009. The thirteen ships of the class will be progressively modernised before being replaced by the new Type 26 Global Combat Ship from around 2021 onwards. *(Conrad Waters)*

a base worldwide whenever our needs require it'.

The RN's new strike carrier will normally embark no more than twelve F-35C fast jets, but could operate up to thirty-six, if these can be found. The carrier will also be able to operate the E-2C/D Hawkeye, helicopters and unmanned aerial vehicles, as well as being interoperable with American and French carriers and naval aircraft.

2. SUCCESSOR SUBMARINE:

The UK's nuclear deterrent is currently provided by four *Vanguard* class submarines, each with sixteen tubes for the launching of Trident II D5 ballistic missiles. The oldest submarine – *Vanguard* herself – commissioned in 1993 and was due to decommission after twenty-five years' service, i.e. by 2019. A review in 2010 showed that class service life could be extended by nine years, but significant work on a 'Successor' class is already being undertaken by the MoD, BAE Systems Submarine Solutions, Babcock Marine and Rolls-Royce.

The 2006 White Paper 'The Future of the United Kingdom's Nuclear Deterrent (Cm 6994)' estimated that four new submarines would cost £11bn–£14bn (c. US$17.5bn–US$22.5bn) at 2006–7 prices, and £687m (US$1.1bn) had been spent by the end of January 2011. The UK has also committed £282m (US$450m) to developing a Common Missile Compartment (CMC) in partnership with the United States, with General Dynamics Electric Boat Corp. as the lead contractor. The UK wants the CMC to have eight or twelve tubes compared to the US Navy's preference for sixteen tubes – saving up to £250m (US$400m). The tubes will initially carry existing Trident missiles, but will be able to accommodate a new missile planned for the 2040s.

On 18 May 2011 it was announced that the government had approved (termed Initial Gate) the commencement of detailed design work on the 'Successor' class, which will have a new propulsion plant called the PWR.3. This will be based on a US design but use UK reactor technology. Including orders for some long-lead items such as specialist steel and nuclear propulsion components, about £3bn (US$ 4.8bn) of expenditure was authorised.

The long-term core of the Royal Navy's escort fleet will be comprised of the new Type 26 Global Combat Ship, on which design work is progressing under a four-year contract. To be built in anti-submarine and general-purpose variants, it is also being designed with export potential in mind. *(BAE Systems)*

An order for the first submarine (Main Gate) is planned for early 2016, after the next UK election. It has not yet been decided whether three or four 'Successor' submarines will be built, but studies have repeatedly shown that a force of three submarines cannot guarantee a continuous deterrent patrol if one experiences an accident or major fault.[5]

Table 2.4A.2: ROYAL NAVY – NEW CLASSES IN THE FUTURE MARITIME FORCE STRUCTURE:

TYPE	CLASS	NUMBER	TONNAGE	DIMENSIONS	PROPULSION	CREW	SERVICE DATE
Carrier (CV/LPH)	*Queen Elizabeth*	2 building	65,000 tons	284m x 73m x 11m	IEP, 25 knots	679[1]	2017
Frigate (FFG)	Type 26	13 planned[2]	5,500 tons	145m x 19m x ?	IEP, 27-30 knots[3]	130	2021
Submarine (SSBN)	'Successor'	3-4 planned	Not Known	Not Known	Nuclear	Not Known	2028
Multi Role Minor Warship	MHPC	8-14 planned	c. 2,000 tons	90/100m x ? x ?	Not Known	30+	c. 2020

Notes

1 Plus accommodation for air crew and embarked forces of up to 921.

2 Official statements suggest replacement of the 13 current Type 23 ships on a one-for-one basis, with 8 ASW and 5 general purpose variants. The latter might be designated Type 27.

3 Diesel or diesel-electric propulsion is a possibility.

3. TYPE 26 GLOBAL COMBAT SHIP:

Since 1994 the Royal Navy has been trying to develop a future surface combatant to replace the Type 22 and 23 frigate classes. Progress was made in March 2010 when BAE Systems Surface Ships was awarded a four-year, £127m (US$200m) Assessment Phase contract to design a RN variant of its modular Global Combat Ship (GCS) concept. Designated the Type 26, it is intended to be a versatile and flexible warship, offering greater capability than the Type 23 but sharing the same anti-submarine warfare bias.

Thirteen Type 26 ships are planned, being built at about one per year. The first eight will share the same anti-submarine warfare bias as the Type 23 class, whilst the final five will have a general-purpose configuration (unofficially referred to as the Type 27). SDSR confirmed that the Type 26 programme will proceed and approval to order the first batch of ships is expected by the end of 2013. Steel for the first vessel will then be cut in late 2015 or early 2016, launch is scheduled for April 2018 and she should enter service towards the end of 2021.

BAE Systems has revealed some details of the Type 26 design – see Table 2.4A.2 – but not their armament. However the images released show a well-armed and well-equipped warship, including:

- A medium-calibre gun, probably 4.5in (114mm) or 5in (127mm).
- A vertical launch silo with sixteen cells, perhaps for Tomahawk or SCALP land-attack missiles.
- The Future Local Area Air Defence System (Maritime) with twenty-four CAMM missiles.
- Two quad Harpoon surface-to-surface missile canisters.
- Two Phalanx close-in weapon systems.
- Two 30mm light cannon.
- Two twin ASW torpedo tubes.
- A large flight desk with a hangar for one Merlin-sized helicopter.
- A small hangar for maritime UAVs.
- Artisan 3D radar.

Although not shown, a Type 2087 towed-array sonar also seems likely, as is an evolution of the CMS-1 combat system.

Affordability is a key design objective and – allowing for inflation – the Type 26 is intended to be similar in cost to the Type 23 – about £400m (U$650m) per ship. However, by the end of 2010 the design team was apparently projecting a cost closer to £500m (US$800m) and changes are being made to reduce this. For example, a stern mission bay has become smaller. The GCS was developed with export markets in mind, and the UK is seeking partners to share the cost of developing the Type 26 design, with Australia, Brazil and Turkey being leading candidates.[6]

CONCLUSION – IMPLICATIONS OF THE SDSR

SDSR gives a low priority to the Royal Navy and sea power. Whilst Afghanistan and the financial situation are offered as reasons, it does seem to reflect a feeling by many British politicians and elements of the public and media that spending money on expensive warships is not necessary at the moment, and that reliance can be placed on allies and in particular the United States of America to fill any gap.

SDSR offers a long-term vision but most of its actual decisions are based upon a desire to cut defence spending in the short term. Before SDSR the Royal Navy could (just) maintain a broadly-balanced fleet with separate Carrier Strike and Amphibious Task Groups. The review ended aircraft carrier operations for at least a decade, shrunk the size of the amphibious force, and imposed a significant reduction on the Naval Service in general. Ironically, just one week after *Ark Royal* decommissioned, the UK government led the imposition by the United Nations of a no-fly zone over Libya. *Ark Royal* had trained for precisely such a task but was put up for sale as scrap on the Internet whilst aircraft from the French *Charles de Gaulle* and American Harriers operating from the *Kearsarge* featured prominently in the military operations.

Between now and at least 2015 the Royal Navy will have to make do with more limited resources, reduced ambitions, fewer deployments around the world, and accept that it is no longer the pre-eminent European navy. A recovery will start if the SDSR 2015 authorises the significant expenditure required to buy F 35C Joint Strike Fighters and to operate a fully-effective carrier strike group. However, at the moment that is more of an aspiration than a reality and without additional funding, the RN's equipment budget will not stretch much beyond the 'Successor' submarines until the 2030s.

Notes:

1. An electronic version of *Securing Britain in an Age of Uncertainty: The Strategic Defence and Security Review – Cm 7948* (London, The Stationery Office, 2010), plus supporting factsheets, is available on the Internet at www.direct.gov.uk. For those who don't want to work through the whole document, the House of Commons Library has published a summary, presumably intended for MPs, by Claire Taylor called *Strategic Defence and Security Review: Defence Policy and the Armed Forces – Standard Note: SN/IA/5743* (London, House of Commons Library, 2010). It can be found at: http://www.parliament.uk/briefing-papers/SN05743

2. The Naval Staff Policy Team has produced an excellent document on the impact of SDSR called *Strategic Defence and Security Review 2010: Royal Navy Internal Communications, Supporting Question and Answer Pack*. At the time of writing a copy can be found at: http://www.rfa-association.org/cms/attachments/309_RN%20SDSR%20IC%20QsAs%20Pack%20_Final_%20v9.pdf.

3. An interesting article on converting the *Queen Elizabeth* class to CATOBAR configuration can be found in 'Converting Carriers to be Conventional', *Marine Engineers Review* – December 2010/January 2011 edition (London, Institute of Marine Engineering Science and Technology, 2010), pp 16–19. The magazine is online at: http://www.imarest.org/Publications/MarineEngineersReview.aspx.

4. In a Parliamentary written answer on 23 May 2011 defence minister Peter Luff stated that '...we will fit one of the *Queen Elizabeth* class aircraft carriers with catapults and arrestor gear to operate the more capable carrier variant joint strike fighter. Investigations into the aircraft launch and recovery systems – and a wide range of other factors – are under way. At this stage, the US Electro-Magnetic Aircraft Launch System (EMALS) catapult and the US Advanced Arrestor Gear (AAG) recovery system appears to be the most promising solution, though we have not ruled out steam catapults or Mk7 arrestor gear'.

5. A primary and revealing source on the progress of the UK's naval construction programme is the *Ministry of Defence: Major Projects Report* published annually by the National Audit Office. Their website is at: www.nao.org.uk.

6. A progress report on Type 26 design development is provided by Richard Scott in 'Type 26 Changes Course as Vision of Global Combat Ship Takes Place', *Warship World* – May/June 2011 edition (Liskeard, Maritime Books, 2011), pp 2–3.

CG50
PORT OF SPAIN
CG50

3.1 SIGNIFICANT SHIPS

BRITISH-BUILT OFFSHORE PATROL VESSELS

Balancing Cost and Capability

Author:
Conrad Waters

INTRODUCTION

Purpose-built offshore patrol vessels (OPVs) are increasingly becoming the day-to-day workhorses of naval forces across the globe. They range from relatively simple vessels built largely to commercial standards and focused on low-intensity constabulary missions through to more sophisticated ships incorporating the weaponry and command systems necessary for higher intensity war-fighting. Many are operated by established fleets looking to replace traditional frigates with more cost-effective assets for surveillance operations. Others are being acquired by fledgling navies in the course of expanding their maritime capabilities. However, all are capable of protecting sovereign interests through the maintenance of a sustained presence in waters that can extend 200 nautical miles (370km) or more beyond a nation's coast.[1]

The competition to service this market is intense. Once largely the preserve of traditional European shipbuilders, yards in emergent economies such as China, India and South Korea are also now making their presence felt. Amongst the key factors for success in this environment is the ability to offer flexible designs that can be readily adapted to support a range of missions. Equally important is a focus on affordability. Initial acquisition cost and on-going economy of operation are both important considerations to potential purchasers. One shipbuilder aiming to fulfil these requirements is the Surface Ships division of BAE Systems Maritime.[2] The unit inherited a considerable OPV-related business when it acquired the former VT Group's shipbuilding interests and is active in both domestic and export markets.

The current BAE Systems' OPV portfolio is largely derived from the former Vosper Thornycroft's EEZ Management Vessel design concept, which was selected by the British Royal Navy to replace its elderly 'Island' class ships in 2001. To date, the design has formed the basis of eight ships in four classes, as set out below:

- 'River' Class (British Royal Navy) – three ships.
- Modified 'River' Class – *Clyde* (British Royal Navy) – one ship.
- *Port of Spain* Class (Trinidad and Tobago Coast Guard) – three ships.
- Modified *Port of Spain* Class (Royal Thai Navy) – one ship.

In addition, there is a degree of commonality with the three larger *Al Shamikh* class vessels currently being completed for the Royal Navy of Oman. This chapter aims to describe these related classes and explain their broader influence on current OPV design.

ROYAL NAVY 'RIVER' CLASS

Project Overview: The origins of the 'River' class date back to the year 2000. Late in that year, the British Royal Navy set up a Future Offshore Patrol Vessel (FOPV) programme in response to an unsolicited bid from Vosper Thornycroft (VT) to replace the five remaining old and unreliable 'Island' class OPVs used principally for fishery protection with more cost-effective units. VT won the subsequent competitive tender and contracts worth c. £60m were finalised in May 2001. A key element in VT's proposal was an arrangement by which it would finance the design and build of the new ships, chartering them to the UK Ministry of Defence for an initial period of five years. Under an associated contract, the company also agreed to supply a comprehensive contractor logistic support (CLS) service that guaranteed a minimum level of operational availability. This arrangement effectively committed VT to making each 'River' class vessel available for 320 days each year compared with around 160 days for the ships they were replacing.[3] As a result, only three new OPVs were required to

Opposite: The BAE Systems-built offshore patrol vessel *Port of Spain* departing Portsmouth in the course of sea trials in May 2010. She is one of a series of offshore patrol vessels and corvettes recently constructed by the company to a broadly similar design philosophy. *(Conrad Waters)*

A view of the 'River' class offshore patrol vessel *Severn* whilst on trials in June 2003. She was the second of the class to be delivered. *(BAE Systems)*

The offshore patrol vessel *Mersey* was the last ship to be built at the former VT Group's Woolston yard in Southampton before the company's shipbuilding operations were transferred to a purpose-built facility within HM Naval Base Portsmouth. This picture was taken off Falmouth in November 2008. *(BAE Systems)*

perform the same duties carried out by the five previous ships.

The first of the new class, *Tyne*, was laid down in September 2001 at VT's Woolston yard in Southampton. Construction was rapid and she was launched on 29 May 2002 prior to official handover in January 2003. The other two vessels followed at roughly six-month intervals and all were in commission by early 2004. *Mersey* was the last ship built at Woolston before VT moved its shipbuilding activities to a new, more spacious facility within the perimeter of HM Naval Base Portsmouth. The CLS concept has proved highly successful in practice and a five-year extension of the contract to 2013 which VT valued at c. £52m was announced in January 2007.

Design: In common with most OPVs primarily intended for peacetime policing, the 'River' class was essentially designed to commercial shipbuilding standards with a minimal overlay of Ministry of Defence specifications in areas such as damage control and stability. The Det Norske Veritas (DNV) classification rules for high speed, light craft and naval surface craft were applied. The steel hull has a double chine hull form to simplify construction, whilst a fine ram bow was incorporated to facilitate good sea-keeping. This is also helped by the overall size of the ships, which – with a full load displacement approaching 1,700 tons – are considerably larger than the vessels they replaced. A general arrangement incorporating four principal decks sees the accommodation areas taking much of the available space amidships from 1 Deck down to 3 Deck, with machinery spaces occupying the rest of 3 Deck and the entirety of the lowest 4 Deck. Propulsion is provided by two medium speed MAN (formerly Ruston) 12RK 270 diesels that are capable of producing a sustained sea speed of around 16.5 knots from two controllable pitch propellers. Range at 12 knots is c. 7,800 nautical miles (14,400km). A bow thruster is also fitted to assist manoeuvrability.

A major consideration in delivering the high levels of availability expected of *Tyne* and her two sisters is careful attention to the human factor. This is reflected in the high-quality modular accommodation provided for a total of up to forty-eight personnel – twelve officers, twelve senior rates and twenty-two junior rates – although the ship is operated by a core crew of only around thirty. The additional berths can be used for an embarked force of soldiers or marines and could also be valuable during a maritime rescue. Officers and senior ratings are provided with single cabins with *en suite* facilities, whilst junior ratings are allocated twin cabins. All accommodation can be used by either male or female personnel. Availability is also boosted by a three-watch manning system under which a pool of forty-five crew is allocated to each vessel, of which only two-thirds are embarked at any one time. Watch handover normally occurs every twelve days but sufficient stores are carried to support deployments of up to twenty-one days without replenishment.

The 'River' class's constabulary role is reflected in a minimal weapons fit, comprising a single 20mm gun mounted forward of the bridge, supplemented by light weaponry. There is no combat management system, only a limited radar suite and no provision

Above: The 'River' class features a double chine hull form to simplify construction combined with a fine ram bow for enhanced seakeeping. This is *Mersey* in June 2011. *(Conrad Waters)*

Below: The first of the Royal Navy's 'River' class offshore patrol vessels, *Tyne*, pictured off Portsmouth in May 2010. In an innovative arrangement, she is leased to the Royal Navy under a series of contracts that also guarantee a predetermined level of operational ability. *(Conrad Waters)*

for helicopter operation. Instead, the focus has been on incorporating facilities necessary for the ships' primary mission, most notably a large working cargo deck aft. This provides space for containers that could incorporate workshops, medical facilities or even diving or mine-countermeasures support equipment. A heavy crane is fitted to ensure these can be embarked without shore-side support. Two Halmatic Jet Pacific 22 rigid inflatable boats (RIBs) are shipped to facilitate boarding operations and these can be automatically tracked through the radar/navigation system. A semi-active stabiliser tank facilitates their launch and recovery. Another area of investment has been the military standard communications suite, including HF/VHF band, UHF band and satellite communications. Provision has also been made for installation of a medium-calibre gun and its associated fire-control system should an upgrade to firepower ever be required.

ROYAL NAVY MODIFIED 'RIVER' CLASS – *CLYDE*

Project Overview: VT always envisaged that the 'River' class design would have wider potential than the FOPV programme, targeting export as well as additional domestic sales. Indeed, a modified variant of the design – including a helicopter deck – was offered to the Royal New Zealand Navy as part of the group's shortlisted but ultimately unsuccessful bid for Project Protector.[4] In the event, it was a further Royal Navy requirement, this time for the Falkland Islands patrol role, which secured the company's first order for a helicopter-capable OPV. As in the case of the initial 'River' class contract, the high level of operational availability at affordable cost provided by the CLS concept was a key element of the successful bid.

The basis of VT's approach to the UK Ministry of Defence was the possibility of securing significant savings by replacing the two 'Castle' class then in use as Falkland Islands guardships with a single modern vessel providing the same level of availability. This proposal resulted in another tender competition during 2004. VT subsequently announced it had achieved preferred bidder status for the deal in December of that year. The essence of the c. £30m contract that was subsequently finalised in February 2005 was very similar to the agreement for the initial batch of 'River' class ships. VT again financed the ship and leased it to the Ministry of Defence for five years, with a linked CLS contract guaranteeing

Clyde pictured in UK waters shortly before departing to the Falkland Islands in 2007. *(Conrad Waters)*

282 days operational availability each year. A particular complication was the need to provide maintenance at considerable distance from UK support infrastructure, requiring careful consideration of the logistical arrangements needed to ensure the contract was delivered.

Construction work on *Clyde* commenced in June 2005 at VT's new shipbuilding facility in Portsmouth. She was floated out almost exactly a year later on 14 June 2006. This complex operation involved her being loaded onto tractor conveyor units for transportation to a barge, which was then floated into a dry dock for the process to be completed.[5] An official naming ceremony followed in September prior to delivery on 31 January 2007. A period of trials and training followed prior to commissioning on 5 July 2007 and departure on the long voyage to the Falklands in August. As for the initial ships, the support arrangements have worked successfully and a £59m, six-year extension of the contract to 2018 has recently been announced.

Design: *Clyde* is a Batch 2 'River' class vessel modified to incorporate a helicopter landing deck, a long-range surveillance radar, a combat management system and a more powerful main armament. The remainder of the design basically mirrors that of the earlier vessels, although there are a number of subtle differences that reflect experience gained with the earlier ships. For example, accessibility of certain equipment has been improved to ease maintenance, more systems are duplicated to ensure continued availability in case of breakdown and higher-grade steels have been used to provide more resistance against corrosion. Whilst still built to commercial standards, a greater level of survivability has been overlaid onto the design.

The ship's combat capabilities, whist still reflecting its essentially constabulary nature, represent a material upgrade to those of the original 'River' class design. Principal armament is a single MSI Defence Systems DS 30B 30mm gun. This has effectively become the Royal Navy's standard small-calibre gun and has a maximum range of over five nautical miles (9.25km). Its potential is enhanced by the installation of the newly-developed Danish Terma Scanter 4001 surveillance radar. This provides air and surface search out to 110 nautical miles (204km) and is claimed to be particularly effective at spotting small targets in all weather conditions. The array is integrated into BAE Systems' own CMS-1 combat

Two images of *Clyde* under construction at the then VT Group's new shipbuilding hall within HM Naval Base Portsmouth. *Clyde* was the first ship to be built within the dockyard since the *Leander* class frigate *Andromeda* was launched in 1967. *(BAE Systems)*

Table 3.1.1.

HMS TYNE ('RIVER' CLASS – BATCH 1) PRINCIPAL PARTICULARS

Building Information:	
Laid Down:	19 September 2001
Launched:	29 May 2002
Delivered:	7 January 2003
Builders:	VT Group (now BAE Systems Surface Ships) at is Woolston facility in Southampton..
Dimensions:	
Displacement:	1,675 tons full load displacement.
Overall Hull Dimensions:	79.5m x 13.6m x 3.8m.
Weapons Systems:	
Guns:	1 x 20mm BMARC KAA.
Aircraft:	No aircraft facilities.
Principal Sensors:	Integrated navigation system incorporating Kelvin Hughes ARPA E/F and I band navigation radars.
Combat System:	No combat management system. Communications include HF/VHF and UHF radio links and Inmarsat B satcoms.
Other:	Cargo deck with space for up to 7 containers with various equipment fits. 2 x Halmatic Pacific 22 RIBs for boarding operations.
Propulsion Systems:	
Machinery:	Diesel. 2 x MAN 12RK 270 medium-speed diesel engines rated at 8.25MW total producing 11,000shp through two shafts. There is also a 280KW bow thruster.
Speed and Range:	Designed maximum speed 20 knots. Sustained speed is c. 16.5 knots. Range is 7,800 nautical miles at 12 knots.
Other Details:	
Complement:	A typical crew comprises c.30 personnel drawn from a total allocated complement of 45. Accommodation is provided for 48.
Class:	Three ships have been delivered: *Tyne* (P281), *Severn* (P282) and *Mersey* (P283).

HMS *Tyne* (2003)
1:500 scale

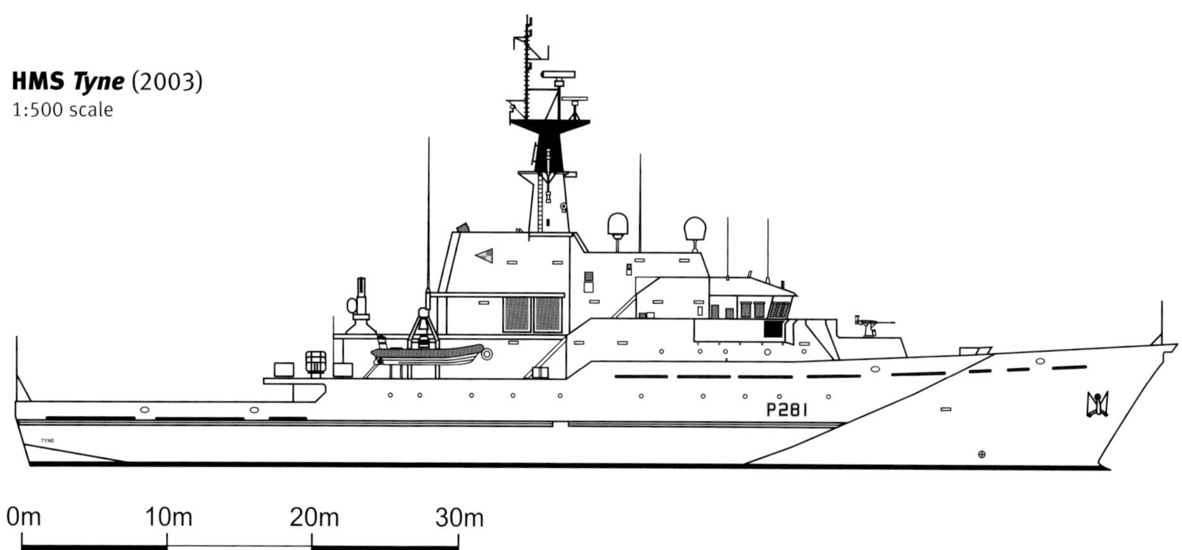

(Drawing © John Jordan, 2011)

Table 3.1.2.

HMS CLYDE ('RIVER' CLASS – BATCH 2) PRINCIPAL PARTICULARS

Building Information:	
Laid Down:	November 2005 (Fabrication commenced June 2005)
Launched:	14 June 2006
Delivered:	31 January 2007
Builders:	VT Group (now BAE Systems Surface Ships) at is facility in HM Naval Base Portsmouth.
Dimensions:	
Displacement:	1,850 tons full load displacement.
Overall Hull Dimensions:	81.5m x 13.6m x 4.2m.
Weapons Systems:	
Guns:	1 x 30mm MSI DS 30B.
Aircraft:	Platform for 1 x helicopter of up to AW-101 Merlin size.
Principal Sensors:	1x Terma 4100 long-range surveillance radar. Navigation radars.
Combat System:	BAE Systems CMS-1 combat system. Communications include HF/VHF and UHF radio links and Inmarsat B satcoms.
Other:	Space for containers with various equipment fits. 1 x Halmatic Pacific 22 and 1 x Rigid Raider MK III RIBs for boarding/insertion.
Propulsion Systems:	
Machinery:	Diesel. 2 x MAN 12RK 270 medium-speed diesel engines rated at 8.25MW total producing 11,000shp through two shafts. There is also a 280KW bow thruster and a 185KW stern thruster.
Speed and Range:	Designed maximum speed 20 knots. Sustained speed is c. 16.5 knots. Range is 7,800 nautical miles at 12 knots.
Other Details:	
Complement:	A typical crew comprises c. 40 personnel. Accommodation is provided for c. 60.
Class:	*Clyde* (P257) is the sole member of the class.

HMS *Clyde* (2007)
1:500 scale

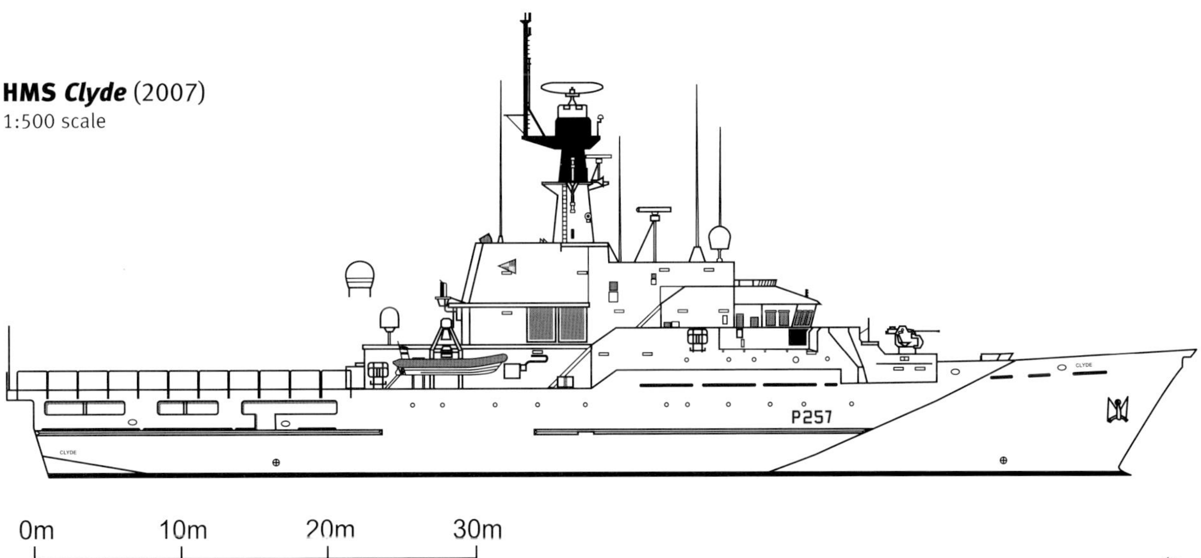

(Drawing © John Jordan, 2011)

Clyde pictured on sea trials in December 2006 shortly before delivery to the Royal Navy. Principal changes from the original 'River' class configuration – the helicopter deck, Terma Scanter surveillance radar and larger, 30mm gun – are all evident in this image. *(Terma)*

management system, which is also used in the vastly more sophisticated Type 45 *Daring* class destroyers. A scaleable system featuring Windows-based software, the version installed in *Clyde* features just one multi-function console compared with more than twenty-five in *Daring* and her sisters.

An important addition to *Clyde*'s capabilities over the Batch 1 vessels is her ability to support helicopter operations through the provision of a landing deck and associated refuelling systems. The deck is large enough to receive Merlin-sized rotorcraft. However, initial landing capability trials were focused on the

An image of *Clyde* in Patagonian waters in June 2008 whilst serving as Falkland Islands guardship. The CLS arrangement supporting her deployment has recently been extended to 2018. *(BAE Systems)*

smaller Lynx. Helicopter operations are facilitated by the incorporation of fin stabilisers, which also ensure enhanced sea-keeping in the rough waters of the South Atlantic. Whilst no hangar is provided on *Clyde*, a telescopic facility has been developed for export versions of the design.

PORT OF SPAIN CLASS

Project Overview: The *Port of Spain* class OPVs were designed to meet a requirement from the Republic of Trinidad and Tobago to improve its Coast Guard's surveillance and interdiction capabilities. A lengthy procurement process saw VT pitch an enlarged version of the 'River' class against competition in the form of the German MEKO 100 OPV design and a derivative of the Italian Navy's 'Comandante' class. Its successful bid incorporated the contracting for availability arrangement pioneered in the Royal Navy vessels, guaranteeing that each of a three-ship class would be operational for 300 days each year. Contracts were signed on 5 April 2007 and had a reported value of over £150m or US$300m at then current exchange rates. According to subsequent Trinidad and Tobago government figures, this was

Above: *Port of Spain* in the course of the complicated process of being rolled out of the main shipbuilding hall at Portsmouth on 7 August 2009. The tractor conveyor units underneath the hull are used to position the ship onto a submersible barge from which floating-off takes place in a dry dock. *(BAE Systems)*

Below: The second *Port of Spain* class vessel *Scarborough* entering Portsmouth for lay up on 11 October 2010 after Trinidad and Tobago's cancellation of the c. £150m contract for the class's purchase and support. *(Conrad Waters)*

Due to delays in the construction process at Portsmouth, fabrication of the second and third members of the *Port of Spain* class was transferred to the former Yarrow facility at Scotstoun in Glasgow. *Scarborough* was launched on 19 November 2009 and *San Fernando* on 16 July 2010. The latter's launch took place at 4 o'clock in the morning to take advantage of the early high tides on the River Clyde in the summer months. *(BAE Systems)*

split between a capital cost of US$230m, training support of US$13m and a five-year CLS package amounting to US$74m.

Construction of the first of class, *Port of Spain*, commenced with a formal ceremony at Portsmouth on 23 January 2008, with delivery expected around the middle of the following year. At this stage all three ships were due to enter service before the end of 2010. However, the construction schedule proved overly ambitious and it was not until early August 2009 that the first of class was floated out, a process followed by the commencement of sea trials at the turn of the year. The terms of the contract had to be revised to take account of the delay and Trinidad and Tobago was allocated compensation as a result. By this time, VT's shipbuilding interests had been merged into the BVT joint venture with BAE Systems that was the forerunner of the current BAE Systems Surface Ships. It was therefore decided to switch construction of the two remaining vessels to the enlarged business's facilities on the Clyde to balance out workloads.[6] Second of class *Scarborough* was subsequently launched from the group's Scotstoun yard on 19 November 2009. The final ship, *San Fernando*, followed on 16 July 2010. By September 2010 the first two ships had completed sea trials and were being prepared for delivery when – on 21 September 2010 – BAE Systems announced that Trinidad and Tobago had given notice to cancel the contract. Although BAE Systems are being tight-lipped about the dispute given that it is subject to on-going arbitration, reports in the local Trinidad and Tobago press have focused on the delays to the contract, as well as a government desire to shift financial resources to other priorities, as key factors behind the cancellation. However, another key influence on the decision seems to have been developments in local politics, as the government administration that had signed the original deal had been voted out of office in May 2010. At the time of writing, the three ships are laid up at Portsmouth pending a resolution to the dispute, although sale to another country seems a likely outcome.

Design: The *Port of Spain* class is officially described as being based on the preceding 'River' class, of which they are essentially an enlarged version. Reflecting BAE Systems' modular approach to OPV design, they include many core platform systems proved on the previous ships built for the Royal Navy but have a modified hull form of greater length (90m

Weaponry on presence-mission offshore patrol vessels tends to be light. This picture shows an MSI Defence Systems DS 30M gun mount, which forms the forward armament of *Port of Spain*. Two 25M versions of this weapon are also shipped, all being controlled by the OSIRIS integrated command and control system. *(BAE Systems)*

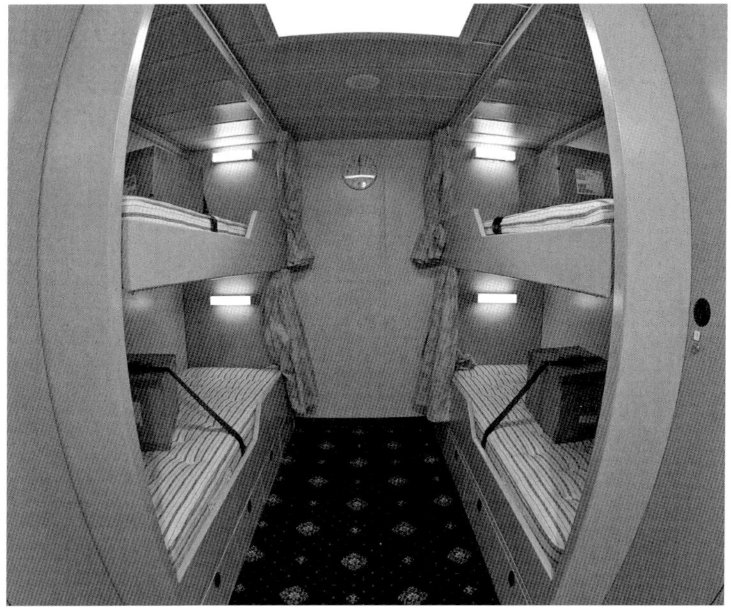

Accommodation in *Port of Spain*. As in other vessels in BAE Systems' OPV range, modular cabins are used to provide a flexible range of accommodation options in line with customer requirements. *(BAE Systems)*

compared with 80m) that owes much to VT's previous experience in constructing corvettes and light frigates. As well as facilitating higher speeds – the class has exceeded the design speed of 25 knots on trials – the longer hull provides a much greater accommodation capacity. This was a particularly important factor for Trinidad and Tobago, which wanted the ability to transport up to fifty additional troops in addition to the normal crew. Stores capacity is also increased and an endurance of up to thirty-five days is claimed.

The class's combat systems have much in common with those fitted to *Clyde*, most notably the Terma Scanter 4100 radar that provides the principal surveillance capability and the MSI Defence Systems 30mm gun that forms the main armament. However, it is understood that the Trinidad and Tobago vessels incorporate the latest DS 30M variant of this mounting, which is also backed by two MSI Defence DS 25M 25mm weapons fitted port and starboard aft of the bridge. Perhaps equally important was the selection of Ultra Electronics' OSIRIS integrated command-and-control system to provide the ships' command-and-control function as opposed to the CMS-1 system installed in *Clyde*. Ultra Electronics specifically designed OSIRIS to provide an integrated surveillance picture from the radars and electro-optical equipment typically fitted to OPVs involved in EEZ policing and it therefore represents a more appropriate system for a fleet that has no requirement for commonality with more sophisticated ships. OSIRIS also provides the class's gun fire-control capability. The provision of a helicopter flight deck – but no hangar – is another area of commonality with the Batch 2 'River' class, the latter facility being accorded a lower priority than additional troop accommodation. The Coast Guard intended to operate AgustaWestland AW-139 helicopters from the ships. Four of these had been ordered before the OPV contract was cancelled.

As for the Royal Navy OPVs, construction is largely to commercial standards. Propulsion is provided by two MAN 16V 28/33D medium-speed diesel engines, each of which drives a controllable-pitch propeller through a single input/output, horizontal offset reduction gear. Introduced as the Ruston RK 280 around the turn of the Millennium, MAN's 28/33D range is effectively the successor of the RK 270 diesel engine series used in the 'River' class and is therefore yet another example of follow-through of previous design concepts to the new class. The propulsion system provides a range of around 5,500 nautical miles (10,175km) at 12 knots. The ships are also highly manoeuvrable – the second ship *Scarborough* completed turning circles in three-and-a-half ship lengths and stopped in less than four ship lengths during trials.

ROYAL THAI NAVY MODIFIED *PORT OF SPAIN* CLASS

The potential of the basic *Port of Spain* design is demonstrated by an order received from the Royal Thai Navy for a modified version, which was announced in June 2009. In contrast to the other OPVs described in this chapter, the contract was for transfer of the design and related technology to Bangkok Dock, which will build the new ship locally. In addition, it has been reported that the vessel will be equipped with a more comprehensive electronics and weapons systems package than those specified for the more basic Royal Navy and Trinidad and Tobago ships. As such, they represent something of an interesting hybrid in so far as they incorporate what is effectively a front-line warship's combat potential in an essentially commercial hull.

Precise details on the combat system installed in the new ship are hard to come by, with official statements referencing only 'a similar combat system to

Port of Spain pictured during sea trials on 18 February 2010. The class has exceeded its designed maximum speed of 25 knots on trials and has also proved highly manoeuvrable. The ships can stop in less than four ship lengths, whilst turning circle is around three-and-a-half ship lengths. *(BAE Systems)*

that being fitted to other ships in Thailand's fleet'. However, it seems that a package of Thales Nederland equipment has been selected. If confirmed, this is likely to include the TACTICOS combat system, a VARIANT medium range surveillance radar with IFF and a LIROD Mk2 fire control radar/optronic director. The last-mentioned will probably be linked to a 76mm Oto Melara compact medium-calibre gun, which is effectively the standard main armament for Thailand's fleet of corvettes and light frigates. Propulsion machinery and other principal equipment will be similar to that in the initial ships.

BAE Systems' role in the project is largely limited to supply of the basic design and subsequent provision of technical expertise to facilitate construction of the ship at Bangkok. As such, tasks such as systems integration and subsequent maintenance and logistical support are the responsibility of local industry. The ship's keel was officially laid in August 2010 and a launch ceremony is planned for the latter half of 2011. Construction of at least one more of the class is a possibility if the initial ship meets expectations.

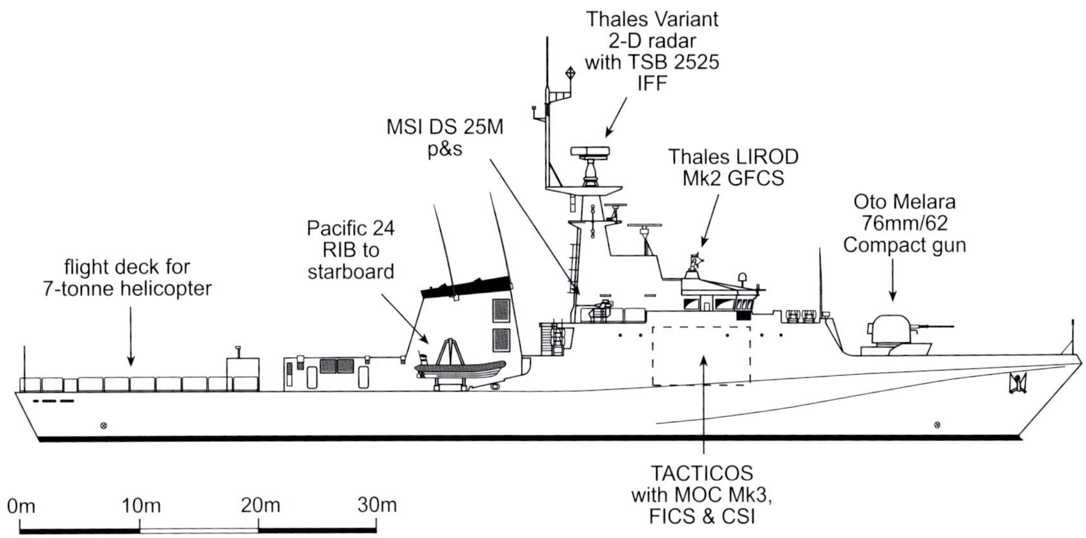

An indicative profile of the modified *Port of Spain* class offshore patrol vessel being constructed in Bangkok with BAE Systems support. It appears that the ship will incorporate a full suite of electronic equipment from Thales Nederland but this has never been officially confirmed. *(Drawing © John Jordan, 2011)*

ROYAL NAVY OF OMAN *AL SHAMIKH* CLASS

Project Overview: Oman's three *Al Shamikh* class corvettes were ordered from VT Group in January 2007. They met a requirement for a new class of oceanic patrol vessels for EEZ surveillance and protection set out in Project Khareef. The contract was allocated after a lengthy competition that saw the size and capability of the required ships expand significantly from what had initially been envisaged, with the VT design selected over proposals from the Dutch Schelde Naval Shipbuilding and South Korea's Daewoo Shipbuilding & Marine Engineering. Costing some £400m (US$800m at then-current exchange rates), the ships are the largest and most sophisticated combatants to serve with the Royal Oman Navy to date.

Work on the new corvettes formally commenced in October 2007 with a steel-cutting ceremony at Portsmouth carried out by the commander of Oman's Navy. The contract envisaged delivery of the first ship in the early months of 2010, with subsequent ships following at roughly six-monthly intervals. Unfortunately, as for the *Port of Spain* class, it became clear that the original construction schedule was overly optimistic. By the time the first of class – *Al Shamikh* – was named on 22 July 2009, the

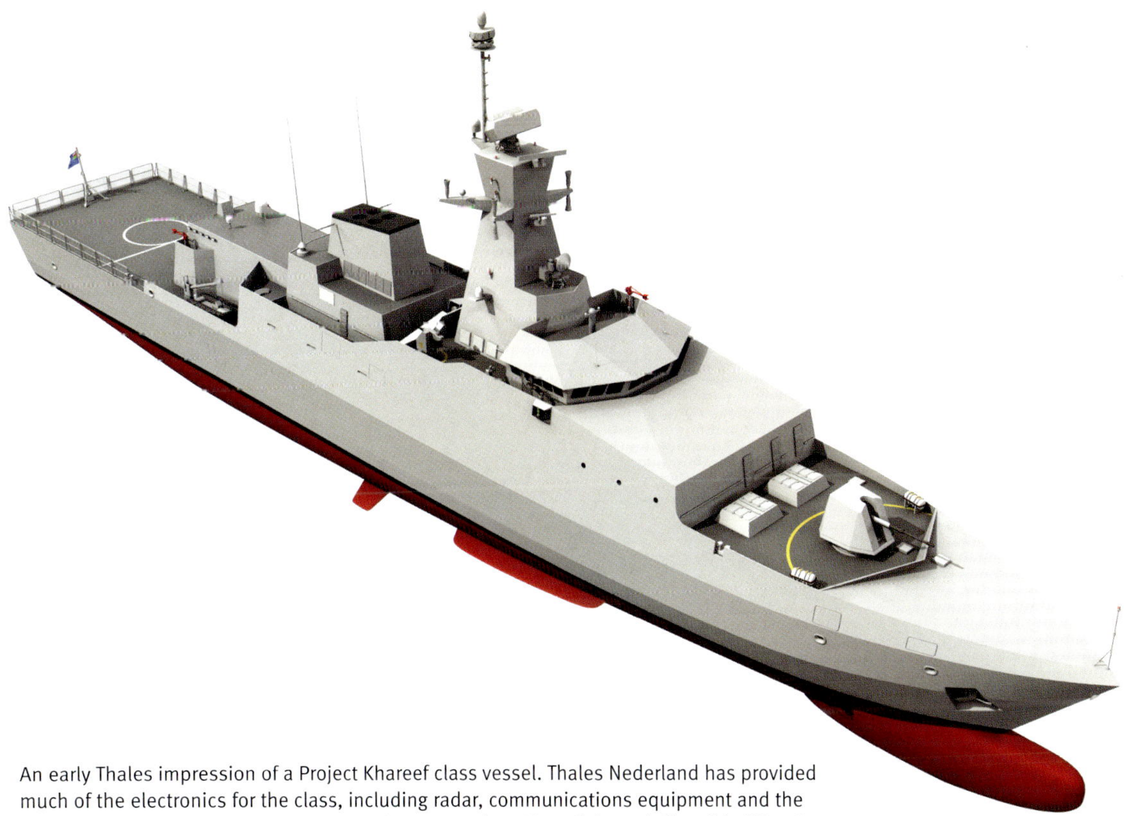

An early Thales impression of a Project Khareef class vessel. Thales Nederland has provided much of the electronics for the class, including radar, communications equipment and the combat management system. It is interesting to note how first of class *Al Shamikh* differs in practice from this early image, for example in the positioning of the secondary guns. *(Thales)*

Table 3.1.3.

PORT OF SPAIN PRINCIPAL PARTICULARS

Building Information:	
Fabrication Commenced:	23 January 2008
Launched:	7 August 2009
Delivered:	1
Builders:	VT Group (now BAE Systems Surface Ships) at is facility in HM Naval Base Portsmouth.
Dimensions:	
Displacement:	1,800 tons full load displacement.
Overall Hull Dimensions:	90.0m x 13.5m x 3.5m.
Weapons Systems:	
Guns:	1 x 30mm MSI DS 30M & 2 x 25mm MSI DS 25M.
Aircraft:	Platform for 1 x medium helicopter of up c. 7 tons in weight
Principal Sensors:	1 x Terma 4100 long-range surveillance radar. Navigation radars.
Combat System:	Ultra Electronics OSIRIS combat system. Integrated communications system.
Other:	Space for up to 6 containers with various equipment fits. 1 x Halmatic Pacific 24 RIB and 1 x fast interceptor for boarding/insertion.
Propulsion Systems:	
Machinery:	Diesel. 2 x MAN 16V 28/33D medium-speed diesel engines rated at 14.6MW total. Two-shaft propulsion arrangement. There are also bow and stern thrusters.
Speed and Range:	Designed maximum speed 25 knots. Range is 5,500 nautical miles at 12 knots.
Other Details:	
Complement:	A typical crew is c. 65 personnel. Accommodation is provided for c. 70 plus an additional 50 troops in more austere facilities.
Class:	Three ships have been completed: *Port of Spain* (CG-50), *Scarborough* (CG-51) and *San Fernando* (CG-51)

Notes

1 Following cancellation of the acquisition contract by Trinidad and Tobago none of the class has yet been delivered.

Scarborough (2010)
1:500 scale

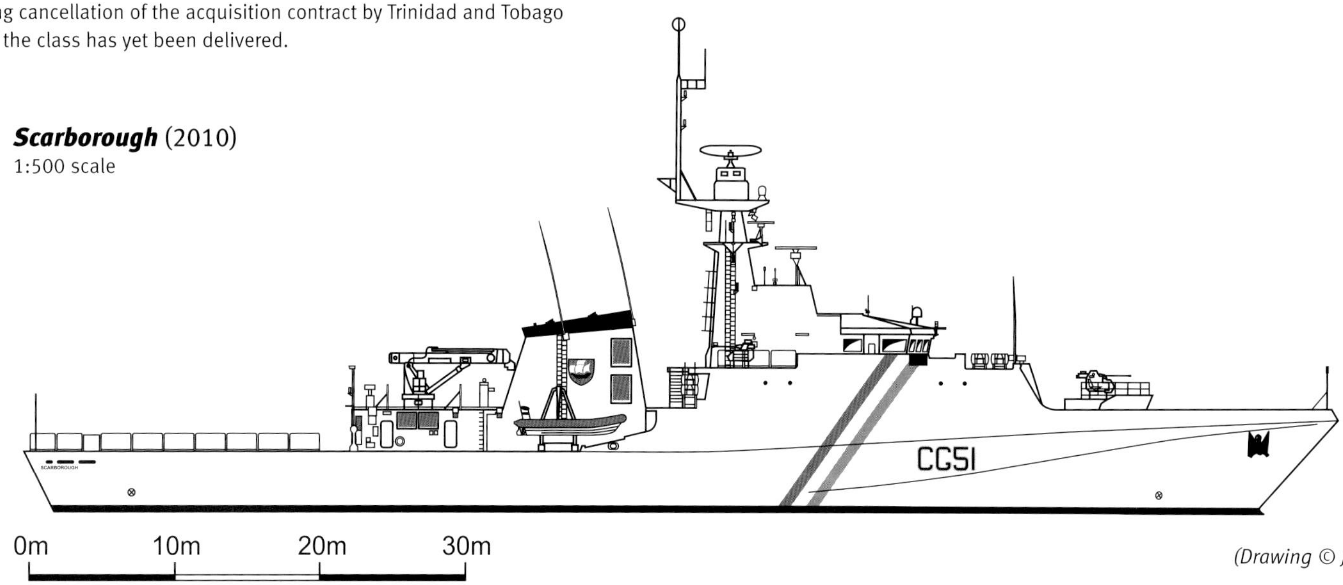

(Drawing © John Jordan, 2011)

Table 3.1.4.

AL SHAMIKH PRINCIPAL PARTICULARS

Building Information:	
Fabrication Commenced:	23 October 2007
Launched:	22 July 2009[1]
Delivered:	[2011 Planned]
Builders:	VT Group (now BAE Systems Surface Ships) at is facility in HM Naval Base Portsmouth.
Dimensions:	
Displacement:	2,500 tons full load displacement.
Overall Hull Dimensions:	99.0m x 14.6m x 4.1m. Length between perpendiculars is 90.0m.
Weapons Systems:	
Missiles:	2 x six-cell VLS modules for MBDA MICA surface-to-air missiles. 2 x quad launchers for MBDA Exocet MM40 surface-to-surface missiles.
Guns:	1 x 76mm Oto Melara Super Rapid. 2 x 30mm MSI DS 30M.
Aircraft:	1 x AgustaWestland Super Lynx 300 helicopter.
Countermeasures:	Vigile 400 electronic support measures (ESM) system. MASS decoys.
Principal Sensors:	Thales SMART-S Mk 2 surveillance radar. Navigation radars.
Combat System:	Thales TACTICOS combat management system. Integrated communications system.
Propulsion Systems:	
Machinery:	Diesel. 2 x Tognum MTU 20V 8000 medium-speed diesel engines rated at 18.2MW total. Two-shaft propulsion arrangement.
Speed and Range:	Designed maximum speed 25 knots. Range is 4,500 nautical miles at 16 knots.
Other Details:	
Complement:	Accommodation for up to 92 personnel.
Class:	Three ships have been ordered: *Al Shamikh*, *Al Rahmani* and *Al Rasikh*.

Notes

1 Date refers to naming ceremony. Floating out took place some days earlier.

Al Shamikh (2010)
1:500 scale

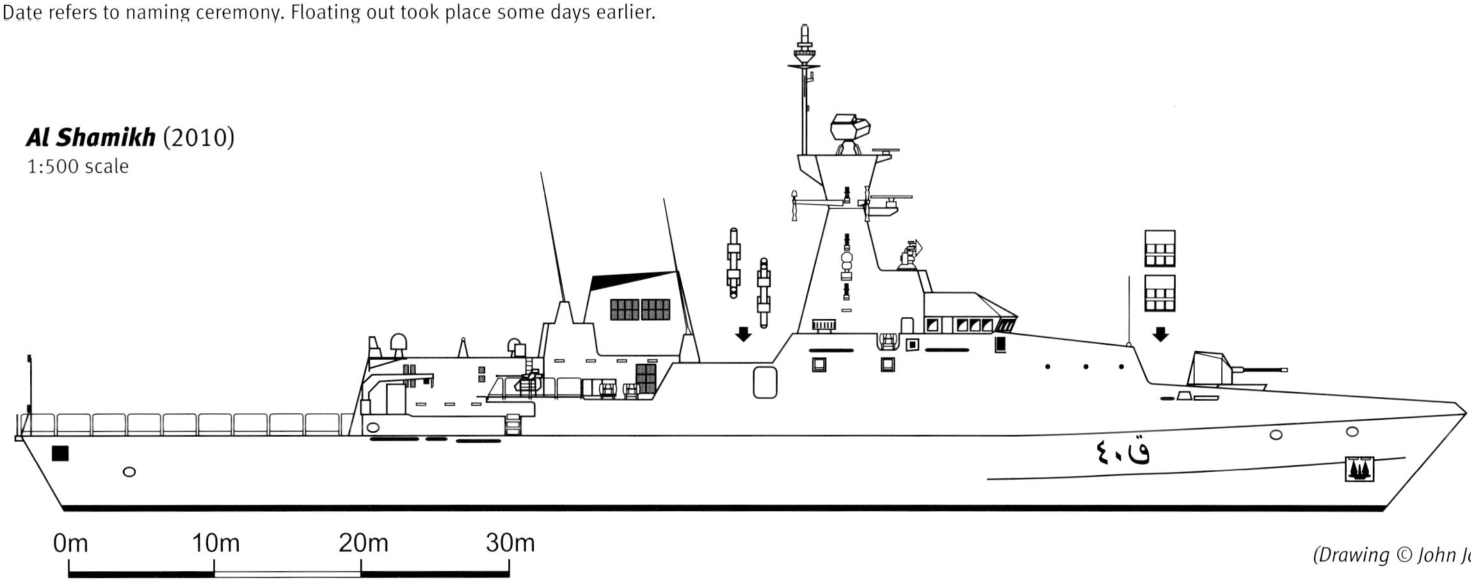

(Drawing © John Jordan, 2011)

Al Shamikh, the first corvette for Oman built under Project Khareef, was formally named in July 2009. This image shows her hull early in the month, shortly after she was floated out. *(BAE Systems)*

contract was running several months behind schedule.[7] In the event, therefore, first-of-class sea trials did not commence until 15 December 2010. Further delays then arose as a result of the emergence of a number of engineering issues during the trials programme. This impacted both the revised planned delivery date of mid-2011 and the timing of training that had been scheduled with the Royal Navy's Flag Officer Sea Training (FOST) organisation. Meanwhile, second of class *Al Rahmani* was launched in July 2010, with the third and final vessel *Al Rasikh* following early in 2011. It now seems likely that it will be around the end of 2012 when all three ships are operational.

Design: In contrast to the other ships that have been described in this chapter, the Project Khareef vessels have been designed and built to full military standards, impacting areas such as steel quality, watertight integrity, blast resistance and overall survivability. The war-fighting role of the ships is also evident in the attention paid to stealth. The hull and superstructure have been laid out to minimise radar cross-section and additional steps have been taken to reduce infrared signature. However, their basic design – which is based on that of the former VT Group's generic multi-purpose ocean patrol vessel – still benefits from the modular approach adopted to the group's smaller warships and there is a distinct 'family resemblance' to the other recent BAE Systems OPVs. For example the hull form adopted by the *Port of Spain* and *Al Shamikh* classes has drawn heavily on the group's extensive lineage of previous light frigates and both have a length-to-beam ratio of c. 6.7:1. The incorporation of a bulb bow to enhance sea-keeping and provide better fuel economy is also common to both classes.

Oman selected Thales Nederland as the principle sub-contractor for the *Al Shamikh* class's combat systems and the company's equipment therefore features prominently in the three corvettes. This includes radar and communications systems, electronic countermeasures and the ships' core command-and-control capability. The combat management system is the well-established TACTICOS, which Thales claims is now in service in more than 150 vessels from over fifteen navies. In common with similar modern combat direction technology such as BAE Systems' CMS-1, TACTICOS is a full distributed system that consolidates information from a range of on-board sensors and tactical data links into a series of multi-function consoles – MOCs or multi-function operator consoles in Thales' terminology. Other core Thales' equipment installed includes a fully-integrated communications system, as well as Vigile 400 electronic support measures (ESM) and the new SMART-S Mk2 long-range surveillance radar. A 3-D array operating in the E/F band (US S-band), SMART-S Mk 2 is claimed to provide coverage out to 135 nautical miles (250km) and is integrated with a Thales IFF interrogator. Each ship is also equipped with a STING-EO Mk2 fire control director.

Armament is also European in origin, with the MBDA consortium providing its MM40 Block 3 Exocet surface-to-surface missiles and short-range VL MICA air-defence system. The latter was developed from the air-to-air missile of the same name and is installed in two six-container modules located forward of the bridge. A fire-and-forget missile using IR or RF seekers and requiring no dedicated fire-control system, it weighs 112kg and has a maximum effective range of c. 20km in vertical-launch mode. It is understood that Oman is the first naval customer for this system. The main gun is a 76mm Oto Melara Super Rapid gun. This is supplemented by two MSI Defence Systems 30mm DS 30M mountings for shorter-range defence located port and starboard in line with the forward end of the hangar. The ships are capable of embarking and supporting a helicopter of up to 12 tons in weight, most likely the AgustaWestland Super Lynx already operated by the Royal Air Force of Oman.

Al Shamikh and her sister-ships have a similar, although more powerful, twin diesel-engine propulsion arrangement to the other recent BAE Systems OPV designs. A contracted maximum speed of not less than 25 knots was met on first of class trials, whilst maximum range is in the order of 4,500 nautical miles (8,325km). An active fin stabilisation system is fitted to assist with aviation and small-boat operations, whilst also improving crew living and working conditions. Careful attention has been paid to ensuring overall habitability, extending to the provision of full temperature control in the accommodation provided for a crew of up to ninety-two personnel.

FUTURE PROSPECTS

With construction of the vessels ordered under previous export contracts drawing to a close, BAE Systems are actively looking for new customers for their OPV range. Although the market for these vessels is growing with the on-going expansion of sovereign responsibilities for oceanic territory, the highly competitive nature of the market means that potential contracts are always hard-fought. Given this situation, BAE Systems believes that its ability to offer prospective customers long-term economic benefits will be essential. These will be achieved by CLS-driven through-life cost-reduction arrangements, as well as building on the group's proven track record in providing 'value-added' benefits to local industry through technology transfer and investment in 'in country' infrastructure, support and training.

BAE Systems are understandably tight-lipped about potential future contracts. However, the basic *Port of Spain* design has featured prominently in a larger warship-procurement package offered to Brazil that also includes a potential industrial partnership in respect of the Type 26 Global Combat Ship and

Two pictures of the first Project Khareef corvette on sea trials off the south coast of England in January 2011. The spent cartridge cases around the forward 76mm gun suggest the impact of firing the main gun on the ship's structure is being tested. Unspecified engineering problems during these trials delayed completion of the programme. *(BAE Systems)*

focuses heavily on both technology transfer and through-life capability management. It is also known that the group are very interested in the United States Coast Guard's requirement for a new Offshore Patrol Cutter, which should see competitive preliminary design contracts allocated during US FY2012 prior to the delivery of the first ship of an extended class towards the end of the decade. Certainly, the extent of BAE Systems' infrastructure and industrial alliances within the United States makes the company a realistic contender for such a contract. In the longer term, the Royal Navy's requirement for a future mine countermeasures, hydrographic and patrol programme (the previous future surface combatant C3 concept) survived the 2010 Strategic Defence and Security Review and could be a further significant opportunity in due course.

CONCLUSION

The portfolio of OPV vessel designs that BAE Systems has inherited from the former VT Group's shipbuilding business has certainly provided the ability to offer a wide range of smaller warships to potential customers. Spanning the full spectrum of capability from basic constabulary duties (the initial 'River' class) through more sophisticated presence and interdiction roles (*Clyde* and the *Port of Spain* class) to the potential to carry out full war-fighting missions (*Al Shamikh* and her sisters), the company has developed what is probably one of the most extensive range of designs currently available in the OPV category. Additionally, whilst each of the classes completed to date exhibits its own specific characteristics, the overall modular approach that has been adopted means that it is relatively straightforward and inexpensive to 'flex' any of these designs to meet particular customer requirements. Whilst most obviously apparent in the different armament and combat systems outfit installed in the *Port of Spain* class and their Thai half-sister, this flexibility also extends to areas such as survivability, propulsion and even the amount and quality of accommodation.

However, it is probably through their role in demonstrating the potential of the contracting for availability concept that were pioneered by the CLS arrangements agreed for the initial 'River' class and *Clyde* that BAE Systems' recent OPVs have been most influential. When the 'River' class CLS agreement was first signed in May 2001, it marked the first time that an approach that had previously been confined to the commercial sector had been extended to operational warships. The new arrangements inevitably suffered from initial teething troubles, for example in engendering a sense of 'ownership' amongst the officers and crew of vessels that were provided to the navy on a leased basis.[8] However, once the early snags were ironed out, CLS has been hugely successful. The 'River' class have achieved amongst the highest availability levels in the whole fleet. In addition, the lessons learned from the initial contracts are also now being fed back into improving subsequent agreements, not least in OPV design. For example, a greater level of duplication was built into *Clyde* than the earlier 'Rivers' to ensure the development of defects with critical equipment did not impact on operational availability. Design changes have even

An unusual bow view of *Al Shamikh* taken at the time of her formal naming ceremony. She forms the 'high end' of a series of modular offshore patrol vessel and corvette designs that BAE Systems has available to offer to potential customers. *(BAE Systems)*

Al Shamikh in the Solent off Portsmouth during initial sea trials shortly before Christmas 2010. *(BAE Systems)*

extended to the level of achieving improved accessibility to certain areas (to reduce maintenance time), as well as to improving paint schemes and the quality of exposed steelwork to limit corrosion. The contract for *Clyde* also involved giving greater consideration to the arrangements needed to ensure availability at a considerable distance from established maintenance facilities. This has resulted in appointment of an on-hand systems manager on six-week rotation in the Falkland Islands, as well as the leasing and local warehousing of certain long lead spares.

Ultimately, the proof of the pudding is in the eating. In this regard, the success of CLS is best-demonstrated by the UK Ministry of Defence's decisions to extend the contracts, firstly, of the 'River' class and, recently, of *Clyde* for lengthy periods. Equally, the general concept of contracting for availability has been spread more broadly across the fleet with the development of Class Output Management (COM) programmes for a number of front-line warship classes.[9] Whilst the collapse of the Trinidad and Tobago order means that CLS has yet to be proved in an export contract, it seems likely that the ability of the cradle-to-grave support arrangements pioneered on BAE Systems' OPVs to offer a defined capability at affordable cost will make them increasingly popular in the years ahead.

Port of Spain in the Solent in 2010. The design is being offered to the Brazilian Navy as part of a larger package of warship designs intended to form the basis of an industrial partnership. The Royal Thai Navy is also building a variant of the class in Bangkok Dock. *(Conrad Waters)*

Notes:

1. National rights and responsibilities in respect of adjacent sea areas are set out in the United Nations Convention on the Law of the Sea (UNCLOS). The current UNCLOS regime was concluded in 1982 but did not come into effect until 1994, a year after the sixtieth signatory – Guyana – ratified the agreement. Amongst its more significant terms was the development of the concept of a national Exclusive Economic Zone (EEZ) extending 200 nautical miles from a country's coastline. The resulting need to police and protect natural resources such as fish and raw materials within these zones has been an important influence driving OPV development.

2. BAE Systems Maritime was formed on 1 January 2011 to bring all BAE Systems' UK-based naval businesses into a common management structure. In addition to Surface Ships, the unit comprises the Submarine Solutions and Mission Systems businesses.

3. More accurately, the CLS contract provides for 960 days operational availability each year across all three members of the 'River' class.

4. The Royal New Zealand Navy's Project Protector envisaged the acquisition of two offshore patrol vessels, four inshore patrol systems and a multi-role support vessel to recapitalise New Zealand's maritime patrol capabilities. The contract was won by the defence division of Australia's Tenix. Somewhat ironically, the division was subsequently acquired by BAE Systems Australia and is therefore now part of a sister division to BAE Systems Maritime.

5. The process represented the first 'launch' at Portsmouth Naval Base since the *Leander* class frigate *Andromeda* entered the water on 24 May 1967.

6. The BVT joint venture was finalised on 1 July 2008 following UK government pressure on BAE Systems and VT Group to merge their shipbuilding interests. At the time the joint venture was created it was expected that BAE Systems would assume full control of the enterprise after three years. In the event, this process was accelerated and BAE became the sole owner of the business in October 2009.

7. Formal naming ceremony dates for the three Royal Navy of Oman ships do not coincide with actual roll-out, which occurred several days, if not weeks, earlier.

8. Some sources have claimed the existence of something akin to a 'company car' mentality amongst certain 'River' class crews when the ships were first introduced, under which lower levels of care and attention were paid to the vessels on the basis that any resultant problems would be for somebody else to resolve. Whether or not these rumours were true in the beginning, it is clear that a strong sense of partnership now exists between naval crew members and commercial maintenance personnel.

9. The editor's chapter on 'UK Warship Support' in last year's edition, *Seaforth World Naval Review 2011* (Barnsley, Seaforth Publishing, 2010), pp 180–8 provides more detail on COM.

10. This chapter has drawn heavily on contemporary defence ministry and industrial press releases, corporate marketing literature and associated press reports. In addition, the assistance of the following BAE Systems personnel in the preparation of the chapter is acknowledged with gratitude:

Garry Lea, Head of Business Development, Small Ships and Global R & S, Surface Ships.

Mark Minshull, Head of CLS & CFA Integration, Surface Ships.

Bill Page, CLS Manager, Surface Ships.

3.2 SIGNIFICANT SHIPS

USS MAKIN ISLAND (LHD-8)

It's What's Inside That Counts

Authors:
Edward Feege
and Scott Truver

INTRODUCTION

Unwanted by the US Navy, beset by construction problems and late to enter service: that was the prevailing image of *Makin Island* (LHD-8) during much of the last decade. However, now she is in service, the ship is setting the pace for future amphibious warship programmes, and for future US warships overall. *Makin Island* might look similar to other amphibious warships in her class, but the contents of her hull are pointing the way to a more cost-effective future US Navy.

Makin Island is the eighth *Wasp* (LHD-1) class amphibious assault ship. With a full load displacement of nearly 42,000 tons, LHDs are second only to large-deck aircraft carriers in size in the front-line USN. They can embark, transport, deploy, command and support an expeditionary unit of approximately 1,700 US Marines. Deploying with an array of aircraft, amphibious vehicles and other equipment, *Makin Island* and her sisters are key to US amphibious power-projection and expeditionary-warfare capabilities. They also have a secondary capability to perform sea control and power-projection missions. Additionally, US amphibious warships have played critical roles in humanitarian assistance and disaster relief (HADR) operations from Haiti through to Pakistan and Japan in recent months.

Until *Makin Island*, however, these highly-capable ships also had operating costs that – in many ways – paced their increasing combat capabilities. According to USN Captain Christopher Mercer, the Amphibious Warfare Program Manager (PMS 377) in the USN's Program Executive Office, Ships, 'with innovative new propulsion, electrical, and other key systems, however, LHD-8 is breaking new ground in reducing operating costs – an integral part of the USN's quest to reduce its fleet's total cost of ownership – while maintaining or even increasing operational usefulness'.[1]

After a relatively long gestation, construction and breaking-in period, in mid-2011 LHD-8 was working up to deploy from her San Diego, California, homeport, most likely to the Western Pacific and Southwest Asian waters. The USN will then have the opportunity to shape her broader future, as its most advanced amphibious assault ship makes its mark. In short, it's what's inside that counts.

AMPHIBIOUS MISSIONS AND TASKS

The 2008 'Capstone Concept for Joint Operations', which sets the tone and direction for other US military doctrine, states: 'The most likely occasions requiring the commitment of joint forces will arise, as they have for the past half-century, in places where few or no forces are permanently stationed. America's ability to project power rapidly and conduct and sustain operations globally thus will remain critically dependent on air and maritime freedom of movement and on sufficient strategic and operational lift.'[2]

The ability to forcibly enter hostile territory also seems certain to remain a critical aspect of overall US power-projection capability. Maintaining the ability to do so from the sea – in an anti-access/area-denial (A2/AD) environment where anti-ship weapons and systems are proliferating globally – is the challenge facing the US Navy and US Marine Corps (USMC). That, in turn, requires advanced amphibious warships able to carry, deploy and support Marines ashore in a hostile environment.

The requirement to conduct amphibious assaults against a defended landmass, however, is not the only driver of the requirement for amphibious ships. Indeed, some say that it is highly unlikely that the US Navy/Marine Corps team would ever attempt an opposed landing along the lines of Iwo Jima during the Second World War. As USMC Commandant General James F Amos pointed out in 2011 congressional testimony, 'The same capabilities that allow an amphibious task force to deliver and support a landing force on a hostile shore enables it to support forward engagement and crisis response.' He noted that US combatant commanders in recent years have increased their demand for forward-deployed amphibious forces able to conduct a range of military operations, from engaging in routine security co-operation activities, providing a highly visible regional deterrent, responding to crises of the mili-

Left: *Makin Island* (LHD-8) pictured on builders' sea trials in December 2008. Although externally quite similar to previous members of the *Wasp* (LHD-1) class of amphibious assault ships, she incorporates some fundamental differences. *(US Navy)*

Above: US Marines pictured embarking onto CH-46E Sea Knight helicopters operating from the deck of *Essex* (LHD-2). The ability to forcibly enter hostile territory – most likely from ships located 25 miles (40km) or more from an enemy's shore – is a critical aspect of overall US power projection capabilities. *(US Navy)*

Left: A landing craft air cushion (LCAC) departs the well deck of the amphibious assault ship *Iwo Jima* (LHD-7) during operations in the Persian Gulf in 2006. The ability to embark and operate vessels that can move vehicles, heavy weapons and supplies to land in addition to supporting aviation operations is a key feature of amphibious assault ships such as *Makin Island*. *(US Navy)*

tary and humanitarian assistance varieties. 'In an era of declining access and strategic uncertainty, I anticipate this demand trend will continue,' Amos added.

Overall, USN and USMC officials have identified five distinct categories of amphibious operations:[3]

- Amphibious assault 'to gain entry and secure a lodgement for additional forces, or support an ongoing campaign'.
- Amphibious raids.
- Amphibious demonstrations to deceive an enemy that an attack from the sea is imminent.
- Amphibious withdrawals, such as the US Navy/Marine Corps operation to evacuate United Nations forces from Somalia in 1995.
- Amphibious support to other operations, to prevent conflict or mitigate crises. This category includes humanitarian or disaster-relief assistance, the evacuation of non-combatants, and security cooperation with foreign militaries.

The amphibious warships that perform these missions cannot be simple 'transports'. Instead, they must have the ability to support US Navy/Marine Corps concepts that see the oceans as a venue for operational manoeuvre. Mobility, flexibility across numerous mission areas, and the ability to 'plug' into broader, joint-service command-and-control networks are vital to their capabilities. And whereas twentieth-century amphibious assaults could be conducted from ships located 1 to 5 miles (1.6 to 8km) from the beach, current and future defences will likely require operations to originate over the horizon, from 25 miles (40km) or more from a hostile shore.[4]

In addition, the USMC is organised to operate and fight in integrated air-ground teams, or Marine Air-Ground Task Forces (MAGTFs). Deploying a MAGTF from the sea requires warships – like *Makin Island* – that can operate and support troop- and equipment-carrying helicopters such as the CH-46E Sea Knight, the hybrid MV-22 Osprey tilt-rotor aircraft and the heavy-lift CH-53E Super Stallion helicopter. MAGTFs also come with a fixed-wing, short take-off/vertical landing (STOVL) aircraft contingent, currently the AV-8B Harrier, later potentially the F-35B Lightning II Joint Strike Fighter. Since amphibious operations usually have air and surface components, assault ships also need to lift the amphibious assault vehicles (AAVs) that carry US Marine combat troops ashore, as well as the

Two images of the *Boxer* Amphibious Ready Group (ARG) comprising the amphibious transport dock *New Orleans* (LPD-18), the amphibious dock landing ship *Comstock* (LSD-45) and *Boxer* (LHD-4) herself in July 2009. The 13th Marine Expeditionary Unit (MEU) was embarked. The 'big deck' LHA and LHD type amphibious assault ships form the core of the ARGs. *(US Navy)*

The amphibious transport dock *Green Bay* (LPD-20) pictured on sea trials late in 2008. It is usual to find an LPD operating alongside an amphibious assault ship during ARG deployments. *(Huntington Ingalls Industries)*

air-cushion landing craft (LCAC) and other vessels that move vehicles, heavy weapons and supplies to the beach.

The US amphibious fleet also must maintain a certain level of strategic and operational lift capacity. The baseline US Navy/Marine Corps requirement is to have enough lift to move the assault echelons of two Marine Expeditionary Brigades (MEBs). A MEB is a MAGTF comprising approximately 14,500 Marines, built around a reinforced infantry regiment, a composite Marine aircraft group, a logistics group and a command element. That same amphibious fleet likewise should be sufficient to build three Amphibious Ready Groups (ARGs), each of which carries a smaller MAGTF, the Marine Expeditionary Unit (MEU). These ARG/MEU combinations deploy to forward areas on a rotational basis, providing US Geographic Combatant Commanders with a flexible, quick-reaction response force for a variety of crises.

Normally, this level of tasking would require an amphibious fleet of thirty-eight warships. Facing a period of tight – and probably shrinking – budgets, the US Navy and Marine Corps agreed in 2009 that a force of thirty-three ships would still be (barely) sufficient to move the MEB assault echelons, although it entails some risk in the movement of MEB logistics elements. However, even that level has been difficult to sustain, with the number of amphibious ships in service falling to thirty-one by the end of 2010. The navy's latest shipbuilding plans show total amphibious warship force levels climbing to thirty-three ships by 2016. Actually accomplishing this – much less getting close to thirty-eight amphibious vessels – will be difficult as the navy looks to retire amphibious ships that are older and more costly to maintain against a difficult budgetary backdrop.

AMPHIBIOUS ASSAULT SHIPS: THE CORE OF USN/USMC EXPEDITIONARY WARFARE

No matter what the eventual shape, size and mix of the US amphibious fleet, it is the large-deck assault ships – the LHAs and LHDs – that comprise the heart of the USN's sea-based expeditionary force.

The dock landing ship *Ashland* (LSD-48) seen alongside at Malta during 2005. LSD type ships such as *Ashland* are the third key component of ARG operations, providing additional space for vehicles, stores and equipment. *(Conrad Waters)*

Makin Island can trace her design origins back to the *Tarawa* (LHA-1) type amphibious assault ships that were ordered in the late 1960s. Only *Peleliu* (LHA-5) of the original five ships in the class remains operational – this picture was taken whilst she was underway off the Californian Coast in May 2010. *(US Navy)*

These are the most capable and operationally flexible amphibious warships by dint of their ability to support a full spectrum of Marine aviation operations, their possession of well decks from which a range of amphibious assault and logistics craft can operate, and their extensive command-and-control, medical and other facilities.

With these capabilities, the 'big decks' are the natural fulcrum of every ARG. They are joined in the ARGs by amphibious transport dock (LPD) ships – increasingly the modern (but initially trouble-plagued) *San Antonio* (LPD-17) class – and dock landing ships of the *Whidbey Island* (LSD-41) class. Whilst ARGs are designed to operate as a unit, the plethora of foreign engagement, training, humanitarian and other routine missions these forward-deployed forces are called upon to accomplish often requires dispersed 'split-ARG' operations by individual ships. The greater the 'slice' of MEU capabilities a ship can support – and the large deck amphibious ships can support the most – the greater its usefulness during these independent operations.

As of mid-2011, nine large-deck amphibious assault ships are in USN service. These comprise one remaining *Tarawa* (LHA-1) class vessel and eight *Wasp* (LHD-1) type ships, including *Makin Island*. In addition, the new LHA-6, based in large part on the LHD-8 design, is under construction. *Peleliu* (LHA-5), the final LHA-1 ship in service, is the survivor of a five-strong class that first entered service in 1976 and which have now been almost entirely supplanted by the newer ships. The LHD's capacity in the areas of embarked landing force personnel, vehicles and cargo is similar to that of the LHA – a LHD has more space for cargo, whilst a LHA can carry more vehicles. However, the *Wasp* class ships can accommodate three LCACs in their well deck, whilst *Tarawa* and her sisters could support only one.

The LHA vessels were followed by the modified *Wasp* (LHD-1) class of amphibious assault ships, which were designed from the start to support LCAC and Harrier STOVL operations. The aft well dock of *Boxer* (LHD-4) is pictured clearly in this March 2011 image. *(US Navy)*

The distinction is important given a LCAC can cross almost 70 per cent of the world's shorelines compared to just 17 per cent for traditional landing craft. However, it is in aviation capabilities where the LHD demonstrates most improvement over the earlier LHA. The *Wasp* class were the first amphibious ships designed from the start to support and operate the fixed-wing AV-8B Harrier aircraft and heavy-lift CH-53E Super Stallion helicopter. They have greater support capacity, including more maintenance and repair space, more storage for spare parts including engines and transmissions, better weapons stowage and handling, and more extensive aircraft command-and-control.

This multi-faceted combat aviation capability, although far less than can be generated by larger, dedicated aircraft carriers such as the USN's *Nimitz* (CVN-68) class, gives the LHD a potent punch in smaller contingencies. This was demonstrated during the opening phase of Operation 'Odyssey Dawn' in March 2011, when Harriers operating from *Kearsarge* (LHD-3) took part in the focused air and missile campaign against the Libyan government of Muammar Gaddafi. While supporting only a limited number of Harrier sorties, the LHD's presence allowed the USN to keep its deployed, large-deck *Nimitz*-class carriers engaged in other, high-priority operations around the world.

LHD-8 DESIGN ORIGINS

The general LHD design is the result of decisions about the threat and nature of amphibious operations that stretch back to the 1960s. During that decade, the US Marine Corps began to re-emphasise the importance of a robust surface element in many (non-nuclear) assault scenarios, and urged the USN to examine ship designs that integrated aviation and surface assault craft operations.[5] A 1965 study resulted in an initial warship design that featured both a flight deck for helicopters and a well deck able to accommodate and load internally landing craft that were protected from the external environment. After numerous iterations and input from both the

Table 3.2.1.

MAKIN ISLAND (LHD-8) PRINCIPAL PARTICULARS

Building Information:	
Keel Laid:	14 February 2004
Launched:	22 September 2006
Delivered:	16 April 2009
Builders:	Northrop Grumman Shipbuilding (now the Ingalls Shipbuilding division of Huntington Ingalls Industries) at its facility at Pascagoula, Mississippi.
Dimensions:	
Displacement:	41,650 tons full load displacement.
Overall Hull Dimensions:	258.2m x 36.0m x 8.6m. Length between perpendiculars is 237.1m
Flight Deck Dimensions:	249.6m x 36.0m. 2 x deck edge elevators. 9 x landing spots for aircraft of up to MV-22 Osprey size.
Weapons Systems:	
Aircraft:	There is space for 45 CH-46 equivalents. A typical air group comprises 12 x CH-46E Sea Knight, 4 x CH-53E Super Stallion, 4 x AH-1W Cobra and 3 x UH-1N Huey helicopters plus 6 x AV-8B Harrier STOVL fast jets.
Missiles:	2 x Mk 29 octuple launchers for Sea Sparrow surface-to-air missiles, 2 x RAM Mk49 launchers for RIM-116 rolling airframe missiles.
Guns:	2 x 20mm Vulcan Phalanx CIWS
Countermeasures:	SLQ-32A (V)3 electronic warfare suite. 6 x SRBOC decoy launching systems. SLQ-25 Nixie towed decoy.
Principal Sensors:	1 x SPS-48E air search radar, 1 x SPS-49 (V)9 air search radar, 1 x SPS-67 surface search radar, navigation and fire control radars.
Combat System:	Ship Self Defense System (SSDS) Mk2. Cooperative Engagement Capability (CEC). Integrated communications include links 4A, 11, 14 and 16.
Propulsion Systems:	
Machinery:	Hybrid Electric Drive (HED). 2 x GE LM2500+ gas turbines rated at 52MW. 2 x Converteam electric motors rated at 7.5MW. Maximum 70,000shp on direct gas turbine drive or 10,000shp on electric motors through two shafts.
Speed:	Designed maximum speed is in excess of 20 knots.
Other Details:	
Complement:	Crew is c. 1,060 including 65 officers. Accommodation is provided for c. 1.200.
Military Lift:	Can accommodate up to 1,687 troops plus a further 190 in surge conditions. Significant vehicle and cargo-carrying capacity. Space in well deck for 3 x LCAC or 2 x LCU.

Navy and the Marine Corps, the USN chose the *Tarawa* LHA design. Litton Shipbuilding in Pascagoula, Mississippi, won the detailed design and construction award for the class in 1968.

With a full-load displacement of nearly 40,000 tons and a combined aviation-surface assault capability, *Tarawa* represented a major advance in amphibious warship design when commissioned in May 1976. However, the LHA design was, in many ways, cramped and not well-suited for a rapid build-up of MAGTF power ashore, particularly given the limited well-deck space that could only support one LCAC.

The USN consequently turned to the LHD design with its greater well-deck capacity, improved aviation logistical support capabilities for helicopter and AV-8B operations, better aviation and amphibious command-and-control capabilities, and other improvements. The new emphasis led to external changes as well, such as moving the LHA's stern elevator to the starboard side of the flight deck and replacing the LHA's 'split' stern gate with one similar to those found on LSD – and LPD – type ships to enhance LCAC operations. The LHD also has a 3 per cent greater displacement and is 24ft (7.3m) longer in overall length than its predecessor. Nevertheless, hangar deck and usable flight deck space is roughly similar onboard both ships, although the older ships have an additional flight deck landing spot (for a total of ten). Most LHDs have room – expressed in 'spots' – for forty-two CH-46 helicopter 'equivalents,' compared with forty-three on the LHAs.

The US Congress approved construction of LHD-1 in fiscal year 1984, and *Wasp* was delivered in May 1989. Six sister ships followed, with the last of these – *Iwo Jima* (LHD-7) – being commissioned in June 2001. LHD-5 through to LHD-7 are 'modified repeats' of the earlier ships in the class, having increased jet fuel storage capacity, as well as improved command-and-control, self-defence, fire-fighting and other damage-control capabilities.

USS *Makin Island* (LHD-8) (2010)
1:1250 scale

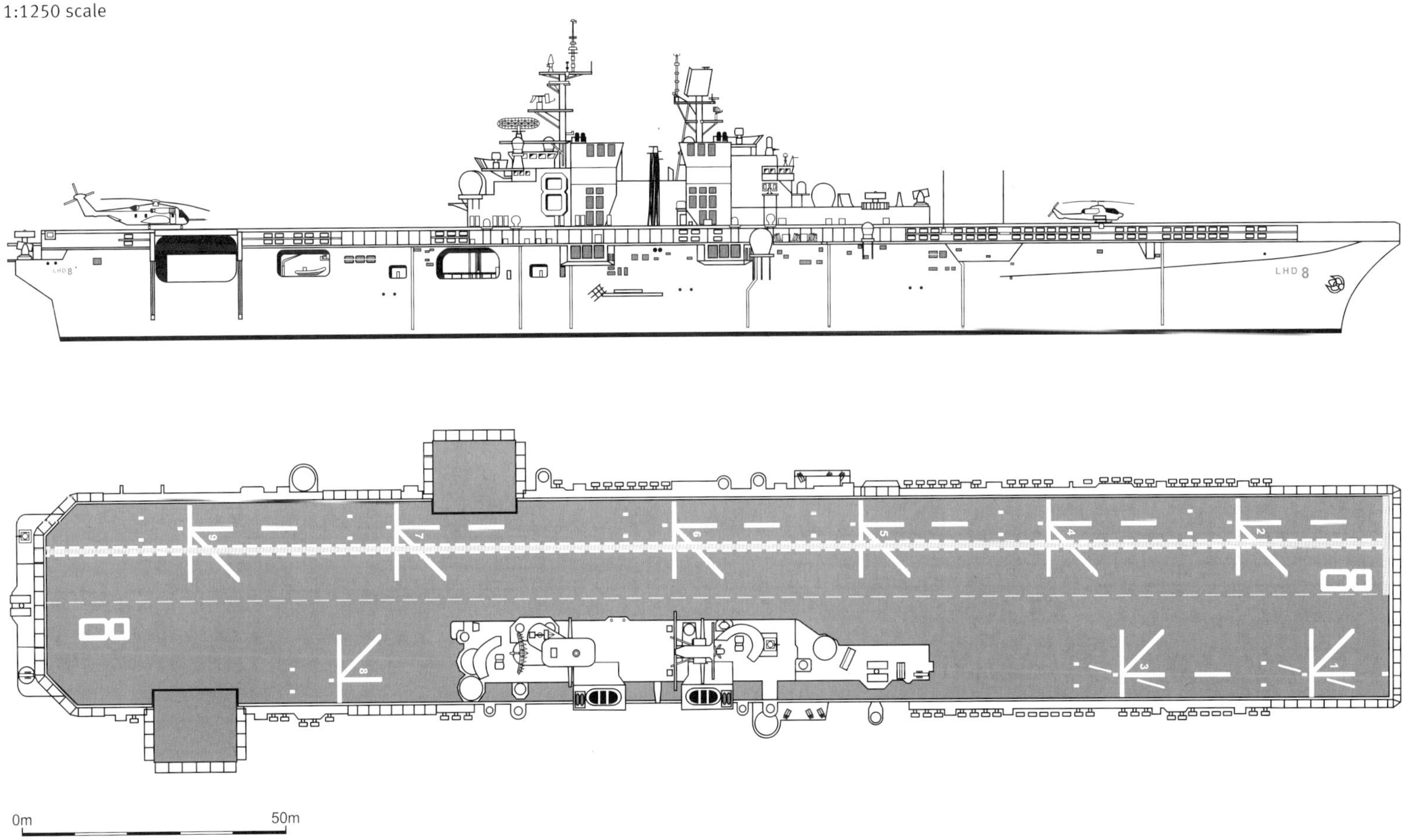

(Drawings © John Jordan, 2011)

Three images of *Makin Island* on sea trials during December 2008 and February 2009. The new amphibious assault ship has broadly similar external features to previous members of the *Wasp* class but has been subject to considerable internal modification that is not readily apparent in these views. A key design feature is the incorporation of hybrid electric drive propulsion (HEP) featuring either direct gas turbine or electric drive as compared with the labour-intensive steam plant of previous amphibious assault ships. The new propulsion system seems to have worked well in practice and offers savings of around US$250m over her projected lifespan. *(US Navy, Huntington Ingalls Industries)*

Wasp (LHD-1) with a full flight deck of MV-22 Osprey tilt-rotor aircraft on their first combat deployment to the Middle East in October 2007. Whilst the LHD type was not designed with this type of aircraft in mind, the Osprey is becoming increasingly common in US Marine Corps service. *(US Navy)*

The USN was considering an eighth LHD in the late 1990s, even as the end of the programme – and the dissolution of at least part of the shipyard workforce that had built the class – loomed. One option discussed was the inclusion of another LHD in its fiscal year 2005 shipbuilding programme. Other alternatives included investment in a new class of ship, the LHX, or upgrades to the existing *Tarawa*-class LHAs to support amphibious lift levels whilst remaining within projected budget levels. Estimates for the cost of a modified-repeat LHD-8 ranged from US$1.5bn to US $2bn. This compared with projections for the LHA service life-extension program (SLEP) within a range of US$1.1bn to US$1.2bn which might have added, at most, only twenty years service life to legacy ships.

Despite official USN silence on LHD-8, the US Marine Corps was enthusiastic about the ship and the capabilities it would bring to the amphibious fleet compared with the aging LHAs. As the then-Commandant of the US Marine Corps, General Charles C Krulak, put it in 1998: 'You cannot SLEP an LHA. That is not being fair to the American people. It is not being fair to take $1.2 billion to SLEP a ship that is not capable to extend its life for 15 to 20 years. For approximately $300 million more you can buy a totally capable, brand-new ship for the 21st century that will last 40 to 50 years. You cannot go to the American people with your hand out for that kind of money and give them such a very low return on their dollar.'[6]

Despite the lack of any USN request for funds for another LHD, the FY1999 defence authorisation bill included US$44m for long-lead time items for LHD-8, due in large part to the efforts of key Mississippi legislators, particularly the then-Senate Majority Leader Trent Lott and Representative Gene Taylor. As noted, Ingalls Shipbuilding (later Northrop Grumman Ingalls, now Huntington Ingalls Industries), which had built the LHAs and the earlier ships in the *Wasp* class, is located in Pascagoula, Mississippi. Thus began a pattern that prevailed for several years: the USN would not request funding for another LHD, but Congress nevertheless would appropriate incremental funding. For example, the FY2000 and 2001 defence appropriations acts, in which a request for LHD-8 was conspicuously absent, contained a provision stating that the Secretary of the Navy was granted authority to contract for an LHD 1-class amphibious assault ship to be funded on an incremental basis. Congress approved the last tranche of funding in FY2006. The USN and the Department of Defense finally recognised the ship as being officially procured in FY2002 at a cost of US$1.37bn, including previously-appropriated advanced funding.

For its part, the USN viewed LHD-8 as a 'bridge' design to a future LHA Replacement class, or LHA(R). Testifying before a Senate subcommittee in April 2002, Marine Corps Major General William A Whitlow, Director of the Expeditionary Warfare Division in the Office of the Deputy Chief of Naval Operations (N85), noted that *Tarawa* class LHAs were rapidly approaching the end of their projected 35-year service lives and faced block obsolescence. From his perspective, LHD-8 played a key role in allowing the USN to retire one of these older warships. As Major General Whitlow observed, however, 'the LHD-8 is a 'transition' ship – a ship designated to develop and demonstrate technology that will be incorporated into the follow-on LHA Replacement ship'.[7]

HYBRID ELECTRIC DRIVE PIONEER

The most significant technologies that LHD-8 would ultimately incorporate were a hybrid electric drive (HED) and advanced electrical generation and distribution systems. USN planners decided in the 1990s to begin phasing out conventional steam plants, which they considered too maintenance- and manpower-intensive. The service also had a long-standing interest in the operational and logistical advantages of all-electric warships. This would ultimately translate into major system improvements in *Makin Island*'s design.[8]

Early feasibility studies concluded that replacing the two steam boilers and two 35,000hp steam turbines fitted in LHD-1 to LHD-7 with two gas turbines could significantly reduce total ownership costs during the course of an eighth LHD's projected forty-year service life. Much of the saving came from the reduced maintenance and manning requirements – seventy to eighty fewer people – associated with the abolition of steam plants. Unfortunately, the USN's

An MV-22 Osprey tilt-rotor landing on *Makin Island* in March 2011. This was the first time landing operations with this rotorcraft had been carried out on a Pacific-coast based amphibious assault ship. The MV-22 will be a key asset within the ship's aviation group in the years to come. *(US Navy)*

The ability to support STOVL fast-jet operations provides amphibious assault ships such as *Makin Island* with considerable flexibility to deal with low- and medium-intensity combat situations. This picture shows AV-8B Harriers from Marine Attack Squadron (VMA) 214 carrying out exercises from the ship's flight deck in February 2011 in preparation for her maiden operational deployment. *(US Navy)*

most commonly-used gas turbine, the 25,000hp General Electric (GE) LM2500, could not meet an LHD's propulsion requirements. A larger engine, moreover, would not fit into the existing LHD's engineering space without a major redesign. Upon further investigation, however, it was discovered that a more powerful LM2500 variant – the 35,000hp LM2500+ that GE was selling to commercial customers – would meet those specifications. The upgraded gas turbine features an additional compressor stage, increased cooling airflow, a hydraulic start system, and digital fuel control, as well as other improvements, according to Captain Mercer. The end result is reliability similar to the long-serving LM2500, but with greater power and efficiency.

The same feasibility studies also found that large-deck amphibious ships spend more than 75 per cent of their underway time at speeds of 12 knots or below. Only 10,000hp of propulsive power or less is required at those speeds, and gas turbines are much less fuel-efficient in that region of the speed-power performance curve compared to other 'primary mover' propulsion systems. The analysis drove the decision to pair each gas turbine on LHD-8 with an electrically-driven auxiliary propulsion motor. The two 5,000hp motors – which, as predicted, have ended up powering *Makin Island* most of the time – draw power directly from the ship's electrical grid, without using battery storage. LHD-8's two shafts are clutched, so that they can be driven either by their dedicated gas turbine or by the auxiliary propulsion motor, and can switch between either one 'on the fly'. Each shaft rotates a controllable-pitch propeller, which in turn gives the ship a handling responsiveness not possible using older steam plants.

The decision to use hybrid electric drive for LHD-8 also allowed designers to tackle another maintenance-intensive system, viz. ship auxiliary power.

Opposite: Two images of *Makin Island* being floated out from what is now Huntington Ingalls Industries' facility at Pascagoula, Mississippi on 22 September 2006. Construction was impacted by the aftermath of Hurricane Katrina in August 2005. *(US Navy)*

Steam has been replaced with electric here as well. In the final evolution, they were able to fit six 4.0MW generators, connected to a 4,160-volt AC zonal electrical distribution system (ZEDS), into the confines of *Makin Island's* hull. Based on distribution systems already installed in some USN destroyers and LPD-17 amphibious dock ships, the ZEDS is both lighter and more survivable than the 'radial' electrical distribution systems found on most previous warships. The system provides speedy fault isolation and power redirection in the event of equipment casualty or battle damage, and requires less upkeep. It also provides operators with the flexibility to route the output of

Makin Island was christened on 19 August 2006, shortly before being floated out. The ship's sponsor was Mrs Silk Hagee, wife of then USMC Commandant General Michael Hagee. This night-time view shows final preparations before the ceremony. *(Huntington Ingalls Industries)*

LHD 8

NORTHROP GRUMMAN
LHD 8

the ship's six diesel generators as needed to match changing propulsion and auxiliary power demands.[9]

The entire electrical system and associated equipment is monitored and controlled by a new fibre-optic machinery control system (MCS) from multi-function workstations located throughout the ship. In addition to the propulsion and auxiliary machinery, the MCS – which constantly processes more than 12,000 input signals – also allows the crew to monitor and control fire-fighting equipment, heating, and ventilation, and to ballast down the well deck for LCAC or AAV operations.

Taken together, the USN has estimated that the cost savings from the totality of these improvements amount to c. US$250m during the ship's expected lifespan. On her two-month maiden voyage from the Gulf of Mexico to San Diego, *Makin Island* already saved more than US$2 million compared with a similar transit by one of her steam-driven sisters. LHD-8 logged 33 per cent of her time on gas-turbine propulsion and 67 per cent of her time on all-electric propulsion during that 2009 voyage, which entailed circumnavigating South America via the Strait of Magellan. Likewise, during a late 2009 at-sea period, the ship's engineering personnel calculated that using the auxiliary motors at full power – which generates 14 knots of speed – saves more than 300 gallons per hour of jet fuel that otherwise would be consumed by gas turbines operating in the same speed range.[10] In some circumstances, that could translate into almost a month of operations before the ship requires refuelling.

On a broader level, the fleet implementation of HED propulsion system on *Makin Island* has served as another step forward in the 'Great Green Fleet' and Navy Energy visions of the current Secretary of the Navy and the Chief of Naval Operations. The insertion of these technologies into LHD-8 – making her the Navy's first 'green 'gator' – and in future warships is key to meeting the CNO's goals outlined in his guidance for 2011, 'We will increase our energy security and operational effectiveness by reducing our reliance on fossil fuels and improving the reach of our afloat forces and the resilience of our shore energy sources.'[11]

Makin Island benefits from an integrated Ship Self-Defense System (SSDS) that controls a defensive armament built around RAM and Sea Sparrow missiles, and the Vulcan Phalanx CIWS. Practice firings of the two last-mentioned systems are seen in these images. *(US Navy)*

SHIPYARD CHALLENGES

Before becoming an exemplar of energy efficiency and a key part of the US amphibious fleet, LHD-8 first served as an unfortunate example of US shipbuilding woes. Whilst *Makin Island* is a modified-repeat of the previous ship in the class, LHD-7, that simple statement can hide a multitude of design changes. By one account, more than 67 per cent of LHD-7 line drawings and nearly 75 per cent of test procedures had to be modified for LHD-8.[12] In effect, builder Northrop Grumman Ingalls (now Huntington Ingalls Industries) was dealing with the construction of a significantly different ship, a situation that often entails a steeper learning curve for a shipyard force, and which is fraught with the risk of delays and overruns – as evidenced by the USN's experience with the *San Antonio* class amphibious transport docks.

In *Makin Island*'s case, nature also conspired against the shipyard and the USN. Fortunately for US taxpayers, the contract to build LHD-8 that the USN awarded to Northrop Grumman Ingalls was of the fixed-price, incentive fee type, and much of the setback fell on the shipbuilder's shoulders.

Makin Island's keel was laid at the Northrop Grumman Ingalls yard in February 2004. A year and a half into construction, in August 2005, Hurricane Katrina struck the Gulf of Mexico region. In addition to the physical damage it wreaked upon Northrop Grumman's facilities, the storm dispersed a portion of the shipyard's labour force. According to one former Northrop Grumman official, before Katrina 20 per cent of the shipyard's work force had twenty-five years of experience; after the storm, less than 5 per cent did. The ranks of electrical workers in particular suffered from this out-migration.[13] Northrop Grumman Ingalls received some compensation for the damage to its yard, but Katrina also consumed a significant part of the company's performance margin on the contract. A four-week strike in 2007 resulted in the company taking another financial hit against the project. Then, in April 2008, Navy inspectors found that shipyard workers were not installing the key electrical and fibre-optic cabling correctly – in many cases the cables were crushed or connected improperly. Northrop Grumman subsequently registered more charges to rework the damaged cables and account for schedule delays on *Makin Island* and other ships. Overall, the yard was forced to muster almost 1,500 workers for the additional six months of work.

Makin Island's delivery date, originally scheduled for 2007, slipped to 2008 and then to 16 April 2009, nearly two years behind schedule. Later, in August 2010, as the ship's final contract trials in Southern California waters drew near, crew members found damage to a turning gear assembly used in conjunction with the propulsion plant. Fortunately, this time

Makin Island's pre-commissioning cruise saw her circumnavigate the coast of Latin America, including port calls in Brazil, Chile and Peru. There was time for exercises with Chile's fast attack craft *Casma* and *Chipana*. *(US Navy)*

An image of *Makin Island* passing through the Magellan Strait on 15 August 2009 during her three-month-long pre-commissioning delivery voyage from Pascagoula to San Diego. *(US Navy)*

Makin Island visited San Francisco in October 2010 to participate in San Francisco Fleet Week 2010. This image shows her approaching the Golden Gate Bridge. *(Mrityunjoy Mazumdar)*

the ship's company and the Navy's Southwest Regional Maintenance Centre were able to perform pier-side repairs at the *Makin Island*'s new homeport of San Diego.

CHARACTERISTICS AND CAPABILITIES

LHD-8's advanced engineering plant sets the ship apart from other warships in the US amphibious and surface fleets, but the amphibious mission is still the ship's *raison d'etre*. Table 3.2.1 lists some of the elements of the ship's 'main battery': the people, aircraft, supplies and equipment of the embarked MAGTF.

In common with her sisters, the ship has an efficient system of six-ton capacity elevators and internal monorails. This system can move equipment and ammunition efficiently – up to 300 pallets per hour – from storage and magazines to areas from which they can be loaded on helicopters, LCACs or other landing craft. Cargo storage, efficient stores and people movement, a flight deck with forty-five CH-46-equivalent spots, and a 267ft (81m) long, 50ft (15.2m) wide well deck allows *Makin Island* to support a range of options for moving MAGTF assets ashore.

In the aviation area, LHD-8 and her sisters increasingly will be hosting the MV-22 Osprey tilt-rotor aircraft in the coming years, although the LHD class was not designed with this aircraft in mind. The Osprey is replacing the aging CH-46E Sea Knight helicopter in the medium-lift role, with two Marine squadrons transitioning to the tilt-rotor each year. Reflecting this change, in March 2011 *Makin Island* became the first West Coast-based amphibious warship to conduct flight operations with the MV-22. The ship is not embarking the Osprey in its 2011 deployment, however, but instead will support a MEU air combat element flying CH-46s.

Like its predecessors, *Makin Island* has command-and-control and other facilities that make the ship a key node in a networked sea base supporting amphibious operations. LHDs in general have one of the more advanced command-and-control suites in the USN's amphibious fleet and can support joint-service, naval commander, and Marine Corps landing force or MAGTF commanders. LHD-8 has even more advanced command spaces, which are fitted out with equipment first assembled and pre-tested at the Space and Naval Warfare Systems Command's Test and Integration Facility in Charleston, SC.

Elsewhere on the ship, the medical facility is second only to those found onboard the USN's hospital ships, consisting of sixty-four beds (including seventeen intensive care unit beds) and six operating rooms. This compares with eighteen beds and six operating rooms in the *Tarawa*-class LHAs. With onboard blood storage, X-ray, and other assets at their fingertips, the medical team onboard the ship is well positioned to care for combat casualties or victims of humanitarian disasters.

Makin Island's water purification facilities likewise could be vital during disaster-response scenarios. The ship has four reverse-osmosis units capable of producing up to 200,000 gallons of fresh water daily. Loaded into bladders, the water can be moved where needed ashore by helicopter or LCAC.

For self-protection, *Makin Island*'s two NATO Sea Sparrow missile systems, two Rolling Airframe Missile (RAM) systems, two Phalanx close-in weapons systems mounts, and six missile decoy launchers are controlled via the Ship Self-Defense System (SSDS). SSDS is a local area network that integrates the ship's sensors and weapon systems for the automated detection, tracking and engagement of air and other threats. The ship also is equipped with Cooperative Engagement Capability (CEC), a sensor network with integrated fire-control capability that combines data from multiple air search sensors into a single, real-time, composite track picture. CEC acts as the primary source of air-tracking data for SSDS Mark 2-equipped ships like *Makin Island*.

These systems generally have been proven effective during testing and real-world operations, but a 2010 report by the Director of Operational Testing and Evaluation also described some problems on *Makin Island* during testing. It noted that, at the time, some elements of the combat system 'continue to have reliability problems' and that 'the LHD 8 combat system had difficulty engaging certain classes of asymmetric threats'.[14] These shortcomings were reportedly corrected by 2011.

OPERATIONS

Makin Island departed her Pascagoula birthplace in July 2009, arrived in San Diego the following September, and was commissioned on 24 October. The crew engaged in a mix of training, ship evaluation and operational duties during the LHD's maiden, pre-commissioning voyage. For example, after conducting early aviation qualifications in the Gulf of Mexico, *Makin Island* supported shipboard training by US Army CH-47 Chinook helicopters operating from Belize. The ship also made port calls in Brazil, Chile and Peru in support of the US Southern Command's regional engagement policy.

After her arrival in San Diego, LHD-8 continued with various certification and training evolutions, before and after her commissioning ceremony. These included Combat System Ships Qualification Trials, flight operations by AV-8Bs, and well-deck operations with Marine Corps AAVs. In early 2010, the ship's Navy inspectors evaluated the SSDS and its associated sensors and weapons. The ship entered a four-month post-shakedown maintenance period in March 2010, during which the turning gear problem was discovered. That, in turn, pushed back final contract trials until the autumn. The ship passed this final set of special trials, which were administered by the Navy's Board of Inspection and Survey, in October 2010. That milestone marked the warship's official designation as a fully-operational fleet asset.

Makin Island has been assigned to the US Pacific Fleet as part of Amphibious Group Five, which includes *New Orleans* (LPD-18) and *Pearl Harbor* (LSD-52). The 11th MEU will embark in the group's ships and forward-deploy to Asian waters during the second half of 2011. Consequently, much of LHD-8's 2011 activities were in preparation for this eventual deployment. In February, 11th MEU Marines and units from the Japanese Ground Self Defence Force's Western Regiment embarked on *Makin Island* to practice coordinated ship-to-shore movements as part of Exercise Iron Fist 2011. In March, the ship took on a full load of ammunition as she moved into her deployment work-up phase, which would continue through the summer.

Soldiers from the Japan Ground Self Defence Force's Western Army Infantry Regiment deploying from rigid-hull inflatable boats from *Makin Island*'s well deck. Operations with Allied units will form a core element of her future service. *(US Navy)*

MODEL FOR THE FUTURE

After the turn of the century, USN planners contemplated a future with eight LHDs and a dwindling number of *Tarawa*-class LHAs, with the last passing from service by 2015. Given the requirement for a minimum number of aviation-capable, large-deck amphibious warships – currently set at eleven – work on the next-generation LHA(R) began. A key driving force in the LHA(R) design was the requirement to handle larger and heavier aircraft such as the MV-22 Osprey and the F-35B Lightning II, as well as the equipment, weapons and fuel to support their operations. The end result was a ship whose hull, propulsion, and many other systems are identical or nearly identical to *Makin Island*'s. However, this focus on air operations has been achieved at the expense of surface assault capabilities, at least initially.

With a notional aviation complement of twelve MV-22 Ospreys, four CH-53 Sea Stallions, four AH-1 Cobras, and six F-35B Lightning IIs, the first ships in the class also will have:

- Nearly 40 per cent more hangar deck space, and more space devoted to aviation equipment and parts storage.
- Larger, armoured magazine spaces, the latter protection being a first for any US large-deck amphibious ship.
- The capacity to carry 1.3 million gallons of JP-5 jet fuel, compared with LHD 8's 585,000 gallons.

In return, the new LHA design deleted the well deck and vehicle-storage space found on the LHDs. That change did not please the Marine Corps and, at its urging, the USN agreed to restore the well deck beginning with the third ship in the class.

The keel of the lead ship, *America* (LHA-6), was laid in July 2009, and the ship should commence fleet operations by April 2015. Meanwhile, LHA-7 is being funded over two years – a process that began in FY 2011 – and will be followed by the well-decked LHA-8 by the end of the decade. To a large extent, all of these ships will look like LHD-8. That will particularly be true inside these ships – in their engineering spaces and combat centres – where it counts, with *Makin Island* clearly in the van.

A computer-generated image of *America* (LHA-6). The new LHA-6 design draws many core design elements from *Makin Island* but places greater emphasis on aviation missions. *(Huntington Ingalls Industries)*

Notes:

1. Captain Mercer was interviewed 25 March 2011. The authors thank Captain Mercer for his insight into the construction, technical and operational details on LHD-8.

2. Admiral Michael G Mullin, USN, Chairman, Joint Chiefs of Staff, *Capstone Concept for Joint Operations*, (Washington DC, Department of Defense, 15 January 2008), p 3.

3. Statement of Assistant Secretary of the Navy Sean J Stackley; USMC Deputy Commandant, Lt. General George J Flynn; and Deputy Chief of Naval Operations, Vice Admiral John Terence Blake, before the House Armed Services Committee, Subcommittee on Seapower and Projection Forces, 26 March 2011

4. Major General Timothy Hanifen, USMC, Director Expeditionary Warfare Division, Office of the Deputy Chief of Naval Operations (N85) briefing to the National Defense Industrial Association, 5 October 2010.

5. Class histories are taken mainly from Norman Polmar, *The Naval Institute Guide to the Ships and Aircraft of the US Fleet* (Annapolis, MD, US Naval Institute, 2005), pp 181–92; Eric Wertheim, *The Naval Institute Guide to Combat Fleets of the World*, 15th edition (Annapolis, MD, Naval Institute Press, 2007), pp 919–24; and Norman Friedman, *US Amphibious Ships and Craft: An Illustrated Design History* (Annapolis, MD, Naval Institute Press, 2002), pp 448–9.

6. Lt. Colonel Arthur P Brill, 'A Defining Moment in Marine Corps History', interview with General Charles C Krulak (CMC), *Seapower* (Arlington VA, Navy League of the United States, November 1998). A copy can be found at www.navyleague.org/seapower/krulak_interview.htm.

7. Statement of Major General William A Whitlow, USMC; Director, Expeditionary Warfare Division, Office of the Deputy Chief of Naval Operations (Warfare Requirements and Programs), before the Subcommittee on Sea Power of the Senate Armed Services Committee on Navy and Marine Corps Operational Requirements for the 21st Century, 9 April 2002.

8. This section draws from Thomas Dalton, Abe Boughner, C David Mako and Commander Norbert Doerry, USN's 'LHD 8: A Step Toward the All Electric Warship', a paper submitted for ASNE Day, American Society of Naval Engineers, 2002; Louis V Dusang, Jr. and C David Mako's 'An Integrated Power System Aboard *Makin Island*,' a paper presented to the ASNE Electric Machines Technology Symposium, 19 May 2010; and Norman Friedman's 'USS *America*: A Different Kind of Gator,' Defense Media Network, 28 October 2010.

9. According to Captain Mercer, the electric plant can parallel the output of five diesel generators in ring-bus mode. In split-plant mode, the ship can use the output of all six generators (three on each auxiliary propulsion motors). The ship also can dedicate a diesel generator to each propulsion motor, while the plant parallels the output of the remaining four diesel generators.

10. USN, '*Makin Island* Completes First CSSQT, Harrier and AAV Ops', press release, 14 December 2009.

11. Admiral Roughead, 'CNO Guidance for 2011: Executing the Maritime Strategy,' October 2010, p 5.

12. Please see 'LHD 8 Ship Delayed, NGC to Foot the Bill', *Defense Industry Daily*, 23 March 2009. It can be found by searching the www.defenseindustrydaily.com website.

13. Grace V Jean, 'Navy Shipbuilding Challenges Loom Large in the 2020s,' *National Defense* (Arlington VA, National Defense Industrial Association, June 2011). A copy can be found in the archives at www.nationaldefensemagazine.org.

14. J Michael Gilmore, Director, *Operational Testing & Evaluation FY 2010 Annual Report* (Washington DC, US Department of Defense, 2010). An electronic copy is located at www.dote.osd.mil/pub/reports/FY2010/.

K32
K31

3.3 SIGNIFICANT SHIPS

Author:
Guy Toremans

SWEDEN'S VISBY CLASS CORVETTES

Stealth At All Levels

INTRODUCTION

In December 2001, a radically different type of surface warship was spotted on trials in the Baltic. It was the Royal Swedish Navy's stealthy corvette *Visby,* lead ship of a five ship class and the first vessel in the world to incorporate fully-developed stealth technology. This was combined with a revolutionary new approach to multi-mission warfare. The amalgamation of high operational versatility with effective stealth characteristics is the hallmark of the *Visby* class. As a result, many commentators consider the design as the ideal multi-purpose surface combatant of the future. Although an extensive programme of trials and modifications encompassed much of the decade, the class is now starting to become fully operational.

PROGRAMME BACKGROUND AND SHIP DESIGN

Due to declining defence budgets in the 1970s, Sweden progressively gave up its cruiser and destroyer-type units in favour of a surface fleet based around a force of missile-armed fast attack craft. At that time, these were judged to be the most cost-effective solution for carrying out surveillance and sea-denial operations in and around the Swedish archipelago. Subsequently, with the end of the Cold War and the consequent reduced threat to Sweden's territorial integrity, priorities changed. As a result, the need arose for modern, multi-purpose surface combatants able to perform a variety of functions in both a national and international environment.

This need coincided with Swedish research on the application of stealth to naval vessels. In 1986 Sweden's Defence Materiel Administration (Försvarets materielverk or FMV) – together with shipyard Karlskronavarvet (KkrV), the National Defence Research Establishment (FOI), the Royal Swedish Navy, Stockholm's Royal Institute of Technology (KTH), and other Swedish institutes of technology and private companies – initiated a concept programme that was ultimately to lead to the Surface Combat Vessel 2000 (YS2000) project. Three main aims were set out, viz:

- To evaluate the effects of different methods of signature reduction on a surface stealth ship.
- To test the integration of weapons and sensors in a stealthy ship.
- To analyse surface-effect-ship (SES) technology.

This project resulted in the launch of the *Smyge*, a stealth demonstration platform incorporating several innovative design features, in 1991. Through this project, the Swedish Navy reached an advanced technological level much faster than would otherwise have been possible.

Subsequently, in 1994, Karlskronavarvet – later to become part of the Kockums group – was awarded a contract to undertake the initial design work required to make YS2000 a reality.[1] After a fairly tough political debate on the need for the new ships, the Swedish government gave the FMV permission to order the initial two units – *Visby* (K31) and *Helsingborg* (K32) – in September 1995. The construction contract for the two vessels was signed in October 1995 and contained options for a second pair. An agreement to build these additional two units – hulls three and four *Härnösand* (K33) and *Nyköping* (K34) – was confirmed at the start of construction ceremony for the first-of-class, *Visby*, on 17 December 1996. The first four ships were laid down at six-monthly intervals between December 1996 and June 1998.

Initially the Royal Swedish Navy planned to acquire as many as fourteen corvettes but this number was cut back to ten units in two variants: four Series I units with an anti-submarine warfare (ASW) and mine countermeasures bias, and six Series II platforms with an anti-surface warfare capability.[2] However, budget cuts and force structure revisions saw the programme further reduced to six

Left: *Helsingborg* and *Visby* operating in company whilst on trials in the Baltic during September 2005. The class provides an amalgamation of high operational versatility with effective stealth characteristics. *(Kockums)*

ships, cutting the number of Series II-variants to two. Total costs for the six ships – including subsystems – were estimated at c. €780m. A contract for the construction of hulls five and six – *Karlstad* (K35) and *Uddevalla* (K36) – was signed on 31 August 1999. Early in 2001, however, Kockums acknowledged that cost overruns since the inception of the programme were endangering its completion within the likely available budget. With the top priority being the safeguarding of the overall programme rather than the specific number of hulls, the FMV agreed to reduce the number of units to five to ensure its continuation. Consequently, construction of the sixth ship – *Uddevalla* – was cancelled in October 2001. All five remaining ships will have full multi-role capabilities.

The FMV received its first *Visby* class corvette from Kockums on 10 June 2002. *Helsingborg* was delivered on 24 April 2006, followed by *Härnösand* on 12 June 2006 and *Nyköping* on 27 September 2006. Delivery of the final corvette, *Karlstad*, was delayed due to gearbox problems and may not occur until planned upgrades are completed. Table 3.3.1 provides further details.

Visby was originally scheduled for delivery by the FMV to the Royal Swedish Navy in early 2005, with its four sister-ships following at approximately ten-month intervals.[3] However, the programme suffered from slippage, caused partly because of capability changes fairly late in the design process. Most notably, the Swedish Parliament mandated a search-and-rescue (SAR) helicopter capability for the class: a requirement necessitating the installation of a retractable deck to lower the embarked helicopter into a hangar beneath the flight deck. This plan was subsequently cancelled. Indecision has also impacted other areas, such as the on/off aim to equip all five units with an anti-air warfare (AAW) system in the form of the South African Umkhonto-IR missile.

Through the *Smyge* technology demonstrator, the Swedish Navy reached an advanced technological level much faster than would otherwise have been possible. Since 2005, *Smyge* has been used to train the *Visby* class crews in damage control and fire-fighting at the Naval Sea Safety Training School. *(Guy Toremans)*

DESIGN – HULL FORM AND STRUCTURE

The corvettes' hull form is a variation on the well-proven planing monohull, specifically designed for water-jet propulsion and with fixed fins for directional stability. The under-body has a fine 'V' entry for slicing through waves together with a variable dead-rise bottom geometry, squared bilges, and a deep spray chine forward to assure a minimal wake and spray. The hull is made of a double-skin, energy-absorbing carbon fibre-reinforced plastic (CFRP) sandwich construction.[4] The platform is assembled from four main modules: Section 10 (aft block); Section 20 (midships block); Section 30 (forward block); and Section 40 (superstructure). The sections are joined together by a bonding technique based on the KVASI (Kockums Vacuum Assisted Sandwich Infusion) process. In areas of high stress concentration, such as the gearbox mountings, titanium reinforcing inserts are laminated into the composite. CFRP provides:

- High strength and rigidity – the material is twice as tough as conventional steel hulls with regard to mine explosions. Shock resistance is also good.
- A dramatic reduction in structural weight – a CFRP sandwich sheet weighs only 10–20 per cent of that of a steel plate yet with the equivalent bending stiffness. This results in greater payload carrying capabilities, higher speeds and longer ranges.
- Integrated stealth qualities.

The seagoing performance of the *Visby* class is superior in all respects to the legacy *Stockholm* and

Table 3.3.1: *VISBY* CLASS LIST

SHIP	NAME		ORDERED	COMMENCED	LAUNCHED	DELIVERY TO FMV	TO NAVY
1.	*Visby*	K31	17 October 1995	17 December 1996	8 June 2000	10 June 2002[1]	[2012]
2.	*Helsingborg*	K32	17 October 1995	June 1997	27 June 2003	24 April 2006	2009[2]
3.	*Härnösand*	K33	17 December 1996	December 1997	16 December 2004	12 June 2006	2009[2]
4.	*Nyköping*	K34	17 December 1996	June 1998	18 August 2005	27 September 2006	[2012]
5.	*Karlstad*	K35	31 August 1999	December 1999	24 August 2006	[2013]	[2013]
6.	*Uddevalla*	K36	31 August 1999	[Cancelled]	–	–	–

Notes:

1 K31 was initially delivered to the FMV prior to installation of her combat system and other core equipment. Final acceptance took place on 12 June 2006.

2 K32 and K33 were commissioned into the Royal Swedish Navy on 16 December 2009 but will be transferred back to FMV and Kockums in 2012 for an upgrade to 'Version 5' standard. K32 will be returned to the Swedish Navy at the end of 2013 and K33 in the middle of 2014. From the middle of 2014, all the *Visby* class ships will therefore have been upgraded to the latest 'Version 5' standard.

A view of the interior of a *Visby* class hull under construction. Water intakes and ducts are bonded into the carbon fibre-reinforced plastic hull to form a homogenous structure of great rigidity. *(Kockums)*

Göteborg class corvettes. During their 'at sea' trials, the corvettes proved to be very seaworthy in all sea states in the Baltic and the North Sea. Class manoeuvrability is also a strength: although 72m in total length, their ability to pivot around their centres makes them broadly equivalent to a 35m vessel. The *Visby*s also have enhanced operational ranges and can remain on station for approximately twenty-one consecutive days. Table 3.3.2 provides further technical detail.

DESIGN – SURVIVABILITY

Whilst the *Visby*s rely on outstanding stealth properties to achieve a fundamental improvement in ship-survivability, much effort has also been put into more traditional damage control. For example, they feature ten water- and gas-tight compartments and can remain afloat even with three adjacent compartments flooded. Due to lean manning, the ships rely heavily on automation such as CCTV, anti-smoke, anti-fire and anti-flood sensors and automatic fire-fighting equipment. The main damage control centre is located in the centre of the ship two decks below the main deck. Should this compartment be damaged, secondary facilities are provided on the bridge and in the Combat Information Centre (CIC).

The class features an integrated solution for damage control – the Integrated Damage Control System (IDCS) – that provides the crew an overview of the ship's status in all aspects and gives them the opportunity to act in a very tight timeframe. In case of damage or general emergency, the system's safety management software collects and distributes relevant information and provides decision-support capabilities. Structural fire protection is ensured thanks to the excellent fire-containment properties of CFRP, supplemented by fire retarding and insulating materials as well as by an advanced Halotron fire-extinguishing system that is installed throughout the ship. The fire alarm system automatically governs the ventilating system, thus giving the ship a high degree of survivability in relation to fire and smoke.

DESIGN – STEALTH TECHNOLOGY

The *Visby* class design concept represents 'stealth all the way'. At Kockums, this is defined as Genuine Holistic Stealth or GHOST. With stealth being the key driver, the design of the *Visby* platform took a comprehensive approach to signature reduction. The aim was to break the classic 'kill chain' of detect–identify–localise–target–engage. What makes the class unique is the very low level of 'signature' in all areas that has been achieved. All signatures and emitted signals in every dimension have been optimised in order to create a protective signature 'shell' around the ship. This encompasses radar cross-section (RCS), infra-red, optical, hydro-acoustic, magnetic, laser, wake and extremely low-frequency electromagnetic (ELFE) elements. Also taken into account are active transmission sources, such as radars and communications, including their directivity. Many of the technologies used in the *Visby* class have been employed in their first maritime application.

Radar Cross-section: The Swedish Navy set out particularly demanding standards for minimising the ships' radar cross-section (RCS) as much as possible. Whereas a conventional non-stealthy corvette will typically be detected by radar at a range of thirty nautical miles (50km), the navy wanted *Visby* to be detectable at only eight nautical miles (13km) in rough seas and thirteen nautical miles (22km) in calm seas. Jamming reduces the detection range even further to five nautical miles (8km) and seven nautical miles (11km) respectively.

A key factor in achieving these aims has been the controlled shaping of hull and superstructure. Through the use of large, flat angled surfaces and sharp edges, radar energy is dispersed in four main

A view of *Visby* on early trials. Her construction at the Karlskrona yard started in December 1996 but she was not delivered to Sweden's FMV Defence Material Administration until June 2002 – and then in incomplete form. Final acceptance was delayed until June 2006 and it will not be until 2012 that she enters operational service. *(Kockums)*

Left: *Karlstad* was the last of the class to be launched when she entered the water on 24 August 2006. She was lowered into the water by means of a ship-lift. This image shows the sleek stealty characteristics of the class's structure to good effect. *(Kockums)*

directions and in a single angle of elevation. The low, sleek characteristics of the class's superstructure greatly reduce the ships' electro-optic/visual signature. The superstructure is constructed as a truncated pyramid, with a sensor radome atop and radar absorbent material (RAM) applied in areas where the required low-signature properties were difficult to achieve – the so-called critical radar 'hot spots'.

The BAE Systems Bofors 57mm/70 Mk3 gun is housed in a specially-designed stealthy cupola. The slab-sides of the turret, manufactured from a reinforced glass-fibre mesh, are inclined to reflect incident radar energy. The barrel itself is concealed inside the turret and only exposed during firing. Similarly, the gun's stealthy CEROS 200 Multi-Sensor fire-control director has also been given a very low RCS by using flat, inclined metallic surfaces with radar-absorbent material (RAM) and a frequency selective surface in front of the antenna.

Similarly, the Sea Giraffe 3D air/surface-search radar and mast-mounted ESM antennae are concealed within the stealthy radome, which has been specifically produced with 'frequency selective surface' material that allows only certain frequencies to pass through. The communications antennae are flush-mounted to the superstructure.

The arrangement and shaping of the majority of other topside structures is such that they are mounted internally, have been made hoistable or retractable, or are hidden behind hatches. As a result, the usual clutter of deck gear, anchors and the like is built into the structure or concealed under hatches. The class's rigid hull inflatable boat (RHIB) and remotely-operated vehicles (ROVs) are stored behind flush-fitting hangar doors and launched from telescopic gantry cranes. In order to store the life-rafts inside the hull, a special raft ejector design was developed. The inte-

Left: Stealth extends to infra-red reduction. For example, the gas turbine exhausts and exhaust pipes are concealed in hidden outlets in the stern, close to the waterline. To reduce heat signature, water is injected into the exhaust pipes, cooling down the exhaust gas from approx. 1,000°C to 40°C – hence the immense cloud of 'smoke'. *(Guy Toremans)*

Two forward views of *Helsingborg*. The hull form is a variation on the proven planing monohull, specifically designed for water-jet propulsion. The under-body has a fine 'V' entry for slicing through waves together with a variable dead-rise bottom geometry, squared bilges and a deep spray chine forward to assure a minimal wake and spray. Note also that the usual clutter of equipment and deck gear is built into the structure or concealed, aiding stealth. *(Guy Toremans)*

gral main weapon and equipment deck also enables the crew to work in a weather-protected environment, allowing for greater endurance and operations in rough weather. All air inlets and outlets are covered with radar reflecting metal meshes, mounted flush to the inclined hull sides.

To improve visual stealth, a new two-tone grey camouflage pattern has been applied, which is designed to 'break up' the appearance of the ship against sea and sky, thereby confusing actual detection and identification. In other words, the paint scheme and pattern reduces the ships' visual signature, making it difficult to detect them from their surrounding environment.

Infra-Red (IR) Reduction: The ships' infra-red (IR) profile is also carefully managed. To reduce the IR-signature, highly advanced masking techniques and water-jet sprays have been incorporated. The CFRP's innate thermo-insulating qualities, coupled with the cooling down of all exhaust emissions with seawater, greatly assist the elimination of cold and hot spots. Thermal-absorbent exterior paint has been selected for optimum heat insulation. The gas turbine exhausts and ventilation exhaust pipes are concealed in hidden outlets in the stern while the triple-cooled engines and generators exhausts vent at the waterline. To reduce heat signature even further, a wash-down system can give the external surfaces a temperature similar to the surrounding environment and water is injected into the exhaust pipes. When the corvettes sail on gas turbine (GT) propulsion, a lot of 'smoke' surrounds the ship. This is, in fact, the steam

Table 3.3.2.

VISBY PRINCIPAL PARTICULARS

Building Information:	
Fabrication Commenced:	17 December 1996
Launched:	8 June 2000
Delivered:	10 June 2002/12 June 2006[1]
Builders:	Kockums at its Karlskrona shipyard.
Dimensions:	
Displacement:	650 tons full load displacement
Overall Hull Dimensions:	72.7m x 10.4m x 2.5m. Length between perpendiculars is 61.5m.
Weapons Systems:[2]	
Missiles:	2 x quad Saab Bofors Dynamics RBS-15 Mk2 surface-to-surface missiles.
	Provision for 1 x 8 cell VLS module for Denel Umkhonto-IR Mk2 surface-to-air missiles.
Guns:	1 x BAE Systems Bofors 57mm Mk3. Light weapons.
Torpedoes:	4 x 400mm fixed anti-submarine torpedo tubes for Saab Underwater Systems Type 45 ASW torpedoes. Mines and depth charges.
Aircraft:	Platform for 1 x AW-109 light helicopter.
Countermeasures:	ES-3701 electronic support measures (ESM) system. MASS decoys.
Principal Sensors:	1 x Saab Sea Giraffe 3D air/surface search radar. 1 x Saab PILOT surface search radar. 1 x Saab CEROS 200 Mk3 fire control radar.
	Hydra multi-sonar system encompassing C-Tech CHMS-90 hull mounted sonar, C-Tech CVDS active variable depth sonar.
	Hydroscience Technologies TAS together with ROV-S and ROV-E remote operating vehicles.
Combat System:	Saab Systems 9LV Mk 3E CETRIS combat management system.
	Saab ICS2000 integrated communications system. Includes Link 16 compatibility.
Propulsion Systems:	
Machinery:	CODOG. 4 x Vericor TF-50A gas turbines rated at 16MW. 2 x Tognum MTU 16V 2000 N90 diesels rated at 2.6MW.
	Provides c .21,500hp through 2 x 125 SII RR Kamewa waterjets. One bow thruster.
Speed and Range:	Designed maximum speed is in excess of 35 knots. No figure for range has been released.
Other Details:	
Complement:	A typical crew comprises 43, including 26 officers and petty officers. Accommodation is provided for 53.
Class:	Five ships have been ordered: *Visby* (K31), *Helsingborg* (K32), *Härnösand* (K33), *Nyköping* (K34) and *Karlstad* (K35).

Notes

1 Dates relate to initial delivery and final acceptance by the FMV. The ship had not been formally handed over to the Royal Swedish Navy as at mid-2011.

2 Details relate to 'Version 5' upgrade.

produced when the 600C° exhaust is cooled down to approximately 40C°. Care has also been taken to reduce possible 'glint' sources. The few windows on the bridge – and the glass over navigation lights – are coated with radar-reflecting material.

Radiated Noise and Hydro-Acoustic Measures: Reduced radiated noise levels and hydro-acoustic signature are achieved through several methods. Again the CFRP provides better structure-borne noise-damping qualities compared with conventional construction materials. The specifically developed Rolls-Royce Kamewa water-jet propulsion generates a lower hydro-acoustic signature than traditional propeller systems. The two propulsion diesels are housed in double elastic resilient mountings, with sound absorbing hoods fitted. Similar measures have been taken with regard to the four gas turbine units and the main auxiliary machinery. Other noise-generating equipment, such as pumps and fans, are mounted on elastic mounts to damp out their natural vibration and fluid-filled pipes are insulated.

Magnetic Signature: Magnetic signature (the so-called DC, AC and Eddy currents) is addressed in a variety of ways. The choice of CFRP sandwich construction resulted in a hull that is completely non-magnetic, so it inherently shields against a wide range of electromagnetic signals. Onboard systems are depermed, equipped with magnetic mine protection coils, or constructed with non-magnetic material. The propulsion plant makes use of low and non-magnetic materials and galvanic interruptions in the frames and pipe systems. All major prime movers

Helsingborg (2010)
1:350 scale

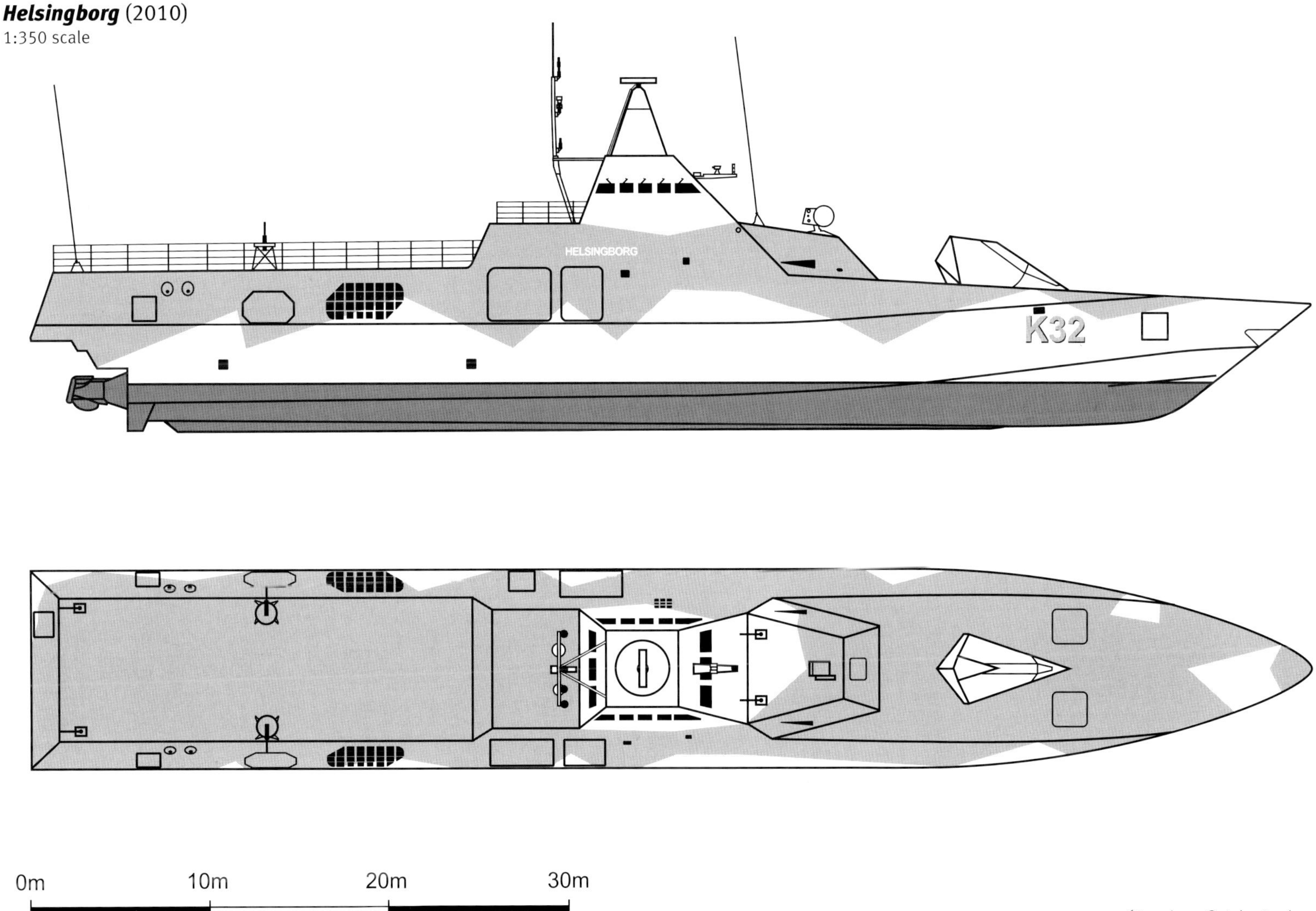

(Drawings © John Jordan, 2011)

have been modified to reduce internal magnetic signature and demagnetised. To reduce the remaining magnetic signature even further, the corvettes have been equipped with an advanced degaussing system, consisting of several current coils in all three dimensions which eliminate the magnetic disturbance induced by the vessel as it moves through the earth's magnetic field. The degaussing control system receives information from the ship's navigation system and from external magnetic sensors. As a back-up, the system can be controlled by stored data from a geomagnetic map.

Electronic Emissions: Radio communications and other essential emissions are, wherever possible, transmitted in selected sectors. They are even bounced off the ionosphere to limit detection to a very small field, confusing opposing surveillance systems by denying them sources to home in on.

WEAPONS SUITE

A key component of the *Visby* class concept is its modularity in terms of different combinations of weapons. Weaponry can be tailored to a specific situation as necessary. This, in turn, places more demands on the crew, though, and – consequently – on operational and maintenance training and on onboard organisation.

Combat Management System (CMS): The heart of the *Visby* class's combat potential is formed by its 9LV Mk 3E CETRIS combat management system, which incorporates modular open-system architecture using Windows NT. As installed on *Visby*, CETRIS provides twelve CeCots multi-function operator consoles, each equipped with dual flat-screen colour displays and incorporating intuitive human/machine interface techniques. The consoles are based on ruggedised commercial off-the-shelf components developed by Saab Systems and the Norwegian company Hitec. The CMS fully integrates the different sensors, weapons, navigation and communications systems within the ship, combining unified operation of the overall combat system with a high degree of automation. It is especially designed to reduce system reaction times and operator workload. It also provides for integration with the common command system of the Swedish Armed Forces, as well as full integration with the Swedish Air Force FSR890 Surveillance Radar and its Saab JAS-39 Gripen multi-role fighters.

Anti-Air and Anti-Surface Warfare Systems: The ships' basic anti-surface and anti-air warfare capabilities are provided by the BAE Systems Bofors 57mm/70 Mk 3 gun. This features all-digital interfaces and new, on-mount computers for performance monitoring, prediction and ballistic calculation. Programmable in six different modes, the cannon's function is programmed individually at the point of firing by an electronic fuse programmer connected to the fire control computer and range sensors on the gun. The six function modes comprise: gated proximity function (main air-defence mode against missiles, strike aircraft, helicopters); gated proximity function with impact priority (large aircraft, helicopters); continuous proximity function (default mode for air targets); time function (designed to fragment above soft ground targets, concealed helicopters, small naval craft); impact function (against trucks,

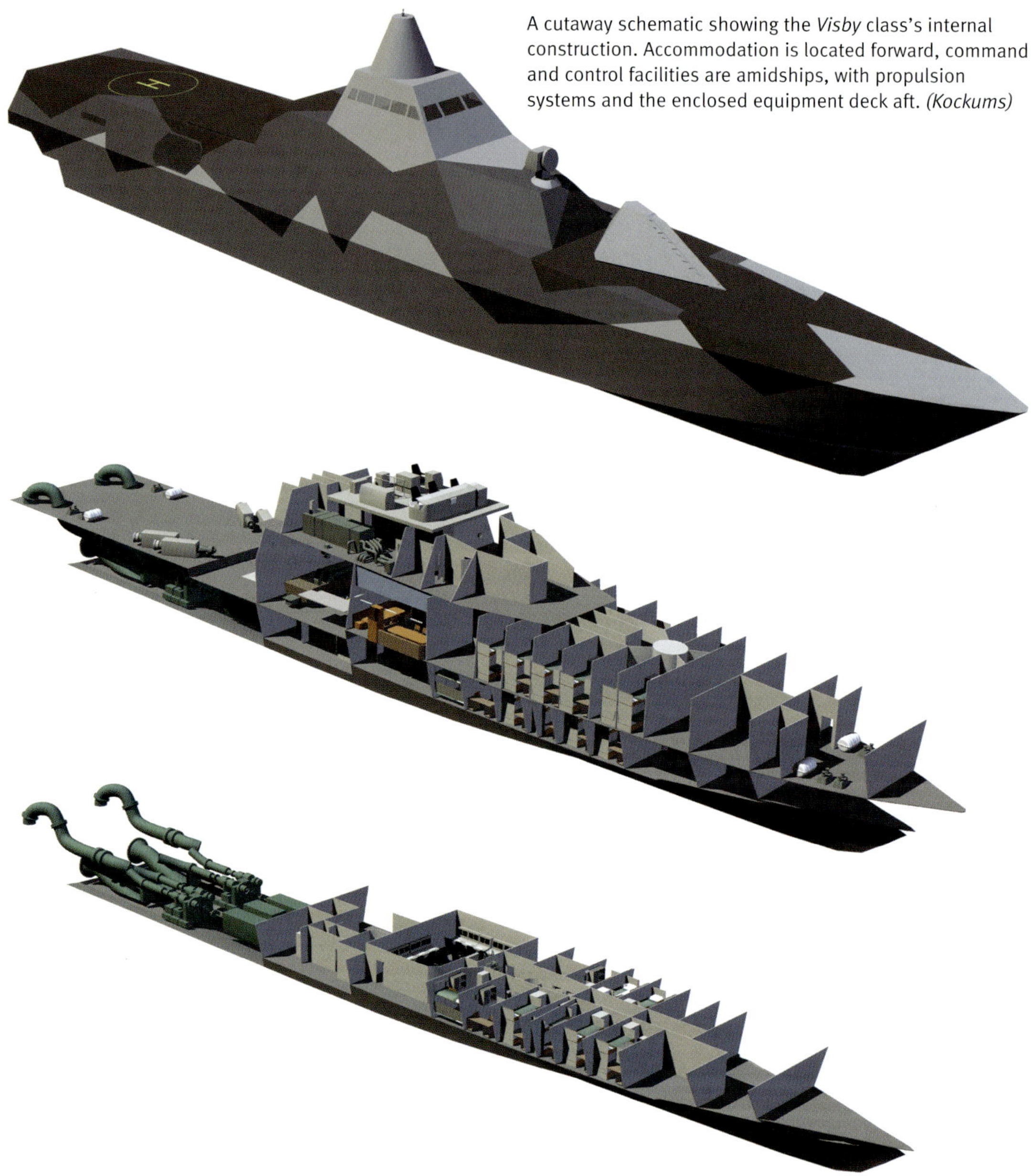

A cutaway schematic showing the *Visby* class's internal construction. Accommodation is located forward, command and control facilities are amidships, with propulsion systems and the enclosed equipment deck aft. *(Kockums)*

personnel carriers, small naval craft); and armour-piercing impact function (lightly-armoured vehicles). Rate of fire is up to 220 rounds per minute.

The cannon is capable of firing the new 57mm 3P (pre-fragmented, programmable, proximity-fused) intelligent all-target ammunition. Each 57mm 3P round weighs 2.4kg. Of this total, 460g comprises high explosive (Octol or PBX) and 560g tungsten pellets (about 2,400 in total).

Subject to funding being provided, it is anticipated that the *Visby* class will be equipped with the South African Umkhonto-IR surface-to-air (SAM) vertically-launched missile system. The system is normally installed in an eight-cell launcher in its naval version and can engage up to eight targets simultaneously. The Umkhonto is a high-velocity missile, with the potential to track and engage aerial threats to a range of 12km and up to an altitude of 8km. Each 3.32m-long missile has a launch-mass of 135kg and a 23kg warhead, can reach a speed of Mach 2 and has a time-of-flight to 8km of just eighteen seconds. The missiles employ radar guidance for initial tracking, IR guidance for the actual intercept, and receive continual updates throughout their course to the target.

The corvettes are already scheduled to be fitted with two quad Saab RBS-15 Mk 2 surface-to-surface (SSM) launchers with smart, rapid hatches to allow for quick weapon launch and minimal compromise of the ship's RCS profile. This long-range, radar-homing subsonic anti-ship missile has a reported range of 100km.

Finally, the units have also been back-fitted with two 12.7mm and two 7.62mm machine guns. These have been installed to combat asymmetric threats and assist international deployment.

Anti-Submarine Warfare and Mine Countermeasures: The *Visby* class ships are fitted with four 400mm torpedo tubes for Saab Underwater Systems Type 45 wire-guided lightweight ASW torpedoes. They will also be equipped with the Saab Underwater Systems Double Eagle Mk 3 remotely-operated vehicle (ROV) for mine-hunting and the expendable Atlas Elektronik SeaFox ROV for mine disposal. Their Hydra sonar suite provides the ability to search the full water column for mines using the ROVs, while the hull-mounted sonar can also be set to detect and classify mine threats. The ships also have a minelaying capability and are able to carry depth charges.

A detailed view of *Helsingborg*'s forward superstructure showing the stealth mounting for the 57mm gun, the stealth CEROS 200 fire-control director and the conical housing for the Giraffe 3D surveillance radar. The gun provides the ship's basic anti-surface and anti-air warfare capability. *(Guy Toremans)*

Left: During forthcoming refits, all ships will receive upgrades to provide a pad and landing system for a light helicopter similar to the Agusta Westland AW-190 already in Swedish service. *(Agusta Westland)*

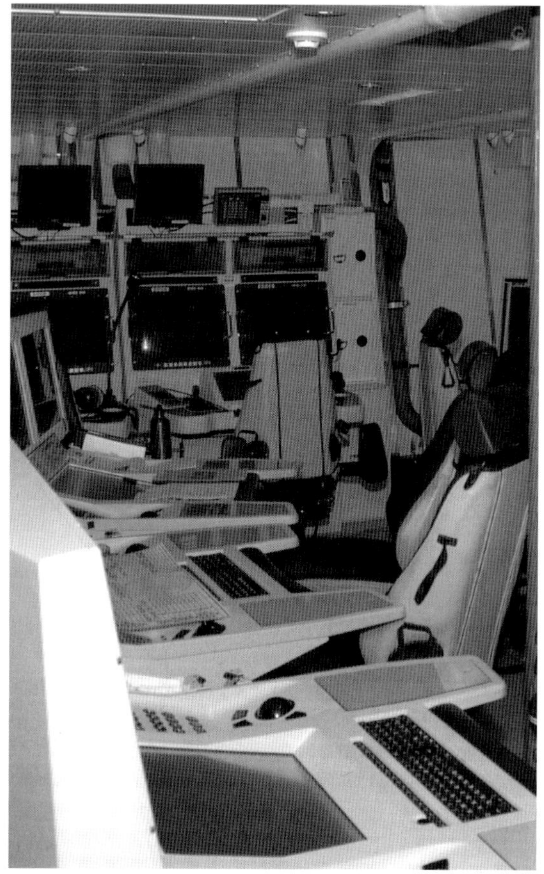

Above: A detailed view of the Combat Information Centre (CIC) on *Helsingborg*, which is equipped with the CETRIS combat management system. Featuring twelve multi-function operator consoles, CETRIS integrates information provided from the ship's radar, sonar system, electronic warfare suite and communications systems to allow weaponry to be used to maximum effect. It provides a high degree of automation and is especially designed to reduce system reaction times and operator workload. *(Guy Toremans)*

Left: The fully-automated BAE Systems Bofors 57mm/70 Mk3 gun is capable of firing 3P (pre-fragmented, programmable, proximity-fused) intelligent, all-target ammunition and provides the ships with a basic AAW capability. The barrel of the gun is protectively concealed inside the cupola and is only exposed when firing. *(Guy Toremans)*

Helicopters: The corvettes incorporate a landing pad for a light helicopter, which is likely to be the AgustaWestland AW-109 LUH (HKP-15) helicopter in Swedish service. Previous plans to install a below-decks hangar (where the vertical-launch air-defence missiles would be fitted) have now been abandoned. The operational ships of the class have not yet been certified for helicopter deployment but this is planned for the 'Version 5' of progressive capability upgrades planned for 2012.

SENSORS AND ELECTRONIC WARFARE

As might be expected, the corvettes' weapons suite is supplemented by a comprehensive range of sensors and communications equipment.

Radar: The ships' primary active anti-air and anti-surface warfare sensor is the Saab Sea Giraffe AMB (Agile Multi-Beam) 3D air/surface search radar. Operating in the 4,000–8,000 MHz G/H (USN C) bands, modes include full 3D detection and tracking, as well as a special air-defence mode for stealth sea-skimmer detection. The radar features low probability of intercept functionality and has several built-in ECM features to deal with jamming. Sheathed in a frequency selective conical 'stealth' radome atop the superstructure, the Sea Giraffe AMB radar rotates at 30rpm in normal surveillance mode and 60rpm in air-defence mode. Elevations of up to 70 degrees can be covered. The Sea Giraffe's surface operating modes include high-resolution surface surveillance with ducting mode and gun fire-control support. This enables improved tracking accuracy against surface targets, and provides precise azimuth and range resolution for fall-of-shot and gunfire corrections.

Other main sensors include the Saab CEROS 200 multi-sensor fire-control director, which operates in the 8,000–12,000 MHz I/J (USN X) bands. It is used to direct the 57mm gun and would also provide missile direction capabilities if surface-to-air missiles are installed. There is also a Saab PILOT Mk2 array for low probability of intercept surface surveillance out to 15–20km, whilst navigation duties are fulfilled by two Terma Scanter radars.

Sonar System: The class incorporates sensors for both passive and active underwater reconnaissance that have been designed for operation in a very harsh hydro-acoustic environment. Computing Devices Canada Ltd, now part of General Dynamics, developed the integrated anti-submarine/mine countermeasures sonar suite. The system, known as the Hydra multi-sonar system, integrates data provided by:

- A Hydroscience Technologies passive towed-array sonar (TAS).
- A C-Tech CVDS-26 dual-frequency active variable depth sonar (VDS).
- A C-Tech CHMS-90 hull-mounted sonar.
- Sonobuoys.
- Sonars in the two types of remotely-operated vehicle (ROV) used in mine countermeasures operations.

This suite is closely integrated into the CETRIS combat management system, and is capable of performing own-ship signature monitoring and threat alert functions. Although intended primarily for mine detection and while not as flexible owing to its fixed depth, the hull-mounted set provides classification against bottom-lying submarines in shallow water conditions where VDS operation is impractical. The remotely-operated vehicles will comprise (i) the ROV-S: the Saab Underwater Systems Double Eagle Mk III incorporating detection and classification sonars, a camera and conductivity, salinity and depth sensors for minehunting and (ii) the ROV-E: the Atlas Elektronik SeaFox with an identification camera and classification sonar for mine disposal.

Electronic Warfare Systems: The electronic support suite is built around ITT Corporation's widely-used ES-3701 (formerly known as the Condor Systems CS-3701) tactical radar ESM (electronic support measures) and surveillance system, which provides the corvettes with surveillance capabilities across the radar spectrum. A Communication ESM or CESM system permits the ships to cover radio signals, whilst an Infra-Red Search and Track (IRST) system enhances overall surveillance potential. To maximise stealth by operating in electromagnetic 'silence', all three systems are passive – they emit no signals.

For defence against guided missiles in both blue-water and littoral environments, the ships will be fitted with the Rheinmetall Waffe Munitions Multi-Ammunition Soft-Kill System (MASS) chaff launchers. Capable of launching up to thirty-two omni-spectral projectiles, MASS operates by firing sequential volleys of decoys, which divert the enemy

Cutaway showing the location of the two quad launchers for RBS-15 Mk II missiles. *(Kockums)*

Helsingborg and *Visby* pictured whilst on sea trials in 2005. *Helsingborg* was first ship of the class to be fully accepted by Sweden's FMV Defence Material Administration – in 2006 – but it was to be a further three years before she was declared ready for operations. *(Kockums)*

The Royal Swedish Navy took delivery of its first operationally-deployable *Visby* class corvettes – *Helsingborg* and *Härnösand* (shown here) – on 16 December 2009 following upgrade work to a 'Version 4' standard intended to allow them to participate in international missions. The high quality of accommodation and general living conditions provided in the class will be particularly important on such extended deployments, assisting the relatively small crew to withstand the inevitable demands and stresses of operating far away from home. *(Guy Toremans)*

Right: The integrated weapons deck conceals most of the corvettes' weapon suite. The ships can be equipped with remotely-operated vehicles (ROVs) for minehunting and mine disposal, as well as mines, depth charges, torpedoes, and surface-to-surface and surface-to-air missiles. Accommodation spaces for up to fifty-three personnel – a typical crew comprises forty-three – are located forward of the bridge. *(Kockums)*

missile from its intended target, eventually causing it to fly harmlessly off into empty space. Thanks to the system's programmable omni-spectral decoys, effective protection is provided across all relevant wavelengths of the electromagnetic spectrum.

Communications: The *Visby*s are equipped with the Saab ICS2000 Integrated Communication System. Integrating voice and data communications equipment by means of a fibre-optic network, it is compatible with the national system for the Swedish Armed Forces, called LIM. If required, provision for other systems such as NATO Links can also be made.

ACCOMMODATION

The living conditions and accommodation provided for the complement of six officers, twenty petty officers and seventeen ratings is excellent. This is partly a reflection of the specialist nature of the crew, who have to maintain high standards of efficiency and flexibility to operate and understand multi-task software and to handle extremely complicated instruments and sensors. The more the crew has to withstand varied demands and stresses on operations, the more important it is to provide them appropriate recreational facilities and time in order to safeguard their long-term reliability and contentment.

Accordingly, officers and chief petty officers have double cabins, whilst the petty officers and ratings are accommodated in four-berth cabin modules. There are also ten extra bunks for additional personnel. Food is prepared in a well-equipped galley, with officers and petty officers sharing a wardroom and the ratings being provided with their own mess. The cabins and working areas are, by corvette standards, very large. The furniture – as well as the decoration of walls and ceilings – provides a cosy atmosphere. The materials used

Right: Officers and petty officers share a wardroom. The furniture – as well as the decoration of walls and ceilings – provides a cosy atmosphere throughout the ship. *(Guy Toremans)*

meet relevant Society specifications, securing good noise-reduction and privacy.

PROPULSION

The propulsion system is provided by a combined diesel or gas (CODOG) configuration. This comprises four Vericor Power Systems (Honeywell) aero-derivative TF-50A gas turbines (providing 16MW output) and two Tognum MTU 16V 2000 N90 diesels (2.6MW output).[5] The power plant drivers are alternatively connected to twin Cincinnati MA-107 SBS gearboxes driving two Kamewa water-jet propulsors. The gas turbines are used for medium and high-speed (35 knots) operations; the diesels for low speed (15 knots) and long-duration operations. The corvettes' main auxiliary plant is made up of three Isotta Fraschini Motori V 1308 T2ME-1550 diesel generator sets each producing about 270KW.

At speed, steering is done by the azimuthing water-jet buckets. During close-quarter manoeuvring, the jets are assisted by a 125KW HRP 200-65 Holland Roer Propeller bow thruster.

OPERATIONAL EXPERIENCE

Although initial delivery of the *Visby* class to the FMV commenced as long ago as 2002, the specification changes referenced above – as well as the extensive trials required for what is virtually a new type of warship – has meant that considerable time elapsed before the new vessels were considered fit for operational service. As such, it was not until 16 December 2009 before the first two operational units – *Helsingborg* and *Härnösand* – were officially commissioned into the Royal Swedish Navy.

During this period, the Royal Swedish Navy had, however, gained valuable experience in international operations that has served to the *Visby* class's benefit. This included the deployment of the existing corvettes *Sundsvall* and *Gävle* in support of the UNIFIL Maritime Task Force 448 off Lebanon in late 2006, as well as that of the corvettes *Stockholm* and *Malmö* and the OPV (former minelayer) *Carlskrona* for counter-piracy operations in the Gulf of Aden during 2009–10 in support of the European Union's Operation 'Atalanta'. As a result, the Royal Swedish Navy decided to back-fit *Helsingborg* and *Härnösand* with an enhancement package that improved the ships' ability to take part in international missions. Both corvettes underwent a modification, known as the 'Version 4' upgrade. This package included the installation of two 12.7mm and two 7.62mm machine-gun mountings for force protection, additional HF and VHF communications equipment, greater fresh-water production capacity, an improvement to the cooling and ventilation systems for operations in warm climates and provision of a NATO-compatible astern replenishment-at-sea (RAS) rig.

From the beginning of 2010, *Helsingborg* and *Härnösand* undertook quite a busy programme of training and exercises to reach full operational readiness by October of that year. In early 2010, both corvettes took part in Basic Unit/Advanced Unit Training (BUT/AUT) manoeuvres together with units of the Danish, German and Norwegian navies. Then followed exercise Brilliant Mariner 2010 during which the ships were evaluated by 'sea-riders' of the NATO MCC (Maritime Component Command) Headquarters. This was the first time the Royal Swedish Navy took part in a NATO exercise with its *Visby* class corvettes. Upon completion, the corvettes sailed to Plymouth for two-weeks of Flag Operational Sea Training with the British Royal Navy's FOST. In August they took part in Danex 2010, followed the next month by exercise Northern Coasts 2010. Their ultimate evaluation followed during the national tri-service Swenex manoeuvre in early October 2010. Upon completion, *Helsingborg* and *Härnösand* were declared fully ready for operations.

Looking forward, it can be anticipated that the Swedish government will decide to earmark both corvettes for international deployment. If so, it is quite possible that the authorities might choose to send the corvettes to the Indian Ocean in support of the EU's Operation 'Atalanta'. If such a mission was launched, the corvettes would embark a Special Forces boarding team and equipment optimised for anti-piracy operations, such as Long Range Acoustic Device (LRAD) systems and additional communications. In the meantime, further exercises are planned to keep their operational readiness at the highest-possible standard. At the time of writing, *Helsingborg* and *Härnösand* are scheduled to participate in a further four-week training period with FOST in May 2011. In September 2011 *Härnösand* is earmarked for participation in the combined Danex/Northern Coasts 2011 exercise, whilst

Helsingborg's superstructure with, from left to right, the retractable mast, the conical stealth radome (concealing the Giraffe 3D surveillance radar) and the CEROS 200 multi-sensor fire-control director. The bridge's high vantage point is ideally located for visual surveillance. Additional HF and VHF communcations equipment has also been provided as part of the 'Version 4' upgrade. *(Guy Toremans)*

Above: An aerial view of *Helsingborg* at speed. CODOG propulsion comprising four Vericor Power Systems TF-50A gas turbines and two Tognum MTU 16V 2000 N90 diesels provides a maximum speed of over 35 knots. *(Kockums)*

Right: A stern view of *Helsingborg*. The ship's acoustic signature is minimised with the aid of water-jet propulsors provided by Rolls-Royce Kamewa. At speed, steering is done by the azimuthing water-jet buckets. During close-quarter manoeuvring, the jets are assisted by a 125KW HRP 200-65 Holland Roer Propeller bow thruster. This view also shows some of the enhanced close-range armament installed under the interim 'Version 4' upgrade to increase the ship's ability to participate in international operations. *(Guy Toremans)*

Nyköping, fourth of the five-strong *Visby* class, will undergo a 'Version 5' upgrade before officially commissioning into the navy in 2012. Modifications will include the enlargement of the enclosed sensor mast, the introduction of new deck structures incorporating conformal antenna arrays, installation of two quad launchers for RBS-15 Mk II missiles and the provision of full helicopter landing systems. *(Royal Swedish Navy)*

Helsingborg will take part in the national Swenex 2011 exercise in October 2011.

CURRENT PROGRAMME STATUS

All five *Visbys* are scheduled to receive an enhancement package in order to make the class compliant with their planned final delivery standard. This is called the 'Version 5' upgrade. It will involve the installation of two quad launchers for RBS-15 Mk 2 surface-to-surface missiles and Rheinmetall MASS missile countermeasures, as well as improvements to the command-and-control system and the incorporation of NATO-standard Link 16 communications, a hull monitoring system and IFF- and weather sensors. Other enhancements include the provision of the ROV-S and ROV-E remotely-operated vehicles, equipment for divers, an in-built replenishment-at-sea rig and ballistic protection.

Physical design modifications encompass the introduction of new deck structures to incorporate conformal antenna arrays.

The Royal Swedish Navy is also planning to equip the ships with a landing-pad and landing-system to operate an AgustaWestland AW-190 LUH (HKP-15) helicopter. Adding this ability also gives growth potential for future deployment of VTOL unmanned airborne vehicles. The FMV began tests to certify the corvettes for helicopter operations as long ago as late October/early November 2006. On 7 November of that year, a Royal Danish Navy AgustaWestland Super Lynx Mk 90B performed the first ever helicopter deck landing on the *Visby* in the Danish Navy's Fredrikshavn Naval Base. This was followed a few days later by a first deck landing out at sea in the waters of the Kattegat. However, the other vessels have yet to be equipped for helicopter operations and this will form part of the planned upgrades.

Visby and *Nyköping* will be the first units to receive the 'Version 5' upgrade package, entering refit in 2011 and returning to service in 2012. *Karlstad* will go into the shipyard between 2011 and mid-2013, followed by *Helsingborg* in mid-2012. She will be ready for operations again by the end of 2013. The final ship to receive the upgrade will be *Härnösand*, which will enter the shipyard early in 2013 and return to service mid-2014.

POTENTIAL FUTURE VARIANTS

At Kockums, development work has been undertaken on a range of *Visby* variants, most notably the larger *Visby* Plus. Its prime functions would encompass anti-submarine warfare, surface attack, air defence, training and patrol.

The *Visby* Plus design takes a modular approach, incorporating a variety of equipment options aimed at the international market. The initial model has a length of 88m, a full load displacement of approximately 1,500 tons and a core crew of seventy-one. Improvements over the standard *Visby* encompass a lower profile for a reduced visual impact, a lighter, more shock-resistant structure as well as lower hydro-acoustic, magnetic, infrared and radar signatures. Equipment includes a helipad and hangar, two universal cranes and two ship's boats. Propulsion comprises four diesel engines of about 7.4MW, driving four water-jets, with the engine room located aft in order to leave appreciable volume amidships for operations. Weapons and command-and-control systems would be NATO-compatible. The design could form the basis for the future combatant that has been mooted as a possible follow-on to the *Visbys* if funding ever permits.

CONCLUSION

The *Visby* class units are a vital step in the Swedish Navy's development towards meeting future tasks and challenges. They are not just futuristic units, but also stand apart as compact multi-mission, network centric-enabled surface combatants capable of flexible international deployment in spite of their modest size. They make for an interesting comparison with the US Navy's two Littoral Combat Ship designs, which share some similarities in operational concept but which are considerably larger.[6] They can switch easily from peacekeeping activities to the conduct of missions under full war-fighting conditions, whilst also being able to undertake classic patrol, surveillance and escort roles as well as participating in maritime interdiction and embargo operations. Versatile platforms well-equipped for war-fighting and designed for survival, the *Visbys* will form the core units of the Royal Swedish Navy's surface fleet.

The Royal Swedish Navy took delivery of its first operationally-deployable *Visby* class corvettes – *Helsingborg* (shown here) and *Härnösand* – on 16 December 2009 following upgrade work to a 'Version 4' standard intended to allow them to participate in international missions. They will return to the shipyard between 2012 and 2014 for modification to the final 'Version 5' delivery standard. *(Guy Toremans)*

Notes:

1. Tracing its origins to the foundation of Karlskrona as a naval base and dockyard in 1679, Karlskronavarvet is Sweden's leading naval shipyard. The rationalisation of Sweden's shipbuilding industry from the late 1970s onwards saw it draw steadily closer to fellow Swedish yard Kockums of Malmö and the two entities – by then both subsidiaries of the larger Celsius group – formally merged in 1998. The enlarged business was combined with German shipbuilding interests in the following year and currently forms part of ThyssenKrupp Marine Systems.

2. Planned class numbers and variants saw on-going change as Sweden's armed forces adapted to changing circumstances and declining funding in a post-Cold War environment. It seems that up to twenty vessels were initially envisaged to replace the bulk of the existing fast attack flotillas but this had fallen to fourteen by 1996. Modernisation of some of the older ships was considered at that stage as partial compensation. Further force structure reductions reflected the effective implosion of the former Soviet fleet in the Baltic, as well as the cost overruns as the programme progressed that are referenced in the main text.

3. The FMV is a civilian agency of the Swedish state responsible for managing procurement activities for the Swedish armed forces. The *Visbys* were handed over to the FMV by Kockums after initial sea trials for further outfitting with combat equipment and systems, as well as detailed operational evaluation and testing. This has included a series of upgrades or 'Versions'. The first ships were delivered to the Royal Swedish Navy only once 'Version 4' specification had been reached.

4. CFRP comprises 100 per cent carbon fibre skins placed over a foam core, manufactured in a vacuum-assisted infusion system.

5. Vericor introduced the TF-50A as an improved engine for the marine market in 1997. The *Visbys* are the first ships to use this maritime application.

6. A potential weakness of the *Visby* design is its relatively small size, which is partly a legacy from the previous era of fast attack craft. Whilst the Royal Swedish Navy does not believe that the inevitable impact on range and open-ocean seaworthiness in comparison with larger types will prove to be a practical impediment to international operations, this has yet to be proven.

4.1 TECHNOLOGICAL REVIEW

DEVELOPMENTS IN MODERN SONAR

Author:
Norman Friedman

INTRODUCTION

When the Cold War ended, the foundations of 'Western' anti-submarine warfare – and with it, sonar – shifted dramatically.[1] Developments since then have been shaped by this different operating environment, as well as by the on-going development of more and more powerful digital processors, driven by Moore's Law (the power of processors doubles about every eighteen months). The first change affected the balance between passive and active sonar.[2] During the 1980s, by far the bulk of the Soviet submarine fleet was nuclear-powered. In contrast to a diesel-electric submarine, which can sometimes simply sit silently on the bottom, a nuclear submarine must constantly run at least its pumps and generators.[3] No matter how well these elements are isolated from the outside, some noise must emerge. The key to much of NATO Cold War anti-submarine warfare was that any man-made device produced a steady sound or sound pattern which could be distinguished from the random natural background. Talk of a submarine so quiet that it is a 'hole in the ocean' is just that; there is no such thing. Sufficient processing, including integration over time (for example, to distinguish a steady signal at a particular frequency), can recover enough of a signal to make it distinguishable. The point of silencing is to make that recovery too difficult to be achieved using electronics of a given power level. The point of Moore's Law is that what cannot be done right now often can be done next year or in five years. That reality was obscured, throughout the Cold War, by the insistence on the part of Western navies to use standardised (military specification) electronics. It took a long time to certify and produce a given computer or processor, and a new generation of equipment never instantly replaced its predecessors.

PASSIVE SONAR DEVELOPMENT DURING THE COLD WAR

For a passive sonar, such as a towed array or a field of sonobuoys, a sonar equation is normally written to show how much signal a given sound source, such as a submarine, produces at a distant receiver. The signal dies off over distance, in a way which depends on factors like water depth and the way in which the water refracts sound. To the real signal are added sea noises corresponding to the clutter with which a radar struggles. The larger the receiver array (in wavelengths, which in turn depend on sound frequency), the larger the fraction of the signal it picks up. This pick-up is measured by receiver gain. Signal processing imposes its own form of gain, so that a much better signal processor can make up for a much worse array. The more that is known about the signal (and the more complicated it is), the better the chance that it can be distinguished from the background noise.

The big discovery which transformed Cold War anti-submarine warfare was that submarines produced characteristic sets of low-frequency emissions (signatures) which were distinguishable hundreds or even thousands of miles away. The signatures were little distorted as they passed through the water. They could, moreover, be recovered by integrating over time. The process was not too different from the one already used by physicists trying to detect cosmic rays by their characteristic energy spectra. In the early 1950s it was also being used by scientists investigating human speech, for example to improve telephones. That is why the Bell Telephone Laboratories in the United States became involved in submarine acoustics. At first the submarines were all diesel-electric, and they could not easily be detected when running using their batteries. However, when snorkelling, the submarine poured liberal amounts of noise into the surrounding ocean, and the sound pattern was set by the very characteristic firing pattern of her diesel engines.[4]

This passive method of detecting weak submarine signatures came to be called LOFAR (Low-Frequency Acoustic Ranging, a largely meaningless phrase adopted only because its acronym resembled RADAR). LOFAR was also called narrow-band operation, because it worked by breaking down signals by frequency and concentrating on a narrow frequency band characteristic of its submarine targets. The narrower the band, the more processing was needed to recover that energy, but also the less extraneous energy the band might contain. By way of contrast, a typical sonar 'ping' is a broad-band signal (in frequency terms). The longer the duration of a signal (hence the greater the uncertainty in target position), the broader the range of frequencies it contains. It is possible, however, to create a long signal out of narrow-frequency elements – if whatever is detected can be processed elaborately enough.

It soon turned out that, in addition to machinery sounds, submarines emitted blade rate sounds caused by the way in which the turning propeller blades hit the wakes of vertical and horizontal submarine surfaces (the vibration travels up the propeller shaft into the submarine, and is worst for modern single-screw submarines). Modern scythe-shaped propellers and pump-jets are ways of eliminating this source of sound. Blade rate was publicised during the Cold War when the Russians obtained Japanese computer-controlled machining equipment specifically to produce quiet propellers. Photographs suggest, incidentally, that most Third World submarines do *not* have quiet propellers, as presumably the details of how to silence a propeller remain classified. Unlike machinery sounds from a nuclear submarine, blade rate depends on how fast the submarine is moving.

In the early 1950s LOFAR was an Anglo-American secret, so closely held that the French were told that it was really nothing more than the use of low-frequency active sonars.[5] The first application was the SOSUS (Sound SUrveillance System) of bottom-mounted arrays looking across the Western Atlantic. Later applications were several generations of passive sonobuoys (usually code-named JEZEBEL) and the towed arrays, installed on board both surface ships and submarines. For example, at least in theory, SOSUS identified an area in which a submarine was probably operating, and a maritime patrol aircraft such as a P-3 or a Nimrod searched the area for the submarine whose signature SOSUS had detected. The US Navy had a special link which sent the signature as detected by SOSUS to the aircraft, for comparison with what the aircraft was detecting.

Passive sonar was so important that from time to time sceptics raised the possibility that the Soviets would catch on and silence their submarines accordingly. For example, in the 1950s the British found a means of silencing their new *Porpoise* class diesel-electric submarines (the direct forebears of the *Oberon* class), even when snorkelling. Surely the Soviets would learn to do as well, and SOSUS would lose its value. The US response was to look more deeply at how sonar worked. A passive sonar relies on whatever the submarine is emitting. The sonar equation for an active sonar is similar, except that the active sonar imposes its signature on the submarine

The British Royal Navy submarine *Astute* pictured prior to launch in June 2007. The design incorporates both active (where the sonar produces a ping, and listens for reflection) and passive (where the sonar simply listens for a noise the target emits) arrays in the integrated Sonar 2076 system. The shrouded pump jet is designed to minimise the submarine's own sound emissions. *(BAE Systems)*

Three P-3C Orion aircraft belonging to the Tridents of Patrol Squadron Two Six (VP-26) stand ready on a rain-soaked airfield on board Naval Air Station Sigonella in January 2006. The SOSUS network of bottom-mounted arrays was intended to identify the general area in which a hostile submarine was operating, which would then be searched by a long-range maritime patrol aircraft such as a P-3. *(US Navy)*

The equivalent to a passive sonar for anti-submarine warfare aircraft is an array of sonobuoys floating in the water. This image shows a P-3C Orion ASW aircraft being loaded. *(US Navy)*

A Russian Project 671 RTM 'Victor III' class nuclear-powered attack submarine pictured at speed during a surface transit. Passive sonar detection of submarines came of age when the Soviets concentrated on nuclear submarines, because, unlike diesel-electric submarines, these craft really did produce consistent signals on a continuous basis. *(US Department of Defense)*

(the signal is whatever is left of the sound pulse emitted in the first place by the active sonar). It would be impossible simply to replace SOSUS altogether, so the US Navy devised an alternative long-range system in which the SOSUS arrays would act as receivers. The only entirely new element would be a series of enormous sonar emitters. The first such emitter was successfully tested after having been lowered from a converted tank on board the tanker *Mission Capistrano*. Keeping long-range performance mattered, because even in the 1950s the navy depended heavily on long-range patrol aircraft cued by some external system, such as SOSUS.

SOSUS was good, but it could not pinpoint a submarine so precisely that a weapon could be dropped on it. Instead, whatever arrived at the indicated area had to search it. In the 1950s, even the analogue electronics used to extract LOFAR signals were too massive for existing aircraft, so the usual method was to drop what amounted to microphones into the water (broadband passive buoys). It was not difficult to imagine that a submarine might be sufficiently silenced to avert detection. The solution paralleled that being applied to SOSUS. The aircraft could drop several sonobuoys and then a practice depth bomb with a small explosive charge. When the charge went off, it produced what amounted to a sound pulse. Any of the pulse hitting the submarine would echo from it, and echoing pulses hitting two or more buoys could be triangulated to find the submarine. This process was called JULIE (or Explosive Echo-Ranging, E2R), and the name was also applied to broadband buoys.

JULIE was not entirely effective, partly because the sound of the explosion would also echo off the bottom. JULIE was therefore unusable in water less than 8,000ft (2,438m) deep. However, by about 1960, it was clear that narrow-band signals could be recovered from sonobuoys using equipment that could fit inside an aircraft of reasonable size. This airborne LOFAR technique was called JEZEBEL. The electronic edge enjoyed by the West at this time is reflected in the fact that the Soviets opted to develop JULIE further. By the end of the Cold War they had large sound sources in which small explosives circled a vertical body much like the line on a barber pole, producing a sound beam that rotated and elevated. In theory this method drastically reduced bottom reflections.

LATE COLD WAR ERA DEVELOPMENTS

LOFAR came of age when the Soviets concentrated on nuclear submarines, because unlike diesel-electric submarines these craft really did produce consistent signals on a continuous basis. For their part, the Soviets seem to have been innocent of LOFAR until the 1970s.[6] At that time they had several possible sources, including the US-based Walker spy ring (one of whose members was a US Navy sonar instructor). The Soviets made a concerted effort to silence their submarines, which included illicitly buying Japanese computer-controlled machine tools. LOFAR having been compromised, it was publicly discussed in the mid-1970s (but without details such as the frequency range involved).

The US Navy's response was twofold. One element was to revive the 1950s idea and add active elements to existing passive systems. For example, in the 1970s the US Navy began to deploy sonar surveillance ships (T-AGOS), which were, in effect, mobile SOSUS arrays. The obvious solution to Soviet silencing was to add a large low-frequency 'pinger' like that proposed as a SOSUS adjunct decades earlier. Similarly, JULIE was revived in modified form, a command-detonated charge being the initial pinger. Later non-explosive pingers which could produce a shaped pulse appeared, an example being Ultra's ALFEA.

The other possibility was that, even though the signatures of Soviet submarines had been reduced dramatically, they had not (because they could never have been) eliminated altogether: there is no such thing as a 'hole in the ocean'. Array gain (and, for that matter, sensitivity) could, therefore, be increased. One example was the new *Seawolf* (SSN-21) class submarine. It had a larger-diameter bow array than previous US submarines, because it had a larger-diameter hull. Sensitivity was increased by splitting the array into active and passive elements. The Russians had long done that, on the theory that it was impossible to produce an array element with sufficient dynamic range to work equally well as transmitter and receiver. Ironically, at just about the same time that the big dual *Seawolf* array was being produced, the Russians were trying to solve about the same problem by mixing transmitting and receiving elements in the same bow array.

The same idea was applied to sonobuoys. In the late 1980s, an aircraft laid sonobuoys and processed whatever they detected individually, buoy by buoy. Each buoy created two broad receiving beams. Typically the bigger the array, the narrower the beams, and the higher the gain. Handling whatever the buoys produced coherently meant creating receiving beams out of the whole field of buoys. Beam-forming required more electronics in the aircraft but, in the late 1980s that was not yet possible in an operational patrol aircraft.

All of this effort was designed to deal with nuclear submarines producing consistent, hence detectable, signals in deep cold water. The Russians did have some diesel-electric submarines, but it was reasonable for NATO anti-submarine warfare efforts to have more limited interest in them; they were essentially a means of coastal defence.

MOORE'S LAW AND THE POST-COLD WAR ENVIRONMENT

Then the Cold War ended, and in effect the roof fell in. One particularly marked change was that there was no longer sufficient money to buy huge new submarines with larger sonar arrays. However, the Russians had finally learned to silence their submarines, and there was no reason to imagine that they would never become a threat in the future. What could be done with the large number of existing submarines and surface ships? The projected big new arrays were one way of buying increased gain to compensate for better silencing, i.e., for a reduced signal. However, there was another way; signals could be processed more effectively. Given Moore's Law, signal processing could get better and better over time, if new processors could be introduced inexpensively into existing systems. How could that be done?

Clearly the Cold War process of developing and certifying specialised military computers could not keep up with the accelerating development of civilian computers driven by Moore's Law. The idea was to insert banks of new processors in generic chassis which could be changed as required. In the US Navy's ARCI (Acoustic Refresh COTS [Commercial Off the Shelf] Insertion) programme, the object is to maintain the hardware 'state of the practice', rather than the more advanced 'state of the art', on the theory that state of the practice means reliable technology. By about 2005 the state of the practice was so reliable that processors typically required no maintenance during a patrol. Hardware and software are refreshed periodically, the software at more frequent intervals. The submarine's arrays are not changed. ARCI began in 1998, and it has continued since. The submarine ARCI programme has proven so successful that it has spread to surface

The *Seawolf* (SSN-21) class submarine *Connecticut* (SSN-22) underway in the Pacific Ocean in November 2009. It has a larger-diameter bow array than previous US submarines, because it has a larger-diameter hull. Sensitivity was increased by splitting the array into active and passive elements. *(US Navy)*

ships and to aircraft, to the point where bespoke signal processors are no longer used.

The two keys to ARCI are the use of digital arrays and the use of a high-capacity bus for the new processors. The submarine's arrays all sense sounds as pressure waves. These waves are then translated into digital data for processing (at one time LOFAR and much other processing was analogue). Ultimately processing decides that whatever some array element has sensed represents a real submarine, as opposed to, say, the noise of schools of fish. The more powerful the processing, the better its ability to tell the difference. The point of ARCI is that this kind of processing pays much higher dividends than building a new submarine large enough to accommodate a larger processor.

ARCI also has a second aspect. A submarine operating passively detects targets at a series of bearings and, perhaps, elevations, over time. Many of those sets of target directions relate to the same target moving through the sea. For many years submarines have used mathematical techniques called Target Motion Analysis (TMA) to turn those strings of data into target tracks. Once the tracks have been created, the submarine has a picture of underwater activity around it, and the picture can be used for decision-making – such as where to fire a torpedo. In effect TMA entails making a first estimate of where a detected submarine is, then projecting it ahead to see whether it fits later data. The more active the area around the submarine (as in littoral operations), the more difficult the analysis. Conversely, a more powerful track-keeping computer (or an adjunct) can apply more sophisticated forms of analysis and can disentangle a more complex situation. Later US Navy *Los Angeles* (SSN-668) class submarines were provided with more powerful (but still military specification) fire-control computers responsible both for track-keeping and for fire control.

Inserting commercial processors into such computers presented a special problem. A submarine fire-control computer can actually fire weapons. At least in the US Navy, and probably in most others, anything which can fire weapons requires special certification. It would be intolerable that a computer software bug could kill people automatically. The US solution, initially in the *Virginia* (SSN-774) class, and back-fitted into other submarines, has been to split the track-keeping (picture-making) function from the fire-control function. Track-keeping is of course tested, but it does not require the sort of certification demanded of a fire-control system. Conversely, there is not nearly as great a demand for fire control to be updated regularly with new processors.

The more powerful track-keeping element of the submarine system can accept a wider variety of inputs. For example, the *Virginia* class boats have photonic periscopes. Computer workstations in the submarine's command centre can display their images. In effect a photonic periscope displays bearings just the way the submarine's passive sonar does (the periscope may also be able to obtain ranges by using a laser rangefinder). The same kind of software which converts sound bearings into tracks can also convert optical bearings into a tactical picture, and it can cross-reference sound and optics for surface craft. Since surface ships produce sound, this kind of cross-reference is at the least a way to help disentangle the submarine's tactical picture.

An early conceptual image of a *Virginia* (SSN-774) class submarine. The class – designed in the post-Cold War environment – split track-keeping (picture-making) and fire-control functions to allow the former to benefit from the accelerating development of commercial computers driven by Moore's Law. *(General Dynamics)*

The *Virginia* (SSN-774) class submarine *California* (SSN-781) under construction at Huntington Ingalls Industries' Newport News facility in May 2010. Later members of the class will have a modified bow that replaces the traditional spherical bow array with co-located active and passive functions with a new large-aperture bow array featuring separate active and passive sonar elements. *(Huntington Ingalls Industries)*

ACTIVE SONAR AND DIGITALISATION

The other side of sonar operation is active pinging. Into the 1980s that was a completely analogue operation. A sonar contained a high-powered pulse generator, whose signals were led into the elements of its array. The great development of post-Second World War sonars was the shift from a single-element 'searchlight' sonar into an array sonar which used a switching network to create a beam from properly-timed pulses sent by its elements. Typically a second network created, in effect, receiving beams.

In a digital sonar, each element of the array is fed (and controlled) separately. As in a digital radar, the sonar signals are created by computer software and amplified for transmission. A digital sonar is a sonar equivalent of a phased-array radar. Using a computer to create the signals makes it possible to code them. Just as SOSUS could recognise the signature of a submarine against a noisy background, a digital sonar can gain considerably by recognising a coded echo. The first US digital sonar was SQS-53, the big hull sonar of *Ticonderoga* (CG-47) class missile cruisers and *Arleigh Burke* (DDG-51) class destroyers. Initially digital operation seems to have been valued mainly because it gained reliability and reduced weight and complexity. SQS-53 operated at much the same frequency as the earlier SQS-26, in its time the most powerful US surface ship sonar.[7]

SQS-53 was part of the US shift to digital combat direction systems; initially it was digital mainly in the sense that it was designed to send its target tracks to a digital underwater combat system, the ancestor of the current SQQ-89. Digital transmission seems not to have been adopted for some time. When it was, in the current SQS-53C, the sonar was credited with an ability to detect a target at two and sometimes three convergence zones – up to 105 nautical miles (194km) away. That would be particularly important for a sonar working against quiet diesel-electric submarines. That having been said, some reports suggest that SQS-53 is not agile enough, or cannot easily depress its beam enough, to detect and track nearby small diesel-electric submarines. That would not necessarily be inconsistent. A sonar relying on coded pings would also rely on protracted signal processing. At short range even a fairly slow diesel-electric submarine will flit in and out of a sonar beam. At long ranges the beam is so wide that it holds the submarine for a protracted time.

The transducer of an SQS-53 sonar is visible in these images of *Port Royal* (CG-73) and *Winston S Churchill* (DDG-81) in dry dock. The size of the transducer is obscured by the sheer size of the ships, although the workers on the dry dock bottom in the photograph of *Port Royal* give some idea of scale. It is often described as being the size of a 60ft personnel boat. *(US Navy)*

The German Type 212A air-independent propulsion (AIP) submarine *U31*. The increased importance of the current generation of quiet patrol submarines in the post-Cold War environment has had a profound impact on sonar operations. *(German Navy)*

Many navies use variable-depth sonars simply to reach beneath the surface layer of the water, which traps sounds. This is the Canadian destroyer *Athabaskan*'s SQS-505 fish pictured in February 2004. The openings in her transom are for her towed array. In a smaller ship, a variable-depth sonar is also valued because it is isolated from hull motion. That makes it possible for a corvette to enjoy the advantages of a large low-frequency transducer. *(Canadian Navy)*

Two images of the British Royal Navy's Sonar 2087, which is deployed in some of the Type 23 frigate class. A low-frequency combined active and passive, variable-depth sonar, it was developed to replace a previous passive-only towed array that had become less effective in the face of noise-quietening advances in modern submarines. It is integrated with the ship's bow-mounted active sonar. *(Thales)*

MODERN ANTI-SUBMARINE OPERATIONS

It was also clear that the end of the Cold War did not end the need for NATO navies to operate in the face of underwater opposition. However, now the old secondary diesel-electric threat was the one which counted. Moreover, these submarines would be encountered not in the deep cold Norwegian Sea but in warm shallowish waters such as the Eastern Mediterranean and the Gulf. Warm shallow waters, particularly those near the outlets of major rivers, present a wide variety of problems. First, water refracts sonar beams, and exactly how that happens depends on the temperature structure of the water. A warm surface layer, for example, can trap signals so that they cannot penetrate to where a submerged submarine may be. That is why many navies operating in warm areas use variable-depth sonars, which can be lowered below the surface layer.

Second, shallow water is difficult because sonar signals can be reflected by both the surface and the bottom. It is difficult to interpret a signal which has bounced many times between the two. The ideal way to solve the problem is to suspend the sonar pinger between the surface and bottom so that it bounces off both at a very shallow angle. That is difficult to arrange. A less happy solution is to adopt so high a frequency that the sonar signal cannot get very far to bounce off either water surface. That is, a navy can adopt the opposite of the SQS-53 approach.

To further complicate matters, torpedo ranges are long, whilst an increasing number of submarines carry anti-ship missiles. Abandoning long-range detection is not a very happy solution. During the Cold War, European NATO navies generally did not adopt hull sonars with frequencies as low as that of the big US sonar, presumably because in a frigate of modest size, such a large a bow sonar would cause real sea-keeping problems in the rough North Sea and Eastern Atlantic. The new passive towed arrays seemed to offer sufficient range. However, by the end of the Cold War it seemed that Russian silencing might render them ineffective. Various NATO navies became interested in towed pingers which would use towed arrays as receivers. A towed pinger does not entail sea-keeping problems; conversely, it can be effective even on board a small ship. The most important current example of this type of sonar is probably the British Type 2087.

Shallow water now adds a third problem. A diesel-electric submarine can hide by sitting on the bottom. A nuclear submarine cannot do the same for fear that she will suck mud into her condensers and thus disable her machinery. By way of contrast, a diesel-electric submarine can close up any openings on her bottom. She does risk contact with whatever debris litters the bottom, but for a submarine under threat that risk is probably well worth running. How does the hunter somehow find a submarine amid what may be complicated bottom topography?

Unlike a nuclear submarine, a diesel-electric submarine operates in several different ways, in each of which it has a different signature. That means, among other things, that integrating its signals over a very long period may prove to be difficult, because the signature may not be consistent. Perhaps worst of all, a diesel-electric submarine can simply lie quietly on the bottom, its batteries powering its sensors and little else. Even then the submarine is not a 'hole in the ocean', but passive sonar is unlikely to be altogether effective. On the other hand, simply pinging also will not solve the problem – among other considerations, a pinging surface ship identifies and localises itself, making it more likely victim than attacker.

An MQ-8B unmanned aerial vehicle (UAV) operating from the flight deck of the USN frigate *McInerney* (FFG-8). Current US thinking involves using a combination of arrays, UAVs and lightweight torpedoes deployed from Littoral Combat Ships to combat submarines operating in coastal waters. *(US Navy)*

RECENT ANTI-SUBMARINE DETECTION TECHNIQUES

One solution, pursued by at least the US Navy and the Royal Navy, is to revive explosive echo-ranging, with an important twist. In the past, processing was limited to measuring the time delay between the pulse announcing the explosion and the pulse reflected by the submarine. Any pulse reflected off the bottom would only confuse matters, which was why JULIE was limited to water more than 8,000ft (2,438m) deep. The current technique is to record the details of the received signal, not just the peak but also any lesser peaks and indeed the entire shape of the received pulse. Moreover, instead of a single receiver, as in JULIE, the new Enhanced Echo Ranging (E2R) technique employs an array of receivers, which may be sonobuoys or ship towed arrays. The key is the post-military specification processor, which can compare data from everywhere in the array. The output is a detailed map of the bottom, including any submarine sitting on it. This technique was first developed under contract with the US Defense Advanced Research Projects Agency (DARPA) in the early 1990s under the project name 'Deep Thunder'. By about 1994 a shoebox-size processor could provide the bottom map in about twenty minutes. Moore's Law suggests that – sixteen years later – processing speed should have increased by a factor of better than thirty-two, in which case a processor ought to provide a map in well under a minute. 'Deep Thunder' first entered service on board destroyers operating near Korea, where they faced a North Korean diesel submarine threat.

'Deep Thunder' would find a submarine on the bottom, but presumably the sound of the small explosion (or the controlled ping) would send it on its way. The US Navy has also been working on a way of tracking a moving diesel-electric submarine without alerting it by pinging. The idea is to strew lines of sensors along the bottom in shallow water. For example, an array of upward-looking sensors can detect the pressure wave of a submarine moving overhead. The array does not track the submarine; all it does is observe where it crosses the array. The array thus acts as an acoustic fence. Recording where and when the submarine crosses a series of such fences does provide the submarine's course and speed, and its position can be predicted. Because the system is entirely passive, it is unlikely that the submarine will manoeuvre deceptively. If it does, it will not get wherever it intends to go, and its mission will be frustrated.

Several technologies are involved here. One is the advent of unmanned surface craft, helicopters and underwater craft which might emplace the arrays. A second is the relatively new technology of digital underwater communications (which is possible thanks to much better processors which can overcome the distorting effect of the water). Communication means, firstly, the ability to determine where the transmitter is, so that whatever the small bottom arrays detect is meaningful. Secondly, of course, it makes it possible for the data they obtain to be collected. Most likely arrays would report mainly by radio, because long-range underwater communication would be limited by the speed of sound. Probably arrays would report to a nearby radio-emitting buoy so as to avoid giving away their positions.

In theory, the combination of arrays would provide sufficient precision that a weapon could be delivered quite close to the submarine. It would not need much endurance to search. Unmanned helicopters offer precise delivery on command. If the weapon need not search, it need not be very large. This combination of possibilities is one reason the US Navy is currently developing an ultra-lightweight 6.75in (171mm) torpedo (the same weapon is also intended to destroy enemy torpedoes).

Current US thinking would put the unmanned helicopters, the arrays and the ultra-lightweight torpedoes on board a Littoral Combat Ship, which would process data from nearby arrays and prosecute any contacts it developed. The submarine tracks it found would also be transmitted to a group command ship, perhaps for further attacks in the event that the initial ones failed.

None of this might work. The US Navy's alternative is the big Active Adjunct pinger for the surveillance ships. This Active Adjunct was generally described as being the size of a stack of full-size automobiles. It has been quite effective in tests, including tests looking into shallow water. The main current drawback is that at its very low frequency it can affect marine mammals such as whales and dolphins. For that reason operations have been limited, and projected production was drastically curtailed. The passive alternatives described above would seem to be simpler, more mobile, and less controversial – but they may not work.

A final point is worth making. During the Cold War, SOSUS, which was eventually installed on both sides of the Atlantic and in the North Pacific, showed extraordinary range. It was the basis of NATO maritime patrol aircraft operations – the aircraft were actually much more interceptors than patrollers. It was also extremely useful in other ways. When the Cold War ended, SOSUS was phased out because it no longer seemed worthwhile to invest so much to contain the Russian submarine fleet, and also because the system was not nearly so effective once the Russians had silenced their submarines. The system left in the Western Atlantic was a string of upward-looking sensors not too different in concept from the bottom arrays now envisaged. Since the Cold War, the US Navy has been interested in deployable arrays which would support patrol airplane operations in forward areas. The ideal is a combination of quick and covert deployment, as an enemy aware of the position of an array would evade or attack it.

Notes:

1. This account emphasises US developments, because the author is most familiar with them. However, the central themes are common to all Western sonars. The views expressed are the author's own, and should not necessarily be taken as those of the US Navy or of any other organisation with which he has been associated. For more details of particular sonars, the reader is directed to the author's *Naval Institute Guide to World Naval Weapon Systems, Fifth Edition* (Annapolis, Naval Institute Press, 2006). The situation in sonars had not changed enormously over the past few years.

2. One great divide in sonar is between active and passive operation. In active operation, the sonar produces a ping, and listens for reflection from the submarine. A passive sonar simply listens for a noise the submarine emits. The quieter the submarine, the more attractive active sonar becomes. However, by pinging an active sonar announces its presence and it may also provide the submarine with a way of locating it for counter-attack. Also, if the passive sonar detects not merely something, but also a distinctive sound (signature), it can recognise the submarine (or at least determine that what it is hearing is a submarine). Attempts to do that with active sonars, e.g. by using a series of very short pulses to visualise the shape of the submarine or other underwater target, have failed.

3. A few nuclear submarines have natural-circulation reactors, which do not need circulating pumps, at least when they are running well below full power. The newest British submarines, and the US *Ohio* class, use them, but it seems that the Russians never adopted this technology because they were unwilling to accept a combination of larger hulls and limited power output per unit weight and volume. The current French strategic submarines reportedly have natural-circulation reactors.

4. It seems that eventually the Russians realised that snorkelling made even more noise than running on the surface, because so much more of the submarine (which emitted noise) was in contact with the surrounding ocean. Snorkelling was originally attractive because it allowed a submarine to charge her batteries without risking detection by an aircraft or surface ship. After the Second World War, 'Western' anti-submarine forces were far less numerous than during the war years; they relied far more on being cued by long-range detectors. The Russians eventually realised that it was generally safer to charge batteries on the surface than to cue patrol planes and other anti-submarine warfare forces by snorkelling at periscope depth. That is probably why the 'Kilo' class had an air-defence position in the sail (for a crewman with a shoulder-fired SAM) and also why the Russians developed a special device to check whether it was safe to surface. The latter was an omni-directional radar source surrounded by radar receivers, to take what amounted to a radar snapshot before the submarine surfaced. This device, unknown until then in the West, was revealed after the end of the Cold War. It was called 'Kodak', because it took a (radar) snapshot. The Russians were also aware that anti-submarine homing torpedoes generally used active sonars, which were ineffective near the surface (their pings reflected from the surface, for example). Late in the Cold War the US Navy took special pains to demonstrate that, because it could operate passively as well as actively, the Mk 46 Mod 5 torpedo could sink surfaced targets.

5. This is evident from French records. The experimental T56 class ASW destroyer *La Gallissonière* began as the LOFAR killer ship, and French design records show that LOFAR referred to her 5kHz hull sonar and the accompanying variable-depth sonar. Other French records show how bitter the French were that their allies, the Americans and the British, were not sharing anti-submarine warfare technology (anti-air warfare technology was an entirely different matter).

6. The best evidence is the Russian account of their towed array. The reason it is housed in a pod is that it was intended for sprint-and-drift broadband operation. To limit drag (and noise) the submarine would retract the array for the sprints, and let it out for the drifts (while it listened). The history of Soviet-era sonar produced by the array's design organisation (Morphizpribor) explains that sprint-and-drift was abandoned as soon as the Russians realised that they had to resort to narrow-band processing, but that it was already much too late to give up the big 'draggy' pod and its overly-elaborate towing winch.

7. Because of both its enormous power and its low frequency (about 3.5kHz, well below that of contemporary foreign sonars), SQS-26 was credited with very long range: 20,000 yards (18,288m) in direct path (i.e., like a radar) and out to first convergence zone (35 nautical miles [65km] – 70,000 yards – in the Atlantic). The convergence zone is where sound bent down and then back up by refraction in the ocean refocuses. Thus, when operating as advertised, SQS-26 could detect a target somewhere in a 5-nautical-mile (9.25km) zone about 35 nautical miles (65km) from the ship, then lose it as it came closer, and then pick it up again 10 nautical miles (18.5km) out. At this time, the 1960s, the next best series of sonars could detect a target reliably at 10,000 yards (6 nautical miles [9.25km]). Unfortunately SQS-26 gained a terrible reputation for unreliability and sheer complexity. It was the first US sonar to use a computer to manage detection, and it had a bewildering number of different operating modes.

4.2 TECHNOLOGICAL REVIEW

Author:
David Hobbs

WORLD NAVAL AVIATION

An Overview of Recent Developments

INTRODUCTION

The previous twelve months have seen significant changes in the sphere of global maritime air power. Most notably, the British Royal Navy has surrendered – at least temporarily – all embarked fast-jet capabilities with the early retirement of the iconic Harrier aircraft on cost grounds. Elsewhere, the outlook is more positive, with both India and China making progress with their own carrier projects. In the longer term, the development of unmanned naval aircraft offers interesting possibilities and this chapter includes a review of current projects in some detail.

The US Navy's amphibious assault ship *Kearsarge* (LHD-3) pictured in the Red Sea in February 2011 shortly before being deployed to the Mediterranean for operations to protect Libyan civilians in support of United Nations Security Council Resolution 1973. The six US Marine Corps Harriers embarked proved ideally suited for this mission. *(US Navy)*

A GLOBAL OVERVIEW OF CURRENT DEVELOPMENTS

CARRIER AVIATION

The UK Strategic Defence and Security Review (SDSR) of October 2010 dramatically reduced the size and capability of the Royal Navy (RN) and, consequently, Britain's ability to project power effectively. The previous Government had halved the operational Harrier force to one RN and one Royal Air Force (RAF) squadron but – before this cut could be fully implemented – the SDSR ordered the immediate withdrawal from service of the only operational British aircraft carrier, *Ark Royal*, and the entire Harrier fleet. 800 Naval Air Squadron, the RN's only remaining fast-jet unit, was disbanded alongside its sister RAF squadrons in Joint Force Harrier on 28 January 2011. The shock with which the measure was received adds credibility to the belief that the Harrier force was sacrificed after a last-minute decision to save the RAF's costlier and less versatile Tornado bomber force, which had been expected to take substantial cuts. Of the remaining fixed-wing carriers, *Invincible* was sold for scrap in 2011, leaving only *Illustrious* refitting at Rosyth. She is to be re-commissioned for use as a helicopter carrier but retains the ability to operate USMC, Spanish or Italian Navy Harriers if required to do so. After 2014, *Illustrious* will also be retired and the RN will retain only the LPH *Ocean* as part of a much-reduced amphibious force.

British carrier-borne aircraft were not, therefore, available to participate in operations off Libya in support of United Nations Security Council Resolution 1973, which began in March 2011.

Conversely, French and Italian carriers were present off the Libyan coast. The USN had no big-deck carrier close by but USMC AV-8B Harriers from the *Kearsarge* (LHD-3) did carry out strikes, demonstrating the developing 'cross-over' capability of amphibious carriers. Although only six Harriers were embarked, they used the advantage of their ideal position and the technical and logistical support within the ship and its ready group to fly several sorties per day. *Ark Royal* – carrying up to eighteen British Harriers – would have been equally ideal for the close air support mission. Her aircraft would have been better suited to the task, have been able to operate from a 'sovereign' British base and would have achieved high sortie generation rates with no need for the extensive air-to-air tanker support required to get distant RAF aircraft into action.

With bizarre logic, the SDSR confirmed the British Government's requirement for a future RN carrier strike capability, thereby continuing construction of the new carriers *Queen Elizabeth* and *Prince of Wales*. However, this might have more to do with punitive cancellation costs and the devastating effect of project termination on British industry than any real commitment to future carrier aviation. It failed to state how the RN was to be expected to maintain the skills needed to operate a big-deck aircraft carrier until the period of what must now be termed 're-armament' later in the decade. There will certainly be no help from the RAF, which both fails to understand the enormous range of capabilities offered by carriers and actively opposes their very existence.

The SDSR also announced that Britain would not buy the 'less capable and more expensive' STOVL (short take off and vertical landing) F-35B version of the Lightning II Joint Strike Fighter and would, instead, procure the F-35C 'tail-hook' version designed to operate from aircraft carriers. However, no numbers were quoted. This would have been the logical version to procure from the outset; the UK's decade-long investment in F-35B development has left it with little value for money. The three prototypes on order are no longer completely relevant and, apparently, might not be renegotiated as F-35Cs. Completion of *Queen Elizabeth* and *Prince of Wales* has been delayed from the previous target of 2016 for the first to about 2020 to give time for the design to be revised to incorporate catapults and arrester wires. Remarkably, no consideration appears to have been given to procuring the F/A-18E/F Super Hornet, which has a unit price about half that of an F-35C.

The British Royal Navy's light aircraft carrier and Falkland Islands' veteran *Invincible* departing Portsmouth *en route* for the shipbreakers at Aliaga in Turkey on 24 March 2011. The decommissioning of *Invincible*'s sister *Ark Royal* and the premature cessation of British Harrier operations were amongst the major developments in world naval aviation over the past year. *(Conrad Waters)*

It would be available 'off-the-shelf' at a known fixed price in time for the new carriers and would still offer commonality with the USN. The Super Hornet has more capabilities than any aircraft at present in British service at an affordable price and, whilst it lacks stealthy features, it and its EA-18G cousin can perform tasks that the F-35 cannot.

Meanwhile, the US Navy continues to make progress with new aircraft and equipment. The first manned aircraft to be launched by the new electro-magnetic aircraft launch system (EMALS), an F/A-18E, was catapulted successfully on 18 December 2010 at NAS Lakehurst, NJ. More than 722 test loads had been launched previously to prove the system at end-speeds up to 180 knots. After further tests, the system will be installed in the new *Gerald R Ford* class carriers from 2015 and – potentially – the *Queen Elizabeth* class from 2020.

The first manned aircraft to be launched from the US Navy's new EMALS electro-magnetic aircraft launch system took to the air on 18 December 2010. The system will be installed in the new *Gerald R Ford* class of aircraft carriers in place of more traditional steam catapults. *(Lockheed Martin)*

Delays with the F-35 Lightning II programme have caused the USN to re-think its procurement strategy for the type. In the short term extra F/A-18s are being procured in a new multi-year buy. This will take the F/A-18 E/F 'program of record' to 515 units, as well as 114 EA-18G Growler electronic warfare variants. When future plans are taken into account, total F/A-18 E/F numbers are likely to exceed 550. In March 2011 the US Navy and Marine Corps also announced the number and types of Joint Strike Fighters to be procured between them. Their combined total is to be 680 F-35s, half of which will be F-35Bs and half F-35Cs. The Marine Corps' share will comprise eighty 'C's and 340 'B's, the Navy taking the balance of 260 'C's.[1] The Marines will form five squadrons, each with twelve aircraft, to operate F-35Cs as part of CVN carrier wings, replacing their existing F/A-18C/Ds.

A F-35C carrier variant of the Lightning II joint strike fighter seen undergoing trials during early 2011. Decisions taken over the past twelve months have seen the British Royal Air Force and US Marine Corps join the US Navy as potential users of this variant. *(Lockheed Martin)*

The Indian Navy's long-standing efforts to modernise its carrier force have gained momentum over the past year, suggesting relief for the elderly *Viraat* (formerly the RN's *Hermes*) is finally on the horizon. India expects to be able to run *Viraat* until about 2020 if necessary, although she will only be useful as long as the steadily-diminishing numbers of remaining Sea Harriers can be kept operational. The 45,000-ton *Vikramaditya* will shortly start to carry out trials and the Indian Navy is optimistic that she will be delivered by December 2012. The indigenously-built *Vikrant* should achieve initial operational capability from 2016. Mig-29K strike fighters procured from Russia should be joined in the latter part of the decade by the naval version of the local Tejas light combat aircraft. Both use the Russian-developed short take-off but arrested landing (STOBAR) system in which the aircraft carries out a free take-off using a ski-jump and is arrested on landing by a tail-hook and arrester wires. Interestingly the Eurofighter consortium has offered a navalised STOBAR version of the Typhoon for potential operation from the Indian carriers. However, given the lack of UK interest in such a variant and the lack of multi-role capability demonstrated by RAF

Two computer-generated images of a navalised Eurofighter in Indian Navy markings over-flying the modernised Russian-built carrier *Vikramaditya*. The carrier should be delivered to the Indian Navy around the end of 2012 but prospects of a navalised Eurofighter taking to the sky seem much less likely. *(Eurofighter)*

Typhoons, an Indian Navy version seems unlikely.

China is also working to complete a STOBAR carrier, the 65,000-ton *Shi Lang* (the former Soviet *Varyag*). Signs of progress with her at Dailan Shipyard since she arrived in 2002 were slow at first but have now gathered momentum, with sea trials said to be imminent. She moved into dry dock in 2009 to allow the installation of heavy equipment and may be completed in 2012. The People's Liberation Army Navy Air Force (PLANAF) has begun training naval aircrew to operate jet fighters from the ship. A 'dummy deck' has been built ashore to train aircrew and aircraft handlers at a naval air station where a runway is marked in the size and shape of *Shi Lang*'s flight deck complete with a ski-jump.

SEA CONTROL HELICOPTERS

The first three French Navy NATO Frigate Helicopters (NFH), a variant of the Eurocopter-lead NH Industries' NH90, were delivered to the *Centre d'Expérimentations Pratiques et de Réception de l'Aéronautique Navale* (CEPA) during 2010 to undergo development flying. A further twenty-four are on order and the type has been named the Caiman after a species of South American crocodile. First deck landing trials were carried out on the LHD *Tonnerre* (L9014) in October 2010.

The Caiman's sensor suite is not yet fully developed and early aircraft are being delivered to a standard designated Step A. This includes a development version of the European Navy Radar, a FLIR turret, some electronic support measures, active and passive sonars, a basic data-link without systems integration and a rescue hoist. The Italian and Royal Netherlands Navies have accepted early aircraft with similar limitations but regard them as being valuable for gathering experience with the new type. Step A aircraft are to equip a single operational unit from 2011. Step B, the full operational standard, will be incorporated in the eighth and subsequent production Caimans delivered from 2012 onwards, introducing integrated production-standard sensors that are expected to give a massive improvement over the Lynx helicopters they will replace. They will also have chaff and flare dispensers, external weapons stations, Link 11 and machine guns fitted to the cabin doors. The first Caiman Step B flight is due to embark in a destroyer during 2012. The French Navy plans, subsequently, to use thirteen of its Caimans in the maritime security and SAR roles fitted with a rear ramp and fourteen in the anti-submarine role with the full sensor suite. Up to 4,600kg of weapons including ASW torpedoes, Marte Mark 2/S air-to-surface missiles and depth charges can be carried on two pylons on Step B aircraft. The numbers are sufficient to maintain up to eight detachments in the destroyer/frigate force and two aboard *Charles de Gaulle* at any one time. The remaining four will be used for training and development flying ashore. Caimans will replace Lynx in the new 'Horizon' class destroyers and *Aquitaine* class frigates but they are too big to operate from the F70 class frigates and Lynx are likely to remain in these until they are retired by about 2020.

A version of the NFH, based on the French Caiman, is one of two contenders for the Royal Australian Navy's (RAN's) Project Air 9000 Phase 8 intended to replace the current S-70B Seahawk and the failed SH-2G(A) Super Seasprite. The rival contender is the Sikorsky MH-60R Seahawk and selection between them leading to procurement of twenty-four helicopters should be announced by 2012. They will form a training and headquarters unit at RANAS Nowra and a number of detached flights able to embark in upgraded *Adelaide* class frigates, *Anzac* class frigates and the new *Hobart* class destroyers.

Both contenders have strengths and weaknesses. The NFH has 80 per cent commonality with the MRH90 which is being built in Brisbane for the Australian Army as a Blackhawk replacement and the RAN as a Sea King replacement by Australian Aerospace, a subsidiary of Eurocopter. Its immature sensor outfit counts against it, however, and the MRH90 programme itself is running twelve months late with all the aircraft delivered being grounded for three months in 2010 after one suffered a failure of one of its two Rolls-Royce Turbomeca RTM322 engines in flight. The type has also suffered from transmission oil-cooler fan failures and shortages of spare parts leading the Government to put the project on its 'Projects of Concern' List.

The MH-60R offers mature airframe and systems designs, commonality with the USN and aircraft from a large production line procured through the US Foreign Military Sales (FMS) Programme. The MH-60R is also more likely to meet the RAN's optimistic target of putting the first flight equipped with the new helicopter to sea in 2014. The definitive sensor outfits of both types are closely comparable but the NFH has more internal space with the role equipment installed. The major weakness of the 'Romeo' is that – procured 'off the shelf' – it would come equipped to fire Hellfire air-to-surface missiles intended for use against fast patrol boats in a littoral environment (since the USN would expect to use carrier-borne fighters to attack larger warships in the open ocean). The 'Romeo' could be modified to carry larger 'ship-killing' missiles but development would have to be funded by the RAN, lessening the advantage of buying a mature design at a known cost and timescale. The NFH is intended to carry the heavier MBDA Marte Mark 2/S missile as an anti-surface vessel option but this is not yet operational with any of the type's customers and might, therefore, also have an element of risk. Following the failure of its attempt to develop a unique strike version of the Seasprite and the current problems with the MRH90, the RAN is wary of choosing a helicopter that would require unique system development.[2]

Meanwhile Lockheed Martin's UK subsidiary is managing the RN AW101 Merlin upgrade to HM2 standard, with development flying carried out at AgustaWestland's facility at Yeovil in Somerset. The contract allows thirty airframes to be modified to HM2 standard but no decision has been announced about the remaining twelve HM1 airframes. Options include their conversion to an ASaC standard with the Cerberus mission system to replace the Sea King ASaC7, modification to the commando assault role, or disposal. The first 'production' standard HM 2 is scheduled to be delivered in mid-2012 and the flight test programme is due to be completed in 2013, followed by the commissioning of the first operational unit in 2014.

The upgrade aims to maintain Merlin viability until 2029, introducing an open-architecture electronic systems structure that greatly improves mission-system processing capability and allows a straightforward introduction of software improvements. The new version will be flown by a crew comprising two observer/weapons system officers and either one or two pilots. The aircrewman responsible for the 'wet' acoustic systems in the HM1 is replaced by the new software. All crewmembers can access both flight and tactical information through large, flat-panel touch-screen displays. Radar, sonar, communications and navigation systems will be improved and integrated into a new tactical system which will use Link 16 to share data with other network-enabled units. Early statements about the programme stated that the HM2 would be able to carry the same future air-to-surface guided weapon as the Wildcat. This would be logical since a Merlin embarked in a deployed frigate or destroyer might be the only UK air asset at the scene of action and it makes little sense for the

Deliveries of interim versions of the NFH variant of NH Industries' NH90 helicopter are now well underway, with France, Italy and the Netherlands all receiving aircraft by mid-2011. These images show a NFH of France's *Marine National* in February 2011 – the type will be known as the Caiman in French service. *(Eurocopter: Anthony Pecchi)*

Thirty of the Royal Navy's existing Merlin HM1 helicopters are being upgraded to HM2 standard. Various options are being considered for a further twelve airframes, with conversion to an Airborne Surveillance and Control (ASaC) configuration incorporating the Cerberus mission system and Searchwater 2000 radar currently utilised in the elderly Sea King one possibility. However, with the operational member of the *Queen Elizabeth* class now to be completed for conventional carrier operations, Northrop Grumman's E-2D Hawkeye might be a more attractive alternative. These concept images were released in July 2010. *(AgustaWestland)*

The AW159 Lynx Wildcat project was one of a number which were previously perceived to be at risk that survived the UK's Strategic Defence and Security Review. Three test aircraft have now been completed. *(AgustaWestland)*

HM2 to have no better anti-surface-vessel capability than a door-mounted machine gun. The new version is also to be fitted with Helicopter Electro Actuation Technology, HEAT; a third generation fly-by-wire system that uses 'maintenance-free' electrical actuators instead of hydraulic units to make control inputs to the main and tail rotors offering greater serviceability and a reduction the type's cost of ownership.

SDSR contained many illogical surprises and continued production of the naval version of the AW159 Wildcat as a Lynx replacement was one of them. After the immediate cuts are implemented, the only remaining big-deck ships, *Illustrious* and *Ocean*, are to operate primarily in the LPH role, leaving a destroyer/frigate force of only nineteen vessels and a small number of Royal Fleet Auxiliaries (RFAs) with facilities to support embarked helicopters. All of these are capable of operating Merlins. Five already do so and not all will be operational at once. Given this situation, it would have been logical to concentrate on the Merlin HM2 as the standard embarked helicopter, if necessary bringing all the available airframes up to HM2 standard. If more were to be needed to support the Type 26 frigates in the next decade it must, surely, be cheaper to build an extra batch of Merlins capable of using the existing training and logistic support systems than to develop a new but less capable helicopter that will require expensive and different training and logistic support. Even the US Navy has said that it cannot afford to operate more than one basic type of helicopter. It is difficult to escape the conclusion that Wildcat is more about providing Government support for AgustaWestland than providing a vital capability for the RN. The money saved might have allowed the RN to maintain a squadron of Harriers in *Illustrious* to fill the gap until the *Queen Elizabeth* class are completed.

AMPHIBIOUS WARFARE

The majority of significant navies continue to expand their amphibious capability but the post-SDSR RN has been forced out of step. The Royal Marines' amphibious brigade is to be reduced in size and several amphibious ships bought recently at considerable expense are to be reduced to reserve or sold. The plan announced in 2009 by the previous UK government to transfer the Merlin HC3 fleet from the RAF to the RN as Sea King HC4 replacements has not been confirmed and may now hinge on whether the RAF is to get all, or indeed any, of the extra Chinooks announced at the same time. Budgetary constraints are also affecting the US Marine Corps (USMC) and have forced it to slow the development of the CH-53K which will not now reach initial operating capability (IOC) until 2018 at the earliest. The new heavy-lift helicopter is intended to allow a brigade-sized expeditionary force with all its equipment to be landed through a single landing zone in a single night.

The most significant amphibious development since the last edition, however, was the announcement by President Dimitri Medvedev that Russia intends to procure two *Mistral* class amphibious assault ships (*bâtiments de projection et de commandement* or BPC) to be built in France with options for two more to be built under licence in Russia. Three similar ships have already been built for the French Navy.[3] The order for the two Russian units was confirmed by DCNS on 17 June 2011. Both will be built at the STX shipyard at St Nazaire for delivery in 2014 and 2015. The initial Russian contribution to construction is set at about 20 per cent, increasing through the course of the project. The *Mistral* class BPCs are capable of embarking up to sixteen NH90-sized assault helicopters, up to seventy vehicles including twelve main battle tanks, and 450 marines. Russia plans to deploy the ships to its Northern and

The French *Mistral* class LHD-type amphibious assault ship (*bâtiment de projection et de commandement* in French terminology) *Tonnerre* pictured whilst exercising with the US Marine Corps. Third of class *Dixmude* commenced sea trials in the first half of 2011 and should be delivered around the end of the year to replace the existing *Foudre* during 2012. Meanwhile on-off negotiations for the construction of up to four variants for the Russian Navy reached a successful conclusion with a formal order for two ships – both to be built in France – on 17 June 2011. As for *Dixmude*, construction work will be carried out by STX Europe's Chantiers de l'Atlantique facility in Saint Nazaire with delivery scheduled for 2014–15. Further units may be built at a proposed new yard in St Petersburg. *(US Marine Corps)*

The Royal Australian Navy amphibious landing ship *Manoora* has been withdrawn from service after defects made her unseaworthy. The fortuitous availability of the British Royal Fleet Auxiliary *Largs Bay* has, however, allowed an amphibious capability to be maintained until new Spanish-designed amphibious assault ships are delivered. *(Royal Australian Navy)*

Pacific Fleets. All four will closely resemble their French counterparts with the substitution of some Russian equipment and hulls that are thickened to navigate through thin ice. The flight decks will be strengthened to cope with the greater all-up mass of Russian assault helicopters.

Australia's amphibious force faces short-term problems, with mechanical defects causing the amphibious landing ships *Kanimbla* and *Manoora* to be declared unseaworthy in September 2010. *Manoora* was subsequently found to be beyond economical repair and has been decommissioned but *Kanimbla* could be repaired to run on until the two *Canberra* class LHD type amphibious assault ships are operational. The heavy landing ship *Tobruk* has also suffered problems. However, the fortuitous availability of the RFA *Largs Bay*, a four-year-old UK *Bay* class auxiliary dock landing ship (LSD) discarded by the SDSR has allowed the RAN to purchase an effective vessel with a flight deck but no hangar, capable of a range of war-fighting and disaster-relief missions that will be useful in the short-term and ideally complement the two *Canberra* class LHDs in the long-term. The first LHD, *Canberra*, was launched on 17 February 2011, marking the beginning of a bright future for amphibious operations by the Australian Defence Force. She will be manned by men and women of all three Services and will operate a mixture of Navy and Army helicopters. Despite having a ski-jump she is not intended to embark STOVL fighters but could, if necessary, operate USMC, Spanish or Italian Harriers. Since there is no Royal Australian Marine Corps, she will rely on specialised amphibious elements of the Army for operations and their initial inexperience will mean that some time will have to elapse after completion before 'best practice' evolves to bring the LHDs to full operational capability.

MARITIME PATROL AIRCRAFT

The decision to abandon the Nimrod MRA4 maritime patrol aircraft programme was another controversial outcome of the SDSR. The UK already had no maritime patrol aircraft in service since the previous Nimrod MR2 fleet was discarded in 2010 but the SDSR conclusion made this capability gap permanent. Within weeks of the decision to cancel the project the incomplete airframes were scrapped, leaving the Boeing P-8A Poseidon as the only significant maritime patrol aircraft in development and production. The MRA4 programme stands out as one of the UK's worst defence failures, being ten years late and with over £4 billion spent on a force that was eventually cut down to only nine aircraft that were not yet developed to operational capability. In contrast, the US $3.89bn P-8A system development and demonstration contract was signed in 2004, first flight was in 2009 and the first aircraft arrived at NAS Patuxent River, Maryland in 2010. There have, inevitably, been hitches but development remains within the planned time-scale and cost estimates and the Navy plans to procure 117 P-8As, with the first unit achieving initial operational capability as predicted in 2013. A low-rate initial production (LRIP) contract for six aircraft was signed on 21 January 2011. The P-8A is the manned element of a US Navy 'system of systems' known as Broad Area Maritime Surveillance or BAMS. It will specialise in anti-submarine search and strike but be fully capable of surveillance, targeting and anti-surface vessel strike. Its BAMS partner, the unmanned MQ-4C Global Hawk, will specialise in surface search and targeting.

The P-8A is based on the commercial Boeing 737-800 airframe, with the strengthened wings of the -900. Unusually for a military aircraft, production is interspersed with commercial aircraft on the same line. Design alterations include structural strengthening and the addition of a weapons bay aft of the wings. Sensors include electro-optical/infrared cameras in a belly turret forward of the wing and a Raytheon AN/APY-10 radar system in the nose. A Northrop Grumman ESM system provides detection, signature recognition and protection against infrared-guided missiles. Air-to-air refuelling was not part of the original specification but the USN decided to take advantage of the system designed by Boeing for the 737-based RAAF Wedgetail AEW & C aircraft and has fitted it. There are five mission work-stations each of which has a 61cm screen with keyboard and mouse controls. Two are intended for acoustic system display; one for non-acoustic system display; one for tactical co-ordination; and one for navigation and communications control. All five can be used for all functions and the two pilots can call up tactical information displays on their screens if necessary. The basics are not forgotten and there are two observers' visual-search windows aft of the cockpit. The P-8A has the internal fuel capacity to fly

Poseidon P-8A data

Span: 37.6m
Length: 39.5m
Maximum launch weight: 85,900kg
Endurance: 4 hours at 1,200nm (2,220km) from base
Propulsion: 2 x CFM56-7B. 54,000lbs (24,000kgf) of thrust
Maximum speed: 490 knots (910km/h)
Ceiling: 41,000ft (12,500m)

1,200 nautical miles (2,220km) from its base, spend four hours on station and then return with standard fuel reserves. Its weapons are designed to be dropped from aircraft flying at high-level to allow the aircraft to conserve fuel. These will include AGM-84K missiles carried on hard points under the wings for use against surface vessels and Mark 54 torpedoes and mines carried in the heated weapons bay. Sonobuoys are dispensed from three pressurised rotary dispensers in the after fuselage.

The USN plans to accept P-8As at the rate of about one a month which means that production will continue for at least a decade and longer when export orders are added. India has already ordered eight Poseidons to P-8I standard, the first of which will be in production during 2012, and has an option to purchase four more. Australia has stated an intention to replace its AP-3s with AP-8s towards the end of the present decade. If the UK seeks to recover a maritime patrol capability, it may eventually have to investigate the lease or procurement of a batch of P-8s once its economy has recovered sufficiently.

CURRENT UNMANNED NAVAL AIRCRAFT PROJECTS IN DETAIL

UNMANNED CARRIER-LAUNCHED AIRBORNE SURVEILLANCE AND STRIKE (UCLASS)

Experience with the QH-50 Drone Anti-Submarine Helicopter (DASH) during the 1960s left the USN averse to the deployment of immature, unreliable unmanned systems.[4] However, the recent dramatic growth in unmanned combat aerial vehicle (UCAV) technology to support operations in Iraq and Afghanistan has allowed it to select mature airframe designs to match new systems in the same way that it has done with manned aircraft. The USN therefore plans to capitalise on the new technology to deploy a

A picture of the fourth P-8 Poseidon test aircraft under construction at a new Boeing final production facility in Seattle that was opened for the project in November 2010. Planned orders for the aircraft from the United States and India total nearly 130 aircraft. *(Boeing)*

A P-8A Poseidon test aircraft flying in US Navy colours. Based on the commercial Boeing 737-800 airframe, the Poseidon's trials programme has made good progress and a low rate initial production contract for six of the jets was signed in January 2011. *(Boeing)*

squadron comprising four to six UCAVs as part of a carrier air wing by 2018. The UCAV selected will demonstrate its value in 'irregular and hybrid warfare situations' and to refuel in flight from both 'probe and drogue' and 'flying boom' technology. UCLASS is expected to offer a radical new approach to naval aviation that is both less expensive and potentially more effective than legacy manned aircraft.

The USN has asked industry to propose alternative air vehicles capable of from eleven to fourteen hours endurance and with an adequate fuel reserve to loiter waiting for recovery. The platform selected must be able to use 'lethal precision weapons to suppress, defeat, destroy, deceive or influence a range of enemy targets' and is to have both folding wings and tie-down points for carrier stowage. The Northrop Grumman X-47B (see below) has been funded under the UCAS-D programme to demonstrate the carrier suitability of a stealthy, tailless unmanned aircraft and autonomous in-flight refuelling and is scheduled to demonstrate carrier launch and recovery in 2013. However, its eventual use for UCLASS is not guaranteed. Naval analysts have put forward the concept of UCAVs in a 'swarm', maintaining aircraft over a potential target for considerable periods with artificial intelligence deciding when to refuel or replace individual aircraft. The unmanned systems would stay 100 per cent alert but humans in the mission control centre would take decisions and accept or veto the use of lethal force. 'Swarms' would provide continuous streams of real-time intelligence to network-enabled forces, if necessary supported by manned fighters. When not required the 'swarm' would have no need for continuation or training flying and would, thus, be much cheaper to operate than conventional aircraft.

Since the unmanned air vehicles will be cheaper to operate, be stealthier and fly further for longer than the F-35C, the degree of success achieved by UCLASS may well impact the eventual number of F-35Cs produced. If UCLASS works as envisaged, there would seem little point in paying for the continued production of an aircraft that would have become the second-best option for stealthy 'first-day-of-conflict' strikes, the niche capability in which the JSF offers advantage over other platforms that are now in service. The F-35 was conceived in the last century when there was little credible alternative to it as a stealthy, first-strike system. With UCLASS at sea only two years after the F-35C's planned IOC in 2016, the new technology may well offer a more immediate and more affordable alternative. Despite USN enthusiasm, there has been no official comment in the UK about the possibility of operating a British UCLASS system from the *Queen Elizabeth* class; another of the surprises in SDSR.

The prototype X-47B commenced initial flight testing in February 2011 – this image was taken during a subsequent flight in 2011. *(Northrop Grumman)*

NORTHROP GRUMMAN X-47B

The X-47B is derived from an earlier X-47A version first flown in 2003 as part of the joint unmanned combat air system (J-UCAS) trials terminated in 2006. It is now a naval programme with Northrop Grumman contracted to demonstrate its safe operation from an aircraft carrier alongside conventional, manned aircraft. Unlike earlier UAVs such as the General Atomics MQ-9 Reaper, X-47B is not 'flown' by a remote pilot but programmed to carry out an autonomous sortie from catapult-launch to arrested recovery. Inputs from a mission controller can change target co-ordinates or accept weapon release but the 'system' carries out the routine 'dull, dirty or dangerous' aspects of the mission.

Northrop Grumman was selected as the prime contractor for the US$636m unmanned combat air system demonstration (UCAS-D) programme in August 2007, being tasked to develop two prototype aircraft. The first X-47B was rolled out in December 2008 and first flew for twenty-nine minutes from Edwards Air Force Base on 4 February 2011; the second aircraft joined the programme later and both will move to NAS Patuxent River, Maryland, to prepare for carrier-suitability trials scheduled for 2013. The X-47 can be fitted with a wide range of sensors including multi-mode synthetic aperture and inverse synthetic aperture radar, electro-optical and infra-red cameras and ESM. Two internal weapons bays are capable of carrying a total of 2,041kg of weapons. In a typical strike sortie each bay could carry six precision-guided small diameter bombs (SDB) and aircraft would have a radius of action of

X-47B data

Span: 18.9m
Length: 11.6m
Maximum launch weight: 20,900kg
Endurance: 9 hours or up to 100 hours with in-flight refuelling
Propulsion: Single Pratt & Whitney F100-PW-220U. 18,000lbs (8,000kgf) of thrust
Maximum speed: 460 knots (850km/h)
Ceiling: 40,000ft (12,200m)

1,600 nautical miles (2,960km) or the ability to loiter for over two hours above a target 1,000 nautical miles (1,850km) from the carrier. Fuel tanks could be fitted in the weapons bays instead of bombs to increase endurance.

NORTHROP GRUMMAN MQ-8B FIRE SCOUT

Derived from a conventional Ryan-Schweizer manned helicopter design which evolved into the RQ-8A evaluated for use by the US Army, the MQ-8B is being procured by the US Navy for operation from Littoral Combat Ships (LCS). A new four-bladed main rotor gives improved lift performance, allowing a mission payload of up to 320kg to be carried. Stub wings provide aerodynamic lift as well as acting as anchor points for podded mission systems and weapons. Sea trials with an RQ-8A were carried out on the *Nashville* (LPD-13) off NAS Patuxent River in January 2006, starting with the first autonomous deck landing by a USN unmanned helicopter with no input from a pilot or controller. A longer deployment and operational evaluation of a MQ-8B in the frigate *McInerney* (FFG-8) followed. The ship was employed in counter-narcotics operations in the Eastern Pacific, culminating in the detection in April 2010 by an MQ-8B of a speedboat smuggling cocaine which was intercepted and arrested.

The MQ-8B forms a key part of the overall LCS package. Weapons – such as Hellfire missiles for attacking small fast vessels – and sensors can be changed rapidly to match a variety of different roles. The initial sensor fit comprises either the Brite Star II electro-optical/infrared camera system mounted in a turret under the aircraft's nose or a pod containing a voice/data communications relay system to extend the range of 'line-of-sight' communications between dispersed ships and aircraft. Alternative payloads

MQ-8B data

Rotor diameter: 8.4m
Length: 7.3m
Maximum launch weight: 1,430kg
Endurance: 8 hours.
Propulsion: Single Rolls-Royce 250-C20W shaft turbine. 450hp (340kw)
Maximum speed: 115 knots (210km/h)
Ceiling: 20,000ft (6,100m)

Whilst unmanned carrier strike operations are still some distance in the future, operation of unmanned rotorcraft from smaller vessels is already a reality. Northrop Grumman's MQ-8B Fire Scout has already been deployed operationally on the FFG-7 class frigate *McInerney* (FFG-8). *(Northrop Grumman)*

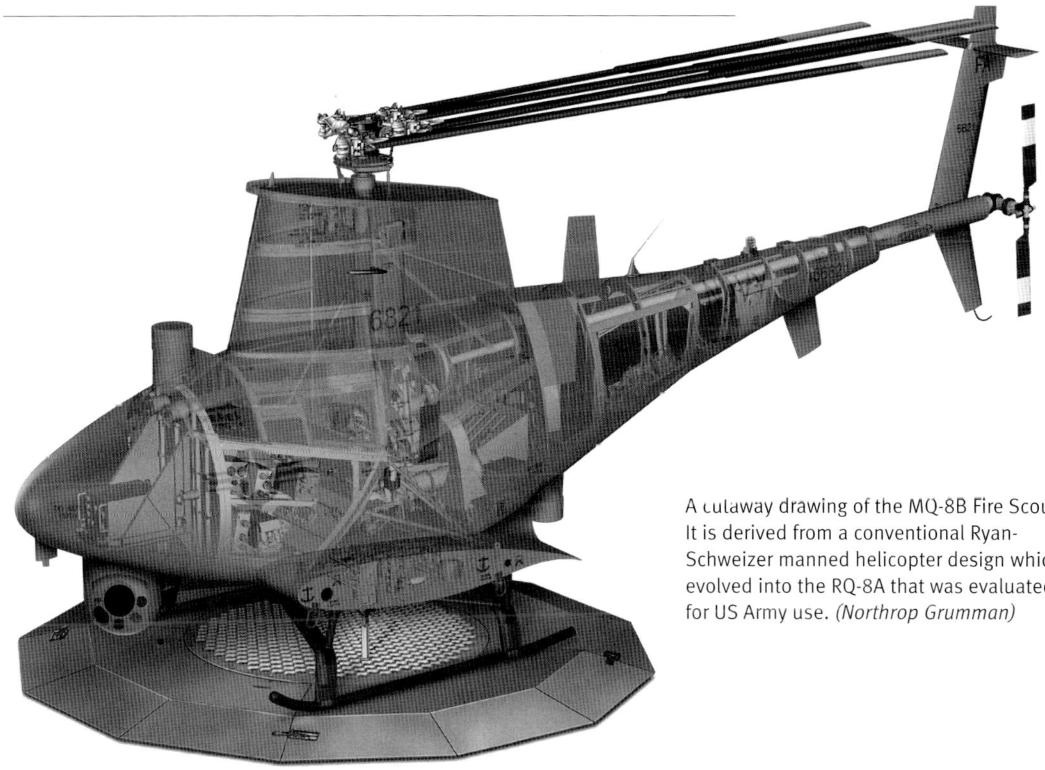

A cutaway drawing of the MQ-8B Fire Scout. It is derived from a conventional Ryan-Schweizer manned helicopter design which evolved into the RQ-8A that was evaluated for US Army use. *(Northrop Grumman)*

being developed include a SIGINT package; tactical synthetic aperture radar and a moving target indicator; sonobuoy delivery; a minefield detection system; and a countermeasures module.

The concept of operations is that the aviation detachment in each LCS will comprise a single MH-60R/S helicopter and a single MQ-8B. The latter will provide up to five hours on station at 100 nautical miles (185km) from the parent vessel allowing the human aircrew to concentrate their efforts into activities for which they are better suited. With its initial sensor fit and weapons, an MQ-8B is capable of surveillance, reconnaissance, over-the-horizon targeting, post-strike analysis and communications relay over a dispersed battle group and light strike against a fast-moving target. Since it is only required to fly on operational tasks, the MQ-8B will be the first UCAV to demonstrate the cost-savings associated with the new transformational UCAVs.[5]

NORTHROP GRUMMAN MQ-4C GLOBAL HAWK

The unmanned element of the USN BAMS system is the MQ-4C, a derivative of the US Air Force RQ-4B Global Hawk. Originally designated the RQ-4N, it is another example of the USN's cost-conscious approach and uses a proven airframe with a sensor outfit completely changed to match the aircraft's new maritime surveillance mission. Whilst the airframe closely resembles its Air Force cousin and has the same Rolls-Royce AE3007 engine, its operational profile is very different. The RQ-4B is designed to remain at high level throughout its mission but the MQ-4C will have to descend below cloud to use its electro-optical/IR cameras to identify individual ships if necessary. Icing could, therefore, be a problem and it has been fitted with sophisticated, commercial 'off-the-shelf' engine and airframe anti-icing systems similar to those fitted to the P-8A. The MQ-4C has the ability to remain airborne for long periods at peak efficiency and is intended to enhance a Fleet Commander's battle space awareness with imagery, multi-function radar and ESM transmitted continuously in real time using a variety of data links including Link 16. Coverage is to be world-wide and could potentially be sustained in the vicinity of a carrier battle group or amphibious ready group for its entire forward deployment. The USN intends to procure a minimum of forty-eight and potentially up to sixty-eight MQ-4Cs to fulfil this task.

Each MQ-4C will have a mission controller who will be able to move the air vehicle to a new area of interest if requested by a force commander. The type's most important sensor is the Northrop Grumman Multifunction Active Sensor (MFAS), active electronically scanned array radar that gives 360-degree track-while-scan coverage. It is capable of tracking hundreds of targets while carrying out multiple reconnaissances, even in high-density target areas such as the Straits of Malacca or the English Channel. Individual identification of targets tracked by MFAS can be made by using the electro-optical/Infrared cameras mounted in a turret under the aircraft's nose or by the sophisticated Sierra Nevada Merlin ESM system. This gives 360-degree coverage out to 300 nautical miles (555km) and has a 'library' of signatures enabling it to identify specific emitters and confirm target identification. BAMS is expected to offer radical improvements since, unlike legacy patrol aircraft which had to return to base for information to be downloaded, analysed and distributed, it can transmit continuous real-time information throughout the network-centric fleet. MQ-4C squadrons are expected to become operational from 2014, initially sharing the same bases as the P-8A fleet.

Germany has procured a version of the RQ-4B with European sensors and Australia has expressed an interest in the MQ-4C to complement its intended purchase of the P-8A. Other nations are monitoring USN progress and once BAMS becomes operational and has set new standards of efficiency and cost-consciousness, a number of export sales are likely.

Unmanned aerial vehicles are also being developed for land-based maritime surveillance. Northrop Grumman's MQ-4C Global Hawk is paired with Boeing's manned P-8A Poseidon in the US Navy's Broad Area Maritime Surveillance (BAMS) concept. *(Boeing)*

MQ-4C data

Span: 39.9m
Length: 14.5m
Maximum launch weight: 14,600kg
Endurance: 28 hours
Propulsion: Single Rolls-Royce AE3007. 7,000lbs (3,100kgf) of thrust
Maximum speed: 430 knots (800km/h). Loiter speed 330 knots (610km/h).
Ceiling: 56,500ft (17,200m)

OTHER SIGNIFICANT UCAV PROJECTS

Three other UCAV air vehicles with the potential to operate from aircraft carriers are in the early stages of development. In 2010 General Atomics proposed its projected turbo-jet powered Sea Avenger, based on the MQ-9 Predator C, to meet the US Navy UCLASS requirement. It represents a low-risk solution with an internal weapons bay capable of carrying the same weapons as the Predator B in service with the USAF. These include Hellfire missiles, Paveway III precision-guided bombs and Joint Direct Attack Munitions (JDAMs). Sensors could include the Lynx synthetic aperture radar and an electro-optical targeting system known as the Advanced Low-observable Embedded Reconnaissance Targeting system (ALERT), based on the system fitted in the F-35. The fuselage incorporates stealth characteristics but it requires a remote pilot to 'fly' it throughout its mission.

Another contender for UCLASS is the Boeing Phantom Ray derived from the X-45C, which originally formed part of the cancelled J-UCAS programme. A tailless delta, it is slightly smaller than the X-47 and the prototype is to undergo a test programme intended to demonstrate its ability to

Although the X-47B is seen as the lead contender for the UCLASS project, there are other potential contenders. These include General Atomics' Sea Avenger (above) and Boeing's Phantom Ray (top), both pictured here. *(General Atomics Aeronautical Systems / Boeing)*

Sea Avenger data

Span: 20.1m
Length: 13.4m
Maximum launch weight: Not available
Endurance: 20 hours; 22 hours with a fuel tank fitted in the weapons bay
Propulsion: Single Pratt & Whitney PW545B. 4,000lbs (1,800kgf) of thrust
Maximum speed: Over 400 knots (740km/h)
Ceiling: 50,000ft (15,200m)

Phantom Ray data

Span: 15.0m
Length: 11.9m
Maximum launch weight: 16,600kg
Endurance: Not stated. Combat radius is more than 1,300nm (2,400km)
Propulsion: Single General Electric F404-GE-102D. 11,000lbs (4,900kgf) of thrust
Maximum speed: 530 knots (980km/h)
Ceiling: 40,000ft (12,200m)

carry out a variety of missions including intelligence, surveillance and reconnaissance, suppression of enemy air defences, electronic attack, attacks on time-sensitive moving targets and autonomous air-to-air refuelling. Like the X-47 it will fly autonomous missions with minimal need for external control.

The Phantom Ray made its first test flight from Edwards Air Force Base on 27 April 2011.

Undoubtedly the United States leads the world in developing and bringing UCAVs into service but other nations have development projects. The BAE Systems Taranis, named after the Celtic god of thunder, is an interesting example that is due to fly and begin its development programme in 2012. A mock-up was displayed by BAE Systems at Farnborough in 2010, where it was described as an autonomous UCAV potentially capable of operating from *Queen Elizabeth* class aircraft carriers as well as land bases. Integrated System Technologies (Insyte) – now part of the Military Air and Information business – is developing command, control, communications, intelligence, surveillance, target acquisition and reconnaissance systems, although the number and type of sensors have yet to be finalised. BAE Systems Australia is developing the flight-control computing system. Like the X-47 it has two weapons bays but the airframe is smaller, about the size of a BAE Systems Hawk, with which its shares the same Adour engine. It is intended to be able to engage aircraft in flight with missiles, a claim that would represent a major step forward if confirmed by trials, as well as strike at targets on the sea or land. BAE Systems also claims that Taranis is the result of ten years' research and development into stealthy airframes, making it 'virtually invisible' to radar.

BAE Systems' Taranis is described as capable of carrier operations. About the size of a Hawk trainer, it is smaller than similar US-based projects. *(BAE Systems)*

Taranis data

Span: 11.4m
Length: 9.9m
Maximum launch weight: 5,500kg
Endurance: Compatible with 'intercontinental' range
Propulsion: Single Rolls-Royce Adour 951 turbofan. 6,500lbs (2,900kgf) of thrust
Ceiling: Not stated

Notes

1. Some commentators have surmised that the US Marine Corps' decision to operate the F-35C is essentially a hedge against outright cancellation of the STOVL 'B' variant. On 6 January 2011, US Defence Secretary Robert Gates announced that he was putting the F-35B on two-year probation because of significant testing difficulties, reducing planned short-term orders and threatening outright cancellation of the variant if performance, cost and scheduling could not be brought back on track. The results of the probationary period will also have significant implications for Italy and Spain, which are counting on the F-35B to sustain their fast-jet carrier operations when their existing Harriers are retired.

2. On 16 June 2011, as expected, Australia announced that the MH-60R had been selected for the new naval helicopter requirement under a contract worth over AS$3bn (US$3.2bn).

3. The initial two members of the *Mistral* class were ordered from DCN (now DCNS) in 2001 and delivered during 2006–7. Construction was shared between DCN's Brest yard and Chantiers de l'Atlantique at Saint Nazaire, which is now controlled by the European branch of Korea's STX group. A third ship, *Dixmude*, was ordered from STX in April 2009 and was floated out on the night of 17/18 December 2010. She should be delivered around the end of 2011. A fourth French ship is planned.

4. The Gyrodyne QH-50 DASH was a small, unmanned helicopter introduced during the 1960s as an anti-submarine weapon delivery system embarked primarily on the US Navy's modernised Second World War destroyers. High attrition rates caused by a combination of electronics failures and training deficiencies resulted in the type being withdrawn from USN service in 1970.

5. Recent reports suggest that the MQ-8B may be superseded by a MQ-8C model. This will incorporate the same software and sensors tested on the current rotorcraft but utilise a Bell 407 light helicopter airframe, doubling endurance and payload.

6. This chapter has been compiled from a wide range of international periodicals, of which *Air International*, *Flight*, *Jane's Defence Weekly*, *Warship World* and *The Navy* (the journal of the Navy League of Australia) provide particularly good sources of further reading. Reference should also be made to the following publications, as well as to the various websites maintained by relevant aircraft maufacturers and navies:

Gunter Endres and Michael J Gething, *Janes's Aircraft Recognition Guide- Fifth Edition* (London, Collins-Jane's, 2007).

Norman Friedman, *The Naval Institute Guide to World Naval Weapon Systems – Fifth Edition* (Annapolis, MD, Naval Institute Press, 2006).

Jane's Fighting Ships – Various Editions (Coulsdon, Surrey, Jane's Information Group).

Contributors

Juan Carlos Arancibia is a journalist based in Southern California, where he lives with his wife, Deb, and children, Alexis and Noah. He has spent most of his career working for business and finance publications, and has also written about Latin American military forces on a freelance basis. In 2007, he started writing a blog: Chile's Defense & Military (chiledefense. blogspot.com). Born in Chile, he immigrated to the United States with his parents and sister in 1974. He graduated in 1987 from California State University Long Beach with a bachelor's degree in political science.

Richard Beedall is a Senior Manager at Mazars Consulting in Ireland. Born in England, he served for fourteen years in the Royal Naval Reserve as a rating and later as an officer, often working with USN and local naval forces around the world. He has a long-standing interest in the Royal Navy and naval affairs in general, and is the founder of the *Navy Matters* website. He has written extensively on naval developments for many organisations and publications, including *AMI International*, *Naval Forces* and *Warships IFR*. He is married with two young daughters.

Edward H Feege is Senior Maritime Intelligence Analyst at Gryphon Technologies LC. He has more than twenty years' experience in maritime intelligence, strategic communications, and market research and reporting in support of a wide range of US government, maritime and other transportation industry customers. A graduate of the US Naval Academy, during his naval career he performed flight, maintenance, safety and operations duties for the USN airborne early warning community and was assistant division officer for the USN aviation manpower branch in the Office of the Chief of Naval Operations. Further qualifications include an MA in National Security Studies, Georgetown University, and MBA, George Mason University.

Norman Friedman is one of the best-known naval analysts and historians in the US and the author of over thirty-five books. He has written on broad issues of modern military interest, including an award-winning history of the Cold War, whilst in the field of warship development his greatest sustained achievement is probably an eight-volume series on the design of different US warship types. A specialist in the intersection of technology and national strategy, his acclaimed *Network-Centric Warfare* was published in 2009 by the US Naval Institute Press. The holder of a PhD in theoretical physics from Columbia, Dr Friedman is a regular guest commentator on television and lectures widely on professional defence issues.

Ross Gillett joined the RAN Reserve in 1982, serving on full-time duties for five years. He completed his career with the RAN as the Senior Public Affairs Officer at Garden Island, Sydney. Ross has edited three Australian magazines, *The Navy* (1978–99), *Australian Sea Heritage* (1986–8) and – currently – *Australian Warship* since early 2011. He has authored fifteen major nautical books and edited ten others. He has also written extensively for other Australian and international naval magazines. He is now a full-time author/editor, working on his sixteenth naval book. Ross who lives with his wife in Sydney, New South Wales, also serves as volunteer guide for the Naval Historical Society around the historic Garden Island Naval Dockyard.

David Hobbs is a well-known author and naval historian. He has written eight books and co-authored eight more. He writes for several journals and magazines and in 2005 won the Aerospace Journalist of the Year, Best Defence Submission. He lectures on naval subjects worldwide and has been on radio and TV in several countries. He served in the Royal Navy from 1964 until 1997 and retired with the rank of Commander. He qualified as both a fixed and rotary-wing pilot and his log book contains 2,300 hours with over 800 carrier landings, 150 of which were at night.

Mrityunjoy Mazumdar, whose father served in the Indian Navy, has been writing on naval matters since 1999. His words and pictures have appeared in many naval and aircraft publications including several of the *Jane's* family, *Ships of the World* and the RINA's *Warship Technology*. He is also a regular contributor to several naval annuals including *Combat Fleets of the World*, *Flottes de Combat*, *Jane's Fighting Ships*, *Seaforth World Naval Review* and *Weyers Flotten Taschenbuch*. Besides his writing, he maintains a comprehensive website on the Indian Navy at www.bharat-rakshak.com. Mr Mazumdar lives in Alameda, California with his wife.

Guy Toremans is a Belgian-based freelance maritime correspondent and member of the Association of Belgian & Foreign Journalists, an association accredited by NATO and the UN. His reports, ship profiles and interviews are published in the English language naval magazines *Jane's Navy International*, *Naval Forces* and *Warships IFR*, as well as in the French *Marines & Forces Navales*, the Japanese *J-Ships* and the Spanish *Fuerza Naval*. Since 1990, he has regularly embarked on on a wide range of NATO, Asian and South African warships, most notably the aircraft carriers *George Washington*, *Harry S. Truman* and *Ronald Reagan* whilst they were deployed in the US Navy's Fifth Fleet's area of operations.

Scott C Truver is Director, National Security Programs, at Gryphon Technologies LC, specialising in national and homeland security, and naval and maritime strategies, programmes and operations. Since 1972, Dr. Truver has participated in numerous studies and assessments – most notably supporting the inter-agency task-force drafting the US *National Strategy for Maritime Security* (2005) – and has also written extensively for US and foreign publications. He has lectured at the US Naval Academy, Naval War College and Naval Postgraduate School, among other venues. Further qualifications include a PhD in Marine Policy Studies and a MA in Political Science/International Relations from the University of Delaware.

Conrad Waters is a lawyer by training but a banker by profession. He was educated at Liverpool University prior to being called to the bar at Gray's Inn in 1989. His interest in maritime affairs was stimulated by a long family history of officers in merchant navy service and he has been writing articles on maritime affairs for over twenty years. This included six years producing the 'World Navies in Review' chapter of the influential annual *Warship*. When not acting as Head of Credit Analysis at the European arm of one of the world's largest banks, Conrad lives with wife Susan and children Emma, Alexander and Imogen in Haslemere, Surrey.

INDEX

Page numbers in *italics* indicate illustrations

Jacket image credits:
Front, main: *Härnösand*, Sweden *(Guy Toremans)*; **top:** *Simpson*, USA *(Conrad Waters)*; F-35C, USA *(USN)*; *Independencia*, Mexico *(Mexican Navy)*; *Dechaineux* & *Waller*, Australia *(RAN)*
Back, left from top: *Akizuki*, Japan *(JMSDF)*; 'Castle' Class, Bangladesh *(A&P Tyne)*; *Arlington*, USA *(Huntington Ingalls Industries)*; **right:** *Nicolas Bravo*, Mexico *(USN)*

MAGNUM LEGACY / INGE MORATH

INGE MORATH

AN ILLUSTRATED BIOGRAPHY / LINDA GORDON

Magnum Foundation

Prestel Munich • London • New York

The Magnum Foundation's Legacy Program preserves and makes accessible materials related to Magnum Photos and the larger history of photography to which it has uniquely contributed. This series explores the creative process of Magnum photographers, from the agency's founders to its contemporary members, through a mix of biographical text, archival materials, and iconic imagery.

Managing Editor: Andrew E. Lewin
Series Editor: Carole Naggar

FRONTISPIECE

1. Inge Morath at 8 Rue de la Chaise, Paris, 1959. Photo by Henri Cartier-Bresson

CONTENTS

FOREWORD

Inge Morath is remembered for her pictures of people—sensitive, humorous, and elegant images that capture an international intelligentsia of postwar Europe and America. Just as fascinating, though, is the story of her own life and how she used photography as a passport to worlds conventionally closed to women.

Born in Austria in 1923, Inge Morath was marked by a childhood in Nazi Germany, World War II, and a harrowing escape from 1945 Berlin. She barely survived, yet was able to reinvent a life for herself, showing a remarkable determination and joie de vivre in postwar Vienna, where she became part of a network of avant-garde artists and intellectuals. Then, together with her friend and colleague photographer Ernst Haas, she arrived in Paris in 1949 as a journalist and soon became part of Magnum's community of leftist, bohemian, often Jewish photographers. Inspired by them, she became a professional photographer whose career would span some fifty years.

One of the first two women to become a full member of the renowned Magnum photographers collective, Morath traveled in Europe with Henri Cartier-Bresson and worked closely with Robert Capa until his death in 1954. When she moved to the United States after a decade of being based out of Paris, she served as an important bridge between Magnum's founding members and its New York branch.

The still relatively new profession of photoreportage was dominated by men, but there was opportunity for a convention-defying woman like Morath to use it to carve her own path. She was remarkable in her willingness to travel to places where a female traveler would stand out and might be vulnerable. Before embarking on any reportage, she studied in depth that country's language and culture (she was fluent in eight languages). She also was a prolific and elegant writer. Traveling alone, she displayed an adventurousness and ambition that challenged what was proper for women at that time. Perhaps drawing on her wartime experiences, she was able to live and work and even thrive in conditions of hardship. Later, as a working mother married to another famous artist, she worked to define her own autonomous creative identity.

She was above all interested in others, always eager to learn what she did not know. This shows in her portraiture and in her focus on the ordinary in unfamiliar cultures. Her images consistently display a respect for others—no matter how unfamiliar the culture, she was able to bond with famous artists, illiterate Chinese peasants, Iranian villagers, and Russian intellectuals.

We are grateful that historian Linda Gordon brought her deep knowledge of postwar women's history and photography to bear on Morath's extraordinary life. This series of biographies of Magnum photographers looks at the lives behind the photographs, and we cannot imagine a more thoughtful, rigorous, and nuanced portrait of this extraordinary figure.

Andrew E. Lewin
Managing Editor, Magnum Legacy series

Chapter One

FORGED BY WAR

We are all shaped by history, but Inge Morath more than most. Her hideous experiences as a teenager in Nazi Germany marked her permanently. Every cell of her body and spirit was tried—in the furnace of affliction, as the prophet Isaiah put it. But Inge was born with a sturdy and adventurous temperament, and her forebears gave her unusual confidence. Her resilience was extraordinary, and everyone who knew her remembers her upbeat spirit and capacity for fun. Still, a darkness remained, visible to her intimates.

Graz, where Ingeborg Hermine Mörath was born in 1923, was at the time second only to Vienna as the cultural center of Austria. Home to a great university and to fine medieval and Renaissance buildings, Graz had been kind to her ancestors: both her mother and father descended from renowned and wealthy members of its German-speaking *haute bourgeoisie*. "My family came from a long Austrian line and tradition in which I always felt secure," she recollected.[1]

In fact, she was not only of Austrian ethnicity. Her mother, Mathilde, née Wiesler, came from Slovenia, then the Duchy of Lower Styria in the Austro-Hungarian empire. National borders were by no means taken as natural or eternal in these areas. In this region, even after the dissolution of the empires into nation-states, borders were anything but fixed; after World War I, much of the area became part of Yugoslavia, later part of the Nazi Third Reich. This borderland heritage helps explain how Morath became so fully cosmopolitan.

Her mother, Mathilde, came from an intellectual family. Distinguished men such as poet Ernst Goll and composer Hugo Wolf were regular visitors. She attended university in Graz where she participated in the *Wandervogel*, a popular movement in which German youth hiked, camped, played guitars, and sang. On one such excursion she met "a very handsome young man," a German student at the Technische Hochschule. By then Edgar Mörath was already a highly decorated World War I pilot who had been wounded in action four times. The two married in 1921, but not before making a remarkable decision—they both converted from their native Catholicism to Protestantism, so that they would be able

2. Inge Mörath, Salzburg, Austria, 1939, photographer unknown

3. Inge's mother, Mathilde (Titti), with microscope, year and photographer unknown

to divorce if necessary. This decision tells us much about Mathilde's unconventional mind-set, and about the relatively minor weight the Möraths placed on religion.

Both Inge's parents were working scientists, and if that wasn't unusual enough for a woman at the time, both of Inge's grandmothers were also educated and unconventional: one an accomplished musician and owner of Picasso drawings, the other a feminist, spiritualist, novelist, and champion bridge player. Edgar worked first in his family's chemical factory, and Mathilde in a veterinary laboratory. Ambitious and inventive, he pursued a series of engineering positions in chemical manufacturing and thus moved his family many times. It was left to Mathilde to make do with what positions she could get, but she was never without some scientific work of her own. Titti, as she was always called, used a state-of-the-art Contax camera in her laboratory, making photographic slides through a microscope, which Edgar used in his lectures (fig. 3). She corrected his papers, but also found time to write her own. She was a fashionista but also a competitive fencer and a free and athletic spirit.[2] Inge recalled a sports competition at her brother Werner's school, where the mothers in attendance wore "sensible shoes, skirts, and blouses," while Mathilde ran around the playing field in a long white organdy dress flying a red kite to celebrate her son's win. She had a "big cloud of curly hair" that she never attempted to tame, gave elegant dinner parties, and traveled frequently to Paris, returning each time with stylish new clothes and perfume. As Inge put it, "She let admirers adore her from a safe distance." Once, after the war, when food was scarce, she sent Inge a care package consisting of a bouquet of snow roses, rather than practical necessities like the food and clothing her friends received. "Titti was sure that I could always find a piece of bread, so she sent me poetry instead."

The intellectualism, connoisseurship, and bohemianism of Inge's female forebears were by no means disreputable qualities among bourgeois women in urban Mitteleuropa.[3] Titti's unconventional approach to child-rearing shows in a surviving photograph: on a beach, she is holding the hand of three-year-old Inge, already tall for her age, naked, with her back to the camera; little Inge had not wanted her picture taken,[4] and Titti was not one to force her daughter into proper behavior (fig. 4).

It was a happy childhood. Inge's imperturbable temperament appears in her memories of contentment despite having been moved frequently around Europe—she changed schools ten times. From Graz they moved to Freiburg, Germany, where her younger brother Werner was born, then to Munich; then came a few years, fondly recalled, in the German countryside near Eberswalde, northeast of Berlin, where the children could play in their large courtyard, climbing on machinery, chasing the chickens and geese. In 1928 they moved to Schirmeck in Alsace, France, near Strasbourg. There they lived in the Villa Isemann, enjoying its grand French garden. Then they relocated to nearby Wisches, also in Alsace. In these years the children were schooled in French, and Inge, because she didn't know the language, was at first placed at the back of the class. But she was "determined to sit in first place, just to show them," she later recalled,[5] an early sign of her ambition. Not only were the languages different, she was "learning totally different views of the same events." This childhood pan-Europeanism contributed to Möraths unusual facility with languages as an adult.

Sometime after 1930, they moved to Darmstadt, Germany, known as a city of science because of its renowned technical university. There Edgar took up a chair professorship and Titti worked as his assistant. A fan of art deco, she no doubt took in the art movement known as Jugendstil (the German version of art nouveau), centered in Darmstadt. Also an aficionada of ballet, she took in dancers as lodgers, and they gave Inge lessons—which may have contributed to her athleticism and later love for yoga.

For the Möraths, life was good and the Nazi regime that took over in 1933 made it better. They credited it for easing the economic depression. Their wealth increased. Edgar took up flying, Mathilde took up fencing. They bought a car, the first in their neighborhood. The children were such good students that they skipped a year of school. Every Sunday morning at eleven, university professors and upper-level employees made courtesy calls, addressing Edgar as Herr Direktor.[6] The Möraths gave fancy-dress parties—with hors d'oeuvres so artistically arranged that Inge feared to take one—attended by Darmstadt's artistic elite and foreign visitors.

Wherever they lived, theirs was a cosmopolitan household, Morath* later recalled, full of students, scientists, artists, and "people of different races . . . Hindus with many spices." Though Edgar Mörath cheered the Nazi seizure of Austria and Czechoslovakia—his prideful nationalism gratified by this alleged uniting of the German peoples—he and his wife did not share in Nazi anti-Semitism, and many of the artists and intellectuals

4. Inge and her mother on the beach, 1926. Photo by J. Haselsberger

they admired and befriended were Jews.[7] One of Inge's uncles was married to a Jew (he sent her to Switzerland). And Inge resisted the growing anti-Semitism: she recalled a Jewish girl in her school who "suddenly showed up with a yellow star . . . But then we all said, we should be showing solidarity with her."[8]

Inge had long loved to look at paintings: "reproductions of Arnold Böcklin and Anselm Feuerbach played enigmatically on my imagination." This would continue throughout her life, as the fine arts, especially painting, underlay the strong sense of composition that would become a core aspect of her photography. Always a reader and a connoisseur of fine art, she became a photographer whose work was deeply influenced by her literary and artistic erudition. But in her teenage years, photography did not interest Inge, because, she recalled, what she saw of photography in the Nazi years was only propaganda.[9] Its contrast with the art she viewed in museums probably contributed to her ambivalence about photography as an art form.[10] It was only after she was exposed to the great photography of Magnum's founding members, such as Robert Capa and Henri Cartier-Bresson, that she saw—and embraced—the medium's power and beauty.

In 1937 Mathilde took Inge to see the famed *Degenerate Art* (*Entartete Kunst*) exhibition, organized by Adolf Ziegler, head of the Reich Chamber of Visual Art. This exhibition contrasted modern art, labeled Jewish and/or Bolshevik art, to the sentimental, heroicized nationalist imagery of official Nazi art. But like many visitors, Inge was attracted to precisely what the Nazis reviled. She lingered over works by Marc Chagall, Paul Klee, Emil Nolde, and Wassily Kandinsky. She fell in love with Franz Marc's *The Large Blue Horses* (1911), and recalled staring at it long enough to "remember it in all its details." "We were supposed to say that it was terrible but I just said nothing, and I learned by heart those paintings that I wanted to remember. I went home and I drew the compositions and then threw them out. So I memorized paintings."[11] The captions on the walls that told viewers what to think about this "Jewish" unconventional art were appalling, she recalled: "Revelation of the Jewish Racial Soul"; "The Ideal—Cretin and Whore"; "Deliberate Sabotage of National Defense." It made the exhibition look like a "tunnel of horror." Mathilde, long interested in modern art, rejected the Nazi condemnations entirely. But the chill was felt: in the Mörath household, the jazz records disappeared, and books once in front on the shelves were moved to the back.[12]

In 1938 the family moved to Berlin. Edgar took a position running a major wood chemistry research institute, where Titti was again his assistant. Berlin was "a swinging town," Werner thought,[13] presumably in contrast to the smaller, less sophisticated places they had lived before. The Möraths all assumed that Germany would win the war. As pan-Germanists and revanchists they saw the Anschluss as the re-creation of the Holy Roman Empire of German Nations.[14] The Treaty of Versailles was redressed. Edgar reenlisted in the Air Force Reserve as a captain.

For Inge there was still breathing room. Now sixteen, she attended the Luisenschule, a high school identified as "humanist," even though it meant spending two hours a day biking there, because her mother had "fallen in love with a house outside the city . . . in a big garden."

*Inge Mörath later changed the spelling of her name to Morath, to make it easier for non-German speakers to pronounce. I do the same: Mörath when referring to the earlier years, and Morath to the years after this change. Additionally, I use Inge when discussing her as a child or in personal relations, and Mörath or Morath when speaking of her as a photographer.

5. Titti and Edgar on Titti's birthday. Captioned on back "The birthday kiss, October 13, 1962," photographer unknown

But they soon bought a big house in Berlin-Wilmersdorf. After graduating, Inge planned to go directly to university to study Romance languages, but because she had skipped a year of school, she was too young to be admitted.[15] From there her life grew steadily worse. She herself wrote, in characteristic understatement, decades later, "The new order of the Nazi regime drew a heavy curtain over my childhood."[16]

That curtain never entirely opened. In 2001, the year before she died, she visited her hometown with her brother Werner and husband Arthur Miller. When her childhood best friend, Renate, whose father had been an SS man, initiated a discussion about their parents' politics, Inge responded, "My mother Titti never liked the Nazis." Werner, however, challenged her. "I see it differently. It was only as the war progressed and was progressively lost that our mother began to rail at the national comrades," specifically because four nephews had been killed in action. He denied that they knew about the annihilation of Jews and other "undesirables." Yet Inge's grandfather had been a surveyor for the Third Reich's expansion to the east, and her father held a high position in the forestry institute. Renate recalled that Inge herself had worked as a translator for the Nazi foreign ministry. Renate had married Imo Moszkowicz, a Jewish concentration camp survivor whose mother and six brothers had died in the camps. He remarked that Renate needed to testify to her parents' guilt "in order to be able to breathe freely herself," and that it pained him that "his friend Inge still has difficulties talking openly about these dark times."[17] In a letter to Inge written shortly after the visit, he compared the two old friends in a phrase that further illuminates this contrast: "the one [Renate] a fervent noncomformist, the other an habitually charming tactician and avoider of conflict."[18]

If Morath had unconsciously reshaped memories

of her parents' attitudes toward the Nazis, doing so expressed love and intimacy. Despite their different paths, geographic and political, the family remained extremely close. As Inge began to share the leftist views of her new postwar friends, Titti was comfortable with that change. She would later spend months at a time living with her daughter, granddaughter, and Jewish leftist son-in-law. A three-generation line of intellectual, unconventional women lay behind Inge's personality and strength—a line that extended to four generations with her daughter, Rebecca Miller.

The Nazi *Arbeiteinsatz* (labor mobilization) program assigned civilians to work for the war effort, and to replace men drafted into the armed forces. Inge was first assigned to a "public social program," in this case to a working-class kindergarten. She found her six months there reasonably agreeable, but her next assignment was miserable. Drafted into the Arbeitsdienst, she was sent to a tiny village in East Prussia, Groß Borken, population about three hundred. There her jobs included milking cows, mowing with a sickle, cleaning pigsties, and pulling the sprouts out of old potatoes while kicking away the mice in the cellars. The farmers distrusted and abused the city girls placed there. The matrons who supervised the girls in their barracks were "bitter women who had it in for 'intellectuals,'" a label they applied to anyone who intended to go to university, and gave them the worst jobs. Inge and her one friend, the only other girl "of this kind," were the ones designated to clean the toilets and privies. The work was supposed to bring them "close to Mother Earth."

6. Inge's brother, Werner, after he joined the air force, 1940, photographer unknown

She returned to a radically different Berlin.[19] Her brother, Werner, had joined the Luftwaffe (fig. 6), and Edgar was flying transport planes all over Europe. In his absence, Titti herself took over the institute (which she ran with "unrelenting" efficiency until it was destroyed by bombing in 1944). In 1943 Edgar "came home with fresh glory . . . adding a second row of medals, an authentic hero," in Titti's words. Four of Inge's cousins were soon killed. Werner was captured by British forces and spent two years in a POW camp in Egypt. Air raids grew in number and severity. Still, Inge managed to enroll at the university with a specialty in Foreign Studies (perhaps a sign of her distaste for Nazi Germany and a yearning for a worldliness that would later become part of her).

Thanks to her family's Nazi connections, she spent a semester in Bucharest where a 1940 coup had installed a Nazi government. But she declined to join the Nazi party when invited, and had a poor attendance record at Nazi rallies.[20] As a result, she was called in for interrogation (by what agency she didn't say), no doubt a terrifying experience. But she put on a show of naïveté and successfully escaped punishment. When she returned to Berlin, she managed to get admitted to the university "in spite of my not exactly flattering Arbeitsdienst certificate." There, as in Romania, she refused to join the Studentenschaft, the student organization now merged with the Nationalsozialistischer Deutscher Studentenbund (National Socialist Student League); when pro-Nazi Professor Pfeffer encountered her later, he snarled, "'We'll get you yet.'" Many years later, when she ran into him on a visit to Germany with Arthur Miller, he asked her to help him get his book published![21]

Meanwhile, conditions in Berlin were rapidly deteriorating. Fresh food was scarce. Fuel for heating was in such short supply that Inge and her mother often slept in one bed to keep warm, saving the coal for cooking. After one Allied bombing raid, Titti and Inge emerged from a shelter to find their house destroyed, its front wall collapsed, leaving "rooms open to the street like those of a doll's house." In a bizarre stroke of fortune, a small red vase of handblown Venetian glass survived intact. Her parents treasured it, and had forbidden the children to touch it, so it was the essence of fragility to Inge; when she saw it now, its ruby glass reflected the flames engulfing Berlin. In a response reminiscent of Titti sending roses instead of food, Inge saw it as an omen that they were "meant to survive."[22] They went upstairs and lay down on the bed to sleep, a bed now entirely in the open. Afterward, Titti fled to Salzburg and she remained in Berlin alone.

By now she had been conscripted to work in a factory producing airplane parts for Lufthansa, near Tempelhof Airport. Most of the other workers were Ukrainian women prisoners. As a military target, the factory was repeatedly bombed, and the work became intermittent and chaotic. Soon rumors warned that the Russian army was approaching. Berlin was in flames. During one air raid in April 1945, Inge decided to join a fleeing exodus of workers. A soldier gave her a salami. She stuck it in her backpack and started walking, intent on reaching Salzburg, a distance of 732 kilometers (455 miles).

She walked among retreating soldiers, fleeing soldiers, refugees coming from the east, refugees heading to the east, and advancing Russians. They all slept in fields. She saved the salami for a long time and then someone stole it in the night. Sometimes she clung to the side of a train, jumping off and "lying flat on the ground to avoid being hit by low-flying spitfires,"[23] her backpack shielding her head. Then she was up and walking again. A woman carried a dead child in her arms. "Dead horses look huge, so bloated. Dead people look small." No place to wash. "The crust between my legs grew painful." Her toes were covered with blisters. At one point, she contemplated jumping into a river to drown herself. Luckily a soldier with a wooden peg leg pulled her down from the bridge railing. As it happened, he was also going to Salzburg. They walked together and arrived, it seemed to her, on just about the last day of the war, but by then she had lost all sense of how long she had been on the road.[24]

Even then, there was no end. The insults to her body and spirit had shut down her memory, and she couldn't recall where her parents lived. She spent several nights with crowds on the floor of the Salzburg railway station.

The peg-leg man walked with her through the city, searching for her family's home, until, when she was on the edge of despair, he took her to the wealthy part of the city where she finally recognized their wartime abode—the baroque Emsburg castle. Amid her exhaustion and relief, peg-leg man—her savior—disappeared and she never saw him again.[25] Once with her parents, she immediately fell ill. A doctor thought she needed her tonsils removed, but he did "a rather butchery job." She bled for days. It took her weeks to recover—from the surgery, the trek, the Nazi years as a whole. Had she not left Berlin when she did, just before the last bridge was blown out, she recalled, she might not have survived. Still, this survival rested as much on steely determination as on lucky timing.

She was in Salzburg on May 4, 1945, when the US Army rolled in. She remembered the Rainbow Division of the US Army National Guard because some of them quartered with the Möraths. The American soldiers introduced the family to peanut butter, of particular value in restoring Inge's health; the rest of their sustenance required waiting in long queues at soup kitchens. She emerged with a permanent disability: having been hungry for so long, her digestion lost some of its powers. She could not digest fats at all, and intermittent stomach pain plagued her throughout her life. Always thin, she ate mainly vegetables, fruit, a bit of fish, sometimes rice, sometimes bread, almost never meat. (It was not a delicate "ladylike" diet; her daughter remarked that she could make a salad big enough to fill a washbasin and then eat half of it.)[26] Such were Inge's invisible scars of war.

In a sign of improving health, she was soon experiencing erotic moments and wrote about one, distancing herself by writing in the third person. A man she had known from childhood came in to her parents' Salzburg home. He was older, "very handsome and known for various love affairs. . . . She saw that he did not look at her any more as a child, there was something liquid in his eyes, aggressive and tender, it was the first time she saw a man's eyes like this. Now he said, you are beautiful, and he carefully lifted a finger and softly drew the outline of her mouth as if to remember it . . . Her mouth started to burn as if outlined in fire. . . ."[27] That reaction, not of fear but of pleasure, signaled her renewed spirit and capacity for joy.

By 1946 Inge needed something to do. She envisioned returning to a university to study philosophy. Her father thought she would be better off working and found an ad from the United States Information Service (USIS) seeking translators. She doubted that her English was good enough but applied anyway, and got hired. "Maybe my English was not so good, but I could write a text and I was young and pretty."

Working for the US occupying forces brought privileges—good food and an opportunity to become familiar with American journalism. *Life* magazine, for example, arrived weekly. She translated into German features on American life, politics, and culture—the details of which were often astonishing to her. She also searched out photographs to accompany the pieces (fig. 7).

When the US Information Service Features Section moved from Salzburg to Vienna, Inge went along. The USIS put her up with coworker Irmgard Walter on the fourth floor of the large home of a Nazi leader, near the beautiful Strudlhof Steps, with its fountain and "magic winding marble sweep of stairs which became my favorite shortcut." (Thirty-five years later she photographed this lovely stairway [fig. 8]). Vienna was "euphoria," she wrote, especially "for young people no longer marching in step . . . everything possible, we were like prisoners

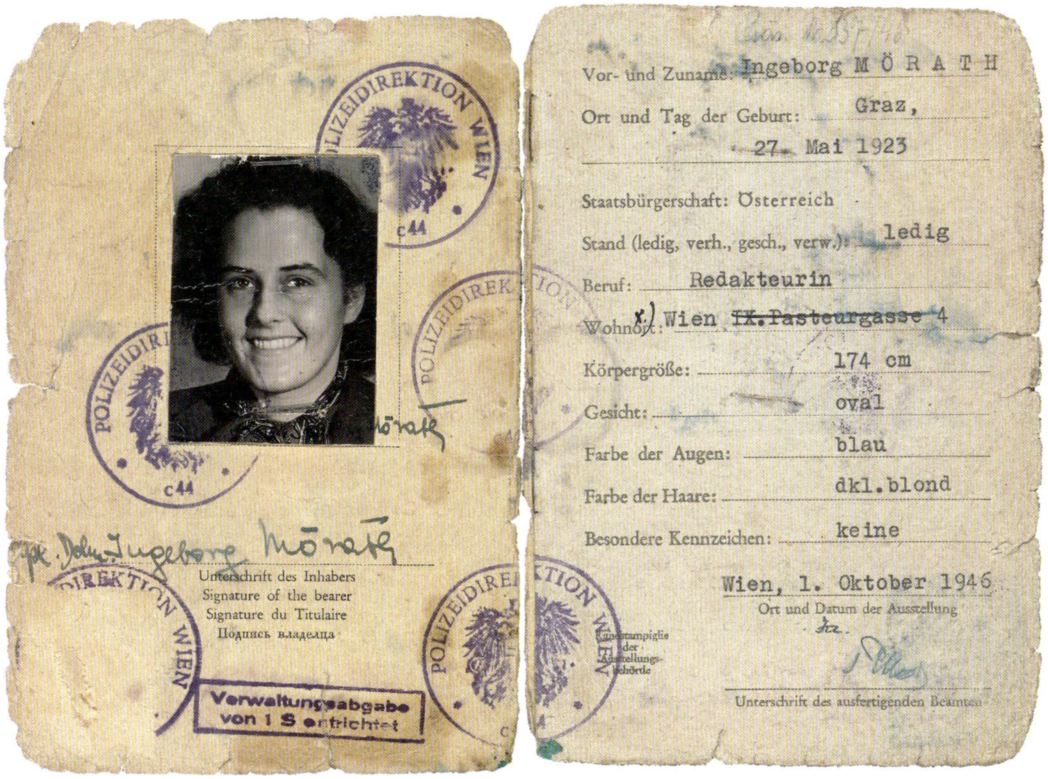

POLIZEIDIREKTION WIEN

Unterschrift des Inhabers
Signature of the bearer
Signature du Titulaire
Подпись владельца

Verwaltungsabgabe von 1 S entrichtet

Vor- und Zuname: Ingeborg MÖRATH
Ort und Tag der Geburt: Graz, 27. Mai 1923
Staatsbürgerschaft: Österreich
Stand (ledig, verh., gesch., verw.): ledig
Beruf: Redakteurin
Wohnort: Wien ~~IX. Pasteurgasse 4~~
Körpergröße: 174 cm
Gesicht: oval
Farbe der Augen: blau
Farbe der Haare: dkl.blond
Besondere Kennzeichen: keine

Wien, 1. Oktober 1946
Ort und Datum der Ausstellung

Unterschrift des ausfertigenden Beamten

7. Inge's Austrian identity card, 1946

freed."[28] "Irmi and I decided to paint our fingernails in red, to show up today very sinful."[29] In later recollections, Morath never commented explicitly on her attitude toward Nazi ideology, or on any other political matter, but there is no mistaking her elation at being liberated from Nazi censorship.

That rebirth shows in the way her later memories of postwar Vienna whited out its devastation. True, Vienna had not suffered the degree of destruction inflicted on Hamburg or Dresden, but she was still living amid a million cubic meters of rubble, three thousand bomb craters, and uncountable homeless. Those lucky enough to have housing were often without heat. Inge asked for her mother's fur coat to wear indoors. Potatoes froze in her kitchen. Thousands searched for lost family members. Electricity blackouts were routine. Bombing had killed most of the zoo's animals. The opera house, the Burgtheater, St. Stephen's Cathedral, and many other public buildings were destroyed or severely damaged (fig. 9). The extent of wartime destruction and hardships in Vienna appeared only occasionally in her many letters to her parents. "The Second World War had been over for four years but its dark cloud of terror and human suffering still hung heavy over us. The smell of burned houses is carried even by spring breezes." More often she kept her complaints light. "A tasty meal out of food cans, with terrible amounts of tea with rum." (Apparently liquor was not in short supply.) She instructed her mother to give up on darning her blouses that were beyond repair.[30]

But for the young Inge, Vienna was not only a place of liberation, it was also a social whirl. "Coffee and even more cognac" at Ibach's coffeehouse. A costume party at Frau Roth's house, which she attended dressed

as a "*schlurf*," "a swing kid with long hair and nonconformist attitude"—a term also applied to "hippies" of 1960s Germany. "The season has started," she wrote, referring to holiday season 1948, "and you can't slip out of it if you don't want to be a stubborn outsider. This is how, in addition to spiritual and alcoholic joys, I can line up a nice dinner for myself." She asked her mother to send her black evening dress because the "first Viennese balls" were about to start. She frequently recounted partying until the wee hours, then sleeping for an hour before heading off for work.[31]

The happier and the more effervescent she became, the more she attracted others. For five years her energy had paid off in the tender of mere survival; now it produced a sparkling, bohemian social life. Groups of friends talked art and ideas endlessly, wherever there was a place to do so, in cafés and, often, in the house of a "wonderful woman, a painter, Hilde Polsterer . . . She lived on the fourth floor . . . and someone had to accompany leaving guests to open and close the house door . . . a lot of kissing was going on on those trips down the stairs." For a time, Inge shared an apartment with her childhood friend Renate, who remembered that "Inge was such a ravishing beauty that she had everyone at her feet. . . . Inge was just amassing marriage proposals."[32]

Vienna's literary/artistic/intellectual sphere became Mörath's scene. She sat for a portrait by painter Julius Mahainz. She socialized with the members of Gruppe 47, a now legendary literary circle that included Hans Weigel, a major Austrian Jewish critic just returned

8. The Strudlhof Steps, made famous by Heimito von Doderer's novel, which has its name as its title, Vienna, 1980

9. Ruins of the Philipshof in Albertinaplatz after a wartime bomb raid in which more than one hundred people died in the shelter, Vienna, 1948. Photo by Erich Lessing

from exile in Switzerland, and whose manuscripts she typed without compensation; poet Ingeborg Bachmann; Austrian Jewish writer Ilse Aichinger, who had survived a slave labor camp. Philosopher Arnold Keyserling, whom her family had known in Darmstadt, introduced her into "the mysteries of Oriental wisdom and Yoga" (the latter becoming a lifelong pastime). She attended lectures at the Forum Alpbach, a network of pan-European anti-Nazi intellectuals including such luminaries as Theodor Adorno, Ralf Dahrendorf, and Max Horkheimer. She met Viktor Frankl, an "existential analyst," and attended his lectures.[33] Prince Josef Schwarzenberg III, of ancient Austrian nobility and one of her boyfriends, introduced her to concerts at the Musikverein, a concert hall that was home to the Vienna Philharmonic.[34] She saw Sartre's *Huis Clos* (*No Exit*) "performed by special permit of the Archbishop." She was a regular at the famous Theater in der Josefstadt, where she saw plays by Brecht and Saroyan and partied with the theater director Rudolf Steinboeck.[35] And at the museums "I never could . . . see enough of painting." As fast as Vienna could revive its modernist culture, Mörath was absorbing it. She was drunk on it, fizzing with energy. What she had only been able to glimpse in the *Degenerate Art* exhibition now surrounded her, transforming her ideas of what art could be.

Vienna's culture helped her think critically about her parents' German nationalism, and recognize the attitudinal difference between them. Referring to the modernist artistic culture she imbibed there, she remarked fifty years later, "These were things my father would have rejected anyway," the "anyway" meaning, even if there had been no Nazi regime. By contrast, she wrote, "Titti took it all in stride, elementary, like nature . . . *ohne kritik*" [without criticism].[36]

Mörath was soon fluent in English—her fourth language—and devoured the American magazines, including the *New Yorker*.[37] Postwar chaos created endless opportunities for ambitious and talented newcomers, at least for those free of previous ideological ties (the Americans were as unsympathetic to former Communists as they were to former Nazis). She began to pitch her own stories to the weekly *Heute*, the propaganda magazine of the US occupation forces in Germany, and then used the connection to help her friends, like when she wrote a piece on the theater that featured her friend, actress Nelly Dreyfuss, a Jew who, Mörath wrote, had been sentenced to death by the Gestapo.[38] She became an active freelancer. She sent articles to daily newspapers such as *Salzburger Nachrichten* and *Wiener Ilustrierte*, and wrote skits for the Austrian radio station Rot-Weiß-Rot (Red-White-Red, the colors of the Austrian flag).

In a remarkably brief span of time Mörath had become a successful journalist. *Der Optimist*, a small literary weekly, offered her a staff position, which she accepted. She wrote stories and reviews, learned about typesetting and layout, placed illustrations. The publication soon folded, but in early 1948 a better job came her way. *Heute* wanted an Austrian editor for photographs and stories. She felt ignorant of photography, but agreed to an interview. Editor Warren Trabant, an American, presented her with a stack of photographs and asked her to pick the ones she liked and tell him why. She passed the test. She concluded that her "painterly education" helped her recognize good composition. Trabant hired her on the spot, then took her to lunch at the Bristol, Vienna's most luxurious hotel, open only to Allied Forces. She ate shrimp in a basket with French fries and ketchup and a Coke. She was ready to be loyal to American propaganda imperatives (fig. 10).

In hindsight, it would be easy to assume that her "painterly education," combined with her experiences researching photographs for print media, destined her to become a photographer. But as a historian looking at her trajectory, and as a biographer striving to be faithful to her life, I have to imagine it with foresight instead of hindsight—that is, to look at what seemed likely in 1948, not to look back from, say, 1970. A full-fledged journalist by 1948, Mörath remained a writer for the rest of her life. She wrote persistently and extremely well—even in English, which was neither her first nor even her second language. Her travel journals and other informal writings shimmer with unanticipated perception and vibrant description, the result of close observation. In fact, to read Mörath's writing is to be reminded that writing and photographing are not so far apart: both depend on seeing; not just looking, but noticing, discerning the patterns and revelations that are typically passed over and conventionalized.

Her *Heute* job involved creating features, not "news"—perhaps the editor would not assign hard news stories to a woman. In fact, the masthead listed by name the editors in Munich and London, but not Mörath, head of the Austrian bureau—perhaps for the same reason. Certainly women seldom reached positions of authority at the time. When she hired a man as her secretary, it was a "big scandal"[39]—and a sign of her confidence. Her *Heute* pieces were usually unsigned so they are hard to trace, but they were mainly cultural features and reviews of performing arts events, designed to suit a magazine required to be upbeat. Her stories included "City on the Danube Open to the Western World," "Wiens Gloria," about a Viennese youth chorus, and "Wiener Walzerseligkeit," Vienna waltz madness.[40]

Part of her job involved finding photographers; since she didn't know any, she searched publications with pictures, read bylines carefully, and asked her artist friends. She found and used work by Lothar Rübelt, an Austrian press photographer known for his dynamic still and moving pictures of athletes; by Hanns Hubmann, who also worked for the American *Stars and Stripes*; and by Franz Hubmann, who went on to become a major documenter of postwar Vienna (and who, coincidentally, founded an Austrian magazine called *magnum*). She discovered Erich Lessing, a Jew who had managed to escape to Palestine in 1939, then returned to Vienna to work for AP; he would become a member of Magnum

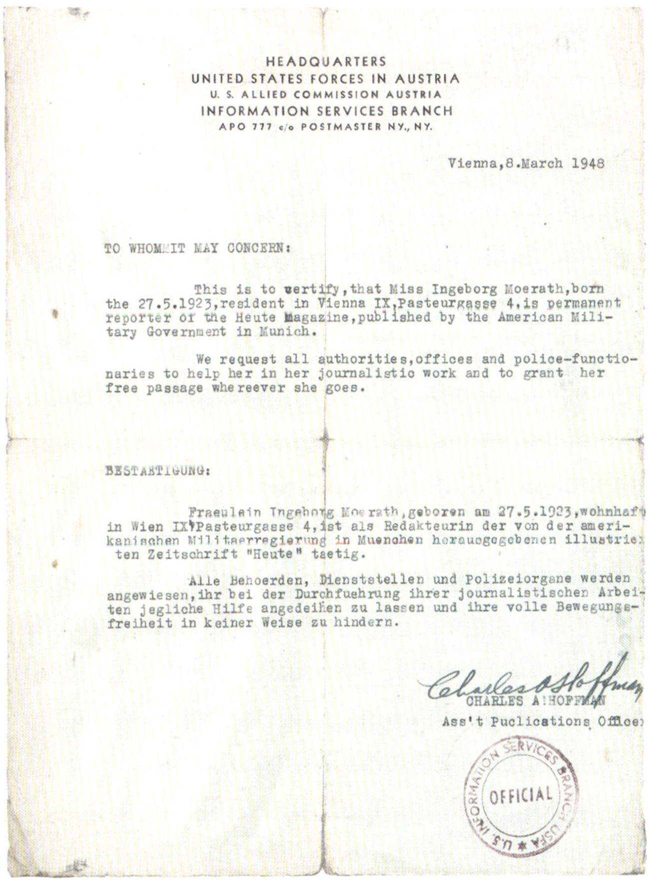

HEADQUARTERS
UNITED STATES FORCES IN AUSTRIA
U. S. ALLIED COMMISSION AUSTRIA
INFORMATION SERVICES BRANCH
APO 777 c/o POSTMASTER NY., NY.

Vienna,8.March 1948

TO WHOMMIT MAY CONCERN:

This is to certify,that Miss Ingeborg Moerath,born the 27.5.1923,resident in Vienna IX,Pasteurgasse 4,is permanent reporter of the Heute Magazine,published by the American Military Government in Munich.

We request all authorities,offices and police-functionaries to help her in her journalistic work and to grant her free passage whereever she goes.

BESTAETIGUNG:

Fraeulein Ingeborg Moerath,geboren am 27.5.1923,wohnhaft in Wien IX,Pasteurgasse 4,ist als Redakteurin der von der amerikanischen Militaerregierung in Muenchen herausgegebenen illustrierten Zeitschrift "Heute" taetig.

Alle Behoerden, Dienststellen und Polizeiorgane werden angewiesen,ihr bei der Durchfuehrung ihrer journalistischen Arbeiten jegliche Hilfe angedeihen zu lassen und ihre volle Bewegungsfreiheit in keiner Weise zu hindern.

Charles A Hoffman
CHARLES A!HOFFMAN
Ass't Puclications Officer

U.S. INFORMATION SERVICES BRANCH USFA
OFFICIAL

10. Inge's identification paper as a *Heute* magazine reporter, 1948

in 1955.[41] All were her beneficiaries, continuing to sell photographs to *Heute* long after Mörath left.[42]

Luckily, her two actress friends at the Theater in der Josefstadt each told her to try Ernst Haas, who had done their portraits. She contacted him, he came by, she was charmed—he was handsome and, if the photos I've seen are indicative, flirtatious.

An Austrian Jew from an upscale family, Haas had planned to attend medical school. When this became prohibited for Jews, he took up photography, teaching himself, washing his prints in his bathtub. When he came to see Mörath in order to sell to *Heute*, he spread his photographs dramatically on her table—showing them "one by one like treasures." A bit self-important, she thought, but they both knew he was good; he went on to become a world-class photographer and pioneer in color photography. "He observed his surroundings with catlike concentration," she later recalled. She sent some of his pictures to Trabant who found them "most extraordinary." Trabant began to send him on shoots around Europe. She had made the connection that sparked Haas's career.

Mörath and Haasi, as he was known, began working together as a photo story team, studying *Life* to get the knack of appealing to an American editor. Their first several pieces were somewhat banal, "dreadful things," as she called them—one on the anniversary of the composer of "Silent Night, Holy Night," several on women's fashions, a major topic for *Heute*.[43] (By late 1948, *Heute* was featuring a pretty girl on every cover.) But they were developing a productive partnership. Their road trips furthered their bonding; they sometimes rode in boxcars and ate nothing but bread, sometimes they were treated

11. Inge and Ernst Haas during their first reportage for Magnum Photos, Capri, Italy, 1949, photographer unknown

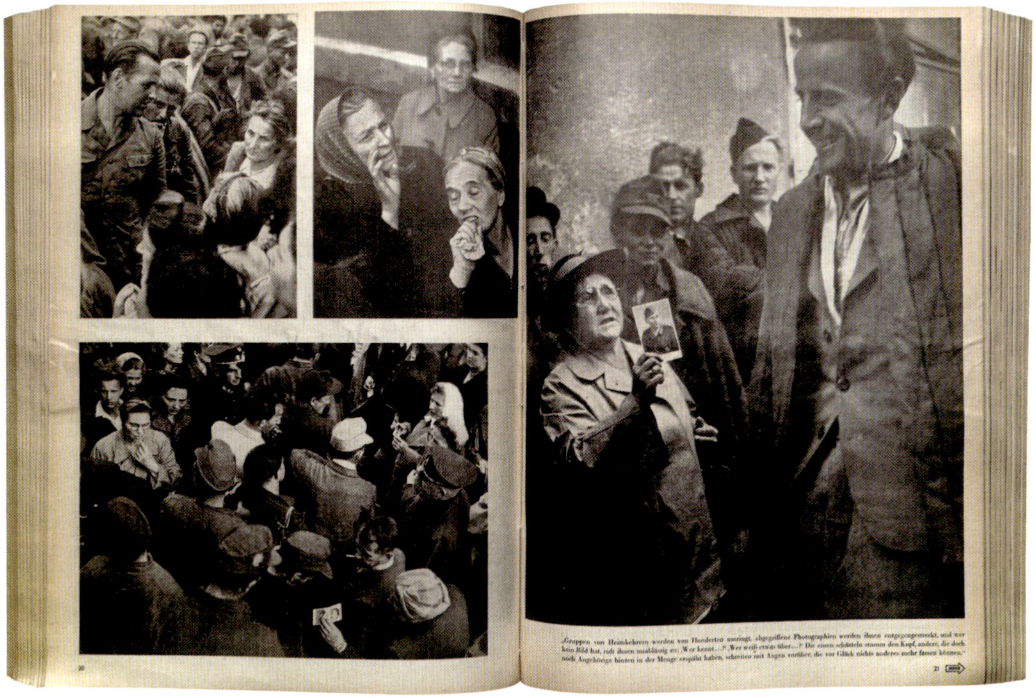

12. Returning prisoners of war, Vienna, 1949. Photos by Ernst Haas

to sumptuous meals. They discussed "text and picture harmony not only for hours and days but for months and even years." Many of their pieces, because they were not time bound, were published after they left *Heute* (fig. 11).

Their greatest joint success treated a serious subject—Austrian soldiers returning from Russian POW camps—from an unusual and dramatic angle: through the eyes of Viennese mothers at the train station searching for their sons. Some of these "hopeful and desperate people" would know relief and happiness, others would suffer excruciating disappointment (fig. 12). Mörath and Haas feared it might be too sad for *Heute*, but Trabant did not flinch; he not only published it, he also sent some of the Haas photos to Robert Capa in Paris, who was creating a photographic agency.[44] Capa invited Haas to come to Paris to work with Magnum, and Haas insisted on bringing Mörath. She had promoted him; now he returned the favor.

Because Haasi had brought her, the Paris group assumed, understandably, that they were lovers. They did, after all, make a beautiful couple. But Inge denied this, "we just weren't interested in sleeping together. We had other loves and in some way did not want to destroy the strong friendship that bound us." Besides, it would have put their working relationship at risk. "You," said Haasi similarly, "you were afraid. I was too. That is wonderful." The result was a friendship that lasted a lifetime. "We could confide in each other as only in a brother or a sister."[45] Maintaining a platonic relationship with Haasi signaled her love for the work—and her increasing ambition.

In retrospect, Mörath recalled finding postwar Vienna too small and too impoverished. On her arrival in Vienna she had been thrilled; after three years it seemed to have shrunk and dimmed. She was "thirsting for the larger world."[46]

Chapter Two

MAGNUM, PARIS

On July 14, 1949, Haasi and Mörath traveled by third class from Vienna to Paris, she with a new hat and a pile of sandwiches supplied by his mother.[47] Short of French money, they walked the two and a half miles from the Gare de l'Est to the address Capa had provided, 125 Rue du Faubourg-Saint Honoré. A sign there announced that the elevator would take you up but not down. Mörath had expected to be greeted by "big shots." No one answered the door for so long that they feared they had made a mistake. Finally a tall thin guy with a hangover and an ice bag on his head came to the door (he turned out to be Carl Perutz, who would become a Magnum member and the most famous photographer of Marilyn Monroe). When they asked for Capa, he responded, "but it's Bastille Day!" He told them to come in and immediately went back inside to sleep. The place had a bedroom—shared, Mörath and Haasi gathered, by the hangover man and anyone else who didn't have a bed, as well as a kitchen, a bathroom, and a front room that also served as the "office." Its furnishings included a long high table for photo editing, a phone on a long cord that could be carried around, a few filing cabinets, and, in the days to come, a couch on which she would often sleep when she had no money. There were no chairs. "Haasi," she wrote, "was a rock or rather a cat—he could just sit down and be quite happy. I had bought a hat and felt a touch betrayed."

That shard of disappointment dissolved quickly. If Vienna had been a liberation, Paris was a paradise. Between the wars, Paris was a magnet for artists and intellectuals throughout the world. French work permits were relatively easy to get.[48] Brassaï, Man Ray, Salvador Dalí, Berenice Abbott, Germaine Krull, Sonia Delaunay, Lee Miller, Philippe Halsman, and Ilse Bing all came to Paris. As Nazi control grew, escaping photographers joined them, including Gisèle Freund, Lisette Model, Fred Stein, and Hans Namuth. Often urban and Jewish, these expats moved easily into Parisian life, in part because the city was full of others just like them; they formed a tribe. Most gravitated toward the French Left. In 1939 many fled yet again, to the United States and England or anywhere safe that they could reach. But

13. Inge, 1956, photographer unknown

after the war many returned and a new cohort arrived. Mörath was among them. She would live in Paris for more than a decade, developing her lifelong identity as a European, an identity that others would recognize even after she had spent forty years in the United States.

For many of these artists, their immigrant status—the fact that their lives had been disrupted and reconstructed, often several times—informed their development as photographers. As photography historian Nissan Perez has suggested, camera and negatives were a perfect artistic apparatus for immigrants because of their portability.[49] And working in new surroundings honed the sharpness of their most valuable tool, their eyes.

Capa finally showed up at the Magnum "office" that first day, accompanied by Len Spooner, editor of London's *Illustrated* magazine, an important Magnum client. His arrival immediately erased Mörath's anxiety about leaving her job in Vienna. Even "while continuing to plan Magnum projects with Mr. Spooner," she recalled, "Capa had picked up the phone, found us cheap hotel rooms, and firmed up a job with UNESCO

14. Inge's Magnum press card

for us" (fig. 14). Then he took them to a restaurant on Saint-Germain-des-Prés, "where we had wine and a glorious dinner. . . . We felt in God's hands." Many drinks later, they went out into the street where they were surrounded by Bastille Day celebrations. Amid the fireworks and dancing, Inge and Ernst showed the others how to do the "waltz-to-the-left" (fig. 15).[50]

Capa's personal narrative, style, and reputation made Magnum what it was in its heady early days. He was the world's first superstar war photographer and the charismatic founder of Magnum. Even before his iconic images of D-day, his photography of the Spanish republican battle against the fascist coup had been published throughout Europe. "He practically invented the image of the globe-trotting war photographer, with a cigarette appended to the corner of his mouth and cameras slung over his fatigues. His fearlessness awed even his soldier subjects," wrote Randy Kennedy of the *New York Times*.[51] To those who knew him, his personality and his way with women surrounded him with an aura that vibrated with energy. He loved women, gambling, horse racing, pinball machines, good food and liquor, but his political commitments and generosity toward others lay not far underneath that high life. His battleground death in Indochina in 1954 further cemented his heroic reputation.

"I only kissed Robert Capa once," Mörath wrote teasingly in one of her several memoir fragments (fig. 16). It was her way of referring to Capa's irresistible attractiveness. "We often met in one or the other of these swank places, sometimes he paid, sometimes an important person with whom he had a date . . . expensive food." Capa always had "big friends."[52] Perhaps he and Inge did more than kiss—we don't know. In any case, she

15. Inge photographing, 1960s, photographer unknown

16. Text by Inge on Magnum's early years

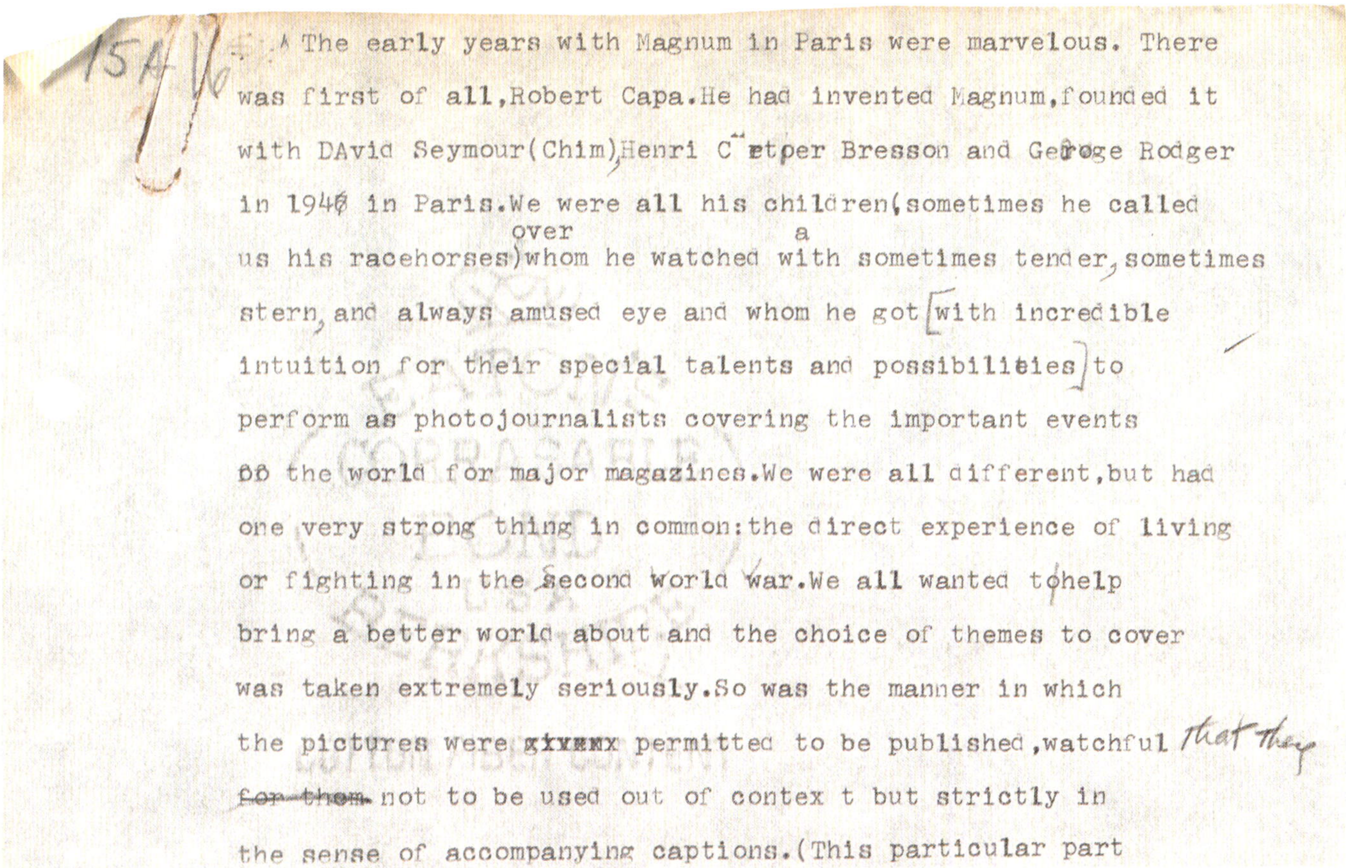

The early years with Magnum in Paris were marvelous. There was first of all,Robert Capa.He had invented Magnum,founded it with DAvid Seymour(Chim),Henri Cartper Bresson and Gerоge Rodger in 1946 in Paris.We were all his children(sometimes he called us his racehorses)whom he watched over with a sometimes tender, sometimes stern, and always amused eye and whom he got [with incredible intuition for their special talents and possibilities] to perform as photojournalists covering the important events of the world for major magazines.We were all different,but had one very strong thing in common:the direct experience of living or fighting in the Second World War.We all wanted to help bring a better world about and the choice of themes to cover was taken extremely seriously.So was the manner in which the pictures were ~~gixwx~~ permitted to be published,watchful that they ~~for them~~ not to be used out of contex t but strictly in the sense of accompanying captions.(This particular part

appreciated the fine food and luxuries he provided. "I had one black woolen skirt which I considered chique [sic] and two white shirts, one just a little more fancy than the other . . . a pair of black Ferragamo pumps . . . hate cheap shoes."[53] This was always to be Mörath's taste and style, already fully formed in 1949; she was quite willing to live penuriously even as she loved elegant decor and couture clothing.

Capa confirmed her tastes and made possible her calling and her career. Beyond his sexiness, he was a master administrator and entrepreneurial promoter; he launched or helped along the careers of many fine photographers. He brought Mörath into a friendship circle that lasted for her lifetime. Irwin Shaw remarked that some people are born to be Parisian and Capa was one of them;[54] so was Mörath.

Born Endre Friedmann in Budapest in 1913, Capa left Hungary at eighteen in exchange for release from imprisonment for his leftist activism. He went first to Berlin, then left for Paris on the night of the Reichstag fire in 1933. There he created a new identity—Capa—to get his photographs published.[55] Leaving just before the Nazis arrived, he returned to Paris in time to photograph the city's liberation. He had long resented his dependence on agents who took too much of his fees and publishers who took ownership of his negatives. He "dreamed of plotting his own stories, owning his own copyright."[56] Already in the 1930s he had talked up a plan to create a photographic agency owned and operated by the photographers themselves. Gradually he drew in three other major photographers—Chim, Henri Cartier-Bresson, and George Rodger.

Chim was the moon to Capa's sun.[57] Born Dawid Szymin in Warsaw, son of a publisher of Jewish books, he was shy and short, Mörath recalled years later, with a "round, bald head, wise smile, and half-moon eyes" that peered owlishly through his thick glasses. In Paris, where he arrived in 1932, he acquired the nickname Chim, pronounced Shim, because the French couldn't pronounce his surname, he said; in the United States he renamed himself David Seymour.[58]

Chim brought Cartier-Bresson into the group, and he became the artistic father to the Magnum family, Mörath especially. Always the defender of Magnum's standards of quality, Cartier-Bresson became its moral and aesthetic consciousness; he was a purist, both politically and aesthetically. He grew up wealthy, served by a white-gloved butler and addressing his father as *vous*, a youthful dilettante who tried his hand at music, acting, filmmaking, and painting, even literature at Cambridge University.[59] He too was a leftist, a member of the Association des Écrivains et Artistes Révolutionnaires, a group dedicated to using art in the struggle against fascism. Its slogan: "There is no neutral art" (fig. 17).[60] Yet he was never strictly a photojournalist or documentary photographer—influenced by the surrealists and cubists, his photography remained the most "artistic" of the Magnum founders. In this respect, his sensibility resembled Mörath's more than that of the other Magnum founders, and she always considered him her master teacher.

George Rodger's influence on her was less direct. At Magnum, it was his contact sheets that she was first assigned to edit, an activity she later remembered as thrilling. Then, too, his vivid stories of experiences around the world kindled a lust for travel that she retained all her life. Born in 1906, Rodger grew up in England and Scotland, joined the UK Merchant Navy while still

17. Ernst Haas and Henri Cartier-Bresson at a Magnum meeting, Paris, 1958

a teenager, then worked as a freelancer until *Life* hired him as a war photographer in 1936. The breadth of his war photography was unmatched. He covered sixty-two wars, including the Blitz in London; West Africa with the Free French; the fall of Burma (where he managed to escape the Japanese by walking three hundred miles through a bamboo forest); the Sicilian and Salerno landings of Allied troops; D-day; and the liberation of Paris.[61]

No one is sure who thought up the name Magnum, but it was perfect: catchy, easy to pronounce in any language, signifying generous quantities of champagne but also the macho toughness and romance of war photography—the source of the group's bonding and passion. It appeared at the right moment. New technical developments, such as quick drying ink, were giving birth to mass-circulation photographic magazines and increasing the popularity of newspaper photographs.[62] The glossies in particular wanted photo stories more than individual photographs.[63] But fine art photography had consisted of single photographs. Cartier-Bresson wrote that prior to Magnum, he had "been engaged in looking for the photo for itself . . . like one does with a poem." With Magnum he had to tell a story.[64] And with stories, explanatory captions became important.[65] It is possible that without this shift toward storytelling and captioning photographs, Mörath would not have become a photographer, as writing them was initially her primary task at Magnum.

Magnum helped magazine and newspaper editors by creating a central agency from which they could obtain fine photography. Nevertheless, corporate publications such as *Life* wanted editorial control over how many and which photographs to publish, what parts of photographs to use, and in what order and context to place them. Magnum resisted complying, defending the integrity of the photographer's work. Eventually Magnum began to stamp the back of each photograph, forbidding its use outside the context indicated by accompanying captions. This stand for "photographic integrity," as Mörath put it, was a major contribution to photojournalistic honesty.[66] At the same time, Magnum's structure allowed photographers considerable freedom to explore their own topics. As fine photography began to be appreciated as art, desirable to collectors, photographers could also market fine prints of their work. Ultimately, this small band changed the working conditions and living standards of photographers everywhere.

In 1947 it went without saying that Capa would be the head of Magnum, not only because it was his idea, but also because of his experience, connections, vision, and "fighting" spirit, in Mörath's words. "There was fire in him, and the spirit of attack, but nothing vile." In addition, she immediately observed his generosity. He was "quick to recognize the potential in people . . . He kept on the lookout for stories for everybody," and his pairings of photographers with assignments seemed always to match photographers' skills and interests.

He rounded up commissions by playing gin rummy with editors and filmmakers.[67] Magnum's success soon attracted more photographers. Werner Bischof joined in 1949.[68] Capa's younger brother Kornél Friedmann soon arrived. He became a darkroom apprentice and picked up skills quickly. He changed his name to Cornell Capa to not only make their relationship clear, but to avoid the notorious French anti-Semitism.[69]

Mörath's recollections mention, but only in passing, that all the Magnum people had "one strong thing in common: we all wanted to help bring a better world about and the choice of themes to cover was taken extremely seriously."[70] Her comment articulated the implicitness of their politics, which were so taken for granted among them, so embedded in body and soul that they did not require articulation. Their anti-fascism was visceral. Capa, Chim, and Cartier-Bresson had all worked for the French Communist Party newspapers from 1937 to 1939.[71] The Magnum photographers were also mostly Jews, urban and urbane men from elite families whose resources helped keep them alive. Their loathing for Nazis and fascists expressed not only anti-anti-Semitism, but also a holistic repugnance for the political Right, which threatened every value they cherished: art, modernism, free speech, sexual freedom, cosmopolitanism, the value of cultural difference. The non-Jews detested fascism just as vehemently.

The Magnum group bonded also through personal experiences of war—as photographers and as casualties. Capa had been photographing war and the Nazi advance since 1933. His first and greatest love, Gerda Taro, another Jewish war photographer, was killed covering the Spanish Civil War in 1937;[72] had she lived she surely would have been central to Magnum.[73] Chim was the first in the group to photograph in Spain, in 1936, and later served in the US Army.[74] Nazis killed Chim's parents and he himself was killed by Egyptian machine-gun fire in the Suez war in 1956. Cartier-Bresson made films for the Spanish Republicans and served in the French army; captured in the Battle of France, he spent almost three years in a Nazi POW camp before escaping. George Rodger, who had served in the Royal Navy, had been nearly unhinged by what he saw photographing the Allied troops' entrance into the Bergen-Belsen concentration camp in April 1945. William Vandivert, a *Life* photographer, had accompanied the Allies into Berlin where he shot the first images of Hitler's bunker. Haas had been in a German army labor camp. And so a current of unarticulated recognition flowed among them, on a wavelength that Mörath and Haas recognized immediately when they arrived.

These war photographers labeled their work photojournalism. Distinctions among categories of photography have long been fuzzy, but Capa's advice was strategic: "Just go on doing what you want to do anyway but call yourself a photojournalist, which puts you into direct contact with everything that is going on in the world. So let it be."[75]

Almost all war photographers were, and remain today, anti-war photographers. Still, they live with a contradiction—between anguish and terror and the fact that they are also pulled by the thrill of action and danger. That contradiction fueled their high-flying life in Paris. It was the flip side of their high-risk work. The whole package was then exclusively a male preserve. Also male was the group's fervor for travel to distant lands, driven by a hankering for adventure and for novel subjects that would sell. To the surprise of the initial group,

Mörath soon demonstrated an equal capacity and love for adventurous travel.

Several other women were crucial members of the close-knit community. Maria Eisner was an entrepreneurial talent who had run the Alliance Photographic Agency in Paris, which had represented Capa and Chim, so she knew how to bargain with publishers. She too was war-scarred. Born in Milan and raised in Germany, she fled with her family in 1933. In a common but bitter irony, she was arrested in 1940 as a German alien and sent to the Gurs concentration camp in France. Returning, she served as Magnum's secretary treasurer, the brains of its business organization. (The "office" was actually her apartment.) Her husband, Dr. Hans Lehfeldt, treated all the many illnesses, aching backs, and muscle sprains of the Magnum family. But soon after Mörath arrived, Eisner and Lehfeldt left for New York where he had taken a job.[76] Rita Vandivert, William's wife, was Magnum's first president, and eventually headed the New York office. Both these women were wives, neither were photographers, and these identities kept them in subordinate positions. Other women, often relatives and friends, volunteered or worked for low pay as editors, researchers, accountants, and cooks. One of them usually prepared a lunch for all. While John Morris, who would become Magnum's executive editor, and Capa's chum Irwin Shaw described the female members as "seductive and dynamic women" who worked "more for love than money," they were in fact exploitable young women scrounging for a meager living while seeking creative opportunities, often in vain.[77]

Mörath, too, had entered in the "wife" status. As Haas's work partner, she continued to travel with him, writing stories and captions to go with his photographs. She also assisted other photographers, typing letters, holding lights and reflectors, enlarging photos, keeping accounts, and translating. She felt that among Magnum's photographers only Haasi treated her with full respect. After the initial excitement of entry into the Magnum world, Mörath chafed at her subordinate position. Neither a real employee nor a member of Magnum, guaranteed no regular salary, she called herself a "standby."[78] She slept on the couch in the office when she couldn't afford a flat. She sought more work from *Heute*, unsuccessfully, and she had trouble collecting from them the money she was already owed.[79]

Mörath shrugged off these inequalities with enough ease to enjoy Magnum socializing. The group ate, drank, and relaxed together. Because the office had no chairs, and the couch was usually covered with boxes of negatives and prints, the bistro downstairs served as an annex, the place to have a conversation, to discuss and distribute jobs and trips, or just to unwind. (It was the last place the group saw Capa alive.) Capa regularly supplied entertainment to all his flock, as if doing so was part of his job as their leader. They often attended the races at Longchamp, where Capa bet on the "hot tips" given him by the concierge at the Hotel Lancaster.[80] Winnings went into the Magnum kitty. They were a family, their bonding made all the tighter since, as Inge shrewdly noticed, few of them were married. The Magnum clan lived and worked in much the same way as did 1960s members of the civil rights movement or New Left activists. Mörath saw them all as Capa's children, and he sometimes called the group his racehorses who required his constant loving care, because, he said, he couldn't "afford the real thing" (fig. 18).[81]

"Through friendships, and also affairs, one got to

know new cultures and languages,"[82] Mörath wrote. True, but being single and good-looking also brought risks. Living on the pittance that Magnum gave her, she often accepted dinner invitations, only to find that her date wanted to get her a hotel room.[83] Beautiful, svelte, and charming, she had no shortage of beaux. But of all her love affairs, the most intense was with Paris. Had it not been for Arthur Miller she would have stayed there forever. Her memories of her first Paris days captured her immediate love for the city. The bistro downstairs from Magnum had "white curtains and brass door handles . . . zinc tables . . . Behind the counter, the wonderful array of bottles shimmering in poisonous colors . . . baskets with hard boiled eggs, salt cellars, toothpicks, paper napkins cut in half and folded into glasses." Describing Capa's favorite pastime, the bistro's pinball machine, she wrote, "He tilted it mercilessly, his whole body participated, hands clasped to the sides while he wiggled along with the way the ball took. To raise his arms in triumph or despair at the end of each sortie."[84] She accumulated friends. June, for example, the subject of a story for *Holiday* about American girls in Paris. She lived on the top floor of a building on the Rue de l'Université, the window of her room jutting out from a mansard roof surrounded by an ornate grille, from which they hung baskets of eggs and onions and spun their lettuce. An Egyptian painter friend who lived nearby had dragged up four huge truck tires that served as chairs. "From the local *boucherie chevaline* . . . he bought the cheapest organs, hearts above all, out of which he managed to prepare succulent dishes" (fig. 19).

18. Magnum Meeting. Burt Glinn, Eve Arnold, Elliott Erwitt, Inge Morath (with paper hat), Ernst Haas, Erich Hartmann, Dennis Stock, early 1960s, photographer unknown

Adventurousness multiplied her pleasures. Once she answered a wrong-number call in the office and, because she was bored, "arranged a rendezvous with the people" on the other end, met them in a bar and had "one of the funniest nights. They are musicians, radio people, painters. They drag me to studios, strange restaurants, and are charming . . . Thank god I met them . . ."[85] For a young woman who had been deprived of her teenage years by war; who had lived through privation, homelessness, bombing, and destruction; who had seen her family hide their books and "Jewish" music; who had walked on aching feet from Berlin to Salzburg—this bohemian world was a dreamland. As Arthur Miller put it, Paris became her second birthplace.[86]

It was all the easier to enjoy Paris because her economic security was never really threatened. Magnum's bohemian poverty was a sort of slumming. However short of cash, they never did without the maid who cleaned the office every morning. They seemed almost proud of being broke, their printer Pierre Gassmann noted,[87] while bits of luxury accumulated in their world. Their photography opened the doors of the rich and famous, as portraits of celebrities became an important part of their photographic work. You could live as you

19. Paris, 1957

liked, Mörath recalled, but also "go to the chicest parties as Capa's friends."[88]

Mörath would remain a Parisian for thirteen years. Halfway through, however, Magnum had to weather a devastating loss—Capa's death in 1954. Mörath remembered their last time together vividly. A premonitory anxiety imbued the occasion. They gathered at the bistro to say farewell just before he left for Japan on assignment for *Life*. "We had seen each other off to so many places for years now, but somehow we were all sadder at this occasion." He seemed uncharacteristically depressed. Inge thought he "had had it with war photography." His back had caused him great pain on and off for several years, despite doses of codeine, one day so bad he lay on the floor and wept.[89] At the bistro that night he "worked hard on the pinball machine and mused about getting old, past forty, an old man. . . . We all embrace in the dark wet street, *Bonne chance, mon vieux*, to a man who had been brother and father to us all." From Tokyo he went to Vietnam to cover the last days of the French war and died there on May 25, 1954, stepping on a land mine just eleven days before the French capitulated.[90] Two days after learning this, they heard that Werner Bischof had also died.[91] As George Rodger remembered hearing the news, "the world stood still."[92]

On June 30, Magnum folk gathered in anguish and anxiety about the future. But if Magnum did not continue, they knew, they "would be like traitors."[93] In their grief-muddled thinking, they decided not to appoint a new president but to leave that position vacant because no one could replace Capa. Instead, they chose three vice presidents: Chim, Rodger, and Cornell Capa.[94] When Chim was killed two years later, Cornell became president. Until 1960 he not only held Magnum together, but with the same level of commitment to the collective that his brother had, he expanded it.

Chapter Three

CHOOSING PHOTOGRAPHY

By 1950 Mörath was an experienced journalist, able to write articles in German, French, and English, but the writing that Magnum required did not take advantage of her journalistic skills. She found editing contact sheets and scrutinizing them through a magnifying glass much more challenging. The task required close inspection, attention to detail, keen judgment, and patience. But doing only that was not satisfying. Besides, Magnum could not afford to keep her on a salary, paying her piece rate for scattered jobs. Yet it was through Magnum that she was accidentally propelled into a new adventure.

One of Magnum's major customers was the London *Picture Post*. Established in 1938 by Stefan Lorant, a Hungarian Jewish refugee,[95] the magazine was a liberal, anti-fascist, British version of *Life*; its writers included George Bernard Shaw, Dorothy Parker, William Saroyan, and J. B. Priestley. It published Capa's photographs extensively.[96] Through his friendship with Lorant, Capa had also connected with one of its writers, Lionel Birch, who became one of his drinking buddies, which eventually led to his meeting Mörath.[97]

Birch descended from two distinguished families: on his mother's side from a prominent Italian banking family, de Bosdari; on his father's, an old English family that included a well-known nineteenth-century landscape painter also named Lionel Birch. The younger Lionel's father, John Somerville Birch, was British Commissioner of State Domains in Egypt, known to his friends as Birch Pasha. Capa's friend Birch, born in 1910 in London and educated at Shrewsbury, an ancient, elite, and snobbish boarding school for boys, resembled in some ways the stereotype of his lineage: he was a cricket player of near professional standard, the author of a book of poems ("vaguely homosexual verse"), and several novels.[98] Tall, lean, beautifully dressed, a member of London's literary circles, he was also distinctly left of center.

As a package, Birch was immediately attractive to Inge—"a very seductive man"—and for a short time she was much in love with him.[99] They married on April 21, 1951, without festivities, at a registrar's office in Kensington. Bobby, as she called him, was forty-one and already thrice divorced, and would ultimately go through

20. Inge, Viale Marco Polo, Rome, 1952. Photo by Titti Mörath

five wives and some gay affairs; Inge was twenty-seven (fig. 21). Decades later, she told her friend Honor Moore that she had married him "in order to be a Madame."[100] Still in many ways a refugee, she might have meant that she yearned for a position and a home. Whatever the motive, she left Magnum and moved to London.

A voracious reader and language acquirer, Mörath seized upon her residence in England with high energy. Birch introduced her to Shakespeare and Shaw, cricket and country pubs. At the Tate Gallery she could "rinse her eyes," one of her many lively metaphors. She evaluated the English "girls" she met in what I take to be positive terms, as more independent, whimsical, willful, and eccentric than those in France. Yet, ever circumspect about personal difficulties, she wrote only that the marriage "was a mistake which Housman, Yeats, Joyce could not mend." And that she was "unprepared for married life. I love to work." "I couldn't possibly wash socks and stuff."[101] She was hinting that Birch did not want her to work.

In hindsight, she described this marriage as "infinitely dull" and "a waste."[102] She also commented that Englishwomen were "sexually more related," a phrase possibly signaling their greater sexual freedom—or Birch's infidelity. Their relationship lasted only a year, although their divorce was delayed until 1954 due to a British law prohibiting divorce within the first three years of marriage. The cause cited was his adultery, but in those days, when grounds for divorce were so limited, we cannot be sure that it was an accurate diagnosis of their difficulties. Still, his reputation labeled him a womanizer, and in his later life, a homosexual—not at all contradictory labels in upper-class British culture at the time.

21. Kurt Hutton (left) and editorial staff writer Lionel Birch on assignment covering a group of Londoners on a weekend horse riding break near Ashdown Forest, Sussex, 1948

One comment about visiting the Tate—"I was not a born painter"—suggests that Mörath experimented in drawing what she had seen at the *Degenerate Art* exhibition. But now that she had seen great photography, a new possibility appeared. She said that it was only when she was in London and no longer surrounded by photography that she realized how much she loved it. It seems equally plausible that it was only when she got away from Magnum's male master photographers, and the discussions in which they analyzed so exactingly the strengths and shortcomings of each other's work, that she dared try it herself—privately, secretly, telling no one in Magnum about her first photographic ventures.

22. Inge in Venice, 1955, photographer unknown

In November 1951 Lionel had taken Inge to Venice, possibly as a honeymoon. One rainy day, she found the quality of the light so stunning that she telephoned Capa and urged him to send someone to photograph in Venice. Her enthusiasm had made her illogical, and Capa pointed out that by the time someone got there, it wouldn't be raining, and besides, he had no paying customer for Venice. He suggested she try capturing the light. She had taken along her mother's Contax camera—a subconscious indication of her yearning?—so she went to a store to buy some film. She was such a "greenhorn," to use her word, that she didn't even know how to load the film, and had to ask the storekeeper to do it for her.[103] He told her that she shouldn't bother, that one couldn't photograph in rain. But she had seen rainy-day photos, so she tried anyway, by following the instructions that came in the box for photographing in cloudy weather: 1/50 exposure at f-stop 4. She stood on a corner, and waited—as she had learned to do from Haasi—until the patterns made by walls, pedestrians, umbrellas, and pigeons pleased her, then pressed the shutter. She instantly knew, she often said in later years, that this was what she should do, "that this was the perfect way for me to express what I had within me." The moment when "eye and feeling coincide." It "totally satisfied me" (figs. 22, 23, 24, 25).[104]

This is a type of origin story—an epiphany story—that often settles into memory because it is dramatic, and through repetition becomes reduced to and cemented around a single moment. My sense is that this turn to photography grew somewhat more gradually, out of many sources: her mother's work; the visual art that she had grown up with, including the artistic tastes that the family had to hide during the Nazi regime; and her years of work alongside Haasi.

FOLLOWING PAGES

23. Venice in the rain, 1954

24. Old neighborhood near the Fondamente Nove, Venice, 1955

Nel decennale
della Liberazione d'Italia
Devoto Settenario
MADONNA del CARMINE
VOTA
VOTA

25. Riva degli Schiavoni, Venice, 1955

Language was another factor that led her to photography. Now that she lived in Paris and London, she was made to feel that German was the language of the enemy. But her command of English and French, she thought, was limited enough that it thinned out her journalism in those languages.[105] She was proud of her acquisition of French, and especially of Parisian argot,[106] but "although I was able to write stories in English and French it did not touch the roots. So turning to the image felt both like a relief and an inner necessity."[107]

Back in London she sought training and found the extraordinary Simon Guttmann, a fellow Viennese and

Nazi refugee who in addition to being a master photographer was a "merciless" teacher.[108] He had founded a photo agency, Dephot, which represented some of the world's most innovative photographers and pioneered the creation of photo-essays (fig. 26). In exile in Paris in the 1930s, his agency represented Capa for a time. In England he created another agency, known as Report. Mörath was nervous—"terrified," she later recalled—when she first approached him and showed him her Venice images. But her bravery paid off, and in becoming his trainee, she had put herself in the hands of a world-renowned artist. He exploited her as an apprentice: she had to write his letters, heat his shaving water, sweep the flat, help him in the darkroom; the tasks multiplied on Saturdays because he was an observant Jew who would not do work on the Sabbath.[109] She complied, always willing to work hard at humble tasks, but she was also restless and ambitious. She bought herself a used Leica and became impatient to try it out. Guttmann's curriculum involved learning how to select subjects, to understand them, to approach them from the right angle and with the right timing, to see how objects and images are related. His approach helped her assimilate her new medium to the older forms of art she was familiar with (figs. 27, 28). He had her practice with a few small photographic assignments, even sending her to Paris to do a photo story. She later reflected that the intensity of working with him helped her to leave her marriage.[110]

26. Simon Guttmann, founder of Dephot agency, outside his London office, 1975. Photo by Romano Cagnoni

She sent out some of her work under a pseudonym—her name reversed, Egni Tharom—so that no one from Magnum would know what she was doing. "I was cutting straight into the territory of the male-dominated."[111] Perhaps she also felt the need to disguise her Germanic name. She sold some photos, and played along when publishers asked how to reach the man who had taken the photos.[112]

In 1953 she made a photo that became widely known under her own name—a portrait of a "fantastic old lady in Mayfair, you would need to see the pictures to believe that something like this still exists."[113] Mrs. Eveleigh Nash was a rich eccentric. Seated in a car, her chauffeur standing just outside the door, she wears a wide-brim hat with a veil over her face, a fur coat and a large fur robe across her lap. From under her veil she

27. Street corner at World's End, London, 1954

28. London, 1953

BY APPOINTMENT
TO THE LATE
KING GEORGE V.
BY
THE
LATE
GENTLE
COURT H

29. Publisher Eveleigh Nash at Buckingham Palace Mall, London, 1953

30. Contact sheet with portrait of Eveleigh Nash, London, 1953

looks directly at the camera with utter confidence and a hint of a sneer.[114] Behind in two converging lines are the arcades of Carlton House Terrace and a path bordered by leafless wintertime trees. The black border of the car's door and window, and the curved top of the window itself, frame both lady and chauffeur, juxtaposing upper-class and working-class Londoners. An elegant picture, and one that communicates some of the British class structure—reminiscent, perhaps, of Lisette Model and Esther Bubley (figs. 29, 30). Mörath later made another portrait of Nash, holding a picture of herself as a "ravishing debutante."[115]

After a year, Guttmann graduated her. She returned to Paris determined to prove herself as a photographer, knowing that she would have to do this with little if any support from Magnum's fraternity. "Being one of the then rather rare women photographers . . . was often difficult for the simple reason that nobody felt that one was serious (what does a pretty girl like you want in this profession). Much male condescension. . . . I certainly do not think that I got the same forceful male brotherhood support the men got." She pointed out that on news assignments, being a woman

COPYRIGHT INGE MORATH
MAGNUM PHOTOS, INC.
53-4-72

31. Memorial Sunday, London, 1953

32. Henry Moore, Much Hadham, Hertfordshire, Great Britain, 1954

was a "terrific drawback . . . I was mercilessly hit by Speed Graphics and blocked by bigger bodies working together."[116] Once years later, while she was photographing Adlai Stevenson, she got down on the floor to get a better angle and the male photojournalists literally stepped on her in order to get closer to the man. But Mörath toughed it out. "I consciously lived alone for a long time in order to be completely independent. . . . More women should have the courage to plunge alone into what they want to do."[117] These comments, made twenty years later, reflect both the influence of 1970s feminism and her awareness of female inequality well before that. They also convey a perspective common among ambitious women in the 1950s—acknowledging prejudice while concluding that women should simply try harder, or "lean in" in twenty-first-century language. Though well aware of male domination—and she would always be a strong supporter of women photographers—she never identified with feminism as a political cause, nor with any other political cause; she did not see the necessity.

She chose as her Magnum "audition" project a photo-essay about the *Prêtres Ouvriers*, worker priests

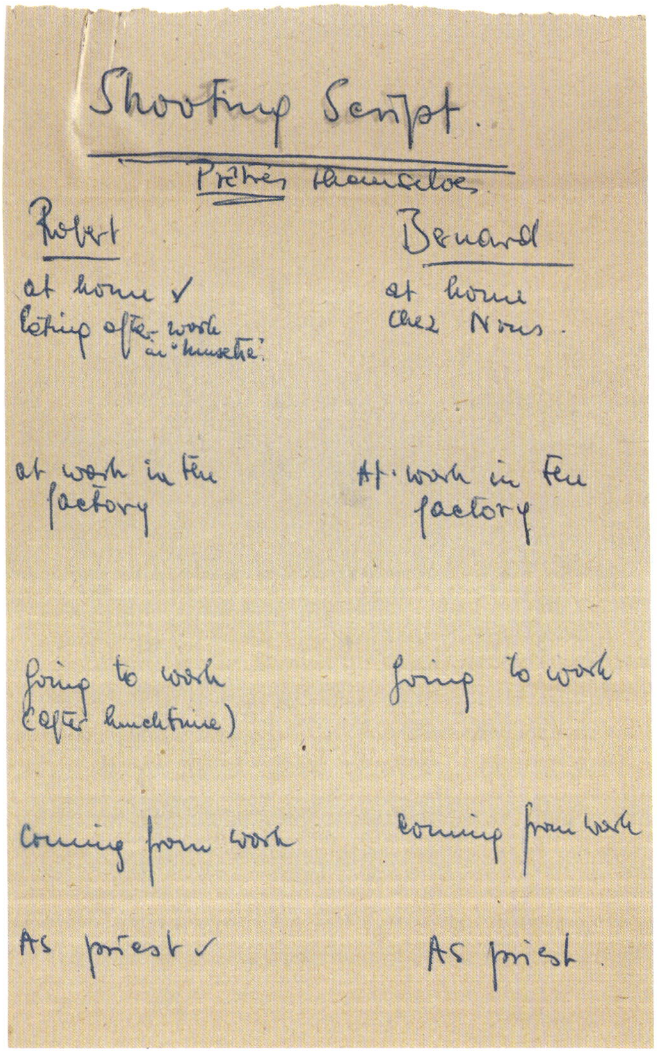

33. Shooting script for worker priests story (*Prêtres Ouvriers*), 1953

34. From worker priests story, Paris, 1953

35. Contact sheet from worker priests story, Paris, 1953

(fig. 33).[118] Derived from the 1920s *Jeunesse ouvrière chrétienne* movement, they preached an urban version of liberation theology. Participants sought to bring workingmen back into the church, at a time when French working-class radicalism and anticlericalism were strong, and at the same time to move the church back toward what they considered its true calling, serving the poor. "They were going around trying to re-evangelize—it was called *la mission intérieure*," like early Christians, Mörath thought (fig. 34).[119] Between 1941 and 1954, a small group of about one hundred young radical priests took working-class jobs and began to live in conditions like those of their coworkers, with the important difference that they were to be celibate. Some hid their clerical identity, some came out to their coworkers as priests. Sharing working-class poverty, industrial injuries, and the threat of being fired at the first sign of protest, they joined campaigns for improved pay and conditions. Some even became strike leaders and supported the Communist labor union, the CGT. Many supported the Algerian anti-colonial struggle.[120]

Mörath connected with a group of worker priests who were willing to let her photograph them. Located in Boulogne-Billancourt, a working-class suburb near the Renault works, the priests kept a bookshop, made offerings to the aged and the poor, and took in strays, including unwed mothers (fig. 35). She moved in, sharing a room with two of their "girl helpers" (apparently even these self-denying priests needed women to do the housework). Ethnographers would call her a participant-observer. She prepared a shooting script featuring two particular priests, identifying them by pseudonyms. She photographed "Bernard" reading the morning Mass in the kitchen.[121] She produced an entire photo-essay, accompanied by thoroughly researched captions (figs. 36, 37).

What she admired in the worker-priest movement was not its Catholicism but its emphasis on self-sacrifice and dedication to the most disadvantaged. Although she never identified as a leftist, her concern for the poor and the victimized aligned her with the Left. Her interest in religious subjects appeared later—she photographed religious emblems often in future decades—cathedrals, shrines, mosques, Zoroastrian ceremonies, and pilgrims on the road to Santiago de Campostela.[122]

In 1953 the worker-priest story won her an associate position with Magnum—a role that lasted two years. The men resented her, she felt. These war-hardened Magnum founding fathers did not easily imagine a woman doing what they did. For the first thirty years of Magnum, only three women became full members—Eve Arnold, Morath, and Marilyn Silverstone. Asked by an interviewer years later how she dealt with that resentment, she responded that

36. From worker priests story, Paris, 1953

37. Children under the care of worker priests, Paris, 1953

"you had to really want to do it," so that you can "make yourself not care" about the resentment. She also pointed out candidly that her "prettiness" was a big advantage. She drew people to her, often seductively, women as well as men—just like Capa.

Making publicity shots for films provided much of Magnum's and Mörath's income throughout the 1950s and 1960s. Mörath's first solo job was making stills on the set of John Huston's film *Moulin Rouge* (1952). Capa had warned her, "It is under my name and I'm sticking my head out. You can't goof."[123] The warning was enough to make anyone nervous, but she emerged triumphant: her photographs got a double-page spread in *Life*, an auspicious start, and she charmed Huston, who became a lifelong friend.

Reflecting the gender culture of the time, her early Magnum work consisted mainly of "feminine" jobs, "the jobs that did not interest the big boys." She covered

38. Cynthia Balfour rehearsing "Fire Vanquished by Snow," Bal d'Hiver, Paris, 1955

39. Empress Catherine the Great enters with sleigh, Bal d'Hiver, Paris, 1955

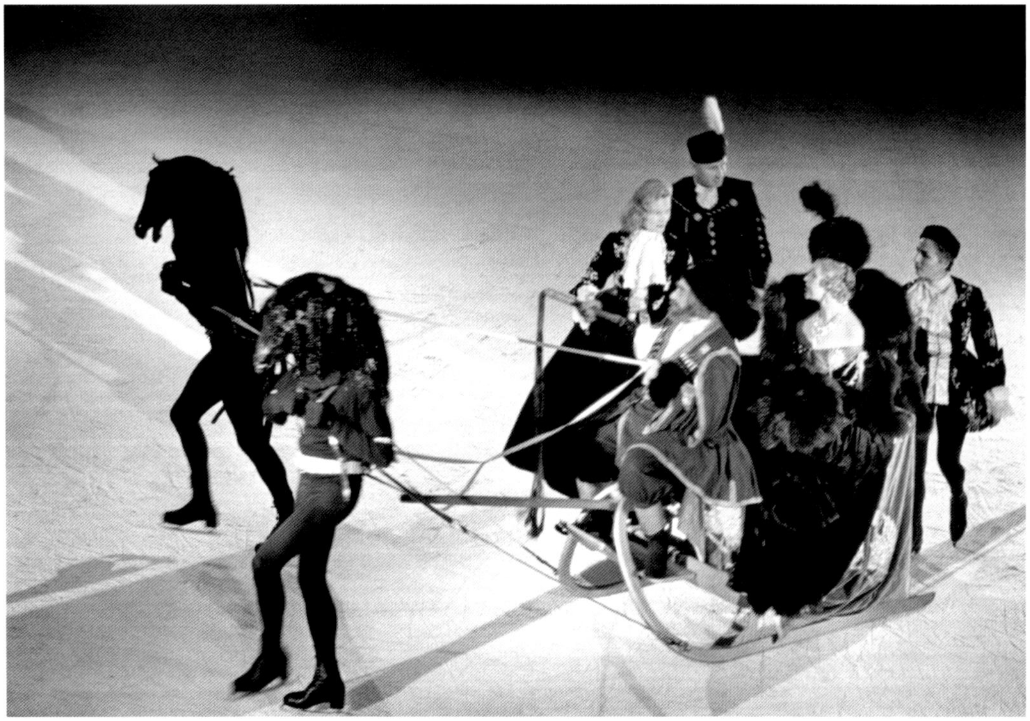

40. Inge and Elliott Erwitt, Paris, circa 1950. Photo by Eve Arnold

debutantes "coming out," dog shows, fashion shows, and produced photographs for features on notable women, such as the Duchess of Marlborough and the Paris editor of *Harper's Bazaar*. One of the more remarkable of these commissions was the 1955 Paris Bal d'Hiver (Winter Ball), an elaborate high-society event to benefit abandoned children (fig. 38). Big contributors watched elaborate tableaux on ice, including members of the Russian nobility costumed to represent historic Russian nobles and rulers: Princess Chavchavadze as the Tsarina Catherine the Great, entering on a sled; Princess Trubetskoy skating as Prince Yusupov. Violet Trefusis, a British socialite best known for her long affair with the poet Vita Sackville-West, performed as the Tsarina Anne (fig. 39).[124] Mörath's photographs of the ornate costumes, props, and headdresses show a surrealist impulse that appeared off and on in her work.

At some point in this period she shifted the spelling of her name from Mörath to Morath, dropping the umlaut to make her byline easier for non-German editors and typesetters, so I will follow the new spelling from now on. In making this change, she was joining scores of other photographers who had made even more drastic name changes—not only the Capas and Chim, but also Brassaï (who had been Gyula Halász), Dora Maar (who had been Henriette Theodora Dorothée Marković) and Magnum photographer Elliott Erwitt (born Elio Romano Erwitt) (fig. 40). All were creating names that better fit the languages used where they lived as well as making their names more recognizable and memorable in the hopes of advancing their careers. Many, too, had been seeking to avoid anti-Semitism. Morath was, by contrast, de-Germanizing her name, from a guilt-shedding impulse. The name change contained the truth: Morath was definitely not German, not fully Austrian, and was becoming, simply, European.

Chapter Four

LEARNING FROM THE MASTER

In 1953 Capa assigned Morath to Henri Cartier-Bresson as assistant and apprentice. She edited, researched, and translated for him. He became not only her mentor and supporter, but also, for almost a decade, off-and-on lover. She told one good friend that he wanted to marry her and offered to divorce his wife, but she refused.[125] Yet, as was characteristic of Morath's equanimity, this entanglement and others like it never impeded their lifelong friendship. Cartier-Bresson treated her as a fellow artistic intellectual, introducing her to culture deemed taboo under the Nazis. His familiarity and comfort with cultural and intellectual rebels was contagious. "In Germany, before," she recalled later, "the silence about all this was profound. . . . So when I met Henri he . . . had taken part, was part of it and yet, as a photographer, an observer. I was naïve, full of feelings and fearless. He could teach me I was open and my eyes could see."[126] He also ordered her to read *Le Monde* daily. Luckily, his politics were anything but doctrinaire, neither constraining nor humorless.

Cartier-Bresson was Magnum's professor of photography. He taught Morath systematically, and she considered him "the hardest taskmaster." Editing his contact sheets in her first years with Magnum had been an important part of this education, because doing so allowed her to examine the images in the sequence that he made them, to see his "rigorous pursuit of an event in clear geometric compositions." Decades later, she summarized her process by writing, "I learned how to photograph myself before I ever took a camera into my hand." She would practice "without a camera, with one eye closed and one open watching the street."[127] Now Cartier-Bresson taught her to see composition by looking at photographs upside-down, a standard teaching method for photographers and painters. He gave her a Vidom viewfinder, which allowed the photographer to view her subject not only upside-down but also reversed right-to-left.[128] He taught her economy and precision in defining her subjects and frames. He was not much interested in darkroom technique, and maintained a hardline rejection of cropping and other manipulation of the original image. For him, what mattered was finding the "simplicity of expression" at the

41. Inge during the filming of *The Journey* by Anatole Litvak, 1959. Photo by Yul Brynner

42. Henri Cartier-Bresson, Léré, Loire Valley, France, 1953

moment of exposure. In one of many autobiographical texts written later, she quoted him as if from memory: "The recognition of a fact in a fraction of a second and the rigorous arrangement of the forms visually perceived which give to that fact expression and significance." She was amazed at how fast he worked, yet remarked also on his patience in searching out the right location and waiting for the moment. "Now I had enough métier to absorb the essence" of his method, she wrote, learning "the conviction of composition, the constant alert, truth to the subject, ruthlessness when there was something to photograph."

During their nine months of joint work, she traveled with Cartier-Bresson on several assignments (fig. 42).[129] *Holiday* magazine wanted a photo story on "Europe," so they took off in 1953, accompanied by Cartier-Bresson's Javanese wife Elie and *Holiday*'s picture editor, Lou Mercier, driving through Germany, Italy, Spain, and England. Cartier-Bresson was demanding and when photographing, somewhat oblivious to others. He required Morath to carry the luggage, keep his cameras loaded with film, make notes for his captions. She had not yet learned to drive, so she sat in the back, waiting for him to stop when he saw something worth photographing. She spent evenings unspooling and cutting bulk film and loading it into cassettes, an activity performed blind with your arms inside a black bag.[130] Doing such scut work cheerfully and uncomplainingly earned her some respect at Magnum, whose members registered her capacity for hard work as a mark of her determination.

Traveling with Cartier-Bresson limited her own photography, however, because "when you are with Henri it's hard to photograph because he would see it first . . . and you can't do the same thing . . . Nothing escaped his lens." Still, she thought it was her "ballsy side" that evoked his respect for her—and attraction to her.[131] In her loving remembrance of this trip she recounted how they went into "every museum in sight" and discussed art passionately. (By contrast he hated to talk photography.)

Capa's decision to provide Morath with such a lengthy internship was simultaneously generous and also, possibly, sexist. None of the men were treated this way. Was admission to Magnum thus not only probationary but "premature," requiring more training to get her to the right level? Or did Capa hesitate to send her out alone? (That would have been ludicrous given her previous experiences.) Whatever the reasons, Magnum was still unaccustomed to a woman photographer.

The highlight of the *Holiday* piece was Spain, and Morath ever after felt a special connection to that country. So Capa got her a Spanish project of her own, another *Holiday* feature, this one on "Women of the World." He had identified the formidable Spanish feminist lawyer Mercedes Formica for one of the profiles.[132] Before Morath left, he urged her to get better clothes—influenced perhaps by the fashion photography he had been doing.[133] Her wardrobe apparently still consisted mainly of a black skirt with different blouses. Capa may have been trying to warn her about Spain's conservative gender culture, and indeed, she met some difficulties in working as a woman there.[134]

For that reason, beginning with Formica was a piece of luck, for she was respectable enough to introduce Morath to the right people and unconventional enough to like her. Born in 1913 to a wealthy family in Cádiz, Formica was an early member and leader of the Falange, a fascist party founded by Primo de Rivera, yet also an outspoken advocate for women's rights. In the fascist Franco regime, she became notorious for defending a woman's right to divorce and challenging the double standard regarding adultery. Morath may not have been surprised at this combination of fascism and feminism, given her mother's support for the Third Reich and rejection of conventional gender standards; in any case, she did not comment on Formica's politics. She spoke with respect of Formica's integration of "emancipation

43. Winter carnival procession, Bad Gastein, Austria, 1955

and femininity," as if a possible loss of femininity produced anxiety—hardly an unusual fear among women in the 1950s.

Arriving in Madrid in 1954, Morath planned to follow Formica through her working days. Upon being admitted to the woman's vast apartment in an exclusive Madrid neighborhood, where the maids wore uniforms and the fine furniture gleamed, she was nonplussed when Formica ignored her and continued signing papers while Morath moved around making photographs. She soon charmed her subject, however, with what an American friend called her "exquisite Old World manners"—a skill that helped her produce many celebrity portraits over the following decades.[135] Her most arresting photograph shows Formica standing on her balcony, the perspective evidently taken from an adjacent balcony. Though at home, the woman carries a small purse and wears a mantilla of lace covering a high pompadour hairdo. She stands at the far left of the image, her black dress and hair and long white earrings completing the vertical line of the building's wall, while two-thirds of the photo shows a Madrid street scene. The composition, combined with Formica's elegance, beauty, and downward gaze onto the street below, accentuates her upper-class standing and her exclusive neighborhood (fig. 44).

Spain promised superb photographic opportunities, so with Magnum's permission and a loan from her brother, Morath extended her stay for three more weeks. She was in love with the country. Over time, she made thousands of photographs in Spain, returning again and again, but even the earliest lot contained many stunning, beautifully composed images. In Cartier-Bresson she had the greatest of teachers, and she was a pupil who not only absorbed lessons, but soon developed her own style and mastery.

Morath delighted in Spain's vivid folk and religious rituals. Formica was being honored by a *falla*, a festive event in which a papier-mâché effigy of the honoree is erected and then, after a few days, burned under a canopy of fireworks. (For this particular festival, Salvador Dalí had made one of the *falles*.) Through Formica she met Gonzalo Figueroa, the Duke of la Torres, who was almost immediately infatuated with Morath—one of many doors that Formica opened for her. Insisting that her plan to travel around Spain by herself was simply impossible, he offered to drive her. He began the trip as he always traveled, with two Cadillacs, one for him, his valet, and secretary, the second one with a library from which his secretary read aloud to him, as he was blind in one eye. When he understood that she wanted to go into the countryside, he switched the Cadillacs for a Land Rover.[136] Morath's beauty and graciousness

44. Dona Mercedes Formica, Madrid, Spain, 1955

45. Gonzalo Figueroa, Inge, and the philosopher Ignacio Olagüe, Córdoba, Spain, 1954, photographer unknown

proved useful in creating photographic opportunities for her (fig. 45).

Back in Madrid, Formica hosted a party that proved to be lucky for Morath. An elegant Spanish man, to whom she had not yet been introduced, asked her what she thought of the clothing of the fashionable women in attendance; she replied that while she admired the styles on display, she would stick to her black skirt until she could afford "something really great." The man turned out to be legendary fashion designer Cristóbal Balenciaga, and he invited Inge to his atelier, where he gave her two suits and a gray dress. Her height and slim build no doubt made her the perfect model for his clothes. When she returned to Paris, she found it delicious to show off her new clothes to Capa. "It was great to see his face," she wrote, "when I showed up in my first Balenciaga." She would wear Balenciaga clothes whenever possible for the rest of her life.

She soon received another Spanish commission from the French art magazine *L'Oeil*—to photograph Picasso's sister at home with some of his early paintings. When she arrived for the shoot at the appointed time, midnight (Spaniards eat supper very late), Lola and her three grown children were drinking and smoking, playing piano and guitar, with a massive Picasso oil of a First Communion in the background.[137] Some of the photographs she made there are like family snapshots, homey, except for one portrait of Lola Ruiz Vilato herself, with the strong facial features we recognize from images of her brother (fig. 46).[138] The family's lack of reverence for the Picasso art they lived with appears in one of these images: a Picasso drawing hanging somewhat casually on a wall, under a broken glass frame, with a little cartoon inserted into a bottom corner of the frame, underneath a large black-veiled marble sculpted head of the Virgin—probably mass-produced—which someone had

46. Lola Ruiz Vilato, Picasso's sister, with her children Jaime and Lolita, Barcelona, 1954

47. Horse market, Pamplona, Navarre, Spain, 1954

crowned with a halo of artificial flowers. More Picasso paintings lay on the floor. Morath evidently enjoyed this nonchalance toward great art.

Returning to Spain later that year, Morath photographed the nine-day-long Fiesta de San Fermín in Pamplona, held yearly in mid-July (fig. 47). She traveled with Dominique Aubier, a French writer who had lived thirty years in Spain, as a guide, and young publisher Robert Delpire, who would produce a book of the photographs Morath made on this trip. (He would also become one of her lovers.) It was Magnum that jump-started Delpire's distinguished career. He got the idea of producing a "luxury review," by which he meant "serious," as he put it, not a "poorness journal with random and badly written articles" (he was speaking in his limited English), but an illustrated journal to be funded by pharmaceutical companies. At twenty-three years old, he had already started and edited the cultural review *Neuf*. Wanting the best, he recalled gathering his courage to approach Capa, Chim, and Cartier-Bresson, who surprised him with their enthusiastic reception.[139] He would return the favor, becoming for a time Magnum's primary book publisher. His press, Éditions Delpire, became the leading French publisher of photography. For sixty years, as both publisher and exhibition organizer, he was a defining force in the careers of the world's greatest photographers.

Morath was elated by the visual flamboyance of the San Fermín festival. It opens with fireworks; rowdy parades called *Riau-Riau* on the second day; a procession with a fifteenth-century statue of San Fermín the next day; followed by "the Roar," when people gather at midnight to make as much noise as possible for several hours with drums, whistles, pots, and pans. Music

48. *Torero* Antonio Ordóñez dressing for combat, San Fermín, Pamplona, Spain, 1954

49. Children celebrating First Communion, La Alberca, Salamanca, Spain, 1955

and percussion are everywhere, and everyone wears costumes and dances—including Morath: "I dance with my cameras in front of the people and behind them and they laugh and let me work."[140] San Fermín's climax is the weeklong "running of the bulls." At 8 a.m. six bulls are let loose in the streets as young men dressed all in white with red scarves try to elude or outrun them. These same bulls then go on to fight *toreros* in the afternoons.

With the help of small bribes and persistence, Morath managed to photograph two *toreros* as they dressed. This was rare access; bullfight culture deemed a woman's presence bad luck, especially at a moment of maximum apprehension. She tried to allay their anxiety about her presence with a hilarious contention: "Look here, I am always wearing pants when I work. Then I am neither man nor woman, just an eye behind the camera. . . ." No doubt she recognized the absurdity of this argument, and yet it symbolized the gender-defying work she was doing. She needed access to the dressing room in order to show, she said, the "transformation of the matador from an ordinary man into the wearer of the *traje de luces*," the shiny threads and sequins of the costumes. The best photographs captured Antonio Ordóñez—one of the most famed bullfighters, a favorite of Hemingway's—as he dressed for combat (fig. 48). They show attendants fussing to get every piece of his costume to fit like a second skin, visually echoing the way his glossy black hair is almost glued to his head. Ordóñez was only half dressed when she photographed him, and Morath thought that "the vulnerability of the naked torso . . . embodies the old symbolic sacrificial aspect of the Cretan bull sacrifices." But he is also sexy, "with the grace of an Andalusian."[141] The man appears focused only within himself, almost as if he did not notice her. We can read his fear. In one image he is praying. Morath wrote that Ordóñez and his dressers were performing "a ritual established over centuries, as in ancient rituals of sacrifice."[142]

The San Fermín photographs appeared in a Delpire book just one year later: *Guerre à la tristesse*, with text by Dominique Aubier (fig. 49).[143] In less than five years since coming to Magnum, Morath had reversed roles so that others were now writing texts for *her* photographs.[144] Royalties from the book bought her an apartment in Paris at 8 Rue de la Chaise. Located in a sixteenth-century building that had once been the Spanish embassy, her apartment had high ceilings and windows overlooking the ancient, tiny street. At last she had a permanent base, and with it a Spanish maid, Florina, who cooked and cleaned and packed for her. A "true pearl," Morath wrote, and "with her presence I continued to enter into some of the secrets of the Spanish soul." (The woman was actually Basque, and thus might have had a rather different soul.) Morath kept the apartment and the maid well into her marriage to Arthur Miller and their resettlement into Connecticut.[145]

Spain long remained her favorite venue and she returned regularly. She photographed there in 1953 to 1954, 1955, 1956, 1957, and 1962. In 1998 she collected photographs for an exhibition at the University of Santiago de Compostela. Beautifully curated, it resulted in a lovely Spanish book focused on the pilgrims who walk to Santiago, a trip considered a once-in-a-lifetime necessity by many religious Spaniards.[146] Images of cathedrals and smaller churches, including an interior shot of the altar of the Santiago cathedral with its over-the-top rococo details, every surface gilded and covered with exuberant curves large and small, in contrast to photographs of pilgrims dressed now not in robes and sandals but in jeans or shorts, hiking boots or sneakers, with modern backpacks, though often still using a walking staff as was traditional. She photographed a procession of *pecadores*, "sinners," walking in all black with veils covering their faces.

There is a touch of orientalism in Morath's fascination with "the Spanish soul," as she called it. That attitude, however unconscious, reflected a more general European belief: "Africa begins at the Pyrenees" had long been a common cliché about Spain,[147] framing it as primitive or exotic. It was folkloric Spain, not high art Spain, that most attracted Morath: the religious festivals and pageantry, the *penitentos* in black pointed hoods, the veiled women, the elaborate headdresses of women in traditional costumes, the preening dances of bullfighters. She wrote that Madrid and Barcelona at first seemed like other European cities, until they did not. "There it was . . . moving, pushing Time out of

50. Public washing, Chinchón, Spain, 1955

51. Still photographer's props, Verbena de San Isidro, Madrid, 1955

52. Fiesta de San Fermín, Pamplona, Spain, 1955

PELUQUERIA

its European pace into an oriental one."[148] She photographed fisherwomen carrying their haul to market on their heads; women washing clothes in a public basin (figs. 50, 51, 52, 53); unplucked chickens for sale at outdoor stands; the elaborate hand embroidery on clothing; the tiny workshops of a carpenter and an *acibeche* carver.[149] She occasionally wore Spanish dresses of brilliant colors with full, tiered skirts and sleeves, though in Paris she returned to her usual understated style. Spain made her feel festive, light-hearted—a step outside the quotidian. Curator Sabine Folie called the mood in Morath's Spanish photographs Dionysian (fig. 54).[150] Admiration for the preindustrial, the traditional, the

53. Romeria del Rocio, Seville, Spain, 1955

people who lived alongside their animals would show in her future work as well.

She was particularly attracted to bullfights, an unusual taste in an Austrian/Parisian woman. Her love of dance allowed her to appreciate the agility and grace of the *toreros*, but she was also thrilled by the danger itself. "It is in the blood, in the young men's dreams of daring," she wrote, perhaps resonating with her own dreams of adventure. She understood "the joy of having been witness to something rare and perfect" that comes with the matador's victory over the bull.[151]

Spain also inspired experimentation with the surreal. At the San Fermín festival, Morath photographed the *gigantes*, weird enormous heads the size of a whole human body, mounted on scaffolding and carried by groups of men whose skirts hide the apparatus, and the *cabezudos*, men wearing large papier-mâché heads. A woman who had just won a doll in a contest has a maniacal grin, while the doll, her face almost as big as the woman's, adds to the fantastic appearance. In the shopwindow of a hairdresser in Madrid, busts of men and women wearing wigs to demonstrate hairstyles resemble severed heads; one of them stares unnervingly at the viewer.

54. Inge in flamenco dress, Spain, 1955, photographer unknown

Neither photographs nor texts referred to Franco's fascist government. Cartier-Bresson spoke to her of García Lorca and the civil war but she never referred to it, or to the Franco dictatorship, in texts or photos. Perhaps Formica's pro-Franco friends made her circumspect while in Spain, but that silence, or avoidance, remained throughout her life (figs. 55, 56).[152] It was her response to trauma. Just as she had no desire to take on war photography when entering Magnum, so she had no desire to relive old pain or confront new sufferings through photography. Perhaps, too, her horrific teenage experience had fused with an inborn personal quality that Imo Moszkowicz noted: a need to be tactful and avoid conflict.[153]

Spain brought Morath another upper-class lover. By the beginning of 1956 she was engaged to Duke Gonzalo Figueroa, whom she had met on the very first trip there, and to whom, she wrote, "I owe my good Spanish."[154] Like Birch he was tall, elegant, rich, and soaked in fine culture. He was smitten. He had fifteen silk shirts made for her, each in a different color.[155] Other gifts were practical: "I could use his huge black car with chauffeur, his

55. Fiesta de San Fermín fairground, Pamplona, Spain, 1954

56. Child reading newspaper, Spain, 1950s

57. Madrid, 1957

secretary held my tripod.[156] The marriage, planned for later that year, was delayed, supposedly because "some papers" that she needed had not arrived.[157] She soon broke the engagement because, she later told her daughter, she realized the life of an aristocratic wife in Spain would have made her feel trapped,[158] perhaps remembering Birch's objections to her roving photographic life. (Still, she remembered the Duke fondly decades later when she wrote of a particular type of bread that Gonzalo had loved[159] [fig. 57].)

During her engagement to Figueroa, Morath was also juggling a relationship with Louis le Brocquy, today considered Ireland's greatest painter. He too wanted to marry her. They had become lovers on one of her photographic trips to Ireland and met frequently thereafter (figs. 58, 59). Never without suitors, she wrote her parents, "I can't decide between the numerous candidates."[160] Yet she and le Brocquy remained friends even as she rejected him. She was too captivating for anyone to remain angry at her.

RAMOS

58. Traveling folk musicians in Killorglin, County Kerry, Ireland, 1954

59. Puck Fair, Killorglin, County Kerry, Ireland, 1954

RADIO
WOODS
ELECTRICAL

Chapter Five

WORLD PHOTOGRAPHER

In the second half of the nineteenth century, photographers from the "West" "discovered" the rest of the world, and travel photography emerged as a popular medium. In an upward spiral, the images, in turn, stimulated tourism, creating a demand for yet more travel photography. *National Geographic*, established in 1888, added to its popularity. Because the photographers were usually European, their photographs often revealed more about their imperial perspective than about their subjects, as they so often focused on the allegedly "primitive," even emphasizing what magazine readers saw as grotesque.[161] Magnum photographers joined those ventures into the global south, but their work was remarkably free of the colonialist eye, reflecting a more democratic and open-minded view of cultural differences. Typically male, travel photographers ventured into barely accessible locations, accepting uncomfortable conditions with a spirit of vagabondage and adventure, much like war photographers. Inge Morath did the same, a most unusual activity for a woman at the time. Somehow the aggravations of travel and alien environments never dulled her zest for far-off places and cultures.

The Spanish photography in *Holiday* and the Delpire book brought her positive notice and more commissions. They inaugurated a decade of "running and flying," as she photographed in Austria, Germany, Basutoland, Iraq, Lebanon, Syria, Tunisia, Italy, Portugal, Romania, Yugoslavia, Mexico, Argentina, England, Switzerland, Sweden, the United States (fig. 61), and that doesn't count the travels to different locations within those countries. Many of these jobs were implicitly marked female—the treasures of the Bavarian Wittelsbach dynasty, the wedding of Princess Furstenberg, the funeral of the Hapsburg Archbishop, the New York City Ballet, Paris boutiques, animals on TV, an excursion of the "Catherinettes" (a French label for young women "still" unmarried at age twenty-five). Whenever possible she tried, however, to expand her subjects and methods beyond the stereotypically feminine. She had been doing color photography from the first moments she held a camera. At first, she used only

60. Robert Delpire and Inge, Paris, 1956. Photo by René Burri

INGE MORATH

1955 - 1 Seine Flood, rolls 355-358.

2 Alcoholism in France, rolls 359-361.

3 Winter Ball in Paris, rolls 362-376 (no #372).
*Princess Chavchavadze (366/16-18), Larrain (367), Charlie Chaplin & Countess of Paris (371/22-31).

4 Archduke Eugen of Hapsburg Funeral, Innsbruck, rolls 377-383.
*Empress Zita of Hapsburg.

5 Austria, Carnival in Snow, rolls 384-391.

6 House of Cezanne, Paris, rolls 392-396.

7 Circus at "Vel d'Hiv", rolls 397-398.

8 Spain - Goya paintings, roll 399.

9 Spain, rolls 400-411.

10 Barcelona, Madrid, Mallorca, rolls 412-427.

11 Corrida in Barcelona, rolls 428-435.

12 Madrid, Verbena de San Isidro, rolls 436-441.

13 Bullfights de San Isidro, rolls 442-450.

14 Dominique Aubier, roll 451.

15 Winefest in Bingen on Rhine, roll 452.

16 House of Ida Rubinstein, roll 460 (no # 453-459,461).

17 Rococo Bavarois, rolls 462,464 (no #463).

18 Iberian Bronzes, rolls 465-466.

19 Rubio de Boston in Madrid, rolls 467-477.

20 Wittelsbach Treasure, Munich, rolls 478-479

21 Spain - Peasant Wedding in Castille, rolls 480-495.

22 Luis Miguel Dominguin, rolls 497-499 (no #496).

23 Marie Louise Bousquet, roll 500.

24 Dominique Aubier, roll 501.
*Dominique Aubier with Robert Delpire.

61. Story list, 1955

62. Zulu tribe, South Africa, 1955

one camera, so she would have to shoot a whole roll of black-and-white before switching to color, which limited her experimentation. Acquiring additional cameras freed her to do more in color, as in Basutoland (today's Lesotho), where she traveled in 1955. There she made a pastoral image of a blanket-clad family resting on green grass with a white horse in the background. Loveliest were her images of African children in the context of the striking Zulu paintings that adorned many houses, walls, and other structures (fig. 62). In Ireland, she made subtle use of color—resisting the way that color can overwhelm composition, yet evoking the green and rainy climate in a delicate evocation of Ireland's feel.

The constant travel caused an injury—in 1954 a taxi collision in Paris "mangled" her right leg. She suffered through great pain and surgery, yet she recalled appreciating the downtime to edit the photographs for the Pamplona book—her memory ever focusing on the positive.

In 1955 she accepted an assignment to do photographs for Mary McCarthy's book *Venice Observed,* to "evoke the Venice in the background of its famous painters." Nothing could have pleased this art lover more, unless it was the resultant friendship with McCarthy that continued for many years. She shot an astonishing three-thousand-plus negatives in a few weeks. It was not, however, until 2003, after her death, that a selection of these could be seen in a book curated by Kurt Kaindl, an Austrian photographer and photography critic.[162]

Her Venetian themes differed from the Spanish. These images focused less on festivals, their tempo was less active, and their atmosphere more muted. Since other photographers were assigned to cover Venice's art and architecture, Morath concentrated on daily life

63. Transport of heavy goods, Venice, 1955

64. Fishermen, Venice, 1955

(fig. 63). This accorded with her desire to get away from the mythical, clichéd Venice, which had already been photographed so extensively. As Karl-Markus Gauß noted in his introduction to the 2003 book, *Venezia*, most people visiting Venice had already seen so many paintings and photographs of it that, once there, they searched out only the places and vistas they had "learned to accept as the real Venice."[163]

Morath resisted these conventions and observed Venice anew, with a different attentiveness and aesthetic. Avoiding the tourist attractions, she documented daily Venetian life. Fish and fishing, the basis of Venice's subsistence and economy, are everywhere in the photographs: women mending nets, fishermen mending nets, fishermen carrying fish to markets (fig. 64), marketers selling fish, buyers haggling about fish prices, women cleaning fish. Also vegetable markets, people hauling vegetables and others buying them, as well as women preparing food out on the sidewalk. She showed people working outside—a street musician, a knife sharpener who propels his turning stone with a bicycle, little girls washing clothes with scrub brushes against boards, women and girls stringing glass beads and pearls. As interested in the rundown tenements as in the palazzos, she photographed eroding walls, revealing intricate textures. Juxtapositions, one of her favorite photographic techniques, showed twentieth-century working-class lives next to battered, centuries old statuary—laundry hanging next to church windows; a grandmother carrying a dirty, bandaged child under a massive stone lion; a young man lugging two heavy cherubs, one on his shoulder, the other with his arm between its legs. A fine leaded glass door on an upper floor of a palazzo opens onto a tiny carved balcony in the foreground, while in the background men struggle to build wooden scaffolding to support the unstable building.

When she could not entirely pass up the familiar, symbolic Venice, her photographs transformed stale motifs. Gondolas appear not as tourist transportation but as part of the lives of the Venetians themselves. She showed men building gondolas, and one striking image shows four men struggling to move a large, heavy machine onto a gondola. She dutifully photographed pigeons on the Piazza San Marco, but defamiliarized them. One image, almost surrealist, showed the pigeons amassed so densely that they appear as a frightening, impenetrable mass of feathered wings.

Most of this photography was black and white, but she used color subtly: a worn sepia brick wall, a barred window with a horizontal stripe of white on the lower windowsill juxtaposed with three vertical whites formed by a painted stripe on the left margin and two little girls dressed in white. What's more, their reddish hair is the same sepia as the wall—a particularly elegant use of color. (Similar color composition will appear in photographs from Iran.)

Morath, ever adventurous, had long dreamed of photographing along Marco Polo's Silk Road, starting from Venice. She broached this idea to *Holiday*, but it was rejected, so she compromised. She knew that Robert Delpire was interested in a book on Iran, and *Holiday* went along with that.[164] Three commissions—from *Holiday*, Standard Oil, and Pepsi Cola—paid for the trip ("pure greed, but necessary," she wrote her parents).[165] In return, the latter two sponsors would receive photographs of their Iranian operations for use in corporate publicity.[166] *Holiday*'s idea of showing Iran was laughable: mosques and carpets, of which the editor wrote, "A color photo of one of these masterpieces . . . might do it for this part of the Near East."[167] Inge's agenda was far more ambitious—and knowledgeable—since she prepared for this trip by reading extensively about Iran and its culture.

In March 1956, Morath and Delpire took off for Tehran on her "longest and most exciting trip so far."[168] She returned only when she ran out of film, propelled as always by irrepressible curiosity to press on to every new location, society, and culture she heard about. The trip lasted six weeks and it shows the fascination with—and respect for—foreign cultures that had been evident in her Spanish photography.

The expedition began with a personal disagreement, one with which she was familiar: she insisted on a separate hotel room; Robert Delpire was unhappy about this. They were lovers, if not now then previously, but Inge was determinedly single.[169] Her complex feelings about that relationship show, perhaps inadvertently, in a remarkable photograph of the two of them by René Burri. She wanted her space and probably did not want to be identified as his partner, which would have placed her as a subordinate, a travel-along. Worse, if they had shared a room in Iran they might have had to pretend to be married. After a few weeks Delpire returned to Paris and Inge moved around the country accompanied only by an interpreter and driver.[170]

Tehran VIPs received Delpire and Morath as prestigious and official guests, perhaps because of their Standard Oil sponsor. A police captain was assigned to protect them.[171] Manouchehr Teymourtash, a member of the old pre-Shah aristocracy, hosted them. The minister of foreign affairs met them and escorted them to the hotel. A captain of the gendarmerie took them on a tour of the city, providing photo opportunities. Morath photographed at the marble Golestan Palace during a reception attended by ministers, generals, diplomats,

65. The Shah and members of the diplomatic corps, Nowruz Reception, Golestan Palace, Tehran, 1956

other unidentified bigwigs and "ladies": she showed the gold chandeliers and candelabra in a silver hall of mirrors (fig. 65); the guards wearing gilded helmets and carrying drawn sabers appeared at every gate, door, and staircase; the diplomats dressed in uniforms with epaulettes and chests full of medals, gold ropes, and sashes; a table "laid with bowls containing seven kinds of fruits and spices, all of whose names start with the letter 'S.'"[172] She photographed the Shah and his cabinet members lined up to kiss Queen Soraya's hand. The photos suggest, perhaps knowingly, that the Queen was challenging the norms of royal splendor, wearing not a gown but a modest knee-length daytime dress with white Peter Pan collar. (She was a modern, secular, cigarette-smoking woman, the daughter of the Iranian ambassador to Germany and a German mother. Perhaps she and Inge conversed in German.)[173]

Morath also photographed the well-to-do at the Abadan Lawn Tennis Club, where expats and elite Iranians played, swam, and drank together, all in Western dress. Today the pictures remind us of the secularism of the Iranian upper classes under the Shah. There is no critique in these images, with one exception: a woman beggar seated on the grounds of the country club, covered in a black chador, holds out her hand for alms as

66. A stall in the market, Tehran, 1956

a group of club members walk by obliviously or with feigned oblivion.

Morath acknowledged her lack of enthusiasm for the industrial photography that her sponsors required. Unlike many earlier documentary photographers, such as Margaret Bourke-White, she did not see beauty in industrial or "mechanical" forms, and was far more interested in the country's natural beauty and rural people.[174] She did, however, illustrate the contradictions of a modernizing Iran, between a state-of-the-art Pepsi Cola bottling factory and vast oil refineries on the one hand, and nomads living in tents with their camels and a mud caravansary in the desert on the other. This is precisely what Morath meant by titling her first Iran book *De la Perse à l'Iran* (from Persia to Iran—i.e., from the traditional to the modern).[175] Yet when the work was published, texts by others supplied the orientalist spin that she so scrupulously avoided. Alan Moorehead wrote in *Holiday* that he found Iran's modernity "repulsive" and longed for the exotic "whiff of the lazy Arabic East." (*Holiday* did not seem to have registered that Iranians are not Arabs.) Edouard Sablier, the French journalist who introduced a second, posthumous book, longed for "the glimpse of dark eyes beneath a deftly fastened veil."[176] Such commentary shows by contrast the respect and lack of sentimentality in Morath's work. The photographs show no laziness, and the veiled women look forthrightly at the photographer. She did comment critically on veiling, notably in a photograph showing three veiled Muslim women next to caged cockatoos with a caption explaining that they were the wives of one man (figs. 66, 67, 68).[177]

In Vanak, an Armenian neighborhood of Tehran, the interior of a small Orthodox church is decorated with rugs, chandeliers, candlesticks, and lace cloths. In Zoroastrian villages, where people practiced a pre-Islamic Persian religion, she photographed the interior of a domed mud-brick home, with seats created by cutting out ledges in the walls. She centered here a framed image of Jesus, complete with halo, hung on the wall amid framed photos of family, no doubt calling attention to this show of ecumenism. In another Zoroastrian home, three seated inhabitants are studiously ignoring the photographer (fig. 69). They remind the viewer of why Morath made few portraits in Iran. Despite her extraordinary linguistic ability, she could not speak Farsi or any of Iran's other languages, and she could not usually get close to subjects. In some photographs we see people not only keeping their distance, but also showing their suspicion or resentment of this intruder. The absence of portraiture characterizes all her photography in North Africa and the Levant, from Tunisia to Jordan; in a rare close-up photograph of two young women of Tunisia, the subject is their exotic costumes, not their individuality.

A technical problem ruined many of Morath's black-and-white photographs. One camera had a light leak, and the disaster was all the worse because, lacking a lab in

67. Inge wearing a chador to hide cameras during work in the streets, Qom, Iran, 1956, photographer unknown

68. Veiled Muslim women and caged cockatoos, Shiraz, Iran, 1956

69. Zoroastrian women washing dishes in the brook that runs through their village, Iran, 1956

Iran, she did not realize the problem until she returned. Consequently, most of her photographs of Iran remained unseen until 2009, when the damaged negatives were scanned and retouched by Steidl's expert digital darkroom for the book *Inge Morath: Iran*. Fortunately the camera loaded with color film functioned perfectly, and the results showed the color sensibility of someone who loved painting. She also used an early instant Polaroid model to create photographic gifts for people she met.[178]

Once outside Tehran, making these photographs required enduring considerable discomforts. At a Standard Oil refinery in Abadan, the air reeked of petroleum and the publicity man who accompanied her was "lazy and keen on gin" and "a fanatic Inshallah." (This

70. Inge photographing in Persepolis, Iran, 1956, photographer unknown

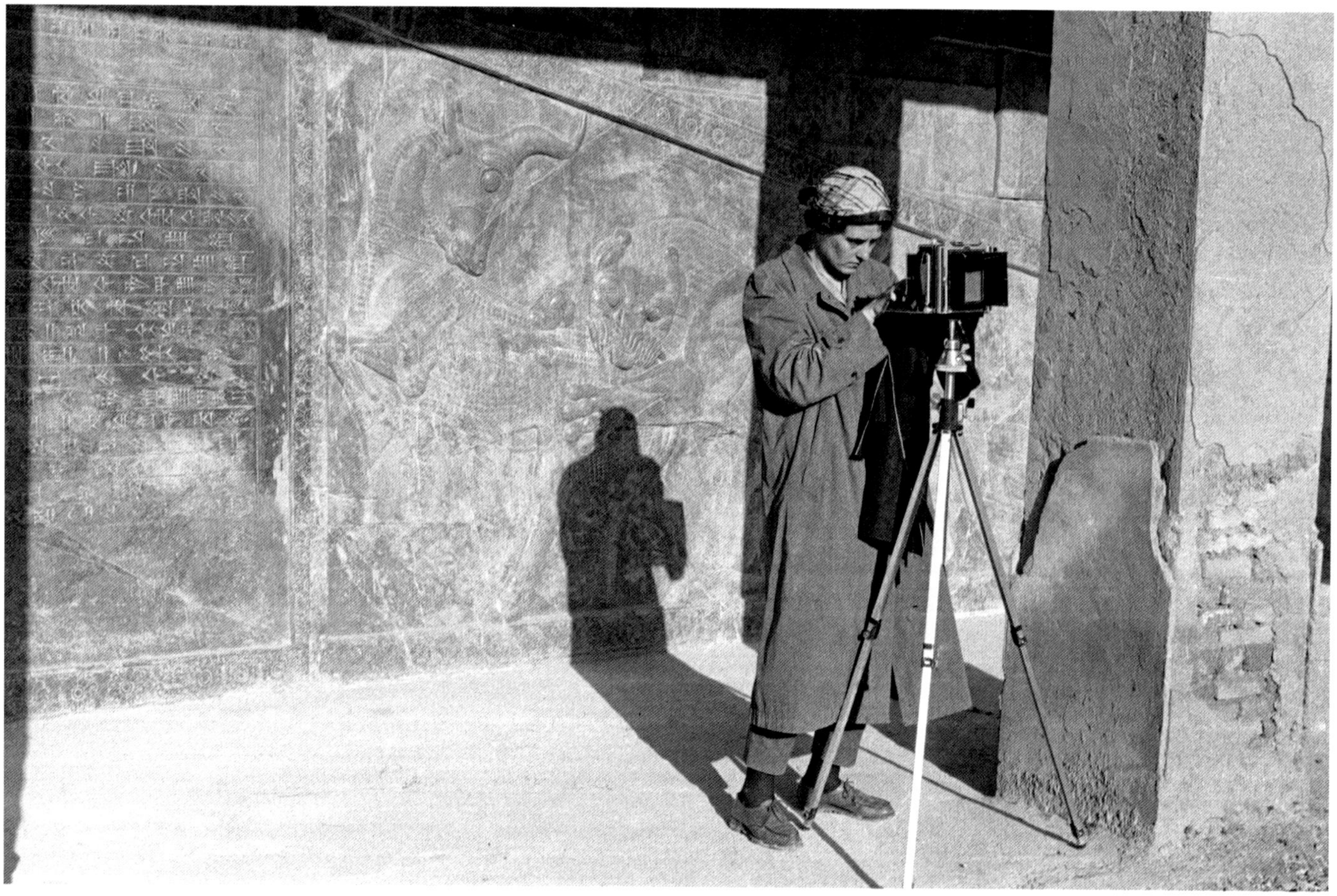

label was no doubt her shorthand for an ultrareligious and preachy Muslim.) The hotels were often miserable, her clothes were dirty and she had no way to wash them, and she suffered from the heat, for which she hadn't brought the right clothing.[179] At times she wore chadors and veils—which of course made her even hotter—as a gesture of respect for Iranian culture, and possibly for her own protection; luckily her Armenian driver showed her how and when to wear them, saving her from some cultural gaffes. But she usually wore trousers. Someone, probably Delpire, photographed her at work in Persepolis, wearing pants, a voluminous wool coat, and flat oxford shoes (fig. 70).[180]

71. *Pahlevani* exercise in *zoorkhaneh*, a domed structure used for practice, Tehran, 1956

Never daunted by harsh conditions, Morath had a curiosity and sensitivity to beauty that produced some of her best work, on a par with her Spanish photography. Leaving Tehran exposed her to entirely different classes of people—peasants, shepherds, nomads, artisans, mullahs, small merchants—and sites: the bazaar, tent dwellings, baths, interiors, mosques, ancient ruins, factories, oil fields, festivals (fig. 71). If there was a trace of orientalism in the Spanish photography, there was none here. She photographed people at work—spinning, dyeing,

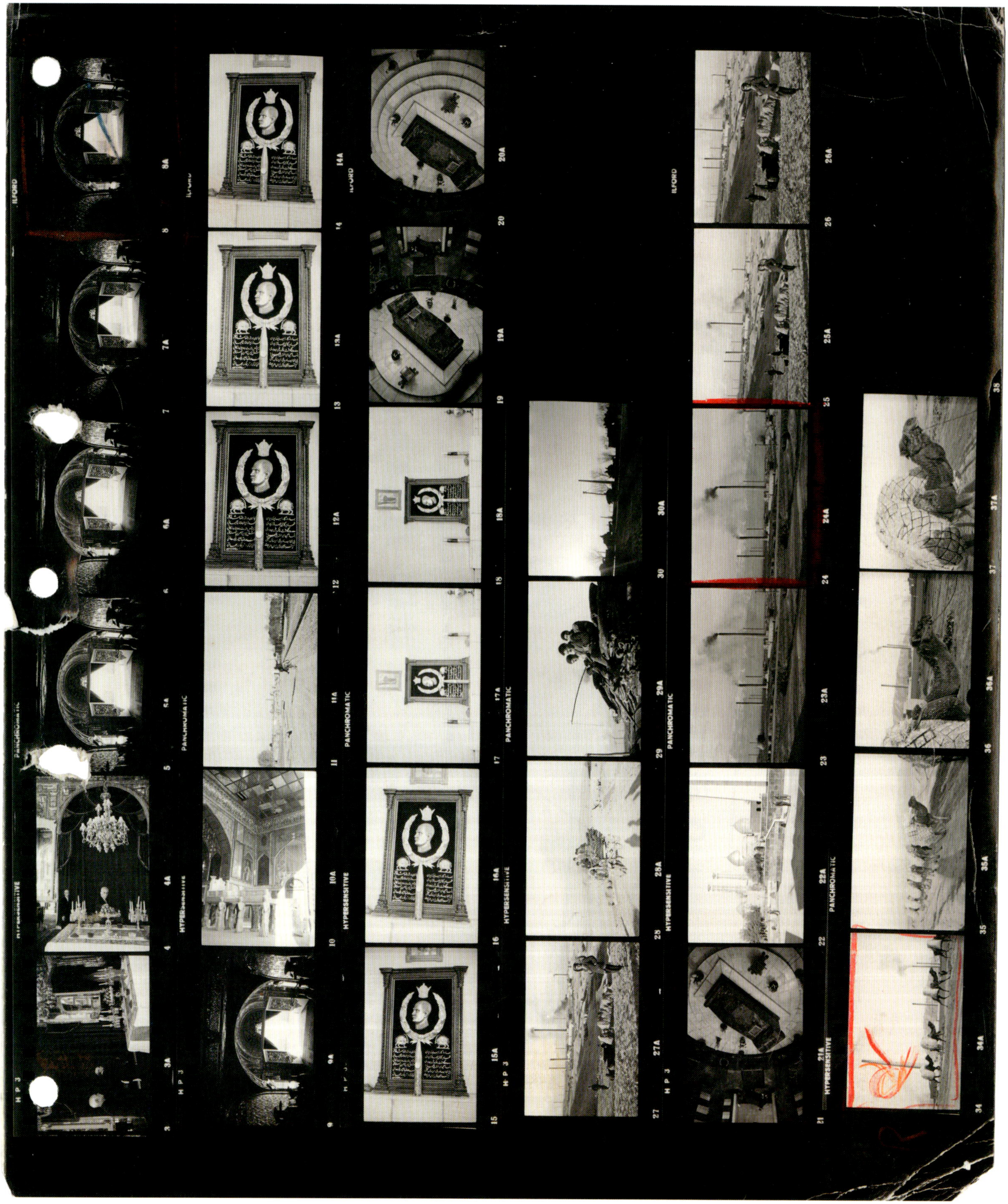

ILFORD
HP3
PANCHROMATIC
HYPERSENSITIVE

72. Contact sheet, Iran, 1956

73. Family waiting for a bus near the Caspian Sea, Iran, 1956

74. Friday mosques, Isfahan, Iran, 1956

carpet-weaving and carpet-knotting, metal-working, brickmaking, cobbling, cooking, baking, laundering, gathering wood, hauling, and in bottling plants, cotton mills, and oil refineries, as well as people at leisure—making music, dancing, drinking tea, smoking hookahs, smoking opium, and celebrating holidays (figs. 72, 73).

In Iran's southern desert regions, near Chum, Yazd, and Pasargadae, she photographed nomads lovingly, perhaps because they presented picture-perfect subjects: women dressed in brilliant printed fabrics contrasting with black tents and multihued earth colors; elaborate headgear and multiple beads; children sitting on camels, children carrying lambs. Her color photography showed the minute variations in the colors of the earth, sand, and mud structures (figs. 74, 75, 76). The earth tones rhyme with those of camels, people's skin, and men's worn, faded clothing—colors punctuated by the bright colors of women's clothing. Together the colors give the viewer a glimpse of why so many love the deserts in the Alborz Mountains.

Many images show young children at work, especially young girls sitting at looms and spinning wheels, both artisanal and industrial.[181] Some commentators have seen these photographs of working children as a criticism of child labor, but in fact they contain no critique; they simply report. With neither judgment nor pity, her photographs offer instead an ethnographic view of cultural and economic life in a foreign country. There is no implication that the children are unloved, neglected, or abused. They are children living in a world in which everyone among the poor must contribute to the family economy, something Morath seems to have understood.

Nothing in the photographs references the CIA/MI6/oil company–backed coup that had deposed the elected Prime Minister Mosaddegh in 1953, after he sought to nationalize the oil industry and guarantee better wages and benefits for Iranian workers. And Morath's photographs reflect only positively on her sponsor Standard Oil's investments there, though the corporation supported and may have instigated that coup. This silence resulted from choice, not ignorance; always studying diligently to learn about what she was to photograph, she had read about the political situation in Iran before arriving.[182] Photography critics Andy Grundberg and Monika Faber criticized Morath's story for its "implicit abandonment of any moral position."[183] But her choice of subjects, while reflecting her response

75. Roof of the bazaar and red towels from the public bath, Isfahan, Iran, 1956

76. Nomads weaving near Pasargadae, Iran, 1956

77. Captions from Iran story, 1956

IRAN 56 ~~-4~~ ~~22~~

Inge Morath 1

Iran Roll Captions

Roll no. 769

Frames 3-10 Reception room and entrance hall inside the Golestan Palace in Teheran. Inside this palace the Shah holds his New Year reception and other state functions. ~~Thexpalacexis~~ ~~openxtoxthexpublicxwhen~~

12 — 22 ~~12 tox20 to 21~~ Photographs taken inside the tomb of Reza Shah, father of the present emperor and founder of the Pahlavi dynasty.

22 Rey, a small town about 10 miles outside Teheran whose Mosque for centuries has been a center for pilgrimages. New walls on the foreground are part of the tomb to the memory ~~ts~~ of Reza Shah.

23 to 37 a Street workers and camels outside the southern industrial suburbs of Teheran. Snow capped mountains in the background are part of the impressive Alborz range, rising steeply behind Teheran.

Roll no. 770

Frames 3-11

3-11 Scenes in various small streets of Teheran: Women wearing the traditional tshador, a heavy veil covering them from head to foot, contrasting sharply with the modern cars; a street vendor counts his money.

12 —27 The private reception room of ~~the~~ His imperial majesty is being prepared for the No Ruz (New Year reception) which takes place on the 21st of March. Mirror inlaid walls and ceilings, crystal chandeliers, precious persian carpets cover the floor. According to an old Aryan tradition, a table is laid with bowls containing 7 kinds of fruits and spices and nuts ~~all~~ whose names must start with s.

28- 33 General view of the throne room in the Golestan Palace with the Peacock Throne in the background. Large alcoves are used to display ~~in~~ some of the precious gifts given to the rulers of Iran by the Kings and emperors of foreign countries.

34 -35 Close up of the Peacock Throne brought back to Iran by Nadar Shah after his victorious campaign to India . The throne is of gold, jewel-inlaid. Above the throne a portrait of the present Shah.

78. Palestinian refugee camp, Gaza, 1960

to trauma, derived also from humility, from demurring to assume that she understood enough to judge (fig. 77). As in all her work, she was a visual ethnographer; she did not go near questions of justice or injustice.

Morath did, however, get involved in a project documenting refugee camps for the United Nations. The commission was doubly appealing in that she would work with film star Yul Brynner, and indulge her curiosity about foreign cultures. But visiting refugee camps must have brought up painful memories of her own wartime trauma. In either case it was a project she was proud of.

She had met Brynner while photographing two of his 1959 films, *The Journey* and *Solomon and Sheba*, and had found him fascinating.[184] It didn't hurt that he was also a fine photographer, his work distributed by Magnum, though he was not a member. When the United Nations declared 1959 "World Refugee Year," Brynner became a special consultant to the Office of the United Nations High Commissioner for Refugees (UNHCR) and asked Morath to join him in documenting refugee camps, with the goal of awakening public support for the agency's work. Once she agreed, they decided to concentrate on the plight of children. The photos were published in Brynner's *Bring Forth the Children* in 1960.

Their trip covered both the remaining WWII European refugees and the new refugees created when the new state of Israel displaced Palestinians. The two traveled together first to a camp for displaced persons—DPs, as refugees were then called—in Ludwigsburg in southeastern Germany. Once a German POW camp, in 1959 it sheltered 420 of the continent's fifteen million refugees. So many children had been there so long, speaking so many different Slavic languages, that they had devised their own pidgin version of a generic Slavic to make playing together possible.[185] Then Brynner and Morath moved on to Camp Parsch in Salzburg;[186] this familiar territory must have reawakened memories of the wartime destruction she had experienced during her Vienna years.

Then on to the Levant, site of approximately 720,000 Palestinian refugees. Near Jericho, then still in Jordan, they visited Aqaba Jaber, which held 46,000 people—and 76,000 in winter.[187] All the photographs sounded a tone of lamentation, but here the conditions were particularly bad: ragged children, women hauling water in jugs due to lack of plumbing, pathways either dusty or muddy, mud-brick shelters built by the refugees themselves. The Palestinians in these Jordanian camps were

79. Gaza, 1960

not served by UNHCR but by the United Nations Relief and Works Administration (UNRWA). It struggled to provide food and clothing and battle malaria and dysentery—with a budget of only seven cents per day per individual, many children did not receive even a minimal daily ration (figs. 78, 79).[188]

At their next stop, Beit Safafa, on the southwestern side of Jerusalem, people became refugees when the Green Line—the border between the new state of Israel and Jordan—cut off their access to Jerusalem, depriving farmers of a market. Camp Muascar, in the old city of Jerusalem, described by UNRWA as "one of our most unsatisfactory," held 5,132 people. Its residents had only

80. Oasis of Tozeur, Tunisia, 1959

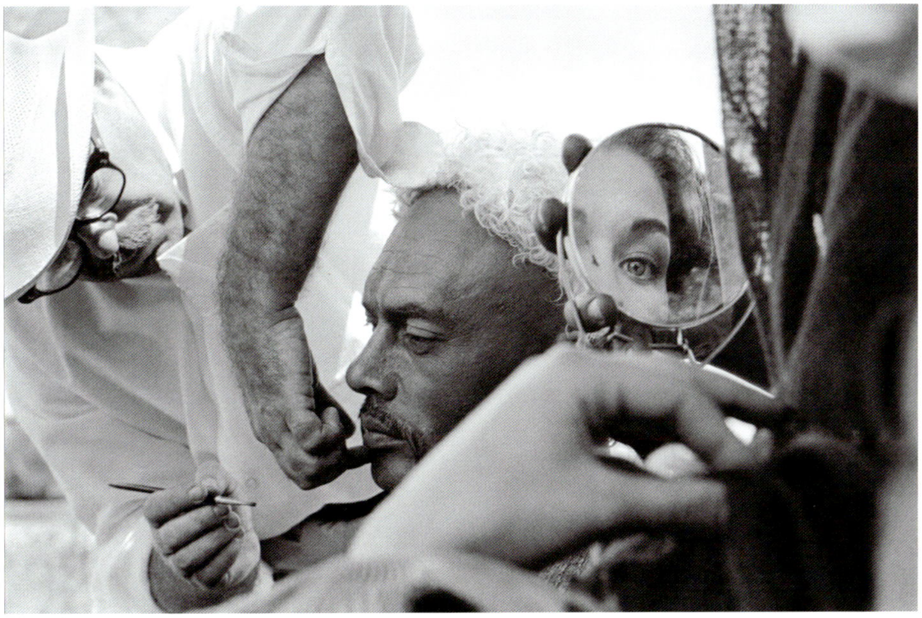

crude shelters that they constructed from rubble; these refugees were not even on UNRWA rolls and depended on private charities. Here, Morath somehow managed to make a powerful photograph in a cave that "housed" an extended family:[189] an old man with one leg holds his handmade substitute for a crutch—a stick with a bit of rag around the top.[190] I can only imagine her feelings in witnessing such deprivation, and the one-legged man surely brought back memories of the peg-leg man who had helped her reach her parents in 1945.

The refugee photographs demonstrate Morath's refusal of sentimentality and sensationalism, a discipline all the more remarkable given her own refugee experience. Every one of these camps could have yielded tear-jerking images of sad or pathetic children, of older faces lined with worry and sorrow. There are a few such children—for example, the image of a young blonde girl, her hair lovingly pulled back with a ribbon and a bobby pin, a sore on her lip and bags under her eyes, though she can be no older than seven—but as always Morath exercised restraint. She rejected bathos and remained both a journalist, reporting the facts, and an ethnographer, always with more curiosity and respect than pity.

81. Yul Brynner and Christine Kaufmann (in the mirror) on the set of the film *Taras Bulba*, Salta, Argentina, 1961

82. Yul Brynner on vacation, Lake Geneva, Switzerland, 1959

The teamwork between Morath and Brynner must have worked well because he not only asked her to photograph his next film, *Taras Bulba* (1962), but also invited her to visit the next year in Geneva, where he had just settled in with his new bride, Chilean beauty queen, model, and actress Doris Kleiner. The photographs Morath made of him on Lake Geneva, driving his motorboat in a revealing white bathing suit, and in action on water skis, captured his image as the sexy hunk he wanted to project. Given her taste, and her taste in men, I suspect her tongue was well in her cheek while making these photographs (figs. 81, 82).

Luncheon • Dinner
MILLS Black Beauty
MILLS Black Beauty
MILLS Black Beauty
MILLS Black Beauty
5¢
5¢

Chapter Six

AMERICA AND ARTHUR MILLER

As Magnum's New York office grew in importance, Morath came to the United States more frequently. She had first been there in 1951 when she and her then husband Lionel Birch both had work in Hollywood. In 1956 she went alone, by ship, in order to have time for the background reading she always did in preparation for photographing. But nothing prepared her for New York City. "It made me dizzy."[191] It quickly captivated her. "Another rhythm," she wrote. "Mary McCarthy, Chelsea Hotel, Jazz, Harlem . . . the Metropolitan, Modern Art, Frick Gallery, Carnegie Hall."[192] She loved riding the subway, populated by such vivid diversity. The Chelsea Hotel would become central to her experience. Built in the 1880s on West 23rd Street, it had become the favored home of artists, writers, bohemians, and Beats.[193] As her American home for several years, it put her just where she wanted to be—with simpatico, out-of-the-mainstream devotees of high and low culture.

Her photography of New York extended over four decades. She did many commercial assignments—fashion, beauty classes at the Helena Rubinstein Salon

84. Beauty class at the Helena Rubinstein Salon, New York, 1958

(fig. 84), the opening of a shopping mall (then a new invention), and celebrity portraits.[194] In a story on animals used in films, her witty shot of a llama peeking out of a car in Times Square became famous (figs. 85, 86). A major advertising job became hers after Cartier-Bresson declined it: Bankers Trust had the idea to commission documentary-style photography instead of posed advertisements to use in its corporate releases (fig. 87). Well paid, the commission allowed her to wander around the

83. Inge, 1960. Photo by Henri Cartier-Bresson

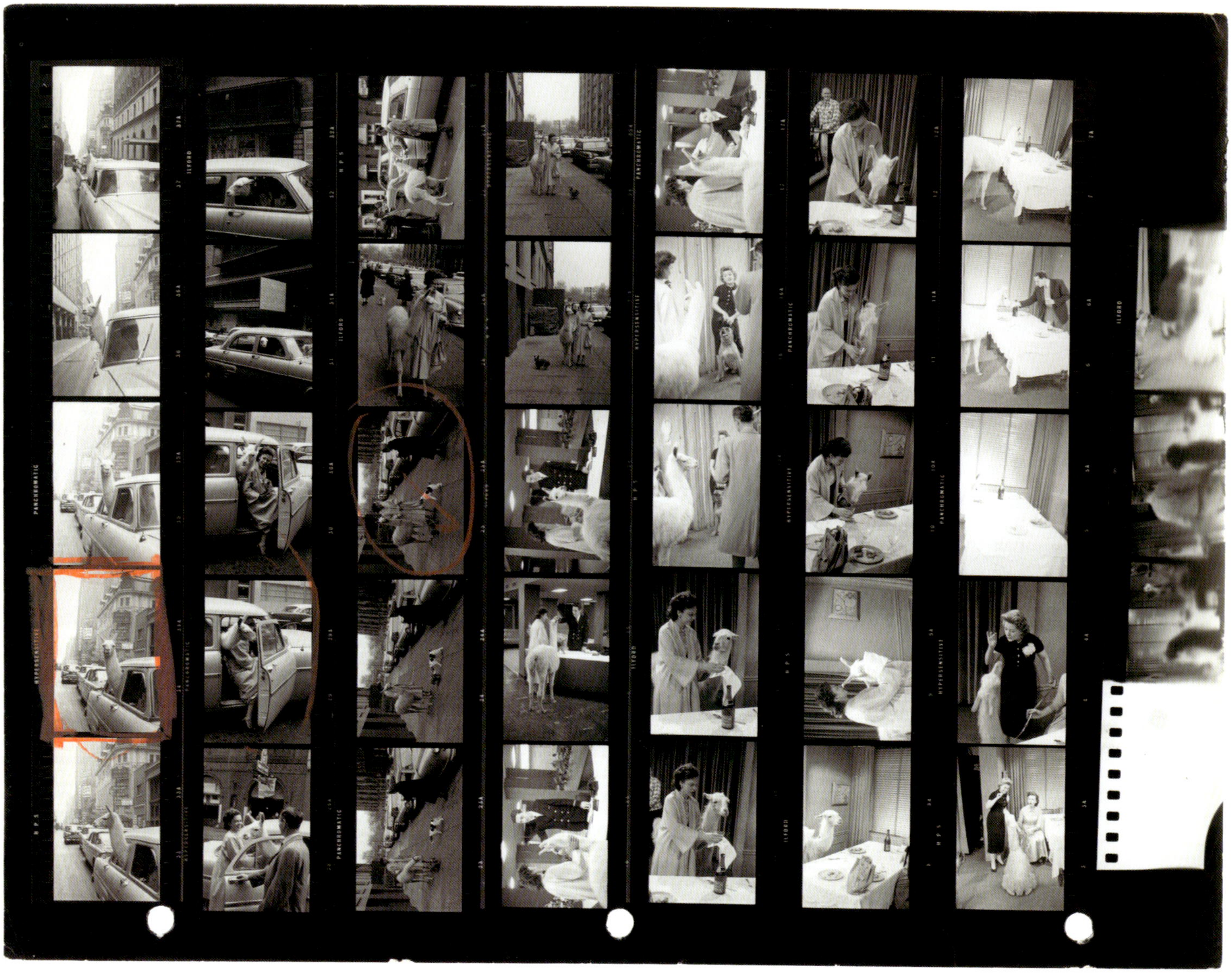

85. Contact sheet, 1957

86. A llama in Times Square, New York, 1957

SHUBERT THEATRE
JUDY
HOLLIDAY
IN
BELLS
THEATRE TICKETS
TAXI

city off and on for several years photographing New York's urban life, including chess players in Washington Square (in those years they were white) and window washers in Midtown (fig. 88).[195]

She also connected with people who helped advance her career (fig. 81). With Gjon Mili, she conversed in Romanian; a great technician, he taught her about strobes.[196] Violinist Alexander Schneider lent her one of his empty apartments where she encountered artist Saul Steinberg's "document" drawings on its walls.[197] That led her to seek out Steinberg (another Romanian), who greeted her from behind a paper mask (figs. 89, 90, 91). This gave birth to a series of photographs created between 1959 and 1962 of Steinberg and friends wearing paper-bag masks; he made the masks and she found the people to wear them. The project questioned, in a playful way, the everyday masks people wear. "A study in impersonation—how am I presenting myself to the world today?" (fig. 92)[198] Years later this yielded the book *Masquerade* (2000).

The Saul Steinberg caper influenced Morath to seek out more portrait work. In modern times, portraiture has been at the core of secular European art, both resting on and strengthening modern individualism; it suggests that individual personality and character can be revealed in a portrait. Portraiture is also a humanist art form, for it presupposes the elevation of human beings to a position that once held only gods. To a historian like myself,

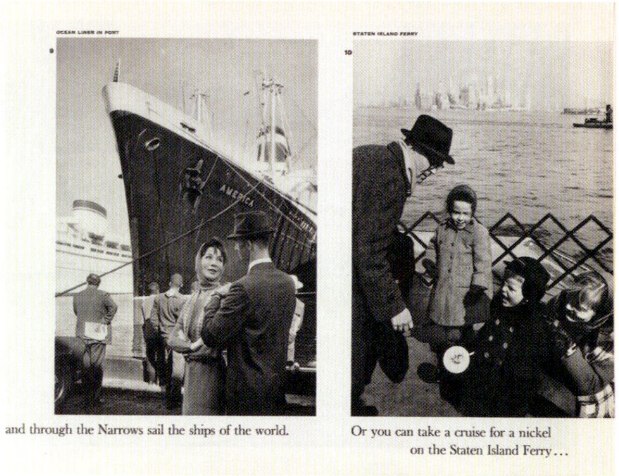

87. Tear sheet of corporate brochure for Bankers Trust, 1958

88. 48th Street window washers, New York, 1958

OPPOSITE

89. Contact sheet from *Carnival chez Saul Steinberg*, 1962

PAGES 104–5

90. Girl in leopard coat and mask from *Carnival chez Saul Steinberg*, 1962

91. Untitled from *Carnival chez Saul Steinberg*, 1962

KODAK TRI X PAN FILM
KODAK SAFETY FILM

92. Arthur Miller peeks out from behind a Saul Steinberg mask, Long Island, New York, 1962

there is a downside to portraiture. As photography critic Andy Grundberg points out, it supports celebrity culture and suggests that a few great individuals make history (figs. 93, 94).[199] The Steinberg masks, however, questioned those assumptions in a postmodern manner, suggesting the unknowability and malleability of individuals, hiding behind masks of self-presentation. I suspect that Morath would have smiled at such a pretentious characterization. Always a woman who enjoyed the humor of the unexpected and the incongruous, she appreciated subjects who could appreciate visual jokes—as, for example, Pablo Neruda in this visual pun on eyes (fig. 95).

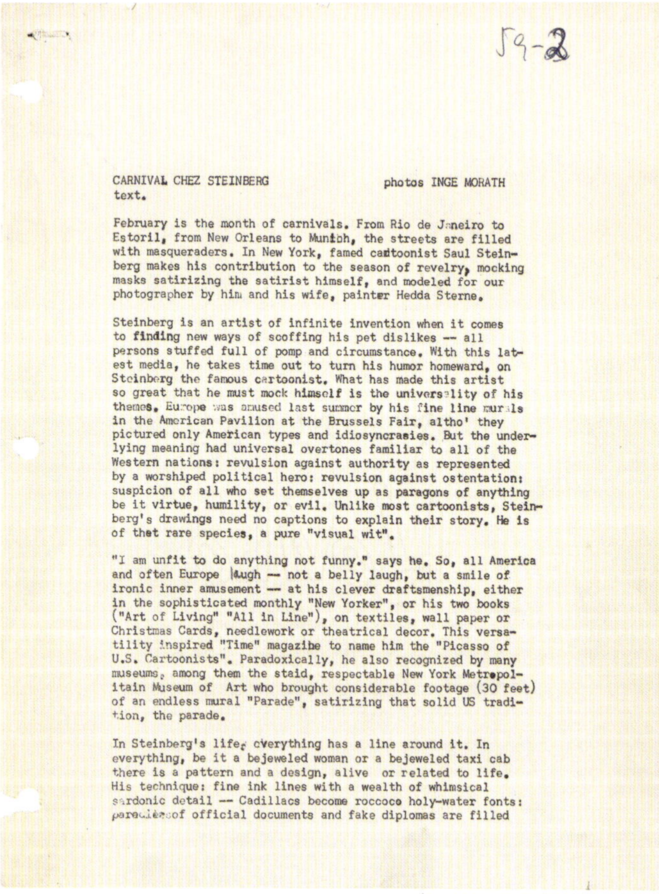

59-2

CARNIVAL CHEZ STEINBERG photos INGE MORATH
text.

February is the month of carnivals. From Rio de Janeiro to Estoril, from New Orleans to Munich, the streets are filled with masqueraders. In New York, famed cartoonist Saul Steinberg makes his contribution to the season of revelry, mocking masks satirizing the satirist himself, and modeled for our photographer by him and his wife, painter Hedda Sterne.

Steinberg is an artist of infinite invention when it comes to finding new ways of scoffing his pet dislikes -- all persons stuffed full of pomp and circumstance. With this latest media, he takes time out to turn his humor homeward, on Steinberg the famous cartoonist. What has made this artist so great that he must mock himself is the universality of his themes. Europe was amused last summer by his fine line murals in the American Pavilion at the Brussels Fair, altho' they pictured only American types and idiosyncrasies. But the underlying meaning had universal overtones familiar to all of the Western nations: revulsion against authority as represented by a worshiped political hero: revulsion against ostentation: suspicion of all who set themselves up as paragons of anything be it virtue, humility, or evil. Unlike most cartoonists, Steinberg's drawings need no captions to explain their story. He is of thet rare species, a pure "visual wit".

"I am unfit to do anything not funny." says he. So, all America and often Europe laugh -- not a belly laugh, but a smile of ironic inner amusement -- at his clever draftsmenship, either in the sophisticated monthly "New Yorker", or his two books ("Art of Living" "All in Line"), on textiles, wall paper or Christmas Cards, needlework or theatrical decor. This versatility inspired "Time" magazine to name him the "Picasso of U.S. Cartoonists". Paradoxically, he also recognized by many museums, among them the staid, respectable New York Metropolitain Museum of Art who brought considerable footage (30 feet) of an endless mural "Parade", satirizing that solid US tradition, the parade.

In Steinberg's life, everything has a line around it. In everything, be it a bejeweled woman or a bejeweled taxi cab there is a pattern and a design, alive or related to life. His technique: fine ink lines with a wealth of whimsical sardonic detail -- Cadillacs become roccoco holy-water fonts: parodies of official documents and fake diplomas are filled

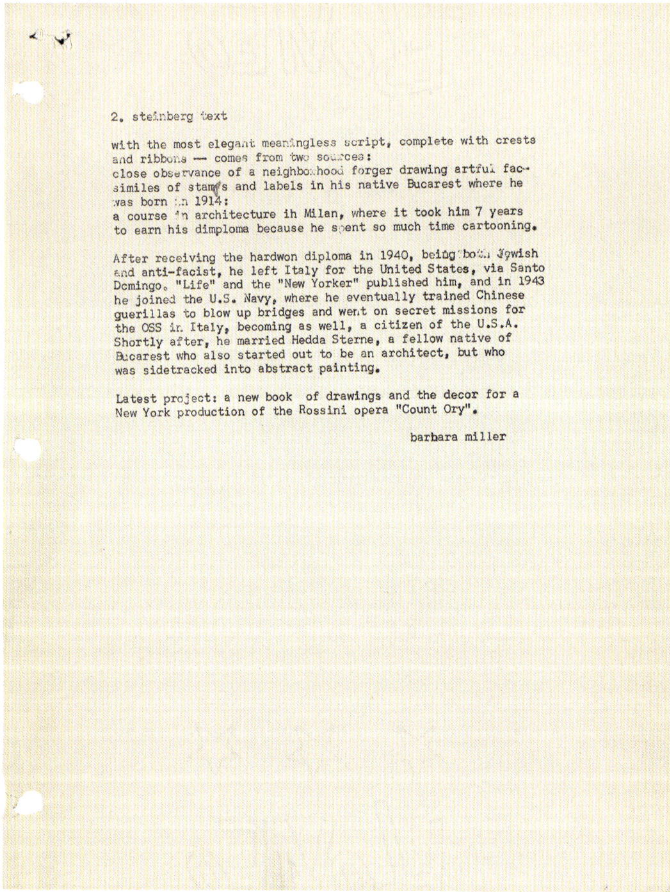

2. steinberg text

with the most elegant meaningless script, complete with crests and ribbons -- comes from two sources:
close observance of a neighborhood forger drawing artful facsimiles of stamps and labels in his native Bucarest where he was born in 1914:
a course in architecture ih Milan, where it took him 7 years to earn his dimploma because he spent so much time cartooning.

After receiving the hardwon diploma in 1940, being both Jewish and anti-facist, he left Italy for the United States, via Santo Domingo. "Life" and the "New Yorker" published him, and in 1943 he joined the U.S. Navy, where he eventually trained Chinese guerillas to blow up bridges and went on secret missions for the OSS in Italy, becoming as well, a citizen of the U.S.A. Shortly after, he married Hedda Sterne, a fellow native of Bucarest who also started out to be an architect, but who was sidetracked into abstract painting.

Latest project: a new book of drawings and the decor for a New York production of the Rossini opera "Count Ory".

barbara miller

93 / 94. Text for the Saul Steinberg story, 1962

95. Pablo Neruda, Pen Club meeting, New York City, 1966

96. British painter and set designer Tom Keogh, Paris, 1958

Or the British painter and set designer Tom Keogh, who appears as a detached head protruding from of a mass of multi-patterned fabric (fig. 96).

Morath's attraction to portraiture reflected both her interest in others and an absence of narcissism. She made very few self-portraits. While the majority of her subjects were celebrities, she preferred to photograph artists,[200] especially nonperformers "because they don't know their best angles."[201] Still, she would ask her subjects to choose their own sites and poses because, as she said, a portrait is a meeting in which two people get to know each other.[202] Or as Arthur Miller wrote, "A portrait embodies two points of view, the subject's and the artist's."[203] As much as possible she photographed her subjects "in the places where they live or where they spend much of their time, places that have absorbed something of their person." She showed musician Paul Tortelier virtually singing to his cello. In 1959 she photographed Habib Bourguiba—a leader of the Tunisian independence struggle and the new country's first president—in the middle of an impassioned campaign speech, his intensity captured in close-up through a powerful lens.[204] She acknowledged exceptions to her usual preparation for these portrait sittings, because sometimes, she admitted, the "best preparation is simply watching someone . . . what Goethe called 'elective affinity.'"[205] Flamboyantly bisexual Vita Sackville-West, for example, owner of the thirteenth-century Sissinghurst Castle, posed in mannish attire, possibly fresh from supervising her famous rose gardens (fig. 97).

Morath gave considerable thought to what constitutes a successful portrait. She prepared meticulously,

CLOCKWISE FROM TOP LEFT

97. Vita Sackville-West, Sissinghurst Castle, Kent, Great Britain, 1961 **98.** Writer Han Suyin, New York City, 1976
99. Mary McCarthy in a New England railway station, 1956 **100.** John Huston on the set of *The Misfits*, Reno, Nevada, 1960

"with the same care as I prepare myself for a trip to a new country." When portraying artists, she studied their work. She developed two general rules for herself: the subjects have to reveal themselves, and the composition must be lively. The photograph can be quiet or loud. The subject's expression, she learned from Cartier-Bresson, is not important—the expression can be happy, sad, thoughtful, engaged, disengaged—because personality can be revealed no matter the mood.[206] Also, "I try to . . . keep that first encounter energy, that moment of sparring while you find out who you are facing and they are casing you." Many of the portraits are tranquil, reflecting her patience in getting subjects to relax (fig. 98). "Most people have a place where they like to sit. If you talk a bit and wait until they sit down, that will happen by itself. . . . I let myself be completely guided by the person . . . In some cases you become friends . . . and get a better portrait later."[207] Like another fine portrait photographer, Dorothea Lange, Morath understood that the body is often more important than the face in expressing character. "You have to observe which movements or postures are typical for a person" (fig. 99). [208]

A 1960 assignment introduced her to the America outside of New York. John Huston (fig. 100) was directing another major film, *The Misfits* (1961), adapted from a short story by Arthur Miller, conceived while he was in Reno waiting to divorce his first wife. There he connected with other would-be divorcers and cowboys whom he saw as misfits, mostly lovable misfits.[209] Huston had a big budget for the film, allowing fifty days for the shoot and featuring three of Hollywood's greatest stars—the aging, now somewhat avuncular Clark Gable; Montgomery Clift, iconized as the sensitive, troubled young man whom women wanted to save; and Marilyn Monroe, the hottest female property in Hollywood.

Monroe had already proved herself a fine comedian, but Huston knew that she was unstable both psychically and physically. Because of his concern that a mass of "paparazzi" on the set could try her nerves, Magnum secured a contract that gave them exclusive access to the shoot. Eight photographers in overlapping teams of two covered the production from beginning to end. Morath and Cartier-Bresson formed the first team.[210] Once lovers, always friends, and a seasoned traveling team, they decided to drive to the Reno, Nevada, location, giving themselves eighteen days to see the "real" America. (Once done by rail, as Morath would travel to Russia five years later, crossing the American continent was by 1960 often an automotive undertaking.)[211] She kept a travel diary that was published, alongside her photographs, posthumously, as *The Road to Reno* (fig. 101).

The road trip is a quintessential and already classic American pastime. From the first European settlers to the intrepid early photographers of the Rocky Mountains to

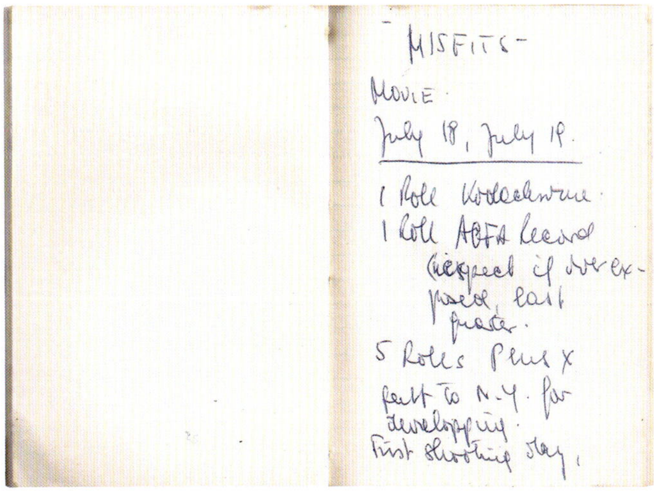

101. A manuscript page from Inge's *The Road to Reno* notebook, 1960

the road sagas of the Beats, crossing the states constituted a masculine motif, identifying the American spirit with mobility. Neither Morath nor Cartier-Bresson had grown up with those values, and neither was sure they liked what they saw. She was unnerved by what seemed to her the isolation of individuals. "I could jump into [the car] at every moment of night or day, turn on the motor, disappear, drive on, without anybody noticing, asking a question, looking up."[212] (This was an isolation peculiar to the automobile, since train travel remained to some extent a group experience.) And unlike the Europe they knew, here one drove through unpopulated distances and saw few people outside. "One glimpses one of the old weather boarded houses with chairs waiting for people to sit and stare . . . But when one finally sees them they have quite a presence. . . . From one of the white old porches a man with a long thin face like a knife and slanted eyes gazes out on things I do not see . . . I cannot penetrate the spirit. It is not for outsiders."

Since they took turns driving, the passenger could "afford to let the road sink below the sightline," as filmmaker Lucy Raven noted in her foreword to *The Road to Reno*, and that perspective brought different things to the attention of their photographic eyes.[213] What they noticed was sometimes landscape, but also roadside commerce; and while the landscape varied, the commerce did not. As the wide ribbons of asphalt and concrete tied the country together like a package, so the facilities along the routes grew ever more standardized, Morath felt, even in these days before travel "plazas." She wrote her journal "each night at the table in a motel room that always was in a different place and always looked the same." The two Parisians were most distraught about the food available on the road, their hopes raised and then dashed, for example, when a cube steak turned out to be just another hamburger. The two of them subsisted mostly on apples.

Morath's photographs from this trip are humorous and ironic, and occasionally—and atypically—disdainful, echoing Robert Frank's *The Americans* (1958), though with a lighter valence. Her pictures condemn the kitschy, mass-culture design, the sameness of commercial signs and spaces, and the typical disrespect for older, often handsomer structures. But they are tempered by humor, unlike the pessimism or sadness in Frank's images. She documented the iconography of billboards and neon (fig. 102). She showed Cherokee Village, North Carolina, with its jammed parking lot, jumble of advertising signs, and Confederate flags. They visited the "reconstructed" Cherokee village, where Indians dressed in "traditional" outfits—a loincloth, in this case—to earn money. Cartier-Bresson photographed Morath mounted on a bronze horse. Looking for an authentic wooden kachina doll, she thought she had found one, bought it, turned it over, and found that it had been made in Japan. She shot color film of twentieth-century Native Americans entertaining tourists by pretending to be nineteenth-century Native Americans.

Ironies continued. In Oak Ridge, Tennessee, birthplace of the atomic bomb used on Hiroshima, they visited an Atomic Museum where radioactivity was presented mainly as a healing agent, with a picture of a sick man being treated with cobalt. In Nashville she photographed a sign advertising whiskey that was next to an ad for Estes Kefauver, running for governor; and she photographed a full-size replica of the Parthenon. Riding a bus in Memphis, she noted that the Negroes—the common label at the time—had to sit in the back; when she sat down next to a Negro woman, it was clear that

102. On the road to Reno, outside Memphis, 1960

nobody liked it. Still, she enjoyed seeing so many African Americans, with "dark, beautiful chocolate" skin and "patent leather high heels with rhinestones . . . and a red parasol. . . ." (I take this comment as expressing enjoyment of creative decoration, but it might also express a disdain for cheap effects.) Then to Oklahoma where "oil derricks grow out of nowhere, complicated, trembling."

Her spirits always rose, however, when they drove through countryside. She appreciated the flowers, the smell of hay, and the roadside stands selling fruit. In New Mexico, unaccustomed sights and smells captured her senses. "Clear cut blue shapes of rock formations . . . stranger insects crush themselves to a hasty death against the windshields, stranger smells of wild grass and passing by animals . . . just before Taos, the Rio Grande cuts deep into the soil, dark blue wound in a soil clad in blue green grass . . . clear silhouettes of mountain cones." In the Taos Pueblo the "strangeness survives the touristic exploitation." Around Gallup, on the Navajo reservation, she encountered fine craftsmanship for the first and only time on this trip—elegant blankets and rugs with natural dyes and stylized images, *real* carved kachina dolls, fine pottery, elegant silver jewelry. But on the street an Indian stopped them and offered, seeing the camera, to let them photograph his wife for fifty cents. He tells his wife to smile but "the eyes of her wide Mongolian face continue to stare unsmilingly straight into the lens."[214]

Just before Reno came Las Vegas, where Morath saw her first slot machines and showgirls allegedly brought from Paris; it seemed a microcosm, perhaps, of her view of the US interior. Las Vegas "receives you, wearing stage makeup in full daylight with the sophistication of a ham actor in an ambulant road show."

Morath was by now an old hand on film sets, particularly Huston's. His respect for her had grown due to her extraordinary rescue of one of his stars on the set of *The Unforgiven* (a 1960 western). During a break in shooting, Audie Murphy fell out of a small boat in the middle of a lake. Morath noticed him flailing in the water, unable to swim or to climb back into the boat. She immediately stripped down to her underwear, dove in, swam a half mile to reach him, then towed him in as he clung to her bra strap. Annoyed at the men who had stood by and done nothing, she called them all bastards, or so Arthur Miller remembered her telling him.[215]

103. Marilyn Monroe and Arthur Miller on the set of *The Misfits*, Reno, Nevada, 1960

When Arthur Miller first saw her on the set, she and Huston were laughing about this incident, so the playwright may have pegged her as somewhat extraordinary from the outset. When she first saw Miller, he was floating on his back in a swimming pool, smoking a cigar, and telling Huston a funny story about a man who sold shoulder pads. She thought he was a good storyteller. She had also expected him to be terribly serious, but was pleasantly surprised by his sense of humor.[216]

The Misfits shoot was plagued by difficulties, most of them caused by Marilyn Monroe, who was habitually late for shooting calls, and frequently did not show up at all. She had trouble remembering her lines, though in her defense it must be said that Miller was constantly rewriting them.[217] Sometimes her intake of drugs—painkillers and barbiturates—left her dulled.[218] One cameraman said, "Her eyes are gone. She can't be photographed."[219] That she'd had two miscarriages added to her suffering. She was in thrall to her personal coach Paula Strasberg, the wife of Lee Strasberg and a teacher of his "Method Acting." The rest of the cast and production staff disliked Paula intensely, and believed she encouraged Monroe's uncooperativeness. When Huston offered direction, Monroe would look to see if Strasberg approved.[220] Cartier-Bresson made a telling photograph of Monroe listening closely to Paula Strasberg, while Miller sits glumly by and Morath frowns at the scene.[221]

Monroe also fought with Miller publicly (fig. 103). His presence throughout the shoot probably didn't help, though he tried to be supportive—"I hoped that by living through this role she too might arrive at some threshold of faith and confidence"[222]—but their marriage was already filled with irrepressible anger, each feeling betrayed by the other. A Bruce Davidson photo of

104. Marilyn Monroe on the set of *The Misfits*, Reno, Nevada, 1960

105. Henri Cartier-Bresson and actor Eli Wallach during the filming of *The Misfits*, Reno, Nevada, 1960

Monroe, Miller, Simone Signoret, and Yves Montand together at a table suggests that betrayal and resultant resentment: Marilyn Monroe, who was engaged in an affair with Montand, flirts extravagantly, mainly with the camera, but her breasts in a clingy dress are touching Montand's arm. Signoret glares at him, and he returns the look with an expression that says, "What of it?" Miller looks glum.[223] It did not help that he had written the play not only for, but also about, Marilyn Monroe, who, as Roslyn, was one of the "misfits." She later expressed her resentment that the film made Roslyn into a sexist stereotype who could express her criticism—of the men's killing of wild mustangs to be sold for dog food—only by screaming hysterically instead of arguing her case.[224]

Despite her distaste for American commercial culture, Morath responded warmly to this woman who was the very symbol of American stardom. Depending on when Morath and Miller began to feel attracted to each other, one might expect some coolness toward the movie star, considering her as a rival. But what shows in Morath's photographs of Monroe is only sympathy, and lyrical beauty. One group of photos shows Marilyn's grace as she danced barefoot and alone in the moonlight (fig. 104).[225] "Once she was ready," Morath said, "she would surpass the expectations of the lens. She had a shimmering quality like an emanation of water. . . ."[226]

And Monroe returned the warmth. Miller recalled that Marilyn "liked her [Inge] at once, appreciating her considerate kindness and the absence—remarkable in a photographer—of all aggression." He added that Monroe sensed "real affection" in the pictures.[227]

It was a struggle to get photographs of Monroe and Miller together, because she refused to pose with him. The best such image emerged by accident—the couple in their hotel room with the door open, it captured Monroe from the back, looking out the window while Miller, cigarette in his mouth and hands in his pockets, looks at her as if at a stranger.[228]

If there was a jinx on *The Misfits*, it did not end when the film wrapped on November 4, 1960. Clark Gable suffered a heart attack the next day, and two weeks later he was dead at fifty-nine (fig. 106). United Artists rushed to release the film on January 11, 1961, taking advantage of the attention created by his death, a move widely criticized as exploitative.[229] The Miller-Monroe marriage was already over; by early November, Marilyn was back in the luxurious apartment on East 57th Street in New York City where she and Miller had lived, while Arthur moved into a hotel on East 86th Street.[230] A year and a half later Monroe was dead.

We don't know how much Inge and Arthur connected on the *Misfits* shoot, but their romance developed quickly afterward. The current of electricity between them was interrupted by separation—they met several times in New York City, and he flew to Paris to be with her—as well as by mutual caution. Inge later recalled that "Arthur . . . was in despair and sought my company. But at the time I just wanted to get away—I had no desire to console a Marilyn Monroe victim."[231] Yet she was powerfully drawn to him. Two decades later her friend Honor Moore told her that the attraction showed in her *Misfits* photographs of Miller. Inge replied that sometimes one's art knows one's soul before the artist does. She later said she was reassured of the possibility of a relationship by a dream in which she was in a bar with Miller, Monroe, and Miller's first wife, Mary Slattery. Marilyn got up and danced and Inge danced with her. The dream, she said, reassured her that her involvement with Miller was safe.[232]

106. Inge and Clark Gable during the filming of *The Misfits*, Reno, Nevada, 1960. Photo by Henri Cartier-Bresson

Publicity about his divorce dogged their courtship. He was hounded by journalists and paparazzi. Inge suggested he move to the Chelsea Hotel—it was shabby but so full of writers that he would be less noticeable. He did and felt liberated there.[233] "The Chelsea in the Sixties seemed to combine two atmospheres," he wrote, "a scary optimistic chaos which predicted the hip future, and at the same time the feel of a massive, old-fashioned, sheltering family." He felt at home there because "it was not part of America, had no vacuum cleaners, no rules, no taste, no shame," and he kept the Chelsea room as a pied-à-terre for many years.[234]

But within a few months after the *Misfits*, Inge was calling their relationship "serious."[235] She accompanied him to Kennedy's inauguration in January 1961, and in March of that year to his mother's funeral. Monroe, just released from a psychiatric clinic, also attended the funeral, where she held onto Miller's father's hand (the two had been quite close). If this encounter made Inge and Arthur tense, neither commented on it. In June, Monroe came to her former home in Roxbury, Connecticut, which she had bought with Miller, to pick up some of her belongings; she saw from the way books were rearranged that Inge was often there. Yet after Arthur and Inge married, Monroe responded to the inevitable journalists' questions with generosity: "Arthur and I could never live together again. It's over. Why shouldn't he get married again." Miller also understood their relationship as hopeless (". . . nothing but destruction . . . A person's got to save himself").[236] Later, after Monroe's passing, he chose not to attend her funeral. To him, "The idea of being photographed next to a stone and in what he anticipated would be a media circus, seemed both pointless and repellent."[237]

During 1960 and 1961, when they were mostly in different locations, Arthur and Inge wrote each other often. He missed her terribly, he wrote, and worried that she didn't get enough rest.[238] Her letters were filled with declarations of love. She wrote him love notes even when they were together (fig. 107). "Your presence to me is like light and clearness." "I know you are next door [at the Chelsea] but your warmth is removed and I would like to just rest against you, where I fit, between your shoulder and your knee." "Why is my whole being moved by you . . . your very maleness." "I would love to give you true joy." Her letters were also sexual. "I have kissed all the wounds of your body and now I feel it live again." "When you make love to me my body remembers it for hours like leaves trembling when the storm has passed." I was surprised by these letters—this is not the restrained Morath I had grown accustomed to.

She knew that he had "loved Marilyn madly,"[239] and that he was fighting depression, his spirits sagging from an accumulation of hurts: the divorce, his mother's death, his persecution by McCarthyites. Worst of all, he felt he wasn't writing well. Inge responded maternally, telling him that his drafts were wonderful ("an extraordinarily perfect and moving piece of poetic prose, unveiling the

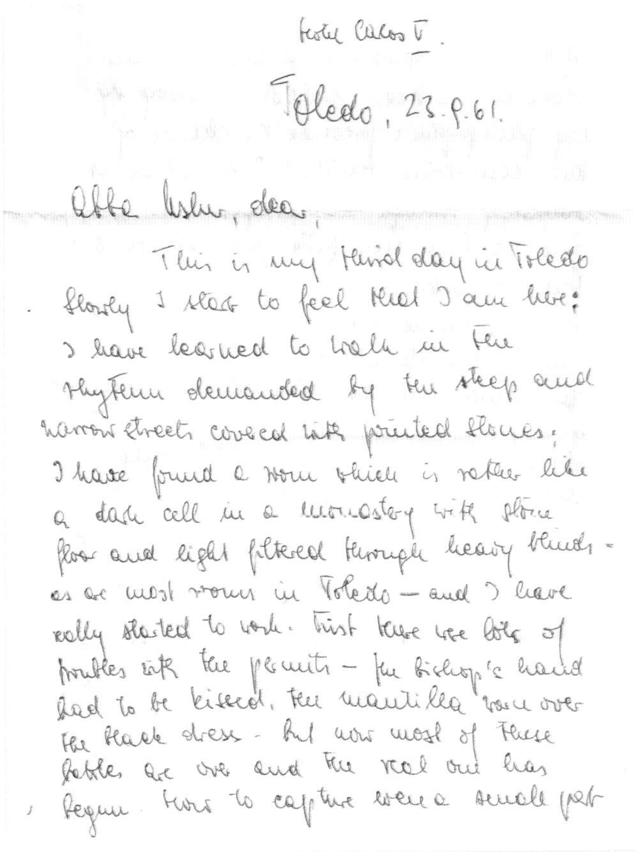
Hotel Carlos V.
Toledo, 23.9.61.
Allerliebster, dear,
This is my third day in Toledo. Slowly I start to feel that I am here; I have learned to walk in the rhythm demanded by the steep and narrow streets covered with pointed stones; I have found a room which is rather like a dark cell in a monastery with stone floor and light filtered through heavy blinds — as are most rooms in Toledo — and I have really started to work. First there were lots of troubles with the permits — the Bishop's hand had to be kissed, the mantilla worn over the black dress — but now most of these battles are over and the real one has begun. How to capture even a small part

107. Manuscript page from letter of Inge to Arthur sent from Toledo, Spain, 1961

human heart with careful fingers"), that he must eat, and that she would like to console him, to help him be less lonely, to make his "difficult life more easy." When the *New Yorker* rejected his short story, "The Prophecy," she told him it was "too good for that kind of market. Your genius needs the unrest of sacrifices . . . your payment for your talent." That kind of support provides a clue to the forty-year duration of their marriage.

Arthur was also smitten. "Your letters are reread many times until I can hear your voice, your reality in my ears. I miss you more than I am able to say, and read of the necessary delays in your coming with some sinking of the heart." And he was protective. "I have a wish to arrange for your feeding; I feel like an old lady—my mother—telling you to get some rest."[240]

The letters show Inge becoming steadily more resolute in coaxing him to marry her, to trust that their relationship would work. Although both had failed marriages behind them, his doubts were greater, and Inge worked to overcome them. "There is pride in me, Abba [the name she would always use with him], that I could offer you all this and there is pride in the hope that it might make you trust that our relationship could be not selfish but a ground to grow towards our aim, in whose moral superiority I will continue to believe." "There is nothing more I want to be than your wife." In mid-November 1961, three months before they married, she became more explicit. "Waiting is only a solution for the falling away of things. I mean in love. Time will not solve feelings—a certain amount of it will clarify but beyond that . . . a decision will have to be made."

"I guess a third marriage always takes some thinking about. I did a lot of thinking," Arthur said later.[241] This hindsight understated his indecision. Though he was always eager for Inge to visit, he was fearful of trusting his attraction. Inge felt at times helpless in her inability to reassure him. "I weep because I love you, because of my impotence." There is a disturbing but unsurprising parallel between the two sets of letters—she writes about him and he writes about himself. "I live on the edge of some ultimate abyss," he agonizes. He has been in analysis where he struggled with his "self-destructive force." He feared that regaining his writing powers would necessarily produce a "compensatory loss" in their relationship, and vice versa—that their love might cripple his writing. These depressions and conflicts visited him for the rest of his life. In his letters to Inge, he wrote that neither of his wives cared enough about his work. He admitted that his egocentricity and self-absorption required from her "a strength, a forbearance, even a disinterestedness worthy of a goddess." He remained uncertain about what to do with their relationship. "I feel haunted sometimes by the question whether anything, any feeling, is eternal."

But he also feared losing Inge. "The whole idea of marrying seemed a little doubtful, but the idea of getting out of her life, or her getting out of mine, was worse."[242] By November 1961, he had made a breakthrough in the play that became *After the Fall*, and this helped him shed some of his doubts. He became convinced that his relationship with Inge would help him. "I think of you as a hope." These hopes were realized, as their marriage lasted for the rest of Inge's life.

They married quietly in February 1962 in Connecticut, in a vain attempt to evade journalists. Fourteen friends and relatives came to a reception at a friend's house. But the media carried the story globally—in papers from Spain, England, Germany, Italy, and

A VIEW FROM THE COUNTRY:
A WEEKEND WITH
THE Arthur Millers
PHOTOGRAPHED BY TONI FRISSELL

"So tell me when you can come? Why don't you come on Friday?" Inge Miller's voice, with its tales-from-the-Vienna-Woods accent, is a welcoming shout on the phone, inviting guests for the weekend...."Four people is ideal," in Inge's view. "One basic dish—you can fill it up with different components. With six, it becomes complicated. It's too much the same without being intimate."

108. Inge, 1970, photographer unknown

109. Tear sheet from "A Weekend with the Arthur Millers," 1963. Photos by Toni Frissell

more—and frequently featured photos of Monroe as well as Miller and Morath (fig. 108).[243]

A month later Inge and Arthur traveled to Austria to see her parents, with whom Arthur soon developed a warm friendship, and then to the former Mauthausen concentration camp in Germany. I presume the camp visit was a way of marking, even honoring, her new relationship with a Jew, for she had not visited a concentration camp previously. The emotional impact must have been heavy. Recalling the visit to her daughter, she commented, "A lot of people don't want to talk about it; it's hard on young people all the time to be judged that way"; she was clearly referencing the guilt that weighed on so many Germans and Austrians who had passively accepted the Nazi regime. But, she added, "Everyone should face the facts."[244] She might have been thinking about her family.

Inge and Arthur lived together in the Chelsea Hotel for a while before moving into the house in Roxbury, Connecticut, that would become their permanent home. With the money from Broadway productions of his plays, he had bought a first house there in 1947, drawn by the numerous other writers who summered there.[245] Intending it as a retreat from urban summer heat, he continued to spend most of his time in New York City. In 1956 he and Monroe purchased an old dairy farm nearby, which he kept after the divorce, while she took possession of their Manhattan apartment. Encompassing 340 acres, the Connecticut property included a pond, hills, pastures, woods, and old fieldstone walls. In addition to the white clapboard house, there were also several outbuildings, one of them a writing studio that Arthur had built for himself. He soon added a darkroom for Inge. "A gorgeous farm," Inge called it, with "a tree nursery with lots of rare and beautiful woods." They rented part of it out to a local farmer but they themselves used the land with great pleasure. They would fish for trout in the pond, cut wood, and ride a horse.[246] They planted vegetables, and Inge cried when rabbits ate them, but they then built a fence to keep out the critters (fig. 109).[247]

With her typical unflappability, Inge did not seem uncomfortable with any remaining Marilyn Monroe associations in the Roxbury property. Still, it would be hard to exaggerate what a drastic rupture this move meant for her. She had been a traveler since childhood, with and without her parents; she was a big-city person, urban to the core; and her only adult home had been a Paris apartment and even that was mostly a pied-à-terre, a place to collect mail, to see friends, and to take a break from uncountable hotel rooms. Her identity was European. She was unskilled in womanly, domestic arts and not monogamous, a beautiful, adventurous, often lone traveler, admired and courted by men nearly everywhere she went. She was accustomed to dealing with artists and celebrities, perhaps catering to them in short bursts of photographic work, but she remained a somewhat guarded, untethered spirit.

It was not that Roxbury changed her. Rather, exerting her formidable will, Inge changed herself and harvested the joys of her new life. Her daughter Rebecca Miller understood that Inge gave up "Paris elegance" and a "gypsy" life for Roxbury settledness "with absolute bravery."[248] Perhaps Morath had uncovered a buried need for a permanent home. She became an avid gardener, and along with Miller, a tree planter, aiming to restore the woods that earlier New England settlers had cut down for farming. Guests hunted for deer on the property and Inge roasted the venison.[249] She took up yoga. She became a fine cook, preparing many dishes that she could not or would not eat. She claimed she was able to cook well because she had honed her taste in many fine restaurants. She became a confident hostess, cooking often for large numbers, with frequent dinner parties. She assigned seats at the table so as to introduce guests to each other and to spark conversation. Arthur, who was a good carpenter and had a complete woodshop, built them a large oval dining table that could seat fourteen (its proportions based on the Fibonacci ellipse). People working on plays with Miller would frequently stay for a week. William Sloane Coffin stayed at their house for five months while in the middle of his divorce ("He is great, but it got long," Inge admitted).[250] This level of domesticity was the gold standard in the 1960s, when countless numbers of women gave up professions for housewifery. And Inge had grown up in such a family, with a scientist mother who did the same, and even served as her husband's assistant.

None of this developed without producing mixed feelings about this drastic change in her life. She wrote to Magnum that she could not travel extensively because "I have to take care of a husband whose superior talents often require my cooking more urgently than my photography."[251] And "my personal problem is, as you know, to give photography its due and be a good wife."[252] Yet she complained of receiving no travel assignments and feeling "*plus en plus isolée*" (more and more isolated).[253] And she felt the need to insist that her "photographic abilities have not necessarily vanished with marriage."[254] Many women live with these contradictions, but few master them with so much success.

The contradictory impulses subsided when their daughter, Rebecca, was born in 1962. True, Inge had some misunderstandings about giving birth. She told

Rebecca that when her labor began, she was high above ground, photographing New York City from the basket of a construction crane; and that she had intended to bring her camera into the labor and delivery rooms to photograph herself giving birth (which did not happen).[255] But once Rebecca arrived, Inge became a devoted, full-time mother (fig. 110). Always visual, she later recalled the pleasures of "the eyes of the child . . . to see again with the eyes of innocence."[256] Staying close to home, Inge began photographing a smaller world. "Possibility of exploration of a small universe, travel of a few steps instead of to another continent. . . . Growing differently now, more plant-like, in one place." One photograph suggests, however, a continuity with her own childhood: toddler Rebecca is wading in their pond with her grandfather Edgar Mörath, and she is naked and shown from the rear, just like the photograph of Inge with her mother at the beach. Inge adored both Rebecca and her own motherhood; just as she would do anything for her own mother, Titti, so she would do anything for Rebecca. Yet, she admitted, "Not easy in beginning—but valuable. Desire to travel elsewhere though exists strongly too" (figs. 111, 112).[257]

On January 7, 1967, Arthur and Inge's second child, Daniel, was born. That he was a child with Down syndrome was immediately apparent, and his parents placed him, first, in a New York City home for infants, and then in the Southbury Training School, a state facility for those with intellectual disabilities. They kept his very existence a secret from almost everyone in their lives. Close friends knew that Inge was pregnant, and at least one visited her a few days after the birth when Daniel was still with her. But it soon became clear to friends and relatives that he was not to be spoken about. He is not mentioned in any of Inge's autobiographical sketches or in Miller's autobiography. One of Inge's assistants, a woman who loved her

110. Rebecca Miller, Roxbury, Connecticut, 1963

111. The Miller family, 1965. Photo by C. Manos

112. Rebecca playing with Arthur while Inge looks on from the hammock, Roxbury, Connecticut, 1963. Photo by Henri Cartier-Bresson

dearly and worked with her in Roxbury for a year and a half, knew about Daniel's existence and surmised that Inge's periodic unexplained absences were visits to him in Southbury.

The problem with secrecy is that when what has been hidden is revealed, it provides fodder for sensationalism. Exposing the cover-up is often far more damaging than the original act. Daniel was outed publicly only after Miller's death in 2005, and the forty-year secrecy made his parents' decisions appear more reprehensible than it was, because it suggested that they felt guilt about those decisions. A journalist writing in *Vanity Fair*, the first to publish a story about Daniel, reported that some of Miller's friends never knew what happened with Daniel. Miller did not mention his son in his autobiography and apparently revealed his existence only to close friends, though he did visit Daniel occasionally. Following the *Vanity Fair* piece, other media then picked it up and made it seem more reprehensible. Some right-wing media even attributed Miller's alleged hard-heartedness to his Left politics. But the original story reported an incident that belies Miller's alleged coldness. In 1995 the father and son met publicly, by accident, at a conference where Miller was speaking and where Daniel arrived with a "self-advocacy" organization for the disabled. When Daniel approached his father, Arthur embraced him warmly. Miller subsequently attended one of Southbury's annual reviews of Daniel's care, to which Inge had always previously gone alone.

Several factors can help explain Arthur's and Inge's decision to institutionalize Daniel. Most important, no doubt, was that in 1967 the majority of doctors advised parents to institutionalize children with Down syndrome. Inge later told one of Miller's biographers that the doctor told her, "'There's nothing you can do. Don't take him home or otherwise you will never be able to make the decision. It is the right decision.' We decided to place him in a home where he would be better off."

Since neither parent ever discussed their decision, I can only infer their motives. As to the secrecy, many parents at this time experienced the birth of a handicapped child as somehow humiliating. The fact that Arthur had a cousin with Down syndrome, Carl Barnett, may have influenced him; the boy was raised at home, quite atypically for the time, and Arthur not only saw the heavy burden this placed on Carl's mother, but had also seen her hit the child in rage and openly mock him. What's more, he observed the hard life of a close friend with a handicapped child. Miller's play *After the Fall*, completed after he married Inge, may reveal some of his anxiety. In it, the character based on Inge has a recurring dream. "I had a child," the fictive Inge says, "and even in the dream I saw it was my life, and it was an idiot, and I ran away. But it always crept into my lap again, clutched at my clothes." The play actually predated Daniel's birth, which suggests that Miller's cousin Carl figured significantly in his consciousness or subconscious. The fact that Miller spoke of his disabled cousin as a "helpless mongoloid" says exactly nothing about Arthur Miller and everything about the way the experts categorized and spoke in the early to mid-twentieth century.

Close family friend Honor Moore felt that Arthur was also driven to institutionalize Daniel out of concern for Inge and Rebecca. He feared that the caretaking demands on Inge could undermine their marriage and potentially bring psychological harm to their adored daughter. Moore thought that Inge, although initially torn about sending Daniel away, soon came to consider it the right decision as well.

Then there is Daniel's own perspective on the story. He seems to have inherited Inge's positive energy—"just a delight, eager, happy, outgoing . . ." in the words of one of his support staff. Everyone who participated in his care adored him. Today he lives in his own apartment connected to the residence of his caretakers and holds down a job. He bears no bitterness toward his birth parents, and his sister, Rebecca, and brother-in-law, Daniel Day-Lewis, consider him part of their family.

Regardless, if we pause to imagine what might have been, losses remain. Had Arthur and Inge funded a less institutional form of care for Daniel, it might have afforded him a private education that could have improved his cognitive skills—though we can only consider this possibility on the basis of subsequent research and advances in treatment. Daniel's sunny presence could have brought another source of love into their family life, along with new insight into the range of rewarding human relationships; and it would have alleviated a burden of guilt.

But raising Rebecca was rewarding enough to compensate for any guilt that lingered. She gave her parents great pleasure, her talents so large and so broad that she might even be called a prodigy. Inge and Arthur began traveling with Rebecca, something they might not have found so easy with two children.

Although motherhood temporarily limited her travels, Inge had joined a community of distinguished artists and intellectuals not unlike what she had had in Europe. In one autobiographical fragment, she listed some of her new friends: Harrison and Charlotte Salisbury, Robert

113. Poet Honor Moore, 1985

and Elodie Osborn, Olga Andreyev and Henry Carlisle, William and Rose Styron, Francine du Plessix Gray and Cleve Gray.[258] In this generation, people mainly socialized as couples, but Inge took pleasure in getting to know "the extraordinary wives Charlotte, Elodie, Francine."[259] She bonded particularly with Francine, a fellow European; they took long walks together and Inge learned to ignore Francine's judgmentalism. Olga Carlisle was also European in orientation—born into a distinguished Russian literary family, she grew up in Paris, accustomed to visits from Marina Tsvetaeva and Isaac Babel, raised on the poetry of Mandelstam and Pasternak. She would soon become Inge's Russian tutor. Inge also became close to two women a generation younger, Martha Clarke, a dancer, choreographer, and director of musicals and opera, and the aforementioned Honor Moore, a memoirist and poet (fig. 113) who became a fictive daughter, nurtured by Inge's encouragement and cooking.[260]

Many of her European friends visited, including some royalty, such as Inge's former boyfriend Josef Schwarzenberg and Mary Inmaculada von Habsburg-Lothringen, daughter of the claimant to the Spanish throne and Archduchess of Austria.[261] An excerpt from Inge's 1966 datebook provides a sense of the social whirl: June 7, Calders for dinner; June 8, Carlisles for dinner; June 9, dinner at Lowells; June 10, dinner with Bill and Jean vanden Heuvel; June 11, Pablo Neruda poetry reading; June 12, dinner with the Nerudas and Carlos Fuentes; June 13, in New York City for a PEN meeting, lunch with John Steinbeck, Saul Bellow, Rosamond Lehmann. While in New York City she took Rebecca to the Statue of Liberty, carrying her for the last sixteen flights of stairs. Inge's energy was prodigious.

Morath found many portrait subjects among their neighbors and visitors (fig. 114).[262] She also began photographing her larger Connecticut environs, often with

Rebecca on her back—wandering with a camera was her way to understand a new environment. The resulting book, *In the Country*, appeared in 1977, with text by Miller. The title is misleading, since it was less about countryside than a lament for the loss of countryside to exurban gentrification, as the farmers sold their land and houses to urban intellectuals who bought "country houses" accessible to New York City (less than ninety miles away). In a passage about nostalgia, Miller wrote that "some have fled cities" to be "renewed by a more ample space, cleaner air, the real contact with revolving seasons," while the remaining farmers "plow and milk in the shadows of nuclear plants."[263] Morath's photographs show those contradictions. We see a sow nursing her piglets, an old-fashioned drug store, and a competition for best sheep, as well as a garden party at the country club and an indoor gathering—presumably at the Miller-Morath house—that includes Yevgeny Yevtushenko and Leonard Bernstein, among other distinguished guests.[264]

Before Inge came into Arthur Miller's life, his career had been threatened not only by Marilyn Monroe's erratic behavior but also by McCarthyism and anti-Red repression. *The Crucible*, his most enduring play and one of his most powerful, directly condemned McCarthyism and more specifically the execution of the Rosenbergs. In retaliation, the State Department denied him a passport in 1956, and he was unable to travel abroad for two years. In 1956 the House Un-American Activities Committee (HUAC) subpoenaed Miller and demanded that he identify his Communist friends. He refused to name names and was convicted of contempt of Congress, a conviction overturned in 1958. The Red-baiting hysteria damaged a close friendship with Elia Kazan, who became a "friendly" witness for HUAC and named eight friends and colleagues of the Group Theater as fellow

114. Sculptor Alexander Calder with a model outside his studio, Roxbury, Connecticut, 1964

Communists. Miller experienced this betrayal as personal as well as political and moral. It was also threatening to him personally: "I was afraid of him. . . . I could still be up for sacrifice if Kazan knew I had attended meetings of Party writers years ago . . . I felt a silence rising around me . . . It was sadness, purely mournful, deadening. . . ."[265] Miller refused to speak with Kazan for years.[266] Through the 1950s and 1960s a virtual vendetta prevented most American productions of his plays: "The abrupt expulsion of Arthur Miller from the living heart of the American theater," wrote one critic.[267] Never backing down, Miller continued to act on his convictions. He marched for civil rights in the 1960s and spoke at anti–Vietnam War rallies in the 1970s. But this time the ever-steadfast Inge was by his side. And his commitment to justice gave her a moral anchor; an integrity that encompassed his writing and their lives together.[268]

Inge Mörath, Christian child of upper-class Austrians who had been Nazi enthusiasts, had married a Jewish leftist with a Brooklyn accent. It was as if this marriage honored her teenage revulsion against the Nazi regime. It was a marriage that might not have worked at the time she married Birch, when she longed for the freedom to pursue an independent career; in Roxbury those longings had shifted toward motherhood and rootedness. And Arthur touched her at a much deeper level than had any previous partner, as did his work. A survivor of trauma herself, she recognized the different traumas he had suffered. His tastes and friends replicated the milieus she had cherished in Vienna and Paris. The Roxbury house gave her back the pleasures of gardens and quiet that she had known in childhood but had done without for almost twenty-five years. Meanwhile, she was becoming an American, both legally—she became a citizen in 1966—and informally, beginning to dress in jeans, cotton shirts, and sneakers.

One can also imagine how Arthur loved her. Inge was graceful and gracious, consistent and calm, resourceful and energetic, never tempestuous or needy. She laughed easily. She was sophisticated and worldly, elegant when she wanted, but informal always. Ambitious, certainly, but already secure in a career that had brought her acclaim and celebrated friends. If she did not share the intensity of Miller's political passions, she did share his aesthetic sensibility, his progressive and antiauthoritarian values, and his commitment to his work. And she both expanded his world—he said once to a friend, "She brought me Europe"[269]—and supported him through his hard times.

For the rest of her life, Morath photographed productions of Arthur's plays, documenting both rehearsals and performances. She saw this as a responsibility and a welcome new challenge. "I work with Arthur when a new play comes out . . . try to get together a photographic record of all the intricate work that goes into the creation of a play." Honor Moore remembers her saying, "We're going into rehearsal soon." She enjoyed the photography work and felt close to Miller's dramas. And as time went on, he realized he was learning to write somewhat differently through her photography, beginning to "visualize" his playwriting in a new way.[270] Still, she subordinated her own professional agenda to Miller's—and to motherhood. It was not until 1977 that she undertook a major trip on her own.

The first Miller play she photographed—*After the Fall*—was possibly the most stressful and certainly the most personally charged (fig. 115). Its thinly disguised plot replicated Miller's marital history: Holga is Inge, Maggie is Marilyn, Quentin is Arthur. To Inge, the play's "lesson" was that "inner awareness" of one's fears, hatreds, and insecurities could "help you face life's problems better." She saw Quentin's process as a form of self-psychoanalysis. In the play he is tempted by a young girl who offers him "a totally consuming love" and "childish adulation," but comes to reject this adoration and to see that it offers him no salvation. As in many Miller plays, the male lead is a wounded, passive, indecisive man. He is then "redeemed," in Inge's words, "only by a new attachment to a 'German girl' whose sense is stronger than her passion." "Unless you recognize the dangerous instincts in yourself . . . you'll end up in disaster," she concluded.[271] (Her words suggest not only her understanding of Arthur but of herself as well.) When asked how she responded to being represented onstage, she commented on the relation between art and life, distancing herself from Miller as playwright. "Unless you are selfish, you have to see the play objectively. . . . I never asked about its source but of course I could feel right away . . . what was happening. I have far too much respect for Arthur's work to want to interfere . . . If he needs something of me for his play, he does with it as he wishes. That's fine with me."[272] No wonder several observers commented about Miller's third marriage that now he had married a grown-up.

But throughout the rehearsals, Miller refused to acknowledge the play's autobiographical character, and his denial confused the cast.[273] He had chosen Elia Kazan as director, in what may have been a gesture of forgiveness. But Kazan's earlier betrayal of Miller and Miller's values contributed to an ambient tension during rehearsals. Inge was present so constantly that she became almost a part of the crew, absorbing the quarrels and fears that swirled around. Dennis Stock hinted

115. Jason Robards and Barbara Loden during rehearsals for the original production of Arthur Miller's play *After the Fall*, New York, 1963

116. Inge and Arthur waiting backstage at Lincoln Center's Repertory Theater on the opening night of *After the Fall*, 1963. Photo by Dennis Stock

at this in an expressive photograph of the couple waiting nervously backstage during the premiere at Lincoln Center's Repertory Theater, sitting on the floor, facing each other, both pairs of long legs extended (fig. 116). Morath photographed *After the Fall* once again when it was made into a film in 1974, starring Faye Dunaway, Christopher Plummer, and Bibi Andersson. No doubt this was a less stressful job.

Morath's photographs leave a remarkable record of Miller's plays and of the group process of creating theater. Many of her images show fine actors—Dustin Hoffman (fig. 117), George C. Scott, Lee J. Cobb, Harvey Keitel, Vanessa Redgrave, Jason Robards and of course Daniel Day-Lewis, her future son-in-law—in mid-rehearsal, and the viewer can see them fully inhabiting their roles. Nowhere was this vision more intense than in her photographs of Vanessa Redgrave in Miller's *Playing for Time* (1980), based on Fania Fénelon's autobiography, *The Musicians of Auschwitz*, about her years in that concentration camp (fig. 118). In 1967 and again in 1990 she photographed *The Price*, a work that begins lightweight but soon transforms into a heavy conflict between two brothers. In 1985 she photographed the film version of *Death of a Salesman* starring Hoffman and John Malkovich. In order to help publicize Miller's autobiography when it appeared in 1987, she joined him in Paris to photograph a television show about him, *Apostrophes*. In 1991 it was *The Ride Down Mt. Morgan*, another work featuring a weak and self-centered man unable to decide between two women. In 1994 she photographed the London premiere of *Broken Glass*, a rather psychoanalytic drama set just as one of the protagonists learns about Kristallnacht. A striking portrait of Peter Falk in Miller's *Mr. Peters' Connections* emerged in 1998 (fig. 119); unusually, Miller wrote this play for the off-Broadway Signature Theater Company and it was apparently never produced on Broadway. The very last job she did for Magnum, while already ill with the lymphoma that would soon prove fatal, was photographing rehearsals for a production of *The Crucible*, starring Liam Neeson and Laura Linney.

117. Dustin Hoffman during the filming of *Death of a Salesman*, New York, 1985

118. Vanessa Redgrave in *Playing for Time*, Pennsylvania, 1979

119. Peter Falk in the production of Miller's *Mr. Peters' Connections* at the Signature Theater, New York, 1998

停

Chapter Seven

HEADING EAST

When Morath became a full member of Magnum in 1955, it was a community in flux. Shaken by the deaths of Capa, Bischof, and Chim, some members doubted its survival. It would take at least a decade to end those doubts definitively, and during that period differences both petty and profound disrupted Magnum's workings. Morath was involved in three capacities—as Magnum's secretary from 1963 on, as a member living close to its new headquarters in New York, and as a photographer who occasionally had her own grievances with Magnum's administration. True to her hardworking and persevering nature, she coped with these demands until 1969. Then she decided to leave Magnum. That leave lasted a decade, until she rejoined in 1980.[274]

Magnum had thrived in the 1950s due to abundant publishing opportunities in print media. These declined with the spread of television. By 1960 even *Life* magazine was losing subscribers. The Magnum cooperative sought to bolster its income in two ways: bringing in more photographers of a wider variety and diversity of locations, and expanding their range of clients through commercial photographic work—advertising, fashion, and annual reports, for example.[275] Both these changes evoked conflicts, particularly about money.

When someone became a full member of Magnum, he or she was required to buy stock in the cooperative. A client commissioning photographs would pay Magnum once its order was received and Magnum would then pay the photographers after subtracting the cooperative's share. But when photographers accepted commissions, they often needed an advance for expenses; Magnum would provide this, to be repaid when the job was completed and the customer had compensated Magnum. Through this system, some photographers ended up with debits, if, for example, the advance they'd received was not immediately recouped through revenue, and Magnum customers did not always pay promptly or might even reject photographs. Other photographers ended up with credits, because they earned more than their advance or had not yet collected their earnings. In this way one photographer's success helped another, a basic function and principle of the cooperative. For

120. Inge in China, 1978, photographer unknown

example, Cartier-Bresson's high credit balance could fund air travel for other photographers.[276] Meanwhile, Magnum accumulated photographs, as photographers deposited work for "second sales"; individual photographers held the copyrights to their work but by keeping it in the Magnum "library," it was available for repeated use and continuing income. Individuals and enterprises seeking photographs on particular subjects would make requests of Magnum, and both Magnum and the photographer would earn from reproduction fees. Thus photographs made decades ago continued to earn income. This practice fulfilled another aspect of Magnum's raison d'être: ensuring that photographers retained rights to and earnings from their own work.[277]

This operating system required complex bookkeeping and accounting and many photographers did not keep track of their credit/debit balance. Moreover, the system exacerbated and called attention to inequalities among the photographers. More well-known and in-demand photographers often accumulated large credits, while others might remain in debit for extended periods. And with Magnum short of cash earnings, some of what it owed to photographers had to be used for operational expenses.[278] Complaints multiplied. Morath herself was overdrawn by about three thousand dollars in 1970, which she paid, possibly a year late.[279] Magnum staff also criticized her for privately selling photographs she made on a trip with Miller to Russia, depriving Magnum of its commission. She admitted blundering in how she had handled these arrangements but defended her right to own the Russian photographs individually since Magnum had not funded her trip.[280]

Meanwhile Magnum's New York executive Gedeon de Margitay, known to the community as Gida, was attempting to balance the books by treating all photographers equally, which sparked fits of pique. Cartier-Bresson complained that Gida had disrespected and insulted him.[281] Some members wanted to check Gida's authority, calling him power hungry, while others defended him, including Wayne Miller, who was president from 1962 to 1966.[282] As Magnum's membership grew larger and more dispersed, the group became looser, the threads of intimacy and trust thinning out. The Paris group grumbled—and Cartier-Bresson shouted—that New York was admitting less-than-superb newcomers. He also condemned the push for commercial work, which he saw as lowering aesthetic standards and compromising political and ethical principles.[283] Morath, perhaps swayed by Cartier-Bresson's arguments, and possibly thinking of her fashion and celebrity photography, worried that she herself was contributing "to the more commercial Magnum."[284]

Morath was in a bind. As secretary, she sought to soothe hurt feelings by letter and telephone, but on at least one occasion even she lost her usual cool, irritably pointing out that she was spending a great deal of time on projects that were "boring" for the sake of Magnum's finances, so others had no right to complain.[285] She was closer to Cartier-Bresson than was anyone else at Magnum. He had been her teacher, her lover, and her friend. Now separated by an ocean, they remained in constant touch, speaking by telephone weekly. He wrote her long letters and when he wrote to Magnum sent copies to her.[286] He took it for granted that she would always agree with him, either because she always had or because he understood that he continued to be her artistic and moral authority. He gave her his "absolute proxy" to vote on his behalf within Magnum, which of course meant that she had to defend the standards he stood for.[287] But she was now an officer of Magnum with accountability to the group as a whole, and she was by nature a bridge-builder, a rational communicator, and one who sought peace, while Cartier-Bresson was explosive. Being close to New York, she knew and valued most of the people there and understood the need for more income. By 1963, Morath saw Magnum as divided between herself, Cartier-Bresson, and Bruce Davidson on the one side, and Wayne Miller and Cornell Capa on the other.[288]

Finally, in 1969, she decided to withdraw from Magnum. She had been more than patient, more than willing to do tedious jobs, and now she wanted the leeway to coordinate her photographic subjects with Miller's work. But quitting was also a consequence of long-simmering discontent. Some in the New York Magnum group considered her a minor photographer, producing lightweight work, a dilettante rather than a professional. Some thought her marriage to a wealthy and famous man showed that photography was not her true calling, and that she had now become a mere wife[289]—a recapitulation of the sexism she faced during her first years with Magnum. She was often the only woman in meetings.[290] Separating from Magnum was not simple, given the cooperative's structure. She hired a lawyer to arrange an agreement in which Magnum would continue to handle the photography she had created as part of the cooperative, but would not handle any new work going forward.[291] This freed her for a decade of travels and joint projects with Arthur Miller. (By 1980, Magnum was urging her to rejoin, and she did.)

For several years after Rebecca's birth, Morath photographed only within driving distance of her new home, but the travel itch never fully left her. As Miller wrote, "For Inge, to see a valise was to start packing."[292] Soon Miller's work brought her new opportunities to explore unfamiliar cultures. His plays were performed all over the world; he liked to see these performances and she liked going along. There was at least one trip to Europe every year, to Hong Kong and Southeast Asia in 1970, Israel in 1972, and again in 1977, Japan in 1977, 1984, and 1996. Morath, ever the ardent traveler, initiated some of these trips, notably to Southeast Asia, which Miller resisted—quite understandably, given his strenuous opposition to the Vietnam War, not to mention the US bombing campaign in Cambodia—but she was determined to see the giant sculptures in Angkor Wat and got her way.

Inge had long dreamed of visiting Russia. As a teenager she had loved its great nineteenth-century novelists and later she discovered the early twentieth-century avant-garde poets. What she yearned to see was "not the Soviet Union. . . . The place I longed to know had no political name."[293] For Miller, Russia did have a political name and a troubled political meaning. Like many American leftists, as a young man he had admired the Soviet Union, an admiration reaffirmed by the Soviet people's valiant defense against the foulest regime imaginable, Nazi Germany. He had never approved of the Stalinist dictatorship or the purges, but his plays had been performed in the USSR for nearly twenty years—usually without his approval. In 1965, with Stalin dead and Gorbachev's perestroika (reconstruction) policy under way, she and Miller embarked on a trip there.

They traveled by train from Düsseldorf to Moscow because, she said, "I had wanted to feel the vastness that separates East from West."[294] Miller, less enthusiastic, remembered what he saw out the train window as snow,

121. A couple returning from Dacha, on the train between Lomonosov and Leningrad, 1989

snow, snow, and more snow for two and a half days. A Morath photo of a middle-aged Russian couple on a train, riding "hard class" on wooden bench seats with their coats on and bundles at their feet, evokes the Soviet working class—poor but dignified (fig. 121). She would return to Russia again and again, as it had joined Spain as one of her favorite places (in what follows I combine the visits into one discussion).[295] "She had fallen in love with Russia," her friend Olga Andreyev Carlisle wrote.[296]

As it happened, Miller's *A View from the Bridge* was being performed in Moscow and they went to see it. They discovered that the script had been altered, compressing a character's gradual transformation into a sudden one. The reason, the director told Miller, was that "we are not interested in all that *psychology*,"[297] expressing the censorious Soviet rejection of "bourgeois" concern with the individual's interiority. Soviet "socialist realism," was actually not realism at all, but a kind of idealism, a notion of socialist man as free of inner conflict. Since Miller and Morath spent much of their time in the USSR meeting with dissident writers, they quickly saw the limits of perestroika and the continuing lack of artistic freedom.

In these meetings, Miller benefited from Morath's many talents. In Roxbury, with the help of her friend

Olga Carlisle, she had studied Russian, and now spoke it fluently.[298] This trip may have been the first occasion on which Miller saw her fully in action as a photographer as well as a polyglot. He valued especially her "way of disarming men of power" through her "romantic playfulness of spirit." He bragged about how Konrad Adenauer, whom she had photographed in the 1950s, had immediately asked her to become his secretary.[299]

In return, Morath benefited from Miller's international connections—many resulting from his position as president of PEN International from 1965 to 1969. "Walking with him in unfamiliar streets . . . led to photographic opportunities in events that at first looked barren of such interest."[300] In yet another turn, Morath's friendship with Olga Carlisle made connections for Miller.[301] Carlisle was the granddaughter of Leonid Andreyev, a Russian novelist and playwright whose work had been staged by Konstantin Stanislavsky. She grew up among Russian émigré intellectuals, including poet Marina Tsvetaeva, writer Andrei Sinyavsky, and Aleksandr Solzhenitsyn (her father had smuggled Solzhenitsyn's second novel, *The First Circle*, out of Russia). Her husband, Henry Carlisle, an editor, translator, and novelist, was Miller's colleague in PEN. Olga's friends in the USSR welcomed the American visitors with typical Russian hospitality, no matter their poverty: tea and cakes, or just vodka. In 1967 Carlisle accompanied Miller and Morath on their second trip to the Soviet Union. In 1976 she published *Pasternak: My Sister, Life and Other Poems*, in which she included some Morath photographs. The two women started work on a joint book on the poet Anna Akhmatova, but it was never finished.

In their meetings with other artists and intellectuals, which took place mostly in people's homes, Morath also made portraits, much valued by the subjects. These number among the best images available of many important Soviet artists. Novelist Vasily Aksyonov, a member of the countercultural movement known as *stilyagi* (the stylish ones), looks the part in his black leather jacket, a ubiquitous-in-Russia cigarette in his hand, his hair combed Marlon Brando style. She captured the weather-beaten face of Valentin Kataev, a playwright who managed to produce subtly subversive plays and edited the journal *Iunost* (Youth) that published Russia's best young literary talent. Sculptor Ernst Neizvestny appeared in his studio, animatedly explaining his work (fig. 122). She made portraits of Yevgeny Yevtushenko on several of her visits, and as a guest in Roxbury (fig. 123).

The most moving portrait is that of Osip Mandelstam's widow, with whom Inge exchanged letters for many years after their meeting (fig. 124). Mandelstam was a symbolist poet during Russia's most fertile artistic period, between 1905 and 1925, a time when artistic creativity and exploration long stifled by the tsarist regime was released. In the 1930s, the Jewish,

122. Russian sculptor Ernst Neizvestny, Moscow, 1989

123. Yevgeny Yevtushenko, 1988

124. Nadezhda Mandelstam, widow of poet Osip Mandelstam, Moscow, 1967

cosmopolitan Mandelstam resisted Stalinist pressure to produce banal, feel-good verse and remained constant to his own poetic truth; sent to a gulag in 1934, he died there in 1938. His wife, Nadezhda Mandelstam, promoted his work and became an intellectual in her own right, publishing two acclaimed memoirs about their lives and resistance.[302] Morath showed her mid-sentence, seated at her table, the inevitable tea in front of her, already a bit frail (though she lived thirteen years more), wrapped in an embroidered black velvet shawl, her beauty still apparent.

Morath delighted in Russia's palaces, churches, museums, and gardens. In photographing Leningrad's eighteenth-century Winter Palace, she used a perspective from on high in order "to get a tsar's view of his subjects," tiny people moving like ants on a chessboard (because the plaza has a checkerboard design). Gardens, filigreed railings, and statuary provide a sense of the luxury in which the nobility had lived. She photographed icons (medieval religious images), as well as churches, mosques, and statues of Russia's writers and composers. She photographed literary sites, such as the street where Dostoevsky's Raskolnikov lived and from where he left to murder the pawnbroker Ivanovna. She spent hours in the Hermitage museum in Leningrad (today St. Petersburg) and the Tretyakov in Moscow. She visited a State Ballet School, always a must in Russia, as well as a gymnastics training facility. In one museum image she showed oil paintings of Pereslavl-Zalessky's nobility and through an open doorway, statues of the saints—thus juxtaposing two kinds of icons. This device, a doorway framing a picture within the picture, was one of her favorites.

The contradictions she had observed in Iran appear also in her Russian photography. Horse-drawn carts, old babas in kerchiefs, and monks in robes contrast with modern art and institutionalized juvenile delinquents, who look the part, but charmingly. She mostly ignored industrial modernity; in contrast to so many images of the USSR, Morath's contained none of turbines, dams, or the other structures of the industrial might of which it was so proud.[303] Nor did she bother with ironic photographs of Stalinist kitsch. As with her work on Spain, what drew her were traditional forms and practices, from medieval icons and bulbous domes to eighteenth-century palaces and gardens. In one photograph she contrasted eras in a single image, showing a distant Kremlin through a delicate wrought-iron art deco grille (fig. 125).

Morath's intellectual restraint showed through contrast with the rhetoric of some of her Russian friends.

125. The Kremlin seen through an art deco grille, Moscow, 1967

Yevtushenko, in his introduction to her 1991 book, *Russian Journal*, was pleased that she "did not humiliate us with insulting sentimentality" and "did not fall for the trite fairy tale about the 'mysterious Slavic soul.'" Yet he indulged in precisely those clichés, writing of "the inexpressible sadness of life" in Russia, and that Morath's sensibility was like "an aristocratic ghost returning to Russia."[304] Carlisle too wrote that her photography made "palpable" the "mysterious force" of Russia.[305] Such vapid characterizations have often figured in Russian nationalism, of all political slants, while Morath avoided them. Unlike the Spanish "soul" she had seen in Spain's folk rituals, her sense of a Russian soul came from its artistic heritage, old and new.

By Morath's second visit in 1967, the Brezhnev repression had arrived. A blacklist, however, made Miller's plays taboo, and was not lifted until 1986. Apparently he had offended Minister of Culture Yekaterina Furtseva because he had spoken out against Soviet anti-Semitism and treatment of writers on behalf of PEN.[306] Morath believed that the ban was also payback for her portrait of Furtseva, published in the 1969 book *In Russia*. (It is difficult to understand why Furtseva was offended; the photo is a sympathetic portrait of a lovely, middle-aged, stressed woman.)[307] Always up for an adventure, however, even at the risk of further offending Russia's rulers, she went with dissident poet Joseph Brodsky onto the roof of the Peter and Paul Fortress in Leningrad, defying a big sign forbidding entry; this fortress had imprisoned generations of dissidents, from Kropotkin to Gorky. (Carlisle went along on this rooftop expedition but spent her time cowering in fear, she wrote.)[308]

In Russia, published jointly by Morath and Miller, is a collection of text and photographs from these visits. Many of the photographs are beautiful, but as a book it is not successful. Miller's narrative is unrelated to Morath's photographs—it is as if he had not looked at them, and as if she had no influence on what he wrote. It is not one book but two. This appears to have been characteristic of their relationship, which may have worked so well precisely because both continued their own work autonomously with no attempt to meld it. Yet the balance was uneven. Inge was deeply involved in Arthur's work, frequently discussed it with him, and worked alongside him as photographer and translator, while he contributed less to hers.

Morath was quite right in her assertion that marriage had not weakened her photographic ability or her thirst for travel. The years 1986, 1989, 1990, and 1993 saw more trips to the USSR. Her photographs from these later visits provide a stronger sense of Russia's underground counterculture, both modern and traditional, as in her images of a small theater production of Bulgakov's *Heart of a Dog*, an astringent satire of the "new Soviet man," and in the photograph of women in babushkas at a Sunday mass at the Zagorsk Monastery outside Moscow. She traveled beyond European Russia, too, photographing writers and artists at a meeting in Kyrgyzstan; a statue of Lenin in silhouette dominating the main square in Yerevan, Armenia. She used one of her favorite visual tropes, a not uncommon compositional technique of photographers, focusing on display window reflections to create double images, as in an exquisite photograph of Leningrad's Nevsky Prospekt reflected in elegant windowed doors—it could stand for the aging elegance she most loved about Russia, as the reflection made the buildings seem liquid, redolent both of their fragility and of a past now more dreamlike than real. In quite another mood is a photograph reminiscent of her evocation of the Miller-Monroe acrimony—this one showing a sullen adolescent, a "juvenile delinquent," being interviewed by a uniformed official, in the background a poster titled *Youth*.

Back home in 1971, Morath thought to try filmmaking—an impulse reflecting both her itch for a new challenge and her pleasure in working with Miller. The project she imagined would be a profile of a playwright, presumably Miller, for the American Film Institute. To prepare, she wanted to study filmmaking at Columbia University with Sumner Jules Glimcher, a documentary filmmaker who had also written a guide to filmmaking. Columbia's application form asked for high school and university transcripts. The letter she wrote the admissions office in response would have evoked bitter laughter to anyone who knew her history, as she explained why she could not produce these documents. Her university in Berlin was, she wrote, "unwilling to give out copies of papers to anybody not living in the East Zone." She offered, seriously I assume, to find former classmates who could attest that she had passed her exams.[309] Apparently nothing came of this project.[310]

In 1977 Morath traveled alone for the first time in fifteen years, to Japan.[311] Some anxiety surrounded her departure. "I am not leaving at a moment of peace, but in a moment of unrest," she wrote in her diary. Arthur always wanted her with him. As her trips became more frequent, she once characterized to Honor Moore the bargain she had made: "I cook his lunch and I can take my trips."[312] The Japan trip was scheduled for a moment when Arthur would be in Washington while Titti would be in Roxbury with Rebecca, but the arrangement did not alleviate Inge's anxiety as she knew that Titti didn't

126. Chojun Otani, Temple Higashi Honganji, Kyoto, Japan, 1977

like to be alone in Roxbury. Though Rebecca was now fifteen, Inge worried about her throughout the trip. As she headed back home she noted how she longed "for the touch and weight of Rebecca on my lap when she cuddles. . . ."[313] And no sooner had she arrived in Japan than she missed "the reassurance of his [Arthur's] strength."[314] Fifteen years in Roxbury as wife and mother had diminished her zeal for traveling solo.

Despite anxiety, Morath savored what she saw of Japanese culture over the ten-day journey—the gardens, pagodas, architecture, public baths, and elegant food presentation—and she would return several times with Miller (fig. 126). But on this first trip, guides also took her to a memorial commemorating the atomic bombing of Hiroshima and Nagasaki, a visit she might not have chosen. There she saw photographs of "the burnt flesh, crushed bodies, terrible wounds on children, women, men, the stare of the victims," she wrote. "Oh God, the horror. I know the feeling of the terrible fear from Berlin, but this is beyond description." These are the only comments about such atrocities that I encountered in her papers, and she was shaken. Her guide, a survivor, did not want to enter the museum and she identified with his feelings: "Like I don't want to see war movies. We have seen the real thing. We know it in our guts."[315]

Hoping again for a relaxation of oppressive state control, Morath and Miller went to China in the fall of 1978. The Cultural Revolution was over and they speculated that this would be a moment when people "felt safe enough to talk freely to foreigners." Some of those they met were indeed willing to recount their sufferings from hysterical and sometimes mob attacks on professionals, intellectuals, artists, and anyone who had questioned the authority and purity of the "Gang of Four."[316] On the other hand, they were dismayed to find that the Chinese remained encased in an ideology and a culture that rejected "Western" liberal norms. Unable to travel freely, moreover, they had to surrender their passports and to accept being guided through a prescribed itinerary designed to display cultural and economic excellence, accompanied by "informative" lectures throughout. Morath, ever compliant, dutifully took notes, though at times she confided her boredom in her journals (fig. 127).

The food was especially trying on this as on her Russian trips. Another "dreaded banquet," she wrote in her China travel journal. Her digestion tolerated only very little and very light food, while Chinese meals for distinguished guests arrived in course after course. She wrote that she "learned a technique of politely refusing, accepting tiny morsels of the more outrageous stuff like black seaweed." She usually traveled with supplies of apples and peanuts, to accommodate her finicky digestion when the food on offer was beyond her limits. In China she managed to get tangerines, the only available fruit that she could tolerate. While Miller drank beer and spirits, she confined herself to Chinese orangeade, of which she drank large quantities. Her eating discipline may have kept her free of the minor ailments that often troubled Miller on these trips, but getting the right food was much on her mind. She recorded in her travel journals not only what she ate but each of the dishes the others ate. Still, accustomed to rough travel conditions, she never complained and even laughed about the hardships. Once, while "squatting on a ladies toilet," she heard over the partition from the men's toilet, someone exclaiming with a German accent, "Aren't you Arthur Miller? So pleased to meet you. Funny place to meet."

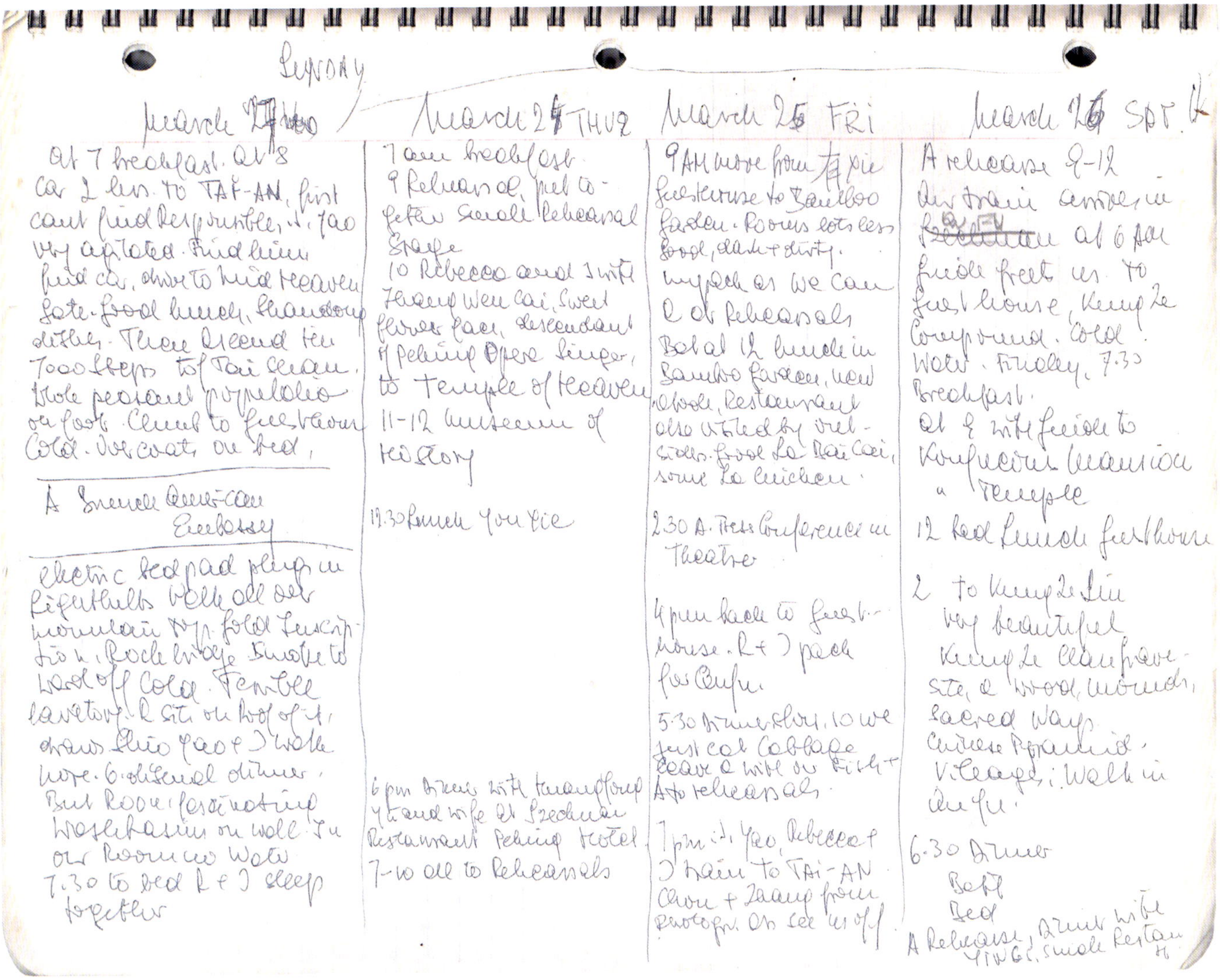

127. A page from Inge's calendar of her trip to China, 1978

And the yoga she now practiced regularly helped her survive uncomfortable nights.[317]

As with the Russia trip a decade earlier, Morath had been preparing herself by studying Chinese for four years, tutored by Vivien H. Y. Lu of Yale. By the time they arrived in Beijing, she was able to converse and to translate for Miller, although he also had a professional guide and translator. (In one of her China travel journals she adopted the Chinese method of organizing text, arranging her notes vertically, from top to bottom, perhaps to accustom herself to reading that way.)[318]

It was Miller's understanding that he and Morath had, as in Russia, fundamentally different agendas in China. He was interested in what had become of the political and social revolution begun in 1949. He already knew Edgar Snow, a journalist and writer sympathetic to the Communist revolution, and fellow McCarthy target; serendipitously, Snow's wife, the actress Lois

128. China, 1978

129. 6:30 a.m., Chang'an Avenue, Beijing, 1978

130. Soldiers on Yuan Dynasty Sculpture at Maitreya, West Lake, near Hangzhou, China, 1978

Wheeler, had performed in Miller's *All My Sons*. Now Miller's fame brought them into meetings with China's greatest writers, artists, and a few political figures whom Morath photographed. He wrote that she, by contrast, was interested in Chinese art and calligraphy.[319] His representation of Morath's interests, however, reduced their breadth. As in Spain and Iran, she was creating a visual ethnography—a light and quick version, of course, but nevertheless insightful (figs. 128, 129). She observed how people lived within their rich, ancient culture, as well as how they modified and ignored it. One delightfully humorous image showed Red Army soldiers climbing and sitting on a thirteenth-century, Yuan dynasty sculpture of a Maitreya, a bodhisattva or future Buddha (fig. 130). One soldier sits on the shoulder of the outsize, laughing, fat-bellied figure with his hand protectively and proudly on its bald head. As in Iran, she noted contradictions between the old and new, between China's "ancientness . . . and her epic struggle to . . . become a modern nation." But while Miller saw its ancientness as filled with "solemnity,"[320] she saw its architecture, sculpture, calligraphy, and painting as rather joyful (fig. 131).

In China, Morath felt obliged to do what she had avoided in Russia: photograph images of turbines and large machinery, as she had done in response to different obligations in Iran. But in one rather mischievous photograph, she juxtaposed machines in a generator factory against the backdrop of a gigantic socialist-realist painting of heroic Chinese soldiers. She dutifully photographed cute, well-behaved schoolchildren bent over their books or lined up clapping and dancing for foreigners. She captured scenes from traditional Chinese opera and theater, which Miller appreciated because it was so openly artificial in contrast to socialist realism's portrayal of stock heroic characters that were meant to be taken as real people.[321] By contrast they found traditional Chinese painting more realistic than they had expected, at least in one region: in the area around Guilin (formerly Kweilin), they found the mountains, waterfalls, bamboo, and mist to be as delicate and dreamy in real life as in the silk scroll paintings.[322]

Morath and Miller's 1979 joint book about China displayed the same failings as the Russian books—lack of integration between text and photography. Miller again wrote a text with no apparent relation to the photographs. His account, complex and fascinating as a stand-alone essay, detailed his earnest and patient but largely unsuccessful attempts to understand how so many Chinese accepted the Cultural Revolution's repression of artists and intellectuals. He also described vividly and somewhat humorously a Western playwright's

131. Prayer flags on the way to the Tiger's Nest Buddhist Shrine, Bhutan, 1993

concern with the dynamics of individual motivation. Morath's images, by contrast, show how the Chinese combined pride in their ancient culture with a hopeful view of a more democratic future. Even the poorest of her subjects, like a woman living in a courtyard in Guilin without electricity or plumbing, watches over her son sitting in a broken, handmade bamboo chair and reading his schoolbook.[323]

They left China via Hong Kong. Met there by a "Rudolf Valentino perfection looking" agent from their hotel, they were whisked into luxury: a bouquet of roses and orchids from the management, a tray of soaps for them to choose from, bottles of scotch and of soda, peanuts and a big box of pralines, and excellent bottles of red and white wines (". . . tastes like Ambrosia") awaited them in their room. Contemplating the contrast with their previous week in China, Morath remarked, "Yet it was wonderful not to need anything like this. Maybe not to be dependent on luxuries was one of the lessons we learned."[324]

For Miller, an enticing theatrical invitation emerged from this visit—an offer to mount a Chinese production of *Death of a Salesman* with Chinese actors. So the two returned in 1983, remaining for two and a half months, Miller staging the play while Morath documented its progress (fig. 132). Miller's 1984 book on the project, *Salesman in Beijing* (this one did not list Morath as joint author), offers not only his frustrations in trying to make his understanding of the play legible to the Chinese but also perceptive insight into the differences between American and Chinese approaches to drama, family conflict, and human nature. *The Crucible* had already been staged in Shanghai, and audiences "had been moved to tears by the memories that the tale evoked of their own sufferings during the Cultural Revolution." But *Salesman* deals with matters foreign to Communist Chinese sensibilities—as they were to Soviet sensibilities: psychological repression, the imperatives of masculinity, and the commercial logic that casts away used-up humans as if they were rubbish.[325] In this book, unlike in their Russian book, the photographs were placed and captioned so as to directly illustrate Miller's text, for example: "Rehearsing the fight scene." But the captions did not identify the actors or associate the images with the problems that Miller describes. And while the photographs might potentially have shown moments of fine acting or cultural differences in theatricality, in the book they were produced in such small sizes and low quality that they are as hard to read as a contact sheet.

While in China, Inge and Arthur received bad news from their daughter: a fire in the Roxbury house. Rebecca deliberately minimized the extent of the damage, thinking there was no point in telling them the worst since her parents had to stay in Beijing for the performance of *Salesman*. So they were shocked when they returned to find much of the house burned out, forcing them to live in the barn for many months.[326] All the silk shirts that the Duke had given her had burned up. Yet Inge saw a gift in the disaster—now she could help design the restoration and realize some of her preferences, a response completely in character.

Amid all these travels, Morath also developed a book with Irwin Shaw, *Paris/Magnum: Photographs 1935–1981*. The project documented the everyday work of the city and its people, from rich to working-class

132. Actor Ying Ruocheng (seated) in a Chinese production of *Death of a Salesman*, Beijing, 1983

neighborhoods, from fashion shows to jazz clubs, from President Mitterrand to Edith Piaf. Morath had become a fine curator. Fifteen years later she helped curate a collective exhibition that represented a quiet challenge to Magnum's typically male reputation, and appeared despite the resistance of some of Magnum's men. Deriving from an idea of Eve Arnold's to gather work by Magnum's six women photographers—Eve Arnold, Martine Franck, Susan Meiselas, Lise Sarfati, Marilyn Silverstone, and Morath—the show was mounted in Edinburgh's National Portrait Gallery (fig. 133). The show became the 1999 book *Magna Brava*.

After Rebecca left home, the pace of travel sped up. By this time, Morath's practice of writing her impressions became less systematic, so the photographs sometimes provide the only evidence of the trips. In 1989 she was in Berlin in time to photograph the dismantling of the wall, though not its initial breach. That same year she traveled to Egypt to photograph a fragile Naguib Mahfouz, who had just won the Nobel Prize in Literature. In Bhutan in 1993 she made exquisite color photographs of a sacred Buddhist temple compound and its prayer flags. Romania/Bulgaria 1994. St. Lucia with Derek Walcott in 1995. Japan 1996. Cuba in 2000,

133. Wedding dresses in the market, Warsaw, 1965

134. Fidel Castro at the Presidential Palace, Havana, March 2000

with Miller and the Styrons, entertained by Fidel Castro himself at a formal dinner, to which he uncharacteristically wore not fatigues but a suit (fig. 134)!

She continued to photograph playwrights, such as Tony Kushner and Wendy Wasserstein, and productions of plays. She also did numerous commercial jobs: Lavazza Coffee, Echo Eyewear, Pentagram. In 1980 she returned to Magnum and took on more of its commissions: a production of Miller's *The American Clock*, a cat show, the Westminster dog show. A somewhat ill-fated project about Jews: Frédéric Brenner, a French photographer, was traveling through thirty-seven countries photographing the Jewish diaspora through portraits of those he called "icons." He gathered a crowd of American Jewish notables on Ellis Island where he had built a temporary labyrinth. Positioned inside it, the participants included Edgar and Charles Bronfman, who funded Brenner's project, along with Betty Friedan, Itzhak Perlman, Mark Spitz, Ruth Westheimer, Roy Lichtenstein, Edward Koch, Philip Glass, Arthur Miller, and many more. (The significance of the labyrinth remains unclear.) Morath was there to photograph the photographer. Brenner published the photographs in 1996 as *jews/america: a representation.*

A few years later she set herself another project: she would go through all her contact sheets to find their "secrets," the small or marginal facts they revealed, even their autobiographical content, however unintentional. After all, "contact sheets are the diary pages of photographers."[327] This did not happen. As her assistant pointed out, Inge had little interest in organizing her past work. Her studio remained chaotic.[328] She was always planning something new.

Chapter Eight

CROSSING BORDERS

An extraordinary opportunity, photographic and personal, arrived in late November 1990. A BBC producer asked Arthur Miller to conduct a filmed interview with Nelson Mandela, just released from twenty-eight years of imprisonment. Miller had never been in South Africa—like many progressives, he would not have traveled to an apartheid state. Morath had been there in 1955 when she visited her former London roommate Toni Scott, now married to a South African diamond mining millionaire.[329] On that trip she made some beautiful color photographs of pastoral people in Basutoland, a stunning and rather surreal image of a dancer wearing ox or buffalo horns, Zulu children and a mother in front of a traditional, colorful abstract painting on the walls of their hut. She showed workers at the Wesselton diamond mines, about ninety miles (145 km) from Kimberley, and children in Johannesburg, some wretchedly poor, some better dressed at a white-funded Christian missionary kindergarten. She also photographed the remarkable Trevor Huddleston, an Anglican bishop who had become, over his thirteen years in South Africa, a respected anti-apartheid activist, earning him the nickname "Makhalipile" (dauntless one). She described him as one of the "most dangerous personalities," referring to his position as an enemy of the South African regime.[330] At the opposite extreme from these images was her photograph of Toni Scott in bed, a glamour shot of her friend leaning back against a satin headboard, wearing a lace bed jacket and reading a novel (fig. 136). I am uncertain about the tenor of this image; through its contrast with images of African people, it could have been intended as a critical comment, and it would likely be read as such by a viewer today. On the whole, Morath's photography on this trip expressed the respect for other cultures that showed in all her work, but it did not emphasize the injustices of apartheid. It may be that her connection to the Scotts, combined with her customary graciousness, held back any overt criticism; on the other hand, shying away from "political" or critical photography was by now part of her identity. Aware that some might find this a reprehensible avoidance, she wrote apologetically

135. Inge at work, 2001. Photo by Stojan Kerbler

136. Toni Scott in her bedroom, Johannesburg, South Africa, 1955

that she "felt unequipped to really plunge into this whole problem."[331]

However "unequipped," the 1990 visit plunged her into it. The Millers' host was Beverley Marcus, an anti-apartheid activist who had been exiled in London. (Her sister, Gill Marcus, was head of the ANC information bureau and an assistant to Mandela.) Beverley had suggested that Miller and Morath first spend several days in beautiful Capetown so as to recover from jet lag. But once she had them there, she was not content to let them admire the city's dramatic landscape. She took them into the "settlements" for those labeled black and coloured in the apartheid racial system. Morath had not seen this poverty and repressiveness on her previous visit. She was even more horrified by Alexandra and Soweto, the "townships" where Johannesburg-area Africans had been confined. "There are a few stand up waterpipes for I don't know how many huts. Cement square behind lined by 2 rows of toilets, on one side no doors, the other behind wooden walk, no doors inside. Men just pee anywhere."[332]

Abba, Inge wrote, was tense on the night before the interview, so she urged him to take a walk in order to relax—she often mothered him; but it poured rain, so they remained inside until they went to Mandela's home in Soweto on the afternoon of December 3. Once inside the brick house, protected by walls and by razor wire, she captured the bustle of an extended family. A Mandela daughter, her rambunctious toddler son, a teenage girl, Mandela's wife, Winnie, and various unidentified relatives and friends, all coming and going, produced a lively background buzz. "Everyone is welcome. All playful," Morath wrote. She noted Mandela's erect posture and that he wore an informal African shirt, not a suit (fig. 137).

Born a chief's son, accustomed to deference, Mandela spoke in long "pronouncements." Miller had to interrupt him to get in his prepared questions. But Mandela did not seem to mind. The interview was interrupted by a large meal and, as usual, Morath listed every dish—shredded lettuce and carrots, whole roast potatoes, rice, stew, and roast beef. But she also noted that Mandela ate none of this rich food but only *mielie* (a porridge of maize, like grits), the staple food of Africans under apartheid and apparently all that Mandela could digest. As the interview continued after the meal, Mandela grew tired and yawned. Still, Morath noted, he "gamely gets back into it."[333] He had been out in the wee hours the night before, he explained, in order to witness the evidence of killings of ANC and Xhosa people by Buthelezi's Inkatha Zulu thugs, a brutality encouraged by apartheid defenders in government. Mandela spoke bluntly of the atrocities being committed, including the fact that the thugs had cut off a man's genitals.

Winnie Mandela had eaten by herself, not with the large dinner group, because, she told Morath, "he counts my calories." Morath gave Winnie her book of portrait photography. Later Morath recalled that when she said to Winnie that it was a pity we didn't get to talk more to her, Winnie responded, "'This is Africa. You talk to him you talk to both of us.'"[334]

In the late 1980s, Morath began developing a productive new partnership with Fotohof, an Austrian photographic gallery and foundation created and led by photographers, critics, and publishers Kurt Kaindl and Brigitte Blüml (the gallery is today located on Inge-Morath-Platz, a testament to her renown in Salzburg). Among her many photographic books, the four published by Fotohof are among the best curated and designed: *Donau* (the Danube), 1995; *New York*, 2002; *Durch Österreich* (Through Austria), 2005; *Venezia*, 2003.[335] This two-decades-long collaboration also gave Morath an outlet outside of Magnum and a chance to work with fellow Austrians. She curated and designed the books together with Kaindl and Blüml, and though two were published after her death, she had been able to select the photographs they contained. The three met several times a year, sometimes in Salzburg, sometimes in Roxbury, where Morath functioned not only as author but also, as always, hostess, housing and feeding her coworkers.

Like creating an exhibition, curating a book is arduous. As Kurt Kaindl recalled their process, the work would begin with choosing 300–400 possible images from contact sheets; from those they would have work prints made, out of which they would narrow the selection to around 150 images; of these Morath would have exhibition-quality prints made, half of which they then rejected; the final cuts they laid out on the floor so that

137. Nelson Mandela, just before he became president, in Julius House, his home in Soweto, 1990

Morath could choose the order and the juxtapositions she wanted, sometimes asking Miller's advice as well (fig. 138). After several years of such joint work, the two Austrians felt that they could predict her preferences. The three grew fond of one another, so much so that Brigitte Blüml accompanied Inge when, in the midst of chemotherapy for her lymphoma in 2001, she went to buy a wig.[336]

The Danube held great resonance for Morath. She had been traveling along or near the river for decades. Europe's second longest river after only the Volga, it was mythologized in the ancient world, fortified by the Romans, and remythologized as the river of the Nibelung by the Nazis. Supporting much of Mitteleuropean commerce, it runs through or along ten nations, more than any other river in the world. She had photographed along the Romanian stretch in 1958, in conditions that were difficult due to the region's poverty and its uniquely oppressive Communist regime—conditions particularly intimidating to a woman traveling alone. Stopped once by authorities, she was told to "rest," then locked inside a hut decorated with a photograph of an open coffin with a dead woman. No explanation offered. Assigned a guide/supervisor/interpreter, a Mr. Cetateanu, she was obliged to follow a set itinerary and suffered frequent interference with her freedom to photograph. "Going crazy," she wrote in her travel journal.[337] "Dinner with a Madame Thalmann. Don't know why." Consoling herself, she wrote, "I go to bed and eat chocolate." Cetateanu criticized her for accepting an impromptu invitation to join a wedding dinner. Soon he declared his love for her. About this she first wrote, "Oh God," and when he "embraces me, I try to remain brotherly." But she also used "his knees as a pillow," and when feeling lonesome, "cried on his shoulder." Accustomed to male adoration and companionship, she might have felt a bit protected

138. Inge working in her studio with Brigitte Blüml, Roxbury, Connecticut, 1992. Photo by Kurt Kaindl

139. Boys in the Street, Nikopol, Bulgaria, 1994

by this small flirtation. Despite the harassment, she was thrilled when she received permission to extend her travel into the Danube delta, which she found enchanting.[338] She shivered on a boat ride there, but came away with a strong photograph of some Romanian folk huddled together against the chill in a manner that could stand as a metaphor for the country's political climate.

In 1993, Kaindl and Blüml proposed creating an exhibition of Morath's work on the Danube for their new gallery; the plan would have her photograph its entire path. She took up the offer and made a full tour of the river the next year, which yielded not only an exhibition but also the book *Donau*.[339] This last Danubian voyage was like a pilgrimage through her homelands, tracing the river downstream from its birthplace to the Black Sea (fig. 139). A startling and, for Morath, most unusual photograph begins the viewer's journey—almost an abstract painting, a bright green close-up of the river's source, where it is such a shallow stream that one sees directly to the bottom. She used diverse images to represent different locations along the way: a Danubian marshland near Diethfurt, a pasture and a bartender in Furtwangen, a bridge in Regensburg, a flea market in Kelheim . . . and onward to the east. A Bulgarian woman washing laundry in the river (fig. 140). In Romania, portraits of an old fisherman and of a peasant woman with two children. This was a variation on her usual "ethnographic" approach, because no one or two images could fully describe a town, still less a region or a culture, still less the range of cultures along the river's route. The book is an homage not only to the river but also to the rich diversity of the region—a diversity Morath regarded as a treasure.

It was important to Morath that all the different religious and ethnic groups along the Danube be valued equally. This priority was shared not only with Kaindl and Blüml, but also by Karl-Markus Gauß, who contributed

140. Dobruja, Danube delta, 1958

a superb introduction. No writer could have better complemented Morath's sensibility. (She met him through Kaindl and for one of their meetings about the book hosted Gauß and his family in Roxbury.) An outspoken critic of racialism and aggressive nationalism, Gauß has written extensively in defense of the minority groups of Mitteleuropa. He used his introduction to condemn the nationalisms and religious bigotry that had created so much violence, even genocide, along the Danubian path. He condemned "the grimace of chauvinism . . . the fanaticism of narrowness, the destruction of nature, the leveling tread of progress" as he reminded the reader of the Danube's "wealth of culture, the multiplicity of its lifestyles which never cease to influence and enrich but do not override . . . art that has retained its frivolity and a passionate love of life."[340]

Gauß also wrote the introduction for *Durch Österreich*, published in 2005, in a parallel manner—that is, he wrote about Austria rather than about the photographs. In this book he is particularly critical of the virulent nationalism that had dissolved Yugoslavia and Czechoslovakia. Born after the war, he had no direct experience of Nazi atrocities. But with the New Left of the 1970s he came to reject "the stately lie that Austria was merely a victim of National Socialism" and that the postwar state was "founded on forgetting." But he criticized another forgetting, too, one in which he had himself participated: that of his generation of young leftists who were so angry about the Austrian lie that they recoiled to the opposite extreme, exiling from their consciousness the priceless achievements of Austrian culture. In this insistence on a complex evaluation of that history, his text fit Morath's sensibility perfectly.

Even as Gauß's introduction is explicitly political in its criticism of Austria's complicity in Nazism, he also saw strengths in Morath's apolitical approach. "Maybe," he wrote, "a photographer can't really do his or her work if they are convinced that the world has been already recognized, correctly seen, and validly interpreted. With Inge Morath . . . I found the conviction that she had seen far too little. . . . This made her appear so young." At the time Morath was in her seventies,[341] but Gauß grasped the humility and curiosity that lay behind her photography.

Durch Österreich, like *Donau*, includes photographs made over many decades from Morath's almost yearly visits to Austria. Portraits showed friends from her postwar days in Vienna, such as psychiatrist Victor Frankl, writer and critic Hans Weigel, and Count Max Thurn, as well as young artists like sculptor Ulrike Truger, actress-singer Erika Pluhar, and poet Barbara Frischmuth. She captured a Viennese ball where guests danced, no doubt, the waltz-to-the-left that she had taught her Paris friends, and Vienna's Belvedere Gardens, where strange sphinxlike sculptures, half woman/angel and half lion, symbolize the fusion of strength and intelligence—the woman has wings and a warlike breastplate, but also the long blond braids that typify the Tyrolean fashion still worn in Morath's youth.

The most revealing of Morath's late-life books is *Grenz.Räume: Last Journey* (2002).[342] It brings together conversations, letters, memories, and photographs to create a kind of *apologia pro vita sua* for Morath, and offers a deep insight into her roots and her feelings for her native land. Elegantly compiled by Austrian filmmaker Regina Strassegger, it contains not only Morath's photographs but also historical images and snapshots of friends and family—including her father in his Imperial WWI uniform—that provide the fullest context for her emotional and visual life.

Already ill with the lymphoma that would end her life, in 2001 Inge made three interrupted trips to her homeland, the Austrian regions of Styria and Slovenia (figs. 141, 142). She was beginning to experience backaches, which were exacerbated, she thought, by all her travels. Most of the time Arthur was with her, her brother and daughter joined her occasionally, and she visited some of her oldest friends as well as relatives.[343] The aging Inge spoke more emotionally than usual of her childhood love for this countryside. She called the local river Mur her "birth river." Expressing, no doubt, her anxiety about her cancer, she added, "May her waters protect me." From a boat ride, she focused her camera onto her own shadow on the water, but never pressed the shutter, remaining true to her abstention from self-portraits.

The book opens and closes with images of folk dance and of Morath behind the camera, astonishingly spry at seventy-nine. As in her Spanish photography, these pictures show her love for carnival—*fasching* in German—including some uncanny images, also reminiscent of her Spanish photographs. At the chateau where her family had summered in Gradišče, Slovenia, she made a surreal photo of an elderly woman, Marija Pečolar, in bed yet animated, her dark, sunken eyes glowing, and above her thirteen deer skulls with full antlers mounted on the wall. Along the Austrian-Slovene border the intrepid photographer went up in a hot-air balloon from which she captured snow-covered fields below. Despite her severe backache, she was up for an adventure.

Crossing borders is surely the great theme of Inge Morath's life and work (fig. 143). To underline that motif, *Grenz.Räume: Last Journey* shows her walking with friends along a road that crossed back and forth between Slovenia and Austria, at times passing farms that actually straddled this border. That these borders could be so easily crossed in 2001 cannot erase a past in which the peoples of the region—Slovenes, Austrians, Germans—have been both victims and perpetrators of nationalist atrocities. In Morath's understanding, furthermore, borders were an internal as well as an external threat. "The decisive issue . . . is to what extent people manage to rid themselves of the border in their heads."[344] Yet borders also promise, she knew, a cultural diversity that enriches. That Inge had married a Jewish leftist and her childhood friend Renate had married a Jewish concentration camp survivor heralded that enrichment, as well as the reconciliation that Inge so cherished.

141. Inge's mother, Mathilde Mörath, and her twin sister, Elizabeth Nowak, celebrating their ninety-second birthdays in an inn near Graz, Austria, 1992

142. Church where Inge's grandparents were married, Slovenia, 1992

But dwelling only on reconciliation, and on silencing the past, had costs. In a reunion with Renate and Imo Moszkowicz in the wine country right at the border, a landscape that represented heaven to Inge, they engaged in awkward conversation about their Nazi-era pasts. Imo loved Inge dearly, but he was not a forgive-and-forget type, and he respected particularly his wife's integrity. He remarked that the "discussion I never conducted with my father-in-law [an SS man] was conducted by Renate, and so violently that I felt she wanted to destroy everything."[345] Inge remained silent during much of these conversations.[346] Regina Strassegger was exasperated by Inge's refusal to engage. "For me, a historian and political journalist . . . I don't want to accept that this worldly and educated woman across from me so ungallantly blocks me . . . because I know this behavioral pattern just in a more extreme form from the generations of the fathers. . . . I can't just have a harmless nostalgic landscape conversation with Inge Morath."[347] What none of

143. Checkpoint into East Berlin, 1989

them articulated was Inge's own burden, the impact of trauma and, possibly, guilt—the place of darkness in her that only her intimates had seen.

While on these trips, Inge's backaches worsened. She stopped frequently to practice yoga, hoping to stretch out her back. Perhaps she strained it playing with her grandson, she thought, or it was a pinched nerve. She refused to see a doctor and they all went to a nightclub where she photographed a rock band. On October 6, 2001, she apologized (!) for holding everyone back. "What a splendid fall day . . . only I, your spoiled guest, am pretty badly out of shape."[348] She finally consulted a physician who was surprised by her mobility despite the severe pain. She returned to the States in a wheelchair, remaining, Regina Strassegger thought, "merry as a lark."[349] The apparent good spirits probably indicated not freedom from pain but rather her self-discipline and determination, and, of course, her graciousness to all around her.

The pain was an effect of Inge's lymphoma, which had been diagnosed over a year earlier. She kept her illness mostly to herself, and in the end, she did not live long enough to see this beautiful book—*Grenz.Räume*—her last, a sort of testament to her life's work and her roots. She died on January 30, 2002.

Inge Morath was not only a superb photographer but also a fine writer, and she frequently articulated her photographic approach in words. At times her thinking reflected what she had learned from the greatest of her mentors, Henri Cartier-Bresson, as when she described "turning round the subject until one finds the right moment."[350] She spoke of the relation between slowness and quickness, between waiting and instantaneousness. "I love the mixture of tension and patience that is involved in approaching a subject. For me 'technique' is only the decision from which height or distance to take the picture, moving a fraction to the right or to the left,

144. Janet Flanner, who wrote the *New Yorker* magazine's "Letter from Paris" column for many years under the name of Genêt, Roxbury, Connecticut, 1973

which lens, which shutter speed and aperture." To be fairly certain of "these decisions taken semiconsciously . . . is probably what makes you a 'professional.'"[351] Often her comments about photography fit her life as well: photography is "yes, yes, yes," she wrote, quoting Cartier-Bresson, "and there's no maybe. All the maybes should go to the trashcan because it's an instant."[352] Her respect for the way Arthur Miller wrote evoked a vivid comparison with her own creative process. In an essay about him she wrote that he "has to take his time to formulate thoughts and words. For me, a missed moment is irretrievably lost."[353]

Morath understood herself as a cosmopolitan and an explorer. "I am a traveler with a camera through whose viewfinder I have been looking at the world and the faces of its people for more than forty years," she wrote in 1996 (figs. 144, 145). Her global photography shows her respect for other cultures, as well as her ability to see beauty in the mundane as well as in fine art. She experienced the two major aspects of her work—portraiture and the exploration of the world's vernacular cultures—as one. Her respect for other cultures, absorbed from her parents and her multicultural homeland, was mirrored in her respect for her every portrait subject. In both genres she accepted but also hoped to illuminate, however partially, the essential mystery, the unknowability of others and other cultures. That she rarely if ever made self-portraits signals her lack of self-absorption and unquenchable interest in others. Confidence, yes; ambition, yes; self-assurance, but no narcissism. Yet she emphasized the subjectivity of every photograph, "Not at random, but as a result of looking outside from inside oneself, with a kind of disciplined enthusiasm."[354]

Just as avoiding political critique in her photography was part of who Inge was, so was her lack of bitterness or self-importance. If she smothered reflections on the Nazi politics of her parents, she never claimed moral superiority, never sought credit for her refusal to comply with Nazism even as a teenager, and saw no reason to announce her values publicly. She expressed those values implicitly, through the cosmopolitanism that saturates her photography. Open to all the world's inhabitants and cultures, and able to see and picture beauty in likely and unlikely places, her work is of particular value in today's world where nationalistic, ethnic, and religious animosities once again threaten.

As a means of recognizing and encouraging photographers who share Morath's globalism, a yearly award in her name was established in 2002, given to a female photographer under the age of thirty to support a long-term documentary project. Its recipients have photographed, to cite a few examples, lives along the oil pipelines in Azerbaijan, Georgia, and Turkey; "girl power" in Iran; the gay scene in Beijing; growing up in Haiti; mental illness in America's prisons. These awards, and the online magazine in which they appear, can be found at www.ingemorath.org.[355]

Twelve years later an extraordinary group photographic project grew out of these awards, celebrating the commitment to internationalism that Morath stood for and exemplified. A group of nine women photographers, all winners of the annual Inge Morath awards, converted an eighteen-wheeler into a mobile gallery of Morath's work and drove it along the course of the Danube. For thirty-five days, beginning on July 5, 2014, they traveled, exhibited, and made their own photographs. Visiting twenty-four towns in ten countries, they brought Morath's photography home to the people of these lands she so treasured. Nothing could have been a finer homage, recognizing both her rootedness in the region and at the same time her rejection of nationalism.[356]

145. French artist Jean Arp with one of his sculptures, Paris, 1956

Photographer Dorothea Lange's favorite quotation was "A camera is a tool for learning how to see without a camera." It fits Morath perfectly. Like all fine photographers, she understood her calling as a means to deconventionalize how we observe. "We can only see, hear, feel what we have been in the habit of seeing, hearing and feeling"—this is what the photographer must work against.[357] In challenging the unavoidable human tendency toward conventionalization, Morath's main instrument was not her camera but her curiosity. And this was indistinguishable from her refusal to claim a comprehension that she knew to be incomplete. "In my heart I like to remain an amateur . . . forever again astonished at the endless possibilities of seeing anew."[358] As Gauß realized, her photographic eye reflected her humility, her strong belief that there was always more to learn. The thrill of discovery gave her energy and fed her lust for travel. Always learning, she wrote, "I still have not tired of it: the discovery . . . remains as exhilarating as ever."[359] Critic Lola Garrido saw this early in Morath's career, and characterized her photographic approach as "the absence of certainties";[360] that quality is all the more impressive given that Morath typically arrived at any photo op with as much knowledge as she could gather about its subject.

Despite her traumatic wartime experiences, Inge had a remarkable capacity for fun, both in her life and her photography. She had the advantage of a happy childhood and loving parents, but then, emerging from

146. Roy Lichtenstein in his studio, New York, 1997

147. Louise Bourgeois in her studio, New York, 1991

an ordeal that might have crippled a less courageous woman, she made her own happiness through a long and satisfying career, marriage, and motherhood. She forged that life through fortitude, high energy, charm, beauty, hard work, and extraordinary talent. Never indulging a sense of entitlement, never retreating from tedium or discomfort, she honed her talent into mastery.

It wasn't always easy. As a young woman Inge willed herself into "a woman's complete independence in work and, intimately connected with it, personal life." Refusing to concede to the male domination of photography, she responded to discrimination and disrespect with grit and a thick skin, ignoring slights and making compensatory connections. In her first ten years as a photographer she made "the choice of living alone . . . in order to be totally free to work and move."[361] After her marriage to Arthur Miller, she prioritized wifehood, motherhood, and his career. Those priorities constituted the female standard at the beginning of the 1960s, as well as the model she saw in her childhood. And those priorities were reinforced by her husband's extraordinary art and renown. When she faced a choice between becoming a superwoman—that is, trying to do Magnum-level itinerant photography while also doing the work of a full-time mother, cook, and hostess—she chose to limit the range and quantity of her photography until her domestic labor was no longer needed. In the 1980s and 1990s she returned to exhausting travels and global photography, reclaiming her youthful energy and adventurousness.

To some extent Morath's career was eclipsed by Miller's. I doubt that she regretted this. She had not only fallen in love with him but had also discovered in herself a desire for home and its many pleasures. She had found a loving partner with whom she could share her tastes, her ideas, and her friends. She respected his work and may have believed it more important than hers—which would not have been a surprising opinion among women at the time. But she was also enriched by her relationship with Miller. He brought her a fresh aesthetic sensibility and unique photographic opportunities. All told, their marriage yielded great satisfactions: a stimulating social community, a brilliant daughter, shared projects, shared travel, and access to the natural beauty of their home and its grounds.

Morath was an unusually intellectual photographer. Her approach involved intensive preparatory study of her subjects, whether individuals or whole cultures, and her images reflected her extraordinary cultural sophistication, particularly about literature and the fine arts. This cultural fluency notably underlay her interest in photographing artists and the revealing images that resulted, as well as her friendships with many of the artists she photographed (figs. 146, 147). Art historian Garrido distilled the essence of Morath's mastery, calling her "the most intellectual, sophisticated and cultivated photographer I have met."[362]

Morath often spoke of the joy of making a good photograph, even of the visceral pleasures of her tools. "I grew to like the shape and the weight of the camera in my hand while walking."[363] "My darkroom is small. It really only can accommodate me, the table with the enlarger and the paper drawer, and the sink with the trays for the chemicals. It is an unshared experience, I mean by another body, but it is densely populated by whatever I wish to conjure up."[364] Many times she resolved to make order of her contact sheets and papers, but she never did. The outside world was too interesting for her to remain inside her studio (fig. 148).

148. Inge's studio in Roxbury, Connecticut, 1992. Photo by Kurt Kaindl

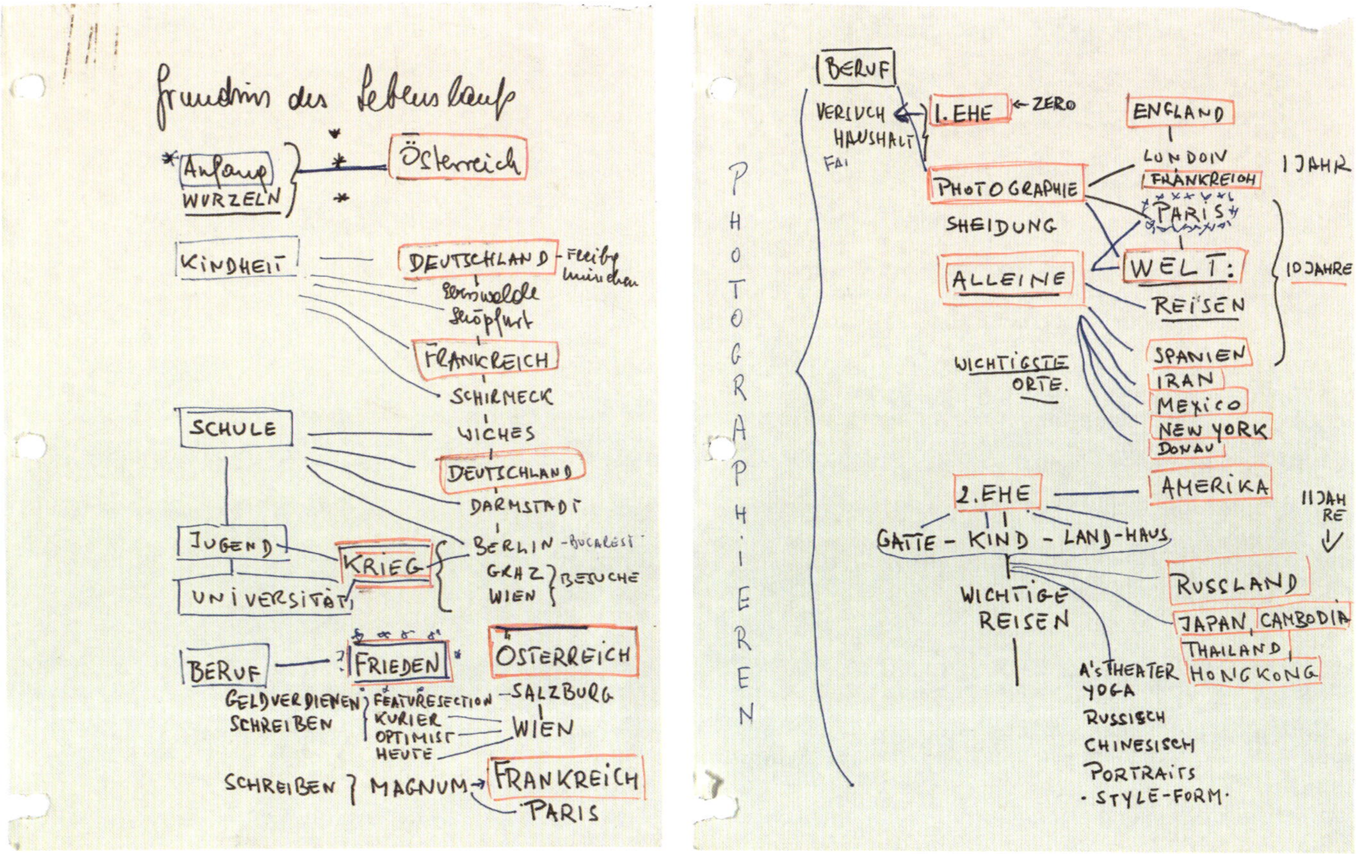

149 / 150. A diagram by Inge showing the main events in her life

TRAVERSING THE ARCHIVES: MAPPING THE LIFE OF INGE MORATH

On two pieces of three-hole-punched paper Inge Morath (b. Austria, 1923) diagrammed her life (figs. 149, 150). It is unclear when or why she undertook this task, but the document is illuminating nonetheless, serving as a visualization of her biography. It shows the conceptual framework of Inge's life as she perceived it, delineates what she considered most *wichtig* (significant), and also speaks to a sense of itinerancy that is intrinsic to her narrative. Written in her native German, the left-hand column lists major life stages and milestones (childhood, university, first and second marriages, etc.) as well as her profession (initially as a writer, then as photographer). In the middle column of the first page, double outlined both in red and blue, she wrote *Krieg* (war, in reference to World War II) and *Frieden* (peace). On the right,

Morath outlined in red all the countries in which she had lived (Austria, Germany, France, England, and America) and underneath, she listed the cities. The second page also includes some of the many countries in which she traveled.

These two pieces of paper are among thousands in Morath's archive, which comprises more than 740 boxes at the Beinecke Rare Book & Manuscript Library at Yale University. Morath began her photographic career at Magnum Photos in 1953, and these boxes are replete with photographs, contact sheets, and captions. But unlike the archives of many of her Magnum colleagues, Morath's also contains an abundance of personal materials. Extending far beyond her career with the agency, there are images, documents, and objects from the various phases of her life. Family photographs span over a century, from nineteenth-century studio portraits of her ancestors posed against painted backdrops in Graz, Austria (fig. 151), to snapshots of Morath's husband, Arthur Miller and daughter, Rebecca, in their home in Roxbury, Connecticut. There are journals and letters in which Morath reflects on her childhood in war-torn Austria and Germany, the trajectory of her career, and her later role as wife and mother. These extensive materials from Morath's life and career were only made publicly accessible in 2015.[1] Beyond the previously published Morath material, a look into the archive grants a new, personal view of the photographer.

151. The Mörath family, 1885, photographer unknown

The collection of family photographs shed light on Morath's personal history and her experiences during World War II. There are photographs of Morath throughout her childhood—as an infant in a carriage, a toddler on her father's knee, and a schoolgirl smiling with her friends in the yard. There are only a few from the war, and some have been annotated. On the back of a 1939 portrait of Morath (in which she wears a swastika brooch and a grimace) (fig. 161), her brother Werner wrote, "No, she didn't like it too much, however, you learned something about the earth—and you came back eager for liberty and studies" (fig. 152).[2] This likely refers to Morath's return from a year spent in a Nazi work program, milking cows and tending fields in East Prussia. Filed with this photograph, there is also a letter from Werner. He reflected, "We were on the threshold then from youth to greater responsibilities and were caught at that time in the inexorable unescapable grip of the beginning of

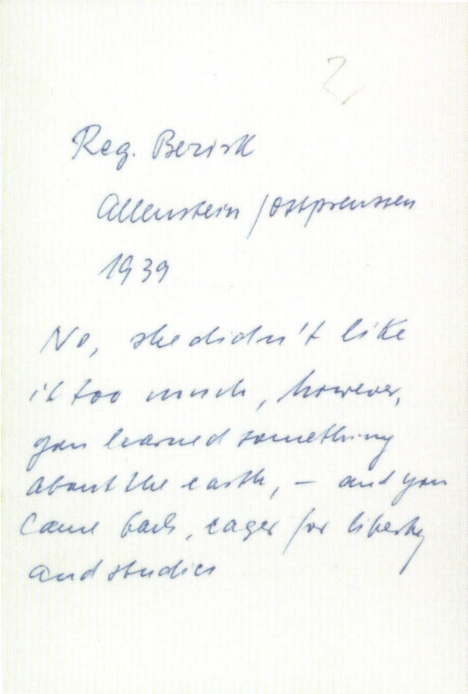

152. Inge, Salzburg, 1939 (verso)

war which finally changed and shaped our lives beyond what we ever imagined possible."[3] He then wrote that later in the war Morath trekked through "rubble and smoke" to get to university, where she studied Romance languages.[4] There are no images in the archive that show this, as Werner explained that they lacked film to take more photographs. But here, the thin carbon letter acts as a surrogate for the absent images. Its presence augments an understanding of Morath's life in the war and enhances our understanding of the surviving visual material.

From the immediate postwar period, Morath saved a yellowed letter with worn fold marks and an official United States Information Branch stamp, verifying her employment as reporter for *Heute*, a German-language picture magazine produced in Munich by the American-occupying government (fig. 10). Her professional beginnings and early prowess as a writer are made evident by *Heute* tear sheets of a 1949 story on Austrian prisoners of war returning from Russian camps (figs. 12, 153). This collaboration with Ernst Haas as photographer features Morath's poignant text and captions describing the desperate crowds and the many women and children waiting in vain for husbands and fathers who never returned. In later writings found in the archive, Morath looked back on her own emotions during this time period. On a piece of paper titled "Ernst Haas," written sometime after his death in 1986, she wrote, "The Second World War had been over for four years but its dark cloud of terror and human suffering still hung heavy over us . . . but there was also the euphoria of newfound freedom, of endless possibilities, of being able to be young."[5] Both her personal reflections and published texts demonstrate Morath's ability to capture the many painful, contradictory, and sometimes even hopeful feelings of the postwar period. This accumulation

153. Returning prisoners of war, 1949. Photos by Ernst Haas

of materials provides a fuller sense of Morath as a person who not only lived through these trying times, but would return to them many times through her writing.

Like those she wrote for Haas's images, Morath's captions for her own photographs amplify the reading of her work. The archive has an extensive collection of caption sheets from throughout her career (figs. 77, 93, 94). For her first photo story on worker priests in 1953, Morath wrote paragraph-length descriptions that detail the priests' daily regimens, providing a rich and informative context for the photographs. Later captions from a 1960 road trip that she took from New York to Reno, Nevada, with Henri Cartier-Bresson are more poetic. To accompany her photograph of cars in an open field (fig. 154), she wrote:

> Tonopah, Nevada. Car Collectors Dreams dying slowly in the dumps above the former gold and silver mining town. Sometimes a miner's hat looks out over their tangled and twisted bodies, the dirty gold of a mine dump behind accentuating the sadness of the rotting luxury of a torn leather upholstery.[6]

154. Outside Tonopah, Nevada, 1960

Morath's journals from this, and many other, trips have also made their way into her extraordinary archive. She traveled with her typewriter and on page twenty-five of her road-trip journal, Morath wrote: "We arrived in Reno on the evening of the 17th. Into a world so different from the loneliness of the trip, the world of a movie being started. It is difficult to describe the last extraordinary days, although when I close my eyes, the road still seems to be passing in front of me, running straight and hot through the desert."[7] Her photographs create a visual diary of the trip but these journals capture experiences that took place beyond the confines of the framed image. These black-type pages were later annotated in blue pen—perhaps she had intended to publish her writing.

Morath's extensive travels and assignments for Magnum are also chronicled in a story list, now stored in a heavy red binder. Under each year, Morath typed the story number, title, and the number of rolls of film she had shot. Her entries from 1955 indicate that in that year alone she photographed in France, Germany, Austria, Great Britain, South Africa, Spain, and Italy (fig. 61). Morath also cataloged her travels alphabetically by country in a Rolodex, and a spin of the wheel shows that she returned to these countries again and again. In preparation for the trips, and to deepen her understanding of other cultures, Morath spent her life learning languages. Her journals and letters demonstrate her staggering command of eight languages, and she sometimes moved fluidly among French, German, and English in a single text. The archive also holds a collection of passports that show Morath's successive Austrian, British, and American citizenships (figs. 155, 156, 157, 158). A "canceled" stamp on the second of these denotes her brief stint as Mrs. Ingeborg Birch (wife of Englishman Lionel Birch), and the last, her subsequent identity as Mrs. Arthur Miller.

In a letter to her Magnum colleague Elliott Erwitt, Morath wrote of how her "life changed considerably" when she married Arthur Miller in 1962.[8] The marriage took primacy in her life, and this is reflected in the predominance of the Miller material in the archive. For example, she saved few professional tear sheets of her photo stories, but there is a collection of tabloid clippings announcing their marriage (which was on the heels of Miller's divorce from Marilyn Monroe). A 1962 *Evening News* article quotes Miller, who "said that the marriage [to Morath] would be totally different from his marriage to Monroe. 'She will mostly be a housewife. There is nothing professional involved. We want to have children.'"[9] There is also an array of correspondence with Magnum, in which Morath requested to downgrade her membership, from full member to "contributor," stating "I have to take care of a husband whose superior talents often require my cooking more urgently than my photography."[10] Despite these remarks, and despite articles like "A Weekend with the Arthur Millers" (*Vogue*, 1972), which portray Morath primarily as a hostess and refined cook (fig. 109), she did continue to photograph and publish extensively until her death in 2002.

The archive holds more than 46,000 of Morath's 35 mm color transparencies, a majority of these from this later, prolific period. She had turned primarily to portraiture and there is an extensive catalog of personalities—artists, authors, and celebrities—that she photographed.

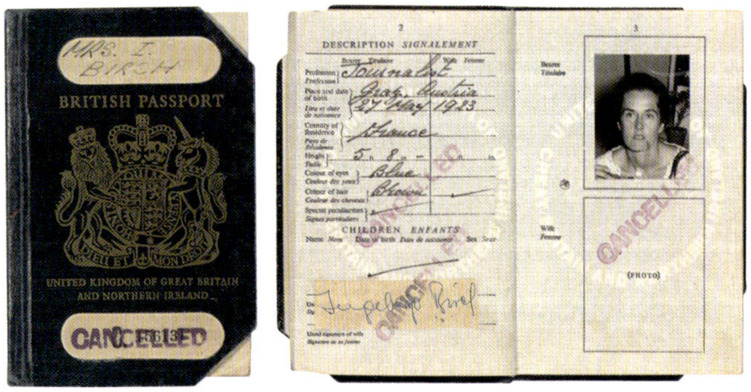

155 / 156. Mrs. I. Birch, British passport, 1958

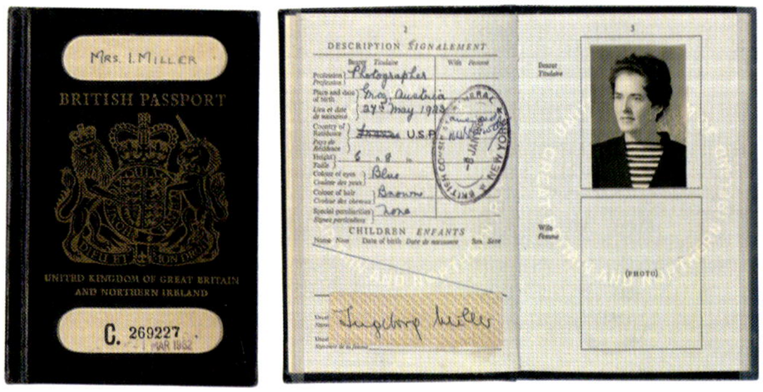

157 / 158. Mrs. I. Miller, British passport, 1962

There are also color photographs she took of Miller's plays such as his production of *Death of a Salesman* in Beijing, and from the couple's extensive international travels. Many binders are filled with personal snapshots of Miller and Morath's life together in Roxbury. Images show Miller doing yard work or the couple reading a newspaper in the kitchen (fig. 159). These offer rarely published glimpses of the well-known couple at ease in their day-to-day routines. In addition to these later photographs, there are also color slides from the 1950s, starting with her first assignment in London for *Holiday* magazine in 1953. Much of her early color work was only recently rediscovered when the Inge Morath Foundation began to organize and digitize her slides in 2007. Of this material, now found at the Beinecke, only a fraction has been published. Here, Morath's personal and professional color photographs from throughout her career are neatly cataloged by subject, demonstrating an expansiveness and inclusiveness characteristic of the archive.

159. Arthur Miller, Roxbury, Connecticut

As charted in the opening diagram, Morath's journey from war-torn Austria to America was extraordinary. Hundreds of boxes of photographs, contact sheets, and slides demonstrate her professional accomplishments from throughout her career. But her archive is also distinctly personal and displays an openness that is rare among photographers, as is her gift as a writer. Morath once stated in an interview that she loved to write and did so every day. But she published very little of her writing in her lifetime and instead, she told the interviewer, she would just file it in a drawer.[11] In the move of the Morath materials from her home in Roxbury, to the Inge Morath Foundation, and finally to the Beinecke, her writings and family photographs have relocated from private spaces to the public sphere. Her newly accessible letters, journals, and drafts of various writings are both eloquent and essential tools to understanding how Morath viewed herself and her work. They reveal her experiences in World War II, her grace at navigating relationships and cultures as well as her devotion to her family. Snapshots too of her grandparents and parents as children and as they aged, and of her husband and daughter, show her familial heritage and the legacy that she passed on. With the archive, Morath has now allowed the lens to be aimed at her. The archival photographs, documents, and objects come together to yield her most intimate self-portrait.

Tessa Hite

160. Inge, Roxbury, Connecticut, 1996, photographer unknown

CHRONOLOGY COMPILED BY TESSA HITE

1920s

1923

Born in Graz, Austria, on May 27 to parents Edgar and Mathilde (Titti) Mörath, both scientists.

Throughout her childhood, lives in various towns in France and Germany including Freiburg, Munich, Schirmeck, and Wisches.

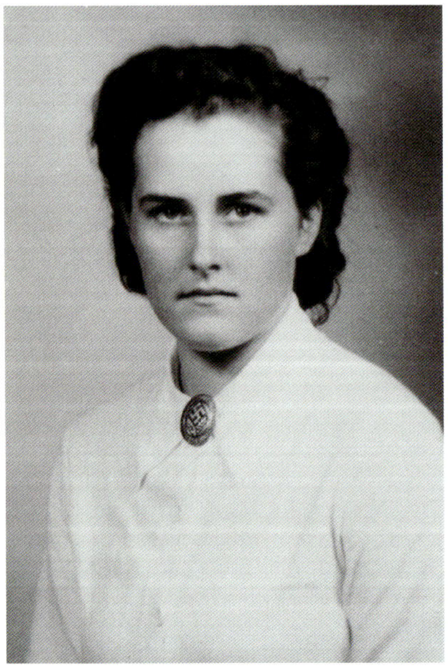

161. Inge, Salzburg, 1939, photographer unknown

1930s

1930

Moves to Darmstadt, Germany.

1937

Sees *Degenerate Art* (*Entartete Kunst*) exhibition in Munich.

All information is derived from materials at the Beinecke Rare Book & Manuscript Library at Yale University.

1938

Moves with her family to Berlin.

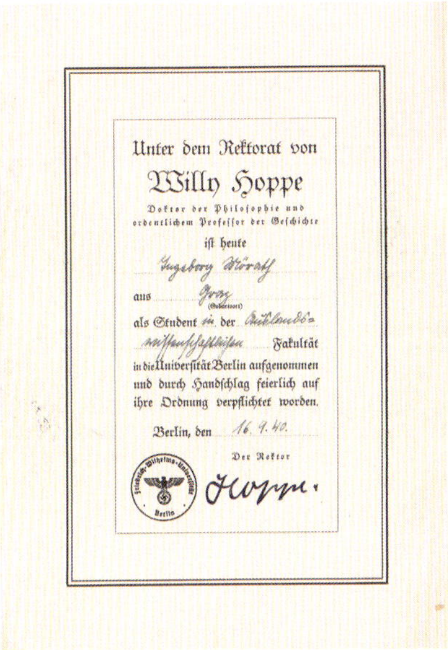

Unter dem Rektorat von
Willy Hoppe
Doktor der Philosophie und
ordentlichem Professor der Geschichte
ist heute
Ingeborg Mörath
aus Graz
(Geburtsort)
als Student in der Auslands-
wissenschaftlichen Fakultät
in die Universität Berlin aufgenommen
und durch Handschlag feierlich auf
ihre Ordnung verpflichtet worden.
Berlin, den 16. 9. 40.
Der Rektor
Hoppe.

162. Inge's diploma, Berlin, 1940

1940s

1940

Graduates from high school in Berlin. Following this, Mörath is sent to East Prussia for a year as part of a Nazi work program.

Upon return, she enrolls in the University of Berlin and studies Romance languages. Spends a semester abroad at University of Bucharest in Romania.

1944

Receives Bachelor of Arts from University of Berlin. After which, she is drafted into war service and works at an aircraft factory at Tempelhof Airport outside Berlin.

1945

Flees Berlin in an arduous trek, mostly on foot, back to Salzburg, and reunites with family.

1945–49

Works for United States Information Service in Salzburg as an editor and translator and then is transferred to the Vienna bureau.

Coeditor for political-literary magazine *Der Optimist* and contributes as a freelance writer to Red-White-Red Radio network.

By 1948 is a reporter for *Heute*, a biweekly picture magazine published by the American-occupying government in Munich. Collaborates with photographer Ernst Haas.

163. "Junge Ärzte" (Young Doctors), text by Inge Morath and Heintze von Kracht, *Heute*, 1949. Photo by Ernst Haas

1949

Haas and Morath publish a story on Austrian prisoners of war returning from Russian camps in *Heute*. It also runs in *Life* and is brought to the attention of Robert Capa, who invites the pair to Magnum in Paris.

Haas joins Magnum as a photographer and Morath continues to work with him, researching, writing, and editing for Magnum.

164. Actress Zsa Zsa Gabor in *Moulin Rouge* by John Huston, 1953

1950s

1951

Marries Englishman Lionel Birch and lives in London.

On a trip to Venice begins to take her own photographs with an old Contax that was a present from her mother.

Submits photographs to publishers under pseudonym Egni Tharom (Inge Morath backward).

1952

Receives photographic training in London from Simon Guttmann, who had worked for *Berliner Illustreite* and founded Dephot photographer agency.

Separates from Lionel Birch.

165. Granada, Guadix, Spain 1954

1953

Photographs her first photo story, "Prêtres Ouvriers" (Worker Priests) in Paris.

Joins Magnum as an associate member.

On her first Magnum assignment, photographs on the set of John Huston's film *Moulin Rouge*. Befriends Huston and continues to photograph on the set of many more of his films.

Lives in Paris and apprentices with Henri Cartier-Bresson. Travels with him on assignment and also researches, edits, and translates for him.

Embarks on first trip to Spain with Cartier-Bresson.

166. Sorting and cleaning diamonds at De Beers, Johannesburg, 1955

1954

Divorces Birch.

Travels to Ireland. Photographs John Huston in his home and Irish travelers in Killorglin, County Kerry.

Photographs sculptor Henry Moore in his studio in Hadham, Hertfordshire.

Capa sends Morath to Spain on assignment for "Woman of the World" series in *Holiday* magazine.

167. Skin dyeing south of Tehran, 1956

1955

Becomes full member of Magnum.

Travels to South Africa and photographs De Beers diamonds.

Spain photographs are published in *Guerre à la Tristesse*, with text by Dominique Aubier (Paris: Robert Delpire). American edition: *Fiesta in Pamplona* (New York: Universe Books, 1956).

1956

Photographs of Venice are published in *Venice Observed*, with text by Mary McCarthy (New York: Reynal & Co).

168. Audrey Hepburn during the filming of *The Unforgiven*, Durango, Mexico, 1959

Spends six weeks in Iran on assignment for *Holiday* magazine, Standard Oil, and Pepsi Cola. Photographs extensively while there.

Breaks engagement to Spanish aristocrat Duke Gonzalo Figueroa.

Sent on first work assignment to United States. While there, photographs heiress Gloria Vanderbilt and actress and model Nancy Berg.

In France photographs Christina Onassis, artist Jean Arp, French minister of culture, and writer André Malraux.

1957

Photographs a llama in Times Square and other TV animals. Photographs neighborhoods in Paris and New York.

Returns to Spain. Photographs flood in Valencia and Holy Friday in Zamora.

Photographs couturier Yves St. Laurent and dancer Zizi Jeanmaire in Paris.

Photographs the Ringling Museum in Florida.

1958

Photographs in Romania, France, Austria, Yugoslavia, and Czechoslovakia.

Publishes Iran photographs in *De la Perse à L'Iran*, with text by Édouard Sablier (Paris: Robert Delpire). English edition later printed: *From Persia to Iran: An Historical Journey* (New York: Viking Press, 1960).

169. George Washington, Hall of Presidents, Gettysburg, Pennsylvania, 1960

1959

Photographs on the set of John Huston film *Unforgiven* in Mexico, starring Burt Lancaster and Audrey Hepburn.

Photographs in Tunisia and images are later included in *Tunisia, from Carthage to Tomorrow*, with text by Claude Roy and Paul Sebag (New York: Orion Press, 1961).

Begins photographing mask series with artist Saul Steinberg.

On a project with actor Yul Brynner for the United Nations, photographs displaced persons in Germany, Austria, Jordan, and Israel. Publishes photographs in *Bring Forth the Children: A Journey of the Forgotten People of Europe and The Middle East*, with text by Yul Brynner (New York: McGraw-Hill, 1960).

170. Inge and Arthur, ca. 1962

1960s

1960

Embarks on an eighteen-day road trip from New York to Reno with Henri Cartier-Bresson.

171. Arthur at his desk with daughter, Rebecca, Roxbury, Connecticut, 1962

172. Moscow State Ballet, 1965

Photographs on the set of *The Misfits*, written by Arthur Miller and starring his wife Marilyn Monroe.

Undertakes commercial work for Bankers Trust and Citroën.

Photographs on the set of *Good-Bye Again*, starring Ingrid Bergman, Yves Montand, and Anthony Perkins.

1961

Photographs on the set of *A View from the Bridge*, written by Arthur Miller.

1962

Marries Arthur Miller. The couple first lives in the Chelsea Hotel and soon moves to Roxbury, Connecticut.

Daughter Rebecca Miller is born.

Continues to photograph mask series with Saul Steinberg.

1963

Photographs a production of Miller's play *After the Fall*.

Continues commercial work for Bankers Trust.

First photographs sculptor Alexander Calder in his studio, continues into the following decade.

Becomes secretary of Magnum.

1964

On assignments for *Vogue*, photographs a gala opening at the Philharmonic, actress Jessica Walter, and singer Marnie Nixon.

Exhibition *Inge Morath Photographs*, Art Institute of Chicago.

1965

Travels with Miller by train from Germany to the USSR, where she photographs extensively. Learns Russian in preparation for the trip.

Photographs a production of Miller's play *Death of a Salesman*, starring Dustin Hoffman.

1966

Becomes US citizen.

Publishes *Steinberg: Le Masque* (Paris: Maeght Éditeur).

173. During Festival of the Grapes, Kaheti Valley, Georgia, USSR, 1967

1967

Returns to the USSR to photograph. Travels there again in 1986, 1989, 1990, and 1993.

Second child, Daniel Miller, is born with Down syndrome.

Photographs a production of Miller's play *The Price*.

174. Mourners queue outside St. Patrick's Cathedral during Robert F. Kennedy's funeral, New York, 1968

1968

Photographs mourners outside Robert F. Kennedy's funeral at St. Patrick's Cathedral, New York.

1969

Publishes *In Russia*, with text by Arthur Miller (New York: Viking Press).

1970s

1970

Files paperwork to downgrade Magnum status to "contributor."

Photographs extensively around home in Roxbury, Connecticut.

Travels to Hong Kong, Japan, and Cambodia.

1971

Lectures at Cooper Union in New York.

Begins to study Mandarin.

1973

Photographs Pilobolus dancers rehearsing in Roxbury, Connecticut.

175. Faye Dunaway during the TV production of *After the Fall* by Arthur Miller, New York, 1974

1974

Photographs TV production of Miller's *After the Fall* with Faye Dunaway and Christopher Plummer.

Travels to Austria, Hungary, and Czechoslovakia.

1977

Travels to Japan on first solo trip since marriage to Miller.

Travels to Israel.

Publishes photographs of Roxbury, Connecticut, in *In the Country* with text by Arthur Miller (New York: Viking Press).

176. Chairman Mao's last cave residence, Yunnan, China, 1978

177. Portrait of sculptor Marisol Escobar in the Sidney Janis Gallery, New York, 1981

1978

Travels to China with Miller and returns there again in 1979 and 1983.

Photographs in Nantucket. Subjects include Dustin Hoffman and director and choreographer Martha Clarke.

1979

Publishes *Chinese Encounters*, with text by Arthur Miller (New York: Farrar, Straus & Giroux).

Exhibition *Inge Morath: Photographs of China*, Grand Rapids Art Museum, Michigan. Publishes accompanying catalog.

1980s

1981

Travels to Egypt.

Photographs, often in color, numerous artists and writers such as sculptor Marisol Escobar, writer William Styron, and fashion designer Pierre Cardin.

1982

Pursues work in portraiture, focusing on women artists, such as Helen Frankenthaler and Louise Bourgeois. Continues to photograph Bourgeois several more times in the years to follow.

Photographs personalities in Caracas, Venezuela.

1983

Photographs production of Miller's *Death of a Salesman* in Beijing.

Photographs author Philip Roth.

1984

Publishes *Salesman in Beijing* with text by Miller (New York: Viking Press).

Awarded doctor of fine arts, University of Connecticut, Hartford.

1985

Photographs on *Death of a Salesman* film set starring Dustin Hoffman and John Malkovich.

1986

Publishes *Portraits* (New York: Aperture).

178. Production of *Death of a Salesman* at Beijing People's Art Theatre. Arthur Miller (center), actor Ying Ruocheng (seated, right), Beijing, 1983

179. Book cover of *Portraits*, 1986

180. Louise Bourgeois and Andy Warhol, New York, 1987

1987

Photographs playwright Edward Albee at his home with Arthur Miller.

1988

Photographs several more writers including Jay McInerney, Tama Janowitz, and Evan Hunter (a.k.a. Ed McBain).

Returns to Spain.

1989

In Berlin for the dismantling of the Wall. Photographs the opening passage at Potsdamer Platz.

1990s

1990

Teaches a portrait course at the International Center of Photography in New York.

Returns to South Africa. Photographs Nelson Mandela.

1991

Photographs production of Miller's play *The Ride Down Mt. Morgan* in London.

Receives Grand Austrian State Award for Photography.

Publishes *Russian Journal: 1965–1990* (New York: Aperture).

1992

Travels to Slovenia. Photographs church where her grandparents were married.

Exhibition *Retrospective* travels internationally. Publishes accompanying catalog.

1993

Travels to Bhutan. Breaks wrist.

Mother Titti dies at ninety-five years old.

1994

Photographs London premiere of Miller's play *Broken Glass*.

Publishes *Inge Morath: España años 50* (Spain in the Fifties) (Madrid: Artecontexto).

Photographs the Danube River in Romania and Bulgaria.

181. Opening of passage at Potsdamer Platz, Berlin Wall, West Germany, 1989

182. Near the Danube delta, Romania, 1994

183. Daniel Day-Lewis on the set of the movie *The Crucible*, Hogs Island, Massachusetts, 1995

184. Arthur next to the studio in which he wrote *Death of a Salesman*, Roxbury, Connecticut, 1998

1995

Photographs on the film set of *The Crucible*, starring Daniel Day-Lewis, who marries Rebecca Miller the following year.

Publishes *Donau*, with text by Kurt Kaindl (Salzburg: Müller Verlag).

1996

Returns to Japan.

1997

Exhibition *Inge Morath: Photographs 1950s to 1990s* at the Tokyo Museum of Photography.

1998

Returns to Spain and photographs a series on the Camino de Santiago pilgrimage.

1999

Honorary Gold Medal of the Federal Capital Vienna.

Retrospective exhibition at Kunsthalle Wien. Publishes accompanying catalog *Inge Morath: Life as a Photographer* (Munich: Kehayoff).

2000s

2000

Travels to Cuba, photographs Fidel Castro.

2001

Photographs around the borderlands of Styria and Slovenia. *Inge Morath: Grenz. Räume: Last Journey*, with text by Regina Strassegger is posthumously published (Munich: Prestel, 2002).

2002

Dies January 30 from lymphoma.

SUGGESTED FURTHER READING

SELECTED BOOKS ON AND BY INGE MORATH

Fiesta in Pamplona. Edited by Robert Delpire. Text by Dominique Aubier. Photos by Morath and others. New York: Universe Books, 1956.

Inge Morath: First Color. Intro by Mary Panzer. Edit and text by John P. Jacob. Göttingen, Germany: Steidl, 2009.

From Persia to Iran. Edited by Robert Delpire. Text by Edouard Sablier. New York: Viking Press, 1960.

Inge Morath: Grenz.Räume: Last Journey. Texts by Arthur Miller, Inge Morath, Renate Moszkowicz, Imo Moszkowicz, Drago Jančar, Werner Morath, Gerhard Roth, Karel Pečko, Gerald Brettschuh, and Regina Strassegger. Munich: Prestel, 2002.

Inge Morath: Iran. Texts by Azar Nafisi and Monika Faber. Edit and text by John P. Jacob. Göttingen, Germany: Steidl, 2009.

Inge Morath: Life as a Photographer. Intro by Sabine Folie and Gerald Matt. Texts by Inge Morath, Rolf Sachsse, Sabine Folie, Olivia Lahs-Gonzales, and Gerald Matt. Munich: Kehayoff Verlag, 1999.

Inge Morath: On Style. Text by Justine Picardie. Edited by John P. Jacob. New York: Abrams, 2016.

Inge Morath: The Road to Reno. Texts by Lucy Raven and Arthur Miller. Edited by John P. Jacob. Göttingen, Germany: Steidl, 2006.

Inge Morath: Venezia. Texts by Peter Weiermair and Karl M. Gauss. Salzburg, Austria: Otto Müller Verlag, 2003.

Portraits. Texts by Arthur Miller, Anna Farova, and Robert Delpire. Salzburg, Austria: Otto Müller Verlag, 1999.

Saul Steinberg: Masquerade. Text by Inge Morath. New York: Viking Studio, 2000.

BOOKS ABOUT MAGNUM

Arnold, Eve, and Martine Franck. *Magna Brava: Magnum's Women Photographers*. New York: Prestel, 1999.

Boot, Chris, ed. *Magnum Stories*. London: Phaidon, 2014.

Coeln, Peter, Achim Heine, and Andréa Holzherr, eds. *Magnum First*. Vienna: Hatje Cantz, 1999.

Miller, Russell. *Magnum: Fifty Years at the Front Line of History: The Story of the Legendary Photo Agency*. Chicago: Avalon Travel, 1999.

Morris, John G. *Get the Picture: A Personal History of Photojournalism*. Chicago: University of Chicago Press, 1998.

Ritchin, Fred, and Naggar, Carole. *Magnum Photobook: Catalogue Raisonné*. London: Phaidon Press, 2016.

NOTES

Chapter One: Forged by War

1. Regina Strassegger, "Kindheit im Hause an der Grenze." In *Grenz. Räume: Last Journey* (London: Prestel, 2002).
2. Inge Morath, "I Trust My Eyes," lecture in Berlin, 1994.
3. Memoirs by Inge's contemporaries, historians George Mosse of Berlin and Gerda Lerner of Vienna, show their mothers similarly, even dabbling in lesbianism and travels on their own; and also show their daughters translating those models into serious careers.
4. *Our Mothers: Portraits by 72 Women Photographers*, edited by Viviane Esders (New York: Harry N. Abrams, 1996), 101.
5. Inge Morath, "Ehrlicher Lebenslauf," Morath Papers, Beinecke Library, Box 710.
6. In Ibid., but Morath put it in French, as "Monsieur le Directeur."
7. Arthur Miller came to attribute Edgar's Nazi loyalty to his ingrained respect for authority, and for military gallantry, but over time the two become quite friendly.
8. Inge Morath, interview by Kurt Kaindl, typescript in author's possession.
9. Inge Morath, "I Trust My Eyes."
10. Arthur Miller, "Inge's New York," in *New York* by Inge Morath (Salzburg: Otto Müller Verlag, 2002), 11.
11. Christopher Bigsby, *Arthur Miller: 1915–1962* (London: Weidenfeld and Nicolson, 2008), 648. In fact the *Degenerate Art* exhibition was far more popular, attracting twice as many viewers as the *Great German Art Exhibition* (*Große Deutsche Kunstausstellung*) mounted nearby to show the "right" kind of art.
12. Inge Morath, interview by Kurt Kaindl, *Magnum Stories*, edited by Chris Boot (London: Phaidon, 2004), 339.
13. Werner Morath, "Titti Remembers through Werner's Ears," Morath Papers, Beinecke Library, Box 710.
14. Official name of the Holy Roman Empire after 1512.
15. Inge Morath, "I Trust My Eyes."
16. Inge Morath, interview by Kurt Kaindl, *Magnum Stories*, edited by Chris Boot (London: Phaidon, 2004), 339.
17. Regina Strassegger, "Kindheit im Hause an der Grenze." In *Grenz. Räume: Last Journey* (London: Prestel, 2002), 133, 137.
18. Ibid., 120, 133, 173.
19. I am unable to date Inge's various wartime experiences, as her memory of these years was understandably imperfect.
20. Linda Gordon interview with Rebecca Miller, March 15, 2017. Inge told her daughter that she had "screaming arguments" with her father because of this refusal to join.
21. Inge Morath, "I Trust My Eyes."
22. Fragment titled "Lilac and ashes," Morath Papers, Beinecke Library, Box 710.
23. Spitfires were the most famous planes of World War II, a British design classic.
24. Regina Strassegger, "Kindheit im Hause an der Grenze." In *Grenz. Räume: Last Journey*, 137.
25. In Morath's autobiographical fragments and interviews she gave various versions of this traumatic trek and final return to her parents, and the difference in her recollections illustrates precisely the loss of memory she noted.
26. Linda Gordon, interview with Rebecca Miller, March 16, 2016.
27. Fragment titled "Lilac and ashes," Morath Papers, Beinecke Library, Box 710.
28. Fragment titled "Perhaps I can do my life like a telegram," Morath Papers, Beinecke Library, Box 600.
29. Inge Morath private papers, February 28, 1946, translation courtesy of Kurt Kaindl.
30. Inge Morath private papers, January 6, 1947, and November 12, 1948, translation courtesy of Kurt Kaindl.
31. Inge Morath private papers, January 6, 1947, October 21, 1946, and November 12, 1948, translation courtesy of Kurt Kaindl.
32. Regina Strassegger, "Kindheit im Hause an der Grenze." In *Grenz. Räume: Last Journey*, 176.
33. In an interview made twenty years later, Morath mentioned that while in Vienna she had taken courses in psychoanalysis, which "involved an analysis of myself. . . . I didn't think anything was particularly wrong with me, I had a more sporting view of it; yet I learned quite a bit from the experience." Inge Morath, interview by Richard Kostelanetz, January 1964, Magnum Archive. Finding these comments surprised me, because there was no mention of it in any other of her interviews or writings, or in any documents from her time in Vienna.
34. In 1959 Schwarzenberg would accompany her on a photographing trip to Tunisia, perhaps renewing their affair.
35. Inge Morath, January 6, 1947, and November 12, 1948, Inge Morath private papers, translation courtesy of Kurt Kaindl; "Perhaps I can do my life like a telegram."
36. Inge Morath, note to Rebecca Miller, July 1993, Inge Morath private papers.
37. Inge Morath, *Saul Steinberg Masquerade* (New York: Viking, 2000).
38. Inge Morath, June 15, 1947, Inge Morath private papers.
39. Inge Morath, interview by Russell Miller, typescript, Magnum Archive, 2.
40. *Heute* February 15, 1947; April 13, 1949, 13–15; and July 6, 1949, 11.
41. Inge Morath, "About Myself," in *Inge Morath: Life as a Photographer* (Vienna: Kunsthalle Wien; Munich: Gina Kehayoff Verlag, 1999), 13.
42. Throughout 1948 and 1949, after which *Heute* ceased publication, it relied heavily on Magnum and other photographers Morath had found, filling its pages with pictures by Robert Capa, David Seymour, Carl Perutz, George Rodger, Erich Lessing, Fenno Jacobs, and especially Ernst Haas.
43. Inge Morath, interview by Russell Miller, 2.
44. The feature was published in *Heute* as "Und die Frauen Warten" in 1949; Steven Hoelscher, "Magnum's Geographies," in *Reading Magnum: A Visual Archive of the Modern World*, edited by Steven Hoelscher (Austin: University of Texas Press, 2013), 162.
45. Morath Papers, Beinecke Library, Box 585.
46. Inge Morath, "Meeting Magnum," in Irwin Shaw, *Magnum, Paris* (New York: Aperture, 1981), 7.

Chapter Two: Magnum, Paris

47. Inge Morath, "Meeting Magnum," in Irwin Shaw, *Magnum, Paris*, 7.
48. Irme Schaber, Richard Whelan, and Kristen Lubben, eds., *Gerda Taro* (New York: International Center of Photography and Steidl, 2008), 14.
49. Nissan N. Perez, "A Century of Migration," in *Displaced Visions: Émigré Photographers of the 20th Century* (Jerusalem: Lund Humphries, 2013), 22.
50. The Viennese Waltz is a particular variation of the generic waltz and is, according to experts, easier to perform to the left than to the right, due to both the alignment between partners and the fact that most people are best at rotating counterclockwise. See https://ascholarlyskater.wordpress.com/2013/12/31/fasching-begins-an-introduction-to-viennese-ball-season/.
51. Randy Kennedy, "The Capa Cache," January 17, 2008, in "The Online Photographer," at http://theonlinephotographer.typepad.com/the_online_photographer/2008/01/the-capa-cache.html.
52. Inge Morath, interview by Russell Miller, 3.
53. Ibid.
54. Irwin Shaw, *Magnum, Paris* (New York: Aperture, 1981), 16.
55. He chose the new name for several reasons: because of growing anti-Semitism in France, because like everyone in Paris he loved American films and his favorite director was Frank Capra, because the name Capa was ethnically ambiguous, and because he preferred a cosmopolitan rather than a French ethnic identification.
56. Carole Naggar, *George Rodger: An Adventure in Photography, 1908-1995* (Syracuse: Syracuse University Press, 2003), 118. In his work for *Life*, despite his friendship with its picture editor John Morris, Capa was disgusted that it frequently lost his negatives and dumbed down his stories.
57. Richard Whelan, *Robert Capa: A Biography* (New York: Knopf, 1985), 56.
58. Tom Beck, *David Seymour (Chim)* (New York: Phaidon, 2005).
59. John G. Morris, *Get the Picture: A Personal History of Photojournalism* (Chicago: University of Chicago Press, 1998), 165.
60. Pierre Assouline, *Henri Cartier-Bresson: A Biography* (London: Thames & Hudson, 2005), 101, 130–31.
61. Carole Naggar, *George Rodger*; Fred Ritchin, "Seeing the World Differently," in *Magnum Photos* (London: Thames & Hudson, 2008), np.
62. A Gallup poll from 1932 found that the rotogravure sections of newspapers were their most popular parts, and that advertisements in those sections brought in the most revenue. In 1936, Henry Luce bought and relaunched *Life* magazine. His first issue carried fifty pages of photos, the text no more than captions for the photographs. The magazine's circulation reached one million just four months after its first issue.
63. Great photographers had produced photo-textual stories and books previously, typically with the writer receiving equal billing. For example, Dorothea Lange and Paul Taylor, *American Exodus*; Margaret Bourke-White and Erskine Caldwell, *You Have Seen Their Faces*; Walker Evans and James Agee, *Let Us Now Praise Famous Men*.
64. Henri Cartier-Bresson, in Mary Panzer, "The Complete Story," in *Inge Morath: First Color*, edited by John P. Jacob (Gottingen: Steidl for Inge Morath Foundation and Magnum, 2009), 11.
65. Capa criticized Cartier-Bresson's earlier practices, demanding fuller texts: "The texts are absolutely insufficient. Never in a picture story can you write captions saying 'Prime Minister' -- 'Policeman' -- 'Club contrasting luxury'. . . " Letter from Capa to Cartier-Bresson and Gail Mayo Vincent, April 21, 1951, in Alison Nordström, "On Becoming an Archive," in *Reading Magnum*, ed. Steven Hoelscher (Austin: University of Texas Press, 2013), 22.
66. Inge Morath, "About Myself," in *Inge Morath: Life as a Photographer* (Vienna: Kunsthalle Wien; Munich: Gina Kehayoff Verlag, 1999), 12. Cartier-Bresson's biographer claims that this stamping originated earlier with Cartier-Bresson, who wrote on his photographs, "This photo may only be reproduced if accompanied by its caption or by a text written expressly in the spirit of the caption"; and that Capa had done this with his photos from the USSR. Pierre Assouline, *Henri Cartier-Bresson: A Biography* (London: Thames & Hudson, 2005), 173.
67. Inge Morath, introduction to Irwin Shaw, *Magnum, Paris*; Inge Morath, "I Trust My Eyes."
68. Capa was awed by his work and the group unanimously invited him to join Magnum. He hesitated, wanting to make sure they were "sound" and "socialist-inspired." Capa reassured him and soon became his photographic father. Tom Beck, *David Seymour (Chim)* (New York: Phaidon, 2005); Richard Whelan, *Robert Capa: A Biography* (New York: Knopf, 1985), 273.
69. In 1937 the brothers got their parents out of Hungary and Kornél went with them to the United States, where he got a job in *Life*'s darkroom.
70. Untitled fragment, Morath Papers, Beinecke Library, Box 585.
71. Peter Galassi, *Henri Cartier-Bresson: The Early Work* (New York: MoMA, 1987), 24.
72. Taro was born Gerta Pohorylle in Stuttgart, Germany, to Jewish immigrants from Galicia. She became Taro when Friedmann became Capa, and for the similiar reasons, and because of their mutual admiration of Greta Garbo.
73. Irme Schaber, Richard Whelan, and Kristen Lubben, *Gerda Taro* (New York: International Center of Photography, 2007); Richard Whelan, *Robert Capa* (New York: Knopf, 1985), 65.
74. Tom Beck, *David Seymour (Chim)* (New York: Phaidon, 2005).
75. Ibid., 11.
76. On Eisner, see John G. Morris, *Get the Picture: A Personal History of Photojournalism* (New York: Random House, 1998), 135–36.
77. Inge Morath, introduction to Irwin Shaw, *Magnum, Paris*; John G. Morris, *Get the Picture: A Personal History of Photojournalism* (New York: Random House, 1998), 136.
78. Inge Morath, undated, Inge Morath private papers, translation courtesy of Kurt Kaindl.
79. Inge Morath to Haas, November 17, 1949, collection of Inge Bondi.
80. Inge Morath, introduction to Irwin Shaw, *Magnum, Paris* (New York: Aperture, 1981).
81. Untitled typescript, Morath Papers, Beinecke Library, Box 585.
82. Regina Strassegger, "Kindheit im Hause an der Grenze." In *Grenz. Räume: Last Journey*, 176.
83. Inge Morath to Ernst Haas, November 17, 1949, collection of Inge Bondi.
84. Inge Morath, various typescripts, Morath Papers, Beinecke Library, Box 585.
85. Inge Morath to Ernst Haas, November 17, 1949, collection of Inge Bondi.

86. Regina Strassegger, "Kindheit im Hause an der Grenze." In *Grenz. Räume: Last Journey*, 15. I would call it her third birthplace, making Vienna the second.
87. Pierre Assouline, *Henri Cartier-Bresson: A Biography* (London: Thames & Hudson, 2005), 75.
88. Inge Morath, introduction to Irwin Shaw, *Magnum, Paris*.
89. John G. Morris, *Get the Picture: A Personal History of Photojournalism* (New York: Random House, 1998), 153.
90. Several friends, including John Morris, tried to talk him out of going to Vietnam, but he was bored and broke and the job for *Life* offered $2,000, or $18,000 in 2016 dollars. John G. Morris, *Get the Picture: A Personal History of Photojournalism* (New York: Random House, 1998), 154.
91. Bischof actually died before Capa, on May 16, 1954, but he was in the Peruvian Andes so it took longer for the news to reach Paris.
92. George Rodger, in Carole Naggar, *George Rodger*, 240.
93. Inge Morath, interview by Russell Miller, 6.
94. John G. Morris, *Get the Picture: A Personal History of Photojournalism*, 163.

Chapter Three: Choosing Photography

95. Lorant had made experimental films in Berlin in the 1920s, edited the *Weekly Illustrated*, and founded the popular *Lilliput*, a magazine made famous by his clever pictorial juxtapositions.
96. Richard Whelan, *Robert Capa: A Biography* (New York: Knopf, 1985), 151.
97. John G. Morris, *Get the Picture: A Personal History of Photojournalism*, 148.
98. One of his novels, *The System*, was so critical of British upper-class education that it was condemned by Shrewsbury; http://levantineheritage.com/note31.htm.
99. Inge Morath, interview by Russell Miller, 4.
100. Honor Moore, interview by Linda Gordon, March 21, 2016.
101. Inge Morath, interview by Russell Miller, 4.
102. Regina Strassegger, "Kindheit im Hause an der Grenze." In *Grenz. Räume: Last Journey*, 176.
103. This was her recollection, but I wonder: could she have spent so much time with Haas and not watched or helped him load film?
104. Kurt Kaindl, *Inge Morath: Fotografien 1952-1992* (Salzburg: Otto Müller Verlag, 1992), 22.
105. Inge Morath, interview by Russell Miller, 2.
106. Inge Morath, December 22, 1951, Inge Morath private papers, translation courtesy of Kurt Kaindl.
107. *Camera Austria*, # 19/20: 1985/1986, 80.
108. Guttmann had been, along with his friend Walter Benjamin, a member of the *Freideutschen Jugendbewegung*, Free German Youth Movement, which had emerged from the *Wandervogel* groups. Another of his friends, Ernst Kirchner, brought him into the *Brücke* school of German expressionist artists. A member of the German communist Spartacists, Guttmann had also visited Russia to take in the revolutionary art movements of the early twentieth century—constructivism, suprematism, anti-art. There he met avant-garde photographers such as Alexander Rodchenko and El Lissitzky.
109. Morath Papers, Beinecke Library, Box 600; Inge Morath, "I Trust My Eyes."
110. Ibid.
111. Inge Morath, interview by Russell Miller, 4.
112. Morath Papers, Beinecke Library, Box 600.
113. Inge Morath, January 9, 1953, Inge Morath private papers.
114. In an article about a show at the Tate Britain that featured this photo, a journalist wrote that "Morath once recalled having lunch with Mrs. Nash at the Ritz, where she leaned across the table and asked, 'Why do these people stare at me so? Do you think I put on too much rouge?'" Lucy Davies, "Another London at Tate Britain," *The Telegraph*, July 17, 2012.
115. Inge Morath, *Portraits* (New York: Aperture, 1986), 94.
116. The Speed Graphic was a large camera, virtually synonymous with photojournalism in the 1930s and 1940s.
117. Morath to Elizabeth Smith, August 7, 1973, Morath Papers, Beinecke Library.
118. She managed to interest a small Catholic magazine in the subject and got a small advance. Morath Papers, Beinecke Library, Box 554.
119. Inge Morath, interview by Russell Miller, 4.
120. Although the Cardinal of Paris supported their work, the Vatican, responding to complaints from factory owners and Cold War politicians, ordered the project ended and the priests returned to their conventional tasks. Only about one-third complied. Emma Bell, "Disruptive Religion: The Case of the Catholic Worker-Priests (1943-1954)," *Journal of Management, Spirituality and Religion* IV #4, 2007, 432–43; Robert F. Byrnes, "The Priest-Workers," *Foreign Affairs* January 1955.
121. Morath Papers, Beinecke Library, Box 554.
122. One photography critic recalled her continued interest in houses of worship; Kurt Kaindl, personal communication, Inge Morath private papers.
123. Morath's recollection was that she did this photography in place of Capa; see her 1994 "I Trust My Eyes" lecture; but John Jacob, former director of the Inge Morath Foundation reports that both Morath and Capa made photographs on the set. *Inge Morath: First Color*, edited by John P. Jacob (Gottingen: Steidl for the Inge Morath Foundation and Magnum, 2009), 193.
124. Inge Morath, "I Trust My Eyes"; Inge Morath, *Bal D'Hiver*," in *Esopus* #17, 2011, 47–67.

Chapter Four: Learning from the Master

125. Linda Gordon, interview with Honor Moore, March 21, 2016.
126. Inge Morath to Rebecca Miller, July 1993, Inge Morath private papers.
127. Inge Morath, "I Trust My Eyes."
128. Inge Morath, "I Trust My Eyes"; Russell Miller, *Magnum: Fifty Years at the Front Line of History* (New York: Grove Press, 1997), 103.
129. Elsewhere she wrote that her work with Cartier-Bresson went on for two years, Morath Papers, Beinecke Library, Box 585; and elsewhere she says a year and a half, in an interview by Russell Miller, 10.
130. Inge Morath, interview by Russell Miller, 9.
131. Inge Morath, interview by Russell Miller, 11; Inge Morath, *Spanien in den Funfziger Jahren* (Altzella, Germany: Batuz Foundation, 2000), 7.
132. Mercedes Formica-Corsi Hezode (her full name) was a prominent figure in Spain: editor of the weekly *Medina* starting in 1944, winner of the Fastenrath Prize from the Royal Spanish Academy. She felt nevertheless that her association with the *Falange* cost her some recognition.
133. Bernard Lebrun and Michel Lefebvre, *Robert Capa: The Paris Years*

1933-1954, trans. Nicholas Elliot (New York: Abrams, 2011), 238.
134. Inge Morath, interview by Russell Miller, 8.
135. Olga Andreyev Carlisle, in "Instantaneous Forever," in Inge Morath, *Russian Journal 1965-1990* (New York: Aperture, 1991), 119.
136. Inge Morath, *Spanien in den Funfziger Jahren* (Altzella, Germany: Batuz Foundation, 2000), 12–13.
137. Ibid., 20.
138. When Ruiz Vilato asked "how do you want me to look?" Morath answered "As you would look at Pablo." Ibid., 20. Critic Sabine Folie calls the images labeled "family snapshots," "mysterious genre" pictures because of their unsettled feeling, as people change places around the small room. Sabine Folie, "Inge Morath: A Visual Historiographer," in *Inge Morath: Life as a Photographer* (Vienna: Kunsthalle Wien; Munich: Gina Kehayoff Verlag, 1999), 29.
139. MB (unidentified) interview by Robert Delpire, Morath Papers, Beinecke Library.
140. The ambition of the Pamplonians, she reported, is "to spend the whole of the *san fermines* without going to sleep." Inge Morath, *San Fermín: Años 50* (Madrid, 1997), 28.
141. Ibid., 29–30.
142. Untitled fragment, Morath Papers, Beinecke Library, Box 600.
143. An English version appeared as *Fiesta in Pamplona* in 1956, and a Japanese version in 1957. Morath made numerous photographs of Aubier while in Spain. Kurt Kaindl, *Inge Morath: Fotografien 1952–1992* (Salzburg: Otto Müller Verlag, 1992), 24.
144. Eventually she would produce more than thirty text-and-photography books. *Inge Morath: First Color*, 189.
145. Arthur Miller, *Timebends: A Life* (New York: Grove Atlantic, 1987), 565.
146. Inge Morath, *Camiño de Santiago* (Santiago: Universidade de Santiago de Compostela, 1999).
147. This idea was enunciated by William Z. Ripley in his 1899 book *The Races of Europe: A Sociological Study* (New York: Appleton, 1899).
148. Untitled fragment, Morath Papers, Beinecke Library, Box 600.
149. Acibeche, also known as lignite or jet, is a form of hard coal used in jewelry. Items of acibeche guard against the evil eye and became the talisman of the pilgrims to Santiago.
150. Sabine Folie, "Inge Morath: A Visual Historiographer," in *Inge Morath: Life as a Photographer*, 35.
151. Inge Morath, *San Fermín: Años 50* (Madrid, 1997), 28, 30.
152. Photographer and curator Olivia Lahs-Gonzales writes of Morath's "distinct lack of didacticism" as a sign of her sensitivity. Olivia Lahs-Gonzales, "To Unseal the Deeper Nature," in *Inge Morath: Life as a Photographer*, 69.
153. Regina Strassegger, "Kindheit im Hause an der Grenze." In *Grenz. Räume: Last Journey*, 133, 173.
154. Ibid., 176.
155. Linda Gordon, interview with Rebecca Miller, March 16, 2016. The gift may have been also a commentary on her simplified mode of dress.
156. Inge Morath, February 27, 1955, translation courtesy of Kurt Kaindl.
157. Morath to Toni Scott in South Africa, January 8, 1956, Morath Papers, Beinecke Library, Box 707; Linda Gordon, interview with Rebecca Miller, March 16, 2016. I was not able to determine what these papers were.
158. Linda Gordon, interview with Rebecca Miller, March 22, 2016.
159. Morath travel journal, labeled "Spain," n.d. but probably 1986 or 1987, Inge Morath private papers.
160. Inge Morath, February 27, 1955, Inge Morath private papers.

Chapter Five: World Photographer

161. These photographs not only illustrated but even advanced an imperial approach to anthropology.
162. *Inge Morath: Venezia* (Wien: Otto Müller Verlag, 2003).
163. Ibid., 8.
164. *Holiday* advanced her $1,200, equivalent to $10,600 today; Louis F. V. Mercier to Morath, March 14, 1956, Morath Papers, Beinecke Library, Box 706.
165. Inge Morath, April 20, 1956, from Abadan, Inge Morath private papers.
166. Edward R. Sammis of Standard Oil N.J., March 9, 1956, to Morath at Magnum Paris, Morath Papers, Beinecke Library.
167. *Holiday* shooting script, Morath Papers, Beinecke Library.
168. Document entitled "cv," in Morath Papers, Beinecke Library, Box 600.
169. Her notes on March 21 say that she slept with him—very unusual for her to put such a personal note in writing; untitled fragment, Morath Papers, Beinecke Library, Box 585.
170. As with many of Inge's ex-lovers, Delpire remained a friend and publisher of her books. Delpire recalled in 2010 that he had stayed for five weeks, only one week less than Morath did; MB (identity unknown) interview with Delpire, Magnum Archive.
171. Inge Morath, March 20, 1956, from Tehran.
172. The Shah and members of the diplomatic corps, Nowruz Reception, Golestan Palace, Tehran, 1956.
173. The Queen would soon become the subject of sensationalist publicity: since their marriage produced no heirs, the Shah wanted to take a second wife; Soraya refused and fled to her parents' home in Cologne.
174. Inge Morath, April 20, 1956, from Abadan, Inge Morath private papers.
175. Inge Morath, *De la Perse à l'Iran* (Paris: Delpire, 1958).
176. John Jacob, "Preface," *Inge Morath: Iran* (Gottingen: Steidl, 2009), 6.
177. Veiled Muslim women and caged cockatoos, Shiraz, Iran, 1956.
178. Robert Delpire wrote that the camera "made the Kachgai nomads think she was an alien with magic powers," an observation quite possibly condescending; Delpire, "Observer, Observed," in Inge Morath, *Portraits* (Salzburg: Otto Müller Müller Verlag, 1999), 125.
179. Inge Morath, April 20, 1956, from Abadan, Inge Morath private papers.
180. Inge Morath, "I Trust My Eyes."
181. One photograph is so reminiscent of Lewis Hine's 1908 shot of a young girl tending industrial spinning machines that one wonders if she had seen it.
182. Inge Morath, April 20, 1956, from Abadan, Inge Morath private papers.
183. Andy Grundberg, "Magnum's Postwar Paradox," in *Crisis of the Real: Writings of Photography, 1974-1989* (New York: Aperture, 1992), 194; also quoted in Monika Faber, "Perplexity and Perpetuity: Inge Morath in Iran," in John Jacob, *Inge Morath: Iran* (Gottingen: Steidl, 2009).
184. Born in Vladivostok to a middle-class family of the intelligentsia, Brynner's father abandoned the family. His mother took her children first to China and then to Paris. There Yul began to hang out with

Romani (gypsy) entertainers and soon began to perform gypsy songs in Paris's Russian ex-pat nightclubs. Expanding his range of performance, he recieved training as an actor from Mikhail Chekhov (nephew of Anton Chekhov the writer) in the Stanislavsky method. Gene Feldman and Suzette Winter, *Yul Brynner: The Man Who Was King*, video (Harrington Park, NJ: Wombat Productions, 2009).

185. Yul Brynner, *Bring Forth the Children* (New York: McGraw-Hill, 1960), 10.
186. On these camps, see http://www.dpcamps.org/austriaP-R.html and http://www.dpcamps.org/salzburg.html.
187. This camp constituted the fourth largest city in Jordan. I have not been able to verify the location of this camp; Brynner puts it near Jericho, but Akaba, i.e., Aqaba, is further south, just across from Eilat on the Gulf of Aqaba. In fact none of the camp names listed in the Brynner/ Morath book correspond to a list of UNRWA Palestinian refugee camps at https://en.wikipedia.org/wiki/Palestinian_refugee_camps.
188. Yul Brynner, *Bring Forth the Children* (New York: McGraw-Hill, 1960), 84.
189. Ibid., 100–106.
190. Photographer John Chillingworth had also photographed in this camp for the 1956 *Picture Post*.

Chapter Six: America and Arthur Miller

191. Untitled fragment, Morath Papers, Beinecke Library, Box 585.
192. Mary McCarthy introduced her to the Chelsea Hotel where Morath stayed on her New York trips. Sherill Tippins, *Inside the Dream Palace: The Life and Times of New York's Legendary Chelsea Hotel* (New York: Simon & Schuster, 2013), 132; Arthur Miller, *Timebends*, 512.
193. It was showcased in several movies and appeared in songs by Bob Dylan and Jefferson Airplane.
194. She also flew to Hollywood several times to do film start portraits of Jayne Mansfield, Charlton Heston, Anthony Quinn, Kirk Douglas in *Spartacus*, and May Britt in *Blue Angel*, among others.
195. These photos were published not only in many advertisements but also as a small photographic book/pamphlet, *New York City*, by Bankers Trust. Morath was able to do this so quickly that the Bankers Trust art director was annoyed that she was being paid so much; Kurt Kaindl, *Inge Morath: Fotografien 1952-1992* (Salzburg: Otto Müller Verlag, 1992), 26.
196. Untitled fragment, Morath Papers, Beinecke Library, Box 600.
197. Steinberg drew many fake documents and diplomas, perhaps parodying the difficulty he had faced in immigrating to the United States.
198. Inge Morath, "I Trust My Eyes."
199. Andy Grundberg, "Magnum's Postwar Paradox," in *Crisis of the Real*, 177.
200. Her portrait subjects included renowned artists and performers Henry Moore, John Huston, King Vidor, Burl Ives, Jules Dassin, André Malraux, Jean Arp, Pablo Picasso, Alberto Giacometti, Bernard Buffet, Harry Belafonte, Arthur Rubinstein, Alexander Schneider, Yul Brynner, Igor Stravinsky, the Budapest String Quartet, Saul Steinberg, Yves Montand, Simone Signoret, Otto Preminger, Audrey Hepburn; artists less well known today, such as Louis le Brocquy, Gael Mayo, Theodora Keogh, Rosanna Schiaffino, Jean Lurçat, Paul Tortelier; royalty—the Princess of Furstenberg, the Duchess of Kent, the Princesses Chavchavadze and Trubetskoi; and fashionistas or simply upper-class people and their festivities, such as Gloria Vanderbilt, Nancy Berg, Christina Onassis, Helena Rubinstein, a debutante ball at Versailles, the Bal d'Hiver in Paris, Cristobal Balenciaga, and Marie-Louise Bousquet, Paris editor of *Harper's Bazaar*.
201. Inge Morath, in Allen Barnett, "Inge Morath," *Poets & Writers Magazine*, May–June 1990, 37.
202. Interview on occasion of Morath portrait show at Aperture, Morath Papers, Beinecke Library, Box 585.
203. Inge Morath, *Portraits*, 6.
204. This image can be found on the Magnum website, ID # PAR298462.
205. Inge Morath, *Portraits*, 95.
206. Inge Morath, "I Trust My Eyes;" untitled fragment, Morath Papers, Beinecke Library, Box 585.
207. Untitled fragment, June 1988, Inge Morath private papers.
208. "A conversation with Inge Morath: Making Contact," Morath Papers, Beinecke Library, 5.
209. Serge Toubiana, "Black Desert, White Desert," in Arthur Miller and Serge Toubiana, *The Misfits: Story of a Shoot* (London: Phaidon, 2000), 50.
210. The others were Eve Arnold, Cornell Capa, Bruce Davidson, Elliot Erwitt, Erich Hartman, and Dennis Stock. Serge Toubiana, "Black Desert, White Desert," in Arthur Miller and Serge Toubiana, *The Misfits* (London: Phaidon, 2000), 67; George Kouvaros, "*The Misfits*: What Happened," *Film Quarterly* 55 #4, 31; Gail Levin, *Making the Misfits* (Chatsworth, California: Image Entertainment, 2002); Alain Bergala, ed., *Magnum Cinema* (London: Phaidon, 1995), 11–12.
211. By 1950 there were 100,000,000 autos in the United States, and in 1956 President Eisenhower approved a huge highway building plan to create the National System of Interstate and Defense Highways, which further encouraged auto travel at the expense of the railroads. David Campany, introduction to *The Open Road* (New York: Aperture, 2014), 23.
212. Inge Morath, *The Road to Reno*, ed. John P. Jacob (Göttingen: Steidl Publishers, 2006), 10.
213. Ibid., 7.
214. I have not been able to find this photograph.
215. Arthur Miller, *Timebends*, 495. Another near-death experience had troubled that production: Audrey Hepburn fell off a horse and broke her back, suffering a miscarriage as a result.
216. Arthur Miller, *Timebends*, 494–95; Enoch Brater, *Arthur Miller: A Playwright's Life and Works* (London: Thames & Hudson, 2005), 87; Rebecca Miller to Linda Gordon, September 2016.
217. James Goode, *The Making of The Misfits* (New York: Limelight, 1963), 64. In both film and stage productions of his plays, Miller took an active part, and often wrote the screenplays himself.
218. Jeffrey Meyers, *The Genius and the Goddess: Arthur Miller and Marilyn Monroe* (Urbana: University of Illinois Press, 2009), 225.
219. Quoted in Jerome Charyn, *Marilyn: The Last Goddess* (New York: Abrams, 2008), 94; Arthur Miller and Serge Toubiana, *The Misfits*, (London: Phaidon, 2000), 70, 72.
220. Gail Levin, *Making The Misfits* (Chatsworth, CA: Image Entertainment, 2002).
221. On one occasion at the end of a day's filming, she and Paula drove off, slamming the car door against Miller, leaving him humiliated. Lois Banner, *Marilyn: The Passion and the Paradox* (London: Bloomsbury, 2012), 354; Barbara Leaming, *Marilyn Monroe* (New York: Crown, 1998), 367–68. Magnum's Dennis Stock photographed two couples

resting on the ground: Marilyn with Paula, going over her lines, and Miller, excluded by the two of them, chatting with Eli Wallach.

222. Arthur Miller and Serge Toubiana, *The Misfits* (London: Phaidon, 2000), 81.
223. Joan Mellen, *Marilyn Monroe* (New York: Pyramid Publications, 1973), 57. Montand and Signoret had been in Los Angeles for pre-release preparations for the film *The Millionaire*; Alain Bergala, ed., *Magnum Cinema* (London: Phaidon, 1995), 32.
224. Jeffrey Meyers, *The Genius and the Goddess: Arthur Miller and Marilyn Monroe* (Urbana: University of Illinois Press, 2009), 224. Monroe's criticism was by no means unreasonable. In Miller's original short story, Roslyn was an educated woman; in the film she tells Gay (Clark Gable) that she never finished high school and he responds, "'Well, that's real good news.'" Henry Popkin, "Arthur Miller Out West," *Commentary* 31, 1961, 436.
225. These photographs are collected in Arthur Miller and Serge Toubiana, *The Misfits* (London: Phaidon, 2000).
226. Arthur Miller and Serge Toubiana, *The Misfits*, 120.
227. Arthur Miller, *Timebends*, 493.
228. Toward the end of the shoot he could do nothing to help her; she would scream in fury if he even approached her. She moved out of their hotel suite and into Paula Strasberg's. Jeffrey Meyers, *The Genius and the Goddess*, 225.
229. Martin Gottfried, *Arthur Miller: His Life and Work* (New York: Da Capo Press, 2003), 339.
230. On November 11, newspapers announced their impending divorce, which took place in Mexico in January 1961. D. David Heyman, *Joe and Marilyn: Legends in Love* (New York: Emily Bestler Books, 2014), 273.
231. Regina Strassegger, "Kindheit im Hause an der Grenze," in *Grenz. Räume: Last Journey*, 176.
232. Linda Gordon, interview with Honor Moore, March 21, 2016.
233. Sherill Tippins, *Inside the Dream Palace*, 137–38.
234. Arthur Miller, "The Chelsea Affect," *Granta* 78; Miller, Arthur Miller, *Timebends: A Life* (New York: Grove Atlantic, 1987), 512–13.
235. *Grenz.Räume: Last Journey*, 176; Arthur Miller, in Don Kirk, "The Girl [sic] Who's now Mrs. Arthur Miller," *New York Post*, clipping in Morath Papers, Beinecke Library, Boxes 585, 707.
236. Martin Gottfried, *Arthur Miller: His Life and Work* (New York: Da Capo Press, 2003), 342.
237. Quoted in Christopher Bigsby, *Arthur Miller: 1915–1962* (London: Weidenfeld and Nicolson, 2008), 642.
238. Both their letters are in Inge Morath private papers.
239. Regina Strassegger, "Kindheit im Hause an der Grenze," in *Grenz. Räume: Last Journey*, 176.
240. Arthur Miller to Inge Morath, June 17, 1961, and August 23, 1961, Inge Morath private papers.
241. Arthur Miller, in Peter Evans, "The woman who follows Marilyn Monroe," *Express Photo News*, clipping in Morath Papers, Beinecke Library, Boxes 585, 707.
242. Arthur Miller, in Christopher Bigsby, *Arthur Miller: 1915–1962* (London: Weidenfeld and Nicolson, 2008), 663.
243. Clippings in Morath Papers, Beinecke Library, Boxes 585, 707.
244. Inge Morath, interview by Rebecca Miller, Inge Morath private papers.
245. Roxbury residents included William Styron, Alexander Calder, Gay Talese, Stephen Sondheim, Frank McCourt, Dustin Hoffman, Jerry Adler of the Group Theater, all of them good portrait subjects. Nearby Connecticut towns had many others—Vladimir Horowitz, Alfred Kazin, Louis Untermeyer, Peter Yarrow, William Sloane Coffin.
246. Inge Morath, interview by Richard Kostelanetz, February 1964.
247. Rebecca Miller to Linda Gordon, September 2016.
248. Rebecca Miller to Linda Gordon, September 2016.
249. Linda Gordon interview with Honor Moore, March 21, 2016.
250. Inge Morath to Werner Mörath, August 23–24, 1976, Inge Morath private papers.
251. Draft of letter to Magnum, n.d., probably 1964, Morath Papers, Beinecke Library, Box 585.
252. Morath to Wayne Miller, May 29, 1963, Morath Papers, Beinecke Library, Box 585.
253. Morath to Marc Riboud, September 6, 1963, Morath Papers, Beinecke Library, Box 585.
254. Morath to Kay Brown, April 13, 1963, Morath Papers, Beinecke Library, Box 707.
255. Linda Gordon, interview with Rebecca Miller, March 16, 2016.
256. Undated fragment, Morath Papers, Beinecke Library, Box 600.
257. Untitled fragments headed "bankers trust" and "perhaps I can do my life like a telegram," Morath Papers, Beinecke Library.
258. "Perhaps I can do my life like a telegram," Morath Papers, Beinecke Library.
259. "Bankers trust," Morath Papers, Beinecke Library.
260. When Honor finished her first book, *The White Blackbird*, Inge brought her a white rose.
261. Linda Gordon, interview with Honor Moore. Inmaculada's father was Archduke Karl Pius of Austria, Prince Royal of Hungary and Bohemia, Prince of Tuscany, called Carlos Pío de Habsburgo-Lorena y de Borbón in Spain, a member of the Tuscan branch of the Imperial House of Habsburg and a Carlist claimant to the throne of Spain under the assumed name of "Carlos VIII." He was the tenth and youngest child of Archduke Leopold Salvator, Prince of Tuscany, and Infanta Blanca of Spain.
262. Some of these portraits became part of a job for the London *Times*, a feature on American Jewish writers, that included Joseph Heller, Alfred Kazin, Norman Mailer, Philip Roth—Susan Sontag unaccountably missing.
263. Inge Morath and Arthur Miller, *In the Country* (New York: Viking, 1977), 68.
264. But neither Miller's texts nor Morath's photographs drew the obvious connection: that it was precisely the arrival of well-to-do urban sophisticates like themselves that pushed out the old farm community.
265. Arthur Miller, *Timebends*, 333–34.
266. "American Masters: Elia Kazan," PBS American Masters film.
267. Adam Kirsch, "The Great Disconcerting Wipeout," *New Republic*, October 5, 2009, https://newrepublic.com/article/69927/the-great-disconcerting-wipeout.
268. Rebecca Miller to Linda Gordon, September 2016 and March 15, 2017.
269. Linda Gordon, interview with Honor Moore, March 21, 2016.
270. "The Way We Live Now," *New York Times*, December 19, 2002.
271. Inge Morath, interview by Richard Kostelanetz, February 1964, Beinecke Library.
272. Inge Morath, interview by Richard Kostelanetz, February 1964, Beinecke Library.
273. Sherill Tippins, *Inside the Dream Palace*, 160.

Chapter Seven: Heading East

274. Letters regarding Magnum problems are in the Morath Papers, Beinecke Library, Box 706.
275. Of course the definition of "commercial" was fuzzy: for example, Werner Bischof, George Rodger, and Henri Cartier-Bresson did work for Standard Oil's magazine *The Lamp* that was not much different from photography they had published in *Fortune*. John G. Morris, *Get the Picture*, 200.
276. Wayne Miller to Inge Morath, June 13, 1963, Morath Papers, Beinecke Library, Box 585.
277. I am indebted to Susan Meiselas for explaining Magnum's processes. I have done my best to accurately convey their practices.
278. Charles Harbutt to Inge Morath, March 10, 1971, Morath Papers, Beinecke Library, Box 585.
279. The correspondence regarding this confirms my sense that she was trying not to take Miller's money for her needs; Paul Gauci, Magnum Controller, to Inge Morath, September 2, 1970; Morath to Gauci, September 8, 1970, Morath Papers, Beinecke Library, Box 585.
280. Jimmy Fox to Russ Melcher, September 22, 1969; Morath to Elliott Erwitt, October 7, 1969; Charles Roth to Russ Melcher and John Hillelson, October 9, 1969, Morath Papers, Beinecke Library, Box 585.
281. Cartier-Bresson to Inge Morath, October 2, 1963, Morath Papers, Beinecke Library, Box 585.
282. Morath to Wayne Miller, September 6, 1963, Morath Papers, Beinecke Library, Box 585.
283. For Cartier-Bresson, there was only one set of standards; his political and aesthetic criteria of quality were fused. He saw himself—ruefully—as Queen Mother, and felt a responsibility for the cooperative even as his removal from the day-to-day operations in New York made him fearful that what he most valued would be lost; this bind only escalated the intensity of his passions. His grievances against commercial work stemmed not simply from an anti-capitalist politics, but also from disdain for mass, industrial-scale production of photography. Magnum should work "on an artisanal (craftsman's) basis," he wrote in 1962. In 1964, even more angrily, he condemned "a world over-saturated with everything, its riches turning into tumors . . . in a world of 'rewriting,' 'productivity' . . . void of true culture. . . ." Cartier-Bresson to Morath, September 2, 1963; Cartier-Bresson to Magnum members, December 19, 1962; Cartier-Bresson to Lee Jones, June 15, 1964, Morath Papers, Beinecke Library, Box 585.
284. Morath draft of letter to Magnum, n.d., probably 1963, Morath Papers, Beinecke Library, Box 585.
285. Morath to "William," June 29, 1962, Morath Papers, Beinecke Library, Box 585.
286. Esther Samra, interview with Linda Gordon. I assume Morath wrote him also, as she was a diligent, often daily writer of letters. I've puzzled over the fact that the archivist of Cartier-Bresson's papers reported no letters from Morath. It is possible Cartier-Bresson didn't save her letters.
287. Morath to Brian Brake, February 18, 1963, Morath Papers, Beinecke Library, Box 585.
288. Morath to Marc Riboud, September 6, 1963, Morath Papers, Beinecke Library, Box 585. She saw Ernst Haas as "tout a fait a part et ne pense au fond pas en terms d'un ensemble de gens."
289. Linda Gordon, interview with Inge Bondi; Kurt Kaindl, interview with Linda Gordon.
290. Eve Arnold lived in England after 1962, and Susan Meiselas and Marilyn Silverstone were not members yet.
291. John C. Taylor to Howard M. Squadron, November 5, 1970, Morath Papers, Beinecke Library, Box 585.
292. Arthur Miller, *Timebends*, 570.
293. "Politics and history aren't my specialty. I'm better as a listener there," she once commented. Inge Morath, *Russian Journal* (New York: Aperture, 1991), 7; Regina Strassegger, "Kindheit im Hause an der Grenze," in *Grenz.Räume: Last Journey*, 29.
294. Inge Morath, *Russian Journal* (New York: Aperture, 1991), 7.
295. Fragment headed "A conversation with Inge Morath," Morath Papers, Beinecke Library.
296. Olga Andreyev Carlisle, "Instantaneous Forever," in Morath, *Russian Journal* (New York: Aperture, 1991), 119.
297. Arthur Miller, *Timebends*, 570.
298. Morath had actually studied Russian, together with her father, coached by a "Russian nobleman" family friend. Regina Strassegger, "Kindheit im Hause an der Grenze," in *Grenz.Räume: Last Journey*, 88.
299. Arthur Miller, *Timebends*, 568.
300. Inge Morath, "I Trust My Eyes."
301. In the 1970s the Carlisles lived in Connecticut and socialized with Morath and Miller.
302. Nadezhda Mandelstam, *Hope Against Hope* (New York: Atheneum, 1970) and *Hope Abandoned* (New York: Atheneum, 1974).
303. Arthur Miller notes this in Inge Morath and Arthur Miller, *In Russia* (New York: Viking, 1969), 14. As reflected in her Iran photography, she was never drawn to industrial forms.
304. Yevgeny Yevtushenko, "A Gossamer Thread," in Inge Morath, *Russian Journal*, 11, 13.
305. Olga Andreyev Carlisle, "Instantaneous Forever," in Inge Morath, *Russian Journal*, 121.
306. Arthur Miller, *Timebends*, 559.
307. In fact, Yevtushenko singled it out for praise. Yevtushenko, "A Gossamer Thread," in Inge Morath, *Russian Journal*, 11.
308. Olga Andreyev Carlisle, "Instantaneous Forever," in Inge Morath, *Russian Journal*, 120.
309. Inge Morath to Columbia University Office of Admissions, June 21, 1971, Morath Papers, Beinecke Library, Box 603. Nothing came of this venture, unclear whether it was due to the film project falling through or the university's bureaucratic mind-set.
310. Their daughter Rebecca Miller's film about Arthur Miller premiered in September 2017.
311. I could find no evidence of what prompted this trip.
312. Linda Gordon, interview with Honor Moore.
313. Inge Morath, 1977 travel journal, Japan; and 1974 diary, both in Inge Morath private papers.
314. Inge Morath, *tagebuch* entry, May 7, 1977, Inge Morath private papers.
315. Inge Morth, 1977 travel journal, Japan, Inge Morath private papers. I cannot tell from the journal whether this visit was in Hiroshima or Nagasaki; and the travel journal does not mention the fire-bombing of Tokyo.
316. During the last years of Mao's rule, a group of Communist Party figures who dictated policy acquired this name. Led by Mao's wife Jian Qing, the gang also included Zhang Chunqiao, Yao Wenyuan, and Wang Hongwen.

317. Inge Morath, 1978 and 1983 travel journals, Inge Morath private papers.
318. Inge Morath, 1983 travel journal, Inge Morath private papers.
319. Arthur Miller, *Chinese Encounters* (New York: Farrar, Straus and Giroux, 1979), 8.
320. Arthur Miller, *Chinese Encounters*, 9.
321. Arthur Miller, *Chinese Encounters*, 71–79. Miller also noted that theater actually had somewhat more leeway in Communist countries than the other arts, because drama could communicate non-explicitly, through metaphor, symbol, gesture, and movement.
322. Arthur Miller, *Chinese Encounters*, 91.
323. Arthur Miller, *Chinese Encounters*, 130–31.
324. Inge Morath, 1978 travel journal, Inge Morath private papers.
325. Arthur Miller, *Salesman in Beijing* (New York: Viking, 1983), viii.
326. Linda Gordon interview with Rebecca Miller, March 16, 2016; Morath, travel journal 1983, Inge Morath private papers.
327. Untitled fragment, February 23, 1978, Inge Morath private papers; Rebecca Miller to Linda Gordon.
328. Regina Strassegger, "Moments in the River of Time: Memories of Inge Morath," trans. from the German version, in Karl Acham, ed., *Kunst und Geisteswissenschaften aus Graz* (Böhlau Verlag, 2009).

Chapter Eight: Crossing Borders

329. Morath Papers, Beinecke Library, Box 707.
330. Morath's typed captions from the trip, 13.
331. Untitled fragment, Morath Papers, Beinecke Library, Box 585.
332. The South Africa trip is documented in Inge Morath, 1990 travel journal, Inge Morath private papers.
333. Ibid.
334. Ibid.
335. These publications received subventions from the Austrian government. The group also published Thomas Joshua Cooper and Harald Waitzbauer, eds., *Salzburg: An Artist's View* (Salzburg: Otto Müller Verlag , 1991), which featured four photographers including Morath.
336. Linda Gordon interview with Kurt Kaindl; Kurt Kaindl communication to Rebecca Miller.
337. The 1958 journal is written in both English and German with occasional French words.
338. Travel journal, covering May 16, 1958, to June 18, 1958, but written decades later, Inge Morath private papers.
339. Kurt Kaindl communication to Rebecca Miller. Although in the last decades she had written fewer and shorter captions for her photographs, on the Danube trips this was not the case and her captions were more extensive.
340. Inge Morath, *Donau* (Salzburg: Otto Muller Verlag, 1995), 15.
341. Inge Morath, *Durch Österreich* (Salzburg: Otto Müller Verlag, 2005), 11.
342. In English, *grenz räume* means border space, but the book's title is rendered as given.
343. She visited the church in Slovenogradec where her grandparents were married.
344. Regina Strassegger, "Kindheit im Hause an der Grenze." In *Grenz. Räume: Last Journey*, 203
345. Ibid., 137.
346. Ibid., 220.
347. Regina Strassegger, "Moments in the River of Time: Memories of Inge Morath," trans. from the German version, in Karl Acham, ed., *Kunst und Geisteswissenschaften aus Graz* (Böhlau Verlag, 2009).
348. Regina Strassegger, "Kindheit im Hause an der Grenze," 224.
349. Ibid., 229.
350. Inge Morath, press release for 1996 Tokyo show, Morath Papers, Beinecke Library, Box 710.
351. Text for an anniversary issue of *Aperture*, 1992, Morath Papers, Beinecke Library, Box 710; part of this repeated in the press release for 1996 Tokyo show.
352. Handwritten fragment, October 1987, Inge Morath private papers.
353. Inge Morath, "About My Photographs," in *Arthur Miller* (a journal), Fall 1998, vol. XXXVII #4.
354. Morath Papers, Beinecke Library, Box 600.
355. These activities were sponsored by the Inge Morath Foundation from 2003 to 2014, when they were folded into the Legacy Program of the Magnum Foundation.
356. The photographs from this project, "Danube Revised: The Inge Morath Truck Project," can be seen at www.danuberevisited.com.
357. Ibid.
358. Text for an anniversary issue of *Aperture*, March 21, 1992, Morath Papers, Beinecke Library, Box 710.
359. Text for press release for an exhibition in Tokyo, 1996, Morath Papers, Beinecke Library, Box 710.
360. Lola Garrido, in "Inge Morath: Medir las Distancias," translator unknown, from a "pocketbook published by Government of Navarra," n.d., Beinecke Library Box 700.
361. Undated fragment, Morath Papers, Beinecke Library, Box 600.
362. Lola Garrido, introduction to "Inge Morath: Medir las Distancias" (Navarra, Spain) n.d., translation unknown, Morath Papers, Beinecke Library, Box 710.
363. Fragment labeled "for Olga for [illeg.] book," October 24, 1974, Morath Papers, Beinecke Library, Box 710.
364. Inge Morath, "Darkroom Monologues," handwritten fragment, late 1980s, Inge Morath private papers.

Traversing the Archives: Mapping the Life of Inge Morath

1. The Beinecke Rare Book & Manuscript Library acquired the archive from the Inge Morath Foundation in 2014.
2. Inge Morath Papers, Beinecke Rare Book & Manuscript Library, Box 523.
3. Letter from Werner Morath to Inge, May 27, 1977. Ibid.
4. Ibid.
5. "Ernst Haas," n.d. Morath Papers, Box 600.
6. "Roll-Captions, 60-15. Motor Trip from New York to Reno/Nevada," 1960. Morath Papers, Box 562.
7. Inge Morath, Lucy Raven, Arthur Miller, and John P. Jacob. *The Road to Reno*. Göttingen: Steidl, 2006, 83.
8. Letter to Elliott Erwitt, October 7, 1969, Morath Papers, Box 585.
9. "Inga Is British," *Evening News*, February 22, 1962. Morath Papers, Box 707.
10. "Rough Draft," n.d., Morath Papers, Box 585.
11. "Arthur Miller: 'Americans Are Freer Than They've Been in a Long Time,'" Interview by Amei Wallach, *LI: Newsday's Magazine for Long Island*, June 12, 1977. Morath Papers, Box 664.

ACKNOWLEDGMENTS

I have never previously worked for hire, and when topics were suggested to me by others, I have almost always rejected them. So I cannot overstate how glad I am that I did not pass on this subject. Getting to know the photography and life of Inge Morath was an unexpected and happy adventure.

This project would not have been possible without the considerable support provided by the Magnum Foundation. Andrew E. Lewin, a discriminating lover of fine photography, passed on his considerable erudition to me. I have enormous gratitude to Carole Naggar for her learned, perceptive, and passionate knowledge of photography, art, and the world. I am also indebted to her for her editing contributions, traveling to Yale to further research Morath's papers and contact sheets, and even getting my shorthand citations into legibility in a rush while I was away. Together Andrew and Carole did everything possible to help bring this manuscript to life.

Thanks also to Tessa Hite and Audrey Sands for shouldering massive amounts of scanning work at Yale; to Magnum archivist Ryan Buckley for his research assistance; to Matthew Murphy for his responsiveness even in the midst of Magnum's daily bustle; to Susan Meiselas who provided wise and insightful memories, not only about Magnum but about photographic context; to Anne Schult, Kurt Kaindl, and Molly Nolan for their support with German translations; to Molly Nolan, Larry Wolff, and Valerie Deacon for helping me better understand wartime and postwar Vienna; to the work-study students for their additional scanning assistance; and to the whole NYU history department for being a wonderful place to work.

A handful of people who knew Inge generously spent time talking to me and in this regard I am extremely grateful to Inge Bondi, Kurt Kaindl, Marion Kozak, Susan Meiselas, Honor Moore, and Esther Samra. Inge Bondi and Susan Meiselas helped me understand Magnum better. Thanks to Joel Beinin and Irene Gendzier for helping me interpret a Middle Eastern photographic puzzle, and to Shireen Hassim and Gay Seidman for hunting down the identities of some South African people.

Rebecca Miller, Inge Morath's daughter, found time in her demanding schedule for two phone conversations with me. She read a draft of the manuscript and her comments, while we did not always agree, saved me from errors. Her assistants photocopied a mass of material for me—it came too late to be fully exploited but the little of it that I could integrate provided insights.

I am grateful to you all.

Linda Gordon

This book was a collaborative process that would not have been possible without the tireless efforts of a talented and devoted team. A warm thanks are due to them all.

At the Magnum Foundation, Kristen Lubben and Susan Meiselas were driving forces; their interns Claire Debost, Elena Kulikova, and Chloe Young also worked diligently on captioning and sequencing images. Linda Gordon brought her passion and her writing skills to this project in a process that made her fall in love with Inge Morath's work. Series editor Carole Naggar worked on text and picture editing, discovering several unknown Morath images in contact sheets in the process. Tessa Hite contributed her research at the Beinecke Rare Book & Manuscript Library at Yale University, where Inge Morath's archives are kept. She assembled a detailed chronology and wrote a thoughtful essay about Inge Morath's archive. Rebecca Miller, Inge Morath's daughter, contributed her intimate knowledge of her mother's work and brought many crucial private documents and images to the project. Kurt Kaindl provided translations of Inge Morath's private letters and several photographs of her at work. Gregory Wakabayashi created a thoughtful and subtle design that wove together text and images. Sarah Chalfant and Rebecca Nagel from the Wylie Agency helped coordinate the project, and Inge Morath Estate representative Sana Manzoor reread text, notes, and captions at every stage. Chris Klatell brought his legal advice when necessary. David Kogan, chief executive at Magnum Photos, helped with the project and Matthew Murphy, archive editor at Magnum Photos, facilitated research at the Magnum Photos New York office. And finally, we would like to thank Holly La Due and the team at Prestel for their belief and support in this project.

Andrew E. Lewin

INDEX

Page numbers in *italics* refer to illustrations.

Published by Prestel
A member of Verlagsgruppe Random House GmbH

Prestel Verlag
Neumarkter Strasse 28
81673 Munich

Prestel Publishing Ltd.
14–17 Wells Street
London W1T 3PD

Prestel Publishing
900 Broadway, Suite 603
New York, NY 10003

www.prestel.com

Library of Congress Cataloging-in-Publication Data

Names: Gordon, Linda, author.
Title: Inge Morath / by Linda Gordon.
Description: Munich ; London ; New York, NY : Prestel, [2018] | Series: Magnum legacy
Identifiers: LCCN 2018007211 | ISBN 9783791382012 (hardcover)
Subjects: LCSH: Morath, Inge. | Photographers--United States--Biography. | Austrian Americans--Biography.
Classification: LCC TR140.M5945 G67 2018 | DDC 770.92 [B] --dc23
LC record available at https://lccn.loc.gov/2018007211

For the Magnum Foundation:
Managing editor: Andrew E. Lewin
Series editor: Carole Naggar
Editorial assistant/researcher: Tessa Hite

For Prestel:
Editorial direction: Holly La Due
Design: Gregory Wakabayashi
Copyediting: John Son
Proofreading: Kelli Rae Patton
Index: Marilyn Bliss
Production: Luke Chase

ISBN 978-3-7913-8201-2

Printed in China

FSC
www.fsc.org
MIX
Paper from responsible sources
FSC® C137129

Verlagsgruppe Random House FSC® N001967

Image Credits
Unless otherwise indicated, all works are by Inge Morath © Inge Morath/Magnum Photos
Additional credits and sources are as follows:
Figs. 1, 83, 106, 112: © Henri Cartier-Bresson/Magnum Photos
Figs. 2, 3, 5, 6, 7, 10, 14, 15, 16, 20, 22, 30, 33, 34, 35, 56, 61, 72, 77, 83, 87, 89, 109, 120, 135, 149–152, 155–59, 161–63, 170: Inge Morath Photographs and Papers, Beinecke Library
Fig. 4: © J. Haselsberger, Inge Morath Photographs and Papers, Beinecke Library
Fig. 9: © Erich Lessing/Magnum Photos
Figs. 12, 153: © Ernst Haas Estate, New York
Fig. 19: © John Hillelson
Fig. 21: © Bert Hardy/Getty Images
Fig. 26: © Romano Cagnoni
Fig. 40: © Eve Arnold/Magnum Photos
Fig. 41: Courtesy Yul Brynner
Fig. 60: © René Burri/Magnum Photos
Figs. 101, 107, 127: Inge Morath private papers, London
Fig. 108: © Wayne Miller/Magnum Photos
Fig. 116: © Dennis Stock/Magnum Photos
Fig. 135: © Stojan Kerbler, Inge Morath Photographs and Papers, Beinecke Library
Figs. 138, 148: © Kurt Kaindl